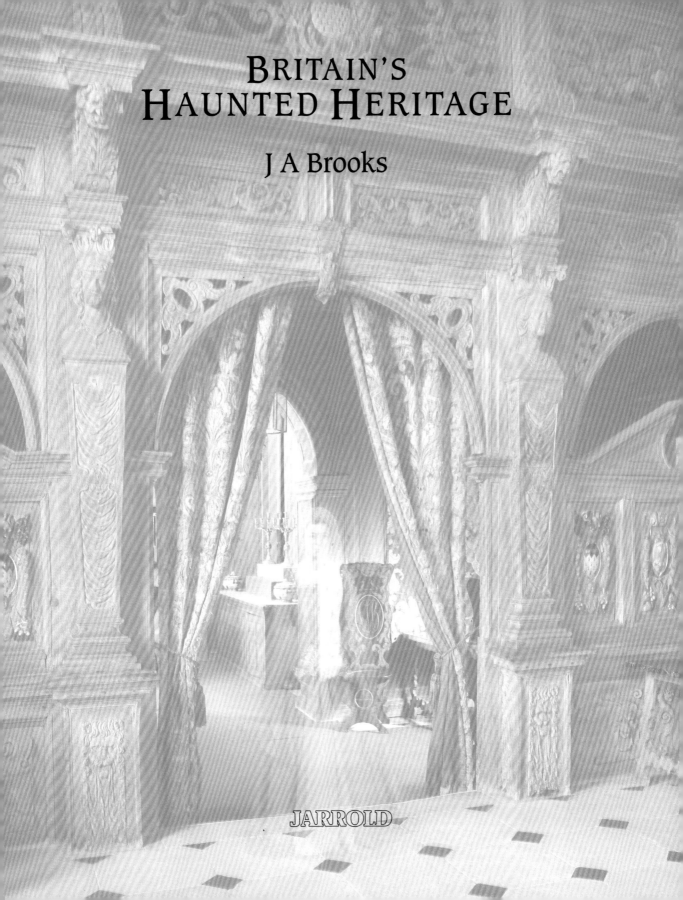

BRITAIN'S HAUNTED HERITAGE

J A Brooks

JARROLD

Contributors

AUTHOR
J A Brooks

INTERVIEWER
Jan Tavinor

RESEARCHERS
Jan Tavinor
Lucy Stone

EDITOR
Helen Thompson

DESIGNER
Geoff Staff

PHOTOGRAPHERS
Dennis Avon, John Brooks, Neil Jinkerson,
Charles Nicholas, Andrew Perkins,
Richard Tilbrook

ILLUSTRATOR
Ryz Hajdul

BRITAIN'S HAUNTED HERITAGE

Designed and produced by Parke Sutton Limited, Norwich
for Jarrold Publishing, Norwich

Copyright © 1990 Jarrold Publishing

ISBN 0-7117-0521-6

Printed in England
Text typeface 10pt Joanna

BRITAIN'S HAUNTED HERITAGE

J A Brooks

Chapter introductions by Jan Tavinor

CONTENTS

JARROLD

INTRODUCTION

Ghost-lore is a fascinating blend of folklore, magic and history. Until the late Middle Ages apparitions were usually regarded as religious phenomena and explained as visions which had a divine purpose. However, one monk living in an obscure monastery in Yorkshire realised that country people looked at them differently. He collected these stories and wrote them down on the backs of old manuscripts in Latin. These are our earliest ghost stories, the beginning of a rich heritage which has inspired such writers as M R James (who first translated the monk's stories), Mary Shelley, and Edgar Allan Poe.

Most genuine ghost stories have pedigrees preserved in print and going back for generations. However much they have been distorted and sensationalised over the centuries there can be little doubt that some sort of highly unusual, if not supernatural, incident lies at their centre. Clues to their authenticity come to light in local history as well as folklore. But in many cases it may just be down to the perception of the visitor to recognise that unique, shivery feeling that 'this place is haunted'.

▽ Hobstones Farm, near Colne in Lancashire. Its hauntings include a ghostly Cavalier and the figure of a monk with a severed arm. Severe poltergeist activity in the 1970s led to an exorcism, which seems to have been successful.

There can be few old buildings in England, Scotland or Wales which are utterly without a ghost. They cling to ancient bricks and mortar like ivy, illuminating history and the personalities from past generations. It is pleasant enough to visit ancestral homes and reflect on the lives of those who have inhabited them through the ages. If you also know that you may be fortunate enough to actually meet an ethereal figure from the past, the outing has added excitement.

Although the motives of ghosts for lingering on the fringes of existence can only be guessed at, there can be little reason to doubt that hauntings occur. After all, most people experience *déjà-vu*, which gives a strong hint of a previous incarnation. Work on this book has spanned more than a year and has involved photographers, researchers, editors and designers. Many of them, especially the photographers began as sceptics but became at least halfway convinced either by strange happenings or feelings experienced on location, or by meeting people who actually have to live with ghosts. Of course if you know already that the place is supposed to be haunted you may be on the way to finding yourself in the middle of your very own ghost story. Our photographer at Chingle Hall, for instance, knew that the place was haunted, but in this

◁ The apparition of a wherry, the flat-bottomed trading ship of the Broads, is said to haunt Oulton Broad, in Suffolk. The ghostly vessel, outlined with a phosphorescent glow, sails round the Broad with a skeleton at the tiller, and a deadly chase taking place on the deck. The story has become accepted as ghost-lore, although it is thought to have been the invention of Charles Sampson, in his 1931 book, *Ghosts of the Broads*.

case it was actually his camera that was affected. He reported that his Nikon inexplicably went completely haywire (the exposure compensation device registering exactly the opposite of what it should) and only returned to normal when he left the house.

The spectral inhabitants of the stately homes of this country are seldom regarded with alarm by their owners. Rather, they seem to tolerate them as part of the furnishings, however disturbing their habits, with a kind of offhand pride. We are very grateful to these people, who allowed us in to photograph their homes and provided details of the hauntings. We met with comparatively few refusals, and most of those who agreed to help looked on their ghosts with affection, and often sent us on to friends living in other, less well-known sites.

It is important to understand that the inclusion of a property in these pages does not necessarily mean that it is open to the public. It is up to the reader to check (perhaps with the local tourist office) to see whether it may be visited. Otherwise please respect the privacy of the owners.

▽ St Michael's Mount, in Cornwall, where two fishermen saw a glowing figure in the year 495. They took it to be a vision of a saint – today, it would probably be called a ghost.

THE
SOUTH WEST

LONGLEAT'S
FAMILY OF GHOSTS

FEW PLACES conjure up a more vivid image of the English aristocracy, its excesses and eccentricities, than Longleat, the Wiltshire home of the Thynnes. Since the time of the Reformation, thirteen generations have added to the tapestry of events, weaving a colourful family history 450 years in the making. Here the avaricious, spendthrift and plain loutish took their turn in the inheritance lottery, as did the enterprising, loved and respected. But whatever their individual characteristics, the Thynne streak of eccentricity was never far from the surface.

Even today, the present (and sixth) Marquess of Bath, Henry Thynne, is remembered as the 'mad Marquess'; how else was the nation to describe the man who sought to launch lions onto the stately home circuit in the 1960s? (The fact that he started a new trend, and snatched his ancestral seat from the jaws of financial ruin might now be more readily recognised as innovative and enterprising.) His eldest son Alexander, Viscount Weymouth, the current occupant of Longleat, has continued to break the mould with a lifestyle that is both individualistic and highly creative; his commanding and often criticised murals, now occupying various rooms and corridors, are in staggering contrast to the quiet dignity of the whole.

Longleat is very dignified. There is an orderliness about it, its three rows of mullioned windows lined up in perfect symmetry presenting a vast, yet uncluttered face to the world. Even its location, in the palm of the valley, speaks of understatement rather than ostentation. But looks

△ The Marquess of Bath.

▷ Longleat House, one of England's most haunted houses.

are one thing, the walls of Longleat contain a hectic past; centuries of superstition, legend and inexplicable events have built a reputation for ghostly activity that puts it high in the most-haunted-house stakes.

Lord Bath has never seen a ghost, but since early childhood has been witness to sufficient strange happenings to leave him open-minded about the subject. 'I believe you are either born able to see or not, and while I haven't seen anything here, my mother could. She also used to have what she called "visions in front of my eyes". She was extraordinary in that way, and these visions, or pictures, always foretold of tragedy or some kind of disaster.'

The fifth Marchioness 'saw' the death of her eldest son, who was killed in action in France, the day before it actually happened. This tragic prediction was heralded by another of Longleat's long-held superstitions; that the Thynnes are doomed to die out if the swans, who have nested there for centuries, fly away. That particular day, in

1916, the Marchioness had seen one of the swans fly away from the house and disappear into the distance. Lord Bath also recalled how on another occasion his mother's psychic senses picked up the noise and general disturbance of workmen in the Great Hall; she even swept aside their dust-sheets. There was no one there, not then. But sometime later a fire broke out in the house, and workmen were subsequently brought in to carry out repairs.

As a small boy, the Marquess was one of five people who succumbed to accidents after coming into contact with a skull uncovered from the grounds by a gardener. Longleat was built on the site of a former monastery and while the location of the monks' burial ground was not known, the discovery of the skull suggested that it had been unwittingly uncovered. In typical boyish fashion, Lord Bath treated the remains to an undignified bike ride. By the evening he was suffering from injuries received after falling off his bike, and the four others involved in the discovery were also nursing wounds.

These, and countless other curious incidents, either first-hand or experienced by others, have left Lord Bath a firm believer – if not in ghosts – in fate, the ultimate agency that predetermines our fortunes. 'I believe it more and more strongly. No matter what we do or say there are things that are fated to happen and we have no free will over them. It makes sense. That fire, for example, it was going to take place and although my mother saw it before it happened, she couldn't do anything to prevent it.'

If Lord Bath is right, fate certainly dealt a poor hand to Lady Louisa Carteret, wife of Thomas Thynne the second Viscount Weymouth, and the subject of Longleat's most sinister legend. Louisa is the Green Lady, the ghost said to wander, grief stricken and wretched, along the corridor that now carries her name. Young, beautiful – and according to some sources, miserably married – Louisa took a lover; Thomas discovered the affair and murdered the man, burying his body beneath flagstones in the house and leaving his unfaithful wife to mourn her misdeeds.

Thomas Thynne became heir to Longleat when his great-uncle died in 1714; he was just four years old. Neglected by his mother and stepfather, he grew into an unpleasant and arrogant youth. Married briefly when barely out of his teens, he promptly left his bride and embarked on a Grand Tour, not even returning after her death to pay his respects. Married again at 22, this time to Louisa, he settled into manhood rather more responsibly, although he certainly believed in living life to its aristocratic limits. He was also the first inhabitant of Longleat to introduce wild-life; vultures, eagles, bears, wolves and lions featured in his private menagerie.

Louisa produced a third son in her third year of marriage. There were problems during the birth and on Christmas Day, 1736, she died; she was just 22. It is not, as legend has it, the untime-liness of her death that causes her to haunt Longleat, but the murder story. And while there is nothing to corroborate this theory, the skeleton of a man was found beneath the floor of the stair-case Thomas is said to have thrown him from. This discovery, in 1915, has never been satisfac-torily resolved, but it seems distinctly unlikely, and somewhat unfair, to associate Louisa with such infidelity, especially when so much of her short married life was spent producing heirs. Given her reputation for grace, discretion and mildness, surely, if she does haunt her home, it is for more spiritual reasons.

Lord Bath is well acquainted with the story, and there are many reported incidences of the Green Lady's presence, as well as a certain amount of confusion with a Grey Lady. He, in fact, refers to her as the Grey Lady – 'I was once told that all ghosts are grey' – adding that it is the colour of Louisa's dress in her portrait that gave rise to the green image. That does not actually add up either, because her dress in the painting is also more grey than green. But whatever shade she is, she certainly seems to add colour to Longleat's haunted heritage.

The Marquess also threw in a possible iden-tity for the murder victim: 'I was always told that the second Viscountess' lover, if he existed at all, was a footman. It was the sort of story you didn't know whether or not to believe, and I don't really know why the man was killed, although there's no doubting the skeleton.'

Whether out of guilt, remorse, or his own grief at losing his wife, Thomas Thynne left

△ **Lady Louisa Carteret, wife of the second Viscount Weymouth, Longleat's Green Lady.**

▷ **The Red Library, where the ghosts of two members of the Thynne family have been seen.**

Longleat soon after Louisa's death and never returned. The death of his youngest son at the age of four only added to his misery. He spent the rest of his life in the nearby village of Horning-sham, leaving his family home to fall into dis-repair.

Dorothy Coates, a former librarian at Longleat, was particularly susceptible to the gloom-laden atmosphere said to surround the Lady Louisa, and was at times unable to walk along the top floor corridor because of the intensity of the misery she felt there. Having gone to work in the house knowing nothing of its ghostly legends, she was soon made aware of other long-dead residents with their own per-sonal reasons for staying on.

In the Red Library she became familiar with Sir John Thynne, buried in 1580, but quite unable to give up his tenure. Sir John was the first occu-pant of Longleat; he bought the tumble-down

priory that paved the way for Longleat as we know it today. He was an enthusiastic builder, which was just as well because the first house was destroyed by fire almost as soon as it was finished. A self-made man and greedy to the point of obsession, John Thynne was not a likeable character – but he appears to have been a far less sinister ghost than the Green Lady. Companionable and friendly, was how Miss Coates found him; and when he was spotted in the same place by Lord Bath's daughter, Caroline, as a child, she merely wondered who the old gentleman was.

More disturbing was the knocking Miss Coates used to hear on the door of a bedroom she once slept in. Every night, and always at about the same time, she would hear one knock. When she opened the door there was no one there. Eventually she stopped responding, but the knocks continued. 'She always hated that room,' Lord Bath remembered. 'I don't know of anyone else who had the same experience but she was certainly glad to move out of there.'

Longleat is beset with ghostly myths and rumours, but the Marquess has no doubts about Miss Coates' experiences. And next to family it is only to be expected that those who spend long hours working inside the house should share the family's brushes with the unexplained. Jean Alpin has been a tour guide at Longleat for some years, and she recounts an incident that took place in November 1984 – on the 8th to be precise – and once again in the Red Library.

'At about three in the afternoon I was taking a small party of visitors around the house. When I opened the door to the Red Library I was surprised to see the room was already occupied. A man was standing behind a desk; he was tall, dark haired and young. He was reading a book and didn't look up when I went in. Normally, as is a guide's practice, I would have asked him what he was doing, but in that same split second something about his bearing told me that he had every right to be there.

'I turned back to my visitors,' she continued, 'and led them towards the next room. When I looked back into the library he had gone; I assumed he had made a discreet exit whilst I was otherwise occupied.' Then in the Breakfast Room, talking to the group about portraits, she realised that the man she had seen was in fact Lord Bath's elder brother, John, killed in action in 1916. 'I remember thinking to myself, "Oh, that's alright then, that's who it was", and still the penny hadn't dropped. It was not until I got down to the Lower Dining Room that it suddenly hit me.'

Miss Alpin is convinced about the identity of the library's visitor. 'He was not ghostly in any sense, but very real. I was not frightened because at the time he looked just as real as any of the people in the party – I don't know if any of them saw him. I can still recall the strong feeling I had that he was related to Lord Bath, and then when I realised who he was I was very relieved that I hadn't challenged him about being somewhere he shouldn't have been.'

Lord Bath has been told that Longleat's ghosts are all independent spirits as it were, each unaware of the existence of the others. But with such a preponderance of hauntings and unaccountable events it's not beyond the bounds of imagination to wonder if the various Thynnes still at large in Longleat ever meet as they wander, browse and mourn around their former home.

Godolphin House,
Cornwall (above), which
has a White Lady among
its ghostly visitors.

Cornwall is England's most western county, and on the map looks as though it is dipping a timid toe into the Atlantic to test the warmth of its water. Because of its position, midway between Brittany and Ireland, it was greatly influenced by the Celts, that race of romantic and warlike people who first settled in Cornwall in the early Iron Age (circa 350 BC), attracted by the easily-worked deposits of tin that had been discovered about seven hundred years earlier, during the Bronze Age. The Cornish language, which is staging an impressive last-ditch revival, had its beginnings at this time, and shares its roots with other Celtic languages such as Breton and Gaelic.

Little wonder, then, that the Cornish developed into an imaginative and passionate people, who felt themselves a race apart from their neighbours to the east, both because of their isolation and because of their temperament. Like all Celts, the Cornish have always had a close and wary relationship with the spirit world, fostered, no doubt, by the dangers of their principal occupations, fishing and mining. Thus an abundance of what we would now call fairy-tales came into being, featuring such spirits and the knockers, who would give warning of impending mining disasters, and the piskies, those mischievous spirits who sometimes stole away human children to leave one of their own kind (usually awkward and noisy) in its place.

A belief in fairies can easily embrace a belief in ghosts, so that it is not surprising that Cornwall lays claim to a wealth of ghost stories. The old houses of the county, built with massive blocks of local granite, seem to be particularly attractive to earth-bound spirits.

Godolphin House is a fine example. Situated in the far west of the county, a little to the east of Penzance, the early Tudor building is approached through a narrow avenue of stunted oaks which, on a dull and damp day, give the full flavour of a Hammer horror film. When these open out to give a view of the house there is a feeling of anti-climax. Godolphin, with its arcade of Tuscan columns, looks open and friendly (as it feels inside) yet it is well haunted, and two of its ghosts have been seen comparatively recently.

The most famous is the White Lady who walks along a path leading from the house to the old chapel. This has been known as the Ghost Path for generations and a spectral funeral procession has also been seen. The White Lady is usually supposed to be the ghost of Margaret, wife of the first Earl of Godolphin, who is supposed to appear here on the anniversary of her funeral. Godolphin was later Queen Anne's Lord Chancellor. Margaret died in childbirth, and on her deathbed insisted that her body should be brought to her husband's home for burial even though she had never lived there.

Her last journey, in a lead coffin, must have been arduous, for it took

Wonson Manor is an ancient house hidden away from curious eyes near Gidleigh on the edge of Dartmoor. The other-worldly forms of four Cavaliers have been seen here playing cards. This ghostly occurrence is a reminder of a time when the owner of Wonson gambled with the deeds of the Manor as a stake – and lost. There is also a ghost here which smooths guests' pillows and tucks them into bed, a homely touch not always welcome!

"UN DIEU, UN AMY".

BENEATH THIS BRASS REPOSE
THE MORTAL REMAINS OF MARGARET GODOLPHIN,
DAUGHTER OF COLONEL BLAGUE OF HORNINGSHEATH,
GROOM OF THE BEDCHAMBER TO KING CHARLES I;
THE WIFE OF SYDNEY GODOLPHIN AFTERWARDS
EARL OF GODOLPHIN, K.G. LORD HIGH TREASURER OF ENGLAND;
AND THE FRIEND OF JOHN EVELYN
WHO HAS TOLD THE STORY OF HER NOBLE LIFE.
SHE WISHED TO REST AT BREAGE, THE CRADLE OF
HER HUSBAND'S RACE.
BORN 2. AUGUST 1652.
SHE DIED IN LONDON, 9. SEPTEMBER 1678.
PLACED TO HER MEMORY BY GEORGE GODOLPHIN OSBORNE, 10TH DUKE OF LEEDS.

A phantom cortège passes along the Ghost Path (top) at Godolphin, bearing Lady Margaret Godolphin to her last resting-place at Breage. Her memorial plaque (left) bears a symbol of magic, a pentacle.

The history of Pengersick Castle, near Penzance, extends back to the twelfth century when it belonged to Henry de Pengersick who seems to have lived such an outrageous life that eventually he suffered 'the Greater Excommunication'. His ghost is probably one of the many which still haunt the ancient building.

two weeks for the cortège to cover the distance from London to the parish church of Breage, close to Godolphin, where a brass plaque marks her final resting-place.

Pengersick Castle is a romantic stronghold occupying an unlikely position amongst the caravans of Praa Sands, to the east of Penzance. Its interior is completely unspoilt, a narrow spiral staircase giving access to a succession of remarkable rooms and leading eventually to the battlements, where the ghost has been known to appear. There is a legend of a wicked crusader haunting Pengersick, but the ghost most frequently seen is supposed to be the shade of Mr Millington who owned the castle during the reign of Henry VIII. He tried to rid himself of a troublesome wife by poisoning her, however she suspected this and managed to switch the goblets so that he died instead.

Jamaica Inn, on the loneliest stretch of the A30 in the middle of Bodmin

Moor, is certainly the most famous pub in Cornwall, immortalised by the romantic novel written by Daphne du Maurier. Naturally there are ghosts here: the best-established one being the motionless figure of a sailor who is seen sitting on the wall surrounding the courtyard. He revisits the scene of his death, which occurred when he was lured outside by a cut-purse, robbed and killed.

Bude is a popular holiday resort on the north coast of Cornwall: the neighbouring town of Stratton is much older, with a lovely medieval church dedicated to St Andrew and many picturesque houses, some as old as the church. **Binhamy Castle** (its name derives from the French *bien aimé*, meaning 'beloved friend') lies between the two places, though hardly any traces of its masonry can be seen, only its moat remaining. This is haunted by the ghost of Sir Ralph de Blanc-Minster who lived at the castle, went to the Crusade, was slain in the Holy Land in 1270, and then returned to haunt his home in the shape of a

The Jamaica Inn is a landmark on the main road which crosses Bodmin Moor from east to west. Such a famous place could hardly lack a haunting, and in fact the Inn has several ghosts.

white hare. His striking effigy may be seen in Stratton church with an epic poem by the Reverend Hawker, a famous figure in this district in the nineteenth century, who is credited with inventing the harvest festival. He wrote:

> Mould me in stone as here I lie
> My face upturned to Syria's sky
> Carve ye this good sword at my side
> And write the legend 'True and Tried'.

The macabre stone figure of Sir Ralph de Blanc-Minster lies in Stratton church: his ghost haunts the nearby site of his castle, in the shape of a white hare.

Penfound Manor is one of the most ancient of Cornish houses, dating back to Saxon times. Its most remarkable feature, apart from its ghosts, is the stream that flows between the kitchen and the Great Hall, the oldest part of the house, occupied by the earliest of the Penfounds. They lived in the Manor until 1759, when the Crown confiscated their property in retribution for supporting the cause of Charles Edward Stuart in the Jacobite uprising of 1745, the last Penfound dying in poverty in 1847. Throughout the previous centuries, however, they had been powerful landowners, reaching the peak of their prosperity in the seventeenth century when the house was considerably enlarged. The family's regular support for losing causes, which caused their ultimate downfall, also brought disaster during the Civil War, when Kate Penfound fell in love with John Trebarfoote, the son and

Beautiful Penfound Manor is not open to the public but can be seen from a nearby right-of-way. The Saxon house is unusual both for having a stream running through it, and for the inexplicable footsteps which occasionally disturb the sleep of its owners.

heir of a neighbouring landowner who followed Cromwell. Elopement was the only way out of this predicament, and at midnight on 26 April (the year is unknown) Kate climbed out of her window in the solar bedroom. Tragically this disturbed her father who, confronting the lovers, killed them both (one version says that he died as well). Kate's ghost appeared at fairly regular intervals on the anniversary of her death up to the First World War, and sometimes the fight was re-enacted as well. Since then there have been glimpses of a white form, and a great many unexplained noises (heavy footsteps tramp steadily through the house, from end to end) but the anniversary seems to have been forgotten. Significantly, Kate's room, the solar, has not been slept in for nearly 70 years.

An earlier member of the Penfound family haunts nearby **Poundstock Church**. In 1357 the district was being

regularly plundered by gangs led by powerful landowners. William Penfound seems to have fallen out with the most successful of these and was brutally cut down at the altar of the church where, as assistant curate, he was helping the vicar say Mass on the feast of St John the Evangelist, 27 December.

Cornwall's neighbour, Devon, can boast an equally impressive array of ghosts. Closest to the boundary with Cornwall in North Devon is the atmospheric old house of **Tetcott**, home of the Arscott family until 1788 when the last of the line, John Arscott, died. He was a famous eccentric, living an almost medieval life complete with a dwarf jester, Black John, whose party trick was to swallow a mouse live, with string tied to its tail, and then pull it out from his stomach. The rumbustuous squire kept a pet toad called 'Old Dawty' which obeyed his call and

fed at the table. Locals believed it to be his familiar. Unfortunately it was eaten by another of his strange pets, a raven. Diversions at church included flies taken in a jar to feed the spiders, and pockets full of apples to throw at the parson. Thus it is hardly surprising to hear that this lively old boy haunts the district, hunting the country mounted on his favourite horse, Blackbird. An earlier member of the family – the Wicked Arscott – was lynched on an oak tree in the park, an event which, legend has it, is still re-enacted.

Further to the east, near Great Torington, is **Frithelstock Priory**. This lovely ruin, situated behind the church, is regrettably no longer accessible without permission. The story furnishes remarkable support for the theory of reincarnation. Shortly before the ruins were excavated a grandmother and her two grandchildren, a boy and a girl, visited the spot for a

The ruins of Frithelstock Priory in North Devon evoke a powerful response from many people. They triggered a remarkable 'out-of-body' experience in a young boy, about 50 years ago.

The White Hart Hotel at Okehampton (right, and below) is a fine example of a West Country coaching inn. It is haunted by Peter, a mischievous young boy.

picnic. Christopher, the seven-year old boy, raced through the gate to be first to climb the crumbling masonry, but paused, bemused, before reaching the walls. When asked what he was waiting for he said that he'd been at Frithelstock before, '. . . long, long ago, when I was a very old man'. Then he ran to the west end of the ruin and cried, 'Oh, what have they done to my tower, my lovely tower – with the steps that went windy up, where I pulled the bell.' He explained that that was before he went to sleep, and then abruptly broke away and began to play about the ruins with his sister in a normal, boisterous, small-boy way.

His grandmother thought the incident strange, but forgot about it until she read that the excavation had revealed that there had been a tower at Frithelstock (which no one had previously suspected) and that it was, very unusually for this period and style, situated exactly where Christopher had located it.

Dartmoor has a fine reputation for legends and ghosts, yet only a few of these come from the moor itself – most are from the towns and villages that surround it. Okehampton has the reputation of being a dull town in a beautiful setting. At its centre is the **White Hart Hotel**, haunted by the ghost of a small boy called Peter. He has been known to open doors to people but if in a bad mood will slam them in their faces. He has played hide-and-seek with the landlord's three-year old daughter (she is nine now) and once, when the family was on holiday and their living quarters locked up, played with her toys and left them scattered about the room in traditional small-boy style. No one knows who he was in his earthly form.

A fine legend tells of the ghost of 'the Wicked Lady Howard' riding in a macabre coach made from the bones of her four husbands, all of whom she is supposed to have murdered. The coach is driven by a headless coach-

'Wicked Lady Howard' rides by Okehampton Castle in a coach made from the bones of her four husbands.

man from Okehampton Park to **Fitz-ford**, her home, where each night she has to bring a blade of grass plucked from the park. This task, to which she was committed by exorcism, will continue until every blade is plucked, when the world will end. Her grim coach is followed by a skeleton hound, a different canine from the black dog which haunts the Castle, a more tradi

tional beast whose glance means death within the year.

Westward from Okehampton, just before the border with Cornwall, is **Lewtrenchard Manor**, now an outstanding country house hotel, previously the home of the Baring-Goulds (the house still belongs to the family who live in America and lease it to the proprietors). Henry Gould, a wealthy

The Long Gallery of Lewtrenchard Manor, a magnificent Tudor house now a luxury hotel, is haunted by the ghost of 'Old Madam'. Another ghost is to be seen outside the house; this is the shade of Susannah Gould who collapsed and died in the driveway immediately after her wedding.

The imperious glance of Margaret Belfield, known as 'Old Madam', of Lewtrenchard, who lovingly restored the house, and whose ghost walks there still.

banker, purchased Lewtrenchard in 1626. The Civil War later in the century divided the family, the Manor being owned by the Royalist branch, who hid secret rooms and passages in and about the property to aid speedy escape. James Gould was at the head of the movement which succeeded in bringing Charles II to the throne, though unhappily he died before he could receive the knighthood that his bravery deserved.

The family fortune was wasted by subsequent owners of Lewtrenchard, notably Captain Edward Gould, nick-named 'the Scamp'. He was addicted to gambling, and on one occasion when he had lost heavily he disguised himself as a highwayman, ambushed the man who had won his money, and shot him. Brought to trial, he was defended by an astute young barrister named John Dunning. When the sole witness to the murder said that he recognised the defendant by moonlight, Dunning was able to produce an almanac in court which showed that there had been no moon on the night in question. He did not reveal that the almanac had been specially printed.

This costly trial brought final ruin on 'the Scamp' and he died in poverty in 1777. Fortunately his mother, Margaret Belfield, had been astute in granting him a 90-year mortgage on the property, which she took up on his death. She put the estate back on its feet financially, and became affectionately known as 'Old Madam' because of the great love that she had for Lewtrenchard and its dependants. She died in her ninetieth year, and her ghost walks the house (particularly the long gallery and the landing corridor on the first floor) while another, the White Lady, haunts the grounds.

The White Lady is the ghost of Susannah Gould who died suddenly of heart failure on her wedding day, 19 March 1729, as she was leaving Lewtrenchard after the ceremony. She usually appears where she died, in the drive opposite the church, still clad in her wedding gown.

A ghost which warns of imminent death belongs to **Berry Pomeroy Castle**, near Totnes. This romantic ruin, standing on a precipitous crag amidst dense woodland, dates from the early fourteenth century, but was enlarged by Edward Seymour, Duke of Somerset, two centuries later. Its ghost is the wicked Lady Eleanor Pomeroy who lived here in the Middle Ages with her sister, Lady Margaret. Insanely jealous of the sister, she locked her up in a dungeon for nineteen years, finally causing her to die of starvation. The crumbling masonry above the cell where she died is still known as St Margaret's Tower.

Another version asserts that the ghost is that of a daughter of the lord whose father forced his attentions on her. She then strangled the child which resulted from this incestuous liaison.

In the eighteenth century this ghost appeared to a physician attending the

Visitors to Berry Pomeroy Castle should take great care – there is a malicious spirit here which may push the unwary off the ramparts to destruction on the rocks far below.

Ghost-hunters who like their comfort will enjoy the Royal Castle Hotel at Dartmouth (right, and below), haunted by the shade of Princess Mary, wife of William III.

wife of the steward of Berry Pomeroy, who subsequently died in childbirth. The doctor wrote:

> If ever human face exhibited agony and remorse; if ever eye, that index of the soul, portrayed anguish uncheered by hope, and suffering without interval; if ever features betrayed that within the wearer's bosom there dwelt a hell, those features and that being were then present to me.

Be very careful if you visit the castle, for apart from her banshee-like abilities one of the ghosts also has the reputation of luring strangers to high, perilous vantage-points where they fall to certain death. Perhaps this is why English Heritage are undertaking such extensive repairs.

Further down the River Dart is Dartmouth where the comfortable **Royal Castle Hotel**, which was built in 1639, is said to be haunted by the ghost of Princess Mary, wife of William III. The sound of the carriage sent by the King to meet her sometimes echoes

through the old courtyard of the hotel: again this is supposed to presage death, though it is most likely to occur in the autumn, and always at two o'clock in the morning. The figure of a ghostly lady has also been seen. If the spirit is that of Mary, why should she commemorate a visit which should have been a pleasurable occasion?

Tavistock is on the western edge of Dartmoor, a beautifully-situated town of granite buildings, many of them ancient. **Betsy Grimbal's Tower** is one of the most picturesque of these. Standing in the grounds of the Vicarage next to the Bedford Arms Hotel it was the western gatehouse of the great abbey which once dominated the town. Poor Betsy is said to have been killed on the spiral staircase by a soldier, leaving bloodstains on the wall which will never disappear (but which are hard to find). Her ghost is supposed to be seen at one of the narrow windows of the tower whenever a national disaster is imminent – in 1966 a policeman saw her shortly before the Aberfan accident.

It is a poor kind of fate to have a historical monument named after you just because you were murdered there. Perhaps that is why Betsy Grimbal haunts her tower at Tavistock (above). She is said to have been killed on the spiral staircase (left).

Kilworthy House is used as a residential school and is situated at the end of a narrow lane above the town. It has a multitude of ghosts – including a White Lady, a Green Lady, and a man who seems to be a sort of supernatural peeping tom, peering in at upstairs windows. Kilworthy appears to be an accident-prone house; built in the sixteenth and seventeenth centuries for the Glanville family, it was originally a large three-storey mansion but after a fire it was left derelict for many years before being rebuilt in its present, modest, form. The incident giving rise to its most famous ghost took place in the early years of the house when it belonged to a powerful, cruel judge, John Glanville. His daughter was forced into marriage with a goldsmith named Page, who was so mean that he immediately sacked all his servants and set his wife and her maidservant to do all the housework and cooking. However the judge's daughter already had a lover, a naval lieutenant, and together with the maid they conspired to kill the husband, a deed that was carried out with great brutality. The miscreants were soon caught and brought before Judge Glanville, who sentenced them to death. The execution took place on the terrace at the top of a steep flight of steps, which still exists today, and is where the White Lady is seen. The Green Lady (there are no clues as to her identity) haunts the rooms upstairs, and yet another ghost occasionally plays classical music on the piano downstairs. The children of Kilworthy House love it, and the ghosts are a frequent subject for projects.

Oxenham Manor near South Zeal marks the last of the ghostly locations surrounding Dartmoor. The stone pillars that stand in front of the house lean slightly and bear the date 1714, when the house was much enlarged. This was the home of the Oxenhams from the thirteenth century until 1814, a family famous for the white bird which foretold of a death in the family through the course of many centuries. The first amazing account of these premonitions came from a branch of the family which lived in Zeal Monachorum in North Devon. In 1635 the eldest son, John Oxenham, unexpectedly fell ill and died after a few days. On his deathbed a bird with a white breast mysteriously came into the room and hovered over him. Within two days Thomazine, the wife of his brother James, also fell ill and died; again the white bird flew into the room before her death. The sickness took two more infant members of the family, and on each occasion the white bird was seen, though it did not visit the surviving members who, though they caught the illness, recovered from it.

The family then remembered that a white bird had been seen when John's grandmother had been on her deathbed in 1618. There were innumerable subsequent occasions when

A White Lady is seen at the top of these steps (above) at Kilworthy House, Tavistock (right). They were the scene of the execution of Judge Glanville's daughter and her lover.

the white bird was seen on the deathbeds of the Oxenhams, in wide-ranging locations from Kensington to (in this century) Canada. There is no written evidence to support its most dramatic appearance which occurred at Oxenham Manor in the eighteenth century. The bird fluttered over the head of Margaret Oxenham on her wedding day, shortly before the ceremony which took place at South Tawton. At the altar of the church she was confronted by a rejected lover, who stabbed her to death.

Almost at the centre of Dartmoor is the lovely village of Widecombe, an essential venue in the Grand Tour of the Moor for every visitor. The **Old Inn** is the picturesque pub at the centre of the village which looks every bit as ancient as its name suggests and dates from the fourteenth century. No one can explain the reason for the activities of either of its ghosts. The first is known as Old Harry, who is often glimpsed in odd corners of the building but vanishes abruptly. His favourite haunt is the new dining-room (once the scullery) between the bar and the kitchen. There is also a child who cries with heart-rending sobs in an empty bedroom upstairs. It has been said that these cries might be the supernatural echoes of Mary Jay, a poor orphan, who, 200 years ago, took her own life when she found herself pregnant by the farmer who employed her. Until 1823 suicides were not

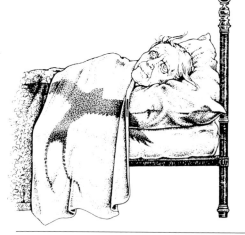

allowed burial in consecrated ground, so poor Mary was buried by the road-side on a lonely part of the moor. There are always flowers on her grave, but nobody seems to know who places them there. Many local people would not go near Jay's Grave at night as it has a fearsome reputation of being haunted, though there are no written accounts of this. It is situated below Hound Tor, by the road from Swallerton Gate to Beetor Cross.

Oxenham Manor near South Zeal on the edge of Dartmoor: the Oxenham family had a famous banshee – a white bird – which attended many of them on their death beds.

Bovey House (below) is a country-house hotel with a headless ghost and a wonderful ceiling (below, right) depicting the escape of Charles II at Boscabel.

To reach Bovey House, close to Beer in East Devon, turn seawards off the main coast road at the **Hangman's Stone** roundabout. This quaintly-named spot celebrates the fate of a man who stole a sheep long ago. He tied the legs of the sheep and slung it on his back. The Stone is shaped something like a chair, and here he rested for a moment, but as his head nodded the sheep slipped off backwards and he was hanged by the beast's strapped legs '... saving the proper hangman a job'. The unfortunate thief was buried by the stone and his restless spirit still haunts the spot.

But that is digression: **Bovey House** has a background of far better pedigree. Now a hotel, it became the home of the Walrond family in 1270 who owned it until the end of the eighteenth century. Soon afterwards it was bought by Lord Clinton (whose family still own the estate) though for many years it stood empty and dilapidated, unfrequented except by the notorious smugglers of Beer, who undoubtedly invented ghost stories to keep strangers away. It is a most attractive house, reached through an avenue of oaks and beech, and the date 1592 on a rainwater head is when the property was enlarged from a medieval manor into the Tudor mansion that we see today.

The King Charles II bedroom is the one most popular with guests, even though there is no private bathroom to go with it. It has a remarkable ceiling, put up soon after the restoration of Charles II, which shows the King hiding in the Boscabel Oak after the battle of Worcester, surrounded by the Cromwellian troopers searching for him. It has been suggested that he stayed in the secret room here during his flight from the Roundheads in 1651.

Bovey's hauntings include a headless ghost probably invented by the smugglers, and the mysterious scent of lavender water which occasionally drifts through its rooms and corridors. I was excited when, watching televi-sion in the King Charles II room, an overwhelming perfume seemed to come from nowhere to envelop me. I knew that this was a feature of the haunting, and next morning men-tioned it to the proprietors. There were very blasé about it, much to my disappointment: 'You probably smelt the chef's aftershave; he usually waits until he's out of the kitchen before he puts it on, and it's pretty powerful stuff.'

A few miles from Beer, to the north of Lyme Regis in Dorset, is the lovely old manor house of **Bettiscombe**, famous for the legend of its screaming skull. Until recently this was the home of the Pinney family, one of whom, having backed the wrong side in the

Serenely beautiful, the façade of Bettiscombe Manor gives no clue to its story of a restless skull.

Bettiscombe's skull must never be removed from the house, or dire consequences follow.

HERMAN THE
GERMAN
Attendants at the Tank
Museum at Bovington
Camp take their ghosts
very seriously, and
many try to avoid
being in the building
after dark. Herman is
said to be the spirit of
a German officer who
commanded the Tiger
tank which is on
exhibition. He has
been seen peering in at
his tank through the
windows, yet they are
eight feet above the
ground! Many of those
who have seen
Herman believe that
he died a sudden
death in the Tiger and,
as is quite common in
such cases, cannot be
reconciled to death.
The RAF Museum at
Hendon has a
comparable ghost of a
Luftwaffe officer.

disastrous Monmouth Uprising of 1685, was lucky not to lose his head, being exiled instead to the West Indian island of Nevis. He prospered there, and in course of time his grandson was able to settle in England, buying the farm at Bettiscombe. He brought with him a faithful negro servant, but the climate soon wrought havoc with the former slave's health and he died of consumption. On his deathbed he won a promise from his master that his body would be taken back to Nevis, but this was ignored and he was buried in the churchyard. The body did not stay in the grave for long, so great were the disturbances that followed. Ghastly screams from the churchyard kept the village awake at night, while the farmhouse shook as doors and windows were slammed and strange noises emanated from all parts of the building. Furthermore, crops failed and stock died. All this

disturbing activity and ill fortune went on until the negro's body was exhumed and the skull brought into the house, where it was kept in a secret room beneath the roof. The story fails to say what happened to the rest of the body, but once the skull was installed in the house, all the disturbances ceased, and were only resumed if the skull was ever taken away, when dire consequences inevitably followed.

There are many other variations of this legend, the most credible, supported by the Pinney family, tells how the skull came from the prehistoric burial-place of Pilsdon Pen, the hill which rises behind Bettiscombe. The people who worshipped the ancient Celtic gods believed that skulls had particular spiritual significance, and sometimes pickled them in honey. The Bettiscombe skull has been given a date corresponding to the Pilsdon burials, so its magical properties may have come from there – most remarkably it is supposed to have sweated blood just before the outbreak of war in 1914. A tale is also told of a ghostly funeral procession that takes place at midnight on the south side of the house and has relevance to the skull. The latter remains in the house today even though the Pinneys have left Bettiscombe.

Further to the east, near Bridport, is the small village of Litton Cheney. **Baglake House** (Bagley House in one old account) is haunted by two ghosts. The oldest is the shade of William Lighte who took his own life in 1748. This account of the ghost gives a pleasing period flavour:

> *Squire Lighte . . . who had been hunting one day, and after reaching home had gone away again and drowned himself. His groom had followed him with a presentiment that something was wrong, and arrived at the pond in time to see the end of the tragedy. As he returned he was accosted by the spirit of his drowned master which unhorsed him. He soon fell violently ill, and never recovered, one of the consequences of this illness being that his skin peeled entirely off. Shortly after Squire Lighte's old house was troubled by noisy disturbances which were at once associated with the evil deed of self-destruction.*

The Squire's ghost was then exorcised, the restless spirit being confined to a chimney of the house for a number of years. Thus the house was quiet for a time, but when the exorcism lapsed the disturbances began again with renewed vigour. Occasionally the shadowy figure of a man in old-fashioned clothes was seen. However the present owner of Baglake House knows nothing of Squire Lighte but says that about twenty years ago a four-year-old boy saw a ghost in the Powder Room. His mother had this ghost exorcised too, since when there has been no sight or sound of a haunting at Baglake.

The country people of Dorset often have a fine, sceptical, attitude to the supernatural. A hundred years ago one told a local newspaper: 'I never knows what they be; because if they was spirits gone to heaven they wouldn't want to come back; and if they was gone t'other place they wouldn't be let come back.'

Once haunted by the ghost of Squire Lightfoot, Baglake House has been free of ghostly activity in recent years.

Many of the old stories need to be taken with a hefty pinch of salt, but often something unusual must have happened to make the event memorable. **Wolfeton House**, west of Dorchester, has several ghostly legends, some more credible than others. The story of a ghostly carriage being driven up the staircase would seem unbelievable until we hear of the account of a wager being won on the successful accomplishment of just such a feat by a member of the Trenchard family. Neither would we give much credence to the story of a judge hurrying away from the Wolfeton dinner table in the seventeenth century, and confessing in his carriage on the way home that he had seen a macabre figure standing behind

Lady Trenchard at the dinner table. It was a mirror image of the hostess, except that she held her severed head, in classic style, beneath her arm. It is not recorded what his steward thought when he heard this story in the carriage, or subsequently when it was learned that Lady Trenchard had killed herself immediately after the dinner party. She still haunts the house, as a headless Grey Lady.

The oldest part of Wolfeton is the remarkable sixteenth-century gatehouse with its two round towers which do not quite match. This is haunted by Cornelius, an Irish Catholic priest who was arrested in 1594. Although he made a very favourable impression on the local gentry, including Sir Walter Raleigh who came from

A spectral carriage is supposed to drive up the staircase (below) at Wolfeton House near Dorchester; and the dining room (below, right) where Lady Trenchard once appeared at a dinner-party holding her head beneath her arm, 'in classic style'.

Sherborne to visit him in captivity here, he would not renounce his Church and so suffered the ultimate penalty, being hanged, drawn and quartered at Dorchester. Yet Wolfeton is the place he haunts: 'His footsteps are still sometimes heard climbing the ancient oak spiral staircase in the Gatehouse to the rooms he occupied on the south side of the first floor. The great door that imprisoned him still remains in place.'

Athelhampton is one of the most historic and beautiful houses of south west England. It dates from the earliest year of the Tudor Age, 1485, when Richard III was vanquished at Bosworth Field. It has an interesting assembly of ghosts, the most unusual being the Spectral Ape – the pet monkey of one of the young ladies of the Martyn family in the sixteenth century. Rejected by her lover, she decided on suicide, and climbed up to a secret chamber above the Great Hall. There she took her life, failing to notice that her pet had followed her

Athelhampton House (below, and right), which has an interesting collection of at least six ghosts.

and was trapped, eventually starving to death. Strange scratching noises on the panelling are never attributed to mice or rats here, but to the ghost of the monkey, still scrabbling to free himself. The Martyn crest incorporates a chained ape, a motif that can be seen in a stained glass window of the Great Hall.

The other ghosts of Athelhampton are a Grey Lady who walks in the Tudor Room, a priest in a black

Athelhampton is one of the most beautiful of West Country houses. A Spectral Ape is probably its most famous ghost. The figure of an ape is incorporated into the Martyn crest, and can even be seen as a statue in the grounds.

cassock, a pair of duellists, and a phan-tom cooper who hammers away in the wine cellar. Thomas Hardy knew and loved Athelhampton, and used it as the location for his chilling story *The Waiting Supper* as well as describing it in verse.

Hardy made use of a different Dorset property in *Tess of the D'Urbervilles*. **Woolbridge Manor** is a fine Tudor house, the ancestral home of the Turberville family, standing by the bridge which crosses the River Frome at Wool on the edge of Hardy's 'Egdon Heath'. Only those with Turberville blood in their veins see the coach, which runs to another of their former properties, the old manor house at Bere Regis. It is particularly likely to appear on Christmas Eve.

The secret passage (far left) and stained glass ape (left) at Athelhampton.

Woolbridge Manor (below) lies at the heart of Hardy Country and is a terminus for the ghostly coach of the Turbervilles which runs between here and Bere Regis.

The sound of an unearthly choir has been heard at Purse Caundle Manor, where King John's pack of hell-hounds also appears twice yearly.

Christmas-time is also the time for supernatural activity at **Purse Caundle Manor**, near Sherborne. On New Year's Eve (and on Midsummer's Eve) King John's Hounds come and tumble and howl on the Bowling Green, until a call from the horn of a spectral huntsman brings them to heel. This story probably dates from the time when John Aleyn lived here (in a earlier house) who tended that bad king's sick and injured hounds. Purse Caundle then belonged to the Crown and was used as a hunting lodge.

The most frequent form of haunting, however, is the sound of plainsong which has been heard by the present owner. Why this should occur is a mystery for the Manor has no obvious religious connections. In 1874 the fine newel staircase was removed because of the often recurring appearance of an apparition on it which frightened the ladies of the house. There is a local legend about a staircase at Purse Caundle being removed by fairies (which causes Americans to raise their eyebrows) so possibly earlier occupants had similar trouble. The lovely building dates from about 1470.

In the east of the county, Shaftesbury is an ancient town with possibly the most picturesque street in Britain – **Gold Hill**. The steep cobbled hill is alleged to be haunted by the cortège of King Edward the Martyr, killed at Corfe in 979. The splendid **Grosvenor Hotel** has a ghostly monk, who enjoys drinking bottled beer kept in the cellar, and a Grey Lady. Is the monk the same one that roams the ruins of the Abbey, unhappy because he died before he could reveal the whereabouts of its treasure? It is doubtful whether the bottled beer of today would cheer him up much.

Wardour Castle is close by, over the county boundary in Wiltshire. Its romantic ruins are haunted by the ghost of Blanche, Lady Arundel, who was besieged by the Roundheads for 25 days. Terms for an honourable surrender were then agreed, but immediately broken by the Puritans, who put Lady Blanche and her followers to the sword. She walks from the castle to the lake at twilight. The appearance of a white owl used to presage a death in the Arundel family, which died out in 1944.

Zeals House could belong to any of three counties: it lies just to the west of Mere, and is actually in Wiltshire, though Dorset and Somerset lie only a mile or so away. Imposing gate pillars topped by talbots (black dogs which were part of the crest of the Chetwynd-Groves family who occupied Zeals until 1898) mark the approach to the ancient house. On the

Lady Blanche often takes a sunset stroll to the lake from Wardour Castle (above) – and she has been dead for 350 years!

Zeals House also has a lake, haunted by a Grey Lady who was murdered nearby.

right is a majestic avenue of lime trees, planted more than 300 years ago. This was the original driveway to the house, but it has not been used since the bolting horses of a driverless landau killed the lodge-keeper's wife about 100 years ago. Zeals House dates mainly from Elizabethan times, though parts of a medieval house were incorporated. It is haunted by a Grey Lady.

The staircase at Zeals House, down which the Grey Lady walks. Another ghost at Zeals is that of a Roundhead put to death for eavesdropping.

She is presumed to be the ghost of a daughter of the house who eloped with a servant. Both vanished mysteriously, but in 1876 a skeleton was found in a shallow grave in the woods above the lake. Since the Grey Lady walks down the staircase of the house, passes out into the grounds and then makes her way to the wood, it has become accepted that her's was the body in the grave, and that she was murdered.

Further, on dark and stormy nights sinister noises come from the Great Hall – ghostly echoes of the occasion when boisterous Royalists billeted at Zeals discovered a spy outside the room and killed him forthwith.

Continuing westwards the keen ghosthunter can make a diversion to the tiny village of Chilton Cantelo, just in Somerset and famous for the skull of Theophilus Brome, who died in 1670 and requested in his will that it should be severed from his body and kept in the farmhouse where he had lived – **Higher Farm**, by the church. The inscription on his tomb in the north transept of the church (by the organ) says nothing of this, but the earliest description of the church, written in 1797, adds this footnote:

> There is a tradition in this Parish that the Person here interred requested that his Head might be taken off before his Burial and be preserved at the Farm House near the Church, where a Head, chop-fallen enough, is still shewn, which the Tenants of the House have often endeavoured to commit to the Bowels of the Earth, but have been as often deterred by horrid noises, portentive of sad displeasure; and about twenty years since (which was perhaps the last attempt) the Sexton, in digging the place for the Scull's repository, broke the Spade in two pieces, and uttered a solemn asseveration never more to attempt an act so evidently repugnant to the quiet of Brome's Head . . .

The only reason ever suggested for Theophilus' weird last request is that

The skull of Theophilus Browne (above), kept at Higher Farm, Chilton Cantelo.

he died at the time of the Restoration when feeling against Roundheads ran so high that some were dug from their graves, their heads being exhibited around the country. Brome had come to Chilton Cantelo from Warwick, and let little slip about his history to the villagers, so possibly he had reason to fear such a grisly reprisal. His skull is still kept at the farmhouse and may be seen if arrangements are made in advance.

Brockley Combe is a famous beauty spot to the south west of Bristol, haunted by a variety of spirits, the most flamboyant being the phantom coach and four which dashes down the narrow lane, causing oncoming traffic to take dangerous avoiding action. A ghostly hunt in full cry with headless huntsman has much the same result. The church at Brockley itself is haunted by a little old lady dressed in brown who used to clean it about 100 years ago. A wicked vicar of Brockley named Hipperson also returns to haunt the village: he painstakingly nursed the squire of the neighbouring village of Chelvey back to health. When the grateful squire changed his will in Hipperson's favour, he was murdered by the evil clergyman. However it is **Brockley Court**, situated in the dark recesses of the Combe, that is most famous for supernatural activity in this district.

The ghost at Brockley Court once attracted the attention of many ghost-hunters, amongst them Sir Arthur Conan Doyle.

In the early years of this century the large Elizabethan house (at present a home for old people) stood empty for some years. Stimulated by the account of a ghost seen by its last occupant, a party of Bristol University students spent the night there hoping to see the ghost. During the course of their vigil they took a hoax photograph which showed one of their number dressed up as monk, double-exposed in one of the rooms. Later this photograph came into the possession of Sir Arthur Conan Doyle, who showed it as evidence for spiritual existence in his lectures. When he projected it to an audience at Nairobi he was dramatically confronted by a man who admitted being the ghost and explained the hoax. (Sir Arthur was rather unfortunate in his choice of photographic material; he was firmly convinced that photographs of fairies taken in 1920 by two young girls in Yorkshire were genuine. Forty years on they confessed on television that the 'fairies' had been cardboard cutouts.)

Yet there are more disturbing stories about the Combe. Soon after the war, two Bomb Recognition Officers with the Civil Defence were driving up the Combe towards Winford. While in the Combe they saw a weird oval light of unnatural yellow-green colour which they began to follow. Jack, the senior officer, left the car to approach the light but as he got nearer it retreated and gradually faded. He thought little more about it until a friend, on hearing the story, told him that it sounded like a 'leader light' which in former times was believed to herald death. Although he scoffed at this at the time, Jack was made uneasy soon afterwards when his colleague who had also seen the light died unexpectedly. The Combe is obviously not the place for the superstitious as there is also the ghost of an old woman who appears every 26 years and brings death or madness to any who see her.

Bath is a city famous for its Roman antiquities, its matchless squares and circles of Regency buildings, and its ghosts, so numerous that Ghost Walks are one of the most popular attractions with tourists. The walks start at the **Garrick's Head** pub, near to the Theatre Royal. The Garrick's Head was once the home, and gaming-house, of Beau Nash. Possibly his may be the shadowy figure that lurks near its entrance, though the most famous ghost is a Grey Lady who haunts the pub and the next-door theatre (which are supposed to be linked by a secret passage). She is supposed to have fallen in love with an actor who her husband killed in a duel. On this she either hanged herself or jumped from a window. Her presence is as often felt as seen, for the temperature drops abruptly to an icy chill and there is a smell of jasmine. When the pub was being altered recently she haunted the nearby Bingo Hall instead, probably disliking the noise and dust. Occasionally this, or another Grey Lady, occupies a box at the **Theatre Royal**.

Bath has many haunted locations and visitors can enjoy an evening tour of them – a 'Ghost Walk'. These start from the Garrick's Head pub (opposite), haunted by a Grey Lady also seen in the Theatre Royal next door (above, and left).

Some owners of historic houses enjoy promoting their ghosts: this is the case with Avebury Manor which has a White Lady and a ghostly Royalist – the skull has no supernatural significance.

Avebury in Wiltshire, some way to the east of Bath, must lay claim to being one of the most remarkable of English villages. It lies within a stone circle of massive standing stones put up more than 4,000 years ago. Unlike those of Stonehenge, these stones

were quarried locally but still weigh up to 40 tons. Their function is not known for certain, but they probably served a religious purpose in fertility rites.

Avebury Manor is a fine Tudor house now dedicated to giving visitors 'the Elizabethan experience' with guides dressed in ruffs and a Torture Chamber built into the basement. Locals are divided on whether this is what tourists need, and the television crews documenting the change seem to have got an opinion from everyone except the resident ghosts. They include a Royalist who haunts the Cavalier Room (once the Crimson Room), who Mr King, the owner of the Manor, believes to be the ghost of Sir John Stawell, who was stripped of his possessions at the end of the Civil War and was heartbroken at the loss of the Manor. A strong smell of roses gives warning of his presence.

The White Lady who has also been seen here is the forlorn spirit of a young girl of the household who loved a Cavalier who died during the conflict. She killed herself by jumping from one of the upstairs windows, though she must have taken quite a risk in believing that such a short drop would be fatal. Recently, Mr King says, she has taken to accompanying visitors to the house through the grounds, which must be confusing when most of the staff are also in bygone costume.

THE
SOUTH EAST

MONASTIC GHOSTS
AT BEAULIEU

ANYONE LOOKING for proof in the largely sceptical court of opinion that judges ghosts to be little more than figments of the imagination, would be overwhelmed by the weight of evidence presented in favour of Beaulieu. Too many witnesses have had their senses alerted by sights, sounds and smells belonging too far in the past to be conjured up by romantic notions or wishful thinking.

You only have to skim the surface of Beaulieu's well-documented history to cream off the essence of its haunted heritage; 334 uninterrupted years of devotion, duty, discipline and prayer. Cistercian Monks arrived here from France in 1204 and were gifted this portion of the New Forest by King John. 'Bellus Locus Regis' – the beautiful place of the king – became the site of Beaulieu Abbey, and for more than three centuries the centre of their universe. Their simple, uncluttered lives were spent solely in the service of God, the outside world as foreign as their roots in Citeaux, France. Such a closed, devout existence could well be considered a breeding ground for spiritual activity; tied to the confines of their

monastic lifestyles where else were the monks to go when their lives came to an end?

The freer spirits among them clearly escaped to wherever it is spirits go, but sufficient numbers have been seen and heard in recent times to force even the most pragmatic non-believer to open his mind to the possibility that ghosts really do exist. Lord Montagu, who inherited Beaulieu and its Cistercian past in 1951, has no first-hand experience of these early occupants, but after a lifetime listening to the stories of others totally accepts the fact that they are around. 'There is nothing sinister about it, they are just here. Most people living in the area accept it without question and don't appear to find it in the least bit unusual.'

That some people see and hear, and others do not, he puts down to their 'receiving apparatus', and his is just not tuned into Gregorian chanting or the sight of monks toiling in the fields, strolling in the ruined cloisters, and generally going about the devotional duties befitting a Cistercian brother. However, his sister, the Hon. Mrs Elizabeth Varley, can well recall hearing the monks for the first time back in her early teens. 'I

◁ Palace House, where a smell of incense lingers.

▽ Lord Montagu and his sister, Mrs Varley.

was sitting by the window of my room quite late at night when I heard it. It was very clear and quite loud enough for me to pick up the notes of the chant. I thought perhaps it was the gipsies living in the Forest, but when I sang the tune the next day to someone staying in the house they recognised it as a Gregorian chant. Over the years I have heard many other people say they have heard the same chanting.'

The church and neighbouring cloisters were at the heart of the Beaulieu Abbey complex; and although next to nothing remains of the church, its size and grandeur are hinted at by the generously spaced pillar bases. It must have been a worthy rival to Winchester Cathedral, and with its squat tower, somewhat similar in appearance. Built by lay brothers (the Abbey's labour force) and hired craftsmen, it took 42 years to complete, and formed the focal point of the monk's life of worship. The cloisters and the odd remains of the church, the archways to nowhere and battered, ancient walls have all been well decorated by nature; wild flowers, mossy outcrops, and grasses meander over and through, and sprout unruly arrangements in the sun spots where centuries before the monks would have sat in quiet contemplation and study. Starkly beautiful, and laden with atmosphere, today's contemplator cannot fail to feel at one with the past.

Beaulieu's monastic life came to an end in 1538 as a result of Henry VIII's Dissolution process. The then Abbot formally surrendered the Abbey to the Crown in return for an annual pension of £66, and between £4 and £6 for the monks. Instructions were issued that the religious buildings were to be destroyed beyond all possibility of repair; the stones and lead from the Abbey being used to build castles at Hurst, Calshot and Cowes to protect England in the event of invasion from France. What was left passed into the ownership of Lord Montagu's ancestor, Sir Thomas Wriothesley, for a knockdown £1,340.6s.8d.

The Palace House, as we know it today, grew from the Great Gatehouse of its Abbey days; an inner hall where the Abbot would have received guests, and two chapels above, where they would be led upstairs to pray. Thomas Wriothesley altered it to create a modest manor house, his son and grandson adding their improvements, until, in 1867, it passed as a wedding present to Edward Montagu's grandfather, Lord Henry Scott, and a major rebuilding programme began. The Victorian Gothic architecture still has a hint of French-influenced late medieval, early Tudor about it, and springs surprises as you round each corner and come across a fresh profile.

Built, as it is, around the Abbot's guest quarters and chapels, it would be logical to assume that Beaulieu's monks put in appearances inside the Palace House; but according to Lord Montagu and Mrs Varley the only trace they have left behind here is the occasional strong smell of incense. 'This is familiar to everyone who knows the house well,' said Lord Montagu, 'but whether it has anything to do with haunting I don't know; it could simply be the result of incense being burned here for hundreds of years and seeping into the woodwork and walls. According to local legend the smell is said to appear when someone dies in the neighbourhood.'

Lay brothers have, however, been sighted in their former dormitory, the Domus, and are in fact so commonplace that when the building was lived in one resident grew to know them so well she even gave them names. 'She would say to me,' said Mrs Varley, '"Brother Augustus was here again yesterday. I knew it was him because his boots squeak".' The Reverend Robert Powles, one time vicar of Beaulieu, was another who knew the brothers by name, she added, and even held special services for them in what is now the Parish Church, but was in their day the Monks' Refectory. 'I often used to wonder', she said, 'what it would have looked like in there, with nearly four centuries of monks packed into the pews.'

'Daddy' Powles, as he was known to the younger Montagu's, was clearly very sensitive to psychic phenomena. It was he who assured Lord Montagus mother that her husband was alive and well after his ship was torpedoed in the Mediterranean during the First World War, and The Times had printed his obituary. 'He told her he was certain father had survived because he had seen him quite clearly walking down a street in the village in front of him. If he had been dead,' said Lord Montagu, 'Reverend Powles said my father would have been walking behind him.' Sure

enough, the news quickly followed that John Montagu was indeed safe.

It is interesting to note that all the sightings reported tell of brown-clad figures, not ghosts. This suggests that what people see are lay brothers as opposed to the white robed monks, and that they look far too real for anyone to consider them anything other than present day workers. But having been assured that Beaulieu has no one from holy orders tending the vineyard or doing other farming chores – and certainly no brothers to smile and wave cheerfully at them as they pass – they do not always find the news very comforting. 'Many people staying in the various houses dotted around the estate have been quite upset when they realise what they have seen are ghosts,' said Edward Montagu, 'and very often they pack up and leave.'

The benign and friendly brothers and the chanting monks are not the whole story. Beaulieu

▽ **The Upper Drawing Room, Palace House**

▷ **The coffin which was said to have been found at Beaulieu with the help of a ghostly monk.**

does have its more sinister and mysterious side. First there is the strange story, said to have been sparked off as the result of a ghostly monk's directions, whereby a coffin was discovered buried beneath the ruins of the Abbey Church. Sir Arthur Conan Doyle is supposed to have been caught up in this discovery (reported in the *Daily Express* of 27 June, 1928), having enlisted the help of his favourite medium to help pinpoint the right spot. Inside were the bones of a man with a hole in his skull, and a crown. What intrigues Elizabeth Varley is the fact that whoever carried out the burial had gone to the trouble of putting a false coffin on top hoping, presumably, that any future discoverers would be satisfied with that. Further down lay a rough wooden coffin from around the thirteenth or fourteenth century.

The crown would suggest that the man was someone of some considerable status, whose death, for some reason, had to be kept a secret. 'Anyone of importance would have been buried in a lead coffin,' pointed out Mrs Varley, 'and not without any means of identification. We can only assume that he was possibly a foreign Prince, smuggled into the country and brought up the river to the Abbey to seek sanctuary.' But how he died, who his enemies were, and who he was will always be a mystery.

Elizabeth Varley also provided the details of another chilling episode. She spent much of her career working in the film world and was back at her old home making a documentary for Columbia about Palace House. 'This would have been in the 1960s,' she said. 'We had been working in the Upper Drawing Room, which was the chapel, when the gaffer went downstairs with some cables. When he came back he was white to the gills; he told us something awful had happened on the way downstairs. He had heard footsteps behind him, and just assumed it was another of the crew, the steps came nearer and nearer, and then passed him – but no one appeared in front of him. After that no one went anywhere on their own.'

Lord Montagu added the final chapter to the hauntings in the Palace House. 'There has only been one really bad ghost, or one that has caused any problems, and this was always associated with the top of the stairs. Sometime during the

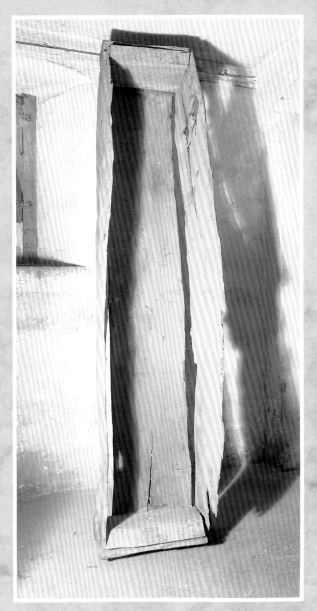

nineteenth century it appears there was a murder, a butler killed a maid, and there were very unpleasant feelings in that part of the house. It was all hushed up, and eventually the problem was taken care of and the unpleasantness disappeared.' He did not explain just how the problem was solved, but suffice it to say there is nothing remotely unpleasant about this magnificent house, and if you detect a hint of incense here and there, or the distant strains of a heavenly choir, you will be in good company.

A vision of the south east of England usually conjures immediate images of rolling downland and snug villages with ancient, picturesque cottages. Further thought might add chalky cliffs and winding estuaries, the shady glades of the New Forest, plus historic towns and cities such as Winchester, Portsmouth, Brighton and Canterbury. The large area embraces a wide span of landscape, history and character – the essential ingredients of heritage.

The Battle of Hastings occupies a watershed in the history of Britain, and this part of the Sussex coastline forms an appropriate and convenient starting point for a tour of the ghostly habitats of South East England.

Only a little crumbling masonry survives of **Hastings Castle**, most of it having fallen into the sea. It was built by Robert, Count of Eu, in 1069 and features as a remarkable apparition for it is said that on occasion it appears over the sea, not as a ruin but 'young and bright, with standards fluttering in the breeze'. This cheerful spectral vision is, however, accompanied by the traditional sounds of clanking chains, screams and groans, and the music of an unearthly choir.

Battle Abbey occupies the spot where King Harold fell, struck by an arrow in the eye. It was built by William the Conqueror as a thanksgiving for his victory, and was a successful and prosperous foundation until 1538 when the abbey was dissolved and given to Sir Anthony Browne, Master of the King's Horse. At the banquet given by Sir Anthony to celebrate his acquisition, an unbidden guest appeared. He was one of the dispossessed monks who cursed Sir Anthony and his successors, condemning them to die by fire or water. The curse has had effect at various times

Hastings Castle (top), now a ruin, and the gatehouse of Battle Abbey (left).

through the centuries, most notably in 1793 when another family property, Cowdray Park, burnt down. More recently, in 1907, a member of the family died by drowning. Opinion is divided about the apparition that has been seen about the abbey: some say that it is the Duchess of Cleveland, who was once a tenant of the house.

Herstmonceux Castle lies to the west of Battle, a vast moated building which, despite appearances, is mainly of the twentieth century. Only the magnificent gatehouse remains of the fifteenth-century castle put up by Sir Roger Fiennes. He was the Treasurer of the Household to King Henry VI, who allowed him to build himself a

A Headless Drummer is the most famous of the ghosts at Herstmonceux Castle and he may well have been invented by smugglers. However there is also a Grey Lady who has a better reason for being here – she was starved to death.

THE GHOUL OF GLADWISH WOOD

Rudyard Kipling, who lived at Burwash, became increasingly interested in the spiritual world towards the end of his life. His biographer, R. Thurston Hopkins, wrote that Kipling felt that the downland surrounding his home was full of pure magic, and that the small area of woodland known as Gladwish Wood was particularly evil. This seems to have been borne out when Hopkins organised a 'Ghost Hunt' through the wood. One of the hunters, separated from the rest of the party, was suddenly confronted by the hideous figure of a man, his flesh decayed, hands clutching his throat. Later research showed that this might well have been the ghost (or maybe ghoul) of David Leary, a labourer wrongly executed in 1825. The body of his 'victim' (who after Leary's execution was shown to have died of natural causes) was hidden in the wood and on the scaffold the condemned man promised to prove his innocence by returning after his execution 'to haunt those people who have hounded me to my death'.

The Drummer's Hall at Herstmonceux Castle.

fortified mansion in gratitude for arranging the coronation. The gatehouse is one of the oldest brick buildings in England and was part of a grand palace that reflected the wealth and high position of the owner. Sir Roger was succeeded by his son, who added to his fortune by marrying into the Dacre family who were prominent landowners in the northern counties (they also seem to have been particularly adept in fostering ghosts, a score or so of restless Dacres infest houses throughout England). Unfortunately many of the succeeding Dacres proved to be rotten eggs, one being thrown into the Fleet Prison for his support of a band of thieves and felons, and another being hanged at Tyburn after a poaching expedition which ended in murder.

In 1708, the estate was sold by Thomas Lennard, Lord Dacre, Earl of Sussex to pay off gambling debts. The castle and its lands were bought by a lawyer, George Naylor, and it is his daughter, Grace, who haunts Herstmonceux as a Grey Lady. She is said to have been starved to death by a wicked governess, but it may be that she was the earliest known victim of *anorexia nervosa*.

Subsequently the castle fell into even steeper decline, being abandoned as a dwelling in 1776, when the building was gutted to provide fabric for a new mansion, Herstmonceux Place, close by. Its shell rapidly became a picturesque ruin, used by smugglers as a hiding-place for contraband. The castle's most famous ghost, the headless Drummer, dates from before this time, but it seems likely that his activities were well publicised by the smugglers as a deterrent to the curious. The Drummer would parade on the battlements, a terrifying glowing figure eight or nine feet tall bearing a drum (this luminescence may have come from a coating of phosphorous). Work on rebuilding Herstmonceux to its former glory began just before the First World War, and was complete by 1939. However it was only used as a residence for a very short time, becoming the Royal Greenwich Observatory in 1946. The castle's future is uncertain since its sale in 1989.

One of the oldest ghosts in the country appears at **Michelham Priory** near Hailsham. This is the apparition of King Harold, who wanders off in the vague direction of Battle Abbey, about ten miles to the east. Michelham

The rustle of silk announces the presence of the Grey Lady at Michelham Priory.

was an Augustinian foundation endowed in 1229. In 1537 the Priory was dissolved, King Henry granting its estate to his henchman, Thomas Cromwell. He only enjoyed Michelham briefly, though, losing the property and his head in 1540. In 1556 the Priory was bought by John Foote, gentleman (a brother of one of the dispossessed Augustinian canons), who converted and enlarged the buildings into an unpretentious Tudor manor. Later owners added more ambitious extensions.

Michelham's best-known ghost is the Grey Lady who is seen (sometimes with a small brown dog) looking sadly into the moat where she is supposed to have drowned. Another theory is that she is the spectre of a Mrs Child, wife of a tenant of the Priory, whose five-year-old son Robert was strangled when his clothing became entangled in the millwheel. In 1969 she was identified (presumably from a portrait) as belonging to the Sackville family: this is surprising since, although they owned the Priory from 1601 until 1896, they never lived there. She has

also appeared inside the house, gliding through walls to enter a bedchamber where she walked to the bed with a rustle of silk, drew the curtain of the four-poster to look down at the occupant, and then turned back, as though in disappointment.

The Priory now belongs to the Sussex Archaeological Society who open it to visitors. The staff can tell of many inexplicable happenings in the house, suggestive of poltergeist activity, though there have been comparatively few sightings of actual ghosts. The last private owner of the house used to talk of a spectral monk who would welcome visitors at the gatehouse, and the ghost of a white stallion which would terrify his horses in their stables.

Ghosts from two East Sussex pubs bring relief from the somewhat sombre ghosts of historic houses. There is an Irish flavour about the ghost that haunts the **Queen's Head** at Icklesham near Winchelsea. At the turn of the century the pub was run by a landlord named Gutsell who enjoyed great popularity with the locals. When

The deceased landlord of the Queen's Head at Icklesham seems to have enjoyed his wake so much that he is reluctant to leave.

The bar at the Queen's Head, Icklesham, the scene of landlord Gutsell's wake. The pub's ghost is described as being like a contented farmer or shepherd, relaxing and chewing on a straw.

'Geranium Jane.'

he died they brought his coffin into the bar so that they might drink his health. Inevitably, the toasting became a fully-fledged wake, and the deceased landlord seems to have so enjoyed the occasion that he is reluctant to leave. There have been many genuine sightings of him, even quite recently, sitting by the fireplace chewing meditatively on a piece of straw.

The **King's Head** at Cuckfield, to the north of Brighton, has a ghost cheerfully known as 'Geranium Jane'. Apparently she has the name through meeting her death when a pot of geraniums fell on her head. It has been suggested that this was not accidental and that she was pregnant with the child of the proprietor at the time. This may be why she often appears to members of the staff indulging in extra-marital adventures. On one occasion an employee was terrified by being pushed around the bedroom while still in bed, the haunting being accompanied by an unnatural chill. Jane only appears to men, though she seems to sponsor many supernatural practical

jokes – hiding things, switching lights on and off, and so on – both men and women can be victims in these cases.

In the West Sussex volume of *Buildings of England*, Nikolaus Pevsner remarked how the wilderness surrounding the remains of **Bramber Castle** suits the spirit of the site. This spirit is grim, for evil events have happened here, reflected in the stories of its ghosts.

William de Braose built the castle here immediately after the Conquest, and it was his successor, another William, who fell foul of King John by supporting reforms which eventually led to the Magna Carta. The King determined to make an example of this troublesome lord, and when William refused to yield his children as hostages, Bramber Castle was besieged and William, his wife, and four of his children were captured and imprisoned in Windsor Castle. Here they were starved to death (though one version of the story, promoted by the King, has it that William escaped to Ireland, deserting his family). But it is at Bramber rather than at Windsor where the ghosts of the children, crying piteously for food, are seen, usually in the month of December.

Arundel Castle, though its silhouette is romantic and imposing, essentially remains an imitation castle, mostly dating from the late nineteenth century. Thus the Duke of Norfolk and his administrators are probably right in discouraging ghost stories, though there are rumours of a Blue Man in the library, a phantom scullion haunting the kitchen, and the restless spirit of a girl betrayed in love who threw herself from Hiorne's Tower in the Park, an eighteenth-century folly.

Petworth has been described as a miniature city, an unspoilt town full of 90-degree bends making it almost a maze which can only be properly explored on foot. The intrepid explorer will find innumerable old

The stark remains of Bramber Castle which echo to the cries of starving children.

Arundel Castle, where stories of the supernatural are not encouraged.

of the open-plan hall, the smoke escaping from a hole in the roof. The ghost of a little old lady is seen sitting by the inglenook, waiting for a friend to come down from upstairs. Tragically, when this friend appeared, she slipped on the stairs and fell to her death. The little old lady died two days later from shock.

The present landlord, David Pellant, has heard and felt the presence of the old lady's ghost in the last year. He has also experienced ghostly footsteps in the upstairs corridor when alone in the hotel: on this occasion the ghost appeared to use the bathroom!

As a contrast to the little old lady, an imperial ghost is claimed to haunt the **King's Arms Royal Hotel** at Godalming, north of Petworth in the county of Surrey. In 1698 the Tsar of Russia, Peter the Great, visited England to inspect the Royal Navy. On his way back to London from Portsmouth, where he had witnessed a mock sea battle, he stopped for two nights at Moon's Hotel, now the King's Arms Royal. The Tsar's party behaved outrageously during their stay, consuming vast amounts of food and wine. For breakfast the entourage (of 21 plus the Tsar) ate half

The ghost of a little old lady is often seen at the Angel Hotel, Petworth (above), where she sits by the great inglenook fireplace (below) awaiting her friend.

buildings that will intrigue and enchant, one of the most interesting being **The Angel Hotel** which is said to date from the late fifteenth century. Its enormous inglenook fireplace replaced the original heating system, which was simply a fire at the centre

a sheep, a quarter of lamb, ten pullets, a dozen chickens, and 87 dozen eggs. Six quarts of mulled wine and three quarts of brandy washed this feast down. In the evening they got through an even more gargantuan menu. The room the Tsar occupied, Room 3, is often troubled by supernatural activity, glasses being thrown about and heavy thumps being heard from the floor, as though boots are being drawn off and dropped. Is it the ghost of the Tsar, trying to find respite from indigestion?

The village of Buriton lies in Hampshire, just to the south of Petersfield off the Portsmouth road. **Buriton Manor** has a kind ghost who seems to have been a nanny to the family. Buriton was the home of the Bonham-Carter family in 1957, when they applied for the rateable value of the house to be reduced because of the haunting. Has anyone yet tried to get poll tax from a household which has a ghostly member? This would be particularly unjust if the ghost was headless. Restless monks haunt the grounds of the manor and the village itself.

A short distance to the west (but east of Winchester) is **Hinton Ampner**, where the old manor was so badly haunted in the eighteenth century that it had to be pulled down. These ghosts were malevolent, and though a lesser form of disturbance carried on in the rebuilt house, this was much less frightening than the original haunting. When the old manor was pulled down a small skull was found beneath the floorboards. This seemed to give a point to the story that had circulated about the origins of the ghost.

Lord Stawell came to live at the manor in 1719. He married a woman ten years older than himself and when she died in 1740 took her sister, Honoria, who was much younger and had lived with them, as a lover. Village gossip told of a child being born of this liaison, and then mysteriously disappearing. However both Lord Stawell and his sister-in-law continued to live at Hinton Ampner in comfort and equanimity until 1754 when Honoria died. Lord Stawell died suddenly in the

The ghost of the family's nanny haunts Buriton Manor.

next year, and his servants were of the opinion that his was the male ghost that was seen subsequently, dressed in his favourite drab coat. The figure of a woman also appeared, but it was the constant clamour of ghostly voices which eventually brought about the demolition of the house, its owners becoming demented by years of sleepless nights.

The murder of a child seems to have been behind the malevolent haunting of the old manor at Hinton Ampner. A less malicious haunting affects the present house.

Two places claim the ghost of Dame Alice Lisle, who was an innocent victim of Judge Jefferies' terrible onslaught on the southern counties after the Battle of Sedgemoor in 1685. Dame Alice was a courageous woman always ready to help those in trouble, whatever their politics. Thus she sheltered two of Monmouth's army in her house, **Moyles Court**, near Ringwood. She was discovered, hauled before the brutal judge, and sentenced to be dragged through the streets on a hurdle before being burned at the stake.

Local opinion was outraged at this sentence, which at length was magnanimously commuted. Instead of being burnt she was beheaded, stepping onto the scaffold from an upstairs window of the **Eclipse Inn** in Winchester on 2 September, 1685.

Both the Eclipse and Moyles Court are haunted by Dame Alice's ghost, and surprisingly she appears with her head on her shoulders in each location, though at **Dibden** where her son lived, fifteen miles from Moyles Court, she carries her head beneath an arm in the approved manner. She is also supposed to be driven in a driverless coach drawn by headless horses from the Court to the church at Ellingham where she is buried. This takes place each year on Midsummer's Eve. Moyles Court is now a school, and the headmaster says that one or two of his staff are firmly of the opinion that the building is still haunted by the ghost of Dame Alice.

Viscount de L'Isle (was Dame Alice a forebear?) lives in one of the loveliest of English houses, **Penshurst Place** near Tonbridge, in Kent, the Garden of England. Replying to an enquiry about

the ghost of Sir Philip Sidney haunting Penshurst, he wrote:

> . . . Penshurst has never been haunted in the literal sense of the word. It is, however, true to say that Penshurst is pervaded by the spirit of Sir Philip Sidney, writer and poet, and one of the best remembered men of his age for the manner of his living and dying, as well as for his literary reputation . . .

However there are well-informed folk at Penshurst who know of a woman in Elizabethan dress who walks up a staircase. A similar figure haunts the lime walk, though unfortunately no one knows who either of them is, or why they return.

Two famous castles are situated close to Penshurst – Hever and Chiddingstone – and both are haunted. At **Hever** it is the ghost of Anne Boleyn (who lived there) that appears on

Penshurst Place, where one might expect the ethereal form of Sir Philip Sidney: however there are other ghosts here.

Anne Boleyn haunts Hever Castle.

Christmas Eve, on the bridge over the River Eden. **Chiddingstone** also has a female ghost who, riding side-saddle and in eighteenth-century costume, canters up the lane leading to the castle.

It is hard to believe that the suburbs of Kent derive from villages that were isolated rural communities before the Railway Age. Bexley was just such a village, and its life revolved around **Hall Place**, the Manor House. Fortunately this beautiful and historic building has been preserved and carefully restored and now serves as the headquarters of the local library. Three ghosts are supposed to haunt it.

Visitors to Hall Place will immediately notice that it was built in two different periods. The core of the house dates from about 1537 and incorporates much second-hand stone in the fabric. This came from the demolition of nearby abbeys and monasteries. Medieval paint has been discovered on some of the carved stonework. Flint was also used to give the pleasing texture that has withstood

the wear of the centuries so well. In the middle of the seventeenth century the house was enlarged with a new south range being built of brick. This blends well with the earlier work. The house is an unexpected gem.

Its ghosts are varied. Two of them seem to predate the present house. The White Lady of the Tower is the ghost of a young woman who was watching her husband, Thomas At-Hall, a medieval owner of the estate, hunting a stag. Having cornered the beast, it turned on him and gored him to death. His wife fell into a deep faint from which she never recovered and is seen wandering about near the chequered and battlemented tower that stands in the middle of the west wing of the house.

Even more picturesque is the shade of the Black Prince which appeared to residents of Hall Place to foretell death and disaster, either to themselves or to the nation. He is said to have courted his wife, Joan, 'The Fair Maid of Kent', in this neighbourhood, and is quite unmistakeable, being clad in the shiny black armour for which he was famous. Furthermore he is supposed to have stayed at the medieval manor before embarking for Crecy. Lady Limerick, who lived at Hall Place from 1917 until her death in 1943, claimed to have seen the Prince on four occasions. Each time sorrow followed for her family.

Finally, the unhappy spirit of a servant girl haunts the attics, which would have been the servants' sleeping quarter. About 30 years ago a psychic expert identified her restlessness with a child that she was seeking, and thought that she may have killed herself there.

Modern **Southfleet**, lying to the east of Bexley and beyond the M25, is on the fringe of Kent's countryside. The **Rectory** here, no longer housing a rector and divided into two dwellings, once had the reputation of being one of the most haunted houses in the

The appearance of the Black Prince at Hall Place, Bexley, usually foretold family or national disaster. The house also has a White Lady and the unhappy ghost of a servant girl.

south east. Neither of today's residents has seen anything of a ghost.

Parts of the Rectory are medieval, and the ghost is reputed to be that of a nun who was walled up alive in the cellars. She was seen by a succession of incumbents over 100 years or so, a short, dumpy woman dressed in brown carrying rustling papers. Even exorcism by the Bishop of Rochester in 1874 failed to lay her spirit – she subsequently became fond of appearing in the room where the exorcism took place – the Monk's Room – in which the latter event is commemorated in stained glass. There is no explanation as to why she has now ceased to walk.

The **Shipwright's Arms**, near Faversham, must be one of the most remote and inaccessible of English pubs. It is situated at the end of a bumpy track at Hollowshore, where one of the muddy creeks on the southern side of The Swale divides into two. Although many boats are moored in the creek (and quite a few rotting hulks) the nearest habitation is more than a mile away. In effect, the weather-boarded old pub makes an ideal habitat for a ghost, not least because this was once fine smuggling country.

The story of the Hollowshore ghost is of a snowy Christmas Eve long ago, when the landlord, having shut the inn behind the handful of lingering customers, took himself off to bed. As the wind whined and moaned around the creaky old building he gradually became aware of another sound, a

Southfleet Rectory, where a nun died after being walled-up in the cellars.

persistent banging that could be a loose board, or someone beating at the door. After attempting to ignore the noise for some time he eventually roused himself to look out of the casement: sure enough a dim figure could be discerned knocking at the door.

Believing this to be one of the late revellers returning to demand one for the road (or finding himself locked out by his spouse) the landlord shouted that he was abed and not stirring for man or devil, and took himself back to the warmth of his sheets. Dimly, on the threshold of sleep, he realised that the knocking continued, but became less insistent and weaker.

In the morning he found a snow-blanketed corpse on the doorstep, the body of a shipwrecked sailor who had struggled through the snow in sodden clothes to summon help and died of exposure. His ghost haunts the pub, sometimes leaving a lingering smell of decay (last experienced by the present landlady on the night of the hurricane in October 1987).

At the eastern end of the coast of north Kent is the town of Margate, a resort which relies on day-trippers for its livelihood today, but which at the turn of the century was a fashionable seaside town with several luxury hotels. At this time the **Theatre Royal** was an important theatrical venue, a formidable lady named Sarah Thorne presenting her company there. She died in 1899 but her ghost still walks regally down the aisle and climbs the steps onto the stage. Other supernatural activity is attributed to an actor who dramatically killed himself in one of the boxes, his lifeless body falling onto the stage. Even after the

The lonely Shipwright's Arms near Faversham – an ideal setting for a Christmas ghost story.

alterations which included the removal of the boxes all sorts of inexplicable happenings continued, including unnatural lights which flickered about the building.

The **Connaught** at Worthing in Sussex is also haunted: its Grey Lady walks past the dressing rooms after performances, a slim, pale-faced figure with 'dark pools of eyes' which drifts sideways through walls and corridors of this comparatively modern building and sometimes moves objects – bibles, mirrors and even sandbags (what were they doing here and why should she bother with them?). She is a friendly ghost, but stagehands speak of another entity here which is far from harmless and just after the Second World War caused fatal injury by dropping a lighting bar on a lady in the audience. There

have been similar incidents since, where disaster has only narrowly been avoided.

Returning to Kent, **Pluckley** to the west of Ashford has the reputation of being England's most haunted village. Certainly its twelve ghosts come in an interesting variety of forms and haunt in unusual ways. The lords of the manor of Pluckley were the Dering family who supply a White Lady to haunt the side of the old manor house, burned down in 1952, and a unique Red Lady who wanders through the churchyard sorrowfully seeking her unchristened baby. The Derings were supporters of King Charles I and at a time of crisis a Dering Royalist managed to escape through one of the narrow, round-arched windows which are a feature of the village. At the end of the last century Sir Edward

The Theatre Royal at Margate is a venue for two ghosts – the shades of an early impresario, Sarah Thorne, and an actor who killed himself by throwing himself onto the stage from one of the boxes.

A Red Lady wanders through the churchyard of Pluckley, England's most haunted village (right), and (below) the Chequers Inn at Smarden, haunted by a soldier.

Cholmeley Dering put up many new buildings in the village, and altered some old ones, accentuating the 'lucky' windows, new and old, by framing them in white brick.

Pluckley's other ghosts are: an unlucky Cavalier who was caught and killed by Cromwell's men; a smiling monk supposed to have been executed at Tyburn by Henry VIII (was it his saintly smile which aggravated his tormentors to sentence him to the scaffold?); the latter sometimes accompanies the ghostly figure of a lady from Rose Court; in Dicky Buss' Lane there is a phantom schoolmaster who committed suicide; a miller's ghost by the site of the old mill; at the same place, a ghostly gypsy woman who was burned to death, some say by falling asleep while smoking her pipe, though her death may have come about by more sinister means; at appropriately-named Fright Corner near Dering Wood there is a ghostly highwayman who was run through and left pinned to a tree by a prospective victim; Park Wood is patrolled by a spectral colonel; Brick Walk has the ghost of a man who worked in the brickworks and fell into a clay-pit; and a phantom coach-and-four haunts the road to Smarden.

The **Chequers Inn** at Smarden is haunted by a soldier who was murdered there nearly 200 years ago and on the road from Pluckley, at a spot known as Three Went-Way, there is the Devil's Bush where the Evil One himself will appear should you run round it three times – but what the Devil will you do with him?

Follow a straight line through Smarden from Pluckley and you will come to **Sissinghurst Castle**, most celebrated for having been the home of Harold Nicholson and his wife, Vita Sackville-West. They came to the lovely Elizabethan house in 1930, when the grounds were virtually a wilderness and in 30 years created one of the loveliest gardens in England. Sir

Harold often spoke of the spectral figure of a priest that wanders along the fragrant paths. Some say that the unfortunate priest met his end at Sissinghurst long ago bricked up alive for some dreadful, but unnamed, crime but it could be that he seeks revenge on 'Bloody Baker', Sir John Baker whose skill in following the right political trends through three stormy reigns (those of Henry VIII, Edward VI and Queen Mary) created the wealth necessary to build the Castle. He was fortunate in dying just as Elizabeth I came to the throne, for she would have condemned his harassment of protestants when Mary was queen. It was this persecution that earned him the title 'Bloody', and a hundred years after his death many sensational tales were circulated about his deeds. He was accused of rape, murder and pillage, and even though he was probably innocent of these crimes, there is no doubt that he supported the torture and burning of heretics. He was appointed by the Queen to investigate the heresies in the Canterbury diocese, where the subsequent burnings were only outnumbered by those in Middlesex. Little wonder, then, that a saintly figure walks here, perhaps praying for the redemption of Sir John's soul.

The grandest of the castles of Kent is that at **Dover**; 'incomparably the finest and most interesting military building in England', according to John Seymour. King Harold had a stonghold here, but the massive keep dates from Henry II's time. The walls are twenty feet thick. Its ghost is a drummer boy who, at the time of the Napoleonic wars, was waylaid by thieves while carrying money for the garrison. As he refused to hand this over he was set

The ramparts of Dover Castle are walked by a ghostly drummer boy.

upon and killed, his head being completely cut from his body. When the moon is full he walks on the battlements.

Westwards along the coast from Dover, and just into East Sussex, is the ancient town of Rye which provides a

The beautiful Mermaid Inn at Rye, site of a ghostly duel.

suitable array of ghosts for a finale. The **Mermaid Inn** is one of the most picturesque pubs anywhere in England. In the early years of this century its proprietor spoke of sitting up with a medium who was certain that the old building would provide a good ghost. In the way of such things, the medium fell asleep, but the owner witnessed an exciting haunting, in which ghostly protagonists fought a duel which ended with one of them running the other through with his rapier, and then disposing of the corpse beneath the floorboards. One would have thought that this would hardly have gone unnoticed, even in those less than fragrant days.

Many visitors to Rye see the gibbet-cage in the Town Hall, which still contains part of the skull of its last occupant, a butcher named John Breeds who was hanged for murder in 1743. It was a bungled crime, however, for instead of killing his intended victim, James Lamb, the mayor, he murdered the mayor's brother-in-law. It is the unfortunate brother-in-law who is said to haunt the scene of the crime, **Lamb House**, which was later the home of Henry James, novelist.

The gobbling sounds of a flock of turkeys which used to trouble The Lane seem to have died out now – appropriately enough their cries were always heard around Christmas, but there are still reports of apparitions of monks being seen near the chapel of the Austin Friars on Conduit Hill. These are said to emanate from an incident in medieval times when Brother Cantator was bricked up alive because of his profane love for a local girl. He went mad before he died and cursed those responsible for immuring him, and it is these cruel ghosts who may still be seen occasionally, gliding towards the site of the Friary. When air-raid shelters were built in its gardens skeletons were found here, some standing up, and one kneeling.

CENTRAL

ETTINGTON'S GHOSTLY GUESTS

A milestone near the gates of Ettington Park tells you precisely where you are:

Six miles from Shakespeare's town whose fame
Resounds o'er all the earth.
The same from Shipston whose name
Boasts no such poet's birth

Hardly his style, of course, but a fitting pointer to the fact that the great man himself lived in the neighbourhood. And while many a house within cantering distance of Stratford-upon-Avon, be it humble or grand, lays claim to its Shakespearean connections, Ettington was in fact well known to the playwright.

Even in his day Ettington Park bore the hall-marks of manorial style, but what lies beyond the gate today is grandeur itself; settled in several acres of gently sculpted Warwickshire country-side, with its vivid green early summer dressing, it is a gold-tinged Gothic extravagance. And for those who can afford it, this stately home turned country house hotel is the perfect retreat. That is, when they can find it. Rhyming milestones are one thing, but modern signs quite another in this well protected rural environment!

As well as being among the most exclusive of English hotels, Ettington Park has a history that puts it in a league of its own; it is generally accepted to be the only property in the country still in the same family ownership as at the time of the Domesday Book. The Shirley family – now spread throughout the world – gathered at Ettington in 1986 to celebrate 900 years; Major Shirley, who divides his time between homes in Ireland and the Isle of Man, still owns the hotel and much of the land around it.

The hotel was a family home until as recently as 1935; from then on it enjoyed mixed fortunes – variously used as a nursing home, public school, POW residence, hotel, even a disco – until it was devastated by fire in 1980, locked up and left to deteriorate even further. Three years later, with an injection of three and a half million pounds from sufficiently interested parties, this Victorian phoenix began to rise from its ashes. Now beautifully restored, it recaptures the romantic and imaginative fancies of the Shirley responsible for its development from manor into mansion in the mid-nineteenth century, Evelyn Philip Shirley. And, in keeping with present-day expectations it also incorporates every modern facility the leisure-seeking guest could wish for.

It also enjoys a legacy of eccentric and unsettling experiences, some of which serve to shake the nerves of those on the receiving end, but not sufficiently to stir them from such superbly appointed surroundings. Ian Davies has spent the last four years at the Ettington Park Hotel, as head bartender and now house manager, a career that could well have been cut short after just a few weeks when his first brush with the hotel's mischief-maker resulted in a tray of drinks

crashing to the floor. Once a self-confessed sceptic as far as the inexplicable is concerned, Ian is now convinced that there are things at Ettington that defy any logical explanation.

The bar is housed in what was once the library, where but for the well-stocked shelves of bottles you could be forgiven for thinking it was still intended for refreshing nothing more than the mind. Ornately carved bookshelves line this long almost church-like room with its stained glass over the fireplace, and big squashy armchairs invite you to relax and drink in the atmosphere. 'I had been working in the bar for only six weeks', Ian said, 'when I got my first surprise; I was carrying a full tray of drinks over to some guests when a book suddenly flew out of the bookcase beside me, I was so shocked I dropped the lot. No-one was standing near the shelf, but somehow the book was picked up and literally thrown into the room.' Although this happened only once to Ian, he knows of five other occasions when the incident has been repeated.

And even more curious than the flying book itself is the fact that it is always the same title, Sir Walter Scott's *St. Ronan's Well*, Volume I – and inevitably it falls open at the same page, the one carrying this verse by Wordsworth

> . . . *A merry place, 'tis said, in days of yore;*
> *But something ails it now, – the place is cursed.*

There has never been any suggestion of a curse of any kind hanging over Ettington, so one can only imagine the mystery book-thrower has a wicked sense of humour.

Given what we know about the thrower, it could well be the same invisible prankster who deliberately knocked bottles off the bar shelves one evening when Ian was sitting with someone finishing a business meeting. 'It was quite late when this happened, and the first thing we both noticed was that the bar had suddenly turned cold, quite shivery in fact. Then it was as though someone was walking along behind the bar flicking off bottles, not at random but one of each of the beers, the juices, minerals and so on, all the way along.'

◁ Ettington Park Hotel.

△ Ettington's house manager, Ian Davies, in the bar, with the mysterious 'flying' book.

One other specific event stands out in Ian's mind, among many reported minor annoyances that defy any commonsense explanations. There was a snooker room in the hotel and during a late night check-up before retiring, Ian tidied up the cues, put the balls away, and locked up. Back in the reception area he heard the unmistakable clack, clack of a snooker game in action and went back to find three balls on the table.

Having learned more about Ettington's past, one discovers that its solitary splendour has less to do with a carefully selected location than with the Shirley family's position in the English aristocracy; in 1795 the head of the family promoted a bill in Parliament which enabled him to enclose the present park and farmland surrounding it.

The fact that the village of Ettington was then centred on what is now the croquet lawn of the hotel meant that it had to be demolished and the villagers unceremoniously shipped a mile and a half away. It is tempting to think that perhaps one spirited local has made it his everlasting duty to remind Ettington's residents of this rude interruption to community life.

All that remains of banished old Ettington is its church tower, a few crumpled walls, a handful of graves, and a stone cross marking the centre of the village. The handsome tower now demands your attention as you sit sipping drinks less than 50 yards away on the terrace; and the cross stands firm on the striped green baize of the sweeping lawns. Its remnants at least are now appreciated.

On a purely historic note, with Shakespearean interests so close at hand, the church once contained an epitaph to a member of the Underhill family, who held the lease of Ettington manor from 1509 until 1641, that might well have been penned by the Bard himself in his aspiring days. Anthony Underhill died when Shakespeare was 23, and the quality of the verse commemorating his life has a rich, poetic ring to it. Shakespeare knew the family well, and did in fact buy his own home in Stratford-upon-Avon, New Place, from the Underhills for the princely sum of £60.

Two of the graves lying in the shadow of the tower belong to two young children of the Shirley family who drowned in the River Stour, which runs through the estate. They are connected with another strange series of events recorded in the last few years. A couple from Hampshire chose Ettington for a weekend break and were given the Stour Suite, overlooking the meadows leading to the river. During the night the woman was woken by the sound of children crying; she got up and looked out of the window and thought she saw figures. After the couple had returned home their nights continued to be disturbed by the sound of crying children. Eventually they sought help from their local vicar who suggested they went back to the hotel to, as it were, break the spell. This they did, and stayed in the same room as on the previous visit. The night passed without incident.

Of all the 48 rooms at Ettington, the Stour Suite appears to have the strongest association with the past. This is where, for no apparent reason, the lights decide to switch themselves on and off, and the phone play up. It is also one of the few rooms where the Grey Lady has been seen. Ian recalled the night when a guest staying there turned up in the bar in his dressing gown, white as a sheet. He said he had been washing his hair when he looked up and saw, reflected in the mirror, a woman in a grey smock, ruff collar and cap sitting on the side of the bath. This figure has been spotted by hotel staff descending the main staircase, but walking above the level of the stairs at the height of the original flight. She is always dressed the same way, and is thought to be the ghost of a servant girl who fell down the stairs and broke her neck.

This is also one of the few ghosts to have been successfully captured on camera. The photographer was an American visiting Ettington early in the 1980s while it was still closed following the fire. After his film had been developed one of the photographs showed a figure in period costume, looking down from a window. It was kept by the company managing the hotel in an album of before-and-after photographs recording the restoration work, but unfortunately this has gone missing (a case of human carelessness as opposed to spectral devilment) and therefore the picture itself could not be reproduced here. Ian Davies is among the many people who have seen the photograph and as far as he is concerned it shows, quite clearly, the Lady in Grey.

◁ Ettington's beautiful library, now the bar.

△ The Shirley family crest. The family have owned Ettington since the time of the Domesday Book.

Herne the Hunter with a pack of spectral hounds.

Windsor Castle was one of the innumerable strongholds put up by William the Conqueror to consolidate his conquest of England. In the later years of his reign it had a dual purpose, also serving as a royal hunting lodge. Succeeding monarchs altered, added and improved to such an extent that today it is the largest lived-in castle in the world.

With such a long history of royal occupation it would be surprising if the castle were to be without illustrious ghosts, and indeed throughout there have been continual reports of apparitions and other phenomena (though predictably today's powers-that-be categorically deny that Windsor is haunted). The oldest of these frequents the Great Park rather than the Castle, and is supposed to have been seen by King Henry VIII himself. It is the frightening figure of Herne the Hunter, whose story is usually said to date from the reign of Richard II. Herne was a forester who saved the King's life during a hunt, but in the process, was fatally injured

Lady Hoby's ghost is said to leave this portrait empty when she walks at Bisham Abbey.

himself. As the King and his attendants tried to help the dying man a magician appeared who offered to save his life. He tied a great set of antlers to Herne's head and asked King Richard that if he recovered Herne should be made chief huntsman. The King agreed to this, and in time Herne took up his new position. For some reason Herne failed in his new post, and was dismissed by the King. In despair he hanged himself from one of the massive oak trees which was known as Herne's Oak until 1796 when it was cut down by mistake. The ghost of Herne, complete with antlers, used to appear swinging from the tree on which he died. Its appearance was said to herald a disaster for England, though it must be said that we have not been without calamities since 1796.

Inside the walls of the Castle itself there is a multitude of ghosts, some of the blood royal, others more mundane. In the cloisters near the Deanery the hesitant dragging footsteps of a lame man have occasionally been heard, accompanied by the groans of someone in severe pain. Since the grossly overweight Henry VIII used the cloisters for exercise when his ulcerated legs finally prevented him from riding, these sounds are said to emanate from his spirit. He died at Westminster on 28 January 1547, but is buried here, in St George's Chapel.

His marriage to Anne Boleyn (and divorce from Catherine of Aragon) brought about the final split with the Pope. However Anne's triumph was short-lived: she was queen for just three years before being executed for treasonable adultery at the Tower of London in 1536. Surprisingly, her ghost shares the same locality as that of her husband, appearing at one of the windows of the cloisters.

Their daughter, who became Queen Elizabeth I, is another of the regal ghosts of Windsor. She haunts the Royal Library (not open to the public), and appears dressed in black in an upper gallery. In her time there was a way out of the building from an alcove in the gallery onto a terrace overlooking the Thames. A famous sighting of this ghost occurred in 1897 when Lieutenant Glynn, an officer of the guard, saw it walk through the library. Fifty years or so previously the apparition had been seen in the same place by Queen Victoria's eldest daughter, later the Empress Frederick.

The reign of George III lasted for 60 years, but for the last 30, the king suffered from intermittent madness and took little part in government. Much of this time he spent at Windsor, where he delighted in taking the salute of the guard. Immediately after his death, the duty guard saluted a vague figure at the window where he normally stood: they had honoured his ghost.

Up-river from Windsor, just outside Marlow, is **Bisham Abbey**, now the National Sports Centre. Its remorseful ghost is Lady Elizabeth Hoby, a formidable woman (Edith Sitwell

The effigy of Lady Elizabeth Hoby in Bisham church, kneeling on the recumbent body of her son.

Bisham Abbey, home of Lady Elizabeth Hoby, confidante of Queen Elizabeth I

described her as being 'a pest of outstanding quality') who was a confidante of Queen Elizabeth and lived to be 81, a great age in those days. She died in 1609 and was the wife of the builder of the house, Sir Philip Hoby. She haunts the house because of her cruelty to the son of her second marriage, William, who she is supposed to have killed in anger over his blotted copybooks. In about 1844 some very untidy and besmirched copybooks were found between the joists by workmen carrying out alterations. Two remarkable features of this haunting are that on occasion she appears to step out of the frame of her portrait that hangs in the Great Hall. In this she is painted in a black dress with a very white face: in haunting mode she appears as a black and white negative to the portrait – with white dress and black face. The painting has often caused problems to galleries when it has been taken from

'Wild' Darrell was the wicked squire of Littlecote House, scene of an infanticide.

Bisham to be exhibited elsewhere.

Littlecote House is actually in Wiltshire, but is within a mile of the Berkshire boundary, close to Hungerford. Its ghost makes certain that one of the great scandals of Elizabethan England is never forgotten. In 1575 it was the home of William Darrell, whose family had lived at Littlecote since 1415. One dark night he sent for a midwife from a nearby village. She was taken blindfold to the house and conducted to an upstairs room where a woman was in labour. When the baby was born a nobleman snatched it from the midwife's arms and threw it to the back of the roaring fire. He then thrust a purse at her, and ordered that she should be driven home, still blindfolded. Astutely, she counted the stairs as she left the upstairs room, and shortly before had surreptitiously snipped a piece of bed curtain after the dreadful event had taken place.

'Courtiers', Clifton Hampden (left), is haunted by the ghost of an unhappy young girl.

The next day she went to the local magistrate and told him the story. From her description it seemed that Littlecote was the likely house, and when the stairs were counted and tallied, and the piece of material matched the hole in the bed curtain, Darrell was arrested. He was already known as 'Wild' Darrell because of his debauched lifestyle, so the barbaric story came as no surprise to the Elizabethan public. However they were scandalised when he was acquitted of the murder, having bribed the judge, Sir John Popham. After this there were few to mourn when Darrell's horse threw him fourteen years later and the squire of Littlecote broke his neck (it was said that the horse reared at the sight of the baby's ghost). The property then passed to Sir John Popham, apparently this being one of the terms of the bribe.

The incident was reported by John Aubrey a century later in *Brief Lives* where he states that the child's mother was Darrell's wife's maid. There was a stronger local belief, however, that she was his sister which would have given a stronger motive for Darrell's drastic action. There are several historical inconsistencies in the story, but the belief in the ghosts that it gave rise to remained strong throughout the succeeding centuries, even being mentioned by Sir Walter Scott in *Rokeby*.

Littlecote's ghosts include the Burning Babe, which appeared at the place where Darrell was killed (this spot, known as Darrell's Stile is now haunted by Wild William himself, with phantom hounds; he is also supposed to appear at Littlecote with coach and horses when an heir is about to die); a sad-faced woman, holding a baby, who walks in the room where the murder took place; a woman in the garden (the most frequently seen ghost in modern times); a lady carrying a rushlight; and Gerald Lee Bevin, who was a tenant of Littlecote in the 1920s when he served seven years for a famous City swindle.

The small village of Clifton Hampden lies a few miles to the south of Oxford, between Abingdon and Dorchester. Here there is a house called **The Courtiers**, where a beautiful, tragically unhappy girl named Sarah Fletcher hanged herself on 7 June 1799.

'Roadie' ghosts are a constantly-recurring phenomenon, reported from all over the world, and can take various forms. Many drivers on the A45 Coventry to Rugby road have been terrified by the sight of a lorry speeding towards them on the wrong side of the road – then, just as a crash seems inevitable, the lorry vanishes.

Sarah was married to a naval officer who was not only unfaithful to her but was proposing a bigamous marriage to his lover, a wealthy heiress. His wife learned of this, and arrived at the church just in time to stop the ceremony. Terrible scenes followed which ended with Captain Fletcher storming out to rejoin his ship which was setting sail for the West Indies. Poor Sarah hanged herself from the curtain rail of her four-poster shortly afterwards, and is buried in the Abbey Church at Dorchester, a plain slab with touching words marking the spot (presumably the Coroner's verdict of lunacy allowed her burial inside the church).

Since this melancholy event nearly 200 years ago many people have been affected by the presence of Sarah's spirit. Its influence has been so strong that at least two have confessed to falling in love with her, one of them a clergyman. He actually saw her ghost '... she seemed tremendously alive. Her eyes were filled with tears and I felt as if she had come to seek my love and pity'. Not everybody shared the reverend gentleman's passion for Sarah, and if she felt that she was not

receiving all their sympathy she could be malevolent, which is why few tenants stayed long at The Courtiers. Later it became a school, and was subsequently divided into cottages. It is now a private residence, considerably altered since Sarah's day.

Cumnor Place lies on the other, western, side of Abingdon, and, like Littlecote, was the scene of an Elizabethan *cause célèbre*. In 1560 Robert Dudley, Earl of Leicester, was embroiled in a passionate affair with the Queen. To him, if not to her, it seemed that the only obstacle to a royal marriage was the existence of his wife, Amy Robsart, the daughter of a humble, but wealthy, Norfolk squire.

Although Amy was uneducated she was no fool, and soon learnt of the reason for her husband's neglect. Putting two and two together she also realised that he would very much like to be rid of her. Thus she became very careful of what she ate and drank and took herself off to the security of a country retreat, Cumnor Place.

Here she met her death on a rare occasion when she was alone in the house (she had sent the servants off to

Amy Robsart died in mysterious circumstances at Cumnor Place and her ghost proved so troublesome that it took twelve clergy to exorcise it.

Abingdon Fair). When they returned they found her at the foot of the stairs, her neck broken. Neither the Queen nor Dudley seemed unduly surprised at the news of Amy's death. Within a short time her ghost was seen on the stairs at Cumnor, which the public took to be a sign that her death had not been accidental. Thus Dudley's aspirations to the throne were ended, but the ghost continued to haunt. The Tudor house was demolished in 1810, and it was hoped that this would put an end to the visitation, but it proved to be a vain hope, for Amy took to walking in the park instead. Eventually twelve clergymen performed a service of exorcism intended to lay the ghost in a small pond. Since then there have been few convincing sightings of Amy though villagers will tell of meeting her. The new Cumnor Place is not generally open to visitors.

Amy Robsart's ghost is also claimed to appear at **Worcester College**, Oxford. The University, as might be expected, is well haunted, both by obscure academics and by important historical figures such as Archbishop Laud. He was Chancellor of the University before being decapitated for treason at the Tower of London in 1645. He appears headless and legless (or almost) in the library of St John's College. The reason why only the upper parts of his legs appear is that the floor level of the library has been raised since he built it.

Libraries are favourite places for the unquiet spirits of Oxford. Sir Thomas Bodley, founder of the famous University Library, haunts **Merton College Library**, while that of **Queen's** has an interesting modern ghost, that of Cuthbert Shields, the *nom de plume* of a cranky clergyman who believed that he was the reincarnation of St Cuthbert, and died at the turn of the century. He had no connections with the college, but nevertheless left the library a collection of papers in a box which was only to be opened 50 years after his death.

This instruction was obeyed in the 1950s, and the librarian left the uninteresting letters, religious tracts, etc., lying on his desk overnight. A colleague letting himself into the library late in the evening was startled to see a clergyman in old-fashioned dress

St John's College, Oxford, is haunted by the ghost of Archbishop Laud, beheaded in 1645. It is said he has been seen bowling his head across the floor of the library.

Queen's College, Oxford, where a ghostly clergyman visits the library.

studying the documents. Since then the ghost of Cuthbert Shields has been seen on many occasions, usually in the upper library at times when there is no daylight. The present Keeper of the Archives has written to us:

The occasion I remember was about twelve years ago. Going into the library one evening I found the then assistant librarian, Mrs Penson, in a state of great alarm; she asked me who the person was who had entered the library just before I did. I said there was no such person, which was the case: the library door is visible for a long way before one reaches it. Mrs P said, however, that an elderly man in a black coat had entered just before me, and had walked up the library. She had left her desk, from which there is a very limited view of the library floor, but when she got to a position from which she could see more, there was nobody in sight.

She was so alarmed that I, and an undergraduate who entered whilst we were talking, volunteered to search the whole library, upper, lower and even the basement stacks. This we did, and found nobody there. It would not have been possible, in the time available between Mrs P leaving her desk and my entering, for a person to have reached the steps, at the far end of the ground floor, which give access to the upper or basement library, and there is nowhere in the building a person can hide. I only took the matter seriously because Mrs Penson (who died a few years ago) was far from being an imaginative person, or prone to 'see things'. I have had a quick look at the collection of letters in the library: they are extremely dull, and show, if they show anything, that the author was somewhat off his head.

Many visitors to Oxford choose to stay out of the city in one of the lovely old market towns close by, such as Woodstock or Thame. The **Bear Hotel** is one of Woodstock's old coaching inns, now a luxury hotel belonging to Trust House Forte. It stands close to the gates of Blenheim Palace, but it is not a Churchill or Duke who haunts the hotel, apparently, but the ghost of a workman who fell from its roof (some say he was pushed). This

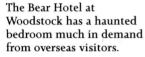

The Bear Hotel at Woodstock has a haunted bedroom much in demand from overseas visitors.

'Mad Maud' is the unfortunate nun who haunts Weston Manor Hotel's (left) best bedroom though she disturbs only a few of those who sleep in the room (above).

occurred about 300 years ago, since when Room 12 has had the reputation of being haunted, though few people today refuse to sleep in the room, and those that do are seldom disturbed by supernatural activities. The last occasion was about eight years ago when an American couple said that they saw a shadow moving about the room and heard strange noises.

Just to the east of Woodstock, at the village of Weston on the Green, is **Weston Manor**, a beautiful and historic Tudor building that has been a hotel since 1945. An abbey was founded here early in the twelfth century, and this gives us the story of 'Mad Maud', a nun who led the monks astray and ended by being burned at the stake. She haunts the best bedroom in the hotel, the lovely Oak Room, which some guests have found to have an atmosphere of lingering malevolence. Weston Manor also has a phantom coach and horses which drives up to the yard at the back of the house, and the ghost of a maid who died after falling from the tower.

The **George and Dragon** at West Wycombe has the sad ghost of a former barmaid named Sukie. In the eighteenth century West Wycombe was notorious as being the home of Sir Francis Dashwood, the founder of the Hell-Fire Club, devoted to orgies and

The George and Dragon at West Wycombe has the restless spirit of a former barmaid, betrayed by a member of the Hell-Fire Club.

debauchery. He had the golden ball built atop the church where he played cards with his cronies and could look down on his park, which he had landscaped to follow the contours of a female body. Members of his club used to frequent the George and Dragon, their wealth and conversation captivat-

West Wycombe Caves, where the barmaid from the George and Dragon slipped and fell.

ing young Sukie, who did not lack for admirers in the public bar. These latter decided to play a practical joke on her. Knowing that she particularly admired one of Dashwood's younger followers, they forged a note from him suggesting an elopement, begging her to meet him at the caves. Wearing a white dress so that she would be ready for instant matrimony she arrived in the caves at the appointed time only to be met by a crowd of jeering yokels.

What happened next is problematical. It may be that her tongue and temper provoked them into stoning her, or she may have simply slipped on the slimy floor of the cave and split her head open. Either way, she was taken back to the inn badly injured and died there soon after. Thus she is still seen about the hostelry, a beautiful girl in a white dress, who usually seems to vanish by a particular bedroom door. The present landlord is sceptical about the supernatural, but nonetheless admits to having heard the sound of a woman sobbing on the night he took over the pub, though he knew there were no guests staying. Also, like his predecessor at the George and Dragon, he has great difficulty in keeping address books: three have disappeared in the short time he has been there.

Today **Great Missenden Abbey** is an adult education centre with residential accommodation. Although its black monks seem to have been infamous for the ways in which they flouted their vows shortly before the Dissolution of the monasteries, it is the ghost of a lady dressed in crinolines which most recently disturbed two lady residents as they read their newspapers by the main staircase. Both agreed that the figure that they had seen floating down the stairs and out through the door was indeed supernatural.

The **White Hart** in the High Street at Chalfont St Peter is haunted by a phantom fiddler, the ghost of a former 'guvnor' of the pub, Donald Ross, land-

A lady in crinolines has been seen recently descending the staircase (left) at Great Missenden Abbey (below).

lord there in the 1920s. He used to enjoy giving impromptu performances on his violin to customers, and had done so on the night he died, standing in front of the huge semi-circular chimney-breast, the most notable feature of the sixteenth-century inn. The landlord, Mr Dan Altass, says that one version of the story is that the only people who hear the music of fiddler Ross are landlords who fail to run the White Hart properly. Since he has never heard of anything he assumes that Ross approves of the present regime, though he says that when a relief couple took over for a fortnight in 1989 the violin was heard together with the noise of barrels

A ghostly fiddler, a former landlord, haunts the White Hart at Chalfont St Peter.

The ruins of Minster Lovell Hall where Lord Lovell was entombed in a secret room.

being rolled across the floor of the cellar. When their two weeks were up the 'temps' left saying that they never wished to see the White Hart again.

Chalfont lies at the foot of the Chilterns, chalky hills which arc across central England north of the Thames. To the west, beyond the Oxfordshire plain, are the Cotswolds, forming another embracing arc. No other part encapsulates so well the rare beauty of the English countryside. The honey-coloured limestone of the buildings in the villages, nestling amidst the folds of the wooded hills, made the Cotswolds uniquely beautiful. Its towns and villages have more than their fair share of history, too, and of course ghosts follow closely in the wake of historical events.

The picturesque ruins of **Minster Lovell Hall** stand close to Burford, a lovely old town that can claim to be the south-eastern gateway to the Cotswolds. Minster Lovell is haunted by Lord Lovell who, in 1487, foolishly chose to support the cause of Lambert Simnel, the pretender to the throne. Simnel's uprising was quashed at the Battle of Stoke and Lord Lovell then fled to Minster Lovell and concealed himself in a secret room at the Hall.

He was cared for by one faithful servant, the only person to know his whereabouts. Unfortunately this servant died unexpectedly, and Lord Lovell remained in his hiding-place until 1718 when his corpse was discovered by workmen. The skeleton was seated at a table and at its feet were the bones of his dog. The impact of this tale is slightly diluted by a similar one which also belongs to Minster Lovell. This tells of a young girl who hid in an oak chest during a game of hide-and-seek. Her triumph in escaping discovery turned to panic when she found herself locked in and slowly suffocating. Her spirit also haunts the ruins of the Hall.

Langston Priory at Kingham, to the north of Burford, is now an old people's home, though previously it had been a hotel. Perhaps it was the activities of the ghost which forced it out of business, for in the 1960s it used to appear every ten days or so, a white shape that could have been a nun wearing a head-dress. Room 1 was particularly favoured by this mysterious entity, which would announce its presence by a polite cough and then proceed in its progress with shuffling footsteps. The foundations of the building are very ancient, and a secret passageway is supposed to link it with Bruern Abbey.

The **Black Horse Inn** at Cirencester has tangible evidence of a haunting. In 1933 the niece of the landlord woke to find her room bathed in an unnatural light: a gentle rustling noise came from a corner. Then she saw the unpleasant face of a stout old lady, who glided across the room towards her with an evil expression. Not surprisingly, the girl screamed, whereupon the ghost vanished, walking through the opposite wall of the room. Panelling had recently been put up on this side, concealing the outside wall and a window. When a search was made of the room the name 'James' was found newly scratched into the glass of the window.

Langston Priory, where the ghost announced its presence with a cough.

The mysterious writing on the window at the Black Horse Inn, Cirencester.

The landlord swore that it had not been there before, and felt so strongly about the incident that, with the help of the local newspaper, a medium was called in to explain the ghost's presence.

She was brought to the inn ignorant of the circumstances of the haunting, but soon a remarkable change came to her posture. As she was shown the rooms she slowly began to assume the

crabbed, bent gait of an old woman, like that seen by the landlord's niece. She was soon able to explain that the old woman had lived here with an old man, whom she had injured in some way. Thus she was earth-bound, but harmless, and would be easy to lay.

The exorcism was simple – at three o'clock in the afternoon on the third day of the month, three white flowers were laid in Room 3, where the medium thought most evil resided. The door was sealed and the room left for three days, and this successfully drove away the lingering spirit.

The village of Uley is situated on the western edge of the Cotswolds, over-looking the River Severn. **Owlpen Manor** stands on the edge of Uley and was the home of refugee children during the Second World War. At the time it was owned by an American lady, and on the morning after the children's arrival she met them for the first time, at breakfast. She was puzzled

when they asked her why she wasn't wearing the lovely clothes that she had on the previous evening. Gradually it dawned on her that they were describ-ing a costume of long ago. Owlpen is supposed to be haunted by Margaret of Anjou who stayed in the house after the Battle of Tewkesbury in 1471. Prince Edward, her brave eighteen-year-old son, was killed in the conflict, and she suffered years of captivity before dying in Anjou in 1482.

Prestbury, a village which manages to retain its identity despite the prox-imity of Cheltenham, rivals Pluckley, in Kent, in the number of its ghosts. It has: a Black Abbot who appears three times a year – at Christmas, Easter and on All Souls' Day; a Cavalier on horseback (a Royalist dispatch rider who was ambushed and executed); a phantom shepherd with ghostly flock of sheep; Mrs Preece's Ghost in Mill Lane; 'Old Moses', a ghost with racing connec-tions; and a malevolent spirit which

A royal ghost, Queen Margaret of Anjou, haunts Owlpen Manor. She stayed here in 1471 after the Battle of Tewkesbury.

haunts a house called Cleeve Corner, close to the church, where a murder was once committed.

North and west, now, to Shelsey Walsh beyond Worcester where the **Court-house** is haunted by Lady Lightfoot's ghost. She was imprisoned and murdered here and returns in a phantom coach drawn by four fiery horses to drive straight through the house uttering the most dreadful shrieks. England's most romantic, and spooky, ruin is situated nearby.

The Welsh Marches, the scene of centuries of bloody strife, were once haunted by a hideous army of the dead or *Herlethingi* until the locals pelted the silent warriors with arrows and spears, since when they seem not to have reappeared. The ghost that haunts **Hergest Court** is supposed to have inspired Conan Doyle to write *The Hound of the Baskervilles*. Sir Thomas Vaughan, known as Black Vaughan, was taken prisoner and beheaded in 1483. His devoted black bloodhound seized his head as it fell and made off with it, since when head and hound have often been seen, both at the Court and on the road to Kington church.

The great border stronghold of Ludlow has an excellent selection of ghosts. **Ludlow Castle** itself is haunted by Marion de Bruyère who was with the castle garrison holding out against a besieging force. Her lover was one of those attacking the castle, but nonetheless it was their custom still to meet, she allowing him to climb up a rope to her chamber. However after one such tryst he neglected to pull up the rope, and his colleagues were able to use it to capture the stronghold. Poor Marion, distraught at betrayal, seized her lover's sword and ran him through, and then threw herself from the battlements. Her ghost walks in the Hanging Tower where laboured breathing is also heard.

Other Ludlow ghosts include a grey-haired lady in a dressing-gown who frequents the rectory and churchyard,

Black Vaughan of Hergest Court.

Sir Thomas Holte of Aston Hall, Birmingham, whose daughter haunts the Hall.

and a soldier named Joe (which seems unlikely, or was he an early GI?) who was executed at the castle in 1553 and returns to haunt the ancient **Globe Inn.**

Birmingham would seem to be an unlikely place for a respectable ghost to play a part in the country's heritage, but **Aston Hall** is proud to be full of very active spirits and the staff enjoy telling visitors of their scary experiences. The rather plain exterior of the house, in red brick, gives no hint of the grandeur of the interior which is breathtaking, rivalling that of Hatfield or Audley End which are of the same period.

Aston Hall was begun in 1618 for Sir John Holte who previously lived at Duddeston Hall. An unhappy story followed him from this house for he was supposed to have run his cook through with the spit and then buried him beneath the floor of the cellar. In 1606 Holte successfully sued a neighbour for spreading this tale which was

revived later when Sir John actively supported the King against Parliament. Most other West Midlanders were ardent Roundheads and such stories (often incorporating ghosts) were useful propaganda. In 1643 Aston Hall was besieged and later taken by force, twelve men being killed in the action.

The portrait of Sir Thomas Holte at Aston Hall shows him standing in front of the newly-built Hall, a sinister figure, looking as though he could well have killed his cook after the serving of a flat soufflé. His cruelty to his daughter Mary inspires one of Aston's ghost stories. She was locked into the Tower Room after attempting to elope, and was kept there for sixteen years before becoming insane and dying. Her ghost, grey but 'solid looking', has been seen by three visitors in the last two years.

There is also the apparition of Mrs Walker, who was housekeeper at Aston in the year of Sir Thomas' death, 1654,

and has been seen by many of the staff wearing a green dress with a high collar. Mr Phillip Bettam, one of the supervisors, saw her in 1988 when he was showing a group of visitors round. She was sitting in an old and fragile chair and he was about to admonish her when she vanished. Another member of staff with Mr Bettam at the time saw his complexion blanch but did not know the reason for it, not being able to see the ghost. When Mr Bettam was chatting about the incident later with a retired member of staff he learned that, unknown to him, the same figure had been seen on previous occasions.

Aston's third ghost is that of Dick, an unhappy houseboy who was accused of theft and hanged himself in the servants' quarters at the top of the house. This room is still known as 'Dick's Garret', and one of the caretakers has seen his ghost swinging there.

The Tower Room at Aston Hall, where Sir Thomas Holte imprisoned his daughter.

'Dick's Garret', which is haunted by the ghost of an unhappy houseboy.

The chair at Aston Hall in which the apparition of a former housekeeper has been seen.

Clopton House, now converted into apartments, has altered since the time of Charlotte Clopton, entombed alive in Stratford church.

Coughton Court (right) has a Pink Lady who visits the room in the south west turret where this sword (above) was found beneath the floorboards during eighteenth-century alterations. The sword was claimed to have been used by Sir Francis Smith at the Battle of Edge Hill, where he bravely rescued the King's Standard.

The physical centre of England is said to lie at Meriden, a village six miles to the west of Coventry. Most people would agree that its spiritual heart belongs to Stratford-upon-Avon, a nearby town inseparable from its connections with William Shakespeare, whose fascination with ghosts is evident from his work. The playwright knew **Clopton House** well: he bought the semi-derelict Great House in Stratford from the Clopton family in 1597 and, having restored it as 'New Place', used it as his residence until his death there in 1616. Shakespeare would have known the macabre story of Charlotte Clopton, and it has been suggested that it inspired the final scenes of *Romeo and Juliet*.

Charlotte was a beautiful young woman who was an early victim of an outbreak of plague when it came to Stratford in 1564. She lived at Clopton House on the outskirts of the town, and as soon as the physician confirmed her death she was hurried off for burial in the family vault at Holy Trinity Church. Within two weeks her mother was also dead from the contagion and the vault reopened to received her remains. To the horror of the pall-bearers Charlotte was found at the entrance, her body bearing the wounds which she had bitten into her own flesh to relieve the agonies of thirst while locked in the tomb. Her spirit is said to walk at Clopton House from where she was taken for premature burial.

In the same year Margaret Clopton was born. She too suffered an unhappy fate, perhaps foreshadowing that of Ophelia. Denied the hand in marriage of the man she loved, she drowned herself in the stream that connected the fish-ponds at the back of the house. Her ghost also used to frequent the house, as did that of a priest, who was murdered in a tiny concealed room at the top of the house that served as an oratory. The blood shed by the unfortunate priest formed a stain that endured over many centuries. Clopton House has now been converted into luxury apartments so it is not known whether the stain still exists, though there are rumours that some ghostly activity continues there.

Coughton Court, to the west, has not suffered this fate and remains open to the public. It has been the home of the Throckmorton family since the early fifteenth century. They suffered greatly for their catholicism, but remained constant to their religion through two dangerous centuries. Throckmorton daughters were wives to Gunpowder Plot conspirators, and the house has genuine priest-holes. Coughton has long been haunted by a Pink Lady who walks from the Tapestry Bedroom, through the panelled dining room, and down the main stairs. One theory is that she is one of the daughters married to a conspirator. They spent many anxious hours in the dining room waiting for news of the outcome of the Plot.

Wootton Hall, at curiously-named Wootton Wawen, was also a Catholic house, the home of the Smith family, one of whom was made Viscount Carrington in 1643 but died in exile, murdered by his valet. It was said that his heart was returned in an oak casket to Wootton and in fact just such a casket was found in the dairy in 1861, containing a shrivelled human heart. For some time this part of the building had been badly haunted, and it was hoped that the discovery of the heart would bring an end to this. In fact the disturbances have continued, spasmodically, right up to the present day but as the presences are all benign they are regarded by the owner as a part of the fittings.

Wootton Hall is haunted by Mrs Fitzherbert, mistress of the Prince Regent.

The portrait of Mrs Fitzherbert at Wootton Hall.

Wootton's most important ghost is the shade of Mrs Fitzherbert, mistress (and probable wife) of the Prince Regent. She once lived here and still manifests herself as a fragrance, sweet and sickly, almost like Blue Grass. There is also a Grey Lady, thought to be the spirit of a servant girl who was killed and secretly buried after having an affair with one of the family. Her remains were discovered when alterations were being made during the middle of the last century.

Warwick Castle has a 'Bogey Room' which is haunted by Sir Fulke Greville, Elizabethan courtier, poet, and Chancellor, murdered in London by his valet who, enraged at learning that he did not benefit from his master's will, stabbed him while helping him to dress. Sir Fulke took a month to die, an agonising time especially since the surgeons of the day insisted that the best medication was to pack the wound with mutton fat.

I was once taking photographs in the castle when there was a power cut and I had to walk through the Bogey Room in semi-darkness. There was a head-high miasma, like cigarette smoke yet odourless, which struck the face with an icy touch – but I have to admit that I did know of the reputation of the room so the experience could be explained by auto-suggestion.

One of the photographers concerned in this book described **Guy's Cliffe** as being the creepiest place he had visited. The ruined mansion stands high above the River Avon on the outskirts of Warwick amidst a jungle of unkempt vegetation. It takes its name from the legendary Guy of Warwick, a bloodthirsty tenth-century hero who having performed countless brave deeds to win the hand of Felice, daughter of the Earl of Warwick, abandoned her in order to live a saintly life as a hermit in a cave above the river. Although Felice provided Guy with

The 'Bogey Room' at Warwick Castle (right), where the presence of Sir Fulke Greville (above) is still felt.

alms, she only discovered his identity after he had died, whereupon she jumped to her death from the precipice above the river.

Many people comment on the unnatural chill of the roofless rooms of the mansion, but there are other mysteries here too. The chapel (now a Masonic Temple) adjoins the ruined mansion and is, at least, sheltered by a good roof. It dates from 1422, and its most remarkable feature is the eight-foot-high figure of Guy which was carved from the living rock and predates the chapel. Beneath the floor is an undercroft which provides

Guy's Cliffe may well be the eeriest location featured in these pages.

committee rooms for the Masons who own the chapel. Below this is a dungeon, reached by six steps which end in a platform ten feet above the floor, the entire chamber being hewn from solid rock. Here a prisoner would be utterly forsaken, no breath of air or gleam of light reaching him as he lay on the damp rock floor without hope of escape. Perhaps it is the tormented souls of those once confined and forgotten here that give Guy's Cliffe its forbidding reputation.

Piers Gaveston, favourite of Edward II, was beheaded on Blacklow Hill

The weather-beaten statue of Guy of Warwick stands in the chapel at Guy's Cliffe.

The stables of Little Lawford Hall, haunt of One-handed Boughton who resisted exorcism.

The spirit of One-Handed Boughton was finally confined in a glass phial.

close to Guy's Cliffe in 1312. Reports of a ghostly procession ascending the hill have been commonplace over the centuries, the tinkling of bells on the horses being most frequently heard (the execution procession was decorated ornately to mock Gaveston's love of finery).

Little Lawford Hall is situated on the outskirts of Rugby. Only the stables of the old house stand today: the latter was haunted by the ghost of One-handed Boughton, an Earl of Boughton who was owner in Elizabethan times.

Lord Boughton got his nickname (devilishly appropriate, as we shall see) when he was caught in his park during a thunderstorm. He was struck to the ground by a terrible bolt of lightning, and his servants all thought that he was killed as they approached his prone figure. To their astonishment he sat up, apparently little the worse for his ordeal except that his hand had been completely burnt off.

There was much talk of his deliverance having been supernatural, a view reinforced when he began showing symptoms of a personality change: having been formerly mild and inoffensive be became violent and unpredictable.

Their suspicions were confirmed after his death. The room where he died became violently haunted by all manner of spirits while the estate was terrorised by a ghostly coach and six with a one-handed passenger. The disturbances became so bad that in 1752 an elaborate exorcism took place involving twelve clergymen, each holding a lighted candle. They mounted the stairs and approached the bedchamber without untoward incident, but as the door was opened a storm of evil was unleashed, threshing about the room and extinguishing all but one of the candles of exorcism. The remaining candle was held by Parson Hall, who kept his nerve and was able to commit the restless spirit in a glass phial which was thrown into a nearby marlpit, though he was forced to allow it to roam abroad 'for a little season'.

Thus the ghost was quietened but not finally tamed. Tragedy followed the family, and soon after the exorcism the young heir to the title was cruelly murdered. In 1784 the Hall was pulled down and for a time the ghost was quiet but it revived early in the nineteenth century when a strange glass phial was dredged from a pond close to the site of the Old Hall. This remained in the family, passed down

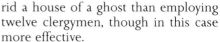

The grounds of Fawsley Park (above) and its ruined Dower House (below) are haunted by a green huntsman.

from father to son through the generations, until it was finally reburied, encased in cement. The owner of Little Lawford Hall today says that when he moved in there was definitely a 'presence' in one of the rooms. However his four children made such a racket through their childhood that the ghost fled, and has never returned. This seems an even more expensive way to rid a house of a ghost than employing twelve clergymen, though in this case more effective.

The county of Northampton, to the east, has a fine array of ghosts, to be found not only in the county's historic houses; a number of them frequent its pubs and hotels.

Fawsley Park, about three miles south of Daventry, is one of Northamptonshire's hidden treasures. The Hall, dating from the sixteenth century, stood empty and derelict for many years but is now handsomely restored. The beautiful medieval church stands between the lakes (where there was once a village until Capability Brown was engaged to create a landscaped park) and has monuments to the Knightley family who lived at the Hall through three centuries. The Knightley Way, a long-distance footpath, passes through the Park, passing close to the **Dower House**, an ivy-clad ruin which has been abandoned since 1702. The reasons for its being haunted have long been forgotten, but this is the ideal setting and sure enough a ghostly huntsman dressed in green appears on New Year's Eve to foretell the death of anyone foolish enough to be about to see him.

In medieval times Northampton was a town of considerable size and importance, but unhappily it suffered a disastrous fire in 1675 when nearly all of its ancient buildings perished. One of these was a pub known as the Plasterers' Arms, which, when it was rebuilt in 1720, was renamed the **Black Lion**. As it is one of the oldest of Northampton's inns it is hardly surprising that it is haunted, though the cause for this is not known. Could an inmate have suffered a terrible death in the fire? Or does the ghost rage against a senseless change of name (scope here for an epidemic of hauntings today when brewers or landlords forsake tried and tested names like the Black Lion for fanciful modern ones every time they put down a new carpet). For all that, the Black Lion has been the scene of persistent supernatural activity for some years – lights being turned on and off, sounds of footsteps across empty rooms, and a cellar which seems to generate a sense of evil and puts the Fear of God into dogs – a succession of landlords have reported such goings-on without discovering a reason for them.

The **Knight's Lodge** is a seventeenth-century manor house at Corby which is now a pub. Situated near the site of a Cistercian monastery, Pipewell Abbey, it is fairly predictable that a ghostly monk should be a regular in the Lancelot Lounge. Yet can this be the same ghost that gave a Sunday tabloid a gleeful headline during the regime of a previous landlord ('Randy Ghost Tickles Pub Girls')? The article went on to describe how the barmaids were persistently being molested by the unseen ghost, which enjoyed lifting their skirts, pinching bottoms, and tickling various parts with something that felt like a feather duster. The present landlord has only been a year or so in the pub, and has never heard a customer or member of staff complain about sexual harassment from a paranormal source.

The Black Lion in Northampton (left) has a presence but no-one knows a reason for its being there!

The Knight's Lodge at Corby has a lecherous ghost that made the Sunday headlines.

An altogether superior ghost haunts the **Talbot Hotel** at Oundle. This is the spectre of Mary, Queen of Scots, who is supposed to haunt the old coaching inn because the staircase where she stood at Fotheringhay Castle when she was told that she was to be executed there the following day, was brought to the Talbot (perhaps illegally) when the Castle was dismantled by her son,

Mary, Queen of Scots haunts Oundle's Talbot Hotel.

For seven years a bloody murder was re-enacted at Rockingham Castle.

James I. Mary reappears at the top of the stairs whenever alterations to the hotel are being carried out, and sometimes haunts the two rooms opposite, now used for conferences. The usual season for her appearances is between February and April, which is also the most likely time for building work. She is dressed in white, with grey shawl and white cap, a sorrowful figure who has also been heard to sob pitifully.

There are countless legends attached to **Rockingham Castle**, and nearly as many ghosts. The present castle dates from 1547 and replaced the Norman castle which was often used by wicked King John. The best-known story is that of Lord Zouch who, told by his best friend that his young wife had taken a lover, rushed back to the castle to find her in the company of her paramour. It was only after he had plunged his sword into the back of this unwelcome visitor that

he found it was his sister Clara, who had fled from a nunnery in order to elope with the man she loved. In order to escape she had disguised herself as a young man – one might have thought that this excused Lord Zouch's hasty action but instead an apparition appeared to warn him of impending death for himself and his family. They would all die within seven days, which they did – and for seven years after that, on the anniversary of the tragedy, the murder would be re-enacted by Lord Zouch's ghost, loud and terrible footsteps giving warning of his vengeance.

Market Bosworth, to the west of Leicester, is a sleepy village whose claim to fame is that the Battle of Bosworth Field took place nearby in 1485. Its ghosts have nothing to do with the Plantagenets, however, but stem from a thwarted love affair and the conflict of faiths.

Bosworth Hall is a house of considerable grandeur, which in this century has served as a hospital and nursing school. It has an indelible bloodstain which resists all attempts of removal. Two explanations are put forward for this: some say that a priest celebrating Mass was disturbed by Cromwellian soldiers. In his haste he broke and cut his hand on the glass chalice, the wine mingling with his blood. The alternative version belongs to the following century when the daughter of the house fell in love with the gardener's son. Her father learned of the assignations and put down a man-trap on the path used by the young man to meet his lover. Instead of catching the boy, the father trapped his daughter, who died a lingering death, since when she has appeared as a Grey Lady.

In 1881 Sir Francis Fortescue-Turville was the squire at Bosworth. A devout Catholic, he married a Protestant widow, Lady Lisger. When one of his faithful Catholic maidservants was dying her ladyship refused to call a priest to administer last rites and so the spirit of the servant still haunts the Bow Room where she died.

Christmas Eve sees a chilling visitation at **Bradgate Park**, in the heart of Charnwood Forest, when Lady Jane Grey drives up to the ruins, her head held on her knees. She is drawn by four headless black horses, and she alights from the carriage and walks towards the remains of the house. This is a beautiful and isolated place, its atmosphere enhanced by the unearthly cries of the resident peacocks, though can they really be responsible for all of the strange howls and wails that emanate from here on wild nights?

A legendary hero features in the most ancient of the ghost stories from **Tamworth Castle** in Staffordshire. Good Sir Lancelot killed Sir Tarquin in a tournament held below the castle walls in Lady's Meadow. The White Lady is one of the ghosts that haunts the castle: she was Sir Tarquin's mistress who watched the conflict from the terrace.

There is also a Black Lady here, who was probably one of the Benedictine nuns expelled by Baron Marmion from their abbey at Polesworth. Marmion did this on receiving the grant of

Tamworth Castle has ghosts which derive from romantic legend.

Both Mortimer's Hole and the Long Gallery of Nottingham Castle are haunted, but by different ghosts.

Tamworth from William I immediately after the Conquest. In 1139 a later, and apparently very wicked, Lord Marmion restored the monastery to the nuns in mysterious circumstances. It is said that a Black Lady appeared to the evil baron on the night following a lavish banquet. She told him that unless the abbey and its lands were restored to her order he would shortly die a horrible death, and on saying this struck his side with her crozier, inflicting a terrible wound. This injury failed to show any sign of healing until Marmion obeyed the Black Lady's demand, though he lived only for a further four years, dying in 1143. Visitors to the castle are shown the Ghost Room where the Black Lady is supposed to have appeared, and a 'Murder Room' which is also said to be haunted.

The appearance of **Nottingham Castle** will have been familiar to generations of smokers who bought Player's Navy Cut. Although the original stronghold has been replaced its history remains and is celebrated by at least one of its ghosts. This is the spirit of Queen Isabella, who with her lover Roger Mortimer had deposed her husband, Edward II, and condemned him to a hideous death in the dungeons of Berkeley Castle.

In 1330 Isabella and Mortimer summoned Parliament to Nottingham Castle, which they considered to be one of their most secure strongholds. However they did not know all of its secrets and rival barons used the secret passageways which riddle the sandstone of its foundations to capture the Queen and her paramour. Mortimer was immediately put to death, but Isabella lived on for another 30 years, a prisoner who later showed remorse for the murder of her husband by joining an order of nuns.

Isabella's ghost is just one of a number which crowd the galleries and corridors of the castle. She calls for her lover through the underground passages known as Mortimer's Hole, from where they were dragged out of the castle. The spirit of a Countess of Nottingham haunts the Long Gallery: if you see her make haste to enjoy yourself – you will be dead within the year!

Another gallery with a stange ambience is the Bonnington Room. Quite recently the alarms went off at night. As is usual, the police were at the castle within minutes, and undertook a search of the premises with the security men and a large black police dog. Nothing was found, but when they entered the Bonnington Room the lights all came on of their own accord, yet no human hand was near the switch. The dog's hackles rose, and big as he was, he showed every sign of fear. No trace of an intruder was found, and the incident was discounted as being just another of the strange events that frequently trouble the night-shift at the castle. However the next day they were amused to hear that the reactions of the police dog had become famous. In the retelling of the story through local pubs and clubs the terror suffered by the black dog was said to have turned it white overnight!

The City of Nottingham also owns **Newstead Abbey**, the ancestral home of Lord Byron, which was bought by the family when the Abbey was dissolved in 1540. The departing Abbot, as is usual in these circumstances, cursed the property and all those who lived there subsequently, and in the case of Newstead this curse seems to have been effective. By the time of the poet's birth the family were impoverished and the house derelict. He saw the ghost, the Goblin Friar, on the eve of his marriage to Anne Millbanke and he knew then that this match would prove to be a disaster. Byron eventually sold the property in 1818 but the curse remained effective, bringing death and

misfortune to later owners (but not to the Corporation as yet). The famous monument to his dog, Boatswain, is supposed to be sited on the Abbey's high altar. Perhaps this is the reason for Boatswain's reincarnation as a phantom black hound, though it may also have had something to do with Byron's request to be buried next to his faithful dog not being fulfilled.

Byron's home was Newstead Abbey where there is an imposing monument to his dog Boatswain who appears here in ethereal form as a black hound.

There is a notice in the drive to **Renishaw**, the home of the Sitwell family just to the south of Sheffield: 'Please do not tread on Mr Sitwell's snakes.' This bizarre warning is reflected in the nature of the ghosts which frequent the house.

The exterior of the house is forbidding, long and low and dark, but inside it is absolutely splendid, though no showhouse for it is obviously lived-in. Sir Reresby Sitwell enjoys telling about Renishaw's other-worldly occupants, of which there are a number. The Kissing Ghost, or Boy in Pink, is Henry, last of the Sacheverells, who died in 1716. He visits one particular bedroom (marked on the bell-board as the 'Ghost Room') where he enjoys kissing a female occupant. Moira Lympany, the concert pianist, was amused by the haunting, noting that he did not just peck her cheek, but kissed her full on the lips. A dark-haired young lady in crinolines, who glides rather than walks has been seen in broad daylight when it was notable that she cast no shadow. A distraught Victorian housemaid and a monk have also been seen.

When asked where the various ghosts appeared, Sir Reresby – a larger than life figure in half-inch-thick tweeds – described thirteen different locations, and concluded that they covered 'the whole blooming place, generally'.

Renishaw, the home of the Sitwell family, has at least thirteen different supernatural locations.

KNEBWORTH'S GHOSTLY RESIDENTS

EDWARD BULWER-LYTTON was an extraordinary man. One of the most prominent and prolific literary talents of his day, a passionate political reformist, an expert in the occult, and the central character in a tortuous domestic saga that spanned more than four decades. His life was the stuff other people's novels are made of, a heady cocktail of love, hate, power, riches, tragedy and revenge.

Having earned a rightful place in history, and a resting place in Westminster Abbey, it comes as no surprise to learn that Edward Bulwer-Lytton (Bulwer to his contemporaries) found eternal rest hard to come by. With so much drama packed into one lifetime, his search for peace, quiet and companionship has brought him back to the one place that offered him sanctuary, his beloved Knebworth House.

And what could be more natural for a man with an abiding passion in the occult, who spent much of his time trying to summon up the departed by means of crystal ball and seance, than to do the very thing he so fervently believed in. His study, virtually unchanged since he completed his final manuscript in 1873 – just days before his death – remains the focal point of his after-life: his published works, mystical texts, crystal ball, favourite pipe all comfortingly familiar to him, if curiously sinister to the casual visitor.

Lady Christine Cobbold, whose husband the second Lord Cobbold is Bulwer's great, great grandson, is matter-of-fact about her forebear's presence; having lived at Knebworth since the early 1970s she is quite accustomed to him. 'It's not as though he's a ghostly figure, and there's no

drifting through walls, it is purely a feeling – a strong sensation of his presence, both in the study and the adjoining drawing room he used. It has never been in the least bit frightening, and never struck me as anything particularly unusual.' Bulwer does not haunt Knebworth, it is simply that he still lives there.

One other member of the family, Lady Cobbold's eldest son, Henry, shares her experiences of Bulwer, and her acceptance of what she considers a far from unnatural phenomenon. 'I grew up in a house with hundreds of years of history attached to it, and have always accepted that old places have vibrations or sensations that we don't necessarily understand. When it comes

to Bulwer's presence here it seems to me to be associated with his great love for the house itself, and a desire to know what is going on today in the lives of his descendants. I feel that if the time ever comes when Knebworth no longer has any family associations, he will just leave.'

It appears, however, that Bulwer's presence proved to be a bit too strong for a couple of cleaning staff Lady Cobbold spoke of – they absolutely refused to go near his rooms, or the main staircase, on their own. Many visitors to Knebworth have also reported 'strange feelings' in and around this part of the house.

Bulwer-Lytton is not the only ghostly resident at Knebworth. Other stories associated with

▷ **Lady Cobbold and her son Henry in the Picture Gallery.**

▽ **Looking across the park to Knebworth House.**

◁ The panelling now in the Queen Elizabeth Room is said to be associated with one of Knebworth's ghosts.

▷ Sir Edward Bulwer Lytton in his study.

the house involve Jenny, the mysterious spinner said to be heard working away in a turret atop the East Wing, where she went mad and died; and another female associated with a secret panel, phial of poison, lock of hair, and no doubt, a dastardly deed or two. Neither carries much weight with Lady Cobbold, though, and she puts these creations down to fiction, and the Victorian drawing room fascination for penning chilling tales to while away the long dark nights.

Having said that, she did recall an incident from last summer when an American guest staying in the Queen Elizabeth room (where the panelling in question is now installed) claimed at breakfast that she had been woken early in the morning by a girl 'with long, blonde hair' leaning over her bed. There was no logical explanation; but is there ever?

Lady Cobbold herself adds another twist to the spiritual concoction that makes Knebworth such a potent mixture. The Picture Gallery, at one end comfy and homely, with its family photos, books and games, but then stretching away to house a sombre collection of seventeenth- and eighteenth-century ancestors and other dignitaries, has been the scene of occasional 'meetings' with a mystery female. This unknown visitor appears to want nothing more than someone to make conversation with, said Lady Cobbold, and is remarkable only by her extreme ordinariness.

But whoever, or whatever else, anyone experiences at Knebworth it is Bulwer-Lytton who commands the most attention. It is also interesting to note that nothing unpleasant has ever been reported, or passed down in the annals of ghostly goings-on, a fact that leads one to the logical conclusion that the chain of gargoyles he had created to encircle the entire building and fend off evil spirits, have more than done their job!

Bulwer did, in fact, do more than add a host of fearsome faces to the outer walls, he changed the entire face of Knebworth. When the once redbrick, Tudor house came into his hands in 1843, he set about refashioning it and creating a Gothic fantasy. 'Iced' in stucco his palace of turrets and domes became as magical and romantic as any of his best-selling literary gems. He lavished attention on the inside as well, turning it into a gathering place for everyone who was anyone in nineteenth-century literary, political and theatrical circles. He clearly loved the place.

Love could also have cost him his dream home. It certainly cost him his peace of mind and blighted his every move from the age of 24 to his death at 70. The favourite son of Elizabeth Bulwer-Lytton, he was 'cut off' when he married against her wishes in 1827. Bulwer's bride, Rosina Wheeler, was a beautiful Irish girl but she was also penniless, and worst of all from a wretchedly unsuitable family background. Marriage put an

end to all financial support, which for a budding writer was an absolute necessity. Success and security was, however, just a few years and a few books away.

Bulwer's outpourings were the blockbusters of the day — *Pelham or the Adventures of a Gentleman*, *The Disowned*, *Devereux*, *The Last Days of Pompeii*, a spell as a playwright, then more novels including the fantastical *Zanoni*.

He wrote twenty-three novels and plays in all. He consolidated his position as one of the country's best-known personalities by becoming a politician, first and somewhat humbly representing St Ives, and eventually rising via his Secretaryship of the Colonies to become Lord Lytton of Knebworth, and take his seat in the House of Lords.

The first cracks in the doomed marriage to Rosina had appeared fairly rapidly and two children later, in 1836, they separated, he to concentrate on writing and politics, she on revenge. Everywhere he went Rosina popped up, with a barrage of abuse here, a tirade there; his political meetings were peppered with domestic debacle. He in his turn had the children, Emily and Robert, taken from her and sent to Ireland, tried to have her committed to a lunatic asylum, and paid off every publisher she went to in an attempt to have her own book published. (*Cheveley*, or *The Man of Honour* – which lampooned her loathed husband – did eventually appear in print.)

By the time Emily (his beloved Little Boots) died of typhoid in 1848, at the tender age of twenty, Bulwer was dogged by poor health, depression, loneliness and the relentless Rosina. She kept it up until finally disappearing off the

scene in 1864. Robert Lytton, who at one time had literary ambitions of his own, was left in no doubt that one writer in the family was quite enough, and turned instead to the diplomatic service. His distinguished career was one of his father's few joys in his old age. Bulwer's last years were spent wandering somewhat aimlessly and sadly abroad, but he remained as creative as ever; his penultimate book, *The Coming Race*, was a bestseller in 1871 and the manuscript for *Kenelm Chillingly* was completed just days before he died on 18 January, 1873.

Knebworth today remains the Gothic fantasy of Bulwer-Lytton's fertile imagination. Mellowed by the years and made more manageable by successive generations, it is a startling sight as it sweeps into view just a minute off the A1M motorway, its spiky pinacles and onion-shaped domes perforating the skyline with an extravagant gesture of grandeur. But it has also moved well and truly into the twenty-first century. It is the perfect film set, romantic, accessible and, thanks to the present occupants, available. As a result it has featured in numerous films and TV series, from *Beauty and the Beast* to *Batman*.

Each June, since the early 1970s, Knebworth has played host to the country's rock fans – the name itself now synonymous with this great annual festival. It is also highly desirable as a photographic location, as the paraphernalia of the advertising 'shoot' demonstrated on the occasion of this particular visit. It was intriguing to imagine what Bulwer-Lytton would have made of it all if he had been there . . . perhaps he was! . . . an immaculately clad 'golfer' teeing off from the green baize of the billiard table in the name of a well-known brand of whisky.

Equally intriguing would be an indication of how he feels every time he passes the portrait of the unforgiving Rosina. For while she never set foot in the house during her lifetime she is there now, on the main staircase leading up to his rooms, her dark hair coiled neatly and the hint of a smile on her face. It is a haunting thought, but if anyone wanders abroad at Knebworth, surely Rosina must. Perhaps Bulwer takes comfort from the fact that today's Rosina, Lady Cobbold's daughter, carries only the name and not the spirit of revenge.

Someone who is a stranger to the region might visualise the east of England as a windswept expanse of flat featureless country, given over to intensive agriculture. In some respects this might be correct, especially in the further-flung parts of the region – the Lincolnshire fens, perhaps, or the breckland of West Norfolk – but here the region extends beyond East Anglia to within fifteen miles of Charing Cross in the south and as far as Peterborough in the north. Thus there is a wide range of countryside as well as a considerable difference in its inhabitants. Original country folk can still be found, but it is becoming harder to do so, as cottages are bought up by commuters spending the greater parts of their lives working in London or the other cities around the region.

Salisbury Hall is a moated house of red brick dating from Tudor and Jacobean times. It lies just fifteen miles from Charing Cross, to the south of St Albans and within a few hundred yards of the M 25. You might expect that the proximity of the motorway alone would be enough to frighten away all but the bravest psychic spirit, but the ghosts of Salisbury Hall must also be disturbed by the upheavals now going on as the ancient building is converted into the 'prestige' offices of a Japanese company (in fact ghosts are sensitive on this score, and many of the most remarkable hauntings follow building work).

Salisbury Hall has always played an important role in history, not least in this century. It was the home of Sir Nigel Gresley when his *Mallard* won the speed record for a steam locomotive, and three years later, in 1940, the prototype of the Mosquito fighter-bomber was unveiled here. It became one of the most efficient of Allied weapons.

King Charles II installed his mistress Nell Gwyn (above) at Salisbury Hall (below) in 1668. She haunts the Hall, as does a young Cavalier.

Lady Randolph Churchill, mother of Sir Winston, made it her home on becoming a widow, and it was here that the young Sir Winston rid the moat of a ravenous pike which was depleting the ducklings: in a most un-British way he shot it with a rifle!

After living at the Hall for a few years Lady Randolph remarried, and in 1905 her second husband encountered its most famous ghost, that of Eleanor 'Nell' Gwyn, the mistress of Charles II. The King installed Nell in the house soon after 1668. She is supposed to have forced the monarch to give their child a title by dangling him over the moat and threatening to drop him: glancing up and seeing the distant tower of the cathedral the King begged her to save 'the Duke of St Albans'.

Nell's ghost appears in a blue fichu (three-cornered shawl). The Hall's other ghost is that of a young Cavalier, who was wounded in a skirmish at South Mimms and sought refuge at Salisbury Hall. However a search-party

located him there, and rather than be captured he took his own life. The previous owners were quite used to hearing his footsteps about the house, just as they often heard the ghostly laughter of, presumably, Nell Gwyn.

Away to the east in Essex, the **Bear Inn** at Stock, south of Chelmsford, has the ghost of Charlie 'Spider' Marshall who was an ostler there in the last century. His party piece was to shin up the chimney in the public bar, pass through the recess between the chimneys where the bacon would be placed for smoking, and emerge down the chimney in the other bar. One Christmas he performed his trick for the last, climbing up the chimney but never appearing again – at least not in earthly form. Some landlords claim to have seen Spider in the past, and there are still regular reports of poltergeist behaviour at the Bear, perhaps caused by his ever-mischievous spirit.

Charlie 'Spider' Marshall haunts the Bear Inn at Stock (below). He climbed a chimney (below, left) for a wager but never came down again.

Edwin's Hall at Woodham Ferrers has a moat haunted by the ghost of a girl who drowned there.

The twin towers of Layer Marney, where the boisterous spirit of Lord Marney rides down a spiral staircase.

A little further to the east is the village of Woodham Ferrers where the lovely moated **Edwin's Hall** takes its name from the man who built it in 1619 – Edwin Sandys, Archbishop of York. Although Sandys had an eventful life before becoming archbishop (he supported the cause of Lady Jane Grey and had to flee the country on the accession of Queen Mary) it is not his ghost who haunts Edwin's Hall. There is a phantom Cavalier (the house suffered a long siege during the Civil War) and the unquiet spirit of a girl who drowned in the moat. The present owner of Edwin's Hall says that he believes that two people have drowned there within living memory and that his dog, Bonnie Blackwag, 'resolutely refuses' to go near the pets' graveyard near the lake.

Lord Marney's ghost haunts the imposing tower of **Layer Marney**, near Tiptree, perhaps because he died in 1523 before the magnificent building was completed. He is said to ride 'dressed in all his grey' down the spiral staircase. An elderly man in the village speaks of having witnessed this terrifying apparition.

The most famous haunted site in Essex used to be **Borley Rectory**, burned down in 1939. The activities of the ghosthunter most involved at Borley, Harry Price, were later exposed as being questionable or even

Tranquil and beautiful in Spring sunshine, who could believe the sinister tales told of Borley church?

Dating from the mid-fifteenth century, The Bull at Long Melford (below) is one of the oldest hotels belonging to Trust House Forte. The corpse of a murdered man vanished from its lounge, and his ghost is supposed to haunt the building, some 350 years after the crime.

dishonest, and the whole business was discredited but to this day there are many psychic researchers (and sensation seekers) who believe that the paranormal disturbances at Borley remain, and are now centred on the church.

For a recuperative drink after Borley visit the splendid **Bull Hotel** at Long Melford. The building was originally put up by a prosperous wool merchant in the middle of the fifteenth century and became an inn about 1530. Later it became an important coaching inn, the 'Norwich Machine' arriving for a change of horses between one and two o'clock in the morning. Its ghost belongs to an earlier period, a reminder of a tragic incident that took place on 26 July, 1648. Richard Evered, a yeoman farmer, was stabbed by Roger Greene in the hall of the Bull. Greene's motive for the crime was never satisfactorily explained, and he duly suffered on the gallows, but the mystery of the incident lies in the disappearance of the murdered man's body. It was laid out in the lounge of the hotel but vanished overnight. It is said that Evered's grave in the church-yard was never occupied, though no attempt was made to search it. Predictably, his ghost walks at the Bull, and is blamed for all the creaks and groans that are customarily heard in a building 500 years old. There is a legend

that there is a secret room at the Bull which was particularly badly disturbed and was sealed up and forgotten long ago, but this seems unlikely at such an establishment today: the rooms here command the price of up to £100 or so per night.

Melford Hall is a National Trust property; a turreted Tudor mansion of red brick, it has been little changed since 1578 when it was built. During the Civil War it was sacked by 3,000 'scum of Colchester' who plundered it because of Countess Rivers' support for the Royalist cause. She was forced to flee for her life, but returns in unearthly form to haunt it from time to time.

The village of Sawston lies in Cambridgeshire, but is within a few miles of both Suffolk and Essex. **Sawston Hall** was the home of the Huddlestone family, staunch Catholics throughout the 400 years that they lived there. The medieval hall of Sawston was burned down the night after Queen Mary slept there in 1553.

Sawston Hall (below) is one of several places haunted by Mary, Queen of Scots, who appears here in the Tapestry Room (above).

She was attempting to reach London to visit her brother, King Edward VI, on his sickbed. Mary did not know that the King had already died and that a powerful group of nobles led by the Duke of Northumberland intended to prevent her from taking the throne, installing Lady Jane Grey instead.

Fortunately she had been fore-warned of pursuit at Sawston and was able to flee the house in time, pausing at a safe distance to watch the fire lit by her enemies engulf the house. She turned to Andrew Huddlestone, her escort, and promised him that she would rebuild his house for him when she became queen. She kept this promise, and rewarded him with high office, but subsequently the Huddle-stones suffered greatly for their faith.

Today the Hall accommodates the Cambridge Centre for Languages: do its foreign students appreciate the rich history of the place, or the multitude of ghosts it generated? It used to be quite common to hear the sound of a spinet being played, yet such an

instrument had not been kept in the house for more than a century. The happy sound of girlish laughter was another ghostly echo, while apparitions included that of Bloody Mary herself and a Grey Lady, both of which haunted the Tapestry Room. The latter was unusual in that she announced her presence with three ominous knocks at the door of this bedroom, which used to contain the bed that Queen Mary is supposed to have slept in.

On the outskirts of Cambridge, Grantchester has enduring memories of Rupert Brooke. Its **Old Vicarage**, now the home of Jeffrey and Mary Archer, was a subject of one of his poems in which he wrote:

> And spectral dance, before the dawn,
> A hundred Vicars down the lawn;
> Curates, long dust, will come and go
> On lissom, clerical, printless toe . . .

The top floor of the Old Vicarage, so it is said, has a restive spirit who wanders about moving books. It is too easy to accept the suggestion that this must be the ghost of Brooke, but no other theory has been put forward.

Rupert Brooke also wrote lines on the ghosts of **Madingley Hall**, just to the west of Cambridge:

> And things go on you'd ne'er believe
> At Madingley – on Christmas Eve.

The ghost referred to is that of Lady Ursula Hynde, wife of Sir John Hynde, who began building Madingley in about 1543. She apparently objected to the way that her son, who carried on with the work after the death of his father, ransacked church properties for treasures which he incorporated in his grand new house. She considered this sacrilege and has haunted the place ever since, usually walking the path between the hall and the church. There is also a young man in Elizabethan clothes with a sickly green face who stands on the upper terrace and looks down at mortals with an

Is it the ghost of Rupert Brooke who haunts the Old Vicarage at Grantchester (above)?

Lady Ursula is one of the ghosts of Madingley Hall, where she walks the path to the church.

expression full of loathing and disgust. Madingley belongs to the University of Cambridge and is used by its Board of Extra-Mural Studies.

Bookshops are an important feature in any university town and Cambridge is no exception, being particularly well-served by the likes of Heffers and, on a slightly smaller scale, **Sherratt and Hughes** in Trinity Street which claims to be the oldest bookshop in Britain. Founded on these premises in 1581 it has known Tennyson, Thackeray and Lewis Carroll amongst its distinguished customers, while in contrast Kim Philby used his account here from undergraduate days until his death in Moscow in 1988. In the 1840s it was owned by Daniel Macmillan who laid the foundations for the famous publishing house.

With so much history it is hardly surprising that Sherratt and Hughes have ghosts on the premises. There is a White Lady whose identity is unknown and a gentleman in Victorian evening dress whom the previous manager once encountered in a stock-room corridor. Perhaps it is this

apparition which delights in opening and closing the drawers of files when the office upstairs is deserted.

The village of Offord Cluny is to be found on the bank of the Great Ouse to the west of Cambridge. Its **Manor House** was built about 1704 and has an unusual haunting – the apparition of a frail old lady who appears when a bride of the owner comes to the house. It is the newly-wed girl who sees the diminutive figure of the old woman who is usually identified as the wife of Mr Deane, owner of the house soon after it was built, who so loved the place that she is reluctant to leave it, and has appeared (always in the drawing-room) to welcome at least four generations of new wives soon after they have taken up residence. Her maiden name was Sismey, and thus she was an ancestor of the present owner, Lieutenant-Colonel Sismey.

A little further down the Ouse is the village of Holywell where the riverside inn, **Ye Olde Ferryboat**, claims to be the oldest pub in England, dating back 1,000 years. Whatever the truth of this – the hostelry probably derived from

The premises of Sherratt and Hughes, Cambridge (below, left), and the Manor House, Offord Cluny (below).

The last thing you'd expect to find in a pub – the gravestone in the bar of Ye Olde Ferryboat, Holywell.

'Old Pork and Lard' is the resident ghost of the Crown Inn at Great Staughton (below).

the shelter for passengers awaiting the ferry run by monks – the story of the ghost is certainly ancient. In one of the bars is an ancient tombstone said to mark the grave of Juliet Tewsley who hanged herself from one of the willows which line the riverbank because of her love for the unresponsive local woodcutter Tom Zoul. Since suicides could not be buried in consecrated ground she was interred where she died and later the pub was built over her grave. In protest at this sacrilege she appears as a White Lady on the anniversary of her death, 17 March, walking to the slab, pointing to it, then drifting through the pub to vanish down the river.

The **Crown Inn** at Great Staughton, to the west of the Ouse and just to the south of Grafham Water, suffered from strange poltergeist activity in 1970 which was said by locals to have been caused by a landlord who had died many years ago. A butcher by day and a publican at night, he was known by

the picturesque nickname 'Old Pork and Lard'. In his seventies he married a young girl but died when she was pregnant. His frustration at not being able to see the baby was the explanation for the haunting.

Woodcroft Castle lies to the north east of Peterborough near the village of Marholm. It dates from the late thirteenth century, its round tower recalling the great castles of Wales put up by Edward I. Subsequent centuries saw many additions and alterations, but it was still a well-fortified stronghold when King Charles I's former guardian, Dr Michael Hudson, was besieged at Woodcroft in 1648. He had carried out several annoying sorties against the Roundheads with his garrison, and the commander of the Cromwellian forces, Colonel Woodhead, decided to root out Hudson from his stronghold. Accordingly he sent his brother-in-law with a strong force to lay siege to the castle. A little later the remnants of this squad returned. Hudson had forestalled them and a chance shot had killed their leader. Enraged by this,

A splendid yet little-known stronghold near Peterborough, Woodcroft Castle has the mangled ghost of Dr Michael Hudson.

Of the scores of abandoned Second World War airfields in Eastern England, RAF Bircham Newton is perhaps the most haunted. Its most poignant apparition is an open car full of happy airmen.

No-one has slept in the haunted room at Hannath Hall since the eighteenth century.

Woodhead quickly gathered as many men as were available and descended on Woodcroft himself.

They found the castle almost undefended, Hudson having considered that the defeat inflicted on the Roundheads would keep them quiet for some time. While most of the garrison were offered surrender, no quarter was given to Hudson, who managed to flee to the battlements. Hearing hot pursuit he climbed over, clinging to the parapet with his fingers. But one of the Roundheads had seen him disappear and slashed at his hands with his sword, cutting both off at the wrists and dropping Hudson into the moat far below.

Yet the worst part of Hudson's ordeal was still to come. Soldiers dragged him from the moat, one named Egborough knocking him unconscious with his musket. Then, not to be outdone, another cut out his tongue. Hudson soon died of his terrible injuries, but achieved immortality both through his ghost, which still appears where he died, and in the pages of *Woodstock* where Sir Walter Scott used the incident for the death of Dr Rochecliffe. Legend has it that both men involved in the killing

suffered ill-fortune, Egborough being killed in a horrible manner soon afterwards when his gun exploded, and Walker, who had cut out the tongue and exhibited it to the morbidly curious for a fee, lost his business and died a pauper.

Hannath Hall is situated four miles to the north of Wisbech, at the village of Tydd St Giles. Built in 1570 it was originally known as Sparrow's Hall but took its present name after the Hannath family moved into the house in the eighteenth century. The Hannaths remained there for more than 150 years, and it was towards the end of their time at the Hall that the events took place that gave rise to the ghost story.

Joseph Hannath was heartbroken at the death of his wife. For six weeks after her death he sent the maid upstairs with food for her. Her corpse lay in the bedroom at the northern end of the house which subsequently became known as 'the haunted room'. At the end of this time he carried her body down and buried it in the garden. It is said that the maidservant subsequently went mad and killed herself and that no one has been able to get a good night's rest in the haunted room since. In the late 1950s there were reports of poltergeist disturbance in the house and investigators flocked there. However they were unable to reveal convincing evidence of paranormal activity though one set of

investigators thought that the coded raps that they heard were from Eliza Cullen, whose fair-haired son had been murdered at Hannath. His apparition has also been reported.

In a village on the other side of Wisbech is **Elm Vicarage**. Now named 'The Old Shires', it is haunted by the ghost of a monk who, at a time of flood, neglected his duty and failed to ring a bell to warn the monastery, which stood close by, of the rising water. The result was that several of the brothers were drowned in their cells, and the watchman still walks in perpetual remorse. The monk is a harmless ghost, but is still active, and the present owners have heard his footsteps in the attics. They are always heard at the same time and, if the pattern of haunting follows its usual course, they herald the appearance of an apparition within a few years.

Like many other historical figures mentioned in these pages, the ghost of Queen Isabella haunts more than one location (see Nottingham Castle). With her lover Roger Mortimer she had plotted to remove Edward III from the throne, and while Mortimer had paid for the conspiracy with his life, Edward was more merciful towards his mother, keeping her, in what passed for luxury in the fourteenth century, at **Castle Rising** in Norfolk. She spent 27 years in the Norman castle, endowed with property which brought in £3,000 per annum, a vast fortune at the time. The King visited her there on several occasions, events full of pomp and pageantry, and though she also spent time at other properties it seems that Castle Rising was her favourite abode. The 'She-wolf of France' died in 1358. For some time previously she had been demented, and it is said that

A careless monk is the ghost at Elm vicarage. He neglected to warn his monastery of an approaching flood which brought calamity to his brethren.

on stormy nights at the lonely castle her crazy laughter echoes over its walls.

The town of Hunstanton boasts of being the only place on the east coast of England where you can see the sun set over the sea (it looks over the Wash to the Lincolnshire shore some twenty miles distant). **Hunstanton Hall**, the ancestral seat of the le Strange family, was once a very grand Tudor mansion, but suffered from two disastrous fires, one in 1853 and another in 1951.

Its ghost is a lady named Armine Styleman, who inherited the estate when her brother Sir Henry le Strange died in 1760. She was particularly fond of a beautiful Persian carpet which had been a present from the Shah. Just before she died in 1768 she made a point of saying that it should never leave the family. However the carpet was packed away and forgotten. After some time, it was discovered by someone who had not heard of Armine's wish, and did not suspect its value. Full of good works, he (or she) cut it up and distributed it about the village to the poor and needy. Armine's ghost was incensed at this and began to haunt the Hall ferociously, until at last the penny dropped and all the pieces were collected and sewn together again.

One of the most magnificent houses in Norfolk is unfortunately never

Castle Rising (below) is haunted by the unhappy Queen Isabella.

opened to the public. This is **Raynham Hall**, which dates from 1630 and contains work by Inigo Jones. It is the seat of the Marquis of Townshend and has one of the most famous of East Anglian ghosts – the Brown Lady. A photograph of her descending the stairs at Raynham appeared in *Country Life* in December 1936. Captain Marryat, author of *The Pirate*, actually fired his pistol at her (whereupon she vanished) and in 1849 the entire staff of the Hall were so frightened that they walked out *en masse*. Lord Charles Townshend replaced them with 'a capable staff of detectives' but the Brown Lady obstinately refused to appear.

Other ghosts at Raynham are a Pink Lady said to be a portent announcing the death of the Marquis, a Red Cavalier (in human form, not on wheels), and two apparitions of children, one of which appears only in the Stone Parlour.

In contrast to Raynham, **Felbrigg Hall** is readily accessible, belonging to the National Trust. It is the library here which is the haunted room, being visited by William Windham who amassed a valuable collection of books at Felbrigg but died in London in 1810, characteristically after attempting to save a friend's library which was in flames. He was frequently seen by subsequent

Felbrigg Hall is haunted by a shy, scholarly ghost.

Armine Styleman as a girl (left), and (above) in old age.

The Library at Felbrigg Hall (right) where William Windham kept his beloved books.

owners of Felbrigg, and even by the first Administrator appointed by the National Trust to Felbrigg after they acquired the property in 1969.

This was a very unobtrusive haunting, however, the ghost returning to his beloved library to browse amongst his favourite books, most notably those that had once belonged to Samuel Johnson. Unfortunately security now means that these valuable items have to be kept elsewhere, and possibly this is the reason why there have been no sightings of William Windham's ghost at Felbrigg for more than twenty years.

Salle church stands between Felbrigg and Blickling, the other great National Trust property of this part of Norfolk. Salle church is vast, beautiful, and always strikes me as very spooky. It is said to be haunted by the ghost of Anne Boleyn as is **Blickling Hall** and much of the surrounding countryside (local legend has it that Salle was her final resting-place).

Blickling Hall (below) belongs to the National Trust, and Anne Boleyn is supposed to haunt its drive in a phantom coach.

It is debatable whether Queen Anne Boleyn knew Blickling, but her father, Sir Thomas Boleyn, certainly lived in the moated manor house which stood on the site before the present magnificent Jacobean mansion, so it is likely that she spent some of her childhood there, as did her brother, Lord Rochfort, who was executed at the same time as Anne. In fear of the King, Sir Thomas betrayed both of his children (one of the charges against the Queen was that of incest with her brother) so it is hardly surprising that all three of the family should frequent Blickling in unearthly form.

On the anniversary of her death, 19 May, Anne is driven up the drive in a carriage with a headless coachman on the box, carrying her head on her knees. She has also been seen inside the house, usually dressed in grey.

Sometimes the unlucky queen is pursued by the ghost of her brother. On the night of his death the headless form of a man being dragged by four horses, also without heads, roamed the countryside around Blickling. Sir Thomas is also driven about the neighbourhood in a spectral coach until he has crossed over twelve (40 in some versions) bridges.

But Blickling's most convincing ghost story comes from comparatively recent times. Before the Second World War the house was divided into flats, though much of the furniture, armour etc. that had belonged to the Marquis of Lothian, the owner, still remained. The son of the house, on his twenty-first birthday, decided to play a joke on his parents dressing up in a suit of armour and climbing the stairs with a din like a mobile dustbin before knocking on their bedroom door with a mailed fist to wake them. A few years later he died in an accident, but his ghost returned on the anniversary of his death to repeat the prank, startling later tenants of the flat.

Banningham Rectory lies quite close to Blickling, on the other side of the market town of Aylsham. It is the home of Bryan Hall, and one of his prized possessions is a remarkable portrait. It is not at all a beautiful painting for the sitter, in her wide-brimmed hat, looks out from the canvas with a disapproving expression. Her name is Miss Henrietta Nelson who died at Yaxley Hall in Suffolk on 4 April 1815. Apart from being ugly, she had another social disadvantage in being illegitimate, in those days a stigma which embarrassed both parents and child alike. Perhaps poor Henrietta had to put up with years of condescension and that accounts for her sour face. Before her sudden death (she fell downstairs) Henrietta

The unpleasant face of Henrietta Nelson stares out from the canvas where her spirit may linger.

The ghostly coach-and-four at Roos Hall.

requested that she should be buried in a mausoleum built for the purpose in the grounds of Yaxley Hall.

This wish was carried out, and for more than 30 years Henrietta lay at peace, until a new owner came to the Hall, disliked the mausoleum and demolished it, moving Henrietta's remains to the family vault in the church. The haunting began soon afterwards, Henrietta's restless spirit roaming the grounds of Yaxley Hall, but when the portrait was moved the ghost followed it. Bryan Hall first encountered it when the portrait hung at a house at Barton Turf, a Broadland village not far from Banningham. He saw Henrietta's face at a bedroom window. Then the painting was moved again, this time to Smallburgh, and again Mr Hall encountered the appari-

tion when it looked in through a kitchen window. He has described her as wearing the same dress as in the portrait, but there is no colour in it, nor in the face which has the texture of parchment. After this he bought the painting and it serves to disconcert his visitors at Banningham, the forbidding eyes of Miss Nelson following them as they move about the room.

As we have seen at Blickling, headless coachmen are a popular feature in East Anglian ghost stories. The device also occurs at **Roos Hall** at Beccles, where a ghostly coach-and-four driven by a decapitated coachman arrives on Christmas Eve. The town gibbet was an oak which stands in the park there: should you wish to meet with the Devil he can be summoned by walking round this tree six times.

Breckles Hall (above and right) is another Norfolk house visited by a spectral coach-and-four.

Two hundred years ago the Breckland of south Norfolk was lonely country, mile after mile of heathland, populated by rabbits and little else. The village of Breckles, as it name suggests, stands on the edge of this wilderness. **Breckles Hall** is a beautiful old manor house that dates from the early sixteenth century when it was the home of the strongly Catholic Woodhouse family. They made sure that there were plenty of hiding-places behind panelling and in the attics. However because of their adherence to the Old Faith they were frequently fined, to such a degree that they were forced to sell the estate in 1599.

The sadness about the subsequent history of the Hall is that no family stayed long enough to be successful, either because of the lack of an heir or because of financial disaster. Perhaps this accounts for its ghost story. On occasion a phantom coach rolls up to the porch. Anyone who sees it is doomed, either being taken off in it to vanish forever or to be left lifeless on the driveway, with no mark on the body to account for sudden death.

Up to the nineteenth century the major industry of Breckland was the production of rabbits, both for their meat and their fur. Just outside Thetford, on the edge of the forest that surrounds the town, in **Warren Lodge**, which at first sight looks like a miniature castle. In fact it dates from the time of King John and was the residence of the Warrener, an important official in those days. Later it served as a leper house and the ravaged face of one of these unfortunates is occasionally seen. One person who met with it wrote:

It had a flat white face and burning eyes, and there was a sound like a running stream. It passed through me making a filthy gust of hot air.

(Quoted in the ghost-hunter's standard reference book, Anthony Hippisley Coxe's *Haunted Britain*.)

The great houses of Lincolnshire were more noted for their support of Catholicism than those of Norfolk, though many a priest travelled secretly between the two counties administering to the faithful. There were many thriving religious foundations in Lincolnshire when Henry VIII began

Look for the grotesque face of a leper at a window of Warren Lodge in Thetford Forest.

the dissolution of the monasteries, none of them greater than **Thornton Abbey**, ten miles to the north-east of Scunthorpe.

Thornton belonged to the Augustinian order, and was a magnificent establishment when it was surrendered to the King in 1539. Remarkably,

It may be the evil Abbot who haunts magnificent Thornton Abbey.

perhaps because of the Abbey's excellent reputation, Henry refounded the house as a college, some of the canons being reinstated to help set it up. He visited Thornton in 1541 where meetings of the Privy Council were held. He intended the Abbey to continue to serve as an educational institution, both religious and secular, and to care for the sick and aged. However it did not long survive Henry's death, being suppressed in the first year of the reign of his son, Edward VI.

Most of the buildings at Thornton remained intact under a succession of owners until the property was acquired in 1602 by Sir Vincent Skinner of Westminster. He pulled down the College and built a mansion within the moat of the Abbey. Immediately it was finished the entire new structure 'fell quite down to the bare ground, without any visible cause'. It was probably at this time that the mysterious walled-up monk of Thornton was discovered. His skeleton was found seated at a table with a book, pen and ink in front of him. Naturally his ghost haunts the Abbey: he is supposed to have been Thomas de Gretham, an evil Abbot who dabbled in black magic and suffered when this was discovered.

It appears that other builders using material from the Abbey also had trouble. Much was incorporated into Ferriby Sluice, another unsuccessful project.

John Wesley was born (in 1703) and grew up at **Epworth**, about six miles to the west of Scunthorpe on the Isle of Axeholme. His father was Rector of this remote parish, and because of his strictness was not well-liked by all of his parishioners. Perhaps a hoax was the cause of a poltergeist bedevilling the household in 1716, or maybe the activity stemmed from the adolescent John Wesley and his eighteen brothers and sisters (children around the age of puberty often seem to trigger poltergeist activity). The family, firm in their

'Old Jeffrey' was the name the Wesley family gave the poltergeist which troubled Epworth Old Rectory.

faith, nicknamed their violent ghost 'Old Jeffrey' and seem to have survived the experience rather better than their dog, a mastiff, who was terrorised by an apparition which was said to have looked like a headless badger.

The remains of **Haverholme Priory** are to be found at Ewerby, not far from Sleaford. Enough remains of the house to show that it would be an ideal habitat for a ghost, and sure enough in his *Ghost Book* Lord Halifax told of

The bridge in the grounds of Haverholme Priory (above) is haunted by an entity making a sudden whizzing sound which has a startling effect on dogs. It takes a brave photographer to take a twilight picture of the actual ruins (left).

Thorpe Hall, Louth, which is haunted by a Green Lady.

mysterious footsteps being heard here in 1905. Apparently even though most of the mansion was dismantled in 1927 the ghost still walks, though it is not known whether it is the same one that troubles the bridge over the Ruskington Beck where a fierce whizzing sound is heard which terrifies dogs. The Priory was a Gilbertine monastery which later became a priest's house and then a country mansion. It was the latter that Dickens described as Chesney Wold in *Bleak House*.

Within these pages there are numerous White, Grey, and even Blue Ladies, but very few that appear dressed in green. An aristocratic Spanish beauty, dressed in a gown of that colour, haunts **Thorpe Hall**, a 400-year old mansion situated on the outskirts of Louth.

In 1596 John Bolle, the builder of Thorpe Hall, was engaged in besieging the port of Cadiz in company with Sir Walter Raleigh and the Earl of Essex. He was awarded a knighthood for his bravery in this action, and at the same time appears to have won the heart of a high-born Spanish lady, Donna Leonora Oviedo. However Bolle was already happily married and, with utmost gallantry, refused to compromise himself with Donna Leonora. When the siege was ended and Sir John left Cadiz she insisted that he took her portrait with him, and gave him a valuable gold chain to present to his wife as a token of her respect. He must have been hard put to explain these presents to a wife who was older than himself and had been married twice before, especially when he began the custom of setting a place at the dinner-table for Donna Leonora, a tradition that continued until the 1920s at Thorpe Hall.

Donna Leonora spent the rest of her days in a convent (an alternative version says she followed Sir John back to England, saw how happy he was with his family at Thorpe Hall, and stabbed herself in the garden there).

Sir John died ten years later, in 1606, aged 46. The Green Lady still looks for the lover who left her, roaming the gardens of the Hall, and even to the hazard of traffic, the road outside.

WALES

PLAS MAWR'S
GUARDIAN SPIRIT

Myth and legend is as much part of Wales as its billowing landscape. This is the land of the Red Dragon, Merlin's magical kingdom, with a heritage steeped in tradition, its own mystifying language and unfathomable place names. Even today, with the once clear cut division between England and Wales smudged together, it has the feeling of somewhere else. And like everywhere else it has its own plentiful supply of ghosts and hauntings.

On the north coast, tucked protectively under the elbow of Llandudno, sits the medieval town of Conwy, snug within its fifteen-feet-thick harp-shaped walls, and watched over by the massive rounded castle that guards the estuary, the mouth of the river, and the surrounding land. They were taking no chances when they built this tough little town. Surrounded by so much muscle-power Conwy itself takes on an almost miniature appearance; and down on the quayside as if to emphasise the point it boasts the tiniest house in Great Britain.

Three bridges span Conwy's estuary, strung out side by side like the strands of a necklace; Thomas Telford's deceptively delicate suspension bridge, with its lace-edged top and trailing strands, now sensibly reserved for pedestrians. Beside it Robert Stephenson created his elegant

▷ Plas Mawr – the Great Mansion – dates from Elizabethan times.

tubular railway bridge, and the modern road bridge making up the trio is, thankfully, as graceful a piece of modern architecture as you could wish for.

Once across and into the town the High Street is almost on top of you, and in it Plas Mawr, the Great Mansion. It is hard to believe that Robert Wynne's dignified Elizabethan home was once set in spacious gardens overlooking the river; the neighbouring streets and cottages are now close enough to touch, and the cluster of roofs that mushroom all around it make it hard to tell where Plas Mawr starts and finishes. But once off the High Street and into the close-walled courtyard, the bustle of everyday life is cut off as abruptly as a radio; it is as if you had stepped straight from the supermarket into church.

Robert Wynne, described as an Elizabethan adventurer, came from a distinguished Welsh

▽ Leonard Mercer, resident curator, outside Plas Mawr.

family and having enjoyed many years travelling the world, bought himself some land in Conwy and set about building Plas Mawr in 1577. The house was passed down the line, eventually coming to rest with another prominent Welsh family, the Mostyns. The present Lord Mostyn, like his father, allows the Royal Cambrian Academy of Art to use Plas Mawr as its head-quarters. But unlike so many of the other buildings written about here, this particular house, even allowing for more than 400 years of occupation, has no tragic, violent or sinister associations to account for its hauntings – or none with any substance to it anyway.

Leonard Mercer and his wife, Sylvia, have been resident curators since 1974, living in one half of the gatehouse and sharing their lives with enough first- and second-hand 'experiences' to have made most people pack their bags years ago. But for some, familiarity breeds acceptance, and this is certainly the case with the Mercers. They have come to terms with the 'guardian spirit' that knocked three times to warn of an impending family mishap, know about the little Girl in Blue who comes to play, have felt the icy-cold places that give visitors the shivers, and take it for granted that they should feel the occasional strong sensation of some unseen, but benign, presence.

There was just one set of unaccountable experiences that Leonard took it upon himself to put a stop to. About five years ago a friend was looking after the office for them, next door to the first-floor Banqueting Hall, when she heard a strange ticking or fluttering sound. When she located the noise, she discovered it came from the goose spit which hangs on a hook on the wall. Occasionally Leonard would wind-up this cooking instrument to show people how it worked, but he had not touched it since June, and this was now September. It carried on rotating for its usual 25 minutes or so, and during that time the phone rang, but no one appeared to be on the other end of the line. When the friend returned home that evening, she had a call telling her her nephew had died suddenly.

Just a week later the woman experienced exactly the same pattern of events; this time she learned of the death of a young woman relative.

Soon afterwards Leonard himself found the goose spit in action and answered the phone to a non-speaking caller, and later suspected this was to let him know of the demise of a distant uncle. That was enough, he said, as far as he was concerned. 'It would have got to the stage where everyone was terrified of the goose spit starting up and what was going to happen, so I made sure it couldn't work any longer. It's still there on the wall, but at least it doesn't move.'

The door knocking heralds less fatal domestic incidents, the type of occurrences not unknown to those living and working in 400-year-old surroundings. Heard at night, and by Sylvia rather than her husband, they have been followed up by falls through ceilings, tripping downstairs, the discovery of dry rot, and collapsing plaster work. The only thing the Mercers can be sure of is that something will happen pretty soon after the knocking. A psychic visitor to Plas Mawr told the couple that these warnings were the work of Mrs Mercer's guardian spirit.

Their everyday acceptance of these curiosities are all part of living where they do, said Leonard. 'You come around to a different way of thinking, I've had so many odd things happen to me you reach the stage when they're not odd any more. If something I've been searching for suddenly turns up where I'd least expect it, I just tend to say "thank you", and carry on with what I was doing.'

Other people, visitors and especially, are not so easily comforted. Sylvia well remembers the day a woman fled downstairs from the second-floor reception room when she realised that the young girl dressed in a blue crinoline was not there just to add a touch of realism. At first sight the visitor appreciated the apparent added extra, but when she looked again and saw that the girl was no longer a solid figure, she made a hasty exit.

As far as the Mercers are concerned, the Girl in Blue goes back to their early days at Plas Mawr, but as to her identity and just how long she has been seen in and around the house, they have absolutely no clues. 'The first we knew of her,' said Leonard, 'was when we had a girl working here in the tea room called Megan Cotton. On a particularly quiet day Megan was sitting reading

when she saw a movement out of the corner of her eye. She went over towards the kitchen, where the movement seemed to come from, and saw what she took to be our daughter, Sharon, standing inside with her back turned.'

Sharon Mercer was about ten years old at the time, and had long copper-coloured hair; the girl Megan saw was of a similar age and also had long reddish hair. 'Megan approached "Sharon", probably wondering why she was wearing such an elaborate dress, but when she went into the kitchen there was no-one there. She was so shaken by the incident that she promptly handed in her notice.'

A fairly regular young visitor to the neighbouring property, Mansion House, actually struck up a friendship with the Girl in Blue. As a three-year-old, Rebecca Roberts, was in the habit of going into the back courtyard to play while her mother enjoyed a chat inside. Nothing untoward ever happened, except that the family dog refused to go outside with his little mistress after dashing in one afternoon with his hair on end. Back in her own home when she heard that another visit was planned, Rebecca was delighted and told her mother she hoped she could play with 'that little girl again'. No other children lived in Mansion House at the time, and the only little girl known to play nearby was the one wearing a blue crinoline.

Another of Leonard and Sylvia's local friends, artist Sandra Holroyde, has witnessed something of this playful apparition. One evening, leaving the curator's office, she remembered she had not switched the phone through to the Mercers' gate-house and popped back. As she walked through the Banqueting Hall she saw a patch of vivid blue, shimmering and swirling across the floor; there was no shape to it, but again the only likely explanation that came to her was the Girl in Blue.

The fact that these extraordinary incidents take place within a step or two of the butcher's, the chemist's, the gift shop, and the endless procession of cars winding up the High Street, makes them all the more bizarre; ghostly girls in mid-nineteenth-century dress, and even guardian spirits, seem distinctly at odds with our twentieth-century lifestyles. Even within the cool confines of the Great Mansion itself, with its sparsely furnished, but still gracious rooms, its bare, creaky floorboards, and leaded windows glazed with what looks like thick ice, you only need to glance outside to see washing lines, TV aerials and camera-wielding tourists walking the walls that wrap themselves around this busy little town.

Having said that, the very emptiness of the rooms, especially those on the upper level, would not encourage you to linger long after dark, especially the Lantern Room. This particular spot brings us back to an earlier reference to un-substantiated stories. The Plas Mawr guide book devotes a full three pages to an account, by a six-teenth-century housekeeper, of a tragic and dreadful night one November. It is a chilling tale, but one Leonard Mercer feels should be taken with a hefty pinch of salt. Sylvia, on the other hand, is inclined to believe something untoward took place in this room at some time in its history, if only because of the intense cold she has experienced in one particular spot, an iciness that has nothing to do with the ambient temperature, or the time of year.

△ A view of Conwy from Plas Mawr's tower, with Conwy Castle in the distance.

The story starts with the then lady of the house, who was pregnant at the time, and her three-year-old child, in the watch tower of Plas Mawr, anxiously awaiting the return of her soldier husband. Disappointed, tired and cold she started to make her way down the steep stairs, child in arms, when she fell. Both were seriously hurt. The old housekeeper put them both to bed, and called the family doctor; he attended his patients and warned the housekeeper to keep a careful watch on them as the situation was critical. Later that night, mother and child began to deteriorate, and the doctor was summoned again. This time his popular but inexperienced assistant, Dr Dick, attended. He found the child on the point of death from concussion and placed her on a couch below the window, while he attended the mother, who by then was showing all the signs of premature labour.

Poor Dr Dick, who had a tendency to be nervous at the best of times, was now in a state of panic, and said he needed to fetch the old doctor. The housekeeper, fearing the worst if the patients were left, locked him in the room to prevent him leaving, saying she would send someone else for the more senior doctor. The 'someone else' mysteriously disappeared en route, and the older doctor never made it to Plas Mawr. The frightened housekeeper heard cries, and then silence from the locked room, but it was not until the husband returned that she dared go near.

By then the Lantern Room had turned into a chamber of horror; Dr Dick was nowhere to be seen, but the wife lay dead on the bed, as did the three-year-old on the couch, and the premature baby was still and lifeless on a window ledge. Stricken with grief the lord of the house dropped dead at the foot of the bed. Dr Dick was never seen again; he is said to have fled from the scene (although not to blame for the tragedy) via the chimney, and been overcome by fumes. His bones, the story says, are still somewhere in the interlinking chimney system, and the soldier husband still paces the room in an agony of torment.

After that, it would be almost a relief to be met on the stairs by the friendly little Girl in Blue, but as yet, neither Leonard nor Sylvia Mercer have had the pleasure. But at least they have their guardian spirit.

Welsh ghosts are creatures of regular habits – according to the ancient books they conform to quite rigid rules:

Ghosts ... are supposed to be mere aerial beings without substance, who can pass through walls and other solid bodies at pleasure. ... the usual time for their appearance is midnight, seldom before it is dark, and no ghosts can appear on Christmas Eve.

'One of the most singular tales of the appearance of a ghost' came from Powis Castle in the mid-eighteenth century.

A ghost has not the power to speak until it has been first spoken to; so that notwithstanding the urgency of the business on which it may come, every thing must stand still till the person visited can find sufficient courage to speak to it.

The mode of addressing a ghost is by commanding it in the name of the 3 persons of the Trinity to tell you who it is and what is its business ... it will in a low and hollow voice, declare its satisfaction at being spoken to, and desire the person addressing it not to be afraid ... it commonly enters into its narrative, which being completed and its requests or commands given, with injunction that they be immediately executed, it vanishes away ...

The 'poor unmarried woman, who was a member of the Methodist Society, and became serious under their ministry' who encountered the Powis Castle ghost in the middle years of the eighteenth century obeyed these rules, followed the instructions given by the apparition, and was well rewarded.

Powis Castle is one of the grandest buildings of Wales. Built of red sandstone, its oldest part is a rectangular tower dating from about 1200. This was considerably strengthened before the end of thirteenth century and much of this fabric survives, together with later work, as the Castle gradually became converted from a border stronghold into a comfortable mansion, home of the Lords Powis. It now belongs to the National Trust.

The poor Methodist spinster of the ghost story was a frequent visitor to the castle, usually being given humble chores such as spinning flax in the servants' quarters. On this occasion, however, she was informed that the family were away and to her surprise at nightfall was conducted to a grand bedroom where a fire had been lit and a candle was burning on the table. She was surprised when the lock clicked

It took seven clergymen to lay the ghost of Maesmawr Hall.

behind the steward as he left the room. Disappointed by his lack of trust, she settled down to read her Bible before preparing for bed.

Before long she was disturbed by hearing the lock turn again, and was startled to see a finely-dressed gentleman enter the room. She knew the members of the Powis family well, but did not recognise his face. He walked across to the window and looked out, then after a few moments returned to the door, opened it and left, locking the door again behind him.

Quite frightened by this episode the woman began her prayers but within minutes the gentleman returned, following the same procedure. When he came back the third time the poor woman decided that he must be a ghost and asked him who he was and what he wanted.

The ghost told her to take her candle and follow him, leading her to a small room where he stooped and lifted a floorboard. A box with an iron handle was revealed. Stepping across the room he pointed to a crevice which hid the key needed to open the lock, and then he spoke to her gravely: 'This box and this key must be taken out and sent to the Earl in London. Do this and I will trouble the house no more.'

The brave woman was quick to give her promise to this, and the ghost nodded and walked from the room, never to be seen again. His instructions were carried out, and the Earl rewarded the woman with a comfortable estate cottage and a pension for life.

At first sight part of this story is puzzling. Why did the ghost need to use the door to enter the room when the usual behaviour would have been to melt through a wall? But then, you realise, the woman would not have been able to follow him to the room where the box was hidden.

The **Maesmawr Hall Hotel** at Caersws, not far from Newtown, is the first of a succession of inviting country house hotels in Wales having a ghost amongst its other attractions. Perhaps it is more debatable at Maesmawr Hall

MORFA, THE UNLUCKY PIT

Miners have good reason to be superstitious, for theirs is a dangerous calling. The miners of South Wales knew many portents of disaster – the most ominous being the sight of a dove, two crows, or any unusual bird above the winding-gear. A large white bird was seen at Morfa Colliery, near Port Talbot, the day before the explosion there which killed 87 miners in 1890. Morfa was always an unlucky pit and ghosts were often seen there, but other phenomena must have been more frightening – like the smell of a rose-garden pervading the coal-face, or the sound of a thunderous roof-fall which proved to be unreal but always served as a warning of impending danger.

because seven able parsons from the neighbourhood are supposed to have laid the ghost in Llyn Tarw, though the proprietors imply that they have reservations about the success of this.

Unusually their ghost has a name, Robin Drwg, and in his prime he caused a lot of trouble. Taking the form of a phantom bull he charged about outside the house shaking it to its foundations. The terrible roars, shrieks and moans that accompanied the visitation so frightened livestock in nearby fields that the cows became dry and poultry egg-bound. Apparently present-day incidents are not so troublesome – perhaps Robin didn't care for having his spirit dampened by the parsons.

Hay-on-Wye is a beautiful town famous for its bookshops. Richard Booth, who was largely responsible for making the town a centre of the second-hand book trade, lived in the

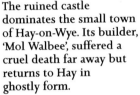

The ruined castle dominates the small town of Hay-on-Wye. Its builder, 'Mol Walbee', suffered a cruel death far away but returns to Hay in ghostly form.

mansion adjoining the castle until it was badly damaged by fire in 1977 (a fire in 1939 had gutted the eastern part of the house). The castle itself was built by Matilda de Breos early in the thirteenth century. Nicknamed 'Mol Walbee', she was a formidable woman both for her size and her spirit and was reputed to have put up the castle in a single night, having made a pact with the Devil. However her black magic did not save her from the vengeance of King John. When she became too 'stomackful' to him in opposing his tyranny he had her and her son entombed at Corfe Castle with a piece of salt bacon and a sheaf of wheat. They lived for eleven thirst-ravaged days, and it is hardly to be wondered that she haunts her castle at Hay-on-Wye.

The **Skirrid Mountain Inn** at Llanfihangel Crucorney near Abergavenny is supposed to be the oldest pub in

Wales and has good cause to be haunted. At least 182 people were executed on its premises, sentenced by the infamous Judge Jefferies after the Monmouth rebellion. The stair-well was used as a gallows and supernatural manifestations have included a lady who, taken ill at the pub, was subsequently found to have a rope-mark imprinted on her neck. The shadows of mysterious helmeted figures sometimes flit across the windows of the inn: in this case it seems more likely that they are the ghosts of Judge Jefferies' guard rather than bikers looking for the gents.

Jefferies stayed at **Llanfihangel Court** while he carried out his ruthless man-hunt. The beautiful house, which dates from the fourteenth century, is haunted by a White Lady who walks from the hall of the house to Lady Wood, where she vanishes.

Many of the numerous castles of South Wales have chilling stories of ghosts and even more sinister entities such as the *Gwrach-y-rhibyn*, the Welsh equivalent of the banshee, but even more fearsome than the Irish variety. Usually she serves as a harbinger of death to long-established Welsh families and appears as a repulsive old crone; her back is hunched and she trails a long black cloak. Sometimes she beats at the window of the sick-room with leathery wings to announce her deadly presence, though there may be confusion here with the *Deryn Corph* (Corpse Bird) which behaves similarly.

Caerphilly Castle (the second largest fortress in Europe, after Windsor Castle) is supposed to be haunted by a *Gwrach-y-rhibyn* who used to enjoy flitting from tower to tower so much that on one occasion some boys (who obviously were not aware of her reputation) almost caught her. She was always seen on occasions when a death was imminent in the Despencer family, even though they had long before abandoned Caerphilly as a residence.

It is only fitting that the oldest pub in Wales should be haunted.

Llanfihangel Court is haunted by a White Lady and a little green man.

The Green Lady of Caerphilly Castle (above) leaves a lingering smell of perfume in the flag tower. Even silver bullets failed to rid Castell Coch (above, right) of its supernatural guardian eagles.

The mighty island fortress is also haunted by a Green Lady, the ghost of Princess Alice who married Gilbert, Lord de Clare, killed at Bannockburn in 1314.

Alice was a French princess who, the story says, fell in love with Tew Teg, a Welsh prince, while her husband was away. In confession, the young prince told the priest of his love for Alice but the priest betrayed the trust of the confessional by informing Lord de Clare of his wife's adultery. She was disgraced and sent back to France, while Tew Teg gave vent to his fury by tracking down and killing the treacherous priest. Princess Alice returns to the castle, dressed in green, eternally seeking the lover that

she lost there nearly seven centuries ago. Perhaps it is her perfume that modern custodians experience in the flag tower, a place where no visitor is allowed.

Gilbert de Clare was responsible for two other great strongholds of this neighbourhood. **Castell Coch** stands at the entrance to the Taff Gorge, a fairytale setting for a fairytale castle. A suitably romantic legend belongs to the building. A medieval Welsh hero, Ifor ap Meurig, had two of his men bewitched and turned into eagles so that they could always stand guard over his treasure which he buried in a tunnel beneath the castle. Centuries later local people learned of the hoard and two gentlemen ventured into the

tunnel but were beaten back by the fierce eagles. The next time they took pistols with them but bullets had no effect on the eagles beyond enraging them further. On the third occasion they took with them silver bullets specially blessed, and a minister to read an exorcism. This served them no better, and after one final attempt, when the eagles flew at them so fiercely that they were lucky to escape, they gave up their efforts.

Castell Coch is one of the treasures of Wales – made a summer palace for the second Marquess of Bute by the architect William Burges who created a colourful extravaganza in high Victorian, mock-medieval, style.

The same patron and architect worked almost the same magic on **Cardiff Castle**, though in a different setting. The result is slightly less spectacular though it still displays a host of colourful styles ranging from Arabian

harem to classical Greek. The second Marquess completed the work at the castle begun by his father. He also made a fortune from developing Cardiff docks, preferring to live in Wales rather than in his other castles in Scotland and Spain. He died at Cardiff, collapsing in his dressing-room in the castle, and his ghost walks through the fireplace of the Library and then passes through a six-feet-thick wall into a corridor leading to the Chapel. From the Chapel he walks to the room in which he died.

The grounds are haunted by a Grey Lady who waves at the castle, some say to attract the attention of Duke Robert of Normandy, eldest son of William the Conqueror who was held prisoner in the Norman castle for eight years. If she does wave at him she does so in vain, for the unfortunate Duke Robert was blinded as soon as he was captured.

High Victorian interior decoration is a fine setting for the noble ghost of Cardiff Castle.

A terrifying glaring eye once appeared in a bedroom at St Donat's Castle, a very haunted building with a variety of ghost stories.

St Donat's Castle lies on the coast to the west of Cardiff. It was the home of the Stradling family from the time of its building in the reign of William Rufus, through 700 years to the reign of George II, when the direct line died out in mysterious circumstances. The Stradlings seem to have been a disaster-prone family through the centuries, and there were two ghosts to warn of the doom that was always in wait for them.

Lady Anne Stradling was left at St Donat's when her husband went to the Holy Land with a crusade. He died defending his honour in a duel. Her wraith, in a long silk dress, would appear before a death in the family, not silently, but with footsteps which sounded loudly on the floor of oak boards. Just to make sure the message was understood the banshee-like *Gwrach-y-rhibyn* would also visit on the night before a death. The evil hag was reported on the night the last of the

Stradlings died, her pack of black hounds with red eyes and terrible teeth following close behind and setting all the neighbourhood dogs and foxes barking.

Sir Thomas was the last of the Stradlings, killed by his travelling companion, the disreputable Sir John Tyrrwhitt in a duel whilst on the Grand Tour. Each had made a pact leaving his estate to the other in the event of an early death. This led to a lawyers' beanfeast – litigation over the Stradling fortune went on for many years. The body of Sir Thomas was brought back to St Donat's and laid out in the Great Hall in funereal pomp. Carelessly the candles at the corners of the bier were left to burn too close to the funeral decorations and the resulting fire cremated five generations of family portraits as well as Sir Thomas and much of the castle.

A nineteenth-century owner, a retired naval officer, found the ghost of St Donat's so troublesome that as a last resort before leaving he called in an exorcist. Four main areas of activity were identified: a panther was seen roaming the corridors; a bright light like a large glaring eye appeared each night in one of the bedrooms; a horrible hag was seen in the library; and the piano, even when closed, was played by invisible hands.

The exorcist set about performing his rites, the culmination of which was a huge gust of wind which swept through the house. After this St Donat's Castle was untroubled, being comprehensively restored in 1925 by the American newspaper magnate William Randolph Hearst who lived there with the film star Marion Davies. Today it is the United World College of the Atlantic, belonging to an organisation promoting international understanding by student contact – in effect an International Sixth Form.

Port Talbot lies a few miles to the north west. It owes its existence to the coal of the Welsh valleys which helped foster heavy industry here in the nineteenth century. The Talbots were the family that made a fortune from this, and in 1840 they built their great mansion at **Margam** and called it a castle, on the site of a Cistercian abbey founded in 1147 (the nave of which survives and is used as a parish

Margam Abbey probably looks better as a ruin than it ever did when it was intact. The curse put on the site by dispossessed monks seems to have been effective.

church). Like most of the abbey, the castle now lies a romantic shell, haunted by a White Lady.

Before the arrival of the Talbots the abbey had belonged to the Mansel family. When the monks had been forced to leave, one of them had placed a curse on the place, saying that if ever the pillars of the abbey gate-house should be dismantled the family would die out. Early in the eighteenth century, young Lord Thomas Mansel inherited the estate and immediately pulled down the gateway, ignoring the entreaties of his steward. Soon after this he died: his uncle succeeded him only to die within the same year. The latter's brother was the last of the line: within five years he too was dead. When they came to the property the Talbots were careful to find the stone the old gate towers had been made from and re-erected them. They are still standing.

A ghostly figure of a Cistercian monk has been seen flitting about the ruins of the abbey. Perhaps it is the ghost of Twm Celwydd Teg (Tom of the Fair Lies), another former monk much given to making prophecies. One day he was asked by a young workmate what the day held for him. Tom replied that his colleague would die three deaths before nightfall. The young man laughed at this, for who could die three deaths, let alone in one day? But the prophecy was fulfilled – hunting for kites' eggs at the top of a tall tree overhanging a river, he put his hand into the nest and was bitten by a viper that the kite had left there for her chicks. On his fall from the tree he broke his neck, landed in the river and was drowned.

The Gower peninsula is an un-expected scenic gem to the west of Swansea. At its western tip, inland cliffs abruptly sweep down to the

Lonely Rhossili Rectory stands dramatically at the tip of the Gower peninsula. Something 'very unpleasant indeed' lurks here.

shore, leaving a narrow plateau fronting the Atlantic. The only house to be seen in this windswept location is **Rhossili Rectory**. Something 'very unpleasant indeed' is supposed to enter the house on a certain winter's night, while in a corridor a sudden chill may be experienced and a low voice urges 'Why don't you turn round and look at me?' As far as is known there has been none brave enough to do so.

On the dunes which engulfed the settlement originally sited here, a phantom coach races across the sands to reach the wreck of a treasure-ship. Another lost village, **Llanellan**, was wiped out when the villagers sheltered the victims of a shipwreck who were fleeing from the plague. A White Lady still haunts the site where the cottages of Llanellan once stood, near Llanrhidian.

The small town of **Laugharne** is most visited by those wishing to pay homage to the life of Dylan Thomas who lived at the Boat House and worked in a shed which gave a view of the castle and river. There have been a few reports of people seeing his ghost about the town, but its more authentic haunt is a rehearsal room at the Shepherd's Bush Hotel in London. However Laugharne does have a quite terrifying, though harmless, phantom mastiff, and in olden days its market was often visited by fairies, the 'little people' coming there from beautiful islands offshore. They always presented the exact money for the goods they bought without being asked, and would return home by a secret underground tunnel.

To the west of Haverfordwest, **Roch Castle** is perched on a small outcrop of rock resembling the remains of a

Laugharne Castle must be one of the few Welsh castles to be ghostless, although the area is visited by a spectral mastiff.

Lucy Walters was the first of Charles II's many mistresses and may well have been his wife. She was born at Roch Castle where she appears as a White Lady.

Dartmoor tor. Legend has it that the tower was built by the first Lord Roch who was warned by a witch that it was his fate to die from the bite of an adder. However if he could survive for a year he would be safe.

He therefore retreated from the world, shutting himself up in the topmost room of his castle and living there safely for almost a year. However the last few days of his exile proved to be very cold, and when his friends arrived to celebrate his release on the next day he persuaded them to send him up brushwood to keep himself warm. An adder was concealed amongst the sticks, the warmth of the fire roused it from hibernation, and it bit him as he slept. When his friends opened the door to release him from self-imposed captivity they found his lifeless body.

The castle is haunted by Lucy Walters, who was born here in 1630. She was the first mistress of Charles II and her apparition has been seen in a white dress, floating through the walls of locked rooms. A mysterious sound

of running footsteps also disturbs the household on occasion, and these can only be explained by supernatural effect.

Nanteos is a magnificent Georgian mansion close to Aberystwyth. It was built between 1739 and 1757 as a home for the Powell family, replacing an earlier house going back to the eleventh century. The Powells lived here until 1952, when the line died out. Nanteos is famous for housing the Holy Grail, the chalice of olivewood used at the Last Supper. Originally one of the treasures of Glastonbury, it was taken to Strata Florida Abbey when Glastonbury was about to be dissolved. Later, when the same fate threatened that remote monastery, three monks brought the precious relic over the mountains to Nanteos for safe keeping. It was taken from the house when the last of the Powells died.

Nanteos went into a sad decline in the ten years from 1980, ending with bank repossession. In 1989 the mansion was bought by a London office equipment company whose main priority is to save the deteriorating fabric. It is unclear what has happened to the ghosts that used to find Nanteos such a pleasing setting. However the building has been saved, so it is to be hoped that they will continue to provide a link with the past. At Nanteos there was said to. be the ghost of Gruffyd Evan, the harpist who played at Nanteos for 69 Christmasses before dying at the age of 92. The sound of his music is heard in the Music Room and in the woods beyond the house. The ghost of Elizabeth Owen is also known to haunt the Pink Room. She was childless, and intensely worried that her hated sister-in-law would inherit her jewellery. Thus she rose from her deathbed and concealed her treasure somewhere in the building. It has never been found, but her shade sometimes walks in this room. Perhaps the extensive new work to be carried out will reveal her secret. A phantom horseman rides up the drive late at night, the ghost of a huntsman who broke his neck while his wife watched from the house, and a Grey Lady holding a candelabra used to appear to warn of an imminent death in the Powell family.

In 1984, a TV crew working at Nanteos refused to work there at night because of a sequence of uncanny incidents including the appearance of a ghostly figure wearing a cloak.

The grand rooms of Nanteos echo to music made by an old harpist who died nearly 200 years ago.

Nannau (above, right) where the discovery of a skeleton in a hollow tree ended a 400-year-old haunting.

Maes-y-Neuadd (below) where a small yellow dog acts as a banshee.

Further to the north, not far from Dolgellau, the mansion of **Nannau** presents a similar picture of sad decay. The beautifully-situated house was once the home of the Vaughan family, which included many great names in the history of Wales. Its most famous legend is that of *Ceubren-yr-Ellyl*, the 'hollow tree of the Spirit'.

In 1402 Owain Glyndwr came to Nannau to try to win the support of his cousin, Hywel Sele, Lord of Nannau, against the forces of Henry VI. Glyndwr knew that his cousin was against his cause, and suggested that they walk in the Deer Park to discuss the conflict of interests. The Lord of Nannau was never again seen alive, but about 40 years later lightning struck the hollow trunk of a great oak, and his skeleton was found inside. The remains of the oak tree survived until 1813, when on a hot sultry night it toppled to the ground, and the ghost of Hywel Sele, which had troubled Nannau over four centuries, was never heard of again.

An interesting haunted hotel is situated in wonderful mountainous countryside at Talsarnau, near Harlech.

This is **Maes-y-Neuadd**, a country-house that seems ideal for the ghost-hunter with a taste for luxury. It is a sixteenth-century house, which Robert Graves said was the most haunted he had ever been in. Apart from quite violent poltergeist activity and ghosts which could only be seen in mirrors, there was also the apparition of a small yellow dog which, on the rare occasions when it was seen – on the lawn early in the morning – heralded a death in the house.

Conwy (Conway) is a town full of ghosts – a cloaked figure appears on the ramparts of the castle where the silhouette of a horseman has also been seen against the night sky; a hooded monk walks in the churchyard and along the waterfront; and a bewhiskered sailor named Albert haunts a house in Berry Street.

Ruthin Castle is another place in Wales to please the ghost-hunter who likes his comforts. Although built on the site of the Plantagenet stronghold, the present building is mainly of eighteenth-century date. George Borrow found the ancient part of the building very disturbing and was particularly impressed by 'that strange memorial of the good old times, a drowning pit' and the whipping-post which stood at the centre of the prison room, or torture chamber. Though catering for all tastes, modern hotels don't gain an extra rosette for these refinements, and they exist no longer.

The hotel's ghosts include the apparition of a man in armour who wears only one gauntlet, a strange glowing ball of light, and (the most usual visitant) a Grey Lady.

She is said to have been the wife of the Deputy Commandant of the Castle when it was occupied by the forces of Edward I. When she found that her husband was being unfaithful she murdered her rival with an axe and was executed for her crime. Since then a grey lady has haunted the castle

The castle is just one of many haunted locations in the walled town of Conwy.

Ruthin Castle (below) is another Welsh hotel having resident ghosts. Parts of the medieval castle still survive (above).

and its grounds – workers at the hotel have claimed to have met her in recent years.

There can be few people driving along the road between Denbigh and Pentre-foelas who are not impressed with the ruins to be seen on the northern side of the road near the Sportsman's Arms. They look the very epitome of a haunted house, surrounded by empty moorland and gnarled trees. These are the remains of **Plas Pren**, a hunting lodge built by Lord Davenport early this century. It was sold in 1925 and then used to accommodate the gamekeepers who looked after the grouse moor until the 1950s when it was left to decay. Apparently locals in the Sportsman's Arms enjoy telling the curious that the ruins are haunted by a terrible luminous skeleton. However it is strange that nobody ever thought it worth-while to renovate such a property, especially when located in such wild countryside.

The **Llindir Inn** is further to the east, at Henllan, two miles from Denbigh. It must be one of the most attractive of Welsh pubs, with its old stone walls and thatched roof. It is supposed to have been an inn since 1229 and so has had plenty of time to acquire a ghost. This is a beautiful blonde – the spirit of a landlady of the inn of three centuries ago who was caught in *flagrante delicto* by her husband when he returned from the sea unexpectedly. As the leaflet in the Llindir says:

> *She is still reputed to roam the older parts of the house in the early hours. Parties and receptions are a speciality.*

How nice to have a ghost that makes herself useful.

The sinister ruins of Plas Pren ('The Hall of Wood') stand on the desolate moorland to the west of Denbigh.

THE
NORTH

ENGLAND'S ORIGINAL GHOST TOUR

BRITAIN'S HAUNTED heritage is not confined to the countryside, nor indeed to the country seat. Every town and city has its haunted heritage, and York certainly enjoys its fair share of spooks and spirits.

Once England's second city and the undisputed capital of the north, York has much to boast about. Influenced in turn by the Romans, Saxons, Danes and Normans it is a treasury of archaeological and architectural gems. Everyone, it seems, left their trademark, bequeathing buildings variously described as the 'finest surviving in Europe' and 'the masterpiece of its age'; while beneath it all lies a rich seam of buried treasure,

△ Peter Broadhead, the man who started England's first ghost tour.

the fragments of ancient everyday life that give real shape and substance to textbook conjecture.

Medieval gateways still stand guard at each point of the compass as you approach the heart of the city, but where they once bristled with defence systems they now welcome all comers, and the never-ending flow of tourists attracted to this history-packed centre.

The first thing the visitor to York needs to do is abandon any form of private transport; engine power here is about as useful as a revolving door with no exit; half a dozen times round and you are back where you started. This is a place for walking. And the purpose of this

▽ The Treasurer's House stands on part of the Roman Via Decumana; a ghostly Roman legion has been seen there.

particular visit was to discover more about a very particular walk.

Among York's many other claims to fame is the fact that it was the first English city to offer guided ghost tours. Since the early 1970s thousands of visitors have enjoyed the experience of tramping around the city streets, well into the night, soaking up the atmosphere of York's darker side . . . its mysteries, murders, gross injustices, and especially its ghosts.

Peter Broadhead, the man behind it all, is now semi-retired from the ghost tour business, but the tours themselves have become so popular that his original company has given birth to a number of others. York was already familiar territory to this former British Rail man when, after what he describes as a 'mid life crisis', he found himself caught up in the city's tourist industry. 'I'd had nothing to do with ghosts in the past,' he said, 'but the idea was put to me and so I did some research into the subject, and I very quickly realised there was a wealth of material available.'

One of his chief sources of local ghost lore was a wonderfully detailed book, *Ghosts of Ancient City*, written by J. V. Mitchell, a former history master at the famous St Peter's School, and after enlisting the author's help in investigating various hauntings even further, Peter Broadhead arrived at those he built into his first special interest tours. 'I was careful to select York ghosts that really stood up to enquiry and had close associations with the city's buildings; I didn't want vague references that couldn't be authenticated, or ghosts no-one could believe in.' The end result was a collection of stories detailed enough to delight the serious ghost-hunter, and give the sceptic plenty of food for thought.

Peter and his storytelling guides took to the streets in 1973, just two nights a week at first, then three, then every evening, and finally two or three times per evening. 'It was popular from day one, and then just grew and grew. In the years I was taking parties around myself I must have had visitors from just about every corner of the world, and it's always fascinated me to see the reactions of people from different countries and cultures. Those from the Far East, for example, with backgrounds steeped in myth and legend, readily accept what they hear, while the German visitor in particular is far less likely to believe.' There are also those, he added, who come with the determination to get their money's worth and see a ghost at all costs – 'and if they've made up their minds they'll see a ghost, then they do!'

On the other side of the coin are those equally determined that the whole thing is nothing more than a jolly evening out with a difference. 'I've known many occasions when someone on a tour is ready to scoff at the whole thing; but then something has happened somewhere along the way and they've left at the end feeling very sober indeed.' But what about the former chief guide himself, a self-confessed steam fanatic with no previous interest in the subject whatever? 'I have not seen a ghost, but I've been to one or two places where my hair has stood on end, and I do believe that when people seriously say they have seen something, they have.'

The magnificent York Minster, the largest medieval cathedral in northern Europe, is a hauntingly beautiful sight in its own right. And in the quiet of late evening when every footstep rings its presence and every murmured word is carried aloft, it takes on a genuinely spiritual quality. Here among tombs and relics spanning 70 years Peter tells a 'modern' ghost tale set in the First World War. A brother and sister who always attended Evensong together shared one last service before the young man went off to war; here in the Minster the brother promised his sister he would come back to her if he was killed.

Walking up the South Choir one evening shortly afterwards the sister and a friend did indeed see the soldier; he was walking towards them, and as he passed by he paused to embrace someone, and was then gone. The sister knew without doubt that her brother had carried out his promise and returned to the Minster to tell her he was in the after life. Some time after that evening she discovered what had happened; the ship he was travelling on sank and he was drowned, at precisely the same time he took his walk up the South Choir of York Minster.

York's great age is evident everywhere you turn in this fascinating walled city, and nowhere more so than in the web of narrow streets that criss-cross the very centre. The Shambles is one of the best preserved of York's medieval thorough-fares, and even in the twentieth century it manages to retain its museum piece appeal. This is also ghost tour territory, and it does not take too much imagination, especially in the moon-light, to peel back the years and let your mind loose on dim distance images of the past. Among the many stories associated with The Shambles, Peter picked on another that hardly qualifies for the history books; it took place within the last 30 years.

Two old farming gents, visiting York for the day, found themselves worn out and soaking wet in The Shambles. Taking shelter from the rain they were invited into one of the houses by an elderly lady. She was extremely hospitable and insisted that while they rested, and dried themselves off as best they could, they share a meal with her. They were very grateful; that is until they started eating. The milk she served was sour, and the soup tasted dreadful. But despite the

The ghost-tour visits York's haunted sites — (right) Clifford's Tower, and (below) St Mary's Heritage Centre.

by piling slabs and stones on their body until they suffocated. Margaret Clitheroe was finally silenced in this way at the bottom of The Shambles, probably within sight of her own home. Peter Broadhead does not suggest that Margaret Clitheroe haunts The Shambles, but her story is typical of several true tales that add a gruesome note to the tours, and keep everyone on the look out . . . just in case.

In contrast the Theatre Royal ghost has been known to exist for at least 100 years. Now theatre ghosts are good news, especially for those whose business it is to keep the theatres full. Actors are a very superstitious breed, and the sight of a ghost is said to indicate a good audience, and hence a successful show. The Royal's Grey Lady was so well known, Peter said, that she had practically become part of the scenery, but some nine years ago a small committee was instituted to investigate the stories surrounding her, and a decision was taken to exorcise the theatre.

'A medium was called in,' Peter explained, 'and successfully called up the ghost. It transpired that she was a novice nun from the time a convent stood on the site in the seventeenth century.' Through the medium the girl talked about her days in the convent, of her enthusiasm, and of how she would see angels hovering over the altar during Mass. There was clearly a little of Margaret Clitheroe about the Grey Lady, since her constant talk of 'hovering angels' soon made the less visionary nuns jealous of her special abilities. The Mother Superior decided on punishment, only allowing the novice back into Mass after she promised to behave herself.

The very next Mass the novice saw her angels again, and told everyone about it. This time her punishment was a lengthy period of solitary confinement, during which she died. Her spirit, according to the medium, had been confined to the building ever since, awaiting forgiveness for her over-enthusiasm. That still begs the question of whether she was telling tall stories in the first place; but since a service of exorcism was arranged, and the Grey Lady released at long last, there will never be another chance of finding out.

But while York is now one ghost less there are many more to fill the night-time shadows and stir up the chill air on these ghostly tours.

quality of the food, the quality of her kindness touched a chord with the farmers, and the next time they visited The Shambles they took a gift of fresh eggs to supplement her poor larder. The only trouble was they could not find the house or the woman, and nor could anyone else. Apparently it did not exist.

This same location shares a less mysterious, and far more brutal story. Margaret Clitheroe, a staunchly Catholic butcher's wife, lived in The Shambles at the time of Elizabeth I. Unfortunately she was altogether too fervent about her religious beliefs and paraded them high and low. As a result she was eventually locked up in prison, and when she appeared to have learned her lesson, released. But Margaret would not be silenced. More short, sharp sentences followed, but to no avail. Finally she was charged with treason and sentenced to death.

One of the fashions of the time when it came to the carrying out the death sentence was for the life to be literally pressed out of the victim

Yorkshire people have the reputation of being somewhat down to earth and taciturn, not given to standing nonsense from anyone, let alone a disembodied spirit. In these circumstances one might think that ghosts would prefer to haunt elsewhere, but there are just as many good, well-documented stories from Yorkshire as there are from other parts.

Sheffield is Yorkshire's biggest city and the ruins of its Manor Lodge stand in unlikely surroundings on the eastern side of the city. It is hard to imagine it as a grand hunting lodge of the Tudor Earls of Shrewsbury seeing its remains today amongst twentieth-century council housing. The only part to survive with roof intact is the **Turret House**, an Elizabethan summer house where Mary, Queen of Scots was accommodated at times during the fourteen years when the Earl of Shrewsbury served as her custodian. It must have made a pleasant change for her to stay here rather than in gloomy Sheffield Castle where she was held for most of the time. Her room at the Turret House contained an unusual incense burner carved from stone in the shape of an evil-looking imp, perhaps designed to frighten away evil spirits. Smoke came from holes where its eyes and mouth should have been. Although very heavy it had the supernatural ability of being able to move about the room without human aid. It is no longer to be seen in Turret House, though it is said that the ghost of the unhappy queen still walks there. The Manor Castle, the pub just below the Manor, has also been troubled by an apparition.

Leeds Corporation bought **Temple Newsam** in 1922, adapting its interior as an art gallery and museum. The great red-brick mansion ('The Hampton Court of the North') had previously been the home of a noted writer of ghost books, Lord Halifax, while in medieval times the demesne was a property of the Knights Templar.

Manor Lodge (right) and its gatehouse, the Turret House (below), stand amongst modern housing on the south side of Sheffield. Mary, Queen of Scots is supposed to have spent some time as a prisoner in the Turret House and her ghost still walks there.

In 1908 Lord Halifax was disturbed by the Blue Lady, an elderly lady wearing a lacy shawl over a blue dress. Perhaps his interest in ghosts sprang from this incident.

All sorts of phenomena have bedevilled Temple Newsam in the past: a famous one has been called The Phantom Ball. This is a noise that seems to come from the floor above, as though heavy furniture is being moved there. The greatest mystery is why this rather mundane haunting should be given such a fancy name.

The ghosts of the Darnley Room (so called because it was the birthplace of the husband of Mary, Queen of Scots) are more conventional. There is a small boy who steps from a cupboard, and the shade of a Knight Templar has also been seen. In the south wing terrible, agonised screams have been heard, yet as with all the Temple Newsam ghosts, no explanation can be given for why these should occur.

Present-day cleaners who work at the house speak of a lady in a long dress who brushes past them while they work on 'the thirteen steps'.

Mary's ghost is also said to haunt the Darnley Room at Temple Newsam House, Leeds.

GHOSTLY SOLDIERS

Phantom armies haunt many parts of Britain from the Welsh Borders to the Highlands of Scotland, where the massacres at Culloden and Killiecrankie are re-enacted by 'armies in the sky'. Yorkshire too has its ghostly legions. Apart from the famous Roman haunting in York itself, a detachment of legionaries also marches past the driveway of Burton Constable Hall. Of course the ghostly soldiers which stumble from the battlefield of Marston Moor belong to a later period; they are Royalists fleeing from defeat at the hands of Cromwell's powerful army. In the 1930s a motorist driving on the main road which crosses the battlefield met with a sad group of dishevelled Cavaliers and was horrified when an oncoming bus drove right through them, with no visible effect.

Calverley, between Leeds and Bradford, has the apparition of Walter Calverley, who, in a fit of jealous rage, killed two of his children, and rides through the village on a headless horse.

On the other side of Leeds is the village of **Calverley**, still bravely trying to maintain its own character against encroaching suburbs of Bradford and Leeds. In the early 1600s the Calverley family had already lived here for 500 years, and the Lord of the Manor at the time, Walter Calverley, was a man of some importance, though through dissipation he had lost much of the fortune that he had inherited. It was probably financial difficulties, combined with his drinking that sparked off a murderous fit of insanity. Convinced that his ever-doting wife was having an affair, he attacked her and the children. Although he only succeeded in wounding his wife, he killed two of his children with a dagger before setting off on horseback to find the third, who was with a wet-nurse in a neighbouring village. Fortunately his horse fell and rolled on him before he could reach this infant and he was captured.

He was sentenced at York Assize, and since he refused to plead was condemned to death by pressing. When a servant obeyed his master's gasped request to add a heavy weight to end his agonies, the authorities had the poor fellow strung up on the gallows in a trice, presumably for contempt of court. Calverley must have felt remorse for his dreadful crime, for by his brave refusal to plea the family retained their estates. Although buried at York, his body was later secretly dug up and taken to Calverley. Here he is said to haunt the village to this day, mounted on a headless horse. His ghost also walked at the Hall, one corridor being so badly affected that it was eventually bricked up. Walter also gave the clergy short shrift: he was blamed when a parson (who was staying at the Hall having preached in the church) was thrown out of bed three times during the course of a night.

Bradford's most famous haunted house is **Bolling Hall** (or Bowling Hall), which, like Temple Newsam at Leeds, serves as a museum today. Part of the building is medieval, but from about 1660 numerous additions were made in a variety of styles, with the delightfully haphazard result to be seen today. In 1643 Bradford, a town strongly supporting Cromwell, was besieged by Royalist forces led by the Earl of Newcastle. He made Bolling Hall his headquarters, but was incensed when the leader of one of his squadrons of horse, the Earl of Newport, was killed in a preliminary skirmish. It was not his death that annoyed Lord Newcastle, but the manner of it. Separated from his men Newport asked the Puritan leader for quarter. The reply was that he would indeed receive quarter, 'Bradford

A female ghost at Bolling Hall saved the citizens of Bradford from massacre at the hands of the Earl of Newcastle. The shade of the industrial reformer Richard Oastler has also been seen.

quarter', and thereupon struck him a fatal blow. Because of this Newcastle swore that he would be avenged and orders were given to '. . . kill all in the town – men, women and children – and to give them all "Bradford quarter" for the brave Earl of Newport's sake.'

Yet with the dawning of a new day the Earl had countermanded this savage order, saying that none of the citizens should be killed in the siege. Rumours soon circulated that this change of heart had come about because of a female ghost that had persistently troubled the commander in the night, three times pulling the sheets from his bed, each time murmuring 'pity poor Bradford' until the Earl promised to be merciful.

Many ghost stories were made up by the propagandists of both sides during the Civil War: most probably this is one of them.

If you are fortunate enough to see a ghost at Bolling now it will probably be the shade of the industrial reformer Richard Oastler. He was a great friend of the Walkers, owners of the house in the mid-nineteenth century, and he promised to return to Bolling after his death to prove that there was a here-after. On the day of his death in 1861 he appeared to the Walkers' son, and there are reports that his ghost still haunts the Hall.

East Riddlesden Hall, near Keighley, is a National Trust property that has three ghosts. The house was

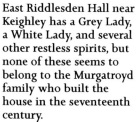

East Riddlesden Hall near Keighley has a Grey Lady, a White Lady, and several other restless spirits, but none of these seems to belong to the Murgatroyd family who built the house in the seventeenth century.

originally built in 1648 for James Murgatroyd, a cloth merchant, whose family is supposed to have been the model for the 'Bad Baronets' in Gilbert and Sullivan's *Ruddigore*.

East Riddlesden's Grey Lady was probably not a Murgatroyd – she is sometimes said to have been a Paslew – but she haunts because her husband found her with a lover. He walled up the young man, and then kept his wife a prisoner in her room, leaving her to starve to death as well. Surprisingly, the Grey Lady is a kindly ghost, who comes to people in trouble.

Another helpful ghost rocks the ornate wooden cradle that can still be seen in an upstairs room. This was used by the Rishworth family who lived at East Riddlesden in the seventeenth century. It is said to rock by itself on New Year's Eve, perhaps because the ghost knows that grown-ups would be too busy celebrating to bother with soothing a baby.

The Scottish Merchant's ghost is a reminder of an incident that happened here in 1790. The owner of the house was away when, on a dreadful night of driving snow, a Scottish wool merchant knocked at the door requesting shelter. The steward welcomed him, but on finding that the Scotsman carried a rich purse, he killed the merchant while he slept. However the crime was discovered and the wicked steward suffered on the gallows at York Castle.

East Riddlesden must be one of the most well-haunted houses in Yorkshire, if not in England, for it also has a White Lady, who was drowned in a fish pond when out hunting and her horse threw her, and a Blue Lady whose identity remains a mystery. The whole district is exceptionally rich in ghosts, but beware – quite a few are dangerous. Be particularly wary of a giant scrawny grey cat and a black dog the size of a donkey – both bring death to those they meet, while a black bear acts as a banshee in these parts, howling around the house of someone shortly doomed to die.

In 1978 the national newspapers took up a story from a restaurant in Haworth where the proprietor had spoken of meeting the ghost of Emily Brontë on 19 December, the anniversary of her death. The ghost, he

The wooden cradle at East Riddlesden – rocked by an unseen hand.

said, climbed upstairs on a staircase that had been removed some time before, and was a small and slim figure who giggled and chuckled happily. The haunting had started twelve years previously and he had been able to identify her from the portrait of the family. However, experts pointed out that Emily was a large lady, invariable morose who would have been little given to giggling. Those who feel that experts are not always right should try patronising **Weaver's Restaurant** at Haworth on the night of 19 December, but be sure to book first in case of a seasonal rush.

A more appropriate place for Emily's apparition to appear is on the moors she loved so well, and indeed her shade is supposed to haunt the path up to the waterfall, a sad figure who walks with head bowed.

The evocatively-named **Old Silent Inn** stands amidst the bleak Brontë moorland near Stanbury. Here the ghost is a kindly old woman, a landlady of the pub long ago who enjoyed feeding the cats that lived off the inhospitable surrounding countryside. She announced feeding time by ringing a bell from a doorway now blocked up, and this is where the ghost has been seen, both by landlords and customers. The present landlord's two dogs will not go near this corner of the bar. Sometimes the sound of a ghostly bell is also heard. An unusual

An old lady who loved cats is the kindly ghost of the remote Old Silent Inn (right).

Is the giggling girl seen at Weaver's Restaurant, Haworth (far right), really the ghost of Emily Brontë?

number of cats still visit the yard at the back of the pub, which apparently takes its name from having served as a secret refuge of Bonnie Prince Charlie after 1745.

The 'tender decay' of **Bolton Abbey** is a scenic gem of the West Riding, immortalised by Turner in paint, by Ruskin in prose. In fact it is an Augustinian priory and not an abbey, a name given it by early railway company publicists, who probably thought it more romantic. Its famous ghost, usually identified as that of an Augusti-

nian canon, does not frequent any particular area of the church or ruins, but can appear anywhere on the demesne of the priory.

The ghost achieved fame by being seen by a prominent member of the aristocracy in 1912. The young Marquis of Hartington was staying at the Rectory, a member of a shooting party. Talk at dinner had been of ghosts, and on retiring to bed the Marquis, still a schoolboy, saw a figure standing by his bedroom door. He was able to describe the figure exactly – a man in

There have been few more detailed descriptions of a ghost than that given by Lord Hartington in 1912 of the phantom monk of Bolton Abbey.

his sixties, with a round, wrinkled face well covered with stubble. He wore a long robe like a dressing-gown, with a hood over his head. The description of the ghost was more or less identical with that given by the Rector of Bolton, who had seen the figure previously. The young Marquis told his story at many dinner parties, King George V showing a great interest, and it was later included in Lord Halifax's Ghost Book. The Rectory once served as the schoolhouse of the Priory, so perhaps the spirit of one of the Augustinian teachers had returned to chide the schoolboy for being up so late (it was 11.15 pm). A phantom monk has been seen at Bolton on several occasions subsequently, and once the angelus was heard many years after the bells had been removed (an Archbishop witnessed this phenomenon).

A Blue Lady haunts Fountains Abbey, where the chanting of a ghostly choir is also heard.

At **Fountains Abbey** a ghostly choir has been heard chanting plainsong in the Chapel of the Nine Altars, but the more interesting incident belongs to the Hall nearby. This was built in about 1611 by Sir Stephen Proctor, 'an unscrupulous and unsqueamish man' (Pevsner), who was so hated because of the cruel way that he extorted fines from practising Catholics that he ended by being murdered on his own doorstep. His daughter witnessed the deed and haunts the house as a Blue Lady – although there is an alternative version suggesting that it was actually the daughter of the house who was murdered on the threshold. In recent years, a member of staff has seen the ghost of a man in Elizabethan costume who walked out of the oak panelling in the Stone Hall.

The Abbey at Byland, far to the east of Fountains on the edge of the North York Moors, does not possess a ghost but is worth mentioning here because one of its monks produced the earliest collection of English ghost stories (actually written in Latin). The tales all came from the neighbourhood and were obviously told to the monk who wrote them down at first hand, using the blank pages at the beginning and end of a missal. They date from the early years of the fifteenth century.

Newburgh Priory was an Augustinian foundation set up within three miles of Byland, but on the other, southern, side of the village of Coxwold. Nothing remains of the Priory, its stones being incorporated into the mansion built on its site for the Lords Fauconberg. Newburgh has two ghosts: a White Lady walks by the lake and is a harbinger of death; and there is a man with an evil expression who is dressed in the silk breeches and wig fashionable in the eighteenth

Newburgh Abbey's ghosts are thought to be connected with a duel once fought there.

Spofforth Castle can only manage half a ghost!

Burton Constable Hall, which has several ghosts.

century. His appearance, and perhaps also that of the White Lady, is connected with a duel that was once fought here.

The unpretentious remains of **Spofforth Castle** can be seen from the road between Harrogate and Wetherby. Once a stronghold of the Percys who controlled much of northern England in medieval times, it has a ghost which throws itself from the battlements. Observant witnesses say that the ghost is female – but why should only half of the figure be visible?

The 46th Lord Paramount of the Seigniory of Holderness, Mr John Chichester-Constable, lives at **Burton Constable Hall** near Hull, Humberside. The grandiose house dates from 1570 though many additions and embellishments were made subsequently, Robert Adam, Wyatt, and Capability Brown contributing their talents.

The Hall is haunted by several ghosts. The grandmother of the present owner saw the ghost of

William Constable, who lived here in the eighteenth century, when she was sleeping in the Gold Bedroom. She recognised him immediately from the portrait that hangs in the house. This was an unusual encounter in that the ghost spoke to her: 'I have come back to see what you have done to my room.' He must have been reassured by what he saw, for he has not been seen since.

The oldest part of the Hall, the North Tower, is haunted by Nurse Dowdall – a much-loved nanny to the children of the household in the nineteenth century. She was so highly regarded that she was buried in the family mausoleum at Halsham. Her apparition is the ghost most frequently seen at Burton Constable.

There is also a nun who floats down the Long Gallery and across the Staircase Hall (where the priest's hole is concealed by a large painting) and a spectral black Labrador which brushes past people on the Tower Stairs. A very recent manifestation has been the

The Gold Bedroom at Burton Constable (above), and (left) seen reflected in one of its ornate mirrors.

Nurse Dowdall, who haunts the North Tower.

'Awd Nance' – Anne Griffith (above), who haunts her old home, Burton Agnes Hall.

appearance of a woman wearing a brown check skirt and brown shoes – the latter appearing very clearly, although the upper part of the body was indistinct. She was seen in the private apartments in the South Wing but remains unidentified at present. Finally, and most spectacularly, a phantom Roman Legion has been seen to march along the road at the top of the drive to the Hall.

It would seem to be asking for trouble to be disrespectful to a ghost, especially to one as gruesome as 'Awd Nance' who haunts beautiful **Burton Agnes Hall**, in Humberside. Hers is a sad story. The youngest of three sisters, Anne Griffith grew up at the Hall as it was being built early in the seven-

teenth century and greatly loved it. One day she rode off to visit the St Quentins, who lived in the neighbouring village of Harpham. Returning to Burton Agnes, she was set upon by footpads or, as we would say today, muggers, and left fatally injured. Five days later she died, having first warned her sisters that unless her head was interred within the house that she loved so deeply her ghost would 'make such disturbance within its walls as to render it uninhabitable for others so long as my head is divorced from my home'.

Thinking her delirious, her sisters ignored this threat and buried her intact in the churchyard at Burton Agnes. A week later terrible night-time disturbances began in the house. There would be six peaceful nights followed by one of bedlam, which increased in violence week by week. Eventually, after a night when it sounded as though a crowd of people were rushing through the corridors and up and down the stairs, the female servants refused to stay in the house any longer. At this the two sisters consulted the vicar who commented that the disturbances always occurred on the day of the week of Anne's burial. They then realised the awful consequences of ignoring her last request and hurried to have her body disinterred. The grave-digger and the vicar were confronted by a fearful spectacle when her coffin was opened:

> The body lay without any marks of corruption or decay, but the head was disengaged from the trunk, and appeared to be rapidly assuming the semblance of a fleshless skull.

Reluctantly, the ladies agreed to the Vicar's suggestion that the skull should be brought back to the house, and when this was done the unwelcome happenings at the Hall ceased. However there were many later attempts to rid the place of its grisly trophy, but all ended with the skull being restored to

its place, terrible upheavals having disturbed the tranquillity of the house. Finally, to avoid any more of this, the skull was bricked up in a wall where it has remained ever since. However the ghost of 'Awd Nance' is said to still walk occasionally, through the rooms that she saw being built and decorated, perhaps to make sure that her successors are caring for the beautiful house with the same love that she had for it.

The ghost of Edward II's favourite, Piers Gaveston, haunts **Scarborough Castle**. He was captured from the castle by the Earl of Warwick who, after besieging it for some time, promised the inmates safe conduct if they gave themselves up. This promise was broken as soon as the gates were opened, and Gaveston was taken back to Warwick and beheaded. His is a dangerous ghost to meet as he walks the castle's battlements at night (not that English Heritage would approve of anyone being in the ruins after dusk). The headless phantom rushes at anyone alone in the ruins, attempting, it seems, to chase them off the battlements to fall to the foot of the cliffs far below.

Scarborough's Pink Lady roams the street where she was murdered in 1804. Her name was Lydia Bell and she was the daughter of a well-to-do York confectioner. There is also a black horse which has haunted the town since Norman times and appears out of a violent thunderstorm.

Count Dracula's dramatic arrival at Whitby might seem to put any self-respecting ghost in the shade (so to speak), but the lovely old fishing-town can parade a fine array of hauntings; like York it has conducted tours on summer evenings to take the curious to haunted locations. The most spectacular of these is **Whitby Abbey**, set high above the town on the clifftop overlooking the harbour. Here St Hilda, who founded the monastery in 657, appears at one of the highest of the empty windows wearing a shroud.

Constance de Beverley, a nun of Whitby who fell for Marmion, the courageous but faithless knight immortalised in verse by Sir Walter Scott, may be met on a twisting stairway leading to a dungeon. She was immured (bricked up alive) for breaking her vows and sobs and pleads with her invisible captors as she is led to the cell where she was left to die.

Beware of the dangerous phantom of Scarborough Castle, said to be the spirit of Piers Gaveston.

The indelible bloodstain on the staircase of Mortham Tower.

Nappa Hall, yet another location for the very restless shade of Mary, Queen of Scots.

Close to the parish church of St Mary, next to the Abbey on the top of the cliff, a coach drawn by four headless horses careers along until it vanishes over the cliff-edge, presumably falling 300 feet to the rocks below.

Away to the west, near Bedale on the far side of the Great North Road, is **Snape Castle** which is said to be haunted by the happy spirit of Catherine Parr, the last wife of Henry VIII. She married Lord Latimer when she was nineteen and spent eleven years at Snape until 1542, when her husband died. Soon afterwards she married the King, and, nursing him through his last illness, proved to be a good wife and queen – rather more than he deserved. She has been seen as a young girl with long fair hair, wearing a blue dress.

Yet further to the west, by Askrigg in Wensleydale, is **Nappa Hall**, the fortified manor house of the Metcalfe family. The house dates from about 1460 and local legend has it that Mary, Queen of Scots stayed here for a night or two in 1568 (perhaps as a break from her six-month stay at Bolton Castle, nearby). In 1878 a visitor was convinced that he had seen the unhappy Queen's ghost here – he wrote:

I . . . was going to touch her when she turned round and I saw her face. It was lovely. Her dress seemed to be made of black velvet. After looking at me for a moment, she went on and disappeared through the door leading to the winding stone staircase in the angle turret of the west tower. Her face, figure and general appearance reminded me of portraits of Mary, Queen of Scots.

Finally, in the far north of the county close to Barnard Castle, the apparition of a headless lady trailing a length of silk has appeared at **Mortham Tower**, a medieval tower house belonging to the Rokeby family. Her story was known to Sir Walter Scott who often stayed at Rokeby Hall, the family's later home. She was the beautiful young wife of a medieval Rokeby who became insanely jealous and, believing her to have been unfaithful, cut off her head and threw the body into the Tees. His dagger dripped blood spots on the spiral staircase and these have proved to be indelible stains to this day, as the present owner of the Tower admits, though he believes that they could have just as well been caused by a nose-bleed.

He has never seen a ghost at Mortham, though many others have experienced strange events here. An eighteenth-century parson met with the ghost beneath the bridge over the River Greta and held a conversation with her in Latin. As an earlier writer has remarked, this was a fair achievement considering that she was without a head!

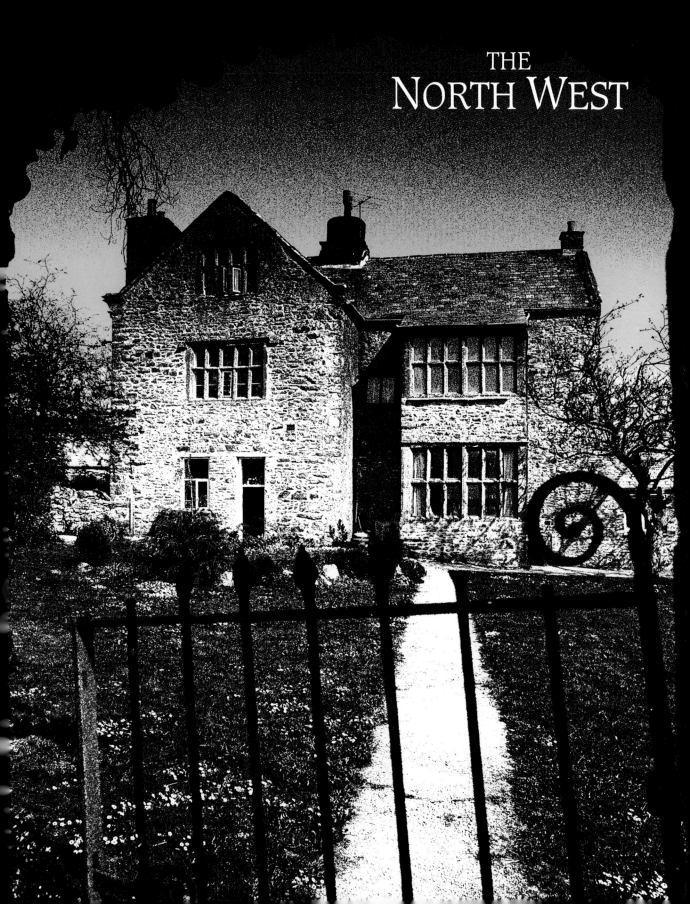

THE
NORTH WEST

THE LEGEND
OF LEVENS

△ Levens Hall.

History does not tell us how the owners of Levens reacted to the curse inflicted on them by a dying gipsy woman, or exactly when it happened. Sometime in the early part of the eighteenth century is suggested. But given the improbable nature of the curse this is hardly surprising; it would have been dismissed as the demented ramblings of a poor, starving wretch. History does, however, record the facts, and the facts state that everything she predicted came true.

Weak and desperate for food, the woman stumbled up to the front door of the Hall begging for help. Horrified that someone of her lowly station should sully the grand portals of Levens the occupants immediately despatched her to the back entrance instead. Unfortunately that proved to be too far for someone in her condition and she collapsed on the way. With her dying breath she cursed the occupants, saying that Levens would never pass from father to son until a white fawn was born in the park, and the River Kent ceased to flow.

Then, as now, Levens Park sported a herd of Norwegian black fallow deer, and if the householders had chosen to believe the gipsy they would have had cause for concern; the likelihood of a white fawn being produced by these darkest of brown creatures was too remote to be thinkable. As for the River Kent, which flows through the estate en route from the Cumbrian Mountains to Morecambe Bay, it was once reputed to be the fastest flowing river in England. A more unlikely pair of prophecies would have been hard to come by. But, whether by coincidence or accursed destiny, it remains a fact that Levens passed only through the female line of the Bagot family for nearly 200 years. It was not until the winter of 1896 that Alan Desmond Bagot was born; and that same year a hind gave birth to a white fawn and the river froze solid. The gipsy's curse was broken at last. Or was it? The most curious aspect of this story is the fact that the two prophecies appear to have continued, while the curse itself

◁ Hal Bagot and one of
his family dogs.

obviously have to wait until the twenty-first century for the next chapter in this intriguing saga.

Curses are one thing, hauntings quite another. But here the two come together because our gipsy appears to have stayed around – perhaps to check up on her predictions, or still in search of food. The Grey Lady of Levens has been seen on a number of occasions over the years, dressed in the unmistakable garb of an early eighteenth-century gipsy, straw hat, heavy skirt, boots and bare legs. 'My sister, Lisa, saw her when she was about seven,' Hal Bagot said. 'At that time she kept a pony and it was while she was out in the stables one night she told us she had seen a woman sidle quietly from the stable and walk right through the woodwork. She was terrified about the whole thing, but was able to tell my parents exactly what the woman was wearing, right down to the boots and no stockings.'

His wife, Susie, also thinks she came across the Grey Lady one night on the drive where the gipsy died on the way to the kitchens. She was driving towards the house when she spotted the figure of a woman rounding a corner in front of her; she fully expected to pass her as she too rounded the bend, but there was no one there. There have also been occasions, even more disturbing than Susie Bagot's, when motorists on the nearby main road have experienced the horror of hitting a female walker who suddenly appears from nowhere. They are relieved, if somewhat shaken, to discover that all they struck was thin air.

The park and grounds of Levens are, despite these sinister sightings, mysterious freezes and snowy fawns, an absolute delight. For well over two hundred years visitors have flocked to experience the wonder and amazement of Colonel James Grahme's horticultural genius. Together with garden designer, Monsieur Guillaume Beaumont, Grahme created a wonderland where nature and man's skill came together to celebrate the art of topiary. It remains today one of the

has long since been replaced by a succession of male heirs. Could it be that the gipsy mellowed in her after-life and forgave her uncharitable 'hosts', but chose to leave a permanent reminder of her suffering?

Hal Bagot, today's owner of Levens, runs his huge estate with the practical efficiency of a chartered surveyor and capable do-it-yourselfer. He is not one to dwell on the uncharted aspects of the supernatural and is slightly dismissive of some of the stories associated with his home. At the same time he knows that when he was born, in February 1946, the River Kent was frozen, and a white fawn was added to the park's numbers. 'The same thing happened again in 1981 when my first son Richard was born. He arrived on December 12, and on that date the river was again frozen solid, and another white deer appeared.' We shall

finest examples of a topiary garden still intact in its original design. Giant beech hedges hide the Disney-like surprise awaiting the first-timer . . . a jostling, bustling crowd of over-sized shapes. Fat, thin, square, round on top, top-hatted, key-holed, king-size, walk-through and corkscrew. Flower-filled beds add a brilliant touch and a feel of order to this uniquely beautiful English garden.

Beyond the estate the coast beckons to the the west and the glorious and much celebrated scenery of the Lake District begins its steady rise northwards. Levens itself offers a somewhat austere backdrop. Clean cut, angular and un-cluttered, its building dates back to medieval times when the de Redman family were granted the land, and its fortunes have been passed, with a few twists and turns, down one branch or other of the family for some 700 years. One previous owner, Alan Bellingham, was careless enough to lose the whole estate in the late 1600s by gamb-ling. His first cousin, the gardening enthusiast, James Grahme, became the next master of Levens. The long-held belief that Levens was won with the turn of the ace of hearts is very possibly true, and it is a fact that the downspouts on the front of the house are decorated with gilded

hearts and the initials of James and Dorothy Grahme.

Inside, Levens has a warmth and friendliness that belies its great age and lofty proportions. The familiar clutter of children's toys, a table-top train set, two sleepy dogs and the TV repair men were all in evidence. 'I've lived here all my life, and it's always been a particularly friendly house', Hal said, 'and certainly not the kind of place anyone would associate with any unpleasantness.' If the Grey Lady occasionally appears to ruffle the com-posure of family and passing motorists on the outside, the most unwelcome sensation reported within is a feeling that someone, or something, is pushing them as they walk down the staircase leading into the Elizabethan Great Hall. Hal Bagot is unconvinced about this – he thinks the angle of the staircase is to blame.

Then there is the dog. A small, black, cheeky little fellow who dashes up the same staircase in front of surprised visitors. Some people staying over at Levens have spent considerable time searching for him after seeing him disappear around their bedroom doors. No one has found him though, because he simply does not exist. 'We've never had such a dog here,' Hal confirmed,

◁ **The famous topiary garden at Levens.** △ **The Hall at night.**

'but people who don't know our own dogs assume he's real enough.' Some ten years or so ago, a visitor was taking photographs of the family on the front steps of Levens when they too spotted the little black intruder, happily wagging his tail and posing for the camera.

An entire touring party witnessed the appearance of the Pink Lady in the 1960s. This particular ghost, in the mop hat, apron and long dress of a maid, has been seen from time to time, although her identity and reason for haunting the house are also unknown. Hal Bagot assumes some kind of traumatic experience befell her and ties her to the house, although she gives no sign of what that might have been and favours no particular spot, appearing instead quite at random.

One final mystery remains, stranger even than the Levens curse. If ghosts are the disembodied spirits of the departed, what are we to call the ghost of someone who still lives? A pre-haunting perhaps, or a sub-spirit. This inexplicable occurrence took place before Hal Bagot was born, and concerns his father, Robin, who no longer occupies Levens but lives close by. On the night in question, a priest staying at nearby Leighton Hall was called to Levens to visit someone who was sick. He duly arrived and let himself in. Passing through one of the rooms on the way to the stairs he heard someone playing the harpsichord, and not wanting to disturb their playing, he tiptoed his way past and made his way to the bedrooms. Mission completed, the priest made his way downstairs again; the harpsichord was still being played and he formed the impression that the musician did not want to be disturbed.

No doubt anxious to report the outcome of his visit, the priest turned instead to the library where although it was brightly lit on the outside, he could see candles burning. Mrs Bagot was taking tea with friends, and explained that as the result of a power cut affecting the whole of the house she was having to entertain by candlelight. So how, the priest asked, was the harpsichord player wreathed in light . . . and who was he anyway. The tea-party rushed to see for themselves. There was no light, and no music.

What struck a real chord of alarm was the fact that the priest could identify the particular tune being played, if not the player. It was a Grand, one of only two or three Robin Bagot knew, and a particular favourite at that time. Mrs Bagot was distraught; she felt certain that what the priest had seen foretold of some dreadful accident and her husband must be dead. He was away on business that day at Cockermouth, and there was no way of making contact, or finding out whether or not he was safe and well. Some time later, to everyone's incredible relief, Robin arrived home at Levens having had a totally uneventful trip. He figured out that at the same time the priest reported him playing the harpsichord, he was in fact driving beside Lake Bassenthwaite with nothing more occupying his mind than land valuations.

There is no reasonable explanation for this unexpected appearance by a living person, and equally no reason to doubt it. But it is surely one of the most enigmatic among the gallery of ghostly sightings at Levens Hall. Hal Bagot's theory is that some people are just born with the ability to see and experience such things: 'I have never seen anything here,' he said, 'and I don't imagine I ever will, I am not made that way.'

The Isle of Man is full of stories of ghosts and witches. Motorists still solemnly say 'Good morning, little people' as they cross a magical bridge beneath which fairies live, and it is accepted that one may meet with a ghostly dapple-grey horse almost anywhere on the island. Probably its best-known ghost is the Mauthe Doog (or Moddey Dhoo). This is the spectral black hound which frequented the guardroom of Peel Castle in the mid-seventeenth century. The soldiers eventually grew used to him, though they avoided meeting him on their own, always going in pairs at night when they delivered the keys of the castle to their captain, a walk which meant passing the Doog's lair.

Because of accidents of geology much of the north west of England was a seed-bed of the Industrial Revolution, and to many people the region immediately conjures up Lowry's scenes of matchstick people dwarfed by factory chimneys. But there is much more to be found here – a good intermingling of history, scenery and legend creating an ideal compost for a wide variety of stories of the supernatural. The convincing tales, the real chillers, are not the most spectacular ones with fearsome boggles appearing out of every nook and cranny, but those that include a morsel of everyday life that everyone can relate to, even though a story may date from times long past.

An example might be the story attached to **Utkinton Hall**, near Tarporley in Cheshire, the home of the Done family – Sir John Done was Chief Forester of Delamere Forest in the reign of Charles I. Some time in the previous century the Hall was plagued by a very unruly ghost whose spirit a priest succeeded in 'consigning' into the body of a blackbird, whose territory included the Hall's walled garden. Today Utkinton Hall is a lovely rambling old farmhouse but the blackbirds that sing around it are supposed to be descendants of the one carrying the trapped spirit (can a ghost's genes be passed on?).

Like York, Chester became a place of importance in Roman times, and its prosperity lasted until the late eighteenth century when its port began to lose trade to Liverpool as vessels became larger and the River Dee silted up. Echoes of the Romans may still be heard in Chester. The modern **George and Dragon Hotel** in Liverpool Road was built on the site of the Roman cemetery and its first floor

Utkinton Hall, Cheshire, where a ghost was laid in the body of a blackbird.

residents sometimes hear the sound of heavy footsteps passing from one end to another, disregarding the innumerable partitions and all the fire doors that would interrupt normal progress.

Lyme Park is a palatial mansion dating from about 1570, and was the ancestral home of the Legh family until 1946 when, with the magnificent deer park, it was given to the National Trust who persuaded Stockport Corporation to maintain and administer the property. Today it is one of the region's showplaces, and an information sheet (much in demand with younger visitors) introduces the ghosts.

The Leghs were an obstinately Catholic family, clinging to the Old Faith through even the most dangerous times. Thus it is perhaps surprising that Lyme was one of the houses where Mary, Queen of Scots was kept a prisoner, but the room she used is named after her and is sometimes mysteriously scented with the smell of oranges. It was the Scottish Queen who introduced the recipe for marmalade from France and it must be a psychic reminder of this that lingers, as a smell from 400 years ago.

An early owner of Lyme, Sir Piers Legh, was badly injured at the Battle of Agincourt in 1415. As he lay on the battlefield with the fighting still raging around him, a large dog came and stood over him, protecting him from further harm. When the battle was

The imposing façade of Lyme Park, haunted by past members of the Legh family.

The George and Dragon Hotel, Chester, built on the site of a Roman cemetery.

Queen Mary's Bedroom at Lyme Park.

The ghost of Martha Legh appears whenever an heir is born at Lyme Park.

his mistress), Lady Blanche, threw herself into the stream by the park entrance and was drowned. She is still seen (three times in the last two years) at the head of a ghostly cortège which winds its way up to the house.

It may be that it is Blanche who also appears inside the mansion as a White Lady, though Lyme is also haunted by a lady called Martha Benet who married the eleventh Piers Legh in 1737. Although they had five children, all of them died in infancy so that there was no direct heir to inherit the estate and the succession went to a nephew whom Martha disliked. After this her ghost has appeared whenever an heir to the property makes his first visit to Lyme Park, presumably to check on his health.

Lyme also has a priest's hole – a secret hiding place beneath floorboards in a room off the Long Gallery – where a skeleton was discovered about 200 years ago. This must explain the phantom of a priest which has haunted these rooms ever since the grisly discovery.

Why were the people who sheltered these priests in the sixteenth or seven-

won and Sir Piers had recovered he took the dog back to England – it hunted with him in Lyme Park, and from it sprang the famous strain of Lyme Mastiffs which were a celebrated hunting breed.

Seven years later Sir Piers went to war again, but this time he was not so fortunate and died of his wounds. When the news of his death reached Lyme, his daughter (some accounts say

A Lyme Mastiff.

teenth centuries so careless of their well-being that they so frequently allowed them to starve? Apparently a common tactic of those employed in seeking them out was to post men at strategic points throughout a suspected house so that the fugitive priest eventually died through hunger and thirst. It seems doubtful that such a speculative, labour-intensive exercise could have been carried out very often, yet it is supposed to have led to the death of the monk who haunts **Tower Grange** near Formby.

Here, too, a skeleton was found in a priest's hole, and the spectre of a small monk, dressed in a black habit, has been seen. The house dates from medieval times, when it was the Grange of farmlands belonging to the monks of Whalley Abbey, so that it is possible that the ghost is of a farming-monk rather than a courageous priest who chose to die of hunger and thirst rather than betray the household who sheltered him.

Between Preston and Blackburn, just to the east of the motorway, is **Samlesbury Old Hall**, haunted by a White Lady known as Sickly Dorothy.

Tower Grange, Formby (left), haunted by a diminutive monk who was sheltered there and starved to death.

Samlesbury Old Hall, the haunt of Sickly Dorothy.

Sickly Dorothy's last resting-place? The Lover's Grave at Samlesbury.

She was the daughter of Sir John Southworth, a leading Catholic who suffered much for his faith during the reign of Elizabeth I. Dorothy imprudently fell in love with a Protestant neighbour, and the plot continues along familiar lines – a brother hearing them planning to elope and then waylaying them, both he and the prospective bridegroom being killed in the ensuing fracas. Poor Dorothy, distraught with grief, joined an order of nuns on the Continent and died a short time after. If the son who betrayed his sister was Sir John's heir, Christopher Southworth, he too came to an uncomfortable end, being beheaded for his adherence to the Old Faith at Tyburn in 1654.

Dorothy returns to haunt the house and grounds, even venturing out onto the main road occasionally which is how she became known as Sickly Dorothy. A motorist who had to swerve to avoid hitting the ghost in 1960 described her as having a green, sickly face.

In 1970 the chapel at Chingle Hall, discovered only ten years previously, filled with smoke. A joist in the blocked-up chimney had ignited spontaneously – by a pyromaniacal ghost perhaps?

Chingle claims to be the most haunted house in England.

The thirteenth-century **Chingle Hall** is to the north of Preston, at Goosnargh. It has a ground-plan in the shape of a cross, and is notable as being the first domestic building in this country to be built of brick. It is also famous for its ghosts, and often claims to be the most haunted house in England. This may be because of its innumerable priest-holes which always seem to foster ghost stories, but Chingle probably needed these, for it was the birthplace of John Wall, one of the last Catholic martyrs, who was executed at Worcester in 1679. His head was taken round the Continent and displayed as a relic for some years before being returned to Chingle: no-one knows of its whereabouts today so it is probably still hidden within the house.

Apparitions of monks are the most usual haunting at Chingle, though there are a variety of other strange happenings which probably belong in the realm of the supernatural. Many people have difficulties with cameras in the house and one photographer had one violently snatched from his hands and flung over a beam in the ceiling.

The **Dunkenhalgh** is a luxury hotel on the outskirts of Accrington. The present building dates from 1815 and was the home of the Petre family until the Second World War. An earlier house on the same site belonged to the Walmesley family who amassed a great fortune in Elizabethan times even though they were Catholics. The two families merged in 1712 when Catherine Walmesley married Robert, seventh Lord Petre. Catherine was fifteen at the time of her marriage, and when her husband died in the following year was left with a baby son. Although she was ardently courted by Lord Stourton she refused to marry him until her son had come of age: a formidable lady, Catherine died in 1785, at the age of 88. It seems most likely that it was during her reign at Dunkenhalgh that the events took place that led to its haunting.

A young French governess was engaged to look after the Petre children. Her name was Lucette, and she was vivacious and attractive. One Christmas a distant relative, a military man, came to visit at Dunkenhalgh and seduced Lucette. Although he had sworn that he loved her and intended to marry her, when his leave was over he returned to his regiment and never returned, leaving her both heart-broken and pregnant.

The spectre of Lucette, a young French governess, haunts the grounds of Dunkenhalgh on Christmas Eve.

Only the outline of the Hall survives at Wycoller, a place exceptionally well-suited for ghostly activity. The wicked Squire Cunliffe is one of its ghosts: he returns each year to re-enact the murder of his wife, whom he whipped to death.

She ended her disgrace by throwing herself off the old bridge into the river which flows through a small ravine in the grounds. Her body was found next day and was wrapped in a shroud and taken back to the house.

The ghost of Lucette haunts Dunkenhalgh on Christmas Eve. Dressed in the white shroud she is usually seen close to the scene of her death, locally known as the Boggart Bridge ('boggart' being a North Country word for ghost).

The ruins of **Wycoller Hall** lie to the east of Burnley amidst bleak moorland close to the Yorkshire boundary and to the moors that surround Haworth and make up the Brontë Country. Charlotte Brontë knew of one of the ghosts of Wycoller and described it in *Jane Eyre*:

> . . . a lion-like creature with long hair, a huge head and with strange preter-canine eyes.

This is the local variety of ghostly black dog called Guytrash Lightfoot which at night roamed the lonely lanes and field paths around the remote ruins of the Hall. Disaster or the death of a loved one was sure to come to anyone unlucky enough to meet the terrifying creature. In *Jane Eyre* Mr Rochester had a painful fall from his horse on meeting Guytrash.

Wycoller Hall was the home of the Cunliffe family, a wild and violent lot whose last member died in 1819, propped up on his deathbed so that he might watch a cockfight. The best-known of the Wycoller ghosts is the Spectral Horseman who is a Cunliffe doomed to ride out once a year to re-enact the terrible murder of his wife. It has to be a night of truly vile weather for him to make an appearance, and then with the wind howling and the rain lashing down the horse is heard galloping up the road to stop at the door of the Hall. The horseman dismounts and enters the house to climb stairs which vanished long ago. Soon after dreadful screams are heard which subside into sobbing groans of agony. The wicked Cunliffe then re-appears, mounts his horse and rides off fiendishly down the lane, his horse breathing flames from its flaring nostrils.

Gisburn is a village on an important crossroads where the **Ribblesdale Arms** was once an important coaching inn. It was built in 1635, and one room contains an ornate bed with carvings of children apparently dressed in shrouds. It is this room which is haunted by a young girl named Mary.

Mary was raped by a lecherous Lord Ribblesdale who was either so vain or so wicked that he was buried in a silver coffin. Having had his evil way he threw her down the back stairs. She later hanged herself.

She is supposed to haunt the bedroom (once numbered 13) and to walk up and down the corridor. All sorts of disturbances have occurred recently – the loo roll in the manager's bathroom was completely unravelled and cassettes turn themselves on and off in the middle of the night. However, Mary responds when she is politely told to leave things alone: the disturbances then die down.

The Forest of Bowland is a paradise for those with a liking for wilderness. Originally it was a royal forest where the hunting was strictly reserved for the king and woe betide those caught red-handed (i.e. with blood on their hands from gutting a carcass). Later it belonged to the Earls of Lancaster, and anyone breaking the forest laws would be brought before one of the Parkers of **Browsholme Hall** for punishment.

Browsholme is a Tudor house that was substantially altered and enlarged in the eighteenth century. It contains many interesting relics from the times when the Parkers (who took their name from being the park-keepers) ruled over Bowland. There is also a skull which is supposed to have magical properties. No one knows where the skull came from, though it seems most likely that it belonged to one of those who died in the Pilgrimage of Grace of 1537-8, the most serious revolt against Henry VIII's reformation.

In the middle years of the last century Edward Parker, a Harrow

The Ribblesdale Arms at Gisburn is haunted by Mary, a maid raped by the thoroughly nasty Lord Ribblesdale. The hotel remains midly troubled by her ghost but the present landlord says disturbances cease when he politely asks Mary to stop. Her ghost is supposed to haunt Room 13 (above), where one version of the story says she hanged herself.

Browsholme Hall, where the removal of a mysterious skull spells disaster. The skull is locked safely away, and we were not allowed to photograph it.

schoolboy at home for the holidays, took the skull from the cupboard where it had been kept for centuries and buried it in the garden. All sorts of mishaps soon followed. The stone facing of the house fell away, revealing the original Tudor work; beams in the chimneys began to smoulder; and there was a succession of unexpected deaths in the family. At length the penny dropped with Edward, and he admitted removing the skull as a prank. When it was put back in its rightful place order was restored, though the Parkers had to move out for a time while the damage to the Hall was being repaired.

The ghost of Sarah Siddons is claimed by Lancaster's **Grand Theatre**. This is not as unlikely as it might seem, for the great actress performed here on several occasions when her brother was the manager and her portrait hangs in the circle. Though the identity of the Grand's ghost may be debatable, there is no denying that the lovely little theatre is indeed haunted. A Grey Lady has been seen on many occasions. She usually appears in the half-darkness of the auditorium, drifting across a person's line of sight, or is spotted from the stage, sitting quietly at the back of the stalls.

Sarah Siddons (opposite page), whose ghost may still walk the boards of Lancaster's Grand Theatre (left) where her brother was once manager.

Kendal is a fine old town standing at the southern entrance to the Lake District, a region which has a wonderful range of ghosts and folklore to match the romance of its scenery. Dobbie stones are tokens of good fortune often found in old houses in the north west of England, though phantom funerals are more likely to be seen in Wales. **Bleaze Hall** at Old Hutton close to Kendal is a 400-year-old house which has both, as well as a haunted bedroom. Dobbie stones are usually three-faced prehistoric hammerheads which also have the power to return to their homes should they be taken away. As the present owner says, the Bleaze dobbie is a most essential part of the house, and his children would never sleep unless

Bleaze Hall has a dobbie stone to protect it from evil spirits. Nevertheless, a phantom funeral used to be seen here.

Thomas Skelton, the Fool of Muncaster, and (right) the fortified side of Muncaster Castle.

The Tapestry Room at Muncaster, the haunt of a headless ghost.

they knew it was safely hanging in the rafters of their attic bedroom.

The phantom funeral has not been seen recently though 'odd, fleeting shadows' are often half-seen passing the windows. The funeral is supposed to be that of a girl who lived in a previous house on this site and died of a broken heart when her lover failed to return from a Crusade seven centuries ago.

Several of the great houses of the Lake District have 'Lucks'. These too are symbols of good fortune, sometimes given to the families by fairies. The Luck of **Muncaster Castle**, however, was a royal gift. It was given to Sir John Pennington by Henry VI who, a fugitive after the Battle of Hexham, was found wandering on the fells and given shelter at Muncaster. In Muncaster Church there is a tablet inscribed

Holie Kinge Harry gave Sir John a brauce wryed glass cuppe . . . whylles the familie shold keep hit unbreken they shold gretely thryve.

Muncaster Castle is supposed to be haunted by the ghost of Thomas Skelton, the last jester of the castle, who died in about 1600. Visitors to the Castle may see the wonderful portrait of 'the Fool of Muncaster' which includes his Last Will and Testament. Apparently Skelton was a mean and vicious man, and was once called upon to dispose of a young man who was paying unwelcome attention to his master's daughter. He brutally killed the would-be suitor and presented his head as proof that the deed had been done. Thus a headless ghost has walked in the Tapestry Room ever since, seeking his lost love. It would be an interesting confrontation should he ever meet with the ghost of the fool who killed him.

Further up the Cumbrian coast, between Whitehaven and Workington, the small village of Moresby has 'the eminently interesting' Hall which dates from 1690. **Moresby Hall** was once the home of the Fletchers who supported the Jacobites in the 1715 uprising. The master of the house was subsequently taken off to London for questioning, without revealing that another Jacobite supporter was concealed within the Hall. This poor man died of thirst and starvation in his hiding-place and is said to haunt one of the bedrooms.

Lowther Castle today stands as one of the most romantic ruins imaginable. The shell is all that remains of the magnificent palace erected between 1806 and 1811 for the second Earl of Lonsdale.

His father was 'Wicked Jimmy', Sir James Lowther, who was created the first Earl Lonsdale in 1784. He was a man of immense wealth (the fortune came from the coal seams of West Cumbria) but chose to live in an outrageous style, terrorising neighbours and servants, and generally making life hell for any unfortunate enough to encounter him.

After an unsuccessful arranged marriage he fell in love with the daughter of one of his tenants and installed her in one of his properties.

Moresby Hall, and the bedroom which is haunted by a man left to die of thirst.

For a short time Sir James was content but his mistress died suddenly, an event which he refused to accept. He would not have her buried, insisting that life in the house should continue as though she was still alive, even bringing her corpse down to dinner.

The dramatic outline of Lowther Castle which replaced the Hall, home of Wicked Jimmy.

Wicked Jimmy's boisterous spirit was eventually laid beneath Wallow Crag.

At last even Wicked Jimmy was forced to accept that his behaviour was anti-social (as well as being a health hazard) and his sweatheart, after spending some time in a coffin with a glass lid, was eventually interred at Paddington Cemetery.

The Earl returned to Lowther where he lived in the manner of a feudal baron of the Middle Ages. He suffered terrible bouts of depression when for days he would wander through his vast estate alone. Then he would return to continue bullying his tenants and servants. He owed the poet Wordsworth's father £5,000, and avoided paying the debt even though the court ruled against him. The sum was still outstanding at his death. Of course this may have been a Good Thing – poverty is usually considered an essential for poets, and had Wordsworth been brought up in affluence he might have deserted the Muse.

Everyone must have been thankful at Lord Lonsdale's death in 1802, though apprehensive when they witnessed the strange events at his funeral:

He was with difficulty buried; and whilst the clergyman was praying over him, he very nearly knocked the reverend gentleman from his desk. When placed in the grave, the power of creating alarm was not interred with his bones. There were disturbances in the Hall, noises in the stables; neither men nor animals were suffered to rest. Jemmy's 'coach and six' is still remembered and spoken of, from which we are probably to understand that he produced a noise, as boggles frequently do, like the equipage of this description. There is nothing said of his shape, or whether he appeared at all; but it is certain he made himself audible. The Hall became almost uninhabitable, and out of doors there was constant danger of meeting the miscreant ghost.

The old account goes on to describe how the Earl's ghost was at last laid beneath Wallow Crag, overlooking Haweswater. Were the disturbances the reason why the second Earl abandoned Lowther Hall and built the splendid Castle in its place? Many local people still believe that 'Wicked Jimmy's' ghostly coach and six careers through the park on wild nights, the cries of its driver mingling with those of the exotic beasts that live there today.

Some families seem to attract supernatural activity, none more so than the Dacres of the Lake District. **Dacre Castle** itself is situated to the west of Penrith, an early fourteenth-century tower that is still occupied, though no longer by the family that gave it its name. Their fortunes were merged with those of the Howards, Dukes of Norfolk, when the male line died out.

The last of the line was Thomas Dacre who thought that the succession was secure when a male heir was born to him after three daughters. Unfortunately Thomas was a philanderer who deceived the young daughter of one of his tenants and then abandoned her when he found that she was with child. The heart-broken maid drowned herself, whereupon her mother, who dabbled in the black arts, called down a curse on the Dacres which promised the extinction of the family. This was fulfilled when Thomas' young son fell from his vaulting-horse and was killed, this death being quickly followed by that of Thomas senior himself. His widow became the third wife of the Duke of Norfolk. The ghost of the wronged maiden walked by the river where she died, until the death of her faithless lover, when she disappeared for good. However, the present occupant of Dacre says the castle is unhaunted. The same story is told of Naworth Castle, another Dacre stronghold, like **Greystoke Castle**, which eventually came to the Howard family, the Dukes of Norfolk, and still belongs to them.

Charles Howard was a Duke who was extraordinarily keen on hunting. He even pursued the sport on the sabbath and on one occasion took a house guest with him. They had a very successful day and after a convivial evening the guest was shown the way to his room – one already haunted by the ghost of a monk who had been bricked up within its walls (he is still supposed to appear, usually in February). Whether the spectral monk had a hand in the subsequent disappearance of the house guest is unknown, but he was never seen again,

Greystoke Castle is haunted by a monk, a White Lady, and the Devil himself.

A sinister aspect of Greystoke Castle which once belonged to the Dacres, a family who seem to have generated a great deal of psychical activity.

though his clothes were found neatly folded and his bed had been slept in.

The incident may have persuaded the Duke to give up sport on a Sunday: certainly the guest room was never used again except by the ghost of the man who disappeared. The present owner of Greystoke says that the Castle is haunted by the monk, a White Lady, and the Devil himself.

Vampires have been described as 'the most awesome features of supernatural dread' and belief in their existence is very fashionable today (Robin Hood is said to be a vampire, escaping from his tomb at Kirklees to

terrorise the district). Probably the best-known vampire in Britain after Count Dracula is the one that roamed about the remote Cumbrian village of Croglin about 300 years ago.

Until 1589 **Croglin Low Hall** was the manor house of an estate owned by the Dacres (vampires as well as ghosts thrive on coincidences). The estate then came to the Howards when the Dacre line died out, and they in turn sold it to a family named Fisher. The Fishers also had estates in the south of England where they preferred to live, and in the latter years of the seventeenth century they let

Croglin Low Hall and its lands to tenants – two brothers and a sister.

At the time the Hall was a long, low single-storeyed building, with the ruins of a church close by in the grounds. For a time the new tenants were content at Croglin, and winter passed uneventfully. It was on a moonlit summer's night that the vampire made its first appearance. The sister had retired to the room, and before preparing for bed glanced out of the window towards the churchyard. At first she saw two lights flickering through the trees, but when they began to come closer she saw that they were fixed in a dark substance,

> . . . a definite ghastly something, which seemed every moment to become nearer, increasing in size and substance as it approached.

The something scratched at the window and eventually gained access to the room. The poor woman seems to have been terror-struck and made little effort to escape as the hideous figure, with its brown shrivelled face and glaring eyes, grabbed her by the hair and sank its fangs into her neck.

At this she managed to scream, and her brothers dashed to her room to find her lying unconscious by her bed, bleeding from a wound in the throat. One brother chased after the fleeing monster, which bounded away with enormous strides, vanishing into the churchyard.

It was hardly surprising that the poor girl was badly shocked at the incident, and the brothers took her to the Continent to recover. At last she insisted she was well enough to return to Croglin, and for some months all was peaceful there.

However, before the next summer events were repeated, though fortunately this time the brothers were more prepared and were able to fire a gun at the figure, hitting it in the leg. It still managed to make an escape but was followed into the graveyard and

seen disappearing into a vault of a family long extinct (most likely a branch of the Dacres).

Croglin Low Hall, famous for its vampire.

The next day all the tenants and neighbours were called to the Hall and told the story. The vault was opened, and the story concludes

> *. . . A horrible scene revealed itself. The vault was full of coffins; they had been broken open, and their contents, horribly mangled and distorted, were scattered over the floor. One coffin alone remained intact. Of that the lid had been lifted, but still lay loose upon the coffin. They raised it, and there, brown, withered, shrivelled, mummified, but quite entire, was the same hideous figure which had looked in at the windows of Croglin Grange, with the marks of a recent pistol-shot in the leg: and they did the only thing that can lay a vampire – they burnt it.*

The story leaves many issues un-answered – surely vampires are only destroyed by impalation with a wooden stake, and what happened to the poor girl – does she, now a vampire herself, still roam the Cumbrian countryside? The present occupant of Croglin Low Hall believes that the story derived from *Robin Redbreast*, a Victorian penny-dreadful. She is used to people coming to the remote farm from all corners of the world to research the story, but can add little to it beyond showing them the bricked up ground floor window through which the vampire is supposed to have escaped (Low Hall is now a two-storey building). She says that the house has never been troubled by ghost or vampire. It may have been the chill of a winter's day, but she struck me as looking almost unnaturally pale . . .

The bricked-up window at Croglin Low Hall, through which the vampire is said to have escaped.

CHILLINGHAM
A CASTLE OF SECRETS

WAY UP in north Northumberland where the wild and heathery Cheviots roll down and unfold before ironing themselves out en route to the coast, you chance upon Chillingham Castle, one of the most important and senior strongholds in this once skirmish-torn region, yet tucked out of sight like a long-forgotten secret.

This is Border country, the furthermost outpost of England where but for a waver of the invisible dividing line you would be well and truly in Scotland; a sentiment clearly adhered to in centuries past by the Scots and much feared by the English. The patchwork foothills now devoted to farming were for centuries little more than bloody battlefields as one side fought to keep the other at bay. Fortresses such as Chillingham played a vital role in these territorial troubles, providing billets for soldiers, stabling for horses, and a stop-over point for visiting monarchs both pre- and post-battle.

From being a twelfth-century stronghold, Chillingham became a fully fortified castle two centuries later, with a considerable amount of new building, only to be smashed in a later rebellion. The reign of Elizabeth I saw extensive reconstruction and adornment; and although the eighteenth century brought further changes, this work took the shape of adaption rather than rebuilding leaving some of this little-known castle's best kept secrets intact within its medieval walls. Some of these skeletons have been uncovered, but the mysteries behind them are not so easily unearthed.

Chillingham's principal apparition, and there are many seen and unseen ghosts here, is the romantically named 'Radiant Boy', a young child sighted in what is now known as the Pink Room. On the stroke of midnight he has been heard crying and moaning, either in pain or fear, close to where a passage cut through the ten-feet-thick wall into an adjoining tower. As the cries fade a bright halo of light is said to appear and anyone sleeping there would see the blue-clad figure of a boy in the light. At the beginning of this century

the bones of a child were discovered within the wall, along with the fragments of a blue dress. The remains were buried with proper ceremony in the churchyard at Chillingham, and for many years the Radiant Boy was quiet. More recently, however, he is reported to have been seen again, emerging from one of the walls high in the north west tower.

Again, at around the turn of the century, the wife of the sixth Earl of Tankerville, the then owner of Chillingham, had the disquieting experience of coming face to face with the skeletons of a man and a child after part of her bedroom wall collapsed. Given the castle's history she felt they

▽ The impressive courtyard at Chillingham Castle.

▷ Sir Humphry Wakefield on the battlements, with the Elizabethan topiary garden below.

could well have been prisoners caught in a border raid, but at least part of this secret is now known; Leonora Tankerville's bedroom was at one time a chapel, and however the pair met their deaths it is likely they were buried here on consecrated ground.

Another skeleton in Chillingham's wardrobe probably does relate to its feuding days, and was found in an altogether more likely location – the dreadful dungeons where many a marauding Scot must have languished and died. Scrawled initials and scratch marks on the walls tell their own poignant story, but the workmen called in to open a sealed-up lower section, sometime in the 1800s, had a real horror story to recount. Having chipped their way through the stonework they came face to face with the figure of a man, perfectly preserved and still sitting in the chair in which he died. And as if that was not enough of a shock the corpse then began to disintegrate before their eyes as the air rushed in.

Less ghastly and more typically ghostly is Lady Mary Berkeley, wife of Lord Grey of Wark and Chillingham and Earl of Tankerville, and next in line to the Radiant Boy when it comes to spiritual activity. Mary became a sad and haunted lady after her philandering husband ran off with her sister, leaving her alone in the castle with just their baby daughter for company. A great scandal ensued, followed by a lawsuit before the infamous Judge Jeffries, all of which did nothing to ease Lady Mary's pain, but perhaps explains why she still anxiously waits and searches for the missing Earl. The rustle of her dress has been heard along corridors and stairs as she wanders aimlessly about, leaving an icy chill in her wake.

The Grey family snatched Chillingham from its previous owners in the twelfth century, and as we will learn, do not appear to have been forgiven for it. The last Grey descendants (by then the Tankervilles) moved out in 1933, leaving this sturdily planted, stern-faced border guard to decay and crumble under the relentless attack of the elements. Roofs and ceilings caved in, floors fell into cellars and the fortress castle became little more than a shadowy shell of its former self. After 50 years of neglect the present owner, Sir Humphry Wakefield, stepped in and expressed his interest in the castle; being married to a Grey himself he eventually won the full approval of the last Lord Tankerville.

'It is really because of my link with the Grey family that I was allowed to take on this place', said Sir Humphry, 'and it is interesting to note that I did not actually have to buy the castle, just the land. Chillingham has never been purchased – admittedly the Greys took it by assault in the first place – but now all these years later it still wasn't actually bought.' What Sir Humphry has set out to do, with tireless enthusiasm and a team of live-in workmen, is restore Chillingham – 'as a flourishing tribute to the many families who have lived here, rather than let it die as a disgrace to the last family.'

If the outer appearance of Chillingham is business-like with its square towers and unfussy entrance, all it takes is a few steps inside to reveal another well-kept secret, the inner courtyard. Ballustraded balconies, pillared arcades, sweeping stairs, garrets and galleries fight for your attention. Italy, Oxbridge, Romeo and Juliet – it lights up your imagination like an outsize stage set. Anything could happen here, and nothing would surprise you. Sitting chatting about history, hauntings and building plans in the late afternoon sun in surroundings like these was almost surreal.

It did not need Sir Humphry's personal accounts of the unexplained to add to the atmosphere, but having taken on the castle he has also taken on a lot more besides. The fact that the resident builders get disturbed by 'things' on a not infrequent basis is mentioned in passing, as is the administrator's report of footsteps where no living person walks. Sir Humphry spelled out in more detail how his elder son, Maximilian, when

△ **Chillingham seen from the gardens.**

staying in the castle alone – 'and armed to the teeth' – heard footsteps coming up the stairs towards his room, continue straight through the door, across the room and out the other side – through a wall.

He went on to tell of his own visit to an Indian sooth-sayer while on a business trip to America. 'During the course of our conversation she happened to say that my heart lay in a haunted house back home, and that I was being overlooked by angry spirits from a long way back. I took that to mean the people the Greys took Chillingham from; but what really put me in a panic was her suggestion that it was not a good place for my younger son Jack. He is the son of my second marriage, and therefore could be considered a member of the Grey family.' On his return home Sir Humphry had the castle exorcised to rid the place of any sinister and unfriendly presences.

While Sir Humphry has not seen a ghost at Chillingham, he accepts with disarming frankness that they exist: 'I think it is very arrogant for people to say ghosts don't exist. To my way of thinking we are like computers, human computers, and we can only talk about or discuss the things we have been programmed for. We're not programmed for the spiritual world, the after-life and so forth, and therefore we don't understand it. I'm not at all fussed by friendly and benevolent spirits, but I would worry about evil ones.' Now that Chillingham has banished any evil associations, the innocent souls like the Radiant Boy, for example, are free to haunt at will as far as their new 'landlord' is concerned.

Visitors already tour this sprawling and shabby castle, local ones in particular taking a delight in seeing just how far work has progressed since the last time. There is a long way to go before the Wakefield family can consider it home, but slowly the once-splendid great halls and state rooms are being brought back to life with antique furniture, tapestries and artefacts. Wandering round amongst the dust sheets and paintpots away from the nearly-finished rooms and on to the not-yet-started, up another spiral stone flight to the next, it is hard not to find yourself looking over your shoulder at the slightest sound, and a great relief to be met by an overalled workman and not something less solid.

One of the starkest contrasts between outside and in is the immaculately laid out Elizabethan topiary garden with its intricately shaped and close-shaved hedges of box and yew. Unlike many such homes Chillingham's gardens do not offer the traditional vista from the front, preferring instead a more private viewpoint with the main driveway coming up at right-angles. And while in the gardens it is worth recalling one or two of the catalogue of strange events recorded by Leonora Tankerville in the early 1900s. Lady Leonora was very receptive to psychic phenomena, and even before she visited Chillingham she was treated to a tour of the grounds by the dead brother of her future husband.

After coming to live in the castle she was sitting one day enjoying the view of the topiary garden when an altogether more worrying scene superimposed itself, accompanied by the sound of distant cannon fire. A woman in the clothes of a Dominican Abbess looked anxiously towards the hills of Scotland before kneeling in prayer; a man also scanned the horizon and sentries paced back and forth. When Lady Leonora spoke the man turned towards her; he had the face of her husband but the clothes of four centuries ago. She assumed, therefore, that the Abbess was herself, but why was she praying, and what was happening? A short time later came the anouncement that the First World War had begun. Leonora had 'tuned in', as she put it, to a similar moment way in the past.

Personal experience aside, in her account *The Ghosts of Chillingham*, Lady Leonora tells the curious story of the family portrait that walked. 'Not only', she writes, 'had our own nursery been disturbed by the restlessness of this picture but the children of friends, and their nurse, declared that she stepped out of her frame and frightened them by following them about.' A well-known psychologist visiting Chillingham expressed an interest in this and decided to sit and watch the portrait; he obviously saw someone but she was not the woman in the picture. The following day he suddenly recognised the woman he had seen from another portrait in the castle and it transpired that it was the same person, but the portraits were painted at different times in her life.

She also mentions a frail figure in white, in what was then the silver store, desperately in need of a glass of water, who vanishes before she can be served; the voices of two unseen men talking in the library; a lady's maid who fled her bedroom to sleep on a sofa in the dining hall because of the oppressive atmosphere. None of this appears to have disturbed Lady Leonora with her total acceptance of such things. When she arrived at the castle as a new bride she says she asked 'Have you any ghosts?', only to be told, 'We do not allow them'. Sir Humphry might have asked the same thing, although he appears to have known the answer all along.

Raby Castle's 'Old Hell Cat', who appears on the battlements, and (below) the castle itself, its stone 'defenders' clearly visible on the skyline.

The Romans were quick to recognise the lawlessness of the border region between England and Scotland: they built a great wall across the neck of this countryside to divide the two ever-warring nations. This may have been effective for the centuries of their occupation but ended as soon as the empire dissolved. Then the region degenerated into its usual turmoil, not helped by frequent, savage, incursions by the Vikings. When these ended the Normans arrived and conflicts between north and south resumed following a familiar pattern of looting and destruction, though often with political motives. This only ended with the defeat of the Jacobites at Culloden.

Such violent events naturally foster stories of the supernatural. Sudden death is often the cause of a haunting and certainly the castles and towers of the north east of England possess their fair share of these.

Raby Castle, to the west of Durham, was one of the great strongholds built by the Nevilles. They were forced to surrender it to Henry VIII after the unsuccessful Northern rising of 1569

(the Pilgrimage of Grace). It then passed to the Vane family whose successors, the lords Barnard, have lived there ever since. Over the centuries, attempts have been made to reconcile the original fortress with everyday comforts, yet Raby with its stone 'defenders' looking out over the countryside from its battlements remains a functional castle, and is all the more impressive because of this.

Its ghost is an eighteenth-century Lady Barnard who was such a virago that she was known throughout the district as the 'Old Hell Cat'. She sits atop the battlements, knitting furiously with needles that glow red-hot.

The environs of Raby are haunted by the victims of the mass-murderer Maria Cotton, executed at Durham in 1873. They pursue each other endlessly in a bizarre game of tag, the ghostly players chasing through fields and over hedges.

Durham's most enduring legend is that of the Lambton Worm – the monster which, though no ghost, certainly possessed supernatural qualities.

Even in earliest times the Lambtons were a proud family and so brave that they feared neither man nor God. John, the heir to the Lambton estates in medieval times, was an unpleasant young man, a braggart who also profaned the Sabbath by liking to fish in the River Wear. On one such occasion he had been fishing for some time without anything to show for his efforts when he felt a strong tug on his line and eventually managed to land his catch. To his dismay he found a repulsive worm-like creature on his hook which he immediately threw down a nearby well. A passer-by, invited to inspect the animal, said that it was not a natural being but an omen of evil to come.

Soon afterwards John left to fight in the Holy Land on a crusade. He was away for seven years and during this time the worm grew and grew, leaving its well to coil itself around **Penshaw Hill**, a conical mound nearby. From here it terrorised the surrounding countryside, eating all the cattle and poisoning the pastures with its reeking breath. Knights came from distant parts to try to kill the monster but all were unsuccessful and most perished in the attempt. Even if they succeeded in cutting it in two the parts reunited immediately and the worm grew even stronger.

When John Lambton returned from the Holy Land he was determined to kill the monster he had spawned. He consulted with a wise woman who first rebuked him for being the cause of the devastation, but said that the worm could be overcome if he wore special armour studded with razors. However the price for this advice was his promise to kill the first living thing that he encountered after slaying the monster. Should he break this vow 'the lords of Lambton for nine generations should not die in their beds'.

The young man duly fought with and killed the worm. He had arranged with his father that when the beast was dead his favourite greyhound would be let loose and this would be killed as the first living creature. Unfortunately in the heat of the moment the old man forgot these instructions and ran forward to embrace his son. Thus, as he was unable to kill his father, the curse was invoked and thereafter nine lords of Lambton died unexpected deaths until 1761 when Henry Lambton managed to die at home and in bed.

Penshaw Hill, topped by the distinctive monument to the Liberal reformer Lord Durham, was where the Lambton Worm rested between forays.

The gloomy façade of Hylton Castle, haunted by the 'Cauld Lad'.

The seventeenth-century stone figure showing the knight slaying the Lambton Worm is now at Biddick Hall, the present home of the Lambtons.

Like Raby, **Hylton Castle**, in Sunderland, is still guarded by stone 'defenders' on its ramparts. Although now only a shell it is an interesting and rare example of a small fifteenth-century castle, only a little larger than some of the elaborate gatehouses of the period. In the eighteenth century it was the core of a mansion but these additions have been removed.

William de Hylton finished the castle in 1410. Its famous ghost is the Cauld Lad, a naked boy who was usually helpful in the running of the place, tidying things away and clearing up, and only occasionally became a nuisance when these tasks were completed and there was nothing else to do. The shivering ghost is said to be Robert Skelton, a stable lad murdered by Baron Robert Hylton in 1609 when, angry at finding his horse not ready, he threw a hayfork at the sleeping boy. The baron disposed of the body in a nearby pond. The spirit of the Cauld Lad was only laid when the servants left out a cloak and hood for him: the lad could not resist trying them, saying

> *Here's a cloak and here's a hood*
> *The Cauld Lad of Hylton will do no*
> *more good.*

Soon afterwards bones found in the pond were buried in consecrated ground and the castle was left in peace.

England has few more unusual pubs than the **Marsden Grotto** which occupies caves once used by smugglers. One of these, nicknamed Jack the Blaster, betrayed his colleagues to the revenue men and it is his spirit which haunts the pub today. He even has his own mug behind the bar which, if it is ever moved, triggers poltergeist activity. The Grotto, situated between Sunderland and South Shields, is reached via a lift from the clifftop to the beach.

Another haunted pub is to be found at Blanchland in Northumberland. This is the **Lord Crewe Arms**, part of the

Model Village created by the trustees of the Forster family in 1752. The village occupies the site of an abbey founded in 1165, only the gatehouse of which survives today, though the Lord Crewe Arms incorporates much of an earlier monastic building, including a priest's hole concealed up a chimney. Tom Forster, one of the leaders of the disastrous Jacobite Rising of 1715, was hidden in the hole before fleeing to France. He had escaped from Newgate Prison in London with the help of his brave sister Dorothy. Her ghost still haunts the hotel, perhaps in the hope of receiving a message from her exiled brother. Guests often feel her presence when they are in bed as a sort of weight on their feet.

Marsden Grotto, haunted by 'Jack the Blaster'.

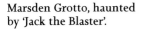

The Lord Crewe Arms at Blanchland (top), with its Priest's Hole (left) where Tom Forster (above) was hidden.

A bridal feast suffered supernatural interruption at Featherstone Castle.

Two more ghosts related to the same rebellion that caused the flight of Tom Forster haunt ruined **Dilston Castle** near Corbridge. Its last occupant, James Radcliffe, Earl of Derwentwater, was beheaded on Tower Hill in 1716. He had been forced to join the Jacobites by his wife who mocked his lack of courage, offering to wield his sword herself. Both the young Earl and his wife haunt Dilston, the former galloping over the surrounding countryside with his men while his remorseful wife roams the castle itself, wringing her hands. Stories were told of amazing events here at the time of the Earl's execution – the gutters of the castle ran with blood while corn ground in the neighbouring mill was tinged red.

Further to the west, beyond Haltwhistle, is the thirteenth-century **Featherstone Castle**. The castle stands at the heart of an exceptionally well-haunted district and is itself haunted by the groans and rattling chains of Sir Reginald FitzUrse who was starved to

death here early in its history. However its most famous story is that of the Ghostly Bridal, which takes place outside the castle.

The Baron of Featherstonhaugh had a lovely daughter named Abigail who was imprudent enough to fall in love with a young man who her father thought was unsuitable, since he was a member of the Catholic Ridley family whereas the Featherstonhaughs were Protestant. The Baron therefore arranged her marriage himself, to a man for whom she did not care at all, but who was of the right faith.

The marriage took place at Featherstone with the greatest pomp and ceremony. Midway through the feast it was decided that the entourage should parade through the demesne, returning later to resume the banquet. The colourful cavalcade left the castle leaving the Baron at the table with his cronies.

When night began to fall and the bridal party had not returned, the Baron became anxious. They were still

missing at midnight when Abigail's father sat alone and distraught amidst the ruins of the deserted feast. Then he heard the sound of the drawbridge being lowered, and the clatter of hooves across its wooden floor. Soon after the bride, groom and guests returned and silently took their seats again at the table. Yet there was no joy in this as their eyes were fixed in stares of death and their complexions were mortally pallid. Worse still they were covered with blood and bore terrible gaping wounds. Horror-struck the Baron made the sign of the Cross, whereupon the whole scene vanished with the sound of a gust of wind.

The Ghostly Bridal is still seen about Featherstone, especially in the ravine known as Pinkeyn Clough where the party were ambushed by the young man Abigail had loved, who with a hired gang slaughtered the entire company.

Another 'Cauld Lad' story is told of **Thirlwall Common** near Greenhead where the pitiful ghost of a six-year-old boy appears with the words:

> Cauld, cauld, aye cauld,
> And ye'll be cauld for ever mair.

Occasionally the touch of an icy hand is felt as well. This must be a very horrible ghost to meet if his words are indeed a curse. This Cauld Lad is said to be an orphan cast out to freeze by a wicked uncle who thus gained his inheritance. He may well have lived in **Thirlwall Castle** which is now a picturesque ruin. Built around 1346 it has not been lived in for nearly 400 years. Its ghost is a dwarf who guards

The remains of Thirlwall Castle – here a ghostly dwarf guards a table made of solid gold.

treasure, in the form of a table of gold, which is buried in a well sealed with a curse. This can only be broken by 'the coming of one who is the only son of a widow'.

Yet another ghost of the district, which must have more hauntings per kilometre than any other in England, belongs to **Blenkinsopp Castle**. A White Lady walks here, eternally seeking her husband who mysteriously went missing after swearing that he would always prefer riches to women. She seems to like appearing to children rather than grown-ups, and her wish is for them to find the treasure that she concealed in a vault beneath the castle so that her husband would not find it.

A hundred years ago, a tunnel was discovered beneath the east wall which leads deep into the rocky foundations of the castle. Two attempts were made to discover where it went but on each occasion the explorer was almost overcome by the foulness of the air and after the second attempt the tunnel was bricked-up. The present owner of Blenkinsopp says that inexplicable footsteps are often heard and that he is convinced that when he was a boy the White Lady tried to get into his room. In the middle of the night footsteps came to his door and the handle turned. Then the footsteps retreated. At the time he thought that his elder brother had approached his room by mistake, but in the morning found that he had spent the night away, and he could only explain the incident by the fondness of the White Lady for children.

A little way to the east the farmhouse of **Hardriding** has a gruesome ghost. The place came by its name because of the almost impenetrable thicket which originally surrounded it. Its ghost is that of a border outlaw who one icy December night

A White Lady haunts the ancient tower at Cresswell.

attempted to climb the curtain wall of the fortified farmstead so that he could let his fellows inside. He was spotted by an alert guard who hacked at him with his sword just before he gained the battlements and dropped him to the ground below. In the morning only his hands and feet were found, the rest of his body having been eaten by wolves. The episode took place 600 years ago, but the outlaw's spirit is still supposed to appear on the anniversary of the unsuccessful raid. Hardriding was troubled by a particularly active boggle (the down-to-earth North Country word for poltergeist) in the 1930s which disrupted the family's Christmas.

Flying with supernatural ease to the other side of Northumberland – its coast – a well-haunted location is **Cresswell** to the north east of Morpeth. Here a White Lady haunts the beach close to the fourteenth-century tower. Her Danish lover was killed while she watched from the tower. Many other ghosts are said to roam this lonely shore, often accompanied by spectral dogs. These are not the usual sort of black hell-hounds but are described as being more like sporting dogs, black retrievers with curly coats.

Warkworth Castle dominates the lovely town which provides its memorable setting. Although many people have seen its ghost there is no clear consensus on its identity, though many believe it to be Margaret Neville, who was the wife of the first Earl of Northumberland and mother of the Harry Hotspur immortalised by Shakespeare. The famous Hermitage was built on her instructions, and the ghostly figure is sometimes seen going in this direction.

Warkworth Castle, home of Margaret Neville who haunts the path to the Hermitage which was constructed according to her wishes.

The dramatic remains of **Dunstanburgh Castle** stand on a remote and precipitous cliff-top site to the north of Alnwick. No road goes near and so the only way to approach the ruin is on foot from Craster village, a delightful walk on springy turf which makes the impact of the castle all the more impressive. It is easy to appreciate why Pevsner called this 'one of the more moving sights in Northumberland'.

The castle was intended to protect a fortified harbour which was never built. Begun in 1314, it was more or less complete eight years later. Dunstanburgh has a White Lady ghost whose story is well suited to the romance of the ruins and their setting.

One stormy night soon after the completion of the castle, a warrior named Guy (known as the Wandering Knight because of his restlessness after

The ghostly ruins of Dunstanburgh Castle.

Dunstanburgh Castle, the magnificent clifftop stronghold which is haunted by Sir Guy and the White Lady of his vision.

the Crusades) rode up to the dark walls of the castle on the smooth grass of the cliffs. As he drew close, he was amazed to see that the drawbridge was lowered. He headed his horse towards it and as the hooves clattered on the wooden planks the portcullis was drawn up and the great doors swung open. Even more startling was the sudden appearance of a glowing disembodied hand holding a lantern. Sir Guy dismounted and followed the hand and its light into the gloomy recesses of the castle. The fearsome sounds of a great bell tolling and various unnerving groans and shrieks accompanied him.

At last they came to a massive and ornate door which opened magically to reveal a scene of splendour. A great chamber, brilliantly lit and lavishly decorated with marble and bronze figures and silken hangings held at its centre a most beautiful woman encapsulated in a wonderful globe of crystal held on a frame of pink coral.

Sir Guy was only able to take in this fantastic scene for a moment before the spectral hand returned, bearing firstly a golden horn, and then a sword of the same metal. At the same time an awesome voice told him that one of these implements would free the maiden from her crystal prison. The knight chose the horn, whereupon the vision abruptly disappeared leaving him alone outside the dark castle. He had been mistaken in his choice, preferring to summon aid rather than attempting to free the incomparable beauty by his own efforts, using the sword to prove his valour. Thus her spirit still awaits release from captivity and she appears on wild nights on the walls of the ruins as a White Lady, while the ghost of Sir Guy also walks, bemoaning his wrong decision.

The border town of Berwick-on-Tweed where the peace of its citizens was disturbed by a vampire in the Middle Ages.

One of Britain's oldest stories of the supernatural comes from the border town of **Berwick-on-Tweed** (though it is also claimed by Alnwick). This is contained in a collection written down by a Yorkshire monk in the Middle Ages, and discovered by M.R. James. For some strange reason this ghost has become known as the Berwick Vampire, even though he seems not to have had any of the properties usually associated with such a creature.

The Vampire was a wealthy merchant of the town who seems to have made his fortune by somewhat shady means. When he died from pestilence all manner of disturbances broke out in the town – the most fearsome being his apparition which regularly roamed the streets of Berwick accompanied by a pack of phantom hounds. This so terrified the citizens that they demanded that the priests and civic authorities put an end to the troubles. It was decided that the only cure would be to disinter the merchant's body, cut it up and burn it. Volunteers were asked to undertake this unpleasant task, and when they came to dig up the corpse it was accidentally hit by a spade, whereupon fresh blood spurted from the wound. This conclusively proved that the merchant had indeed been a vampire, but the incineration of his body put an end to further disturbances.

SCOTLAND

GLAMIS
WHERE FACT AND FICTION MEET

'This castle hath a pleasant seat; the air
Nimbly and sweetly recommends itself
Unto our gentle senses.'

William Shakespeare, *Macbeth*

ACT ONE, scene six of one of the greatest tragedies ever written introduces the doomed King Duncan, lighthearted and lyrical, as he approaches Glamis Castle. Hours later he is brutally murdered, and the 'sweet and nimble' air turns black and sinister . . . 'Glamis hath murder'd sleep . . . Macbeth shall sleep no more' . . . as Shakespeare crafts his grim and ghostly masterpiece, and fact and fiction become bonded together for all time.

It hardly matters that Duncan actually met his death miles to the north near Elgin; Shakespeare succeeded in shifting Scotland's geography and history when he chose Glamis as his literary location. And after all, it is here that the unfortunate King's death is commemorated,

▷ **Historic Glamis Castle**

◁ **The Countess of Strathmore.**

in the ancient and eerie Duncan's Hall. All Shakespeare did was select a stage already groaning under the weight of violence, death and family feuds and add a new twist to its turbulent life and times.

Had the Bard been looking to follow up his gory story of the Scottish crown, he would have found sufficient material here alone for a whole series of sequels; and given the fascination of his times for witchcraft, sorcery and the supernatural, there is one particularly unpleasant episode in Glamis' past sure to have appealed to his audience's tastes. It also gives rise to one of the castle's cast of phantom figures.

Tragedy struck the Lyon family, holders of the thaneage of Glamis since 1372, following the death of John, sixth Lord Glamis. John Lyon had been fortunate enough to marry Janet, a charming, popular woman of impeccable character; his misfortune, or more to the point hers, was the fact that she was a Douglas. King James V had been dominated by a Douglas stepfather, and manipulated by the rest of the Clan, to the extent that the very name eventually conjured up an obsessive hatred. He embarked on a ruthless vendetta against them, and as the widow of Lord Glamis, Janet no longer enjoyed the protection of marriage.

In his determination to rid himself of all living Douglases the King stopped at nothing. Charges of witchcraft were concocted against the innocent woman, and bolstered up by an equally unsubstantiated plot to poison him. Convicting her was not so easy; Janet was well respected by everyone, but James succeeded and the poor woman spent so long in the condemned cell that she was almost blind by the time she was led to a stake outside Edinburgh Castle, and burned alive. Her young son, John, was also condemned to death and imprisoned, but happily he was released when the vicious and obsessive James himself died. Perhaps as a result of such a ghastly death the Earl's widow prefers to recall happier times by returning to Glamis. As the Grey Lady she has been seen from time to time within the castle.

Glamis has a past to be reckoned with, and many have tuned into the echoes of its haunted heritage with its heavy overtones of mystery, and talk of monsters. The very place that inspired Stratford-upon-Avon's famous son left Scotland's favourite poet and novelist, Sir Walter Scott, full of misgivings. After a night's stay in the castle he wrote: 'I must own that when I heard door after door shut, after my conductor had retired, I began to consider myself as too far from the living, and somewhat too near the dead'!

Home now to Mary, Countess of Strathmore and Kinghorne, Glamis reflects a far more lively atmosphere. And while she charmingly brushes aside any talk of ghosts, she does confess to a touch of Sir Walter Scott's nervousness when she herself was a newcomer to the castle. 'We came here to live in 1975, but for some time before that I would often be here clearing up and doing all the things you need to do before a move. Just occasionally, on dark winter nights, I would find myself wondering if all the stories I had heard were true.' But with three young children and her husband (the seventeenth Earl, who died in 1987) to occupy her mind, such thoughts were soon forgotten and nothing has occurred since to resurrect them.

For any other newcomer, arriving at Glamis is one of those once seen, never forgotten experiences. Approached down a mile-long, gently dipping avenue, the castle slowly emerges from its tree-lined foreground as if being unveiled. Grey-capped turrets, towers and spires break the suspense. Then as the curtain drops further the illusion changes; the castle appears to rise upwards as the blue-grey mountains drop behind its rounded pinkish-grey, pointed towers. By the time you break out of the trees and onto the forecourt you have to stop to draw breath – Glamis is a glorious sight, everything you ever expected, and more.

The Glamis granted to Sir John Lyon in 1372 was little more than a hunting lodge; he set to work on a new house suited to the dignity and importance of his position as Chamberlain of Scotland, and husband of King Robert II's daughter, Joanna. Much of what he created is incorporated into the fabric of the present castle. Sir John, incidentally, was yet another victim of Glamis's violent past; he met his end at the hands of Scotland's ambassador to England, being undiplomatically murdered in his bed. Many subsequent Lords of Glamis added, altered and improved the red sandstone structure, none more than the third Earl of Kinghorne.

When Lord Patrick came to the castle in 1670 he was burdened with debts amounting to £400,000, still a huge sum now, but a staggering amount in his day. Undaunted, he set about changing Glamis's fortunes, and not only managed to balance the books, but embark on the rebuilding programme that created very much the Glamis of today with its heavily influenced French chateau style, a fashion that caught on elsewhere in these parts and became known as Scottish baronial.

Glamis was the childhood home of the Queen Mother; her father Claude was the fourteenth Earl. Although not born at Glamis, she spent most of her formative years there, and indeed, still visits her old home. It was one of the Queen Mother's sisters, Lady Rose Bowes Lyon, who is said to have spotted the Grey Lady in the castle Chapel as she sat playing the harmonium. But any talk of ghosts while the Queen Mother and her nine brothers and sisters were children was quickly scotched. 'With such a large family the last thing anyone was going to do was talk about ghosts', said Lady Strathmore, 'and their mother always insisted that there were no ghosts at Glamis. And while I'm well aware that this is the one thing visitors always want to know about, I think it's got more to do with tradition than anything else. To me Glamis is far too friendly and welcoming a place for any lingering feelings of unpleasantness.'

And welcoming it is, its grand stately style contrasting with homely touches like the extra heaters to take off the chill, the smell of fresh paint, and bowls of fresh flowers. The Countess welcomes interest in Glamis, but is far more inclined to joke about her ghosts than dwell on them; the antique, and unconnected, telephone above her desk at the window in the Queen Mother's Sitting Room is used to call up the castle's ghosts and ask them to put in an appearance when curious young visitors are around! Even the phantom page boy, said to sit on the stone stool just inside the doorway, has a sense of mischief. He is given to tripping people up as they walk past his unseen and outstretched foot.

The Glamis of today is not at all the gloomy and ghost-ridden Glamis of yesterday. But there still remains the mystery of the sealed room, its inhabitants, and Lord 'Beardie' Crawford. These alleged hauntings, and the suggestion of a shameful family secret, share the same location, the crypt. This particular crypt defies its subterranean definition, and is in fact reached by going *upstairs*, not down. Long and tunnel-shaped with bare stone walls and floor, the atmosphere here is distinctly chilly.

It is here in one of the oldest, strongest and most impregnable parts of the castle, with walls thick enough to swallow a mini-bus, that a secret chamber exists. Its most written and talked about legend refers to a hideous monster, a child of the Strathmore family born some 200 years ago and doomed to be hidden away to live out its life in isolation so as to protect the family from shame. Depending upon the account you read, this monster-child managed to live until the 1920s –

△ The chapel at Glamis, where the Grey Lady is said to have been seen.

it easier on this occasion, a barred and bricked up window was pointed out to us from the outside. So that part of the mystery at least was solved, even if it remains impossible to locate it from the inside.

As for Lord 'Beardie' Crawford, he was a one-time Earl of Strathmore, renowned for his love of gambling. One winter Sunday night, bored and restless, he called for a pack of cards, but this being the Lord's Day all such activities were forbidden. No one would join him, and in his anger Lord 'Beardie' struck the chaplain who, in return, branded the cards 'deevil's bricks'. Eventually Lord 'Beardie' retreated to his chamber saying, as he stamped off, he would play with the Devil sooner than not play at all. Who then should turn up but the Devil himself proposing such high stakes that the Earl agreed he would sign a bond for whatever the Devil might ask. A fast and furious night of gambling followed, before the Devil disappeared, taking the bond with him.

Lord 'Beardie' lived five years before he paid his bond; but afterwards on every Sunday evening, the old chamber was filled with the sound of raging, wrangling and swearing. For a time these unearthly noises were endured, but finally everyone had had enough and the room was sealed up, never to be found again. There is a slight variation to this in which Lord 'Beardie', losing badly, swore an oath that he would play until the Day of Judgement. At that very moment the Devil appeared, taking Lord 'Beardie' and all his gambling cohorts with him. The room they were in disappeared with them, but they are still to be heard on occasions ranting and raging over their 'deevil's bricks'.

A little fanciful perhaps, but who knows. Wild, winter nights at Glamis are also reputed to bring out a ghostly madman to walk the roof along the so-called 'Mad Earl's Walk', the much-maligned Janet is said to prefer the Clock Tower (when not visiting the Chapel), and the spectre of a man has been seen at the Malcolm Stone close by in the village. Even Macbeth, the real Macbeth as opposed to Shakespeare's creation, returns to wring his hands over the murder of Duncan, adding a further twist to the fact and fiction written into this place of distant memories, everlasting secrets and haunting shadows.

with each successive Earl taken to the chamber and told the awful truth as he reached the age of 21 – or, alternatively, a number of monsters have been born in succession.

Again, according to some sources, the fifteenth Earl is supposed to have fuelled speculation by saying: 'If you could only guess the nature of the secret, you would go down on your knees and thank God it was not yours.' Since his time the Strathmores have, perhaps not surprisingly, chosen to steer clear of so distasteful a subject, and certainly the present Countess made no bones about her feelings on the matter. It was simply not a subject for discussion. She did, however, admit to having heard about the towels-out-of-the-windows experiment. Apparently this was once attempted in a bid to discover exactly where the missing room was located. However, to make

Spedlin's Tower, for many years a ruin, has been painstakingly restored, and (below, right) the Jardine Bible, no longer kept at the tower.

All around England and Wales there are many recognisable plots or themes which are common to ghost stories from different locations, often far apart. The pattern continues in Scotland where the theme of the forgotten prisoner is a special favourite, being found at a tower-house of the Borders as well as in other places further north.

Spedlin's Tower is situated close to Lockerbie and was built in about 1480, presumably by Spedlin, though by the end of the century it was the headquarters of the Jardine family who later made a fortune from the tea trade.

The events giving rise to its ghost took place in the early years of the Jardine occupancy when a dispute broke out between Porteous, the local miller, and the laird. The laird locked the poor man in the dungeon and rode off to Edinburgh, forgetting that he carried the only key in his pocket.

No-one in the tower heard Porteous' pitiable cries for help, and the laird only realised the plight of his prisoner when he reached Edinburgh and discovered the key. By this time the miller was beyond help, but his hatred of the Jardine family endured beyond death, and his restless spirit plagued the family continuously with all manner of activities.

In the end the Jardines were forced to have the ghost exorcised, and he was committed to return to the dungeon in which he had starved. The Bible used in the service (a beautiful Cranmer edition of 1548) was placed in a niche of the stairway to ensure

that he remained there. For all this the ghost still managed to generate sounds in his prison, in particular his cry 'Let me out, let me out, for I'm deeing' o'hunger', and if a twig was pushed through the lock its bark was stripped off, so ravenous was the ghost.

In time the Jardines prospered in trade and moved to a mansion on the other side of the river (Jardine Hall, now demolished). The Bible was left in its niche for a while, but when it was found that its binding was deteriorating it was sent to Edinburgh for restoration. At this the ghost of Porteous (affectionately known to the family as 'Dunty') made haste into the new Hall, announcing his presence there by tipping the baronet and his wife from their bed.

The penny soon dropped as to the cause of the disturbances which daily grew more violent until a messenger was sent to Edinburgh and the Bible restored to its rightful place. However, the Tower became more dilapidated over the years and eventually the Bible followed the Jardine family to their new home in Cumbria. Recently Spedlin's Tower has been restored as a dwelling and it now seems to have been deserted by the ghost of the unfortunate miller.

Of all Scottish castles there is none more sinister and forbidding than the one guarding Liddesdale, in the middle of the bleak and lonely moorland that was once the lawless preserve of the Border rivers. This is **Hermitage Castle**, which has in the past served as a fitting location for a film of Shakespeare's 'Scottish play'. Its name derives from Brother William who lived in this forsaken spot in the twelfth century as a hermit – his cell may still be seen close to the castle.

The first stronghold was a tower put up by the Dacres, but ownership soon passed on, firstly to the Comyns and then to Nicholas de Soulis who, though its lord for only a short time, managed to establish an unwholesome

reputation as a man of evil who ravaged local beauties, abducted children, and dabbled in the black arts. Although history insists that he died a prisoner at Dumbarton, it is believed locally that his tenants eventually turned against him and killed him by throwing him into a cauldron of boiling lead. Either way, Hermitage is haunted

Robin Redcap was the repulsive familiar of the evil Lord de Soulis who practised the black arts at Hermitage Castle. Both Robin and the wicked earl haunt the lonely and sinister castle.

by the ghost of Lord Soulis accompanied by his familiar, Robin Redcap, to whom he gave the key to retrieve the buried treasure which still remains somewhere within the grim stronghold.

The next occupant of the castle was Sir William Douglas, who, though he enjoyed a rather better reputation than his predecessor, was still capable of barbarity. He locked a neighbour, Sir Alexander Ramsay, in a dungeon and starved him to death, his agonies being prolonged to seventeen days by the supply of grains of wheat which trickled into his cell from the corn-store next door.

The most romantic incident in the castle's history took place in 1566 when Mary, Queen of Scots rode from Jedburgh to visit the Earl of Bothwell who lay injured at Hermitage after being wounded in a Border skirmish. She spent less than 30 minutes with the Earl (whom she married a year later after the assassination of her despised husband, Lord Darnley) before returning to Jedburgh on the same day, a ride of 50 miles. It is perhaps not surprising that she became very ill after such an arduous excursion, and nearly died.

The most ancient of Scottish ghost stories comes from Jedburgh. In 1285 Alexander III was married to Iolande of Dreux, the ceremony taking place in the Abbey. Afterwards the guests returned to **Jedburgh Castle** for the wedding-banquet, which was dramatically interrupted by the appearance of a hooded, masked figure, wearing a shroud. Believing that the figure which glided amongst them was a trickster, the guests grabbed at his clothing which came away to reveal . . . nothing. For a moment it lay at their feet, then it too vanished. The older guests recognised this as a portent of disaster and were proved right when the King died five months later, falling from the cliff top at Kinghorn in Fife, when his horse stumbled during a terrible storm. Jedburgh Castle was demolished in 1409, the site later being occupied by the county gaol which now serves as a museum. Edgar Allan Poe was inspired to write *Masque of the Red Death* on hearing the story.

Newark Castle is a simple border keep dating from about 1450, and is picturesquely situated in the heart of the Scott Country. Sir Walter made this the setting for the recitation of *The Lay of the Last Minstrel* by the Bard of Abbotsford. Its courtyard was the scene of a terrible massacre in 1645 when about 300 survivors of the Battle of Philiphaugh (mainly the supporters of Montrose's army, female cooks and stable boys) were butchered by the victorious Convenanters. The soldiers were encouraged in their killing of the

This monument stands at Kinghorn in Fife where King Alexander III fell to his death.

Catholics by the ministers of the Kirk, and it is said that the ghostly echoes of the massacre may still be heard here on its anniversary. Joan Forman, an expert investigator of the supernatural, was engulfed in a feeling of 'frantic misery and desperation' when she visited Newark, and identified the precise location where the atrocities took place without previous knowledge. Her family is actually related to the Grahams, who fought with Montrose at Philiphaugh.

Only Edinburgh can rival **Stirling** in the dramatic situation of its castle. As in the capital, the castle is built on a volcanic rock which rises an almost sheer 250 feet above the surrounding countryside, guarding the route between Lowlands and Highlands. The Romans had a fortress here, and by the twelfth century the castle had become a favourite residence of Scottish monarchs, and Alexander I and William the Lion both died here, in 1124 and 1214 respectively.

Newark Castle where a dreadful massacre gave rise to a haunting.

A Pink Lady haunts Stirling Castle.

Saddell Castle was built from the fabric of Saddell Abbey, which is its name again today. Headstones from the monks' graves were incorporated into the fireplaces – which may have been one of the grievances remembered by its ghosts.

It is probably from these times that Stirling's ghost originates. She is a Pink Lady who walks, enveloped in a pink aura, between the Castle and Lady's Rock, near the church. The rock was once a grandstand for ladies of the court wishing to watch tournaments which took place on the level ground below. It is known that in the time of James II (of Scotland), Scottish lords took on those of Burgundy at a tourney here *à outrance* (to the last man). Perhaps the Pink Lady's lover perished in this encounter.

When Anthony Hippisley-Coxe visited **Saddell Abbey** on the Kintyre peninsula about twenty years ago he was told that the place was haunted – 'I'm nae sure aboot monks', said a local, 'but by giants and beasties sairtainly!' – and indeed he found the atmosphere there powerful and unhappy. At the time, the building had not yet been restored and looked a hundred times more menacing than it does today. Fabric from the abbey was later used in building the castle, the headstones from the abbots' graves being used as firebacks. Not surprisingly this angered the spirits of the long-dead monks and accounted for the disturbances which later troubled the castle.

Away over on the east side of the country, on the seaward tip of Fife, is **Balcomie Castle.** This was where Mary, Queen of Scots' mother-to-be, Marie de Guise-Lorraine, rested in 1538 after her voyage from France. She had come to Scotland as the bride of King James V.

Balcomie's ghost belongs to a time when the castle was garrisoned and in the command of a somewhat crusty colonel who was responsible for controlling the entrance to the Firth of Forth from Balcomie and from Dunbar on the southern side. The colonel liked his dram but was plagued by a servant who was always playing the penny whistle (or, more appropriately, fife, as it is known in these parts).

One morning, after a particularly heavy evening's drinking, he was awoken by the shrill notes of his man's music-making. With his throbbing head made even worse by the sound, the colonel had the servant thrown into an isolated dungeon and returned to his chamber to catch up on his disturbed rest. As is usual in these tales, the garrison was then called away to Dunbar, the unfortunate prisoner being left on his own in an empty castle. Four days later the garrison returned and the man was found dead, since when the plaintive sound of his whistle has often been heard around the castle.

To my mind the abandoned control tower of the wartime airfield on the other side of the road is far more sinister than the castle, and probably has many more ghosts.

Balcomie Castle resounds to a ghostly player of the fife, a Scottish whistle. Appropriately the castle stands at the tip of Fife.

Balcomie airfield awaits redevelopment and its control tower has an aura of desolation typical of many of the haunted wartime stations.

Montrose lies on the other side of the Firth of Tay: like Balcomie there was an important air station here throughout both World Wars. There are many hauntings associated with deserted airfields but few more intriguing than that of Montrose which seems to have acquired its ghost soon after opening as the headquarters of the Second Squadron of the Royal Flying Corps early in 1913.

On 27 May of that year, Lieutenant Desmond Arthur crashed on take-off and died from his injuries. One theory is that it was his ghost that was often seen about the station, in bloodstained flying gear. He was greatly disliked by his fellow officers and the ground crew and on his deathbed claimed that his plane had been tampered with. Another version has it that the ghost is

that of a young pilot who was forced into his first solo flight against his will. He insisted that he was not ready, and when he crashed and was killed his spirit returned to haunt his instructor's room. Eventually this had to be sealed up.

Many aircraft were lost from Montrose, and local people believe that the site of the old airfield is still haunted. Indeed, before its closure in the 1950s, printed handouts given to newcomers to RAF Montrose boasted that the station was haunted by the Force's youngest ghost, Lieutenant Arthur.

Cardinal David Beaton (1494-1546) lived for a time at **Ethie Castle**, which is situated just to the north of Arbroath. He was a ruthless and vicious man, a scourge to Protestants, many of whom were sent to be burned at the stake on his orders. His mistress (or 'chief lewd' as he called her) was Marion Ogilvie who bore seven of his children. Beaton was cruel and greedy as well as licentious, and it was the former sins which eventually brought about his downfall at St Andrew's Castle. He had gone to the castle to see the burning of an enemy, the Reformer George Wishart, who prophesied before execution that the Cardinal too would shortly come to grief 'in as much shame as he now shows pomp and vanity'. Soon afterwards a group of Protestant lairds staged a guerrilla action to enter the castle, stabbed him to death, and displayed his body from the battlements where he had watched the burning of Wishart.

The wicked Cardinal's ghost has been seen at Ethie, but more usually it is heard. At the end of his life Beaton suffered from gout which was treated by binding the affected leg in

The ghost of Cardinal Beaton haunts Ethie Castle. A sufferer of gout, he shuffles down its spiral staircase.

The restored chapel at Ethie Castle where Beaton, ungodly though he was, worshipped, and where his ghost also walks – or rather limps.

bandages. Thus only the sound of one foot is heard on the spiral stairs, the other noise being the faint rustle of loose bandages.

The castle is built in two distinct parts, the newer dwarfing the original, smaller tower. Once a governess came to Ethie and was put in one of the small rooms in the old building. Her sleep was disturbed by the sound of a child sobbing and a wheeled toy being dragged across the floor of the room above. It transpired that this room had been sealed up, but when it was opened a child's bones were found, along with the crumbling remains of a toy cart.

For more than 1,000 years Ethie was the seat of the Earls of Northesk. A ghostly Green Lady acts as a banshee, warning of a death in the family. She has actually appeared at Ethie quite recently, since the Northesks have left, just before the Earl died in London.

Today the castle is the home of Ann and Alistair Forsyth, heads of the Clan Forsyth. Mrs Forsyth believes that another ghost that haunts here is that of the last Earl to live at Ethie. He was keen on photography, like Ann Forsyth. Recently she was engrossed in printing, locked in her darkroom in the old tower. She was terrified to hear heavy footsteps approach the door and pause outside, then they went away. She summoned courage to look outside but found no-one there, but the break in concentration was enough to make her remember that she had left the sandwich-toaster on in the kitchen half an hour before, and ran down just in time to prevent the whole room going up in flames. Mrs Forsyth is convinced that it was the ghost of Lord Northesk who came to warn her of impending disaster.

A little way inland, at the mouth of Glen Clova, is the picturesque **Cortachy Castle**, 'baronialised' in the nineteenth century. The seat of the Earls of Airlie, it is haunted by the ghost of a fine young drummer boy

A handsome young drummer boy, imprisoned within his drum, was thrown from the top of Cortachy Castle.

The tinker's curse continues to be effective at Ashintully Castle – its succession has followed the female line throughout the twentieth century and this pattern looks set to continue.

Green Jean roams the private (and very spooky) graveyard at Ashintully.

who was caught *in flagrante delicto* with Lady Airlie. He was seized, boxed up in his own drum, and flung off the highest tower to his death. Since then drumming is supposed to be heard outside the castle when one of the family is about to die.

Kirkmichael is a remote Tayside township in Stratharole: **Ashintully Castle** lies just to the north east, and is haunted by three ghosts. First there is Crooked Davie, a hunchback servant who was ill-treated and finally killed by a member of the wicked Spalding family, who were the lairds of Ashintully.

Then there is Green Jean. This is a favourite name for Scottish ghosts; another one haunts **Inverawe House** in the Western Highlands, where she acts the perfect hostess, putting out fresh soap and towels for guests: at Ashintully her fate is to wander in the private graveyard of the castle. Apparently she was murdered by an uncle, greedy for her inheritance.

Last of the ghosts of Ashintully (there are probably more, for this has the reputation of being the most haunted house in Scotland) is a tinker

who was arrested for trespassing and summarily executed. As the noose was slipped over his neck he cursed the Spaldings, saying that the family would be extinct within a generation, as indeed it was.

From Kirkmichael it is necessary to pass through Pitlochry to reach the next haunted house, Ballechin near Logierait. It would be hard to resist a visit to the **Pass of Killiecrankie** from Pitlochry, and this is easy to excuse since the battlefield (which is also a beauty-spot) is haunted on the anniversary of the conflict, 27 July. All sorts of manifestations have been reported on this date, the most usual being a strange red light that bathes the scene of the fighting. Perhaps this is because the battle took place at dusk, the fighting only lasting a matter of minutes before the Highlanders under 'Bonnie Dundee' put William III's army to flight. Dundee (Graham of Claverhouse) was killed by one of the last shots fired: the night before he had been visited by a ghost whose head poured with blood.

Edinburgh has a fine array of ghosts, best enjoyed at twilight when 'Alexander Clapperton, deceased: Cemetery Director' conducts his Ghosts and Gore Tours. He relishes the city's innumerable ghost stories, including those of Major Weir, a pillar of the establishment who later confessed to being a wizard and was strangled and then burned at the stake. Weir's ghost is reputed to haunt West Bow, his skeletal figure being seen in a coach drawn by six headless horses.

The Pass of Killiecrankie (left), where strange things happen on the anniversary of the battle.

Ballechin House, the scene of a famous nineteenth-century haunting: (above) the house as it is today, and (right) Ballechin as it was at the height of its notoriety.

Ballechin House became famous in 1899 when a book was published detailing a vast miscellany of hauntings which had taken place there. In the four months of 1897 when the Marquess of Bute rented the house on behalf of the Society for Psychical Research at least seven different apparitions were seen. These included a black dog, a lame man, a shuffling man, a nun and companion, a priest, and the forms of two old women, one without legs. These manifestations were said to be due to an owner of the house who had died in 1872 and promised to return after death in the form of his black spaniel.

Only the east wing of Ballechin House survives today, the haunted part having been pulled down. However quite a lot of ghostly activity took place in the grounds so there is still scope for research here and the investigator might encounter the nun (sister of the black spaniel) who is still said to walk.

The National Trust for Scotland own many beautiful properties but there can be few with a more interesting history than **Crathes Castle**, on Deeside. Part of the estate was given by Cardinal Beaton as a wedding present to Janet Hamilton who married Alexander Burnett of Leys. In 1550 Alexander began the building of Crathes, a task which continued over 40 years. It is one of the most picturesque of Scottish castles, its roofline a tumble of turrets, gables and chimneys.

The fourth baronet Burnett probably fostered belief in the famous ghost of Crathes, its Green Lady. He was intensely superstitious, having a 'boodie fear' of ghosts, especially after the death of his son who was killed by a splinter of rock during blasting operations. The Green Lady was already a well-established spectre when a reason for her presence in the Green Lady's Room was discovered early in the nineteenth century. Building work revealed a child's skeleton beneath the hearthstone – and accounts had already spoken of the Green Lady carrying a baby on her appearances. It is said that the Lady was ill-used while under the Laird's protection, and the resulting bastard child was taken from her, and it is this which causes her to haunt the room. It is an unusually persistent affair, however: Queen Victoria is supposed to have seen her, as have many more before and since, including sightings in recent years since the castle has been open to the public.

Ben Macdhui is the second-highest mountain in Britain, and the major summit of the Cairngorms. It has its very own ghost which seems to have affinities with the yeti of Tibet or Bigfoot of North America. The ghostly figure has been encountered by those who, for reasons of their own, have been on the mountain at night. Known as Bodach Mor (Giant Old Man) he is described as a shadowy figure who is

Crathes Castle, where a Green Lady appears, carrying a baby.

The Cairngorm range from near the Boat of Garten (below). The summit of Ben Macdhui is hidden by lesser peaks.

Andrew Carnegie rebuilt Skibo Castle, once disturbed by ghostly noises.

seen just below the skyline, usually in the vicinity of the Larig Ghru Pass. On one occasion the sighting was accompanied by the sound of scrunching footsteps.

Bodach Mor seems to have an identity quite different from the other famous ghost of the mountains, the Brocken Spectre, which only appears in daylight. This is explained as being the shadow of one's own figure, hugely enlarged, projected onto a bank of mist, usually by a low winter sun.

Castle Grant, now happily restored, also lies within the Cairngorms and was the seat of the Earls of Seafield and clan centre for the Grants. One of its towers is known as Babetts Tower after Barbara Grant, a beautiful daughter of one of the chiefs who refused to marry the man her father chose. Finally, in exasperation, he thrust her into a 'blackness' (cupboard) that was reached by a secret doorway from the Tapestry Room at the top of the tower. There she remained until she starved to death, her ghost returning to haunt the tower.

Further north, near Dornoch, is **Skibo Castle**, which now belongs to an investment company. Andrew Carnegie built the present castle in the early years of

this century for use as a holiday retreat. The predecessor on the same site belonged to the bishops of Caithness, and later to the Mackays and Dempsters. Skibo was haunted by the ghost of a woman who used to visit a servant left in sole charge of the castle when the owner was absent. After one such visit she failed to return to the village and the man gave up his post and went abroad. Although no trace of her was found, the theory that she had come to no good was reinforced when the gloomy chambers and passageways began to resound with unearthly skrieks and groans. These only ceased when bones were found beneath some plaster. When these were given a Christian burial the disturbances ceased.

Crossing to the west coast, the classic Scottish scene features the romantic silhouette of **Eilean Donan Castle** against the calm waters of Loch Duich. The castle is haunted by a Spanish mercenary murdered there during the siege of 1719. The meticulous reconstruction of Eilean Donan was inspired by a vision experienced by a local stonemason, Farquhar MacRae. Later research confirmed that the restoration which followed the vision was historically correct.

To the north, a fine new bridge spans the narrows of Loch Cairnbawn to allow speedy access to Durness and the coast beyond. Until a few years ago a small ferry transported cars across the little strait. This could be unreliable, and if the ferryman had enjoyed a good party the night before cars could wait some time for his appearance. This was bearable on the southern side because of the warming hospitality offered by the hotel there.

The **Kylesku Hotel** was once known as the Old Ferry House and has a fine reputation for being haunted, though the ghost seems to have become inactive recently. Perhaps this is because his favourite haunt is now the Pool Room. Formerly it was the ladies' lavatory, and the ghost would peer down at the inmates from a trapdoor in its ceiling. In bygone days, before the room was a loo, this was the Snuggery of the hotel, forbidden to women, and locals have suggested that the ghost is chauvinistically trying to maintain men's rights. Women point out that he was probably just a peeping tom. He has been identified as being the brother of Miss Mackay, who was landlady in the 1890s and was tricked into losing her licence by a policeman from Stoer. She is remembered as being a fine fiddle player. Perhaps her brother found her personality over-powerful and resents women taking over the cosy drinking den where he was safe from her nagging. The famous broadcaster Professor Joad saw the ghost in the 1950s – presumably before the Snuggery had been converted.

In the early days of this century a couple stopped at the hotel and proposed to walk on to Inchadamph. One of the locals, who had the gift of second sight, begged them not to attempt this, as he had dreamed of a drowning in the loch on three successive nights. They ignored his warning and were indeed drowned, but their spirits linger on to haunt this desolate stretch of road.

The haunted Kylesku Hotel, where a ghost peered through a trap door into the ladies' lavatory.

Eilean Donan Castle – a vision inspired a local craftsman to begin its restoration.

INDEX

ACKNOWLEDGMENTS

The majority of illustrations in this book were
specially commissioned; others supplied to us or
requiring acknowledgment are listed below.
We would also like to thank the many people, too
numerous to mention here, who kindly gave us
permission to photograph their properties.

8-11 By kind permission of the Marquess of Bath. 19 By permission of English Heritage.
21 By kind permission of Mrs Ellis. 23 By permission of Tavistock Town Council.
29 By permission of Robin Barbour. 33 (bottom) By permission of Mordern Estates Company.
35 (top left and right) By permission of English Heritage. 40 Reproduced by kind permission of
Mr King. 42-45 Reproduced by permission of Lord Montagu and the Photographic Library,
Beaulieu. 55 (bottom) National Portrait Gallery, London. 64-67 By permission of Ettington
Park Hotel. 68 (bottom) and 69 By permission of Bisham Abbey National Sports Centre.
73 By permission of Queen's College, Oxford. 78 (bottom) By permission of English Heritage.
82 (top) Reproduced by permission of Birmingham City Art Galleries. 84 (bottom left and right)
By permission of the National Trust. 85 By kind permission of Mr J Allen. 86 (bottom left and
right) By permission of Warwick Castle. 87 By permission of Guy's Cliff Masonic Rooms.
92 (top) National Portrait Gallery, London. 93 By permission of Tamworth Castle. 94 and
95 By permission of the City of Nottingham. 96 By kind permission of Sir Reresby Sitwell.
98-101 By kind permission of Lady Cobbold. 102 (top) National Portrait Gallery, London.
106 By permission of the Cambridge Centre for Languages. 107 (top) By kind permission of
Mr & Mrs J Archer. 107 (bottom) National Portrait Gallery, London. 108 By permission of the
University of Cambridge Board of Extra-Mural Studies. 114 (left) By permission of English
Heritage. 114 (bottom, right) and 115 (bottom, left) Reproduced by permission of Paul Mellon and
the Le Strange Estate. 116 By permission of the National Trust. 118 By kind permission of Mr
& Mrs Archdale. 119 and 120 By permission of English Heritage. 121 (bottom) By permission
of Bernard Thorpe and Partners. 124-127 By kind permission of Mr L H Mercer.
128 By permission of the National Trust. 132 (left) By permission of CADW. 135 By
permission of West Glamorgan County Council. 149 By permission of Leeds City Art Galleries.
151 By permission of Bolling Hall Museum. 152-3 By permission of the National Trust.
156 By kind permission of Mr L Belcher. 158 (top) By permission of English Heritage.
158 (bottom) and 159 By kind permission of Mr J Chichester-Constable. 160 By permission of
Burton Agnes Hall Preservation Trust. 164-167 By kind permission of Mr H Bagot. 176 (right)
and 177 (top) By kind permission of Mr P Hother. 186-189 By kind permission of Sir
Humphry Wakefield. 193 (middle, right) Reproduced by permission of R G Bolam and Son.
194 By permission of Mr J Clark. 202-205 By kind permission of the Countess of Strathmore.
207, 208 and 209 (bottom) By permission of Historic Buildings and Monuments. 210 By
permission of the Landmark Trust.

Every effort has been made to obtain the
appropriate rights or permission to publish all
copyright material. The publishers would be pleased
to acknowledge any omission in future editions.

The publishers would like to express their gratitude
to the many individuals and organisations whose
specialised knowledge was invaluable in the
preparation of this book.

ADOBE® ILLUSTRATOR® CS2
REVEALED
DELUXE EDUCATION EDITION

Chris Botello

Adobe | Approved Certification Courseware

THOMSON

COURSE TECHNOLOGY

Adobe® Illustrator® CS2—Revealed, Deluxe Education Edition

Chris Botello

Managing Editor:	**Production Editor:**	**QA Manuscript Reviewers:**
Marjorie Hunt	Danielle Slade	Jeffrey Schwartz, Chris Carvalho
Product Manager:	**Developmental Editor:**	**Text Designer:**
Jane Hosie-Bounar	Ann Fisher	Ann Small
Associate Product Manager:	**Proofreader:**	**Illustrator:**
Emilie Perreault	Harry Johnson	Philip Brooker
Editorial Assistant:	**Indexer:**	**Cover Design:**
Shana Rosenthal	May Hasso	Steve Deschene
	Composition House:	
	Integra-Pondicherry, India	

Revealed Series Vision

The Revealed Series is your guide to today's hottest multimedia applications. These comprehensive books teach the skills behind the application, showing you how to apply smart design principles to multimedia products such as dynamic graphics, animation, Web sites, software authoring tools, and video.

A team of design professionals including multimedia instructors, students, authors, and editors worked together to create and then refine this series. We recognized the unique learning environment of the multimedia classroom and created a series that:

- Gives you comprehensive step-by-step instructions
- Offers in-depth explanation of the "why" behind a skill
- Includes creative projects for additional practice
- Explains concepts clearly using full-color visuals

It was our goal to create a book that speaks directly to the multimedia and design community—one of the most rapidly growing computer fields today. We think we've done just that, with a sophisticated and instructive book design.

—The Revealed Series

Author's Vision

Hands-on is the best way to explore any software application. You can study every chapter of an instruction manual, but reading about Adobe Illustrator and drawing in Adobe Illustrator are two very different things indeed.

This book is a series of exercises that will take you on a fully guided tour of Illustrator CS2—from basic concepts to advanced techniques—all with a hands-on approach. You will learn by doing, and you'll have fun, which is an essential skill not covered in any instruction manual.

I had fun writing this, and that was possible because of the focus and hard work of my editor and long-time friend Ann Fisher. Ann kept the project on track but left me enough room to bounce around the application and share with you some of my favorite tips and tricks. Her dedication—combined with a great capacity for laughter— brought out the best in both of us. Special thanks also go to Marjorie Hunt, Managing Editor for this series and others, and Jane Hosie-Bounar, the Product Manager.

I also want to acknowledge the QA manuscript reviewers for their input: Jeff Schwartz and Chris Carvalho

—Chris Botello.

SERIES & AUTHOR VISION

Introduction to Adobe Illustrator CS2

Welcome to *Adobe Illustrator CS2—Revealed, Deluxe Education Edition*. This book offers creative projects, concise instructions, and complete coverage of basic to advanced Illustrator skills, helping you to create polished, professional-looking illustrations. Use this book both in the classroom and as your own reference guide.

This text is organized into thirteen chapters. In these chapters you will learn many skills, including how to draw illustrations, transform objects, work with layers, patterns, brushes, and filters, use effects, create graphics for the Web, create graphs, work in 3D, and prepare files for print production.

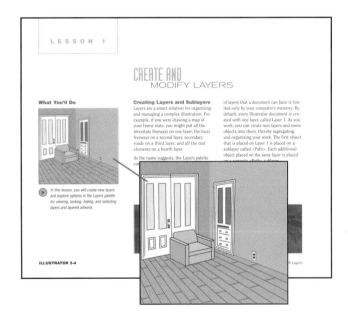

What You'll Do

A What You'll Do figure begins every lesson. This figure gives you an at-a-glance look at what you'll do in the chapter, either by showing you a page or pages from the current project, or a tool you'll be using.

Comprehensive Conceptual Lessons

Before jumping into instructions, in-depth conceptual information tells you "why" skills are applied. This book provides the "how" and "why" through the use of professional examples. Also included in the text are tips and sidebars to help you work more efficiently and creatively, or to teach you a bit about the history or design philosophy behind the skill you are using.

Step-by-Step Instructions

This book combines in-depth conceptual information with concise steps to help you learn Illustrator CS2. Each set of steps guides you through a lesson where you will create, modify, or enhance an Illustrator CS2 file. Step references to large colorful images and quick step summaries round out the lessons.

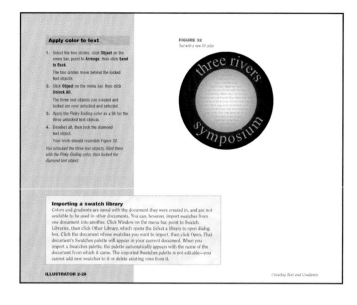

Projects

This book contains a variety of end-of-chapter materials for additional practice and reinforcement. The Skills Review contains hands-on practice exercises that mirror the progressive nature of the lesson material. The chapter concludes with four projects: two Project Builders, one Design Project, and one Group Project. The Project Builders and the Design Project require you to apply the skills you've learned in the chapter. Group Projects encourage group activity as students use the resources of a team to address and solve challenges based on the content explored in the chapter.

What Instructor Resources Are Available with This Book?

The Instructor Resources CD-ROM is Thomson Course Technology's way of putting the resources and information needed to teach and learn effectively into your hands. All the resources are available for both Macintosh and Windows operating systems, and many of the resources can be downloaded from *www.course.com*.

Instructor's Manual

Available as an electronic file, the Instructor's Manual includes chapter overviews and detailed lecture topics for each chapter, with teaching tips. The Instructor's Manual is available on the Instructor Resources CD-ROM, or you can download it from *www.course.com*.

Syllabus

Prepare and customize your course easily using this sample course outline (available on the Instructor Resources CD-ROM).

PowerPoint Presentations

Each chapter has a corresponding PowerPoint presentation that you can use in lectures, distribute to your students, or customize to suit your course.

Figure Files

Figure Files contain all the figures from the book in bitmap format. Use the figure files to create transparency masters or use them in a PowerPoint presentation.

Data Files for Students

To complete most of the chapters in this book, your students will need Data Files. The Data Files are available on the CD at the back of this text book. Instruct students to use the Data Files List at the end of this book if they need to understand how the files are organized. We also include a list of the Data Files needed for each chapter in the Instructor's Manual.

Solutions to Exercises

Solution Files are Data Files completed with comprehensive sample answers. Use these files to evaluate your students' work. Or distribute them electronically so students can verify their own work. Sample solutions to all lessons and end-of-chapter material are provided.

Test Bank and Test Engine

ExamView is a powerful testing software package that allows instructors to create and administer printed, computer (LAN-based), and Internet exams. ExamView includes hundreds of questions that correspond to the topics covered in this text, enabling students to generate detailed study guides that include page references for further review. The computer-based and Internet testing components allow students to take exams at their computers, and also save the instructor time by grading each exam automatically.

BRIEF CONTENTS

C O N T E N T S

CHAPTER 4 **TRANSFORMING AND DISTORTING OBJECTS**

CHAPTER 5 **WORKING WITH LAYERS**

CHAPTER 6 WORKING WITH PATTERNS AND BRUSHES

CHAPTER 7 WORKING WITH FILTERS, GRADIENT MESHES, ENVELOPES, AND BLENDS

CHAPTER 8 · WORKING WITH TRANSPARENCY, EFFECTS, AND GRAPHIC STYLES

CHAPTER 9 · CREATING GRAPHS IN ILLUSTRATOR

CHAPTER 10   DRAWING WITH SYMBOLS

CHAPTER 11   CREATING 3D OBJECTS

Measurements

Measurements on the artboard and measurements referring to an object are given in inches, not points or picas. In order to follow the exercises, it's important that the General Units Preference in the Preferences dialog box be set to Inches. To set this preference, click Edit on the menu bar, point to Preferences, and then click Units & Undo.

Text attributes are given in points.

You may or may not prefer to work with rulers showing. You can make rulers visible by clicking View on the menu bar, then clicking Show Rulers, or by pressing [Ctrl][R] (Win) or ⌘[R] (Mac). You can hide visible rulers by clicking View on the menu bar, then clicking Hide Rulers or by pressing [Ctrl][R] (Win) or ⌘[R] (Mac).

Document Color Mode

Documents in Adobe Illustrator CS2 can be created in one of two color modes—RGB or CMYK. You can determine the color mode in the New dialog box when you create a document. You can also change a document's color mode by clicking File on the menu bar, then clicking Document Color Mode.

The color mode for each document is identified in the title bar at the top of the Illustrator window.

Whenever you are asked to create a new document, the color mode will be specified. Many menu commands, such as those under the Effect menu, are available only in RGB mode. If you run into a situation in which a specified menu command is not available, first check the color mode.

Fonts

Whenever fonts are used in Data and Solution Files, they are chosen from a set of very common typefaces that you will most likely have available on your computer. If any of the fonts in use are not available on your computer, please make a substitution.

For variety and typographic appeal, we have used other typefaces in Data and Solution Files that are not standard; however, we have converted those fonts to outlines. When a font is converted to an outline, the letterform is simply a vector graphic, like all other vector graphics.

Quick Keys

Quick keys are keyboard shortcuts that can be used in place of clicking the command on the menu. [Ctrl][X], for example, is the quick key for Cut on the PC platform. Mastering basic quick keys is essential for a smooth work flow in Illustrator. It's a good idea to start with the commands on the Edit and Object menus as candidates for quick keys.

Certification

This book and its online content cover the objectives necessary for Adobe Illustrator certification. Use the Certification Grid at the back of the book to find out where an objective is covered. Online content (for example, the "Adobe Bridge Appendix") is available to supplement the material in this book. Go to www.course.com/revealed/illustratorcs2dee to access online content.

1

GETTING STARTED
WITH ILLUSTRATOR

1. Create a new document.

2. Explore the Illustrator window.

3. Create basic shapes.

4. Apply fill and stroke colors to objects.

5. Select, move, and align objects.

6. Transform objects.

7. Make direct selections.

chapter 1

GETTING STARTED
WITH ILLUSTRATOR

Getting to Know Illustrator

Adobe Illustrator CS2 is a professional illustration software application created by Adobe Systems Incorporated. If this name is familiar to you, it's because Adobe is a leading producer of graphics software for the personal computer. Along with Illustrator, Adobe produces an entire suite of applications, including InDesign, Acrobat, Type Manager, GoLive, and, of course, the revolutionary and award-winning Photoshop.

With Illustrator, you can create everything from simple graphics, icons, and text to complex and multilayered illustrations, all of which can be used within a page layout, in a multimedia presentation, or on the Web.

Adobe Illustrator offers dozens of essential tools. Using them in combination with various menu commands, you have the potential to create any illustration that your imagination can dream up. With experience, you will find that your ability to create complex graphics rests on your ability to master simple, basic operations.

Tools You'll Use

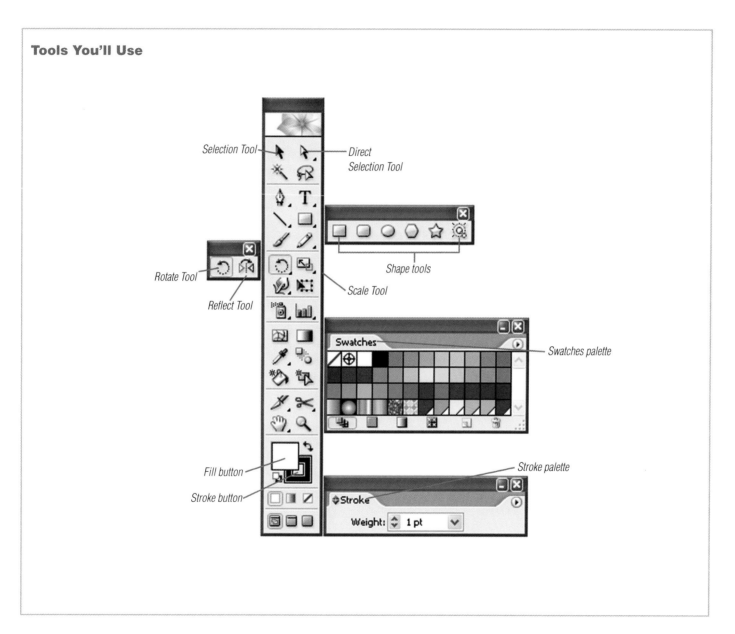

Selection Tool

Direct
Selection Tool

Rotate Tool

Reflect Tool

Scale Tool

Shape tools

Swatches

Swatches palette

Fill button

Stroke button

Stroke palette

⊕Stroke

Weight: 1 pt

CREATE A
NEW DOCUMENT

What You'll Do

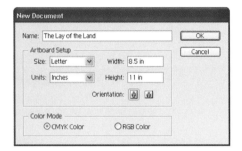

 In this lesson, you will start Adobe Illustrator and create a new document.

Creating a New Document

When you are ready to create a new document in Illustrator, you begin in the New Document dialog box. In the New document dialog box, you specify the name of the document, which appears in the title bar when you close the New Document dialog box. You also specify the document size—the width and height of the finished document. In addition, you can choose the page orientation, landscape or portrait, and the unit of measure you would like the rulers to display. Some designers like to work with inches; others prefer points or picas. Finally, you can choose whether you want to work in CMYK Color or RGB Color by clicking the appropriate option button.

Choosing Color Modes and Document Size

Generally, CMYK Color (Cyan, Magenta, Yellow, and Black) is the color mode used for print projects, and RGB Color (Red, Green, and Blue) is the color mode used for

---

Understanding native file types

The "native" Illustrator file format is noted as an .ai suffix. Native Illustrator files can be opened and placed by other Adobe software packages, such as Photoshop and InDesign. If you want to save an Illustrator file for use in QuarkXPress, save the file as an Illustrator EPS (Encapsulated PostScript). QuarkXPress does not recognize nor does it import Illustrator files in the native .ai format.

projects that will appear on a screen, such as a monitor or television. Once a document is created, you may change the size and color mode settings by clicking File on the menu bar, pointing to Document Color Mode, then clicking CMYK Color or RGB Color.

Choosing a Unit of Measure

Precision is often a key to good design, and many designers choose points and picas as units of measure. A point is $\frac{1}{72}$ of an inch. A pica is 12 points, or $\frac{1}{6}$ of an inch. Defining your artboard in points and picas versus inches is a matter of personal preference. As a designer, you're probably familiar with points and picas, but would you really refer to a letter-size page as 612×792 points? Using measurements such as $\frac{29}{32}$ of an inch gets a bit ridiculous. Working with a combination of the two is the best bet for most people.

You can use more than one unit of measure when working in Illustrator. To set your measurement preferences, click Edit on the menu bar, point to **Preferences,** then click Units & Display Performance. Click the General, Stroke, and Type list arrows to choose your preferred unit of measure. You'll certainly want to measure your strokes and type in points. Imagine setting type in $\frac{3}{4}$" Garamond!

QUICKTIP

If you are using a Macintosh, you will find preference settings on the Illustrator menu.

Saving files in legacy format

When you save a file in Illustrator CS2, it cannot be opened by older versions of Illustrator, such as Illustrator 9 or Illustrator 10. Earlier versions of the Illustrator file format are called "legacy Illustrator formats." If you want to save a file in Illustrator CS2 as an older legacy format, open the file, click File on the menu bar, then click Save As. Name the file, then click Save. The Illustrator Options dialog box opens. Click the Version list arrow, choose the version of Illustrator you want, then click OK. Remember that older versions of Illustrator may not support certain features such as layers, gradients, and transparency.

Create a new document (Windows)

1. Click the **Start button** 〔start〕 on the taskbar, point to **All Programs**, then click **Adobe Illustrator CS2**.

2. Click **File** on the menu bar, then click **New**.

3. Type **The Lay of the Land** in the New Document dialog box.

   TIP Note that you have *named* the file in the New Document dialog box, but you have not yet *saved* it.

4. Click the **Size list arrow** in the Artboard Setup section to view the available sizes, then click **Letter**, if necessary.

5. Click the **Units list arrow**, then click **Inches**, if necessary.

   The size of your artboard will be 8.5" × 11".

6. Click the **left icon** next to Orientation (Portrait as opposed to Landscape) as the page orientation.

7. Click the **CMYK Color option button** as the color mode for your document.

   Your New Document dialog box should resemble Figure 1.

8. Click **OK** to create a new document with these settings.

9. Click **File** on the menu bar, click **Close**, and don't save the document.

You started Illustrator in Windows, then created a new document.

FIGURE 1
New Document dialog box (Windows)

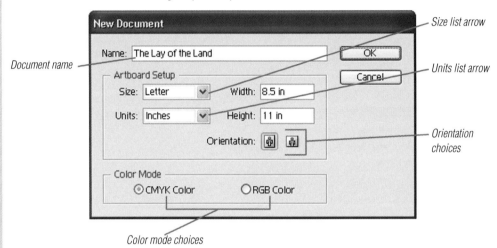

Document name — Size list arrow — Units list arrow — Orientation choices — Color mode choices

FIGURE 2

New Document dialog box (Macintosh)

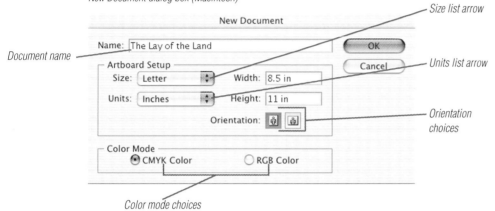

Document name

Size list arrow

Units list arrow

Orientation choices

Color mode choices

1. Double-click the **hard drive icon**, then navigate to and double-click the **Adobe Illustrator CS2 folder**.

2. Double-click the **Adobe Illustrator CS2 program icon**.

3. Click **File** on the menu bar, then click **New**.

4. Type **The Lay of the Land** in the New Document dialog box, as shown in Figure 2.

   TIP Note that you have *named* the file in the New Document dialog box, but you have not yet *saved* it.

5. Click the **Size list arrow** in the Artboard Setup section to view the available sizes, then click **Letter**.

6. Click the **Units list arrow**, then click **Inches**, if necessary.

   The size of your artboard will be 8.5" × 11".

7. Click the **left icon** next to Orientation (Portrait as opposed to Landscape) as the page orientation.

8. Click the **CMYK Color option button** as the color mode for your document.

   Your New Document window should resemble Figure 2.

9. Click **OK** to create a new document with these settings.

10. Click **File** on the menu bar, click **Close**, and don't save the document.

You started Illustrator in Macintosh, then created a new document.

EXPLORE THE
ILLUSTRATOR WINDOW

What You'll Do

 In this lesson, you will learn about the key architecture of the Illustrator window and practice some basic Illustrator skills.

Touring the Illustrator Window

Let's take a few quick minutes to get the lay of the land. It all starts here. If you want to get really good at Illustrator, it's critical that you understand the workspace and learn to how to manage it. Nothing will slow down your work—and dull your creativity—like wrestling with the application. Moving around the window should become second nature.

The Illustrator window includes the artboard, scratch area, toolbox, and "floating" palettes, all of which are described below. Figure 3 shows some of the more commonly used palettes.

The **title bar** contains the name of your document, magnification level, and color mode; it also contains the Minimize, Maximize, and Close buttons.

The **menu bar** includes all of the Illustrator menus. If a menu item leads to a submenu, a black triangle will be positioned to the right. If a menu item requires you to enter information into a dialog box, it is followed by an ellipsis.

The **artboard** is the area, bound by a solid line, in which you create your artwork; the size of the artboard can be set as large as 227" × 227".

The **scratch area** is the area outside the artboard where you can store objects before placing them on the artboard; objects on the scratch area will not print.

The **toolbox** is a palette containing tools that let you create, select, and manipulate objects in Illustrator. A tiny black triangle beside a tool indicates "hidden" tools behind that tool. Press and hold a tool to expose the palette of hidden tools behind it. Click the tearoff tab (the tiny black triangle next to the last tool in the palette) to create a floating toolbar.

The **Zoom text box** in the lower-left corner of the Illustrator window displays the current magnification level. To the right of the Zoom text box is the Zoom menu, which you access by clicking the Zoom list arrow. The Zoom menu lets you choose another magnification level to work in.

FIGURE 3
Illustrator window

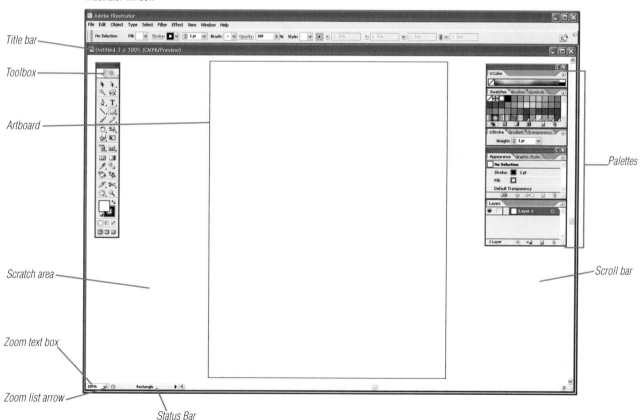

Title bar

Toolbox

Artboard

Scratch area

Zoom text box

Zoom list arrow

Status Bar

Palettes

Scroll bar

The **status bar** contains a list arrow menu from which you can choose a status line with information about the current tool, the date and time, the number of undo operations, or the document color profile.

Scroll bars run along the bottom and right sides of the window; dragging the scroll boxes, clicking in a scroll bar, or clicking the scroll arrows changes the portion of the document displayed in the Illustrator window.

Palettes are windows containing features for modifying and manipulating Illustrator objects.

Some palettes are categorized into groups and appear that way by default. For

example, if you choose the Gradient palette, it appears along with the Stroke and Transparency palettes. If you drag the top of the palette window, all palettes in the group move together. You can separate palettes from their group by simply dragging the palette name tab to a new location. You can also merge two palettes together by dragging a palette name tab into a new group. Docking palettes allows you to arrange multiple palettes or palette groups vertically. Like grouped palettes, docked palettes move together. To dock a palette or a palette group to another palette group, drag one of the palette name tabs in the group to the bottom edge of another palette then release when the bottom edge is high-

lighted. Palettes can also be collapsed to save room in the document window by clicking the collapse/expand button in the palette window.

QUICKTIP

You can temporarily hide all open palettes and the toolbox by pressing [Tab]. Press [Tab] again to show the palettes and the toolbox.

QUICKTIP

You can restore the default arrangement of palettes by clicking Window on the menu bar, pointing to Workspace, then clicking [Default].

Using Quick Keys in Illustrator

Along with the various tools in the toolbox, the commands on the menu bar are essential for performing both basic and complex operations in Illustrator. Many of the menu commands execute operations that you will use over and over again. For that reason, it is a smart idea to memorize the quick keys associated with the basic menu commands. When a quick key is available, it is listed beside the command in the menu.

Many make the mistake of associating quick keys with speed. True, using quick keys will speed up your work, but the real benefit of them is that they help your work flow with fewer disruptions. Leaving your keyboard, moving your mouse, and clicking on a menu command all disrupt the essential flow of your work. Quick keys allow you to quickly execute a command without taking your hands off the keyboard or your eyes off the monitor.

Quick keys are not for 'power users' only; anybody working in Illustrator can use them beneficially. Make learning quick keys a fun part of your work; test yourself along the way. They are so intuitively assigned that you may even find yourself guessing correctly!

In Illustrator, the best place to start memorizing quick keys is with commands in the File, Edit, and Object menus, especially for Open, Close, Save,

Copy, Paste, Paste in Front, Paste in Back, Bring to Front, Send to Back, Hide, Show All, Lock, and Unlock All. When you have mastered those commands, keep going. Memorize the keys you use often, and know when to stop. There's no need to memorize the quick key for Clear Guides, unless you find yourself doing it often. Table 1 and Table 2 list essential quick keys for Windows and Macintosh.

QUICKTIP

Illustrator automatically positions crop marks at the artboard size that you choose. Although the crop marks may be turned on or off, Illustrator regards your artboard size as your trim size.

QUICKTIP

The imageable area is the area inside the dotted line on the artboard, which is intended to represent the portion of the page that your default printer can print. Most designers find this dotted line annoying and irrelevant. It can be hidden or shown using the View menu.

TABLE 1: Essential Illustrator Quick Keys (Windows)

command	Windows	command	Windows
Outline	[Ctrl][Y]	Deselect	[Ctrl][Shift][A]
Preview	[Ctrl][Y]	Cut	[Ctrl][X]
Fit in Window	[Ctrl][0]	Copy	[Ctrl][C]
Zoom In	[Ctrl][+]	Paste	[Ctrl][V]
Zoom Out	[Ctrl][-]	Paste in Front	[Ctrl][F]
Access Hand Tool	[Spacebar]	Paste in Back	[Ctrl][B]
Access the Zoom In Tool	[Ctrl][Spacebar]	Undo	[Ctrl][Z]
Access the Zoom Out Tool	[Ctrl][Spacebar][Alt]	Redo	[Ctrl][Shift][Z]
Select All	[Ctrl][A]		

TABLE 2: Essential Illustrator Quick Keys (Macintosh)

command	Macintosh	command	Macintosh
Outline	⌘[Y]	Deselect	⌘[Shift][A]
Preview	⌘[Y]	Cut	⌘[X]
Fit in Window	⌘[0]	Copy	⌘[C]
Zoom In	⌘[+]	Paste	⌘[V]
Zoom Out	⌘[-]	Paste in Front	⌘[F]
Access Hand Tool	[Spacebar]	Paste in Back	⌘[B]
Access the Zoom In Tool	⌘[Spacebar]	Undo	⌘[Z]
Access the Zoom Out Tool	⌘[Spacebar][option]	Redo	⌘[Shift][Z]
Select All	⌘[A]		

Navigate the Illustrator artboard

1. Click **File** on the menu bar, click **Open**, navigate to the drive and folder where your Data Files are stored, click **AI 1-1.ai,** then click **Open**.

2. Click **File** on the menu bar, click **Save As**, type **Window Workout** in the File name text box (Win) or the Save As text box (Mac), navigate to the drive and folder where your Data Files are stored, click **Save**, then click **OK** to close the Illustrator Options dialog box.

3. Click **View** on the menu bar, note the quick key for Outline, then click **Outline**.

   As shown in Figure 4, outline mode shows the skeleton of your work—the lines and curves that you have drawn. Outline mode can be useful for making very specific selections.

4. Click **View** on the menu bar, note the quick key for Preview, then click **Preview**.

   Preview mode shows your work complete with the colors and styles you used.

5. Toggle between outline and preview modes using the quick key, then return to preview mode.

6. Click the **Zoom Tool** in the toolbox, then click the **circle** four times.

7. Click the **Selection Tool** in the toolbox.

8. Click **View** on the menu bar, then click **Fit in Window**.

(continued)

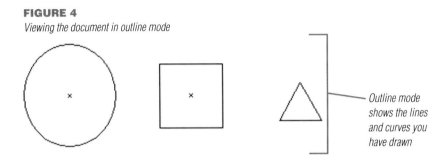

FIGURE 4

Viewing the document in outline mode

Outline mode shows the lines and curves you have drawn

Introducing Adobe Bridge

Adobe Bridge is a new, stand-alone software package that ships with the Adobe Creative Suite 2 software package. Bridge, as it is referred to, is a file browser that works with Illustrator CS2, Photoshop CS2, Illustrator CS2, InDesign CS2 and Go Live CS2. Bridge allows you to locate, browse, and organize files more easily. It also allows you to categorize your files using labels and/or ratings. Using the Sort command on the View menu, you can sort your files in a variety of ways, including, By Date Created, By File Size, and By Resolution. You can also choose numerous ways to view your files, such as thumbnails, details, and filmstrip. You can search for assets with common metadata attributes, such as files that call for a certain font or a specific Pantone color. You can even embed additional metadata into an asset in Bridge—without opening the file itself. To access Bridge, click File on the menu bar, then click Browse. Adobe Bridge may be the perfect tool to help you organize your design projects. For more information about Adobe Bridge, see the online Appendix at www.course.com/revealed/illustratorcs2dee.

FIGURE 5

Moving the artboard with the Hand Tool

Exploring the Adobe Illustrator CS2 Welcome Screen

When you start Adobe Illustrator CS2 for the first time, the Welcome Screen appears. The Welcome Screen includes links to sample art and lots of templates. Templates can really help you jump-start a project if you're running out of time or need some creative guidance. Templates are categorized into topics, such as Restaurant, Spa, and Extreme Sports. Within those folders, you'll find a variety of templates, such as Gift Certificate, Shopping Bag, and Business Card. Perhaps the most important link in the Welcome Screen is the What's New in Illustrator. If you are upgrading to Illustrator CS2, this link offers a handy list of the new features available to you, as well as demonstrations of how they work. It's definitely worth your time to check it out. If you've already installed CS2 and the Welcome Screen doesn't open when you launch the application, fear not! Simply click Help on the menu bar, then click Welcome Screen. If you do not want the Welcome Screen to appear each time, simply remove the check mark in the Show this dialog at startup checkbox in the Welcome Screen dialog box.

9. Click **View** on the menu bar, note the quick keys for Zoom In and Zoom Out, then release the menu.

10. Use the quick key to zoom in to 200%.

> TIP The current magnification level appears in the title bar and the Zoom text box in the lower-left corner.

11. Use the quick key to zoom out to 66.67%.

12. Press and hold **[Spacebar]**, notice that the pointer changes to the Hand Tool ✋, then click and drag the **artboard** with the Hand Tool, as shown in Figure 5.

The Hand Tool allows you to move the artboard in the window; it's a great alternative to using the scroll arrows. Always press [Spacebar] to access the Hand Tool, so as not to interrupt the flow of your work.

You opened an Illustrator document, saved it with a new name, and used menu commands and the Zoom Tool to change the view size of the artboard. You then used the Hand Tool to move the artboard around.

Work with objects

1. Click **Select** on the menu bar, then click **All**.
2. Click **View** on the menu bar, then click **Show Bounding Box**, if necessary.

   The bounding box is a box with eight hollow white squares that appears around an object or objects when selected.

   > TIP If you see Hide Bounding Box on the View menu, the bounding box is already showing.

3. Click **View** on the menu bar, then click **Hide Bounding Box**.
4. Click **Select** on the menu bar, then click **Deselect**.
5. Click the **Selection Tool** ▶ in the toolbox, then move each shape—one at a time—to the bottom of the page.
6. Click **Edit** on the menu bar, then click **Undo Move**.

   The last object you moved returns to its original position, as shown in Figure 6.

7. Undo your last two steps.
8. Click **Edit** on the menu bar, then click **Redo Move**.
9. Redo your last two steps.
10. Click the **artboard** to deselect, click the **red triangle**, click **Edit** on the menu bar, then click **Copy**.
11. Click **Edit** on the menu bar, then click **Paste**.

(continued)

FIGURE 6
Undoing your last step

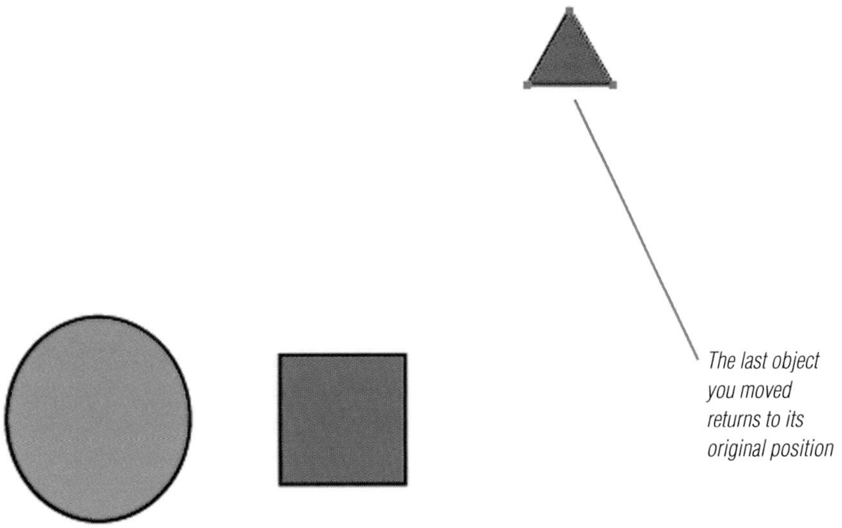

The last object you moved returns to its original position

FIGURE 7
Copying and pasting the triangle

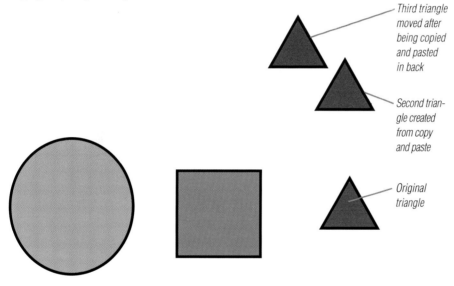

Third triangle moved after being copied and pasted in back

Second triangle created from copy and paste

Original triangle

12. Copy the new triangle, click **Edit** on the menu bar, then click **Paste in Back**.

The Paste in Front and Paste in Back commands paste the copied object from the clipboard in front or in back of a selected object. If you select an object, copy it, and then choose Paste in Front; the copy will be pasted above the original in exactly the same location.

13. Move the top red triangle to expose the copied triangle pasted behind it, as shown in Figure 7.

14. Save your work, then close Window Workout.

You moved objects on the artboard and used the Undo and Redo commands on the Edit menu. You selected and copied objects, then applied the Paste in Back command to position a copy precisely in back of its original.

CREATE BASIC SHAPES

 In this lesson, you will examine the differences between bitmap and vector graphics. Then you will use the Rectangle Tool to examine Illustrator's various options for creating simple vector graphics.

Getting Ready to Draw

Are you eager to start drawing? Do you want to create complex shapes, special effects, and original art? Perhaps you are a self-taught user of Adobe Illustrator, and your main interest is to graduate to advanced techniques and add a few of those cool special effects to your skill set. Good for you! Enthusiasm is priceless, and no book can teach it. So maintain that enthusiasm for this first exercise, where you'll start by creating a square. That's right . . . a square.

Consider for a moment that Mozart's sublime opera Don Giovanni is based primarily on eight notes, or that the great American novel can be reduced to 26 letters. Illustrator's foundation is basic geometric shapes, so let's start at square one . . . with one square.

Don't rush. As you work, keep in mind that the lessons you will learn here are the foundation of every great illustration.

Understanding Bitmap Images and Vector Graphics

Computer graphics fall into two main categories—bitmap images and vector graphics. To create effective artwork, you need to understand some basic concepts about the two.

Bitmap images are created using a square or rectangular grid of colored squares called **pixels**. Because pixels (a contraction of "picture elements") can render subtle gradations of tone, they are the most common medium for continuous-tone images—what you perceive as a photograph. All scanned images are composed of pixels. All "digital" images are composed of pixels. Adobe Photoshop is the leading graphics application for working with digital "photos." Figure 8 shows an example of a bitmap image. The number of pixels in a given inch is referred to as the image's **resolution**. To be effective, pixels must be small enough to create an image with the illusion of continuous tone. Thus, bitmap images are termed **resolution-dependent**.

The important thing to remember about bitmap images is that any magnification—resizing the image to be bigger—essentially means that fewer pixels are available per inch (the same number of pixels is now spread out over a larger area). This decrease in resolution will have a negative impact on the quality of the image. The greater the magnification, the greater the negative impact.

Graphics that you create in Adobe Illustrator are vector graphics. **Vector graphics** are created with lines and curves and are defined by mathematical objects called vectors. Vectors use geometric characteristics to define the object. Vector graphics consist of **anchor points** and **line segments**, together referred to as **paths**.

For example, if you use Illustrator to render a person's face, the software will identify the iris of the eye using the mathematical definition of a circle with a specific radius and a specific location in respect to other graphics. It will then fill that circle with the color you have specified. Figure 9 shows an example of a vector graphic.

Computer graphics rely on vectors to render bold graphics that must retain clean, crisp lines when scaled to various sizes. Vectors are often used to create logos or "line art," and they are the best choice for typographical work, especially small and italic type.

As mathematical objects, vector graphics can be scaled to any size. Because they are not created with pixels, there is no inherent resolution. Thus, vector graphics are termed **resolution-independent**. This means that any graphic that you create in Illustrator can be output to fit on a postage stamp or on a billboard!

FIGURE 8
Bitmap graphics

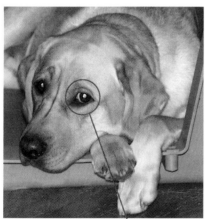

FIGURE 9
Vector graphics

Use the Rectangle Tool

1. Click **File** on the menu bar, click **New**, create a new document that is 8" wide by 8" in height, name the file **Basic Shapes**, then click **OK**.

2. Click **File** on the menu bar, click **Save As**, navigate to the drive and folder where your Data Files are stored, click **Save,** then click **OK** to close the Illustrator Options dialog box.

3. Click **View** on the menu bar, then click **Hide Page Tiling**, if necessary.

4. Click the **Swap Fill and Stroke button**  in the toolbox to reverse the default colors.

   Your fill color should now be black and your stroke color white. The **fill color** is the inside color of an object. The **stroke color** is the color of the object's border or frame.

5. Click the **Rectangle Tool**, in the toolbox.

6. Click and drag the **Rectangle Tool pointer** on the artboard, then release the mouse to make a rectangle of any size.

7. Press and hold **[Shift]** while you create a second rectangle.

   Pressing and holding [Shift] while you create a rectangle constrains the shape to a perfect square, as shown in Figure 10.

8. Create a third rectangle drawn from its center point by pressing and holding **[Alt]** (Win) or **[option]** (Mac) as you drag the **Rectangle Tool pointer**.

   TIP Use [Shift] in combination with [Alt] (Win) or [option] (Mac) to draw a perfect shape from its center.

You created a freeform rectangle, then you created a perfect square. Finally you drew a square from its center point.

FIGURE 10
Creating a rectangle and a square

Square created by pressing [Shift] while creating a rectangle

1. Click **Select** on the menu bar, then click **All** to select all of the objects.
2. Click **Edit** on the menu bar, then click **Cut** to remove the objects from the artboard.
3. Click anywhere on the artboard.

   When a shape tool is selected, clicking once on the artboard opens a dialog box, which allows you to enter precise information for creating the object. In this case, it opens the Rectangle dialog box.
4. Type **4** in the Width text box, type **4** in the Height text box, as shown in Figure 11, then click **OK**.
5. Save your work.

Using the Rectangle Tool, you clicked the artboard, which opened the Rectangle dialog box. You entered a specific width and height to create a perfect 4" square.

FIGURE 11
Rectangle dialog box

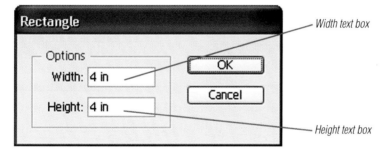

Width text box

Height text box

APPLY FILL AND STROKE
COLORS TO OBJECTS

What You'll Do

In this lesson you will use the Swatches palette to add a color fill to an object and apply a stroke as a border. Then you will use the Stroke palette to change the size of the default stroke.

Activating the Fill or Stroke

The Fill and Stroke buttons are at the bottom of the toolbox. To apply a fill or stroke color to an object, you must first activate the appropriate button. You activate either icon by clicking it, which moves it in front of the other. When the Fill button is in front of the Stroke button, the fill is activated, as shown in Figure 12. The Stroke button is activated when it is in front of the Fill button.

As you work, you will often switch back and forth, activating the fill and the stroke. Rather than using your mouse to activate the fill or the stroke each time, simply press [X] to switch between the two modes.

FIGURE 12
Fill and Stroke buttons

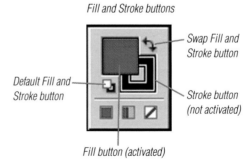

Swap Fill and Stroke button

Default Fill and Stroke button

Stroke button (not activated)

Fill button (activated)

Applying Color with the Swatches Palette

The Swatches palette, as shown in Figure 13, is central to color management in the application and a simple resource for applying fills and strokes to objects.

The palette has 48 preset colors, along with gradients and patterns. The swatch with the red line through it is the None swatch. "None" is a color in Illustrator, used as a fill for a "hollow" object. Any object without a stroke will always have None as its stroke color.

When an object is selected, clicking a swatch in the palette will apply that color as a fill or a stroke, depending on which of the two is activated in the toolbox. You can also drag and drop swatches onto unselected objects. Dragging a swatch to an unselected object will change the color of its fill or stroke, depending upon which of the two is activated.

FIGURE 13
Swatches palette

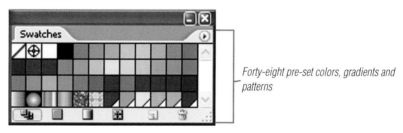

Forty-eight pre-set colors, gradients and patterns

Apply fill and stroke colors

1. Verify that the new square is still selected.

2. Click **Window** on the menu bar, then click **Swatches**.

   Your Swatches palette may already be available.

3. Click any blue swatch in the Swatches palette to fill the square.

   Note that the Fill button in the toolbox is now also blue.

   | TIP When you position your pointer over a color swatch in the Swatches palette, a tooltip appears that shows the name of that swatch.

4. Click the **Selection Tool** ▶, then click anywhere on the artboard to deselect the blue square.

5. Drag and drop a **yellow swatch** onto the blue square.

   The fill color changes to yellow because the Fill button is activated in the toolbox. Your colors may vary from the colors shown in the figures.

6. Press **[X]** to activate the Stroke button in the toolbox.

7. Drag and drop the **red swatch** in the Swatches palette onto the yellow square.

   As shown in Figure 14, a red stroke is added to the square because the Stroke button is activated in the toolbox.

8. Click **Window** on the menu bar, then click **Stroke** to display the Stroke palette.

   Your Stroke palette may already be available.

   (continued)

FIGURE 14
Red stroke is added to the yellow square

FIGURE 15

Yellow square without a stroke

9. Select the square, click the **Weight list arrow** in the Stroke palette, then click **8 pt**.

   TIP Illustrator positions a stroke equally inside and outside an object. Thus, an 8 pt stroke is rendered with 4 pts inside the object and 4 pts outside.

10. Click **[None]** ☑ in the Swatches palette to remove the stroke from the square.

   Your screen should resemble Figure 15.

11. Save your work.

You filled the square with blue by clicking a blue swatch in the Swatches palette. You then changed the fill and stroke colors to yellow and red by dragging and dropping swatches onto the square. You used the Stroke palette to increase the weight of the stroke, then removed the stroke by choosing [None] from the Swatches palette.

SELECT, MOVE, AND
ALIGN OBJECTS

What You'll Do

In this lesson, you will use the Selection Tool in combination with Smart Guides to move, copy, and align four squares.

Selecting and Moving Objects

When it comes to accuracy, consider that Illustrator can move objects incrementally by fractions of a point—which itself is a tiny fraction of an inch! That level of precision is key when moving and positioning objects.

Before you can move or modify an Illustrator object, you must identify it by selecting it with a selection tool, menu item, or command key. When working with simple illustrations that contain few objects, selecting is usually simple, but it can become very tricky in complex illustrations, especially those containing a large number of small objects positioned closely together.

Two very basic ways to move objects are by clicking and dragging or by using the arrow keys on the keyboard, which by default move a selected item by 1-pt increments. Pressing [Shift] when dragging an object constrains the movement to the horizontal, the vertical, and 45° diagonals. Pressing [Alt] (Win) or [option] (Mac) when moving creates a copy of the object.

Grouping Objects

Many of the illustrations you create will be composed of a number of small objects. Once you have established the relationships among those objects, grouping them allows you to select them all with one click of the Selection Tool and then move or modify them simultaneously. To group objects, select them, select Object on the menu bar, then click Group.

Making a Marquee Selection with the Selection Tool

By now, you're familiar with using the Selection Tool to select objects. You can also use the Selection Tool to create a marquee selection, a dotted rectangle that

Getting Started with Illustrator

disappears as soon as you release the mouse. Any object that the marquee touches before you release the mouse will be selected. Marquee selections are very useful for both quick selections and precise selections. Practice, and make this part of your skill set.

Working with Smart Guides

Smart Guides are temporary guides that can be turned on and off on the View menu. Smart Guides help you move and align objects in relation to other objects or in relation to the artboard. With Smart Guides turned on, you will see words, called Smart Guides, that identify visible or invisible objects, page boundaries, intersections, anchor points, paths, and center points as you move your mouse along the objects on the artboard. When you move an object, Smart Guides give you a visual reference for precise alignment, as shown in Figure 16. For example, if you want to align two squares exactly side by side, Smart Guides will signal you when the two items come into contact, using the word "intersect."

FIGURE 16
Using Smart Guides

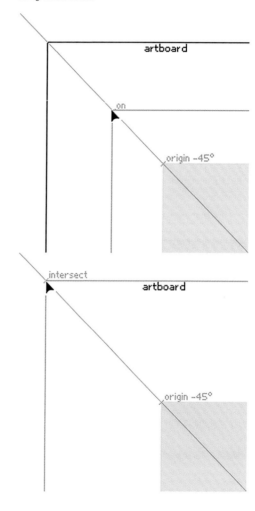

Select and move an object using Smart Guides

1. Click **View** on the menu bar, then click **Fit in Window**.

2. Click **View** on the menu bar, then verify that both Smart Guides and Snap to Point are checked by verifying that there is a check mark to the left of each menu item.

   TIP If you do not see a check mark next to Smart Guides or Snap to Point, click View on the menu bar, then click each item, one at a time, to turn these two features on.

   Snap to Point automatically aligns points when they get close together. When dragging an object, you'll see it "snap" to align itself with a nearby object (or guide).

3. Click the **Selection Tool** ▶ in the toolbox, then click the **yellow square**.

4. Identify the anchor points, line segments, and center point, as shown in Figure 17.

5. Move the Selection Tool pointer over the anchor points, over the line segments that connect the points, and over the center point.

6. Position the pointer over the top-left anchor point, click and drag so that the anchor point aligns with the top-left corner of the artboard, as shown in Figure 18, then release the mouse.

   The Smart Guide changes from "anchor" to "intersect" when the two corners are aligned.

You used the Selection Tool in combination with Smart Guides to position an object exactly at the top-left corner of the artboard.

FIGURE 17
Anchor points, line segments, and center point

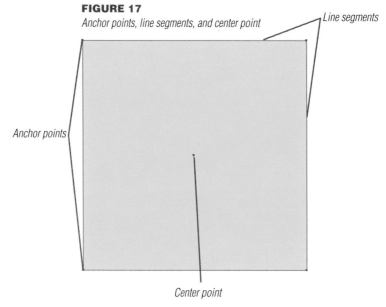

Line segments

Anchor points

Center point

FIGURE 18
Intersecting two points

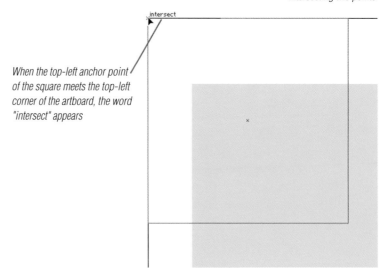

When the top-left anchor point of the square meets the top-left corner of the artboard, the word "intersect" appears

Getting Started with Illustrator

FIGURE 19

Duplicating the square

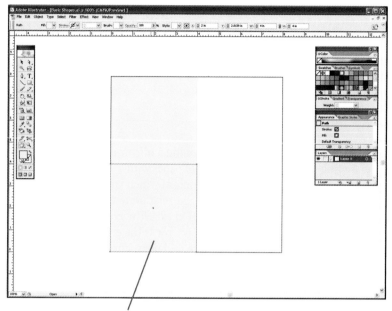

FIGURE 20

Four squares created using drag and drop

A copy of the original square

Duplicate objects using drag and drop

1. Click the **top-left anchor point**, press and hold **[Shift][Alt]** (Win) or **[Shift][option]** (Mac), drag straight down until the top-left anchor point touches the bottom-left anchor point (the "intersect" Smart Guide will appear), then release the mouse.

   When moving an object, pressing and holding [Shift] constrains the movement vertically, horizontally, or on 45° diagonals. Pressing [Alt] (Win) or [option] (Mac) while dragging an object creates a copy of the object, as shown in Figure 19.

   > TIP   When you press [Alt] (Win) or [option] (Mac) while dragging an object, the pointer becomes a double-arrow pointer. When two anchor points are directly on top of each other, the Selection Tool pointer turns from black to white.

2. With the bottom square still selected, press and hold **[Shift]**, then click the **top square** to select both items.

3. Click the **top-left anchor point** of the top square, press and hold **[Shift][Alt]** (Win) or **[Shift][option]** (Mac), drag to the right until the top-left anchor point touches the top-right anchor point, then release the mouse.

4. Change the fill color of each square to match the colors shown in Figure 20.

5. Save your work.

You moved and duplicated the yellow square using [Shift] to constrain the movement and [Alt] (Win) or [option] (Mac) to duplicate or "drag and drop" copies of the square.

TRANSFORM OBJECTS

What You'll Do

 In this lesson, you will scale, rotate, and reflect objects, using the basic transform tools. You will also create a star and a triangle.

Transforming Objects

The Scale, Rotate, and Reflect Tools are the fundamental transform tools. As their names make clear, the Scale and Rotate Tools resize and rotate objects, respectively. Double-click a transform tool to open the tool's dialog box. When you use the tool's dialog box, the objects are transformed from their centerpoints. This can be a useful choice, because the object's position essentially doesn't change on the artboard or in relation to other objects.

Use the Reflect Tool to "flip" an object over an imaginary axis. The best way to understand the Reflect Tool is to imagine positioning a mirror perpendicular to a sheet of paper with a word written on it. The angle at which you position the mirror in relation to the word is the reflection axis. The reflection of the word in the mirror is the end result of what the Reflect Tool does. For example, text reflected across a horizontal axis would appear upside down and inverted. Text reflected across a vertical axis would appear to be inverted and running backwards, as shown in Figure 21.

You can transform an object using the desired tool or its dialog box. Each transform tool has a dialog box where you can enter precise numbers to execute the transformation on a selected object. You can access a tool's dialog box by double-clicking the tool. Click the Copy button in the dialog box to create a transformed copy of the selected object. Figure 22 shows the Scale dialog box.

Repeating Transformations

One of the most powerful commands relating to the transform tools is Transform Again, found on the Object menu. Unfortunately, it is a command often overlooked by new users. Whenever you transform an object, selecting Transform Again repeats the transformation. For example, if you scale a circle 50%, the Transform Again command will scale the circle 50% again.

The power of the command comes in combination with copying transformations. For example, if you rotate a square 10° and copy it at the same time, the Transform Again command will create a second square, rotated another 10° from the first copy. Applying Transform Again repeatedly is very handy for creating complex geometric shapes from basic objects.

FIGURE 21
Reflected text

FIGURE 22
Scale dialog box

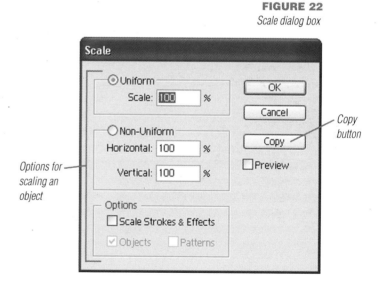

Options for scaling an object

Copy button

Use the Scale and Rotate Tools

1. Select the **green square**, double-click the **Scale Tool** , type **50** in the Scale text box, then click **OK**.

2. Click **Edit** on the menu bar, then click **Undo Scale**.

   TIP You can also undo your last step by pressing [Ctrl][Z] (Win) or [⌘][Z] (Mac).

3. Double-click the **Scale Tool** again, type **50** in the Scale text box, then click **Copy**.

   The transformation is executed from the center point; the center points of the original and the copy are aligned.

4. Fill the new square created in Step 3 with blue.

5. Double-click the **Rotate Tool** , type **45** in the Angle text box, then click **OK**.

6. Apply a 22 pt, yellow stroke to the rotated square, deselect, then compare your screen to Figure 23.

You used the Scale Tool to create a 50% copy of the square, then filled the copy with blue. You rotated the copy 45°. You then applied a 22 pt, yellow stroke.

FIGURE 23
Scaling and rotating a square

FIGURE 24

Using the Transform Again command

1. Click the **Ellipse Tool** in the toolbox.

    TIP   To access the Ellipse Tool, press and hold the Rectangle Tool until a toolbar of shape tools appears, then click the Ellipse Tool.

2. Click the **artboard**, type **3** in the Width text box and **.5** in the Height text box, then click **OK**.

3. Change the fill color to [None], the stroke color to blue, and the stroke weight to 3 pt.

4. Click the **Selection Tool**, click the **center point** of the ellipse, then drag it to the center point of the yellow square. (*Hint*: The center Smart Guide appears when the two centers meet.)

5. Double-click the **Rotate Tool**, type **45** in the Angle text box, then click **Copy**.

6. Click **Object** on the menu bar, point to **Transform**, then click **Transform Again**.

    TIP   You can also access the Transform Again command by pressing [Ctrl][D] (Win) or ⌘[D] (Mac).

7. Repeat Step 6 to create a fourth ellipse using the Transform Again command.

    Your screen should resemble Figure 24.

8. Select the four ellipses, click **Object** on the menu bar, then click **Group**.

You created an ellipse, filled and stroked it, and aligned it with the yellow square. You then created a copy rotated at 45°. With the second copy still selected, you used the Transform Again command twice, thus creating two more rotated copies. You then grouped the four ellipses.

Create a star and a triangle, and use the Reflect Tool

1. Select the **Star Tool** ☆, then click any-where on the artboard.

   The Star Tool is hidden beneath the current shape tool.

2. Type **1** in the Radius 1 text box, type **5** in the Radius 2 text box, type **5** in the Points text box, as shown in Figure 25, then click **OK**.

   A star has two radii; the first is from the center to the outer point, and the second is from the center to the inner point. The **radius** is a measurement from the center point of the star to either point.

3. Double-click the **Scale Tool** ⛶, type **25** in the Scale text box, then click **OK**.

   When you create a star using the Star dialog box, the star is drawn upside down.

4. Fill the star with white, then apply a 5 pt blue stroke to it.

5. Click the **Selection Tool** ▶, then move the star so that it is completely within the red square.

6. Double-click the **Reflect Tool** ⛫, click the **Horizontal option button**, as shown in Figure 26, then click **OK**.

   The star "flips" over an imaginary horizontal axis.

   TIP   The Reflect Tool is hidden beneath the Rotate Tool.

   (continued)

FIGURE 25
Star dialog box

Radius 1 text box

Radius 2 text box

FIGURE 26
Reflect dialog box

Horizontal option button

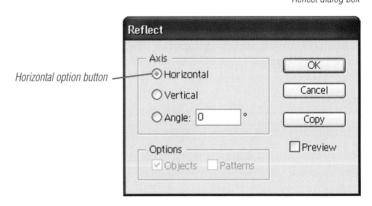

FIGURE 27

Reflecting the star horizontally

FIGURE 28

The finished project

7. Use the Selection Tool ▶ or the arrow keys on your keyboard to position the star roughly in the center of the red square.

    Your work should resemble Figure 27.

    > TIP Arrow keys move a selected item in 1 pt increments, known as the Keyboard Increment. You can change this amount by clicking Edit (Win) or Illustrator (Mac) on the menu bar, pointing to Preferences, clicking General, then typing a new value in the Keyboard Increment text box.

8. Click the **Polygon Tool** ◯ in the toolbox.

    The Polygon Tool is hidden beneath the current shape tool in the toolbox.

9. Click anywhere on the blue square.

10. Type **1.5** in the Radius text box, type **3** in the Sides text box, then click **OK**.

11. Fill the triangle with red.

12. Change the stroke color to yellow and the stroke weight to 22 pt.

13. Position the triangle so that it is centered within the blue square.

    Your completed project should resemble Figure 28.

14. Save your work, then close Basic Shapes.

You used the shape tools to create a star and a triangle and used the Reflect Tool to "flip" the star over an imaginary horizontal axis.

Selecting

The Select menu offers some powerful selection commands under the Same submenu. There you have commands to select by the same fill, the same fill and stroke, the same stroke color, and the same stroke weight, among others. When it comes to selecting multiple objects, using the Select menu is much faster than Shift-clicking!

MAKE DIRECT SELECTIONS

What You'll Do

 In this lesson, you will use the Direct Selection Tool and a combination of menu commands, such as Add Anchor Points and Paste in Front, to convert existing shapes into new designs.

Using the Direct Selection Tool

The Direct Selection Tool selects individual anchor points or single paths of an object. Using [Shift], you can select multiple anchor points or multiple paths. You can also select multiple points or paths by dragging a direct selection marquee. The tool also selects individual objects within a group, which can be very useful for modifying just one object in a complex group. Figure 29 demonstrates the Direct Selection Tool selecting one piece of a grouped object.

Clicking the center of an object with the Direct Selection Tool selects the entire object. Clicking the edge selects the path only. You will know you have made this direct selection successfully if the anchor points on the object all appear white. A white anchor point is not selected.

The Direct Selection Tool gives you the power to distort simple objects such as squares and circles into unique shapes. Don't underestimate its significance. While the Selection Tool is no more than a means to an end for selecting and moving objects, the Direct Selection Tool is in itself a drawing tool. You will use it over and over again to modify and perfect your artwork.

Adding Anchor Points

As you distort basic shapes with the Direct Selection Tool, you will often find that to create more complex shapes, you will need additional anchor points to work with.

The Add Anchor Points command creates new anchor points without distorting the object. To add anchor points to an object, click the Object menu, point to Path, then click Add Anchor Points. The new points are automatically positioned exactly between the original anchor points. You can create as many additional points as you wish to use.

Turning Objects into Guides

Guides are one of Illustrator's many features that help you to work with precision. Any object you create can be turned into a guide. With the object selected, click the View menu, point to Guides, then click Make Guides. Guides can be locked or unlocked in the same location. It is a good idea to work with locked guides so that they don't interfere with your artwork. Unlock guides only when you want to select them or delete them.

When an object is turned into a guide, it loses its attributes, such as its fill, stroke, and stroke weight. However, Illustrator remembers the original attributes for each

guide. To transform a guide back to its original object, first unlock, then select the guide. Click the View menu, point to Guides, then click Release Guides.

FIGURE 29
Using the Direct Selection Tool

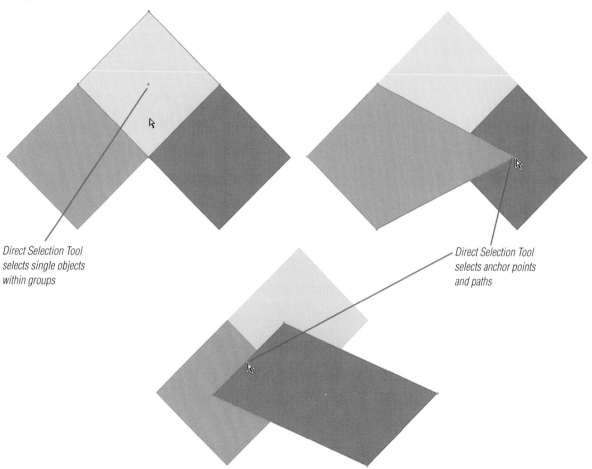

*Direct Selection Tool
selects single objects
within groups*

*Direct Selection Tool
selects anchor points
and paths*

Make guides and direct selections

1. Open AI 1-2.ai, then save it as **Direct Selections**.

   TIP Each time you save a Data File, click OK to close the Illustrator Options dialog box.

2. Click **View** on the menu bar, then click **Smart Guides** to turn this feature off.

3. Select the **green polygon**.

4. Click **View** on the menu bar, point to **Guides**, then click **Make Guides**.

   The polygon is converted to a guide.

   TIP If you do not see the polygon-shaped guide, click View on the menu bar, point to Guides, then click Show Guides.

5. Convert the purple starburst to a guide.

6. Click **View** on the menu bar, point to **Guides**, verify that there is a check mark to the left of Lock Guides, then release the mouse.

7. Click the **Direct Selection Tool** , then click the edge of the red square.

   The four anchor points turn white, as shown in Figure 30.

8. Click and drag the anchor points to the four corners of the guide to distort the square.

   Your work should resemble Figure 31.

You converted two objects into guides. You then used the Direct Selection Tool to create a new shape from a square by moving anchor points independently.

FIGURE 30
Red square selected with the Direct Selection Tool

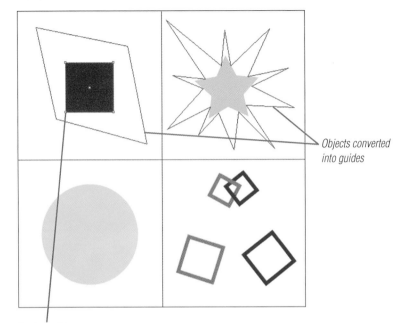

Objects converted
into guides

Anchor points
are hollow

FIGURE 31
Red square distorted

Getting Started with Illustrator

FIGURE 32
Star selected with Direct Selection Tool

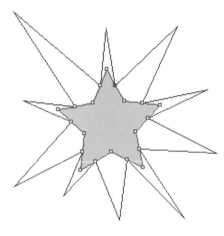

FIGURE 33
Completed starburst

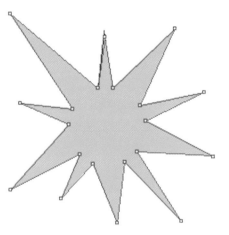

Add anchor points

1. Using the **Direct Selection Tool** ↘. click the center of the light blue star, and note the anchor points used to define the shape.

2. Click **Object** on the menu bar, point to **Path**, then click **Add Anchor Points**.

3. Click the **artboard** to deselect the star, then click the edge of the star.

   All the anchor points turn white and are available to be selected independently, as shown in Figure 32.

4. Move the top anchor point on the star to align with the top point of the guide that you made earlier.

5. Working clockwise, move every other anchor point outward to align with the guide, creating a ten-point starburst.

   Your work should resemble Figure 33.

6. Select and move any of the inner anchor points to modify the starburst to your liking.

You used the Add Anchor Points command and the Direct Selection Tool to create an original ten-point starburst from a generic five-point star.

Making a direct selection marquee

When you create a marquee selection with the Selection Tool, any object the marquee touches is selected in its entirety. You can also use the Direct Selection Tool to create selection marquees. A Direct Selection Tool marquee selects only the anchor points and the paths that it touches. A Direct Selection Tool marquee is very useful for selecting multiple points or paths in one step.

Select paths

1. Click the edge of the yellow circle.

   The yellow circle is comprised of four anchor points and four line segments, as shown in Figure 34. Clicking the edge selects one of the four segments.

2. Copy the segment.

3. Click **Edit** on the menu bar, then click **Paste in Front**.

   A copy is pasted directly on top of the selected segment.

4. Change the fill color to [None].

5. Change the stroke color to dark blue and the stroke weight to 14 pt.

6. Moving clockwise, repeat Steps 1, 2, 3, and 4 for the next three line segments, choosing different colors for each.

   Your finished circle should resemble Figure 35.

You selected individual segments of a circle, copied them, and then pasted them in front. You then created a special effect by stroking the four new segments with different colors.

FIGURE 34
Viewing the path of the circle

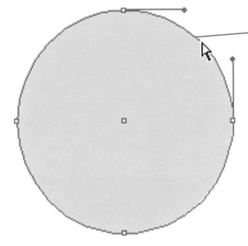

Clicking the edge of an object with the Direct Selection Tool selects one line segment of the entire path

FIGURE 35
Completed circle

FIGURE 36

Completed linked squares

1. Click the Selection Tool ▶, then overlap the large orange and blue squares so that they resemble the small orange and blue squares, then deselect.

2. Click the Direct Selection Tool ▶, then select the top path of the orange square.

3. Copy the path.

4. Select the intersecting path on the blue square.

5. Paste in front, then save your work.

   Your work should resemble Figure 36.

6. Close the document.

You learned a classic Illustrator trick. Selecting only a path, you copied it and pasted it in front of an intersecting object to create the illusion that the two objects were linked.

Start Illustrator and create a new document.

1. Create a new document and name it **Funky Flag**.
2. Make the size of the document 6" × 4".
3. Select Inches for the type of units, and CMYK Color for the color mode, then click OK.
4. Click File on the menu bar, click Save As, navigate to the drive and folder where you store your Data Files, then click Save.
5. Click View on the menu bar, then click Hide Page Tiling, if necessary.
6. Create a circle at the center of the artboard.
7. Click the Selection Tool.

Explore the Illustrator window.

1. Click View on the menu bar, then click Outline.
2. Click View on the menu bar, then click Preview.
3. Click View on the menu bar, then click Zoom In.
4. Click View on the menu bar, then click Zoom Out.
5. Press and hold [Spacebar] to access the Hand Tool, then move the artboard.
6. Click View on the menu bar, then click Fit in Window.
7. Select the circle, click Edit on the menu bar, then click Copy.

8. Click Edit on the menu bar, then click Paste in Front.
9. Move the new circle to the bottom of the artboard.
10. Click Edit on the menu bar, then click Undo Move.
11. Click Edit on the menu bar, then click Redo Move.
12. Click Select on the menu bar, then click All.
13. Click Select on the menu bar, then click Deselect.
14. Select all of the objects, click Edit on the menu bar, then click Cut.
15. Save your work.

Create basic shapes and apply fill and stroke colors.

1. Set the Fill and Stroke buttons in the toolbox to black and [None], respectively.
2. Create a rectangle that is 3" × 1".
3. Show the Swatches palette, if necessary.
4. Fill the rectangle with a light yellow.

Select, move, and align objects.

1. Click View on the menu bar, then click Smart Guides, if necessary.
2. Move the rectangle so that its top-left anchor point intersects with the top-left corner of the artboard.
3. Click the top-left anchor point, press and hold [Shift][Alt] (Win) or [Shift][option] (Mac), drag straight down until the top-left anchor point touches the bottom-left anchor

point (the "intersect" Smart Guide appears), then release the mouse.
4. Click Object on the menu bar, point to Transform, then click Transform Again.
5. Repeat Step 4.
6. Change the fill color of the second and fourth rectangles to a darker yellow.
7. Save your work.

Transform objects.

1. Select the four rectangles.
2. Double-click the Reflect Tool, click the Horizontal option button, then click Copy. The four rectangles are copied on top of the original rectangles.
3. Move the four new rectangles to the right so that they align with the right side of the artboard.
4. Click the Rectangle Tool, click the artboard, and create a square that is .75" × .75".
5. Apply a 1-point black stroke to the square and no fill.
6. Click the Selection Tool, click the edge of the square, then position it at the center of the artboard.
7. Use the Rotate dialog box to create a copy of the square rotated at 10°.
8. Apply the Transform Again command seven times.
9. Save your work.

Make direct selections.

1. Use [Shift] to select each of the nine black squares.
2. Click Object on the menu bar, then click Group.
3. Scale the group of squares 200%.
4. Create a 3.75" × 3.75" circle, fill it with Pumpkin, add a 1-point black stroke, then position it at the center of the artboard.
5. Cut the circle from the artboard, click the group of black squares, click Edit on the menu bar, then click Paste in Back.
6. Adjust the location of the circle, as needed.
7. Click Object on the menu bar, point to Path, then click Add Anchor Points.
8. Deselect the circle by clicking anywhere on the artboard.
9. Click the Direct Selection Tool, then click the edge of the circle.
10. One at a time, move each of the four new anchor points to the center of the circle.
11. Switch to the Selection Tool, then select the Pumpkin-filled shape.
12. Double-click the Rotate Tool, type **22** in the Angle text box, then click Copy.
13. Apply the Transform Again command two times.
14. Save your work, then compare your illustration to Figure 37.
15. Close Funky Flag.

FIGURE 37
Completed Skills Review

The lady who owns the breakfast shop that you frequent knows that you are a designer and asks for your help. Her nephew has designed a sign for her store window, but she confides in you that she doesn't like it. She thinks that it's "boring" and "flat." She wants to redesign the sign with something that is "original" and feels "more like a starburst."

1. Open AI 1-3.ai, then save it as **Star Sign**.
2. Click the Direct Selection Tool, then click the edge of the star.
3. Move two of the outer anchor points of the star farther from its center.
4. Move four of the inner points toward the center.
5. Select the entire star.
6. Reflect a copy of the star across the horizontal axis.
7. Fill the new star with an orange swatch and reposition it to your liking.
8. Group the two stars.
9. Copy the group, then paste in back.
10. Fill the copies with black.
11. Using your arrow keys, move the black copies five points to the right and five points down.

12. Select only the orange star.
13. Copy the orange star, then paste in back.
14. Fill the new copy with black.
15. Rotate the black copy 8°.

FIGURE 38
Completed Project Builder 1

16. Apply a yellow fill to the orange star, then apply a 1-point black stroke to both yellow stars.
17. Save your work, then compare your illustration to Figure 38.
18. Close Star Sign.

Iris Vision Labs has contracted with your design firm to bid on a design for their logo. Researching the company, you learn that they are a biotech firm whose mission is to develop cures for genetic blindness and vision problems. You decide to build your design around the idea of an iris.

1. Create a new document that is 6" × 6".
2. Save the document as **Iris Vision Bid**.
3. Create an ellipse that is 1" wide × 4" in height, and position it at the center of the artboard.
4. Fill the ellipse with [None], and add a 1-point blue stroke.
5. Create a copy of the ellipse rotated at 15°.
6. Apply the Transform Again command 10 times.
7. Select all and group the ellipses.
8. Create a copy of the group rotated at 5°.
9. Apply a red stroke to the new group.
10. Transform again.
11. Apply a bright blue stroke to the new group.
12. Select all.
13. Rotate a copy of the ellipses 2.5°.
14. Create a circle that is 2" × 2".
15. Fill the circle with Charcoal.
16. Remove the stroke from the circle.
17. Position the Charcoal-filled circle in the center of the ellipses.

18. Cut the circle.
19. Select all.
20. Paste in back.

FIGURE 39
Completed Project Builder 2

21. Save your work, then compare your illustration to Figure 39.
22. Close Iris Vision Bid.

The owner of Emerald Design Studios has hired you to design an original logo for her new company. She's a beginner with Illustrator, but she's created a simple illustration of what she has in mind. She tells you to create something "more sophisticated." The only other information that she offers about her company is that they plan to specialize in precise, geometric design.

1. Open AI 1-4.ai, then save it as **Emerald Design**.
2. Select all four diamonds and group them.
3. Select the group of diamonds on the artboard, then create a 75% copy.
4. Use the Transform Again command five times.
5. Use Smart Guides or Outline mode to help you identify each of the seven groups.
6. Rotate one of the groups 75°.
7. Select two other groups of your choice and repeat the last transformation, using the Transform Again command.
8. Apply a dark green stroke to all groups. Figure 40 shows one possible result of multiple transformations. Your illustration may differ.
9. Save your work, then close Emerald Design.

FIGURE 40
Completed Design Project

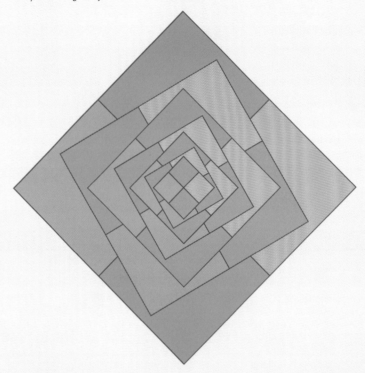

You attend a design school, and you're part of a team that is responsible for the artwork placed throughout the common areas of the school. One of the most admired professors brings you a file that he created in Illustrator, admitting that he's a beginner. Your team opens the file and notices that the file is poorly built—everything is misaligned and uneven. After consulting with the professor, your team decides that the file needs to be rebuilt from scratch.

1. Open AI 1-5.ai, then save it as **Rings N Things**.
2. Distribute copies of the file to the members of your group.
3. Discuss with the group the areas of the file that are misaligned and poorly constructed.
4. Assign one member the task of pulling apart the file, object by object, to see how the effect was achieved.
5. Have the group create a "game plan" for reproducing the artwork with precision. Where's the best place to start? What's the best methodology for recreating the professor's design?
6. Have a group discussion about the art itself. If the professor is open to new ideas, how would the group suggest that the design could be improved?

7. Have one member work on the original Illustrator file.
8. Work as a group to rebuild the file, using precise methods.

9. Save your work, then compare your illustration to Figure 41.
10. Close Rings N Things.

FIGURE 41
Completed Group Project

CREATING TEXT AND
GRADIENTS

1. Create and format text.

2. Flow text into an object.

3. Position text on a path.

4. Create colors and gradients.

5. Apply colors and gradients to text.

6. Adjust a gradient and create a drop shadow.

2 CREATING TEXT AND
GRADIENTS

Working with Text

When it comes to creating compelling and dramatic display text, no other software package offers the graphic sophistication that you'll find with Adobe Illustrator. You can quickly change fonts, font size, leading, and other text attributes in the Character palette. You can make tracking and kerning measurements with a level of precision that would satisfy even the most meticulous typographer. For the designer, Illustrator is the preeminent choice for typography. Powerful type tools offer the ability to fill objects with text, position text on lines—curved or straight—and set type vertically, one letter on top of the next. Once the text is positioned, the Create Outlines command changes the fonts to vector graphics that you can manipulate as you would any other object. For

example, you can apply a gradient fill to letter outlines for stunning effects.

Creating and Applying Gradient Fills

A **gradient** is a graduated blend between two or more colors used to fill an object or multiple objects. Illustrator's sophistication for creating gradients and its ease of use for applying them to objects are a dream come true for today's designers. You can create linear or radial gradients between multiple colors, then control the way they fill an object. Moreover, a single gradient can be used to fill multiple objects simultaneously! The unique gradient fills that you create can be saved with descriptive names, then imported into other Illustrator documents to be used again.

Tools You'll Use

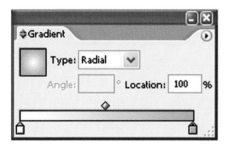

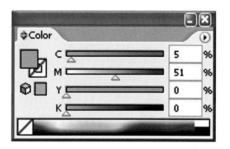

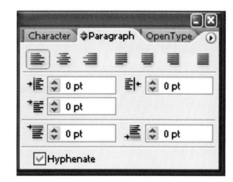

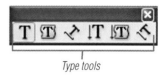

Type tools

CREATE AND
FORMAT TEXT

What You'll Do

 In this lesson, you will use the Type Tool to create the word BERRY as display text. You will use the Character palette to format the text and perfect its appearance. You will also create a vertical version of the text.

Creating Type

You can create text anywhere on the artboard simply by selecting one of the type tools, then clicking the artboard to start typing. You can enter text horizontally or vertically. The ability to type vertically is rather unusual; most text-based applications don't offer this option.

Text generated by the Type Tool is positioned on a path called the **baseline**. You can select text simply by clicking anywhere on the text. This feature is a preference that you can turn on or off: Click Edit on the menu bar, point to Preferences, click Type, then remove the check mark in the Type Object Selection by Path Only check box, if necessary. When this feature is checked, you must click the baseline to select text.

Formatting Text

The Character and Paragraph palettes neatly contain all of the classic commands for formatting text. Use the Character palette to modify text attributes such as font and type size, tracking, and kerning. You can adjust the **leading**, which is the vertical space between baselines, or apply a horizontal or vertical scale, which compresses or expands selected type. The Paragraph palette applies itself to more global concerns, such as text alignment, paragraph indents, and vertical spaces between paragraphs. Figure 1 shows examples of formatting that you can apply to text.

Tracking and kerning are essential (and often overlooked) typographic operations. **Tracking** inserts uniform spaces between characters to affect the width of selected words or entire blocks of text. **Kerning** is used to affect the space between any two characters; it is particularly useful for improving the appearance of headlines and other display text. Positive tracking or kerning values move characters farther apart; negative values move them closer together.

Illustrator can track and kern type down to $1/1000$ of a standard em space. The width of an em space is dependent on the current type size. In a 1-point font, the em space is 1 point. In a 10-point font, the em space is 10 points. With kerning units that are $1/1000$ of an em, Illustrator can manipulate a 10-point font at increments of $1/1000$ of 1 point! Figure 2 shows examples of kerning and tracking values.

Hiding Objects

Two factors contribute to difficulty in selecting text and other objects: the number of objects in the document and proximity of objects. Multiple objects positioned closely together can make selections difficult and impede productivity.

Hiding an object is one simple solution. Hidden objects are safe; they won't be deleted from the document when you quit.

Also, they won't print. Just don't forget that they're there!

The Hide Selection command is under the Object menu, as is Show All, which reveals all hidden objects. When hidden objects are revealed, they are all selected; you can use this to your advantage. Simply press [Shift] as you click to deselect the object you want to see, then hide the remaining objects.

FIGURE 1
Examples of text formatting

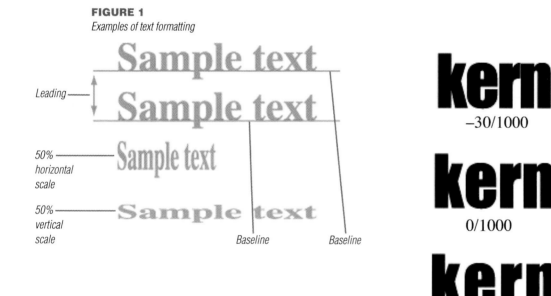

FIGURE 2
Examples of kerning and tracking

Create text

1. Open AI 2-1.ai, then save it as **Berry Symposium**.

2. Click **View** on the menu bar, then click **Hide Bounding Box**, if necessary.

3. Click the **Type Tool** T, then click anywhere on the artboard.

4. Type **BERRY** using all capital letters.

   TIP By default, new text is generated with a black fill and no stroke.

5. Click the **Selection Tool** ↖, then drag the **text** to the center of the artboard.

   TIP Hide Smart Guides, if necessary.

6. Click **Window** on the menu bar, point to **Type**, then click **Character** to show the Character palette.

7. Click the **Character palette list arrow**, then click **Show Options** to view the entire palette as shown in Figure 3.

You used the Type Tool to create the word BERRY, showed the Character palette, then expanded the view of the Character palette.

FIGURE 3
Character palette

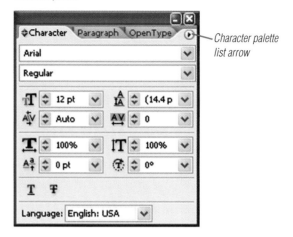

Character palette list arrow

DESIGNTIP **Tracking and kerning**

Typography, the art of designing letterforms, has a long and rich history that extends back to the Middle Ages. With the advent of desktop publishing in the mid-1980s, many conventional typographers and typesetters declared "the death of typography." Cooler minds have since prevailed. The personal computer and software such as Adobe Illustrator have made vast libraries of typefaces available as never before. Imagine the days when the typewriter ruled—its single typeface and two point sizes the standard for literally millions of documents—and you get a sense of the typographic revolution that has occurred in the last 20 years. Many designers are so eager to tackle the "artwork" that they often overlook the type design in an illustration. Tracking and kerning—the manipulation of space between words and letters—are essential elements to good type design and are often woefully ignored.

Illustrator's precise tracking and kerning abilities are of no use if they are ignored. One good way of maintaining awareness of your tracking and kerning duties is to take note of others' oversights. Make it a point to notice tracking and kerning—or lack thereof—when you look at magazines, or posters, or especially billboards. You'll be amazed at what you'll see.

FIGURE 4
Character palette

Set the font size list arrow (Font size)

Set the kerning between two characters list arrow (Kerning)

Horizontal Scale text box

Underline button

Strikethrough button

Set the font family list arrow (Font family)

Set the font style list arrow (Font style)

Set the leading list arrow (Leading)

Set the tracking for the selected characters list arrow (Tracking)

Vertical Scale text box

Character Rotation text box

Set the baseline shift list arrow (Baseline)

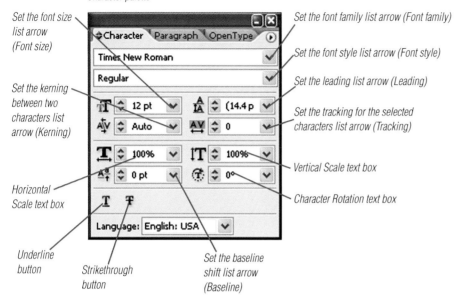

1. Click the **Font family** (Win) or **Font menu** (Mac) **list arrow**, then click **Times New Roman PS MT**, or a similar font, as shown in Figure 4.

   TIP   Figure 4 shows the full name of each setting in the Character palette. The steps in this chapter refer to the shorter name provided in parentheses.

2. Click the **Font size text box**, type **150**, then press **[Enter]** (Win) or **[return]** (Mac).

3. Click the **Horizontal Scale text box**, type **90**, then press **[Enter]** (Win) or **[return]** (Mac).

4. Deselect all.

5. Compare your text to Figure 5.

You used the Character palette to modify the font, the font size, and the horizontal scaling of the word BERRY.

FIGURE 5
Formatted text

BERRY

Track and kern text

1. Select the text, if necessary.

2. Using the Character palette, click the **Tracking text box**, then type **-30**.

   | TIP Click the Character palette list arrow, then click Show Options, if necessary.

3. Click the **Type Tool** T, then click the cursor between the B and the E.

4. Using the Character palette, click the **up and down arrows** in the Kerning text box to experiment with higher and lower kerning values, then change the kerning value to -40.

5. Using Figure 6 as a guide, change the kerning to -20, 0, and -120 between the next three letter pairs.

6. Click the **Selection Tool**, click the **Paragraph palette name tab**, then click the **Align center button** ≡, as shown in Figure 7.

   When text is center-aligned, its anchor point doubles as its center point, which is handy for aligning it with other objects.

   | TIP If you do not see the Paragraph palette, click Window on the menu bar, point to Type, then click Paragraph.

7. Click **Object** on the menu bar, point to **Hide**, then click **Selection**.

   You used the Character palette to change the tracking of the word BERRY, then you entered different kerning values to affect the spacing between the four letter pairs. You center-aligned the text, then hid the text.

FIGURE 6
Kerning and tracking applied to text

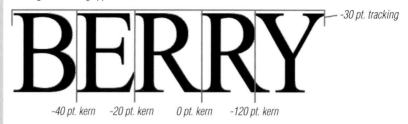

-30 pt. tracking

-40 pt. kern   -20 pt. kern   0 pt. kern   -120 pt. kern

FIGURE 7
Paragraph palette

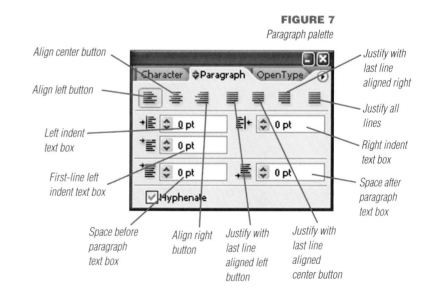

Align center button

Align left button

Left indent text box

First-line left indent text box

Space before paragraph text box

Align right button

Justify with last line aligned left button

Justify with last line aligned center button

Justify with last line aligned right

Justify all lines

Right indent text box

Space after paragraph text box

Creating Text and Gradients

FIGURE 8

Vertical text

B E R R Y

Using the Glyphs palette

The Glyphs palette contains various type characters that aren't necessarily available on your keyboard. Examples of these characters include trademarks, copyright marks, accented letters, and numbers expressed as fractions. Click Window on the menu bar, point to Type, then click Glyphs to display the Glyphs palette. To access a glyph, click the Type Tool, click the artboard as you would to type any character, then double-click the glyph in the Glyph palette that you wish to use.

Create vertical type

1. Click the **Vertical Type Tool** ⵑT , then click anywhere on the artboard.

   TIP   The Vertical Type Tool is hidden beneath the Type Tool.

2. Type the word **BERRY** using all capital letters.

   TIP   The type tools retain the formatting attributes that were previously chosen.

3. Click the **Selection Tool** ▶ , select the text, then move it to the center of the artboard.

   TIP   When any tool other than the Selection Tool is selected in the toolbox, you can press [Ctrl] (Win) or ⌘ (Mac) to switch to the Selection Tool. When you release [Ctrl] (Win) or ⌘ (Mac), the last chosen tool will be active again.

4. Using the Character palette, change the font size to 84 pt.

5. Change the tracking value to -160.

6. Set both the horizontal and vertical scales to 100%, then deselect the text.

   Your screen should resemble Figure 8.

7. Delete the vertical text, then save your work.

You used the Vertical Type Tool to create a vertical alternative to the first word you typed. You adjusted the tracking and kerning to better suit a vertical orientation, and then deleted the text.

FLOW TEXT INTO
AN OBJECT

What You'll Do

rasp
straw blue
cran straw tea
straw checker cran
blue boysen black tea straw
blue boysen checker cran tea rasp
boysen blue black straw tea boysen
checker cran rasp boysen blue black rasp straw
blue black straw tea boysen checker cran rasp straw
blue tea black rasp straw blue black straw tea
boysen checker cran rasp straw blue black
rasp straw blue cran straw tea straw
checker cran straw boysen
black tea straw blue
boysen checker
cran tea
rasp

 In this lesson, you will use the Area Type Tool to flow text into an object.

Filling an Object with Text

Using the Area Type Tool and the Vertical Area Type Tool, you can flow text into any shape you can create, from circles to birds to bumblebees! Text in an object can be formatted as usual. You can change fonts, font size, alignment, etc., and the text will be reflowed in the object as you format it.

When text is flowed into an object, you can manipulate the object as you would any other object. Apply fills and strokes and transformations; use the Rotate Tool, or the Scale or Reflect Tools. You can even use the Direct Selection Tool to distort the shape. Best of all, you can apply those operations to the text or to the text object independently! Figure 9 shows an example of an object, in this case a star, filled with text.

QUICKTIP
You can underline text and strike through text using the Underline and Strikethrough buttons on the Character palette.

Locking Objects

Working in tandem with the Hide command, the Lock Selection command on the Object menu allows you to exempt an object from selections and affix its position on the artboard. The Lock Selection command is useful simply as a device to protect objects from accidental modifications.

Locked objects can be selected only after they are unlocked by choosing the Unlock All command on the Object menu. The Unlock All command unlocks every locked object on the artboard. When locked objects are unlocked, they are all selected. Simply press [Shift] while you click to deselect the object you want to work with, and relock the remaining objects.

Making Guides

Guides are one of Illustrator's many features that help you to work with precision. You can select any object and make it into a guide with the Make Guides command on the View menu. You can also create guides by clicking and dragging the mouse pointer from each ruler to the artboard.

FIGURE 9

An object filled with text

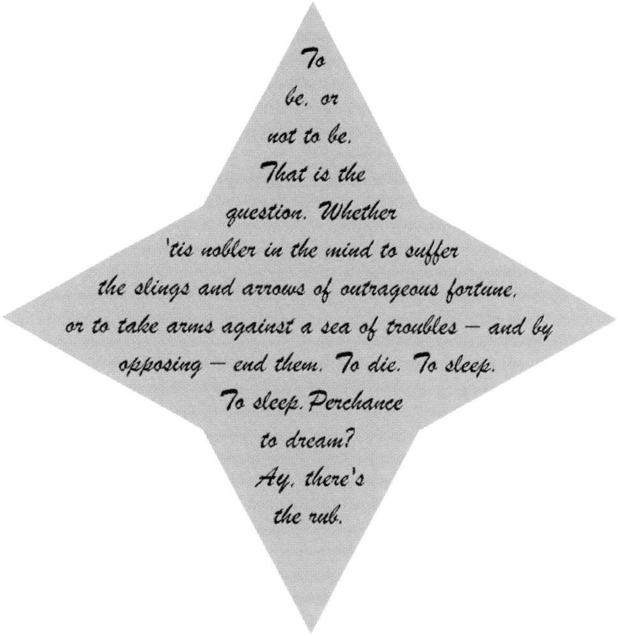

To be, or not to be. That is the question. Whether 'tis nobler in the mind to suffer the slings and arrows of outrageous fortune, or to take arms against a sea of troubles — and by opposing — end them. To die. To sleep. To sleep. Perchance to dream? Ay, there's the rub.

Fill an object with text

1. Open AI 2-2.ai, then save it as **Diamond Text**.

2. Select the yellow square, double-click the **Rotate Tool** ⟳, type **45** in the Angle text box, then click **OK**.

3. Click the **Area Type Tool** ⊤, then click the block of text.

   TIP The Area Type Tool is hidden beneath the current type tool.

4. Click **Select** on the menu bar, then click **All**.

   TIP When you click a type tool cursor on text and apply the Select All command, all the text is selected—not the object that contains the text, and not any other text or objects on the page.

5. Copy the text.

6. Click the **Selection Tool** ▶, select the yellow square, then change the font size to 12 using the Character palette.

   TIP When you are working with a Type Tool, you can press [Ctrl] (Win) or ⌘ (Mac) to access the Selection Tool temporarily and remain in Area Type Tool mode.

7. Click the **Area Type Tool** ⊤, if necessary, then click the edge of the yellow square.

   A flashing cursor appears, and the square loses its fill color, as shown in Figure 10.

8. Paste the copied text into the square.

   Your work should resemble Figure 11.

You rotated the yellow square, then filled it with text by first copying text from another object, then clicking the edge of the square with the Area Type Tool before you pasted the text into the square.

FIGURE 10
Applying the Area Type Tool

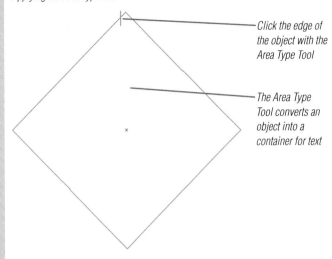

Click the edge of the object with the Area Type Tool

The Area Type Tool converts an object into a container for text

FIGURE 11
Text pasted into an object

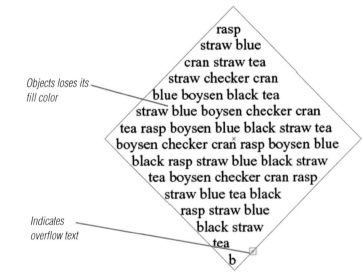

Objects loses its fill color

Indicates overflow text

rasp
straw blue
cran straw tea
straw checker cran
blue boysen black tea
straw blue boysen checker cran
tea rasp boysen blue black straw tea
boysen checker cran rasp boysen blue
black rasp straw blue black straw
tea boysen checker cran rasp
straw blue tea black
rasp straw blue
black straw
tea
b

Creating Text and Gradients

FIGURE 12

Centered text in an object

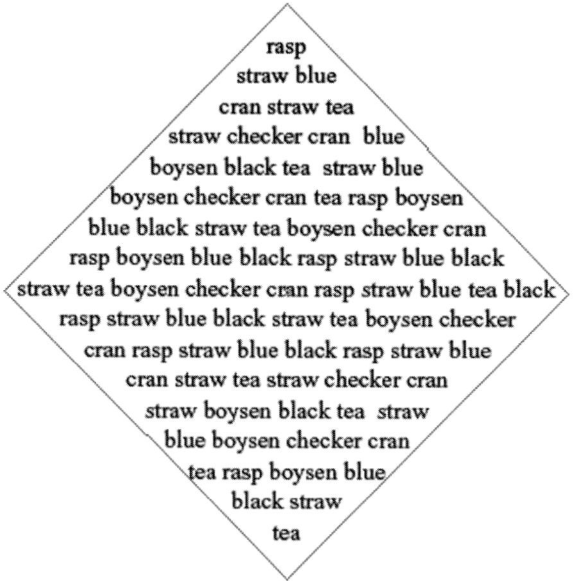

```
                    rasp
                 straw blue
               cran straw tea
           straw checker cran  blue
         boysen black tea  straw blue
       boysen checker cran tea rasp boysen
     blue black straw tea boysen checker cran
   rasp boysen blue black rasp straw blue black
 straw tea boysen checker cran rasp straw blue tea black
   rasp straw blue black straw tea boysen checker
     cran rasp straw blue black rasp straw blue
       cran straw tea straw checker cran
         straw boysen black tea  straw
           blue boysen checker cran
             tea rasp boysen blue
                 black straw
                    tea
```

Using Character and Paragraph Styles

A style is a group of formatting attributes, such as font, font size, color, and tracking, that is applied to text. You use the Character Styles palette to create styles for individual words or characters, such as a footnote, and you use the Paragraph Styles palette to apply a style to a paragraph. Paragraph styles include formatting options such as indents and drop caps. Using styles saves you time, and it keeps your work consistent. If you create styles for an Illustrator document, the styles are saved with the document and are available to be loaded for use in other documents.

Format text in an object

1. Select all of the text in the rotated square.

2. Click the **Align center button** ≣ in the Paragraph palette.

   TIP   When filling an object other than a square or a rectangle with text, centering the text is often the best solution.

3. Click the **Character palette name tab** next to the Paragraph palette name tab, then change the font size to 9 pt.

4. Click the **Leading text box**, type **11**, click the **artboard** to deselect the text, then compare your work to Figure 12.

   It's OK if the line breaks in your document differ from the text in the figure.

5. Click the **Selection Tool** , then click the **diamond-shaped text**.

   Both the text and the object that contains the text are selected.

6. Copy the text object.

   Both the text and the object are copied.

7. Click **Window** on the menu bar, then click **Berry Symposium** at the bottom of the menu.

   TIP   All open Illustrator documents are listed at the bottom of the Window menu

8. Paste the text object into the Berry Symposium document.

You used the Paragraph and Character palettes to format text in the object. You used the Selection Tool to select the text object, and then you copied and pasted it into the Berry Symposium document.

Make guides and use the Lock command

1. Click **View** on the menu bar, then click **Show Rulers**, if necessary.

2. Using Figure 13 as a reference, position your pointer in the top horizontal ruler, click and drag the pointer straight down to the 5" mark on the vertical ruler, then release the mouse to create a guide.

   TIP   You may need to move the toolbox out of the way to see the vertical ruler.

3. Position a vertical guide at the 5" mark on the horizontal ruler.

   TIP   To change the color or style of guides, click Edit (Win) or Illustrator (Mac) on the menu bar, point to Preferences, then click Guides & Grid. The Guides & Grid Preferences dialog box is shown in Figure 14.

4. Click **View** on the menu bar, point to **Guides**, then verify that Lock Guides is checked.

5. Click the **Selection Tool** , if necessary.

(continued)

FIGURE 13
Making guides

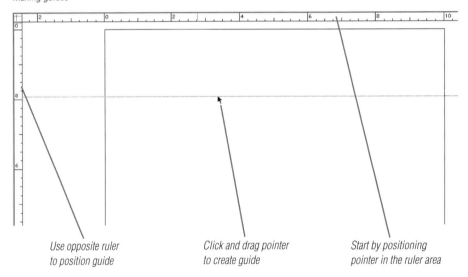

Use opposite ruler
to position guide

Click and drag pointer
to create guide

Start by positioning
pointer in the ruler area

FIGURE 14

Guides & Grid Preferences settings

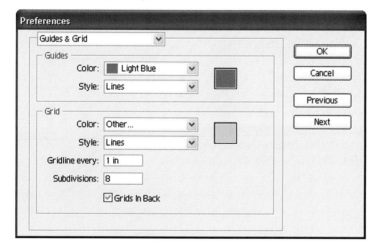

6. Select the text object, then align the center point of the text object with the intersection of the guides.

TIP Use the arrow keys on your keypad to nudge the selection right, left, up, or down.

7. Click **Object** on the menu bar, point to **Lock**, then click **Selection**.

TIP Locking objects is standard practice. You can also lock a selection by first selecting an object, then pressing [Ctrl][2] (Win) or ⌘ [2] (Mac). Make it a point to remember the quick key.

8. Save your work.

You created a horizontal and a vertical guide that intersect at the center of the artboard. You then aligned the center of the diamond text object with the intersection of the guides, and locked the diamond text object.

POSITION TEXT
ON A PATH

What You'll Do

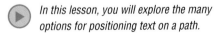

three rivers

rasp
straw blue
cran straw tea
straw checker cran
blue boysen black tea straw
blue boysen checker cran tea rasp
boysen blue black straw tea boysen
checker cran rasp boysen blue black rasp straw
blue black straw tea boysen checker cran rasp straw
blue tea black rasp straw blue black straw tea
boysen checker cran rasp straw blue black
rasp straw blue cran straw tea straw
checker cran straw boysen
black tea straw blue
boysen checker
cran tea
rasp

symposium

▶ *In this lesson, you will explore the many options for positioning text on a path.*

Using the Path Type Tools

Using the Type on a Path Tool or the Vertical Type on a Path Tool, you can type along a straight or curved path. This is the most compelling of Illustrator's text effects, and it opens up a world of possibilities for the designer and typographer.

You can move text along a path to position it where you want. You can "flip" the text to make it run in the opposite direction—on the opposite side of the path. You can

also change the baseline shift to modify the distance of the text's baseline in relation to the path. A positive value "floats" the text above the path, and a negative value moves the text below the path. You can modify text on a path in the same way you would modify any other text element. Figure 15 shows an example of text on a path, whereas Figure 16 shows an example of text flipped across a path.

FIGURE 15
Text on a path

ROLLERCOASTER

FIGURE 16
Text flipped across a path

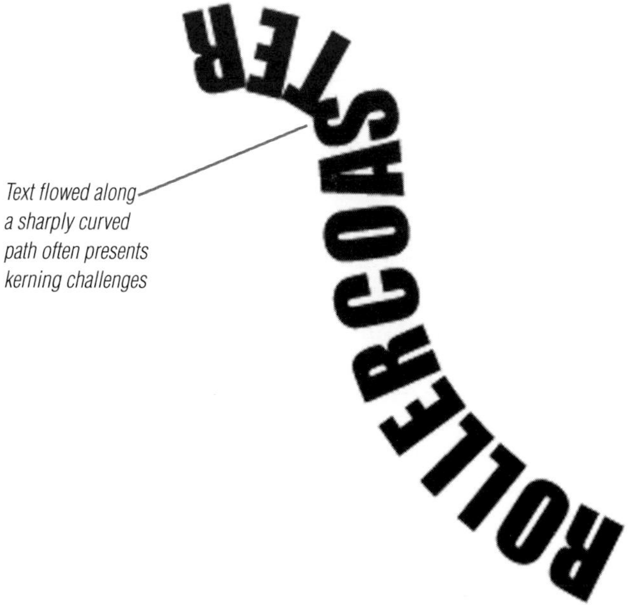

*Text flowed along
a sharply curved
path often presents
kerning challenges*

ROLLERCOASTER

Flow text on a path

1. Click the **Ellipse Tool** 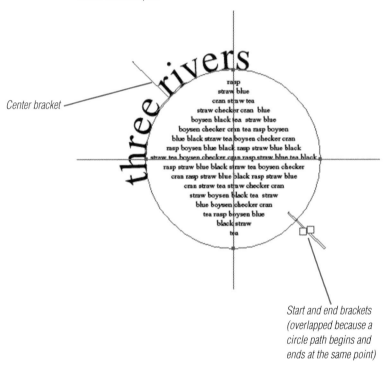, press **[Alt]** (Win) or **[option]** (Mac), then click the center of the artboard.

   Pressing [Alt] (Win) or [option] (Mac) while you click a shape tool on the artboard ensures that the center of the shape will be drawn from the point that you clicked.

2. Enter **2.9** in for the width and the height of the circle in the Ellipse dialog box, then click **OK**.

3. Click the **Type on a Path Tool**, then click anywhere on the edge of the circle.

   ⏐ TIP The Type on a Path Tool may be hidden beneath the current type tool.

   A flashing cursor appears, and the circle loses its fill color.

4. Type **three rivers** in lowercase, using Times New Roman PS MT for the font.

   ⏐ TIP If you do not have Times New Roman PS MT, substitute a similar font.

5. Click the **Selection Tool** to select the text by its baseline, then change the font size to 47 pt.

   You will see three brackets—one at the beginning of the path, one at the end of the path, and one at the midpoint between the two brackets. These brackets allow you to move text along a path.

   ⏐ TIP Text flowed on a circle will often require kerning, especially when it is set at a large point size.

6. Compare your screen to Figure 17.

You created a 2.9" circle from its center, then typed along the circle's path using the Type on a Path Tool. You changed the font and font size using the Character palette.

FIGURE 17
Text on a circular path

Center bracket

Start and end brackets
(overlapped because a
circle path begins and
ends at the same point)

FIGURE 18

Moving text on a path

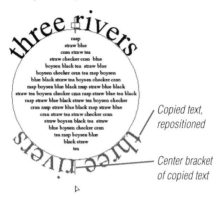

Copied text,
repositioned

Center bracket
of copied text

FIGURE 20

Modifying a baseline shift

Baseline shift

FIGURE 19

Flipping text across a path

Center bracket of copied text

FIGURE 21

Flipped text positioned below the path

Move text along a path

1. Click **View** on the menu bar, point to **Guides**, then click **Hide Guides**.

2. Using the Selection Tool ▶, drag the **center bracket** until the text is centered at the top of the circle.

3. Click **Edit** on the menu bar, click **Copy**, click **Edit** on the menu bar, then click **Paste in Front**.

4. Drag the **center bracket** of the copied text clockwise to move the copied text to the position shown in Figure 18.

5. Drag the **center bracket** of the copied text straight up to flip the text across the path, as shown in Figure 19.

   TIP   Enlarge your view of the artboard if you have trouble dragging the bracket.

6. Click the **Baseline text box** in the Character palette, type **-21**, as shown in Figure 20, then press **[Enter]** (Win) or **[return]** (Mac).

7. Click the **Type Tool** T, highlight **three rivers** at the bottom of the circle, then type **symposium**.

8. Click the **Selection Tool** ▶, then drag the **center bracket** to center the text at the bottom of the circle, if necessary.

9. Lock the two text objects, save your work, then compare your image to Figure 21.

You moved and copied text along a path, flipped its direction, changed the baseline shift, then locked both text objects.

CREATE COLORS AND
GRADIENTS

What You'll Do

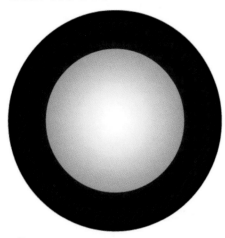

In this lesson, you will use the Color palette, the Gradient palette, and the Swatches palette to create, name, and save colors and gradients.

Using the Gradient Palette

A **gradient** is a graduated blend between colors. The Gradient palette is the command center for creating and adjusting gradients. In the palette, you will see a slider that represents the gradient you are creating or working with. The slider has at least two colors. The leftmost color is the starting color, and the rightmost color is the ending color.

The colors used in a gradient are represented in the Gradient palette by small house-shaped icons called **stops**. The Gradient palette, shown in Figure 22 shows a two-color gradient.

The point at which two colors meet in equal measure is called the **midpoint** of the gradient. The midpoint is represented by the diamond above the slider. The midpoint does not necessarily need to be positioned evenly between the starting and ending colors. You can change the midpoint by moving the diamond.

The Swatches palette contains standard gradients that come with the software. To create your own original gradients, start by clicking an object filled with an existing gradient. You can then modify that existing gradient in the Gradient palette. You can change either or both the beginning and ending colors. You can change the location of the midpoint. You can also add additional colors into the gradient, or remove existing colors.

> **QUICK**TIP
>
> As you work to perfect a gradient, you can see how your changes will affect the gradient automatically, by filling an object with the gradient that you are working on. As you make changes in the Gradient palette, the changes will be reflected in the object.

You can define a gradient as linear or radial. A linear gradient can be positioned left to right, up and down, or on any angle. You can change the angle of the gradient by entering a new value in the Angle text box in the Gradient palette.

Think of a radial gradient as a series of concentric circles. With a radial gradient, the starting color appears at the center of the gradient. The blend radiates out to the ending color. By definition, a radial gradient has no angle ascribed to it.

Using the Color Palette

The Color palette, as shown in Figure 23, is where you move sliders to mix new colors for fills, strokes, and gradients. You can also use the palette to adjust the color in a filled object. The palette has five color modes: CMYK, RGB, Grayscale, HSB, and Web Safe RGB. The palette will default to CMYK or RGB, depending on the color mode you choose when creating a new document. Grayscale mode allows you to create shades

of gray in percentages of black. If you select a filled object and choose the HSB mode, you can adjust its basic color (hue), the intensity of the color (saturation), and the range of the color from light to dark (brightness). If you are designing illustrations for the Internet, you might consider using Web Safe RGB mode to create colors that are in accordance with colors defined in HTML.

Rather than use the sliders, you can also type values directly into the text boxes. For example, in CMYK mode, a standard red color is composed of 100% Magenta and 100% Yellow. The notation for this callout would be 100M/100Y. Note that you don't list the zero values for Cyan (C) and Black (K). In RGB mode (0-255), a standard orange color would be noted as 255R/128G.

Adding Colors and Gradients to the Swatches Palette

Once you have defined a color or a gradient to your liking, it's a smart idea to save it by dragging it into the Swatches palette. Once a color or gradient is moved into the Swatches palette, you can name it by double-clicking it, then typing a name in the Swatch Options dialog box. You can't, however, modify it. For example, if you click a saved gradient and adjust it in the Gradient palette, you can apply the new gradient to an object, but the original gradient in the Swatches palette remains unaffected. You can save the new gradient to the Swatches palette for future use.

FIGURE 22
Gradient palette

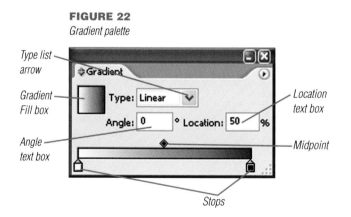

Type list arrow

Gradient Fill box

Angle text box

Location text box

Midpoint

Stops

FIGURE 23
Color palette

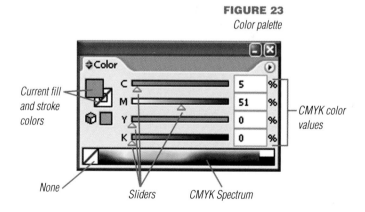

Current fill and stroke colors

None

Sliders

CMYK Spectrum

CMYK color values

Create a gradient and a color

1. Show the guides.

2. Create a 4" circle at the center of the art-board, then apply a yellow fill to the circle.

   The most recently drawn object is automatically placed above the other objects on the artboard.

3. Hide the guides, click **Window** on the menu bar, then click **Gradient** to select it, if necessary.

4. Click **Window** on the menu bar, then click **Color** to select it, if necessary.

5. Click the **Rainbow swatch** in the Swatches palette.

   The yellow fill changes to the Rainbow fill.

6. Click the **Gradient palette list arrow**, then click **Show Options**, if necessary.

7. Click the **yellow stop** on the gradient slider, and drag it off the palette to delete it.

8. Delete the green, aqua, and blue stops.

   | TIP   The changes you make to the gradient slider are reflected in the circle.

9. Click the bottom edge of the gradient slider to add a new color stop, then drag the stop along the slider until you see 50% in the Location text box in the Gradient palette as shown in Figure 24.

10. Verify that the new stop is selected, press and hold **[Alt]** (Win) or **[option]** (Mac), click **Squash** in the Swatches palette, then compare your circle to Figure 25.

(continued)

FIGURE 24
Adding and deleting stops

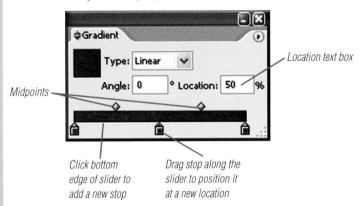

Location text box

Midpoints

Click bottom edge of slider to add a new stop

Drag stop along the slider to position it at a new location

FIGURE 25
The color Squash is added to the gradient

Creating Text and Gradients

FIGURE 26

Black starting and ending colors

FIGURE 27

Changing the location of the midpoint of two colors

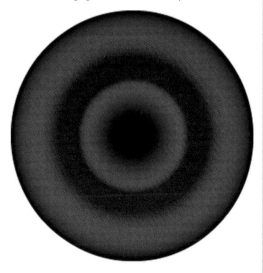

You must select a stop in order to change its color.

> TIP If you don't press [Alt] (Win) or [option] (Mac), as you choose a swatch for your gradient, you will change the selected object's fill to a solid color.

11. Click the **first stop** on the gradient slider, press **[Alt]** (Win) or **[option]** (Mac), then click **Black** on the Swatches palette.

12. Repeat Step 11 to apply Black to the third stop, then compare your circle to Figure 26.

13. Click the **Squash stop** to select it, then drag each slider in the Color palette until the new CMYK values are 5C/95M/95Y/3K.

> TIP Expand the view of the Color palette, if necessary.

14. Click the **Type list arrow** in the Gradient palette, then click **Radial**.

15. Click the **diamond** at the top of the gradient slider between the first two stops, then drag it to the 87% location on the slider.

16. Compare your circle to Figure 27.

You applied the Rainbow gradient to the yellow circle. You created a new gradient by deleting the four intermediary stops and adding a new stop to the gradient. You changed the gradient from linear to radial, then adjusted the midpoint of the blend between the starting color and the red intermediate color.

Add gradients and colors to the Swatches palette

1. Double-click the **Scale Tool** 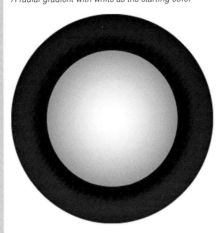, type **65** in the Scale text box, then click **Copy**.

2. Keeping the smaller circle selected, delete the red stop on the gradient slider in the Gradient palette.

3. Change the first stop starting color to White and the ending stop to 0C/40M/50Y/0K.

   | TIP   Press [Alt] (Win) or [option] (Mac).

   When a stop is selected on the gradient slider, the color of that stop appears in the Gradient Stop Color box in the Color palette.

4. Position the midpoint on the gradient slider at 65%.

   Your screen should resemble Figure 28.

5. Drag the **Gradient Fill box** from the Gradient palette to the Swatches palette, as shown in Figure 29.

6. Double-click **New Gradient Swatch 1** (the gradient you just added) in the Swatches palette to open the Swatch Options dialog box.

7. Type **Pinky** in the Swatch Name text box, then click **OK**.

8. Click the **last color stop** on the gradient slider.

   (continued)

FIGURE 28
A radial gradient with white as the starting color

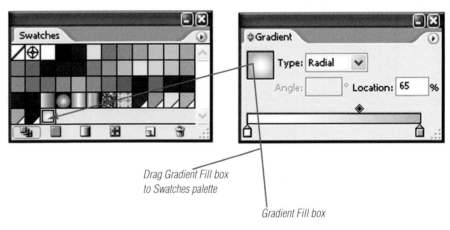

FIGURE 29
Adding a gradient to the Swatches palette

Drag Gradient Fill box
to Swatches palette

Gradient Fill box

Creating Text and Gradients

FIGURE 30

Adding a gradient to the Swatches palette

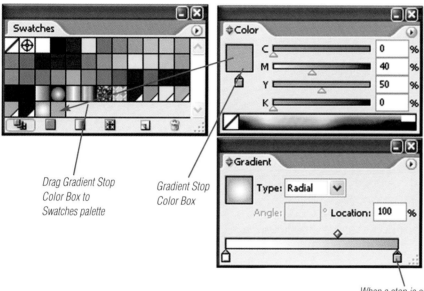

Drag Gradient Stop
Color Box to
Swatches palette

Gradient Stop
Color Box

When a stop is selected,
the color appears in the
Gradient Stop Color Box
in the Color palette

9. Drag the **Gradient Stop Color box** from the Color palette to the Swatches palette to add this color to the Swatches palette, as shown in Figure 30.

10. Click the **Selection Tool** ▶.

11. Click the **artboard** to deselect the smaller circle.

12. Name the new color swatch **Pinky Ending**, then click **OK**.

13. Click the **large circle**, drag the **Gradient Fill box** in the Gradient palette to the Swatches palette, then name the new gradient **Crimson Gradient**.

14. Save your work.

You used the Gradient palette to create a new gradient. You added the gradient fills from the two circles to the Swatches palette and gave them descriptive names. You added a color named Pinky Ending to the Swatches palette, then created a new gradient called Crimson Gradient.

APPLY COLORS AND
GRADIENTS TO TEXT

What You'll Do

 In this lesson, you will apply colors to text, convert text into objects, and fill the objects with a gradient.

Applying Fills and Strokes to Text

Regardless of the fill and stroke colors shown in the toolbox, new text is generated by default with a black fill and no stroke. To change the color of text, you must either select the text by highlighting it with a type tool, or switch to a selection tool. When you switch to a selection tool, the text is selected as a single object (a blue baseline and anchor point are revealed). Any color changes you make will affect the text globally. If you want to change the fill or the stroke of an individual character, you must select that character with a type tool.

Converting Text to Outlines

About the only thing you can't do to Illustrator text is fill it with a gradient. To create the effect, you first need to convert the text into objects. You can do this by selecting the text, then using the Create Outlines command on the Type menu. The letterforms, or outlines, become standard Illustrator objects with anchor points and

Working with the stacking order

The stacking order defines how objects will be displayed when they overlap. Illustrator stacks each object, beginning with the first object. Each successive object you create overlaps the previously drawn objects. You can change the stacking order by moving objects forward and backward through the stack, one object at a time. You can also move an object to the very top or the very bottom of the stack with one command. Grouped objects are stacked together behind the top object in the group. If you group two objects that are separated in the stack, the objects in between will be positioned behind the group.

paths able to be modified like any other object—and able to be filled with a gradient. Figure 31 shows an example of text converted to outlines.

Create Outlines is a powerful feature. Beyond allowing you to fill text with a gradient, it makes it possible to create a document with text and without fonts. This can save you time in document management when sending files to your printer, and will circumvent potential problems with missing fonts or font conflicts.

Once text is converted to outlines, you can no longer change the typeface. Also, the type loses its font information, including sizing "hints" that optimize letter shape at different sizes. Therefore, if you plan to scale type, change its font size in the Character palette before converting to outlines.

FIGURE 31
Text converted to outlines

Apply color to text

1. Select the two circles, click **Object** on the menu bar, point to **Arrange**, then click **Send to Back**.

   The two circles move behind the locked text objects.

2. Click **Object** on the menu bar, then click **Unlock All**.

   The three text objects you created and locked are now unlocked and selected.

3. Apply the Pinky Ending color as a fill for the three unlocked text objects.

4. Deselect all, then lock the diamond text object.

   Your work should resemble Figure 32.

You unlocked the three text objects, filled them with the Pinky Ending color, then locked the diamond text object.

FIGURE 32
Text with a new fill color

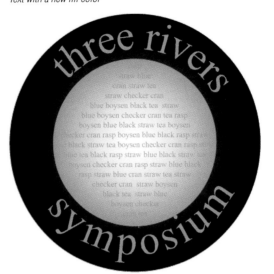

Importing a swatch library

Colors and gradients are saved with the document they were created in, and are not available to be used in other documents. You can, however, import swatches from one document into another. Click Window on the menu bar, point to Swatch Libraries, then click Other Library, which opens the Select a library to open dialog box. Click the document whose swatches you want to import, then click Open. That document's Swatches palette will appear in your current document. When you import a Swatches palette, the palette automatically appears with the name of the document from which it came. The imported Swatches palette is not editable—you cannot add new swatches to it or delete existing ones from it.

FIGURE 33

Outlines filled with a gradient

*Each outline is filled
with the gradient*

1. Show the guides.

2. Click **Object** on the menu bar, then click **Show All**.

3. Select the **BERRY** text, click **Object** on the menu bar, point to **Arrange**, then click **Bring to Front**.

4. Click **Type** on the menu bar, then click **Create Outlines**.

5. Apply the Steel gradient in the Swatches palette to fill the text outlines, then deselect the outlines.

6. Using Figure 33 as a guide, position the BERRY text outlines so that they are centered within the entire illustration, then hide the guides.

7. Save your work.

You showed the BERRY text, moved it to the front, converted it to outlines, then filled the outlines with a gradient.

ADJUST A GRADIENT AND
CREATE A DROP SHADOW

What You'll Do

▶ *In this lesson, you will use the Gradient Tool to modify how the gradient fills the outlines. You will then explore the effectiveness of a simple drop shadow as a design element.*

Using the Gradient Tool

The Gradient Tool is used to manipulate gradient fills that are already applied to objects; it affects only the way a gradient fills an object. To use the tool, you first select an object with a gradient fill. You then drag the Gradient Tool over the object. For both linear and radial gradients, where you begin dragging and where you end dragging determine the length of the blend from starting to ending color. For linear gradients, the angle that you drag in determines the angle at which the

blend fills the object. If you apply the same gradient to multiple objects, you can select all the objects and use the Gradient Tool to extend a single gradient across all of them.

If you select and fill multiple objects with a gradient, each object is filled with the entire length of the gradient, from beginning color to ending color.

When you convert text to outlines and apply a gradient fill, the gradient automatically fills each letter independently. In other words, if you fill a five-letter word with a rainbow gradient, each of the five letters will contain the entire spectrum of colors in the gradient. To extend the gradient across all the letters, drag the Gradient Tool from the left edge of the word to the right edge. Figure 34 shows examples of different angles and lengths of a gradient fill created with the Gradient Tool.

Adding a Drop Shadow

Applying a shadow behind text is an effective design tool to distinguish the text from other objects and add dimension to the illustration. To apply a drop shadow to text, copy the text, then paste the copy behind it. Fill the copy with a darker color, then use the keyboard arrows to move it so that it is offset from the original text. See Figure 35.

FIGURE 34
Using the Gradient Tool

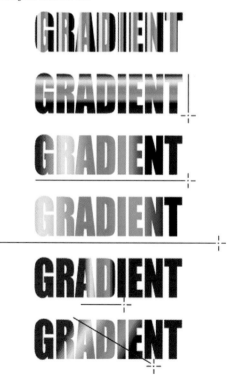

FIGURE 35
Drop shadow created using the Paste in Back command

Use the Gradient Tool

1. Select the **BERRY text outlines**, if necessary.

2. Click the **Gradient Tool** ▣, then position the pointer at the top of the B.

3. Drag straight down to the bottom of the B, then release the mouse.

   Your work should resemble Figure 36.

   > TIP Pressing and holding [Shift] while you drag the Gradient Tool pointer allows you to drag in a perfectly straight line.

4. Switch to the **Selection Tool** ▸, then click the large circle filled with the Crimson Gradient fill behind the text.

5. In the Gradient palette, reposition the red center color stop so that the value in the Location text box reads 82%.

   The red stop in the blend is now positioned behind the three rivers and symposium text, as shown in Figure 37.

You used the Gradient Tool to flow the gradient from top to bottom in the word BERRY. You adjusted the red stop in the Gradient palette to move the red highlight behind the three rivers and symposium text.

FIGURE 36
Gradient Tool applied top to bottom

FIGURE 37
A highlight behind the text

Red stop in a
radial gradient

Creating Text and Gradients

*Drop shadow added
to symposium*

FIGURE 40

The finished illustration

Add a drop shadow to text

1. Select the word **BERRY**.

2. Apply a 1 pt Black stroke to the outlines.

3. Copy the word, then paste in back.

4. Change the fill of the copied object to Black.

   TIP   Even though you can't see the copy
   of the text in back, it is still selected.

5. Press ↓ three times and ← three times to
   move the copied text 3 pts down and 3 pts to
   the left, as shown in Figure 38.

6. Copy the word symposium, then paste in back.

7. Change the fill of the copied text to Black.

   TIP   Since the copy is still selected, you only
   need to click Black in the Swatches palette.

8. Using the arrow keys, move the copied text 2 pts
   down and 2 pts to the left, as shown in Figure 39.

9. Apply the same drop shadow to the three
   rivers text.

   TIP   You might find it easier to select the
   three rivers text if you first lock the symposium text and the symposium shadow text.

10. Unlock all, select everything on the artboard,
    then rotate the illustration 15°.

11. Click the **Selection Tool** ▸, then click the
    artboard to deselect all.

    Your work should resemble Figure 40.

12. Save your work, then close and save each
    document.

*You applied a black stroke to the display text and then
pasted a copy behind. You filled the copy with black,
then offset the copy to create a drop shadow effect.
You then applied a drop shadow to symposium and
three rivers. Finally, you rotated the entire illustration.*

Create and format text.

1. Open AI 2-3.ai, then save it as **Hole In One**.
2. Using a bold font, type **NOW OPEN** on two lines, using all capital letters. (*Hint*: The font used in Figure 41 is Impact.)
3. Change the font size to 29 pt and the leading to 25 pt.
4. Change the baseline shift to 0.
5. Change the alignment to center and the horizontal scale to 75%.
6. Position the text in the center of the white circle.
7. Hide the text.
8. Save your work.

Flow text into an object.

1. Copy the beige circle.
2. Paste the copy in front of it.
3. Click the Type Tool, then select all of the green text at the bottom of the artboard, with the Type Tool.
4. Copy the green text.
5. Click the Selection Tool, then click the top beige circle.
6. Click the Area Type Tool, click the edge of the top beige circle, then paste.
7. Center-align the text in the circle.

8. Change the baseline shift to -4 pts.
9. Fill the selected text with the same fill color as the beige circle (50% Orange).
10. In the Color palette, drag the Magenta slider to 40% to darken the text.
11. Hide the text.
12. Save your work.

Position text on a path.

1. Select the dark gray circle.
2. Click the Type on a Path Tool, then click the top of the circle.
3. Using a bold font, type **THE HOLE-IN-ONE** in all capital letters across the top of the circle. (*Hint*: The font in Figure 41 is Techno Regular.)
4. Change the font size to 34 pt and the fill color to white. (*Hint*: You may need to use a smaller font size, depending on the font you choose.)
5. Click the Selection Tool, click Edit on the menu bar, click Copy, click Edit on the menu bar, click Paste in Front, then move the center bracket clockwise to position the copied text across the bottom of the circle.
6. Highlight the copied text, then type **RESTAURANT & BAR** with the Type Tool.

7. Drag the RESTAURANT & BAR text across the path to flip its direction.
8. Apply a negative baseline shift to move the text below the path. (*Hint*: The baseline shift used in Figure 41 is -27 pts.)
9. Copy both text objects, then paste them in back.
10. Fill the back copies of the text with black, then move them 2 pts up and 2 pts to the right.
11. Save your work.

Create and apply gradient fills to objects.

1. Apply the White, Black Radial gradient to the small white circle.
2. Change the ending color stop on the Gradient palette to Smoke. (*Hint*: Press [Alt] (Win) or [option] (Mac) while you select Smoke from the Swatches palette.)
3. Save the new gradient in the Swatches palette.
4. Name it **Golf Ball**.
5. Fill the large green circle with the Golf Ball gradient.
6. Change the starting color stop to Pure Yellow.
7. Change the ending color stop to Little Sprout Green.

8. Move the midpoint of the two colors to the 80% location on the gradient slider.
9. Save the new gradient as **The Rough**.
10. Save your work.

Adjust a gradient and create a drop shadow.

1. Click Object on the menu bar, then click Show All.
2. Deselect all by clicking the artboard.
3. Select NOW OPEN and convert the text to outlines. (*Hint*: Use the Type menu.)
4. Fill the text with the White, Black gradient.
5. Change the starting color stop to black.
6. Create an intermediary white color stop at the 50% mark on the gradient slider.
7. Drag the Gradient Tool starting at the top of the word NOW to the bottom of the word OPEN.
8. Change the middle color stop of the gradient to Latte.
9. Save the new gradient as **Flash**.
10. Deselect the text.
11. Delete the green text from the bottom of the artboard.
12. Convert the remaining text objects into outlines.
13. Select all, then lock all objects.
14. Save your work, compare your illustration to Figure 41, then close Hole In One.

FIGURE 41
Completed Skills Review

Creating Text and Gradients

An eccentric California real-estate mogul hires your design firm to "create an identity" for La Mirage, his development of high-tech executive condominiums in Palm Springs. Since he's curious about what you'll come up with on your own, the only creative direction he'll give you is to tell you that the concept is "a desert oasis."

1. Create a new 6" × 6" CMYK Color document, then save it as **La Mirage**.
2. Using a bold font and 80 pt for a font size, type **LA MIRAGE** in all capitals. (*Hint*: The font shown in Figure 42 is Impact.)
3. Change the horizontal scale to 80%.
4. Change the baseline shift to 0.
5. Apply a -100 kerning value between the two words.
6. Convert the text to outlines, then click the White, Black gradient in the Swatches palette.
7. Using the Color palette, change the first color stop to 66M/100Y/10K (*Hint*: Press and hold [Alt] (Win) or [option] (Mac) when creating the new color.)
8. Create an intermediary color stop that is 25M/100Y.
9. Position the intermediary color stop at 70% on the slider.
10. Save the gradient in the Swatches palette, and name it **Desert Sun**.
11. Drag the Gradient Tool from the exact top to the exact bottom of the text.

12. Create a rectangle around the text and fill it with the Desert Sun gradient.
13. Drag the Gradient Tool from the bottom to the top of the rectangle.
14. Send the rectangle to the back of the stack.

15. Apply a 1-point black stroke to LA MIRAGE.
16. Type the tagline: **a desert oasis** in 14 pt lowercase letters.
17. Apply a tracking value of 500 or more to the tagline, then convert it to outlines.
18. Save your work, then close La Mirage.

FIGURE 42
Completed Project Builder 1

Creating Text and Gradients

Your friend owns Loon's Balloons. She stops by your studio with a display ad that she's put together for a local magazine and asks if you can make all the elements work together better. Her only direction is that the balloon must remain pink, the same color as her logo.

1. Open AI 2-4.ai, then save it as **Loon's Balloons**.
2. Save the pink fill on the balloon to the Swatches palette, and name it **Hot Pink**.
3. Fill the balloon shape with the White, Black Radial gradient from the Swatches palette.
4. Change the black stop on the gradient slider to Hot Pink.
5. Using the Gradient Tool, change the highlight point on the balloon shape so that it is no longer centered in the balloon shape.
6. Copy the balloon, then paste it in front.
7. Click the Selection Tool on the block of text that says "specializing in etc.", then cut the text.
8. Click the top balloon with the Selection Tool, then switch to the Area Type Tool.
9. Click the top edge of the top balloon, then paste.
10. Center the text and apply a -4 baseline shift.
11. Adjust the layout of the text as necessary. (*Hint*: You can force a line of text to the next line by clicking before the first word in the line you want to move, then pressing [Shift][Enter] (Win) or [Shift][return] (Mac).)

12. Move the headline LOON'S BALLOONS so that each word is on a different side of the balloon string.

FIGURE 43
Completed Project Builder 2

13. Apply a 320 kerning value between the two words.
14. Save your work, compare your screen to Figure 43, then close Loon's Balloons.

specializing in all
your balloon needs - for
birthdays, weddings,
anniversaries, graduations,
halloween, new year's eve
parties, or just to
say hello - we've got the
balloon for you.
call
555-7717

LOON'S BALLOONS

You work in the marketing department of a major movie studio, where you design movie posters and newspaper campaigns. You are respected for your proficiency with typography. Your boss asks you to come up with a "teaser" campaign for the movie *Vanishing Point*, a spy thriller. The campaign will run on billboards in 10 major cities and will feature only the movie title, nothing else.

1. Create a new 6" × 6" CMYK Color document, then save it as **Vanishing Point**.
2. Type **VANISHING POINT**, using 100 pt and a bold font. (*Hint*: The font used in Figure 44 is Impact.)
3. Change the horizontal scale to 55%.
4. Convert the text to outlines.
5. In the Swatches palette, click the White, Black gradient.
6. Drag the Gradient Tool from the exact bottom to the exact top of the letters.
7. Copy the letters, then paste them in front.
8. Fill the copied letters in front with white.
9. Using your arrow keys, move the white letters 2 pts to the left and 8 pts up.
10. Save your work, then compare your text with Figure 44.
11. Close Vanishing Point.

FIGURE 44
Completed Design Project

Firehouse Chili Pepper Company, a local specialty food manufacturer, has hired your team to design a label for its new line of hot sauces. Since this is a new product line, they have no existing materials for your team to start from.

1. Create a new 6" × 6" CMYK Color document, then save it as **Firehouse**.
2. Assign two team members to search the Internet to get design ideas. They should use keywords such as chili, pepper, hot sauce, barbecue, and salsa. What have other designers created to convey these concepts? Is there a broad range of ideas, or are they all pretty much different versions of the same idea? If so, can your group think of something original that works?
3. Assign two other members to go to the grocery store and return with some samples of other products in this niche. Be sure they purchase both products that you've heard of before and products you've never heard of before. Are the known products' design concepts better than the unknown products'? Have the group discuss any correlation between the successful products and better design, if it is evident.
4. Two other team members should be in charge of typographic research and should work closely with the design team. Again, have the group discuss whether it sees a variety of typefaces used in relation with this concept, or whether they are all pretty much the same.
5. While everyone else is researching, the design team should begin brainstorming and sketching out ideas. Although there are no existing materials, the product line's name is very evocative. The team should create design ideas that spring from the concepts of "firehouse" and "chili pepper," as well as from more broad-based concepts such as salsa, Mexico, and fire.

FIGURE 45
Completed Group Project

6. Use the skills that you learned in this chapter to create the label. (*Hint*: Fill text outlines with a gradient that conveys "hot." Use reds, oranges, and blacks. Use a bold font for the text so that the gradient will be clearly visible. Position the stops on the slider so that the "hot" colors are prominent in the letterforms.)
7. Save your work, then compare your results with Figure 45.
8. Close Firehouse.

chapter

3

DRAWING AND COMPOSING
AN ILLUSTRATION

1. Draw straight lines.

2. Draw curved lines.

3. Draw elements of an illustration.

4. Apply attributes to objects.

5. Assemble an illustration.

6. Stroke objects for artistic effect.

7. Use Live Trace and the Live Paint Bucket Tool.

Drawing in Illustrator

You can create any shape using the Pen Tool, which is why it's often called "the drawing tool." More precisely, the pen is a tool for drawing straight lines, curved lines, polygons, and irregularly shaped objects. It is, however, no *more* of a drawing tool than the shape tools—it's just more versatile.

The challenges of the Pen Tool are finite and able to be grasped with no more than 30 minutes' study. As with many aspects of graphic design (and of life!), mastery comes with practice. So make it a point to learn Pen Tool techniques. Don't get frustrated. And use the Pen Tool often, even if it's just to play around making odd shapes.

To master Illustrator, you must master the Pen Tool.

All artists learn techniques for using tools—brushes, chalk, palette knives, etc.

Once learned, those techniques become second nature—subconscious and unique to the artist. Ask yourself, was Van Gogh's mastery of the palette knife a triumph of his hands or of his imagination?

When you draw, you aren't conscious of how you're holding the crayon or how much pressure you're applying to the paper. Much the same goes for Illustrator's Pen Tool. When you are comfortable and confident, you will find yourself effectively translating design ideas from your imagination straight to the artboard—without even thinking about the tool!

When you work with the Pen Tool, you'll want complete control over your artboard. Using the Zoom Tool and the New View feature, you can create custom views of areas of your artboard, making it easy to jump to specific elements of your illustration for editing purposes.

Tools You'll Use

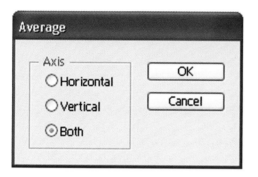

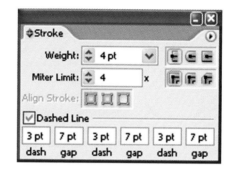

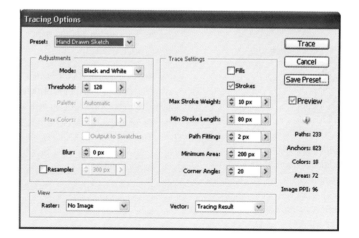

DRAW STRAIGHT LINES

What You'll Do

In this lesson, you will create three new views, then explore basic techniques for using the Pen Tool as you prepare to draw a complex illustration.

Viewing Objects on the Artboard

If you are drawing on paper and you want to see your work up close, you move your nose closer to the paper. Computers offer more effective options. As you have already seen, the Zoom Tool is used to enlarge areas of the artboard for easier viewing. When you are working with the Pen Tool, your view of the board becomes more critical, as anchor points are tiny, and you will often move them in 1 point increments.

Instead of clicking the Zoom Tool to enlarge an area, you can click and drag it over the area you want to zoom in on, creating a **marquee**, a rectangular, dotted line that surrounds the area you drag over. When you release the Zoom Tool, the marquee disappears, and whatever was in the marquee is magnified as much as possible while still fitting in the window.

The New View command allows you to save any view of the artboard. Let's say you zoom in on an object. You can save that view and give it a descriptive name, using the New View command. The name of the view is then listed at the bottom of the View menu, so you can return to it at any time by selecting it. Saving views is an effective way to increase your productivity.

Drawing Straight Segments with the Pen Tool

You can use the Pen Tool to make lines, also known as paths; you can also use it to create a closed shape such as a triangle or a pentagon. When you click the Pen Tool to make anchor points on the artboard, straight segments are automatically placed between the points. When the endpoints of two straight segments are united by a point that point is called a **corner point**. Figure 1 shows a simple path drawn with five anchor points and four segments.

Perfection is an unnecessary goal when you are using the Pen Tool. Anchor points and segments can be moved and repositioned. New points can be added and deleted. Use the Pen Tool to create the general shape that you have in your mind. Once the object is complete, use the Direct Selection Tool to perfect—or tweak—the points and segments. "Tweaking" a finished object—making small, specific improvements—is always part of the drawing process.

QUICKTIP

When the Pen Tool is positioned over an anchor point on a selected path, the Delete Anchor Point Tool appears. To remove a point from a path without cutting it, always use the Delete Anchor Point Tool. If you select a point and cut it, the path becomes broken.

Aligning and Joining Anchor Points

Often, you will want to align anchor points precisely. For example, if you have drawn a diamond-shaped object with the Pen Tool, you may want to align the top and bottom points on the same vertical axis and then align the left and right points on the same horizontal axis to perfect the shape.

The **Average** command is a simple and effective choice for aligning points. With two or more points selected, you can use the Average command to align them on the horizontal axis, on the vertical axis, or on both the horizontal and vertical axes. Two points aligned on both the horizontal and vertical axes are positioned one on top of the other.

Why is the command named Average? The name is appropriate, because when the command moves two points to line them up on a given axis, that axis is positioned at the average distance between the two points. Thus, each moves the same distance.

The **Join** command unites two anchor points. When two points are positioned in different locations on the artboard, the Join command creates a segment between them. When two points are aligned on both the horizontal and vertical axes and are joined, the two points become one.

You will often use the Average and Join commands in tandem. Figure 2 shows two pairs of points that have each been aligned on the horizontal axis, then joined with the Join command.

FIGURE 1

Elements of a path composed of straight segments

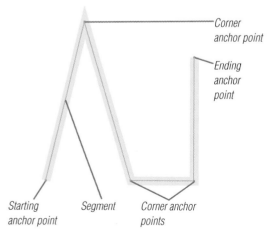

Corner
anchor point

Ending
anchor
point

Starting
anchor point

Segment

Corner anchor
points

FIGURE 2

Join command unites open points

Points to be joined

Points to be joined

Two paths created by
the Join command

Create new views

1. Open AI 3-1.ai, then save it as **Straight Lines**.

2. Click the **Zoom Tool** , then position it at the upper-left corner of the artboard.

3. Click and drag a **selection box** that encompasses the entire yellow section, as shown in Figure 3.

   The area within the selection box is now magnified.

4. Click **View** on the menu bar, then click **New View**.

5. Name the new view **yellow**, then click **OK**.

6. Press and hold **[Spacebar]** to access the Hand Tool , then drag the **artboard** upward until you have a view of the entire pink area.

7. Create a new view of the pink area, and name it **pink**.

   TIP   If you need to adjust your view, you can quickly switch to a view of the entire artboard by pressing [Ctrl][0] (Win) or [0] (Mac), then create a new selection box with the Zoom Tool.

8. Create a new view of the green area, named **mint**.

9. Click **View** on the menu bar, then click **yellow** at the bottom of the menu.

   The Illustrator window changes to the yellow view.

   TIP   You can change the name of a view by clicking View on the menu bar, then clicking Edit Views.

You used the Zoom Tool to magnify an area of the artboard. You then named and saved the new view of the artboard. You named and saved two other views.

FIGURE 3

Drag the Zoom Tool to select what will be magnified

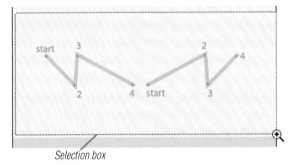

Selection box

FIGURE 4
Four anchor points and three segments

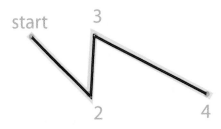

FIGURE 5
Click the path with the Pen Tool to add a new point

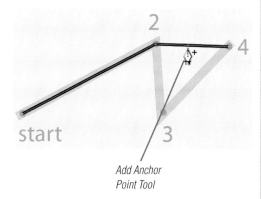

Add Anchor
Point Tool

FIGURE 6
Move an anchor point with the Direct Selection Tool

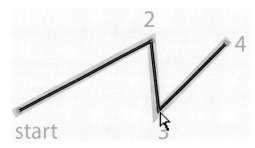

Draw straight lines

1. Verify that you are still in the yellow view, then click the **Pen Tool** ✎.

2. Set the fill color to [None], the stroke color to Black, and the stroke weight to 1 pt.

3. Using Figure 4 as a reference, click **position 1 (start)**.

4. Click **position 2**, then notice the segment that is automatically drawn between the two anchor points.

5. Click **position 3**, then click **position 4**.

    TIP   If you become disconnected from the current path you are drawing, undo your last step, then click the last anchor point with the Pen Tool and continue.

6. Press **[Ctrl]** (Win) or ⌘ (Mac) to switch to the Selection Tool ▸, then click the artboard to stop drawing the path and to deselect it.

    You need to deselect one path before you can start drawing a new one.

7. Click **position 1 (start)** on the next path, then click **position 2**.

8. Skip over position 3 and click **position 4**.

9. Using Figure 5 as a guide, position the Pen Tool anywhere on the segment between points 2 and 4, then click to add a new anchor point.

    TIP   When the Pen Tool is positioned over a selected path, the Add Anchor Point Tool appears.

10. Click the **Direct Selection Tool** ▸, then drag the **new anchor point** to position 3, as shown in Figure 6.

Using the Pen Tool, you created two straight paths.

Close a path and align the anchor points

1. Click **View** on the menu bar, then click **pink**.

2. Click the **Pen Tool** 🖋, click the **start/end position** at the top of the polygon, then click **positions 2 through 6**.

3. Position the Pen Tool over the first point you created, then click to close the path, as shown in Figure 7.

4. Switch to the **Direct Selection Tool** ▲, click **point 3**, press and hold **[Shift]**, then click **point 6**.

   | TIP Use the [Shift] key to select multiple points.

   Anchor points that are selected appear as solid blue squares; anchor points that are not selected are white or hollow squares.

5. Click **Object** on the menu bar, point to **Path**, then click **Average**.

6. Click the **Horizontal option button** in the Average dialog box, then click **OK**.

   The two selected anchor points align on the horizontal axis, as shown in Figure 8.

7. Select both the start/end point and point 4.

8. Use the Average command to align the points on the vertical axis.

9. Select both point 2 and point 5, then use the Average command to align the points on both axes, as shown in Figure 9.

You drew a closed path, then used the Average command to align three sets of points. You aligned the first set on the horizontal axis, the second on the vertical axis. You aligned the third set of points on both axes, which positioned them one on top of the other.

FIGURE 7
Close a path at its starting point

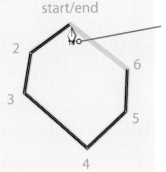

A small circle appears next to the Pen Tool when you position it over the first anchor point

FIGURE 8
Two points aligned on the horizontal axis

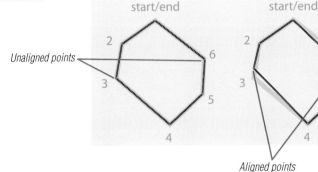

Unaligned points

Aligned points

FIGURE 9
Averaging two points on both the horizontal and vertical axes

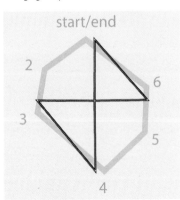

FIGURE 10

Cutting points also deletes the segments attached to them

FIGURE 11

Join command unites two distant points with a straight segment

FIGURE 12

Joining the two open anchor points on an open path closes the path

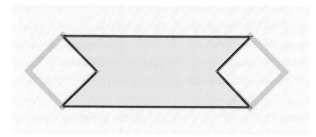

Join anchor points

1. Switch to the mint view of the artboard.

2. Use the Pen Tool [⬧] to trace the two diamond shapes.

   TIP   Remember to deselect the first diamond path with the Selection Tool before you begin tracing the second diamond.

3. Click the **left anchor point** of the first diamond with the Direct Selection Tool [▶], click **Edit** on the menu bar, then click **Cut**.

   Cutting points also deletes the segments attached to them.

4. Cut the right point on the second diamond.

   Your work should resemble Figure 10.

5. Select the top point on each path.

6. Click **Object** on the menu bar, point to **Path**, then click **Join**.

   The points are joined by a straight segment, as shown in Figure 11.

   TIP   The similarity of the quick keys for Average and Join makes them easy to work with in tandem.

7. Join the two bottom points.

8. Apply a yellow fill to the object, then save your work.

   Your work should resemble Figure 12.

9. Close the Straight Lines document.

You drew two closed paths. You cut a point from each path, which deleted the points and the segments attached to them, creating two open paths. You used the Join command, which drew a new segment between the two top points and the two bottom points on each path. You then applied a yellow fill to the new object.

DRAW CURVED LINES

What You'll Do

 In this lesson, you will use the Pen Tool to draw and define curved paths, and learn techniques to draw lines that abruptly change direction.

Defining Properties of Curved Lines

When you click to create anchor points with the Pen Tool, the points are connected by straight segments. You can "draw" a curved path between two anchor points by *clicking and dragging* the Pen Tool to create the points, instead of just clicking. Anchor points created by clicking and dragging the Pen Tool are known as **smooth points**.

When you use the Direct Selection Tool to select a point connected to a curved segment, you will expose the point's **direction lines**, as shown in Figure 13. The angle and length of the direction lines determine the arc of the curved segment. Direction lines are editable. You can click and drag the **direction points** at the end of the direction lines to reshape the curve. Direction lines function only to define curves and do not appear when you print your document.

A smooth point always has two direction lines that move together as a unit. The two curved segments attached to the smooth point are both defined by the direction lines. When you manipulate the direction lines on a smooth point, you change the curve of both segments attached to the point, always maintaining a *smooth* transition through the anchor point.

When two paths are joined at a corner point, the two paths can be manipulated independently. A corner point can join two straight segments, one straight segment and one curved segment, or two curved segments. That corner point would have zero, one, or two direction lines, respectively. Figure 14 shows examples of smooth points and corner points.

FIGURE 13
Direction lines define a curve

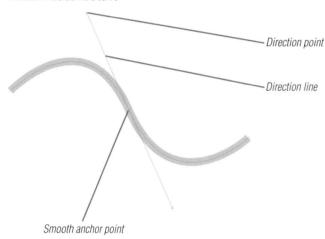

Direction point

Direction line

Smooth anchor point

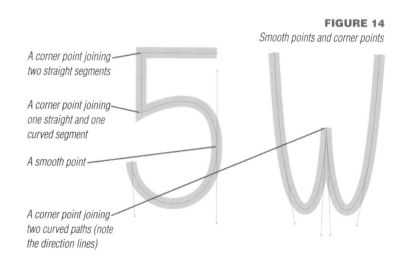

FIGURE 14
Smooth points and corner points

A corner point joining two straight segments

A corner point joining one straight and one curved segment

A smooth point

A corner point joining two curved paths (note the direction lines)

When a corner point joins one or two curved segments, the direction lines are unrelated and are often referred to as "broken." When you manipulate one, the other doesn't move.

Converting Anchor Points

The Convert Anchor Point Tool changes corner points to smooth points and smooth points to corner points.

To convert a corner point to a smooth point, you click and drag the Convert Anchor Point Tool on the anchor point to *pull out* direction lines. See Figure 15.

The Convert Anchor Point Tool works two ways to convert a smooth point to a corner point, and both are very useful when drawing.

FIGURE 15
Converting a corner point to a smooth point

Corner point converted to a smooth point

Corner point

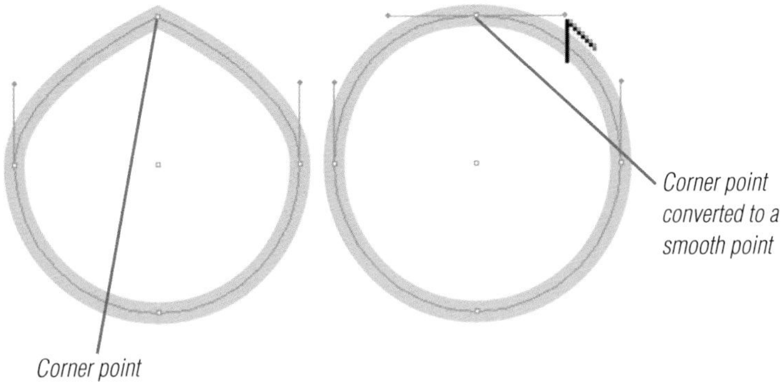

When you click directly on a smooth point with the Convert Anchor Point Tool, the direction lines disappear. The two attached segments lose whatever curve defined them and become straight segments, as shown in Figure 16.

You can also use the Convert Anchor Point Tool on one of the two direction lines of a smooth point. The tool "breaks" the direction lines and allows you to move one independently of the other. The smooth point is converted to a corner point that now joins two unrelated curved segments.

Once the direction lines are broken, they remain broken. You can manipulate them independently with the Direct Selection Tool; you no longer need the Convert Anchor Point Tool to do so.

FIGURE 16
Converting smooth points to corner points

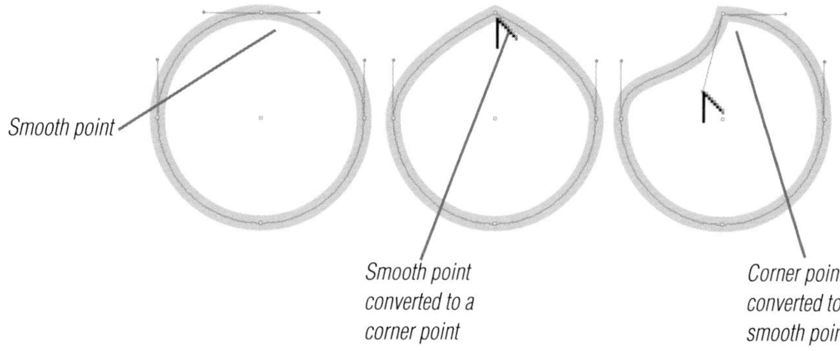

Smooth point

Smooth point converted to a corner point

Corner point converted to a smooth point

Toggling between the Pen Tool and the selection tools

Drawing points and selecting points go hand in hand, and you will often switch back and forth between the Pen Tool and one of the selection tools. Clicking from one tool to the other in the toolbox is unnecessary and will impede your productivity. To master the Pen Tool, you *must* incorporate the keyboard command for "toggling" between the Pen Tool and the selection tools. With the Pen Tool selected, press [Ctrl] (Win) or ⌘ (Mac), which will switch the Pen Tool to the Selection Tool or the Direct Selection Tool, depending on which tool you used last.

Draw and edit a curved line

1. Open AI 3-2.ai, then save it as **Curved Lines 1**.

2. Click the **Pen Tool** 🖋, then position it over the first point position on the line.

3. Click and drag upward until the pointer is at the center of the purple star.

4. Position the Pen Tool over the second point position.

5. Click and drag down to the red star.

6. Using the same method, trace the remainder of the blue line, as shown in Figure 17.

7. Click the **Direct Selection Tool** ▷.

8. Select the second anchor point.

9. Click and drag the **direction handle** of the *top* direction line to the second purple star, as shown in Figure 18.

   The move changes the shape of *both* segments attached to the anchor point.

10. Select the third anchor point.

11. Drag the **bottom direction handle** to the second red star, as shown in Figure 19.

12. Manipulate the direction lines to restore the curves to their appearance in Figure 17.

13. Save your work, then close the Curved Lines 1 document.

You traced a curved line by making smooth points with the Pen Tool. You used the Direct Selection Tool to manipulate the direction lines of the smooth points and adjust the curves. You then used the direction lines to restore the line to its original curves.

FIGURE 17
Smooth points draw continuous curves

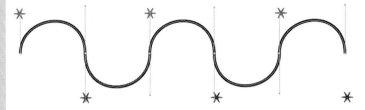

FIGURE 18
Moving one direction line changes two curves

Click the Direct Selection Tool on any smooth point to expose its direction lines

FIGURE 19
Round curves are distorted by moving direction lines

FIGURE 20
Smooth points are converted to corner points

FIGURE 21
Smooth points restored from corner points

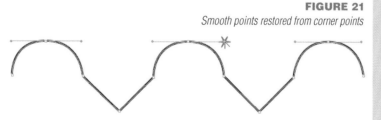

1. Open AI 3-3.ai, then save it as **Curved Lines 2**.
2. Click **View** on the menu bar, then click **View #1**.
3. Click the **Direct Selection Tool** anywhere on the black line.

   Six anchor points become visible.
4. Click **Object** on the menu bar, point to **Path**, then click **Add Anchor Points**.

   Five anchor points are added that do not change the shape of the line.
5. Click the **Convert Anchor Point Tool**, then click each of the five new anchor points.

   > TIP   The Convert Anchor Point Tool is hidden beneath the Pen Tool.

   The smooth points are converted to corner points, as shown in Figure 20.
6. Click the six original anchor points with the Convert Anchor Point Tool.
7. Starting from the left side of the line, position the Convert Anchor Point Tool over the sixth anchor point.
8. Click and drag the **anchor point** to the purple star.

   The corner point is converted to a smooth point.
9. Using Figure 21 as a guide, convert the corner points to the left and right of the new curve.

You added five new anchor points to the line, then used the Convert Anchor Point Tool to convert all 11 points from smooth to corner points. You then used the Convert Anchor Point Tool to convert three corner points to smooth points.

Draw a line with curved and straight segments

1. Click **View** on the menu bar, then click **View #2**.
2. Click the **Pen Tool** 🖊, position it over the first point position, then click and drag down to the green star.
3. Position the Pen Tool over the second point position, then click and drag up to the purple star, as shown in the top section of Figure 22.
4. Click the **second anchor point**.

   The direction line you dragged is deleted, as shown in the lower section of Figure 22.
5. Click the **third point position** to create the third anchor point.
6. Position the Pen Tool over the third anchor point, then click and drag a direction line up to the green star.
7. Position the Pen Tool over the **fourth point position**, then click and drag down to the purple star.
8. Click the **fourth anchor point**.
9. Position the Pen Tool over the fifth position, then click.
10. While the Pen Tool is still positioned over the fifth anchor point, click and drag a direction line down to the green star.
11. Finish tracing the line, then deselect the path.

You traced a line that has three curves joined by two straight segments. You used the technique of clicking the previous smooth point to convert it to a corner point, allowing you to change the direction of the path.

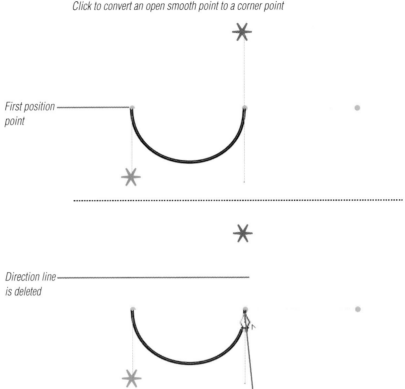

FIGURE 22
Click to convert an open smooth point to a corner point

First position point

Direction line is deleted

Clicking the last smooth point you drew converts it to a corner point

FIGURE 23

Use the Convert Anchor Point Tool to "break" the direction lines and redirect the path

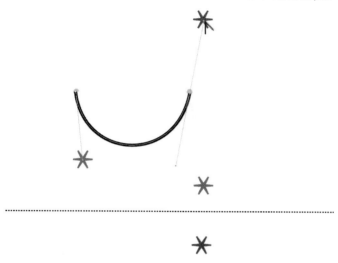

1. Click **View** on the menu bar, then click **View #3**.

2. Click the **Pen Tool** ✎, position it over the first point position, then click and drag down to the purple star.

3. Position the Pen Tool ✎ over the second point position, then click and drag up to the red star, as shown in the top section of Figure 23.

4. Press and hold **[Alt]** (Win) or **[option]** (Mac) to switch to the Convert Anchor Point Tool ⌐, then click and drag the **direction handle** on the red star down to the second purple star, as shown in the lower section of Figure 23.

   TIP Press [Alt] (Win) or [option] (Mac) to toggle between the Pen and the Convert Anchor Point Tools.

5. Release [Alt] (Win) or [option] (Mac), then continue to trace the line using the same method.

   TIP If you switch between the PenTool and the Convert Anchor Point Tool using the toolbox, instead of using [Alt] (Win) or [option] (Mac), you will disconnect from the current path.

6. Save your work, then close the Curved Lines 2 document.

You used the Convert Anchor Point Tool to "break" the direction lines of a smooth point, converting it to a corner point in the process. You used the redirected direction line to define the next curve in the sequence.

DRAW ELEMENTS OF
AN ILLUSTRATION

What You'll Do

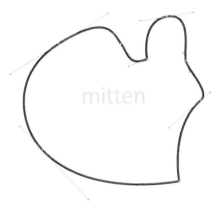

In this lesson, you will draw 14 elements of an illustration. By tracing previously drawn elements, you will develop a sense of where to place anchor points when drawing a real-world illustration.

Starting an Illustration

Getting started with drawing an illustration is often the hardest part. Sometimes the illustration will be an image of a well-known object or a supplied sketch or a picture. At other times, the illustration to be created will exist only in your imagination. In either case, the challenge is the same: How do you translate the concept from its source to the Illustrator artboard?

Drawing from Scratch

Drawing from scratch means that you start with a new Illustrator document and create the illustration, using only the Illustrator tools. This approach is common, especially when the goal is to draw familiar items such as a daisy, a fish, or the sun, for example.

Illustrator's shape tools (such as the Ellipse Tool) combined with the transform tools (such as the Rotate Tool) make the program very powerful for creating geometric designs from scratch. The Undo and Redo commands allow you to experiment, and you will often find yourself surprised by the design you end up with!

Typographic illustrations—even complex ones—are often created from scratch.

Many talented illustrators and designers are able to create complex graphics off the cuff. It can be an astounding experience to watch an illustrator start with a blank artboard and, with no reference material, produce sophisticated graphics—graphics with attitude and expression and emotion, with unexpected shapes and subtle relationships between objects.

Tracing a Scanned Image

Using the Place command, it is easy to import a scanned image into Illustrator. For complex illustrations—especially those of people or objects with delicate relationships, such as maps or blueprints—many designers find it easier to scan a sketch or a photo and import it into Illustrator as a guide or a point of reference.

Tracing a scanned image is not "cheating." An original drawing is an original drawing, whether it is first created on a computer or on a piece of paper. Rather than being a negative, the ability to use a computer to render a sketch is a fine example of the revolutionary techniques that illustration software has brought to the art of drawing. Figure 24 shows an illustration created from scratch in Illustrator, and Figure 25 shows a scanned sketch that will be the basis for the illustration you will create throughout this chapter.

FIGURE 24

An illustration created from scratch

FIGURE 25

Place a scanned sketch in Illustrator, and you can trace it or use it as a visual reference

Draw a closed path using smooth points

1. Open AI 3-4.ai, then save it as **Snowball Parts**.

2. Click **View** on the menu bar, then click **Arm**.

3. Verify that the fill color is set to [None] and the stroke color is set to Black.

4. Click the **Pen Tool** ✎, position it over point 1, then click and drag a **direction line** to the green star on the right side of the 1.

5. Go to position 2, then click and drag a **direction line** to the next green star.

    TIP   Watch the blue preview of the new segment fall into place as you drag the Pen Tool. This will help you understand when to stop dragging the direction line.

6. Using the same method, continue to draw points 3 through 6, then compare your screen to Figure 26.

7. Position the Pen Tool over point 1.

8. Press and hold **[Alt]** (Win) or **[option]** (Mac), then click and drag to position the ending segment and close the path.

You drew a curved path. To close the path, you used a corner point, which allowed you to position the ending segment without affecting the starting segment.

FIGURE 26
Points 1 through 6 are smooth points

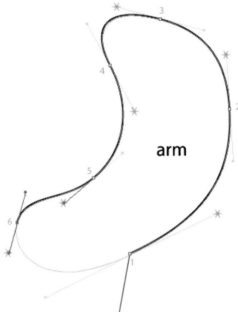

arm

When closing a path, pressing [Alt] (Win) or [option] (Mac) converts the end/start anchor point to a corner point

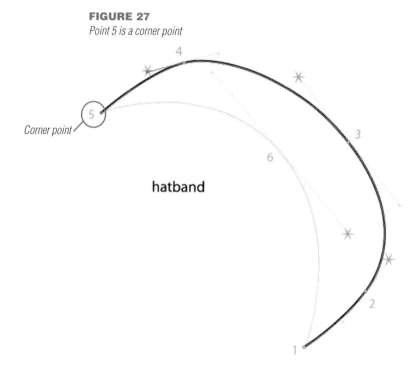

FIGURE 27
Point 5 is a corner point

Corner point

hatband

Begin and end a path with a corner point

1. Click **View** on the menu bar, then click **Hatband**.

2. Verify that the fill color is set to [None] and the stroke color is set to Black.

3. Click the **Pen Tool** 🖋, then click **position 1** to create a corner point.

4. Draw the next two curved segments for positions 2 and 3, using the green stars as guides.

5. Position the Pen Tool over position 4, then click and drag to the green star.

6. Click **position 5** to create a corner point, as shown in Figure 27.

7. Position the Pen Tool over position 6, then click and drag to the green star.

8. Click **position 1** to close the path with a corner point.

9. Click the **Selection Tool** ▶, then deselect the path.

You began a path with a corner point. When it was time to close the path, you simply clicked the starting point. Since the point was created without direction lines, there were no direction lines to contend with when closing the path.

Redirect a path while drawing

1. Click **View** on the menu bar, then click **Nose**.

   The Nose view includes the nose, mouth, eyebrow, and teeth.

2. Click the **Pen Tool** 🖊️, then click **point 1** on the nose to start the path with a corner point.

3. Create smooth points at positions 2 and 3.

   The direction of the nose that you are tracing abruptly changes at point 3.

4. Press and hold **[Alt]** (Win) or **[option]** (Mac) to switch to the Convert Anchor Point Tool Ⴖ, then move the top direction handle of point 3 down to the red star, as shown in Figure 28.

5. Release [Alt] (Win) or [option] (Mac) to switch back to the Pen Tool, click and drag **position 4** to finish drawing the path, click the Selection Tool 🔺, then deselect the path.

   The nose element, as shown in Figure 29, is an open path.

Tracing the nose, you encountered an abrupt change in direction, followed by a curve. You used the Convert Anchor Point Tool to redirect the direction lines on point 3, simultaneously converting point 3 from smooth to corner and defining the shape of the curved segment that follows.

FIGURE 28
Use the Convert Anchor Point Tool to redirect the path

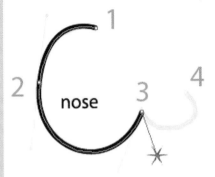

FIGURE 29
Nose element is an open path

Drawing and Composing an Illustration

FIGURE 30

Use a scanned sketch as a reference or for tracing

1. Click **View** on the menu bar, then click **Fit in Window**.

2. Click **File** on the menu bar, then click **Place**.

3. Navigate to the drive and folder where your Data Files are stored.

4. Click **Snowball Sketch.tif**, then click **Place**.

   A scan of the Snowball Sketch illustration is placed in a bounding box at the center of the artboard.

5. Use the Scale Tool 🔲 to scale the placed file 115%.

   | TIP   You can apply all of the transform tools to placed files.

6. Click the **Selection Tool** ▶ , move the placed file into the scratch area, then lock it.

7. Draw the remaining elements of the illustration, referring to the sketch in the scratch area or to Figure 30 for help.

   | TIP   The mouth, eyebrow, and teeth are located in the Nose view.

8. Save your work after you complete each element.

You placed a file of a scanned sketch to use as a reference guide. You scaled the object, dragged it to the scratch area, locked it, then drew the remaining elements of the illustration.

APPLY ATTRIBUTES
TO OBJECTS

What You'll Do

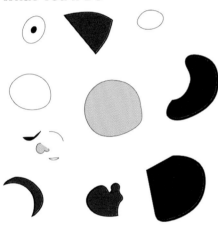

▶ *You will create four new colors in the Color palette and apply each to one of the illustration elements. Using the Eyedropper Tool, you will paint the remaining items quickly and easily.*

Using the Eyedropper Tool

Illustrator uses the word **attributes** to refer to that which has been applied to an object that affects its appearance. Typographic attributes, for example, would include font, leading, horizontal scale, etc. Artistic attributes include the fill color, stroke color, and stroke weight.

The Eyedropper Tool is handy for applying *all* of an object's attributes to another object. Its icon is particularly apt: The Eyedropper Tool "picks up" an object's attributes, such as fill color, stroke color, and stroke weight.

> QUICKTIP
>
> You can think of the Eyedropper Tool as taking a sample of an object's attributes.

The Eyedropper Tool is particularly useful when you want to apply one object's attrib-
utes to another. For example, if you have appplied a blue fill with a 3.5 pt orange stroke to an object, you can easily apply those attributes to new or already-existing objects. Simply select the object that you want to format, then click the formatted object with the Eyedropper Tool.

This is a simple example, but don't under-estimate the power of the Eyedropper Tool. As you explore more of Illustrator, you will find that you are able to apply a variety of increasingly complex attributes to objects. The more – and more complex – the attrib-utes, the more the Eyedropper Tool reveals its usefulness.

You can also use the Eyedropper Tool to copy type formatting and effects between text elements. This can be especially useful when designing display type for headlines.

Adding a Fill to an Open Path

You can think of the letter O as an example of a closed path and the letter U as an example of an open path. Although it seems a bit strange, you are able to add a fill to an open path just as you would to a closed path. The program draws an imaginary straight line between the endpoints of an open path to define where the fill ends. Figure 31 shows an open path in the shape of a U with a red fill. Note where the fill ends. For the most part, avoid applying fills to open paths. Though Illustrator will apply the fill, an open path's primary role is to feature a stroke. Any effect that you can create by filling an open path you can also create with a more effective method by filling a closed path.

FIGURE 31
A fill color applied to an open path

Apply new attributes to open and closed paths

1. Verify that nothing is selected on the artboard.

2. Create a royal blue color in the Color palette.

3. Fill the arm with the royal blue color, then change its stroke weight to 6 pt.

   TIP Use the views at the bottom of the View menu to see and select each element you need to work with. The mouth, eyebrow, and teeth are located in the Nose view.

4. Deselect the arm, then create a deep red color in the Color palette.

5. Fill the hatband with the deep red color, then change its stroke weight to 3 pt.

6. Deselect the hatband, then create a flesh-toned color in the Color palette that is 20% magenta and 56% yellow.

7. Fill the head with the flesh tone; don't change the stroke weight.

8. Fill the pompom with White; don't change the stroke weight.

9. Fill the mouth with Black; don't change the stroke weight.

10. Compare your work with Figure 32.

You applied new attributes to five closed paths by creating three new colors, using them as fills, then changing the stroke weight on two of the objects.

FIGURE 32
New attributes applied to five elements

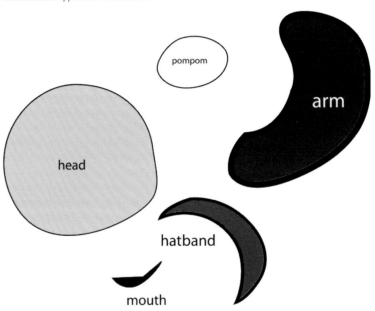

Drawing and Composing an Illustration

FIGURE 33
Use the Eyedropper Tool to apply the attributes of one object to another . . . with one click!

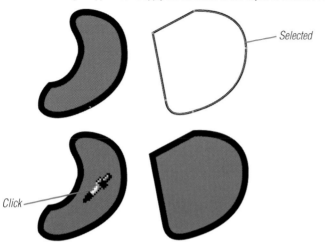

Selected

Click

FIGURE 34
All elements ready to be assembled

Copy attributes with the Eyedropper Tool

1. Select the torso.

2. Click the **Eyedropper Tool** , then click the **blue arm**.

   As shown in Figure 33, the torso takes on the same fill and stroke attributes as the arm.

3. Switch to the Selection Tool , select the hat, click the **Eyedropper Tool** then click the **hatband**.

4. Using any method you like, fill and stroke the remaining objects using the colors shown in Figure 34.

You applied the same attributes from one object to another by first selecting the object you wanted to apply the attributes to, then clicking the object with the desired attributes, using the Eyedropper Tool.

ASSEMBLE AN ILLUSTRATION

What You'll Do

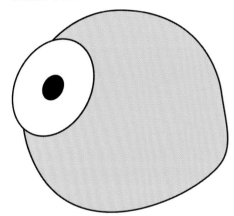

In this lesson, you will arrange the elements that you drew in Lesson 4 to create a composed illustration.

Assembling an Illustration

Illustrator's basic stacking order design is sophisticated enough to compose any illustration. Assembling an illustration with multiple objects will test your fluency with the stacking order commands: Bring to Front, Send to Back, Bring Forward, Send Backward, Paste in Front, Paste in Back, Group, Lock, Unlock All, Hide, and Show All. The sequence in which you draw the elements determines the stacking order (newer elements are in front of older ones), so you'll almost certainly need to adjust the stacking order when assembling the elements. Locking and hiding placed elements will help you to protect the elements when they are positioned correctly.

FIGURE 35
Eye positioned on the head

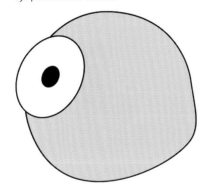

FIGURE 36
Second eye is a copy of the first

FIGURE 37
Nose pasted in front of the left eye

The nose behind
the left eye

The nose in front
of the left eye

FIGURE 39
All elements in position

Lesson 5   Assemble an Illustration

FIGURE 38
Eyebrow positioned over the right eye

Assemble the illustration

1. Select and copy all the elements on the artboard.
2. Create a new CMYK Color document that is 9" × 9", then save it as **Snowball Assembled**.
3. Paste the copied elements into the Snowball Assembled document.
4. Deselect all objects, select the head, click **Object** on the menu bar, point to **Arrange**, then click **Send to Back**.
5. Group the eye and the iris, then position the eye on the head as shown in Figure 35.
6. Click the **eye**, press **[Alt]** (Win) or **[option]** (Mac), then drag to create a copy of it, as shown in Figure 36.
7. Position the nose on the face, cut the nose, select the left eye, then paste in front.

   The nose is pasted in the same position, but now it is in front of the eye, as shown in Figure 37.
8. Select the teeth, then bring them to the front.
9. Position the teeth over the mouth, then group them.
10. Position the mouth and the teeth on the head, and the eyebrow over the right eye, as shown in Figure 38.
11. Finish assembling the illustration, using Figure 39 as a guide, then save your work.

   TIP   Use the Object menu and the Arrange menu command to change the stacking order of objects, as necessary.

You assembled the illustration, utilizing various commands to change the stacking order of the individual elements.

ILLUSTRATOR 3-29

STROKE OBJECTS FOR
ARTISTIC EFFECT

What You'll Do

In this lesson, you will experiment with strokes of varying weight and attributes, using options in the Stroke palette. You will then apply pseudo-strokes to all of the objects to create dramatic stroke effects.

Defining Joins and Caps

In addition to applying a stroke weight, you use the Stroke palette to define other stroke attributes, including joins and caps, and whether a stroke is solid or dashed. Figure 40 shows the Dashed Line utility in the Stroke palette.

Caps are applied to the ends of stroked paths. The Stroke palette offers three choices: Butt Cap, Round Cap, and Projecting Cap. Choose Butt Cap for squared ends and Round Cap for rounded ends. Generally, round caps are more appealing to the eye.

The projecting cap applies a squared edge that extends the anchor point at a distance that is one-half the weight of the stroke. With a projecting cap, the weight of the stroke is equal in all directions around the line. The projecting cap is useful when you align two anchor points at a right angle, as shown in Figure 41.

FIGURE 40
Stroke palette

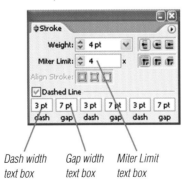

Dash width
text box

Gap width
text box

Miter Limit
text box

FIGURE 41
Projecting caps are useful when segments meet at right angles

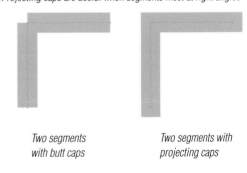

Two segments
with butt caps

Two segments with
projecting caps

When two stroked paths form a corner point, **joins** define the appearance of the corner. The default is a miter join, which produces stroked lines with pointed corners. The round join produces stroked lines with rounded corners, and the bevel join produces stroked lines with squared corners. The greater the weight of the stroke, the more apparent the join will be, as shown in Figure 42.

Defining the Miter Limit

The miter limit determines when a miter join will be squared off to a beveled edge. The miter is the length of the point, from the inside to the outside. The length of the miter is not the same as the stroke weight. When two stroked paths are at an acute angle, the length of the miter will greatly exceed the weight of the stroke, which results in an extreme point that can be very distracting.

QUICKTIP
You can align a stroke to the center, inside, or outside of a path using the Align Stroke buttons on the Stroke palette.

The default miter limit is 4, which means that when the length of the miter reaches 4 times the stroke weight, the program will automatically square it off to a beveled edge. Generally, you will find the default miter limit satisfactory, but remain conscious of it when you draw objects with acute angles, such as stars and triangles. Figure 43 shows the impact of a miter limit on a stroked star with acute angles.

FIGURE 42
Three types of joins

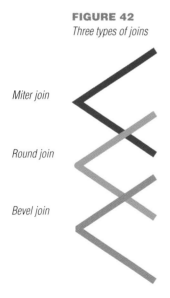

Miter join

Round join

Bevel join

FIGURE 43
Miter limit affects the length of stroked corner points

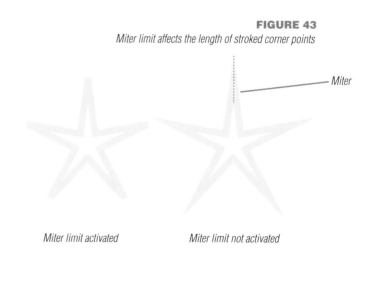

Miter

Miter limit activated   *Miter limit not activated*

Creating a Dashed Stroke

A dashed stroke is like any other stroked path in Illustrator, except that its stroke has been broken up into a sequence of dashes separated by gaps. The Stroke palette offers you the freedom to customize dashed or dotted lines; enter the lengths of the dashes and the gaps between them in the six dash and gap text boxes. You can create a maximum of three different sizes of dashes separated by three different sizes of gaps. The pattern you establish will be repeated across the length of the stroke.

When creating dashed strokes, remain conscious of the cap choice in the Stroke palette. Butt caps create familiar square dashes, and round caps create rounded dashes. Creating a dotted line requires round caps. Figure 44 shows two dashed lines using the same pattern but with different caps applied.

Creating Pseudo-Stroke Effects

Strokes around objects—especially black strokes—often contribute much to an illustration in terms of contrast, dimension, and dramatic effect. To that end, you may find the Stroke palette to be limited.

Sometimes, the most effective stroke is no stroke at all. A classic technique that designers have used since the early versions of Illustrator is the "pseudo-stroke," or false stroke. Basically, you place a black-filled copy behind an illustration element, then distort the black element with the Direct Selection Tool so that it "peeks" out from behind the element in varying degrees.

This technique, as shown in Figure 45, is relatively simple to execute and can be used for dramatic effect in an illustration.

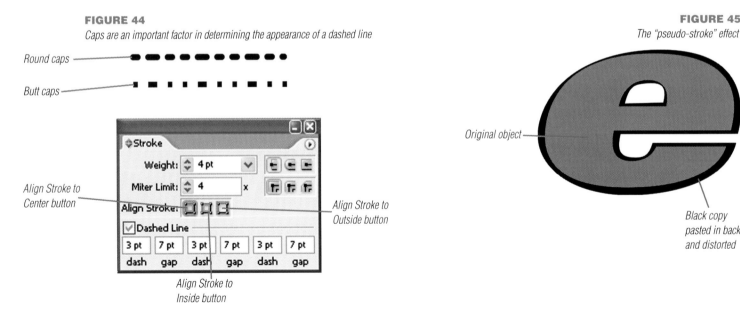

FIGURE 44
Caps are an important factor in determining the appearance of a dashed line

Round caps

Butt caps

Align Stroke to Center button

Align Stroke to Outside button

Align Stroke to Inside button

FIGURE 45
The "pseudo-stroke" effect

Original object

Black copy pasted in back and distorted

FIGURE 46

Bevel joins applied to paths

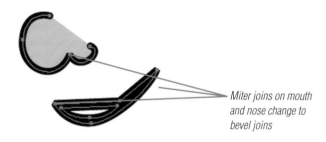

Miter joins on mouth
and nose change to
bevel joins

FIGURE 47

Round joins applied to paths

Bevel joins on mouth
and nose change to
round joins

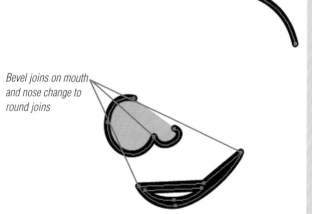

Modify stroke attributes

1. Select the eyebrow, the nose, and the mouth.

2. Click **Select** on the menu bar, then click **Inverse**.

   The selected items are now deselected, and the deselected items are selected.

3. Hide the selected items.

4. Select all, then change the stroke weight to 3 pt.

5. Click the **Stroke palette list arrow**, click **Show Options** if necessary, then click the **Round Cap button** ☜.

   The caps on open paths are rounded.

6. Click the **Bevel Join button** 🔳.

   The miter joins on the mouth and nose change to a bevel join, as shown in Figure 46.

7. Click the **Round Join button** 🔳.

   The bevel joins on the mouth and nose change to round joins, as shown in Figure 47.

8. Remove the stroke from the teeth.

   TIP Use the Direct Selection Tool to select the teeth, since they are grouped to the mouth.

You hid elements so you could focus on the eyebrow, nose, and mouth. You applied round caps to the open paths and round joins to the corner points.

Create a dashed stroke

1. Show all objects, then select all.

2. Deselect the snowball, then hide the selected items.

   The snowball should be the only element showing.

3. Select the snowball, then change the stroke weight to 4 pt.

4. Click the **Dashed Line check box** in the Stroke palette.

5. Experiment with different dash and gap sizes.

6. Toggle between butt and round caps.

   The dashes change from rectangles to ovals.

7. Enter 1 pt dashes and 4 pt gaps.

8. Click the **Round Cap button** ⊑, compare your snowball to the one shown in Figure 48, then show all of the objects that are currently hidden.

You applied a dashed stroke to the snowball object and noted how a change in caps affected the dashes.

FIGURE 48

Creating a dashed stroke using the Stroke palette

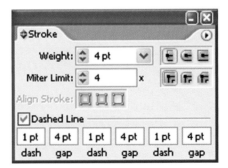

Drawing and Composing an Illustration

FIGURE 49
A black copy peeking out beneath the front object

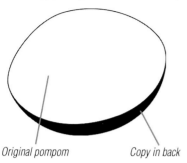

Original pompom   Copy in back

FIGURE 51
Completed illustration

FIGURE 50
Pompom with the pseudo-stroke effect

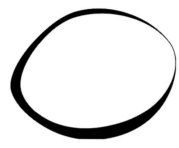

Create pseudo-strokes

1. Copy the pompom, then paste in back.

2. Apply a black fill to the copy.

   TIP The copy is still selected behind the original white pompom, making it easy to apply the black fill.

3. Click the **white pompom**, then remove the stroke.

4. Lock the white pompom.

5. Using the Direct Selection Tool ▸, select the bottom anchor point on the black copy.

6. Use the arrow keys to move the anchor point 5 pts down, away from the white pompom, using Figure 49 as a reference.

   The black copy is increasingly revealed as its size is increased beneath the locked white pompom.

7. Move the left anchor point 4 pts to the left.

8. Move the top anchor point 2 pts up, then deselect.

   Your work should resemble Figure 51.

9. Using the same methods, and Figure 52 as a reference, create distorted black copies behind all the remaining elements except the torso, the mouth, and the eyebrow.

10. Save your work, then close Snowball Assembled.

You created black copies behind each element, then distorted them, using the Direct Selection Tool and the arrow keys, to create the illusion of uneven black strokes around the object.

USE LIVE TRACE AND THE
LIVE PAINT BUCKET TOOL

What You'll Do

In this lesson, you will use the Live Trace and Live Paint features.

Introducing Live Trace

Have you ever roughed out a sketch on paper, only to have to recreate it from scratch on your computer? Or, have you ever wished that you could convert a scanned photograph into editable vector graphics to use as the basis of an illustration? With Live Trace, you can have Illustrator trace a graphic for you.

Live Trace is a new tracing feature in Illustrator CS2 that traces bitmap artwork and converts it into Illustrator vector graphics. Adobe is touting the new feature as being "ground-breaking," and in truth, it is. If you are familiar with Adobe Streamline,

another tracing utility from Adobe that has been around for years, you know that tracing a bitmap graphic and converting it to vector graphics is nothing new. However, Live Trace takes the utility to a new stage.

Live Trace offers a number of built-in tracing presets that help you fine-tune your tracing results from the start. Additional presets, such as Hand Drawn Sketch, Comic Art, and Detailed Illustration, help create even extra special effects.

So what is the "live" in Live Trace, you ask? The live aspects of Live Trace occur in the Tracing Options dialog box, shown in Figure 52. Here, you can click the Preset

FIGURE 52
Tracing Options dialog box

Hand Drawn
Sketch preset

list arrow to choose which type of preset you want to use to trace the bitmap (in the figure, Hand Drawn Sketch is the chosen preset). To see the resulting artwork before you close the dialog box, click the Preview check box. You can also continue to manipulate the graphic by changing the many settings in the Adjustments and Trace Settings sections of the dialog box. Illustrator will continually retrace the graphic to preview the final effect. That's the live part of Live Trace!

Tracing a Line-Art Sketch

Figure 53 shows a magic marker sketch of a dog that has been scanned into

Photoshop and placed in Illustrator CS2. Figure 54 shows the artwork after it has been traced using the default Live Trace settings. Not much difference, you say? Well, that's a good thing, a testament to how accurately Live Trace does its job.

As you were undoubtedly taught years ago, appearances can be deceiving. Though the artwork in 53 and 54 appears similar, they couldn't be more different, because the artwork in 54 is a vector graphic that has been traced from the bitmap graphic shown in 54.

Expanding a Traced Graphic

When a bitmap image is selected in Illustrator, the Live Trace button becomes available on the Control palette. After Live Trace has been executed, the Expand button becomes available in the Control palette. In order to select and modify the paths and points that make up the new vector graphic, you must first click the Expand button. Once done, the illustration is able to be selected and modified, as shown in Figure 55.

QUICKTIP

Figure 55 shows the artwork in Outline mode so that you can better see the paths and points.

FIGURE 54
Traced graphic

FIGURE 53
Bitmap graphic placed in Illustrator CS2

FIGURE 55
Expanded traced graphic, in Outline mode

Tracing a Photograph

You use Live Trace to trace a bitmap photo the same way you trace a sketch. With photographic images, however, the settings in the Tracing Options dialog box can be used to create some very interesting illustration effects.

Figure 56 shows a scanned photograph that has been placed in Illustrator CS2. Clicking the Live Trace button instructs Illustrator to trace the photo using the default Black & White setting. The result is shown in Figure 57.

TIP
The default Black & White setting is 128 Threshold.

The resulting graphic is not the only result possible—not by a long shot. Rather than use the default setting, you can click the Tracing presets and options list arrow on the Control panel and choose from a variety of styles, such as Comic Art or Technical Drawing. The Tracing presets and options list arrow is also available in the Tracing Options dialog box.

FIGURE 56
Scanned photograph placed in Illustrator CS2

FIGURE 57
Photograph traced at default Black & White setting

Introducing Live Paint

Adobe is touting the Live Paint Bucket Tool as being "revolutionary," and it's not an overstatement. The Live Paint Bucket Tool breaks all the fundamental rules of Illustrator, and creates some new ones. For that reason, when you are working with the Live Paint Bucket Tool, it's a good idea to think of yourself as working in Live Paint *mode*, because Illustrator will function differently with this tool than it will with any other.

Essentially, the Live Paint Bucket Tool is designed to make painting easier and more intuitive. It does this by changing the basic rules of Illustrator objects. In Live Paint mode, the concept of layers no longer applies—selected objects are all on the same level. The Live Paint Bucket Tool uses two new Illustrator object types called regions and edges. Regions and edges are comparable to fills and strokes, but they are "live." As shown in Figure 58, where two regions overlap, a third region is created and can be painted with its own color. Where two edges overlap, a third edge is created. It too can be painted its own color.

Adobe likes to say that Live Paint is intuitive—something that looks like it should be able to be filled with its own color can indeed be filled with its own color. As long as you have the Live Paint Bucket Tool selected, selected objects can be filled using the new rules of Live Paint mode. Once you leave Live Paint mode, the paint that you have applied to the graphic remains part of the illustration.

FIGURE 58
Identifying regions and edges in an illustration

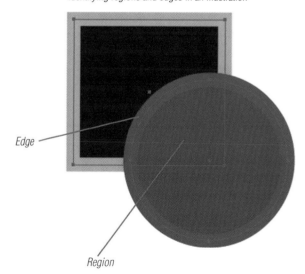

Edge

Region

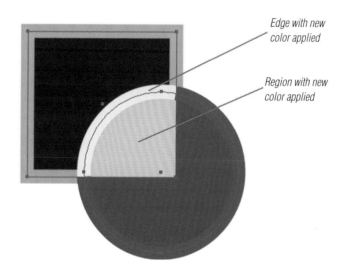

Edge with new
color applied

Region with new
color applied

Live Painting Regions

To paint objects with the Live Paint Bucket Tool, you must first select the objects you wish to paint. Figure 59 shows three selected rectangles that overlap each other. The selection marks show various shapes created by the overlapping. As stated earlier, these overlapping areas or shapes are called regions. To fill the regions, click the Live Paint Bucket Tool, click a color in the Swatches palette, then click a region that you want to fill. As shown in Figure 60, when you position the Live Paint Bucket Tool pointer over a region,

that region is highlighted. Click the Live Paint Bucket Tool and the region is filled, as shown in Figure 61.

As shown in Figure 62, each region can be filled with new colors. But that's not all that the Live Paint Bucket Tool has to offer. The "live" part of Live Paint is that these regions are now part of a **live paint group**, and they maintain a dynamic relationship with each other. This means that when any of the objects is moved, the overlapping area changes shape—and fill—accordingly. For

example, in Figure 63, the tall thin rectangle has been moved to the left—note how the overlapping regions have been redrawn and how their fills have updated with the move.

FIGURE 59
Three overlapping selected rectangles

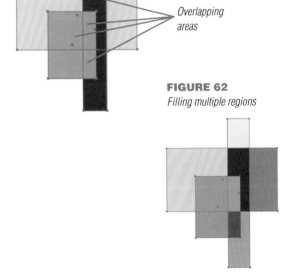

Overlapping areas

FIGURE 60
Positioning the Live Paint Bucket Tool pointer

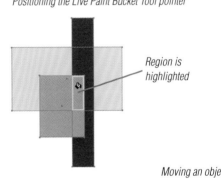

Region is highlighted

FIGURE 61
Filling a region with a new color

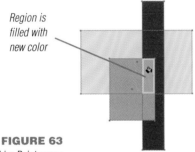

Region is filled with new color

FIGURE 62
Filling multiple regions

FIGURE 63
Moving an object in a Live Paint group

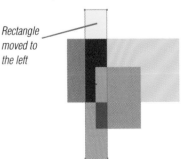

Rectangle moved to the left

Painting Virtual Regions

The intuitive aspect of Live Paint mode goes one step further with virtual regions. Figure 64 shows six Illustrator paths. Each has a 1-point black stroke and no fill—and each is selected. With the Live Paint Bucket Tool, the regions that are created by the intersection of the paths are able to be filled—as though they were objects. Figure 65 shows four regions that have been filled with the Live Paint Bucket Tool.

In this case, as in the case of the overlapping rectangles, the dynamic relationship is maintained. Figure 66 shows the same six regions having been moved, and the filled regions have been redrawn and their fills updated.

FIGURE 64
Six paths

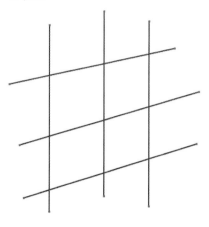

FIGURE 65
Four regions between paths filled

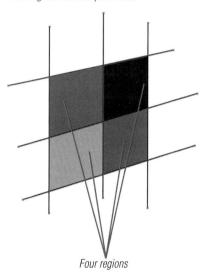

Four regions

FIGURE 66
Moving paths in a live paint group

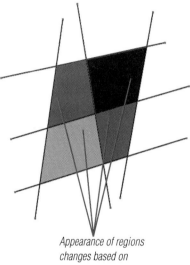

Appearance of regions changes based on paths being moved

Inserting an Object into a Live Paint Group

New objects can be inserted into a live paint group. To do so, switch to the Selection Tool, then double-click inside any of the regions of the group. As shown in Figure 67, a gray rectangle appears around the group, indicating that you are in **insertion mode**. Once in insertion mode, you can then add an object or objects to the group.

As shown in Figure 68, another tall rectangle has been added to the group. It can now be painted with the Live Paint Bucket Tool as part of the live paint group. Once you've added all that you want to the live paint group, exit insertion mode by double-clicking the Selection Tool outside of the live paint group.

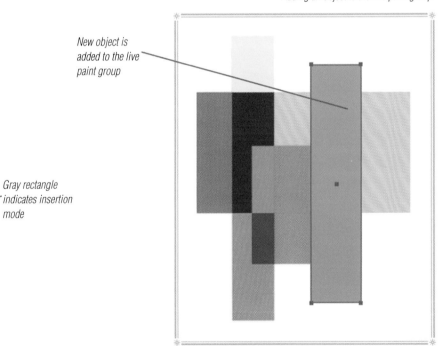

Gray rectangle indicates insertion mode

New object is added to the live paint group

Expanding a Live Paint Group

When you deselect a live paint group, the deselected group does not change its appearance. Additionally, you have the option of using the Expand command to release the Live Paint group into its component regions. Simply select the live paint group, then click the Expand button on the Control palette. Each region will be converted to an ordinary Illustrator object.

Live Painting Edges

In Live Paint mode, if regions are akin to fills, then edges are akin to strokes. With the Live Paint Bucket Tool, you can paint edges as well as regions.

Figure 69 shows two overlapping objects, each with a 6-point stroke. To paint edges (strokes), double-click the Live Paint Bucket Tool, then click the Paint Strokes check box in the Live Paint Bucket Options dialog box, as shown in Figure 70.

When you position the Live Paint Bucket Tool over an edge, its icon changes to a paint brush icon. The edge is highlighted and able to be painted as though it were its own object, as shown in 71.

FIGURE 69
Two overlapping rectangles

FIGURE 70
Specifying the Live Paint Bucket Tool to paint strokes (edges)

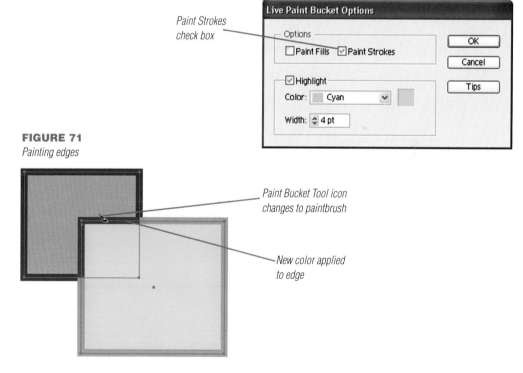

Paint Strokes check box

Paint Bucket Tool icon changes to paintbrush

New color applied to edge

FIGURE 71
Painting edges

Use Live Trace to trace a sketch

1. Open AI 3-5.ai, then save it as **Live Trace Sketch**.

   The file contains a placed marker sketch that was scanned in Photoshop.

2. Click **Window** on the menu bar, then click **Control Palette**, if necessary.

3. Click the **Selection Tool** then click the **placed graphic**.

   When the placed graphic is selected, the Live Trace button on the Control Palette becomes visible.

4. Click the **Live Trace button** on the Control Palette.

5. Click the **Expand button** on the Control Palette.

   As shown in Figure 72, the traced graphic is expanded into vector objects.

6. Deselect all, then using the Direct Selection Tool , select and fill the illustration with whatever colors you like.

   Figure 73 shows one example.

7. Save your work, then close the Live Trace Sketch document.

You used the default settings of the Live Trace utility to convert a placed sketch into Illustrator objects.

FIGURE 72
Expanding the traced graphic

FIGURE 73
One example of the painted illustration

Drawing and Composing an Illustration

FIGURE 74
Photo traced with default Black and White

Use Live Trace to trace a photo

1. Open AI 3-6.ai, then save it as **Live Trace Photo.ai**.

   The file contains three copies of a placed photo that was scanned in Photoshop.

2. Zoom in on the top photo, click the **Selection Tool**, click the **top photo,** then click the **Live Trace button** on the Control Palette.

   Using default Black and White settings, Live Trace creates the trace shown in Figure 74.

3. Deselect the image, then zoom in on the middle photo.

4. Click the **Selection Tool**, click the **middle photo**, click the **Tracing presets and options list arrow** to the right of the Live Trace button, then click **Tracing Options**.

5. Click the **Preview check box**, if necessary, to place a check mark.

6. In the Adjustments section, click the **arrow** to the right of current Threshold value, then drag the **Threshold slider** until the Threshold value reads 200.

   Live Trace redraws the graphic.

7. Drag the **Threshold slider** until the Threshold value reads 160, wait for Live Trace to redraw the graphic, then click **Trace**.

8. Drag the **middle graphic** to the right of the top graphic, then compare the two graphics to Figure 75.

FIGURE 75
Comparing a Black and White trace using different threshold values

Lesson 7   Use Live Trace and the Live Paint Bucket Tool

9. Deselect all, zoom in on the bottom photo, select it, click the **Tracing presets and options list arrow**, then click **Color 6**.

   Color 6 is a tracing preset.

10. Click the **Expand button** in the Control Palette, then deselect all.

11. Click the **Direct Selection Tool** , then select and fill the objects that make up the illustration.

   Figure 76 shows one example.

12. Save your work, then close the Live Trace Photo.

You used Live Trace to trace a photo three different ways. First, you simply clicked the Live Trace button, which executed the default Black and White trace. Next, you opened the Trace Options dialog box and specified the threshold value for the Black and White trace. Finally, you traced with the Color 6 preset.

FIGURE 76
Applying fills to the traced photo

FIGURE 77
Painting the region that is the overlap between two circles

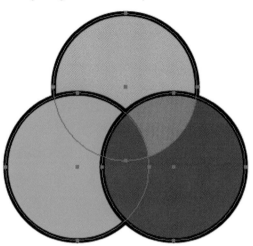

FIGURE 78
Viewing seven painted regions

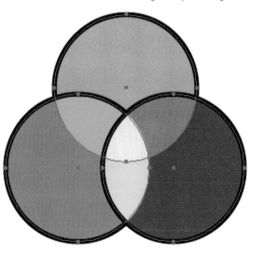

Use the Live Paint Bucket Tool

1. Open AI 3-7.ai, then save it as **Live Paint Circles**.

2. Fill the top circle with red, fill the left circle with green, then fill the right circle with blue.

3. Select all, then double-click the **Live Paint Bucket Tool** to open its options dialog box, verify that both the Paint Fills and Paint Strokes check boxes are checked, then click **OK**.

4. Click any of the orange swatches in the Swatches palette.

   Note that because you are in Live Paint mode, none of the selected objects changes to orange when you click the orange swatch.

5. Position the Live Paint Bucket Tool pointer over the red fill of the red circle, then click.

6. Click any pink swatch in the Swatches palette, position the Live Paint Bucket Tool pointer over the area where the orange circle overlaps the blue circle, then click.

   As shown in Figure 77, the region of overlap between the two circles is filled with pink.

7. Using any colors you like, fill all seven regions so that your artwork resembles Figure 78.

8. Change the Stroke button on the toolbox to any purple, position the Live Paint Bucket Tool pointer over any of the black strokes in the artwork, then click.

When positioned over a stroke, the Live Paint Bucket Tool pointer changes to a paintbrush icon.

9. Using any color you like, change the color of all twelve edges then deselect all so that your artwork resembles Figure 79.

10. Click the **Direct Selection Tool** , then, without pulling them apart, move the circles in different directions so that your artwork resembles Figure 80.

The components of the live paint group maintain a dynamic relationship.

11. Select all, click **Expand** on the Control palette, deselect all, then pull out all of the regions so that your artwork resembles Figure 81.

The illustration has been expanded into multiple objects.

12. Save your work, then close the Live Paint Circles document.

You used the Live Paint Bucket Tool to fill various regions and edges of three overlapping circles. You then moved various components of the live paint group, noting that they maintain a dynamic relationship. Finally, you expanded the live paint group, which changed your original circles into multiple objects.

FIGURE 79
Viewing twelve painted edges

FIGURE 80
Exploring the dynamic relationship between regions in a live paint group

FIGURE 81
Dissecting the expanded live paint group

Drawing and Composing an Illustration

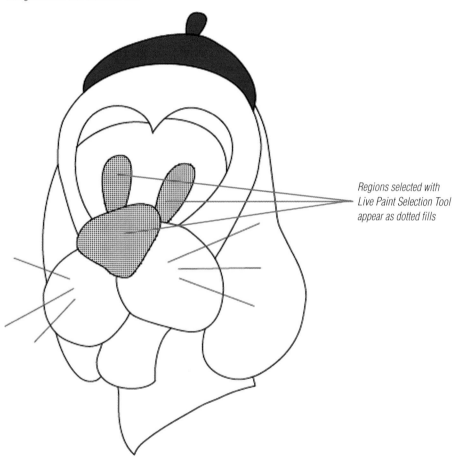

FIGURE 82
Using the Live Paint Selection Tool

*Regions selected with
Live Paint Selection Tool
appear as dotted fills*

1. Open AI 3-8.ai, then save it as **Live Paint Dog.**

2. Click the **Selection Tool** , then click the different colored strokes so that you understand how the illustration has been drawn.

   The illustration has been created with a series of open paths. The only closed path is the nose.

3. Select all, then change the stroke of all the paths to Black.

4. Click the **Live Paint Bucket Tool** , then click a **red swatch** in the Swatches palette.

   Note that because you are in Live Paint mode, none of the selected objects changes to red when you click the red swatch.

5. Fill the hat and the knot at the top of the hat with red, then click **Black** in the Swatches palette.

6. Click the **Live Paint Selection Tool** , click the **nose,** press and hold **[Shift]**, click the **left eye**, then click the **right eye.**

   Your illustration should resemble Figure 82.

   > TIP   When you select multiple areas with the Live Paint Selection Tool, the areas are filled with a dot pattern until you apply a color.

7. Click **Black** in the Swatches palette.

8. Using the same method, select both eyelids, then fill them with a lavender swatch.

9. Click the **Live Paint Bucket Tool** , click a **yellow swatch** in the Swatches palette, then paint the illustration so that your illustration resembles Figure 83.

   Note the small areas between the whiskers that must be painted yellow.

10. Using the Live Paint Bucket Tool , paint the right jowl light brown, paint the left jowl a darker brown, then paint the tongue pink.

11. Click the **Stroke button** in the toolbox to activate the stroke, then click a **gray swatch** in the Swatches palette.

12. Double-click the **Live Paint Bucket Tool** , click the **Paint Stroke check box** in the Live Paint Bucket Options dialog box, then click **OK**.

FIGURE 83
Painting the yellow regions

FIGURE 84
Viewing the finished artwork

13. Paint the edges that draw the whiskers.

> TIP You will need to click 14 times to paint the six whiskers.

14. Deselect, compare your work to Figure 84, save your work, then close the Live Paint Dog document.

You used the Live Paint Bucket Tool to fill regions created by the intersection of a collection of open paths. You also used the tool to paint edges.

Draw straight lines.

1. Open AI 3-9.ai, then save it as **Montag**.
2. Place the Montag Sketch.tif from the drive and folder where your Data Files are stored into the Montag document.
3. Position the sketch in the center of the art-board, then lock it.
4. Set the fill color to [None] and the stroke to 1 pt black.
5. Use the Pen Tool to create a four-sided poly-gon for the neck. (*Hint*: Refer to Figure 53 as a guide.)
6. Draw six whiskers.
7. Save your work.

Draw curved lines.

1. Using the Pen Tool, draw an oval for the eye.
2. Draw a crescent moon shape for the eyelid.
3. Draw an oval for the iris.
4. Save your work.

Draw elements of an illustration.

1. Trace the left ear.
2. Trace the hat.
3. Trace the nose.
4. Trace the left jowl.
5. Trace the right jowl.
6. Trace the tongue.
7. Trace the right ear.
8. Trace the head.
9. Save your work.

Copy attributes between objects.

1. Unlock the placed sketch and hide it.
2. Fill the hat with a red swatch.
3. Fill the right ear with 9C/18M/62Y.
4. Fill the nose with black.
5. Fill the eye with white.
6. Fill the tongue with salmon.
7. Using Figure 53 as a guide, use the colors in the Swatches palette to finish the illustration.
8. Save your work.

Assemble an illustration.

1. Send the neck to the back of the stacking order, then lock it.
2. Send the head to the back, then lock it.
3. Send the left ear to the back, then lock it.
4. Bring the hat to the front.
5. Bring the right ear to the front.
6. Select the whiskers, group them, then bring them to the front.
7. Select the tongue, then cut it.
8. Select the right jowl, then apply the Paste in Back command.
9. Bring the nose to the front.
10. Select the eye, the eyelid, and the iris, then group them.
11. Drag and drop a copy of the eye group. (*Hint*: Press and hold [Alt] (Win) or [option] (Mac) as you drag the eye group.)
12. Select the right jowl.
13. In the Color palette, add 10% K to darken the jowl.
14. Use the Color palette to change the fills on other objects to your liking.
15. Save your work.

Stroke objects for artistic effect.

1. Make the caps on the whiskers round.
2. Change the whiskers' stroke weight to .5 pt.
3. Unlock all.
4. Select the neck and change the joins to round.
5. Apply pseudo-strokes to the illustration. (*Hint*: Copy and paste the elements behind themselves, fill them with black, lock the top objects, then use the Direct Selection Tool to select anchor points on the black-filled copies. Use the arrow keys on the keyboard to move the anchor points. The black copies will peek out from behind the elements in front.)
6. Click Object on the menu bar, then click Unlock All.
7. Delete the Montag Sketch file behind your illustration.
8. Save your work, compare your illustration to Figure 53, then close Montag.

FIGURE 53
Completed Skills Review

The owner of The Blue Peppermill Restaurant has hired your design firm to take over all of their marketing and advertising, saying they need to expand their efforts. You request all of their existing materials—slides, prints, digital files, brochures, business cards, etc. Upon examination, you realize that they have no vector graphic version of their logo. Deciding that this is an indispensable element for future design and production, you scan in a photo of their signature peppermill, trace it, and apply a blue fill to it.

1. Create a new 6" × 6" CMYK Color document, then save it as **Peppermill Vector**.
2. Place the Peppermill.tif file into the Peppermill Vector document. (*Hint*: The Peppermill.tif file is in the Chapter 3 Data Files folder.)
3. Scale the placed image 150%, then lock it.
4. Set your fill color to [None], and your stroke to 2 pt black.
5. Using the Zoom Tool, create a selection box around the round element at the top of the peppermill to zoom in on it.
6. Using the Pen Tool, trace the peppermill, then fill it with a blue swatch.
7. When you finish tracing, tweak the path if necessary, then save your work.

8. Unlock the placed image and cut it from the document.

FIGURE 54
Completed Project Builder 1

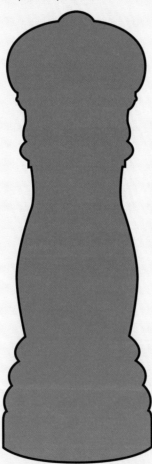

9. Save your work, compare your illustration to Figure 54, then close Peppermill Vector.

USAchefs.com, your client of three years, contacts you with bad news. They have accidentally deleted their Illustrator "chef logo" from the backup server. They need the vector graphic to produce many of their materials. Their first designer has all the original files, but he has retired to a small island in the Caribbean and cannot be contacted. They want to know if there's anything you can do to recreate the vector graphic.

1. Connect to the Internet, go to *www.course.com*, navigate to the page for this book, click the Online Companion link, then click the link for this chapter.
2. Right-click (Win) or [control] click (Mac) the logo of the chef, click Save Picture As (Win) or Save Image As (Mac), then save it in your Chapter 3 Solution Files folder, keeping the same name.
3. Create a new 6" × 6" CMYK Color document, then save it as **USAchefs Logo**.
4. Place the chef logo file into the document and lock it.
5. Zoom in on the chef logo so that you are at a comfortable view for tracing. (*Hint*: Use the Zoom Tool to create a selection box around the logo.)
6. Set your fill color to [None] and your stroke to 1 pt red.
7. Use the Ellipse Tool to trace the head.

8. Use the Pen Tool to trace the hat and the perimeter of the body.
9. Trace the two triangles that define the chef's inner arms.
10. Unlock the placed image and cut it from the document.
11. Fill the head, the hat, and the body with White.

FIGURE 55
Completed Project Builder 2

12. Fill the triangles with Starry Night Blue.
13. Remove the strokes from the objects.
14. Create a rectangle that encompasses the chef objects, then fill it with Starry Night Blue.
15. Send the rectangle to the back of the stacking order.
16. Save your work, compare your illustration to Figure 55, then close USAchefs Logo.

Drawing and Composing an Illustration

Your design firm is contacted by a company called Stratagem with a request for a proposal. They manufacture molds for plastic products. The terms of the request are as follows: You are to submit a design for the shape of the bottle for a new dishwashing liquid. You are to submit a single image that shows a black line defining the shape. The line art should also include the nozzle. The size of the bottle is immaterial. The design is to be "sophisticated, so as to be in visual harmony with the modern home kitchen." The name of the product is "Sleek."

1. Go to the grocery store and purchase bottles of dishwashing liquid whose shape you find interesting.
2. Use the purchases for ideas and inspiration.
3. Sketch your idea for the bottle's shape on a piece of paper.
4. Scan the sketch and save it as a TIFF file.
5. Create a new Illustrator document, then save it as **Sleek**.
6. Place the scan in the document, then lock it.
7. Trace your sketch, using the Pen Tool.
8. When you are done tracing, delete the sketch from the document.
9. Tweak the line to define the shape to your specifications.
10. Use the Average dialog box to align points to perfect the shape.
11. Save your work, compare your illustration to Figure 56, then close Sleek.

FIGURE 56
Completed Design Project

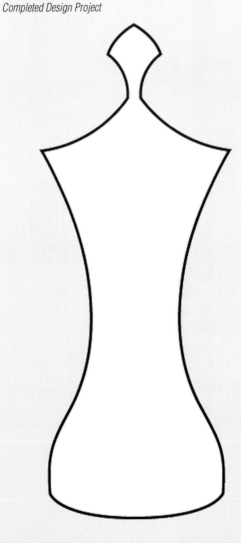

You teach a class on digital graphics to junior designers. To stimulate a discussion on shape and design theory, you show the 20-minute "Dawn of Man" sequence of the classic sci-fi movie *2001: A Space Odyssey*.

Note: The central point of this exercise—a group discussion of shapes and their role in the history of mankind—can be had with or without screening *2001: A Space Odyssey*. Should you choose to not show the film, simply omit questions 1 and 2. Rephrase Question 8 so that individuals are instructed to draw any abstract shape from their own imaginations.

The sequence begins millions of years ago with a group of apes, presumably on the African plains. One day, *impossibly*, a tall, black, perfectly rectangular slab appears out of nowhere on the landscape. At first the apes are afraid of it, afraid to touch it. Eventually, they accept its presence.

Later, one ape looks upon a femur bone from a dead animal. With a dawning understanding, he uses the bone as a tool, first to kill for food, and then to kill another ape from an enemy group. Victorious in battle, the ape hurls the bone into the air. The camera follows it up, up, up, and—in one of the most famous cuts in film history—the image switches from the white bone in the sky to the similar shape of a white spaceship floating in space.

1. Have everyone in the group share his or her feelings upon first seeing the "monolith" (the black rectangular slab). What percentage of the group was frightened? Does the group sense that the monolith is good, evil, or neutral?
2. Discuss the sudden appearance of the straight-edged, right-angled monolith against the landscape. What words describe the shapes of the landscape in contrast to the monolith?
3. Have the group debate a central question: Do perfect shapes exist in nature, or are they created entirely out of the imagination of human beings?
4. If perfect shapes exist—if they are *real*—can you name one example? If they are not real, how is it that humankind has proven so many concepts in mathematics that are based on shapes, such as the Pythagorean theorem?
5. What advancements and achievements of humankind have their basis in peoples' ability to conceive of abstract shapes?
6. Can it be said legitimately that the ability to conceive abstract shapes is an essential factor that distinguishes humankind from all the other species on the planet?
7. Create a new document, then save it as **Shape**.
8. Give the members of the group 10 minutes to draw, in Adobe Illustrator, any shape that they remember from the opening sequence, *except* the monolith. When the group has finished, take a count: How many rendered a shape based on the bone?
9. Save your work, compare your results to Figure 57, then close Shape.

FIGURE 57
Completed Group Project

chapter

chapter

4

TRANSFORMING AND
DISTORTING OBJECTS

1. Transform objects.

2. Offset and Outline paths.

3. Create compound paths.

4. Work with the Pathfinder palette.

5. Create clipping masks.

Putting It All Together

Think about a conventional toolbox. You've got a hammer, nails, a few different types of screwdrivers, screws, nuts, bolts, a wrench, and probably some type of measuring device. That set of tools could be used to build anything from a birdhouse to a dollhouse to a townhouse to the White House.

A carpenter uses tools in conjunction with one another to create something, and that something is defined far less by the tools than by the imagination of the carpenter. But even the most ambitious imagination is tempered by the demands of knowing which tool to use, and when.

Illustrator offers a number of sophisticated transform "tools" in the "toolbox," and the metaphor is apt. Each "tool" provides a basic function: a rotation, a scale, a precise move, a precise offset, or a reflection. It is you, the designer, who uses those tools in combination with each other, with menu commands, and with other features, to realize your vision. And like the carpenter's, your imagination will be tempered by your ability to choose the right tool at the right time.

This is one of the most exciting aspects of working in Illustrator. After you learn the basics, there's no map, no blueprint for building an illustration. It's your skills, your experience, your smarts, and your ingenuity that lead you toward your goal. No other designer will use Illustrator's tools quite the same way you do. People who appreciate digital imagery understand this salient point: Although the tools are the same for everyone, the result is *personal*. It's *original*.

Tools You'll Use

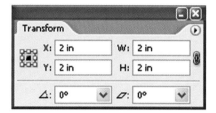

Shear Tool

Rotate Tool   Reflect Tool

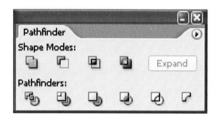

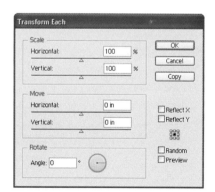

TRANSFORM
OBJECTS

What You'll Do

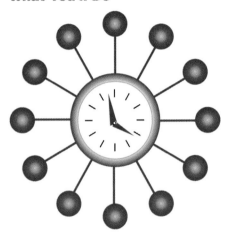

▶ *In this lesson, you will explore options for transforming objects with the transform tools.*

Defining the Transform Tools

When you change an object's size, shape, or position on the artboard, Illustrator defines that operation as a transformation. Transforming objects is a fundamental operation in Illustrator, one you will perform countless times.

Because transformations are so essential, Illustrator provides a number of methods for doing them. As you gain experience, you will naturally adopt the method that you find most comfortable or logical.

The toolbox contains five transform tools: the Rotate, Scale, Reflect, Shear, and Free Transform Tools. The essential functions of the Rotate and Scale Tools are self-explanatory. The Reflect Tool "flips" an object across an imagined axis, usually the horizontal or the vertical axis. However, you can define any diagonal as the axis for a reflection. In Figure 1, the illustration has been flipped to create the illusion of a reflection in a mirror.

The Shear Tool slants—or skews—an object on an axis that you specify. By definition, the Shear Tool distorts an object. Of the five transform tools, you will probably use the Shear Tool the least, although it is useful for creating a cast shadow or the illusion of depth.

Finally, the Free Transform Tool offers you the ability to perform quick transformations and distort objects in perspective.

Defining the Point of Origin

All transformations are executed in relation to a fixed point; in Illustrator, that point is called the **point of origin**. For each transform tool, the default point of origin is the selected object's center point. However, you can change that point to another point on the object or to a point elsewhere on the artboard. For example, when a majorette twirls a baton, that baton is essentially rotating on its own center. By contrast, the petals of a daisy rotate around a central point that is not positioned on any of the petals themselves, as shown in Figure 2.

There are four basic methods for making transformations with the transform tools. First, select an object, then do one of the following:

- Click a transform tool, then click and drag anywhere on the artboard. The

object will be transformed using its center point as the default point of origin.

- Double-click the transform tool, which opens the tool's dialog box. Enter the values by which you want to execute the transformation, then click OK. You may also click Copy to create a transformed copy of the selected object. The point of origin for the transformation will be the center point of the selected object.
- Click a transform tool, then click the artboard. Where you click the artboard defines the point of origin for the transformation. Click and drag anywhere on the artboard, and the selected

object will be transformed from the point of origin that you clicked.

- Click a transform tool, Press [Alt] (Win) or [option] (Mac), then click the artboard. The tool's dialog box opens, allowing you to enter precise values for the transformation. When you click OK or Copy, the selected object will be transformed from the point of origin that you clicked.

QUICKTIP

If you transform an object from its center point, then select another object and apply the Transform Again command, the point of origin has not been redefined, and the second object will be transformed from the center point of the first object.

FIGURE 1
The Reflect Tool flips an image horizontally or vertically

FIGURE 2
All transformations are executed from a point of origin

A baton rotating around its own center

Petals of a daisy rotate around a central point

Working with the Transform Again Command

An essential command related to transformations is Transform Again. Whenever you execute a transformation, such as scale or rotate, you can repeat the transformation quickly by using the Transform Again command. This is also true for moving an object. Using the Transform Again command will move an object the same distance and angle entered in the last step. The quickest way to use the Transform Again command is to press [Ctrl][D] (Win) or ⌘[D] (Mac). To remember this quick key command, think D for *duplicate*.

A fine example of the usefulness of the Transform Again command is its ability to make transforming in small increments easy. For example, let's say you have created an object to be used in an illustration, but you haven't decided how large the object should be. Simply scale the object by a small percentage—say 5%—then press the quick key for Transform Again repeatedly until you are happy with the results. The object gradually gets bigger, and you can choose the size that pleases your eye. If you transform again too many times, and the object gets too big, simply undo repeatedly to decrease the object's size in the same small increments.

Using the Transform Each Command

The Transform Each command allows you to transform multiple objects individually, as shown in Figure 3. The Transform Each dialog box offers options to move, scale, rotate, or reflect an object, among others. All of them will affect an object independent of the other selected objects.

Without the Transform Each command, applying a transformation to multiple objects simultaneously will often yield an undesired effect. This happens because the selected objects are transformed as a group—in relation to a single point of origin—and are repositioned on the artboard.

FIGURE 3

Multiple objects rotated individually

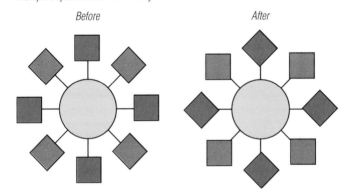

Before   *After*

The eight squares are rotated on their own center points

Using the Free Transform Tool

The Free Transform Tool applies an eight-handled bounding box to a selected image. You can move those handles to scale and shear the object. You can click and drag outside the object to rotate the object.

With the Free Transform Tool, transformations always use the selected object's center point as the point of origin. In general, the role of the Free Transform Tool is to make quick, inexact transformations. However, the tool has a powerful, hidden ability. Moving the handles in conjunction with certain keyboard commands allows you to distort the object or distort the object in perspective, as shown in Figure 4. Press and hold [Shift][Ctrl] (Win) or [Shift]⌘ (Mac) to distort the image. Press and hold [Shift][Alt][Ctrl] (Win) while dragging to distort in perspective. On a Macintosh, press and hold [Shift][option]⌘ to execute the same transformation.

Using the Transform Palette

The Transform palette displays information about the size, orientation, and location of one or more selected objects. You can type new values directly into the Transform palette to modify selected objects. All values in the palette refer to the bounding boxes of the objects, whether the bounding box is visible or not. You can also identify—in the Transform palette—the reference point on the bounding box from which the object will be transformed. To reflect an object vertically or horizontally using the Transform palette, click the Transform palette list arrow, then choose the appropriate menu item, as shown in Figure 5.

FIGURE 4
Use the Free Transform Tool to distort objects in perspective

FIGURE 5
Transform palette

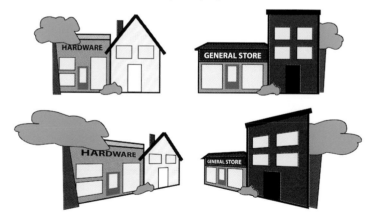

Transform palette list arrow

Rotate text box

Height text box   Width text box   Shear text box

Rotate an object around a defined point

1. Open AI 4-1.ai, then save it as **Mod Clock**.

2. Click the **Selection Tool** , click the **brown line**, then click the **Rotate Tool** .

3. Press and hold **[Alt]** (Win) or **[option]** (Mac), then click the **bottom anchor point** of the line to set the point of origin for the rotation.

   With a transform tool selected, pressing [Alt] (Win) or [option] (Mac) and clicking the artboard defines the point of origin and opens the tool's dialog box.

4. Enter **30** in the Angle text box, then click **Copy**.

5. Press **[Ctrl][D]** (Win) or **[D]** (Mac) ten times so that your screen resembles Figure 6.

   [Ctrl][D] (Win) or [D] (Mac) is the quick key for the Transform Again command.

6. Select all twelve lines, group them, send them to the back, then hide them.

7. Select the small orange circle, click **View** on the menu bar, then click **Outline**.

(continued)

FIGURE 6
Twelve paths rotated at a point

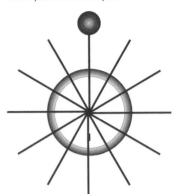

X and Y coordinates

The X and Y coordinates of an object indicate the object's horizontal (X) and vertical (Y) locations on the artboard. These numbers, which appear in the Transform palette, represent the horizontal and vertical distance from the bottom-left corner of the artboard. The current X and Y coordinates also depend on the specified reference point. Nine reference points are listed to the left of the X and Y text boxes in the Transform palette. Reference points are those points of a selected object that represent the four corners of the object's bounding box, the horizontal and vertical centers of the bounding box, and the center point of the bounding box. (You do not need to have the bounding box option turned on to view any of the reference point coordinates.)

FIGURE 7
Twelve circles rotated around a central point of origin

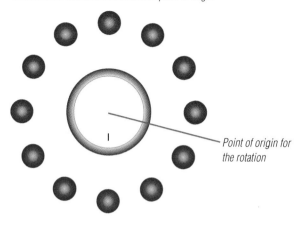

Point of origin for
the rotation

FIGURE 8
Completed illustration

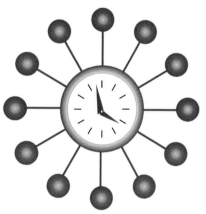

8. Click the **Rotate Tool** ⟳, press and hold **[Alt]** (Win) or **[option]** (Mac), then click the **center point** of the larger circle to set the point of origin for the next rotation.

   The small circle will rotate around the center point of the larger circle.

   > TIP Outline mode is especially useful for rotations; center points are visible and easy to target as points of origin.

9. Enter **30** if necessary, click **Copy**, apply the Transform Again command ten times, then switch to Preview mode.

   Your screen should resemble Figure 7.

10. Select the small black vertical dash, then transform again eleven times.

    The dash is also rotated around the center point of the larger circle, since a new point of origin has not been set.

11. Unlock the hands in the scratch area, then move them onto the clock face.

12. Show all, then deselect all to reveal the twelve segments, as shown in Figure 8.

13. Save your work, then close the Mod Clock.

You selected a point on the brown line, then rotated eleven copies of the object around that point. Second, you defined the point of origin for a rotation by clicking the center point of the larger circle, then rotated eleven copies of the smaller circle and the dash around that point.

Use the Shear Tool

1. Open AI 4-2.ai, then save it as **Shear**.

2. Select all, copy, paste in front, then fill the copy with 60% Black.

3. Click the **Shear Tool** ⬚.

   | TIP   The Shear Tool is hidden behind the Scale Tool.

4. Press and hold **[Alt]** (Win) or **[option]** (Mac), then click the **bottom-right anchor point** of the letter R to set the origin point of the shear and open the Shear dialog box.

5. Enter **45** in the Shear Angle text box, verify that the Horizontal option button is checked, then click **OK**.

   Your screen should resemble Figure 9.

6. Click the **Scale Tool** ⬚.

7. Press **[Alt]** (Win) or **[option]** (Mac), then click any bottom anchor point or segment on the sheared objects to set the point of origin for the scale and open the Scale dialog box.

8. Click the **Non-Uniform option button**, enter **100** in the Horizontal text box, enter **50** in the Vertical text box, then click **OK**.

9. Send the sheared objects to the back.

10. Apply a 1 pt black stroke to the orange letters, deselect, then compare your screen to Figure 10.

11. Save your work, then close the Shear document.

You created a shadow effect using the Shear Tool.

FIGURE 9
Letterforms sheared on a 45° axis

The objects are sheared on a 45° angle in relation to a horizontal axis

FIGURE 10
Shearing is useful for creating a cast-shadow effect

The shadow is "cast" from the letters in the foreground

FIGURE 11
Use the Reflect Tool for illustrations that demand exact symmetry

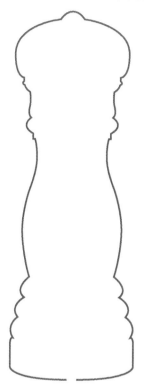

FIGURE 12

Selecting two anchor points with the Direct Selection Tool

Selection box ——

Selected anchor points

Use the Reflect Tool

1. Open AI 4-3.ai, then save it as **Reflect**.
2. Select all, then zoom in on the top anchor point.
3. Click the **Reflect Tool** .

   The Reflect Tool is hidden behind the Rotate Tool.
4. Press **[Alt]** (Win) or **[option]** (Mac), then click the **top anchor point** to set the point of origin for the reflection.
5. Click the **Vertical option button**, then click **Copy**.

   A copy is positioned, reflected across the axis that you defined, as shown in Figure 11.
6. Deselect all, then click the **Direct Selection Tool** .
7. Using Figure 12 as a guide, drag a selection box around the top two anchor points to select them.
8. Click **Object** on the menu bar, point to **Path**, click **Average**, click the **Both option button**, then click **OK**.
9. Click **Object** on the menu bar, point to **Path**, click **Join**, click the **Smooth option button**, then click **OK.**
10. Select the bottom two anchor points, average them on both axes, then join them in a smooth point to close the path.
11. Save your work, then close the Reflect document.

You created a reflected copy of a path, then averaged and joined two pairs of open points.

OFFSET AND OUTLINE PATHS

What You'll Do

 In this lesson, you will use the Offset Path command to create concentric squares and the Outline Stroke command to convert a stroked path into a closed path.

Using the Offset Path Command

Simply put, the Offset Path command creates a copy of a selected path set off by a specified distance. The Offset Path command is useful when working with closed paths—making concentric shapes or making many copies of a path at a regular distance from the original.

Figure 13 shows two sets of concentric circles. By definition, the word **concentric** refers to objects that share the same centerpoint, as the circles in both sets do. The set on the left was made with the Scale Tool, applying an 85% scale and copy to the outer circle, then repeating the transformation ten times. Note that with each successive copy, the distance from the copy to the previous circle decreases. The set on the right was made by offsetting the outside circle -.125", then applying the same offset to each successive copy. Note the different effect.

When you offset a closed path, a positive value creates a larger copy outside the original; a negative value creates a smaller copy inside the original.

Using the Outline Stroke Command

The Outline Stroke command converts a stroked path into a closed path that is the same width as the original stroked path.

This operation is useful if you want to apply a gradient to a stroke. It is also a useful design tool, allowing you to modify the outline of an object more than if it were just a stroke. Also, it is often easier to create an object with a single heavy stroke—for example the letter S—and then convert it to a closed path than it would be to try to draw a closed path directly, as shown in Figure 14.

FIGURE 13
Two sets of concentric circles

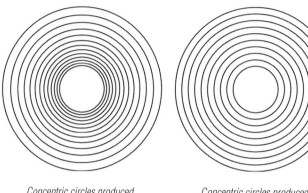

Concentric circles produced by the Scale Tool

Concentric circles produced by the Offset Path command

FIGURE 14
The Outline Stroke command converts a stroked path to a closed object

Offset a path

1. Open AI 4-4.ai, then save it as **Squares**.

2. Select the square.

3. Click **Object** on the menu bar, point to **Path**, then click **Offset Path**.

4. Enter **-.125** in the Offset text box, then click **OK**.

   | TIP   Be sure that your General Units Preference is set to inches.

   A negative value reduces the area of a closed path; a positive value increases the area.

5. Apply the Offset Path command four more times, using the same value.

   | TIP   The Transform Again command does not apply to the Offset Path command because it is not one of the transform tools.

6. Deselect all, save your work, compare your screen to Figure 15, then close the Squares document.

You used the Offset Path command to create concentric squares.

FIGURE 15
Concentric squares created with the Offset Path command

Transforming and Distorting Objects

FIGURE 16

The Outline Stroke command converts any stroked path into a closed path

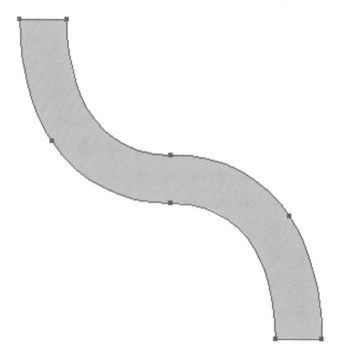

1. Open AI 4-5.ai, then save it as **Outlined Stroke**.

2. Select the path, then change the weight to 36 pt.

3. Click **Object** on the menu bar, point to **Path**, then click **Outline Stroke**.

   The full weight of the stroke is converted to a closed path, as shown in Figure 16.

4. Save your work, then close the Outlined Stroke document.

You applied a heavy weight to a stroked path, then converted the stroke to a closed path, using the Outline Stroke command.

CREATE COMPOUND
PATHS

What You'll Do

In this lesson, you will explore the role of compound paths for practical use and for artistic effects.

Defining a Compound Path

Practically speaking, you make a compound path to create a "hole" or "holes" in an object. As shown in Figure 17, if you were drawing the letter "D," you would need to create a hole in the outlined shape, through which you could see the background. To do so, select the object in back (in this case, the black outline that defines the letter) and the object in front (the yellow object that defines the hole) and apply the Make Compound Path command. When compounded, a "hole" appears where the two objects overlap.

The overlapping object still exists, however. It is simply *functioning* as a transparent hole in conjunction with the object behind it. If you move the front object independently, as shown in Figure 18, it yields an interesting result. Designers have seized upon this effect and have run with it, creating complex and eye-catching graphics, which Illustrator calls compound shapes.

It is important to understand that when two or more objects are compounded, Illustrator defines them as *one* object. This sounds strange at first, but the concept is as familiar to you as the letter D. You identify the letter D as one object. Although it is drawn with two paths—one defining the outside edge, the other defining the inside edge—it is nevertheless a single object.

Compound paths function as groups. You can select and manipulate an individual element with the Direct Selection Tool, but you cannot change its appearance attributes independently. Compound paths can

be released and returned to their original component objects by applying the Release Compound Path command.

FIGURE 17
The letter D is an example of a compound path

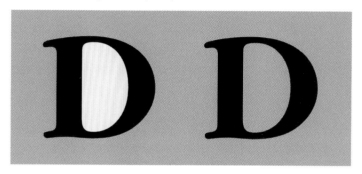

FIGURE 18
Manipulating compound paths can yield interesting effects

Create compound paths

1. Open AI 4-6.ai, then save it as **Simple Compound**.

2. Cut the red circle in the middle of the illustration, then undo the cut.

   The red circle creates the illusion that there's a hole in the life-preserver ring.

3. Select the red background object, then change its fill to the Ocean Blue gradient in the Swatches palette.

   The illusion is lost; the red circle no longer appears as a hole in the life preserver.

4. Select both the white "life preserver" circle and the red circle in the center.

5. Click **Object** on the menu bar, point to **Compound Path**, then click **Make**.

   As shown in Figure 19, the two circles are compounded, with the top circle functioning as a "hole" in the larger circle behind it.

6. Move the background object left and right, and up and down behind the circles.

   The repositioned background remains visible through the compounded circles.

7. Deselect all, save your work, then close the Simple Compound document.

You selected two concentric circles and made them into one compound path, which allowed you to see through to the gradient behind the circles.

FIGURE 20

A simple compound path

FIGURE 21

A more complex compound path

Each of the five small
circles is scaled, using
its own center point as
the point of origin

FIGURE 22

Simple compound paths can yield stunning visual effects

Create special effects with compound paths

1. Open AI 4-7.ai, then save it as **Compound Path Effects**.

2. Select all.

   The light blue square is locked and does not become part of the selection.

3. Click **Object** on the menu bar, point to **Compound Path**, then click **Make**.

4. Deselect, click the **Direct Selection Tool**, then click the **edge** of the large blue circle.

5. Click the **center point** of the circle, then scale the circle 50% so that your work resembles Figure 20.

6. Click **Select** on the menu bar, then click **Inverse**.

7. Click **Object** on the menu bar, point to **Transform**, then click **Transform Each**.

8. Enter **225** in the Horizontal and Vertical text boxes in the Scale section of the Transform Each dialog box, click **OK**, then deselect all.

   Your work should resemble Figure 21.

9. Using the Direct Selection Tool, click the edge of the center circle, click its center point to select the entire circle, then scale the circle 120%.

10. Apply the Transform Again command twice, then compare your screen to Figure 22.

11. Deselect all, save your work, then close Compound Path Effects.

You made a compound path out of five small circles and one large circle. You then manipulated the size and location of the individual circles to create interesting designs.

WORK WITH THE
PATHFINDER PALETTE

What You'll Do

▶ In this lesson, you will use pathfinders to create compound shapes from simple shapes.

Defining a Compound Shape

Like a compound path, a **compound shape** is two or more paths that are combined in such a way that "holes" appear wherever paths overlap.

The term compound shape is used to distinguish a complex compound path from a simple one. Compound shapes generally assume an artistic rather than a practical role. To achieve the effect, compound shapes tend to be composed of multiple objects. You can think of a compound shape as an illustration composed of multiple compound paths.

Understanding Essential Pathfinder Filters

The **pathfinders** are a group of preset operations that help you combine paths in a variety of ways. Pathfinders are very useful operations for creating complex or irregular shapes from basic shapes. In some cases, the pathfinders will be a means to an end in creating an object; in others, the operation they provide will be the end result you want to achieve.

Illustrator offers ten pathfinders. Pathfinders can be applied to overlapping objects using the Effect menu or the Pathfinder palette. For the purposes of drawing and creating new objects, the following five pathfinders are essential; compare each with Figure 23.

- **Add to shape area**: Converts two or more overlapping objects into a single, merged object.
- **Subtract from shape area**: Where objects overlap, deletes the frontmost object(s) from the backmost object in a selection of overlapped objects.
- **Intersect shape areas**: Creates a single, merged object from the area where two or more objects overlap.

- **Minus Back**: The opposite of Subtract; deletes the backmost object(s) from the frontmost object in a selection of overlapped objects.
- **Divide**: Divides an object into its component filled faces. Illustrator defines a "face" as an area undivided by a line segment.

FIGURE 23

Five essential pathfinders

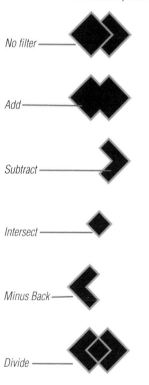

No filter

Add

Subtract

Intersect

Minus Back

Divide

Using the Pathfinder Palette

The Pathfinder palette contains ten buttons for applying pathfinders and for creating compound shapes, as shown in Figure 24. As you learned earlier, a compound shape is a complex compound path. You can create a compound shape by overlapping two or more objects, then clicking one of the four shape mode buttons in the top row of the Pathfinder palette, or clicking the Pathfinder palette list arrow, then clicking Make Compound Shape. The four shape mode buttons share the *same* buttons as four essential pathfinders: Add to shape area (Add), Subtract from shape area (Subtract), Intersect shape areas (Intersect), and Exclude overlapping shape areas (Exclude). To apply one of these four pathfinders, you must press and hold [Alt] (Win) or [option] (Mac), then click the desired pathfinder button.

FIGURE 24
Pathfinder palette

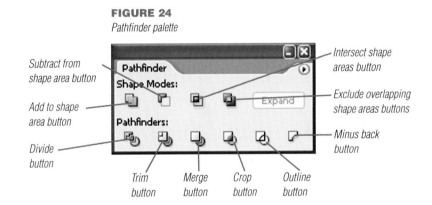

Subtract from shape area button

Add to shape area button

Divide button

Intersect shape areas button

Exclude overlapping shape areas buttons

Minus back button

Trim button

Merge button

Crop button

Outline button

Applying Shape Modes and Pathfinders

Figure 25 shows a square overlapped by a circle. If you apply the Subtract pathfinder, the overlapped area is deleted from the square. The circle, too, is deleted, as shown in Figure 26. The result is a simple reshaped object.

With the same starting image, if you apply the Subtract shape mode, the same visual effect is achieved. However, the resulting

object is a compound shape, as shown in Figure 27. This time, the circle is not deleted; it is functioning as a hole or a "knockout" wherever it overlaps the square. The relationship is dynamic: You can move the circle independently at any time to change its effect on the square and the resulting visual effect.

That dynamic relationship is the essential factor that distinguishes applying a pathfinder from applying a shape mode.

When pathfinders are applied to objects, the result is final. When shape modes are applied to objects, the resulting compound shape can be manipulated endlessly.

Figure 28 shows a group of objects converted into a compound shape using the Make Compound Shape command in the Pathfinder palette.

FIGURE 25
Two overlapping objects

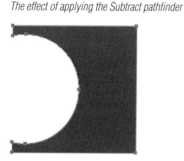

FIGURE 26
The effect of applying the Subtract pathfinder

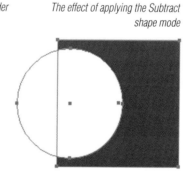

FIGURE 27
The effect of applying the Subtract shape mode

FIGURE 28
A compound shape

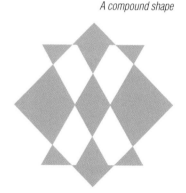

Apply the Add to shape area pathfinder

1. Open AI 4-8.ai, then save it as **Heart Parts**.

2. Click **Window** on the menu bar, then click **Pathfinder**, if necessary.

3. Select both circles, press and hold **[Alt]** (Win) or **[option]** (Mac), then click the **Add to shape area button**  in the Pathfinder palette.

   The two objects are united. For brevity's sake, Add to shape area will be referred to as Add.

4. Move the diamond shape up so that it overlaps the united circles, as shown in Figure 29.

5. Click the **Delete Anchor Point Tool**, then delete the top anchor point of the diamond.

6. Select all, press and hold **[Alt]** (Win) or **[option]** (Mac), then click the **Add button** so that your screen resembles Figure 30.

7. Remove the black stroke, then apply a red fill to the new object.

8. Draw a rectangle that covers the "hole" in the heart, then fill it with black, as shown in Figure 31.

9. Select all, press **[Alt]** (Win) or **[option]** (Mac), then click the **Add button**.

10. Double-click the **Scale Tool**, then apply a non-uniform scale of 90% on the horizontal axis and 100% on the vertical axis.

You created a single heart-shaped object from two circles and a diamond shape using the Add to shape area pathfinder.

FIGURE 29
A diamond shape in position for the Add pathfinder

FIGURE 30
The diamond shape and the object behind it are united with the Add pathfinder

FIGURE 31
A heart shape created by applying the Add pathfinder to three objects

FIGURE 32

Circle overlaps the square

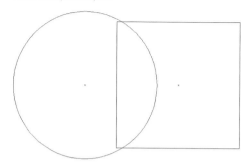

FIGURE 33

Right circle is a reflected copy of the left one

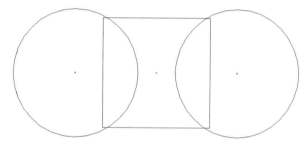

FIGURE 34

The final shape, with all elements united by the Add pathfinder

1. Rotate the black heart shape 180°, then hide it.
2. Create a square that is 1.5" × 1.5" without a fill color and with a 1 pt black stroke.
3. Create a circle that is 1.75" in width and height.
4. Switch to Outline mode.
5. Move the circle so that it overlaps the square, as shown in Figure 32.
6. Verify that the circle is still selected, click the **Reflect Tool** 🔲, press **[Alt]** (Win) or **[option]** (Mac), then click the **center point** of the square.
7. Click the **Vertical option button**, then click **Copy** so that your work resembles Figure 33.
8. Select all, press **[Alt]** (Win) or **[option]** (Mac), then click the **Subtract from shape area button** 🔲 in the Pathfinder palette.
9. Switch to Preview mode, then apply a black fill to the new object.
10. Show all, then overlap the new shape with the black heart shape to make a spade shape.
11. Select all, apply the Add pathfinder, then deselect.

    Your work should resemble Figure 34.

You overlapped a square with two circles, then applied the Subtract from shape area pathfinder to delete the overlapped areas from the square. You used the Add to shape area pathfinder to unite the new shape with a heart-shaped object to create a spade shape.

Apply the Intersect shape areas pathfinder

1. Click the **Star Tool** ☆, then click the **artboard**.

2. Enter **1** in the Radius 1 text box, **3** in the Radius 2 text box, and **8** in the Points text box, then click **OK**.

3. Apply a yellow fill to the star and remove any stroke, if necessary.

4. Use the Align palette to align the center points of the two objects, so that they resemble Figure 35.

5. Copy the black spade, then paste in front.

   Two black spades are now behind the yellow star; the top one is selected.

6. Press and hold **[Shift]**, then click to add the star to the selection.

7. Click the **Intersect shape areas button** ▣ in the Pathfinder palette.

   The intersection of the star and the copied spade is now a single closed path. Your work should resemble Figure 36.

8. Save your work, then close Heart Parts.

You created a star and then created a copy of the black spade-shaped object. You used the Intersect shape areas pathfinder to capture the intersection of the two objects as a new object.

FIGURE 35
Use the Align palette to align objects precisely

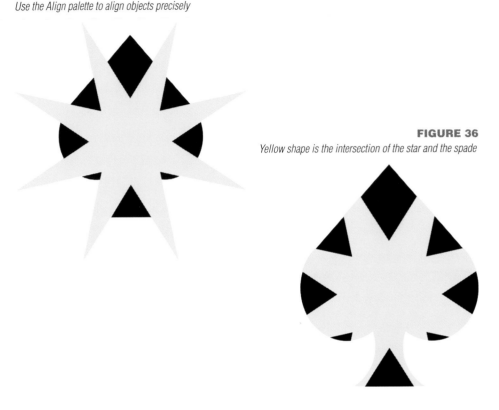

FIGURE 36
Yellow shape is the intersection of the star and the spade

Working with the Align palette

The Align palette offers a quick and simple solution for aligning selected objects along the axis you specify. Along the vertical axis, you can align selected objects by their rightmost point, leftmost point, or center point. On the horizontal axis, you can align objects by their topmost point, center point, or bottommost point. You can also use the palette to distribute objects evenly along a horizontal or vertical axis. In contrasting the Align palette with the Average command, think of the Average command as a method for aligning anchor points and the Align palette as a method for aligning entire objects.

FIGURE 37

Blue star is divided into twelve objects by the Divide pathfinder

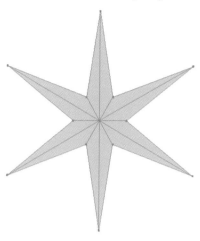

FIGURE 38

Divide pathfinder is useful for adding dimension

Apply the Divide pathfinder

1. Open AI 4-9.ai, then save it as **Divide**.

2. Select the red line, then double-click the **Rotate Tool** ⟳.

3. Enter **30** in the Angle text box, then click **Copy**.

4. Repeat the transformation four times.

5. Select all, then click the **Divide button** 🔲 in the Pathfinder palette.

   The blue star is divided into twelve separate objects, as defined by the red lines, which have been deleted. See Figure 37.

6. Deselect, click the **Direct Selection Tool** ▸, select the left half of the top point, press **[Shift]**, then select every other object, for a total of six objects.

7. Apply an orange fill to the selected objects.

8. Select the inverse, then apply a yellow fill so that your work resembles Figure 38.

9. Save your work, then close the Divide document.

You used six lines to define a score pattern, then used those lines and the Divide pathfinder to break the star into twelve separate objects.

Create compound shapes using the Pathfinder palette

1. Open AI 4-10.ai, then save it as **Compound Shapes**.

2. Click **View** on the menu bar, then click **Yellow**.

3. Select the two yellow circles, then click the **Exclude overlapping shape areas button** 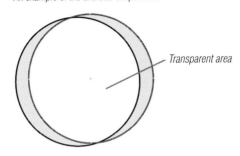 in the Pathfinder palette.

   The area that the top object overlaps becomes transparent.

4. Deselect, click the **Direct Selection Tool** , then move either circle to change the shape and size of the filled areas.

   Figure 39 shows one effect that can be achieved.

5. Select **Green** from the View menu, select the two green circles, then click the **Intersect shape areas button** in the Pathfinder palette.

   The area not overlapped by the top circle becomes transparent.

6. Deselect, then use the Direct Selection Tool to move either circle to change the shape and size of the filled area.

   Figure 40 shows one effect that can be achieved.

7. Save your work, then close the Compound Shapes document.

You applied shape modes to two pairs of circles, then moved the circles to create different shapes and effects.

FIGURE 39
An example of the Exclude shape mode

Transparent area

FIGURE 40
An example of the Intersect shape mode

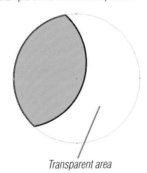

Transparent area

FIGURE 41

A compound shape

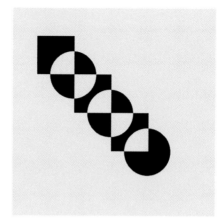

FIGURE 42

A compound shape

FIGURE 43

A compound shape

FIGURE 44

A compound shape

Create special effects with compound shapes

1. Open AI 4-11.ai, then save it as **Compound Shape Effects**.

2. Select all, then click the **Exclude overlapping shape areas button** in the Pathfinder palette.

   Your work should resemble Figure 41.

3. Deselect all, click the **Direct Selection Tool**, select the three squares, then move them to the right, as shown in Figure 42.

4. Drag and drop a copy of the three squares, as shown in Figure 43.

   TIP   Use [Shift][Alt] (Win) or [Shift][option] (Mac) to drag and drop a copy.

5. Scale each circle 150% using the Transform Each command.

6. Scale the center circle 200%, then bring it to the front of the stacking order.

7. Click the **Intersect shape areas button** in the Pathfinder palette.

   Figure 44 shows the results of the intersection. Your final illustration may vary slightly.

   TIP   The topmost object affects all the objects behind it in a compound shape.

8. Save your work, then close Compound Shape Effects.

You made three squares and three circles into a compound shape by excluding overlapping shape areas. You then manipulated the size and location of individual elements to create different effects. Finally, you enlarged a circle, brought it to the front, then changed its mode to Intersect. Only the objects that were overlapped by the circle remained visible.

CREATE CLIPPING
MASKS

What You'll Do

 In this lesson, you will explore the role of clipping masks for practical use and for artistic effects.

Defining a Clipping Mask

As with compound paths, clipping masks are used to yield a practical result. And as with compound paths, that practical result can be manipulated to create interesting graphic effects.

Practically speaking, you use a clipping mask as a "window" through which you view some or all of the objects behind the mask in the stacking order. When you select any two or more objects and apply the Make Clipping Mask command, the *top object* becomes the mask and the object behind it becomes "masked." You will be able to see only the parts of the masked object that are visible *through* the mask, as shown in Figure 45. The mask crops the object behind it.

Using Multiple Objects as a Clipping Mask

When multiple objects are selected and the Make Clipping Mask command is applied, the top object becomes the mask. Since every object has its own position in the stacking order, it stands to reason that there can be only one top object.

If you want to use multiple objects as a mask, you can do so by first making them into a compound path. Illustrator regards compound paths as a single object. Therefore, a compound path containing multiple objects can be used as a single mask.

Creating Masked Effects

Special effects with clipping masks are, quite simply, fun! You can position as many objects as you like behind the mask, and position them in such a way that the mask crops them in visually interesting (and eye-popping!) ways. See Figure 46 for an example.

FIGURE 45

Clipping mask crops the object behind it

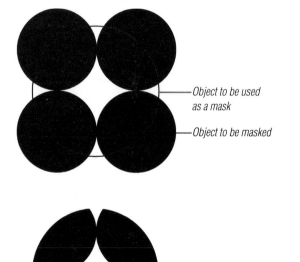

—Object to be used as a mask

—Object to be masked

—The result after applying the Make Clipping Mask command

FIGURE 46

Masks can be used for stunning visual effects

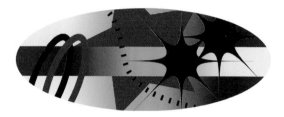

Create a clipping mask

1. Open AI 4-12.ai, then save it as **Simple Masks**.
2. Click **View** on the menu bar, then click **Mask 1**.
3. Move the rectangle so that it overlaps the gold spheres, as shown in Figure 47.
4. Apply the Bring to Front command to verify that the rectangle is in front of all the spheres.
5. Select the seven spheres and the rectangle.
6. Click **Object** on the menu bar, point to **Clipping Mask**, then click **Make**.
7. Deselect, then compare your screen to Figure 48.
8. Click **View** on the menu bar, then click **Mask 2**.
9. Select the three circles, then move them over the "gumballs."

   The three circles are a compound path.
10. Select the group of gumballs and the three circles, then apply the Make Clipping Mask command.
11. Deselect, click **Select** on the menu bar, point to **Object**, then click **Clipping Masks**.
12. Apply a 1 pt black stroke to the masks.

    Your work should resemble Figure 49.
13. Save your work, then close the Simple Masks document.

You used a rectangle as a clipping mask. Then, you used three circles to mask a group of small spheres, and applied a black stroke to the mask.

FIGURE 47
Masking objects must be in front of objects to be masked

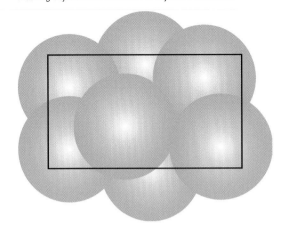

FIGURE 48
The rectangle masks the gold spheres

FIGURE 49
A compound path used as a mask

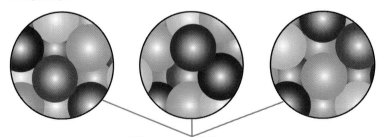

A black stroke applied to a mask

FIGURE 50
Lining up the letter g

FIGURE 51
Positioning the magnifying glass

The two objects that make
up the magnifying glass are
not grouped

FIGURE 52
A fill and stroke are applied to a mask

The mask

By default, a fill is positioned behind the
masked elements, and the stroke is in
front of the mask

FIGURE 53
Large text is masked by the magnifying glass

When a fill is
applied to a mask,
the fill is positioned
behind all the
objects that are
masked

As the mask moves, different
areas of the large text
become visible, creating the
illusion of a magnifying
glass moving over a word

Apply a fill to a clipping mask

1. Open AI 4-13.ai, then save it as **Magnify**.

2. Move the large outlined text over the small outlined text so that the *g*s align as shown in Figure 50.

3. Select the smaller text, then hide it.

4. Select the magnifying glass and the handle, then drag them over the letter *g*, as shown in Figure 51.

5. Deselect all, select only the circle and the text, click **Object** on the menu bar, point to **Clipping Mask**, then click **Make**.

   The circle is the masking object.

6. Deselect, click **Select** on the menu bar, point to **Object**, then click **Clipping Masks**.

7. Use the Swatches palette to apply a light blue fill and a gray stroke to the mask.

8. Change the weight of the stroke to 8 pt, so that your work resembles Figure 52.

9. Show all, deselect, then compare your screen to Figure 53.

10. Select the mask only, press and hold **[Shift]**, then click the **magnifying glass handle.**

11. Press the **arrow keys** to move the magnifying glass.

12. Save your work, then close the Magnify document.

You used the circle in the illustration as a clipping mask in combination with the large text. You added a fill and a stroke to the mask, creating the illusion that the small text is magnified in the magnifying glass.

Use text as a clipping mask

1. Open AI 4-14.ai, then save it as **Mask Effects**.

2. Select the four letters that make the word MASK.

   The word MASK was converted to outlines and ungrouped.

3. Make the four letters into a compound path.

4. Select the compound path and the rectangle behind it.

5. Apply the Make Clipping Mask command, then deselect.

6. Save your work, then compare your text to Figure 54.

You converted outlines to a compound path, then used the compound path as a mask.

FIGURE 54
Outlined text used as a mask

Transforming and Distorting Objects

FIGURE 55
Curvy object in position to be masked by the letters

FIGURE 56
Object behind the mask is selected

The rectangle behind
the mask is selected

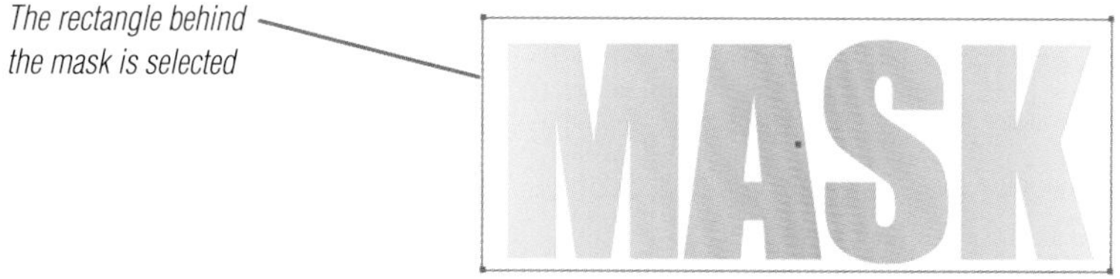

FIGURE 57
Curvy object is masked by the letters

FIGURE 58
Pasting multiple objects behind a mask yields interesting effects

Lesson 5   Create Clipping Masks

Use a clipping mask for special effects

1. Position the curvy object with the gradient fill over the mask, as shown in Figure 55.

2. Cut the curvy object.

3. Use the **Direct Selection Tool** to select the original rectangle behind the mask.

   TIP   Click slightly above the mask until you see the rectangle selected, as shown in Figure 56.

4. Paste in front, then deselect so that your screen resembles Figure 57.

   The object is pasted in front of the masked rectangle and behind the mask.

5. Click the **Selection Tool**, select the purple dotted line, position it over the letter K, then cut the purple dotted line.

6. Select the mask (rectangle) with the Direct Selection Tool, click **Edit** on the menu bar, then click **Paste in Front**.

7. Using the same technique, mask the other objects on the artboard in any way that you choose.

   When finished, your mask should contain all of the objects, as shown in Figure 58.

   TIP   Add a stroke to the mask if desired.

8. Save and close Mask Effects.

You created visual effects by pasting objects behind a mask.

Transform objects.

1. Open AI 4-15.ai, then save it as **Transformations**.
2. Select "DIVIDE."
3. Scale the text objects non-uniformly: Horizontal = 110% and Vertical = 120%.
4. Rotate the text objects 7°.
5. Shear the text objects 25° on the horizontal axis.
6. Save your work.

Offset and outline paths.

1. Ungroup the text outlines.
2. Using the Offset Path command, offset each letter -.05".
3. Save your work.

Apply Pathfinder filters.

1. Select all.
2. Apply the Divide pathfinder.

3. Fill the divided elements with different colors, using the Direct Selection Tool.
4. Select all, then apply a 2-point white stroke. Figure 59 is an example of the effect. (*Hint*: Enlarge the view of your document window, if necessary.)
5. Save your work, compare your image to Figure 59, then close the Transformations document.

FIGURE 59
Completed Skills Review, Part 1

Create compound paths.

1. Open AI 4-16.ai, then save it as **Compound Paths**.

2. Select all, then click the Exclude overlapping shape areas button.

3. Create a 20% copy of the small square, then transform again three times.

4. Save your work, compare your image to Figure 60, then close the Compound Paths document.

FIGURE 60
Completed Skills Review, Part 2

You are entering a contest to design a new stamp. You have decided to use a picture of Mona Lisa, which you have placed in an Illustrator document. You have positioned text over the image. Now, to complete the effect, you want to mimic the perforated edges of a stamp.

1. Open AI 4-.17.ai, then save it as **Mona Lisa Stamp**.
2. Select all the circles, then make them into a compound path.
3. Add the rectangle to the selection.
4. Apply the Subtract from shape area pathfinder, then deselect all.
5. Save your work, compare your image to Figure 61, then close Mona Lisa Stamp.

FIGURE 61
Completed Project Builder 1

Transforming and Distorting Objects

You're contracted to design the logo for Wired Gifts, an online gift site. Your concept is of a geometric red bow. You feel that your idea will simultaneously convey the concepts of gifts and technology.

1. Open AI 4-18.ai, then save it as **Wired Gifts**.
2. Switch to Outline mode.
3. Select the small square, click the Rotate Tool, press and hold [Alt] (Win) or [option] (Mac), then click the center of the large square.
4. Type **15** in the Angle text box, then click Copy.
5. Repeat the transformation 22 times.
6. Delete the large square at the center.
7. Switch to Preview mode.
8. Select all, then fill all the squares with Caribbean Blue.
9. Apply the Divide pathfinder to the selection.
10. Fill the objects with the Red Bow gradient.
11. Delete the object in the center of the bow. (*Hint*: Use the Direct Selection Tool to select the object.)
12. Select all, then remove the black stroke from the objects.
13. Save your work, compare your illustration with Figure 62, then close Wired Gifts.

FIGURE 62
Completed Project Builder 2

You are a fabric designer for a line of men's clothing. The line is known for its conservative patterns and styles. You are asked to supervise a team that will design new patterns for men's ties. You will present your recommended new patterns using Illustrator.

1. Create a new CMYK Color document and name it **Ties**.
2. Create a square, rotate it 45°, then reshape it using the Direct Selection Tool by dragging the top anchor point straight up to create the shape of a tie.
3. Use a square and the Subtract from shape area pathfinder to square off the top of the diamond.
4. Draw a second polygon to represent the tie's knot.
5. Lock the two polygons.
6. Create a small circle, then copy it using the Move dialog box to create a polka dot pattern that exceeds the perimeter of both polygons.
7. Unlock the polygons, then bring them to the front.
8. Create a compound path out of the two polygons.
9. Select all, then use the polygons to mask the polka-dot pattern.
10. Apply a fill to the mask, save your work, compare your image to Figure 63, then close Ties.

FIGURE 63
Completed Design Project

Transforming and Distorting Objects

You are the design department manager for a toy company, and your team's next project will be to design a dartboard that will be part of a package of "Safe Games" for kids. The target market is boys and girls ages six to adult. Your team will design only the board, not the darts.

1. Create a new CMYK Color document and name it **Dartboard**.
2. Have part of the group search the Internet for pictures of dartboards.
3. Have two members research the sport of throwing darts. What are the official dimensions of a dartboard? Is there an official design? Are there official colors?
4. The other team members should discuss which colors should be used for the board, keeping in mind that the sales department plans to position it as a toy for both girls and boys.
5. The team should also discuss whether they will use alternate colors even if the research team learns the official colors for a dartboard.
6. Using the skills you learned in this chapter, work together to design a dartboard, using Figure 64 as a guide.
7. Save your work, compare your image to Figure 64, then close Dartboard.

FIGURE 64
Completed Group Project

5 WORKING WITH LAYERS

1. Create and modify layers.

2. Manipulate layered artwork.

3. Work with layered artwork.

4. Create a clipping set.

Designing with Layers

When you're creating complex artwork, keeping track of all the items on the artboard can become quite a challenge. Small items hide behind larger items, and it becomes difficult to find them, select them, and work with them. The Layers palette solves this problem. Using the Layers palette, you organize your work by placing objects or groups of objects on separate layers. Artwork on layers can be manipulated and modified independently from artwork on other layers. The Layers palette also provides effective options to select, hide, lock, and change the appearance of your work. In addition, layers are an effective solution for storing multiple versions of your work in one file.

Tools You'll Use

Layers palette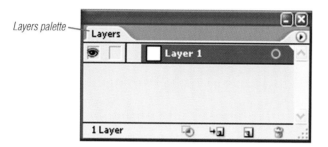

CREATE AND
MODIFY LAYERS

What You'll Do

In this lesson, you will create new layers
and explore options in the Layers palette
for viewing, locking, hiding, and selecting
layers and layered artwork.

Creating Layers and Sublayers

Layers are a smart solution for organizing
and managing a complex illustration. For
example, if you were drawing a map of
your home state, you might put all the
interstate freeways on one layer, the local
freeways on a second layer, secondary
roads on a third layer, and all the text
elements on a fourth layer.

As the name suggests, the Layers palette
consists of a series of layers. The number
of layers that a document can have is limited only by your computer's memory. By
default, every Illustrator document is created with one layer, called Layer 1. As you
work, you can create new layers and move
objects into them, thereby segregating and
organizing your work. The first object that
is placed on Layer 1 is placed on a sublayer
called <Path>. Each additional object
placed on the same layer is placed on a
separate <Path> sublayer.

Importing an Adobe Photoshop file with layers

When you use the Open command to import a layered Photoshop file into Illustrator
CS2, you have the option to open that file with its layers intact. In the Photoshop
Import dialog box that appears, select *Convert Photoshop layers to objects and make
text editable where possible*. When you see the Photoshop file on the Illustrator
artboard, open the Illustrator Layers palette and you will see that Illustrator has
preserved as much of the Photoshop layer structure as possible.

Each layer has a thumbnail, or miniature picture of the objects on that layer, to the left of the layer name. Thumbnails display the artwork that is positioned on all of the sublayers in the layer. You can change the size of the rows in the Layers palette using the Layers Palette Options dialog box on the Layers palette menu. Layers and sublayers can also be given descriptive names to help identify their contents.

The stacking order of objects on the artboard corresponds to the hierarchy of layers in the Layers palette. Artwork in the top layer is at the front of the stacking order, while artwork in the bottom layer is in the back. The hierarchy of sublayers corresponds to the stacking order of the objects within a single layer.

Illustrator offers two basic ways to create new layers and sublayers. You can click the New Layer or New Sublayer command in the Layers palette menu, or you can click the Create New Layer or Create New Sublayer button in the Layers palette. Figure 1 shows a simple illustration and its corresponding layers in the Layers palette.

Duplicating Layers

In addition to creating new layers, you can duplicate existing layers by clicking the Duplicate command in the Layers menu, or by dragging a layer or sublayer onto the Create New Layer button in the Layers palette. When you duplicate a layer, all of the artwork on the layer is duplicated as well. Note the difference between this and copying and pasting artwork. When you copy and paste artwork, the copied artwork is pasted on the same layer.

FIGURE 1
Layers palette

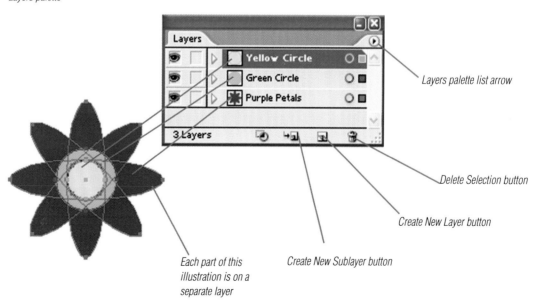

Layers palette list arrow

Delete Selection button

Create New Layer button

Create New Sublayer button

Each part of this illustration is on a separate layer

Setting Layer Options

The Layer Options dialog box offers a wealth of options for working with layered artwork, many of which are not available to you unless you are working with layers. You can name a layer, and you can also set a color for the layer. When an object is selected, its selection marks will be the same color as specified for the layer, making it easy to differentiate layers of artwork on the artboard.

Also in the Layer Options dialog box are options for locking, unlocking, showing, and hiding artwork on the layer. When you lock a layer, all the objects on the layer are locked and protected. When the Show check box is checked, all the artwork that is contained in the layer is displayed on the artboard. When the Show check box is not checked, the artwork is hidden.

Buttons in the Layers palette represent ways to lock, unlock, hide, and show artwork on each layer, making it unnecessary to use the Layer Options dialog box to activate these functions. The Toggles Visibility button (the eye) lets you hide and show layers, and the Toggles Lock button (the padlock) lets you lock and unlock layers.

The Preview option displays all the artwork on a layer in Preview mode. When the Preview option is not activated, the artwork is displayed in Outline mode. Thus, with layers, some elements on the artboard can be in Preview mode, while others are in Outline mode.

The Print option allows you to choose whether or not to print a layer. This feature is useful for printing different versions of the same illustration. The Dim Images to option reduces the intensity of bitmap images that are placed on the artboard. Dimming a bitmap often makes it easier to trace an image.

Use the Template option when you want to use the artwork on a layer as the basis for a new illustration—for example, if you want to trace the artwork. By default, a template layer is locked and cannot be printed.

Selecting Artwork on Layers and Sublayers

When you select an object on the artboard, its layer is selected (highlighted) in the Layers palette, and the Indicates Selected Art button appears, as shown in Figure 2. Selecting a layer or sublayer in the Layers palette does not select the artwork on that layer.

Changes that you make to layers in the Layers palette affect the artwork on those layers. For example, if you delete a layer, the artwork on the layer will be deleted. The artwork on a layer will be duplicated if the layer is duplicated. Changing a layer's position in the layers hierarchy will move the artwork forward or backward in the stacking order.

Duplicating the artwork on the artboard does not duplicate the layer that the artwork is on. If you delete all the artwork on a layer, you are left with an empty layer. *A layer is never automatically created, copied, or deleted, regardless of what you do to the artwork on the layer.*

The same is *not* true for sublayers. If you delete or copy artwork that is on a sublayer, the *sublayer* is deleted or copied, respectively.

Selecting All Artwork on a Layer

The Select All command makes it easy to select every object on the artboard in one step. At times, however, you will want to select every object on a layer or sublayer, not every object on the artboard. To select all the artwork on a single layer or sublayer, select the Click to target, drag to move appearance button to the left of the Indicates Selected Art button, shown in Figure 2, or [Alt] (Win) or [option] (Mac) click the layer. All objects on that layer will become selected on the artboard.

FIGURE 2
The chair on the artboard and in the Layers palette

Selection marks for chair are red, the Chair layer's assigned color

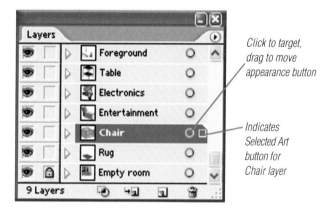

Click to target, drag to move appearance button

Indicates Selected Art button for Chair layer

Create a new layer

1. Open AI 5-1.ai, then save it as **Living Room**.

2. Open AI 5-2.ai, then save it as **Showroom**.

   You will work with two documents during this lesson.

3. Click the **Selection Tool** ▶, select the chair, then copy it.

4. Click **Window** on the menu bar, then click **Living Room**.

   | TIP   Using the Window menu is an easy way to switch between open documents.

5. Click **Window** on the menu bar, then click **Layers** to select it, if necessary.

   The Layers palette opens, showing two layers. The Empty room layer contains the artwork you see on the artboard. The objects on the Foreground layer are hidden.

6. Click the **Create New Layer button** ▤ in the Layers palette.

   A new layer named Layer 3 appears above the Foreground layer.

7. Click **Edit** on the menu bar, then click **Paste**.

   The chair artwork is pasted into Layer 3.

8. Position the chair on the artboard as shown in Figure 3.

You created a new layer using the Create New Layer button in the Layers palette, then pasted an object into that new layer.

FIGURE 3
Chair positioned on its own layer

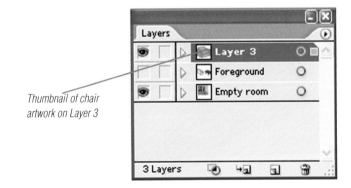

Thumbnail of chair artwork on Layer 3

Working with Layers

FIGURE 4
Layer Options dialog box

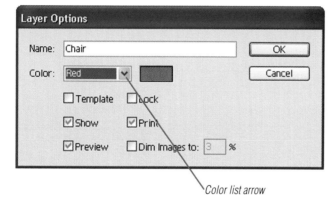

Color list arrow

1. Double-click **Layer 3**.
2. Name the layer **Chair**, then click **OK**.

   The Layers palette reflects the name change.
3. Double-click the **Chair layer**.
4. Click the **Color list arrow**, click **Red**, as shown in Figure 4, then click **OK**.

   Note that the selection marks on the chair are now red, reflecting the new selection color for the Chair layer.
5. Deselect the chair.

You used the Layer Options dialog box to rename Layer 3 and assign it a new selection color.

Select items on a layer and lock a layer

1. Click the **chair** with the Selection Tool.

    Note that the Indicates Selected Art button appears when the chair is selected, as shown in Figure 5.

    | TIP   The Indicates Selected Art button is the same color as its layer.

2. Deselect the chair.

    The Indicates Selected Art button disappears.

3. [Alt] (Win) or [option] (Mac) click the **Chair layer** in the Layers palette.

    The chair artwork is selected.

4. Click either of the two mauve walls in the illustration.

    When an object is selected on the artboard, the layer on which the selected object is placed is highlighted in the Layers palette.

5. Double-click the **Empty room layer**, click the **Lock check box**, then click **OK**.

    The Toggles Lock button 🔒 appears on the Empty room layer, indicating that all the objects on the Empty room layer are locked. See Figure 6.

You noted the relationship between a selected item and its corresponding layer in the Layers palette. You activated the Indicates Selected Art button and selected the artwork on the Chair layer. You then locked the Foreground layer.

FIGURE 5
Indicates Selected Art button identifies the layer of a selected object

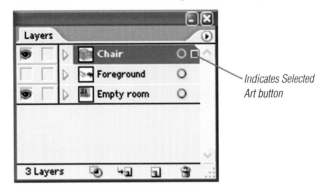

Indicates Selected
Art button

FIGURE 6
Toggles Lock button identifies a locked layer

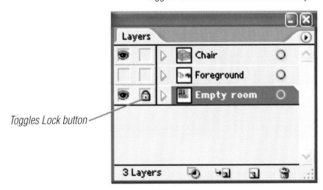

Toggles Lock button

1. Double-click the **Foreground layer**.

2. Click the **Show check box**, then click **OK**.

   The objects on the Foreground layer become visible, and the Toggles Visibility button 👁 appears on the Foreground layer.

3. Click the **Toggles Visibility button** 👁 on the Foreground layer to hide the objects.

4. Click the **Toggles Visibility button** (in its off state) ☐ on the Foreground layer to show the objects.

   TIP The Toggles Visibility and Toggles Lock buttons appear as empty gray squares in their off state.

5. Click the **Toggles Lock button** (in its off state) ☐ on the Foreground layer.

   The **Toggles Lock button** 🔒 appears.

6. Click the **Toggles Visibility button** 👁 on the Foreground layer to hide the objects.

   Your Layers palette should resemble Figure 7.

7. Save your work.

You used the Toggles Visibility button in the Layers palette to toggle between showing and hiding the artwork on two layers. You also locked the Foreground layer.

FIGURE 7
Foreground layer is locked and hidden

The absence of the Toggles Visibility button indicates that this layer is hidden

The Toggles Lock button indicates that this layer is locked

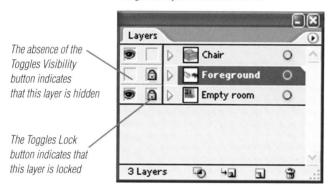

MANIPULATE LAYERED ARTWORK

What You'll Do

 In this lesson, you will learn methods for manipulating layers to change the display of layered artwork. You will change the order of layers in the palette, merge layers, work with sublayers, and move objects between layers.

Changing the Order of Layers and Sublayers

The hierarchy of the layers in the Layers palette determines how objects on the artboard overlap. All the objects on a given layer are behind the objects on the layer above it and in front of the objects on the layer beneath it. Multiple objects within a given layer overlap according to their stacking order and can be repositioned with the standard stacking order commands.

To change the position of a layer or sublayer in the hierarchy, simply drag it up or down in the palette. Small black triangles and a heavy horizontal line identify where the layer will be repositioned, as shown in Figure 8. When you reposition a layer, its sublayers move with it.

Merging Layers

When you have positioned artwork to your liking using multiple layers and sublayers, you will often want to consolidate those layers to simplify the palette. First, you must select the layers that you want to merge. Press [Ctrl] (Win) or $\mathcal{H}$ (Mac) to select multiple layers. Once you have selected the layers that you want to merge, apply the Merge Selected command in the Layers palette menu. When you merge layers, all the artwork from one or more layers moves onto the layer that was last selected before the merge.

Be careful not to confuse merging layers with condensing layers. Condensing layers is simply the process of dragging one layer into another. The repositioned layer becomes a sublayer of the layer it was dragged into.

Defining Sublayers

Whenever you have one or more objects on a layer, you by definition have **sublayers**. For example, if you draw a circle and a square on Layer 1, it will automatically have two sublayers—one for the square, one for the circle. The layer is the sum total of its sublayers.

As soon as the first object is placed on a layer, a triangle appears to the left of the layer name, indicating that the layer contains sublayers. Click the triangle to expand the layer and see the sublayers, then click it again to collapse the layer and hide the sublayers.

Working with Sublayers

When you place grouped artwork into a layer, a sublayer is automatically created with the name <Group>. A triangle appears on the <Group> sublayer, which, when clicked, exposes the sublayers—one for every object in the group, as shown in Figure 9.

Dragging Objects Between Layers

Sublayers are the easiest objects to move between layers: You can simply drag and drop a sublayer from one layer to another.

You can drag artwork from one layer to another by dragging the Indicates Selected Art button. Select the artwork on the artboard that you want to move; the layer is selected, and the Indicates Selected Art button appears. Drag the button to the destination layer or sublayer, as shown in Figure 10. If you drag the Indicates Selected Art button to a layer, the artwork becomes the top sublayer in the layer. If you drag the Indicates Selected Art button to a

sublayer, the artwork is grouped with the object already on the sublayer.

If you don't feel comfortable dragging artwork between layers, you have two other options for moving objects between layers. You can simply cut and paste artwork from one layer to another by selecting the object that you want to move, cutting it from the artboard, selecting the layer you wish to place it on, then pasting. You can also use the Send to Current Layer command. Select the artwork you want to move, click the name of the destination layer to make it the active layer, click Object on the menu bar, point to Arrange, then click Send to Current Layer.

FIGURE 9

A <Group> sublayer

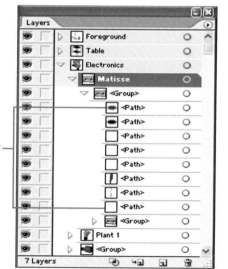

Each object in a group is placed on its own sublayer

FIGURE 8

Changing the order of layers

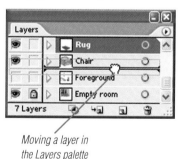

Moving a layer in the Layers palette

FIGURE 10

Dragging a sublayer to another layer

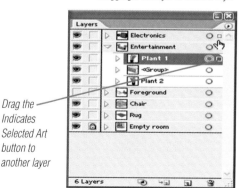

Drag the Indicates Selected Art button to another layer

Change the hierarchy of layers

1. Use the Window menu to switch to the Showroom document, copy the rug, then return to the Living Room document.

2. Press **[Ctrl]** (Win) or ⌘ (Mac), then click the **Create New Layer button** ⬛ in the Layers palette.

   Pressing [Ctrl] (Win) or ⌘ (Mac) creates a new layer at the top of the layer list.

3. Click **Edit** on the menu bar, then click **Paste**.

   The rug is pasted into the new layer because it is the active—or "targeted"—layer.

4. Name the new layer **Rug**, then position the rug artwork with a corner of it hanging slightly off the artboard, as shown in Figure 11.

5. Click and drag the **Rug layer** and position it below the Chair layer until you see a double black line with small triangles beneath the Chair layer, as shown in Figure 12, then release the mouse.

   The rug artwork is now positioned below the chair artwork.

You created a new layer at the top of the Layers palette. You pasted artwork into that layer, then moved the layer below another layer in the hierarchy so that the artwork on the two layers overlapped properly on the artboard.

FIGURE 11
The Rug layer is at the top of the layers hierarchy

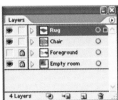

FIGURE 12
Changing the hierarchy of layers

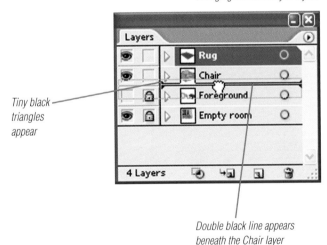

Tiny black triangles appear

Double black line appears beneath the Chair layer

FIGURE 13

Sculpture artwork positioned on top of the end table

Merge layers

1. Switch to the Showroom document, copy the sculpture, then return to the Living Room document.

2. Press **[Ctrl]** (Win) or ⌘ (Mac), then click the **Create New Layer button** 🔲 .

3. Paste the sculpture into the new layer, then name the layer **Sculpture**.

4. Show the Foreground layer, then position the sculpture artwork on the brown end table, as shown in Figure 13.

5. Deselect the sculpture, then drag the **Foreground layer** above the Sculpture layer in the Layers palette.

6. Unlock the Foreground layer.

7. Click the **Sculpture layer** to select it, press **[Ctrl]** (Win) or ⌘ (Mac), then click the **Foreground layer**.

   When merging layers, the last layer selected becomes the merged layer.

8. Click the **Layers palette list arrow**, then click **Merge Selected**.

   The objects from both layers are merged into the Foreground layer; the Sculpture layer is deleted.

   | TIP   Layers must be showing and unlocked in order to be merged.

9. Compare your screen to Figure 14.

   Don't worry that your sculpture is temporarily behind the table.

You merged the Sculpture and the Foreground layers.

FIGURE 14

Foreground and Sculpture layers merged

Merged layer

Work with sublayers

1. Expand the Foreground layer by clicking the **triangle** ▷ to the left of the layer.

   Three sublayers, all named <Group>, are revealed.

2. Expand the sofa <Group> sublayer by clicking the **triangle** ▷ to the left of it.

   The five paths that compose the sofa are revealed.

3. Select the sofa artwork on the artboard.

   The Indicates Selected Art buttons appear for each of the selected paths, as shown in Figure 15.

4. Click the **triangle** ▽ to the left of the sofa <Group> sublayer to collapse it, then deselect the sofa.

5. Double-click the **sofa <Group> sublayer**, name it **Sofa**, then click **OK**.

6. Name the sculpture sublayer **Sculpture**, then name the end table sublayer **End Table**.

7. Move the Sculpture sublayer above the End Table sublayer so that your Layers palette resembles Figure 16.

   Notice that the sculpture artwork is on top of the end table.

8. Click the **triangle** ▽ to the left of the Foreground layer to hide the three sublayers, then hide the Foreground layer.

You viewed sublayers in the Foreground layer. You then renamed the three sublayers in the Foreground layer and rearranged the order of the Sculpture and the End Table sublayers.

FIGURE 15
Each path in the sofa <Group> sublayer is selected

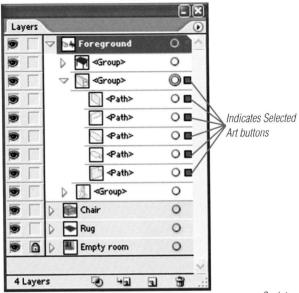

Indicates Selected
Art buttons

FIGURE 16
Sculpture layer moved above the End Table sublayer

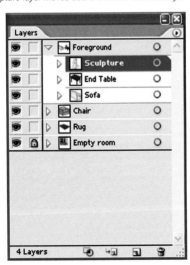

FIGURE 17

Cabinet and plant are on the same layer

FIGURE 18

Moving the Plant 2 sublayer

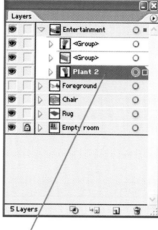

Plant 2 sublayer

FIGURE 19

The reflected copy of the plant in position

The new plant is positioned
behind the cabinet

FIGURE 20

The reflected copy of the plant, scaled and pruned

Create new sublayers

1. Switch to the Showroom document, copy the cabinet, then return to the Living Room document.

2. Press **[Ctrl]** (Win) or ⌘ (Mac), then click the **Create New Layer button** 🔲.

3. Name the new layer **Entertainment**, select Violet as the layer color, then click **OK**.

4. Paste the cabinet artwork into the new layer.

5. Copy the plant from the Showroom document, then paste the plant artwork into the Entertainment layer.

6. Position the cabinet artwork and the plant artwork as shown in Figure 17.

7. Deselect all, expand the Entertainment layer, then select the plant artwork on the artboard.

8. Double-click the **Reflect Tool** 🔄, click the **Vertical option button**, then click **Copy**.

   The reflected copy of the plant is placed on a new sublayer above the original plant sublayer.

9. Rename the new sublayer **Plant 2**.

10. Move the Plant 2 sublayer to the bottom of the Entertainment sublayer hierarchy, as shown in Figure 18.

11. Click the **Selection Tool** ➤, then move the new plant artwork into the position shown in Figure 19.

12. Scale the new plant artwork 85%, delete or move some leaves on it so that it's not an obvious copy of the original plant, then compare your screen to Figure 20.

You created and moved new sublayers.

Move objects between layers

1. Switch to the Showroom document, copy the electronics images, then return to the Living Room document.

2. Create a new layer at the top of the hierarchy, name it **Electronics**, choose Magenta as its color, then click **OK**.

3. Paste the electronics on the Electronics layer, then position the electronics artwork on the cabinet.

   The plant on the right needs to be positioned in front of the electronics for the visual to be realistic.

4. Name the top sublayer in the Entertainment layer **Plant 1**, then select the Plant 1 artwork on the artboard.

   The Indicates Selected Art button appears in the Plant 1 sublayer.

5. Drag the **Indicates Selected Art button** from the Plant 1 sublayer to the Electronics layer, as shown in Figure 21.

   The Plant 1 sublayer moves into the Electronics layer. The Plant 1 sublayer automatically becomes the top sublayer in the Electronics layer.

6. Switch to the Showroom document, copy the Matisse, return to the Living Room document, then create a new layer at the top of the hierarchy, named **Matisse**.

7. Paste the Matisse artwork into the new layer, then position it as shown in Figure 22.

   (continued)

FIGURE 21
Moving a sublayer from one layer to another

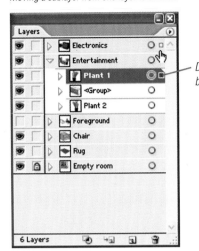

Drag the Indicates Selected Art button to the Electronics layer

FIGURE 22
The Matisse in position on its own layer

Working with Layers

FIGURE 23

Moving the Matisse layer into the Electronics layer

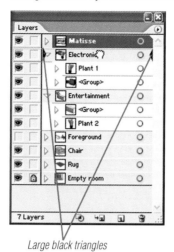

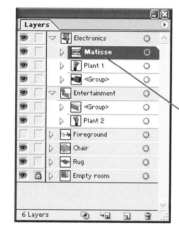

The Matisse layer becomes a sublayer of the Electronics layer

Large black triangles

FIGURE 24

The lamp and table in position

New Table and Lamp layers

8. Drag the Matisse layer on top of the Electronics layer.

Two large, black triangles appear on the Electronics layer when the Matisse layer is on top of it, as shown in Figure 23. The Matisse layer is moved into the Electronics layer as the topmost sublayer.

9. Create new layers for the lamp and the table, copy and paste the lamp and table artwork from the Showroom document to the new layers, then position the artwork so that your illustration resembles Figure 24.

10. Save your work.

You created a new layer named Electronics, dragged the Plant 1 sublayer into the Electronics layer by dragging its Indicates Selected Art button to the Electronics layer. You then moved the Matisse layer into the Electronics layer by dragging it on top of the Electronics layer and created new layers for the table and the lamp.

WORKING WITH LAYERED
ARTWORK

What You'll Do

▶ *In this lesson, you will explore options for managing your work using the Layers palette.*

Using the View Buttons in the Layers Palette

The view options available in the Layers palette make working with layers a smart choice for complex illustrations. The options are targeted: You can apply specific viewing options to each layer in the document. Without layers, your options for viewing your work are limited to the Hide and Show All commands on the Object menu.

The Toggles Visibility button makes it easy to quickly change what can be seen on the artboard. Clicking this button once hides all the artwork on a layer, and the button disappears. Clicking the empty gray square where the button was shows all of the artwork on the layer, and the button reappears. Pressing [Alt] (Win) or [option] (Mac) and clicking the button once shows all layers; clicking a second time hides all layers except for the layer you clicked.

Pressing [Ctrl] (Win) or ⌘ (Mac) and clicking the button toggles between Outline and Preview modes; all the artwork on the layer will switch between outlined and filled objects. Pressing [Alt][Ctrl] (Win) or [option] ⌘ (Mac) and clicking the button switches all other layers between Outline and Preview modes.

Locating an Object in the Layers Palette

With complex illustrations, layers and sublayers tend to multiply—so much so that you will often find it easiest to work with collapsed layers, those in which you hide the sublayers. Sometimes it can be difficult to identify an object's layer or sublayer, especially if there are multiple copies of the object in the illustration. The Locate Object command offers a simple solution. Select an object on the artboard, click the Layers palette list arrow, then click Locate Object. The layers expand, revealing their sublayers, and the selected object's layer or sublayer is selected.

Reversing the Order of Layers

Another option that the Layers palette offers for managing your artwork is the ability to reverse the order of layers. Select the layers whose order you want to reverse. Press [Shift] to select multiple contiguous (those next to each other in the palette) layers. Press [Ctrl] (Win) or ⌘ (Mac) to select multiple noncontiguous layers. Click the Layers palette list arrow, then click Reverse Order.

Making Layers Nonprintable

The ability to choose whether or not the artwork on a specific layer will print is a useful function, especially during the middle stages of producing an illustration. For example, you could print just the text elements and give them to a copy editor for proofing. You could print just the elements of the illustration that are ready to be shown to the client, holding back the elements that still need work.

Another value of the print option is the ability to print different versions of a document. Let's say you're working on the design of a poster for a client, and you've finalized the artwork but you're still undecided about the typeface for the headline, after narrowing down the choices to five typefaces. You could create five layers, one for the headline formatted in each typeface. Then you would print the illustration five times, each time printing only one of the five different headline layers. This is a smart and simple way to produce comps quickly.

QUICKTIP

You can export Illustrator layers to Photoshop by clicking File on the menu bar, clicking Export, clicking the Save as type list arrow (Win) or the Format list arrow (Mac), clicking Photoshop (*.PSD) (Win) or Photoshop (psd) (Mac), then clicking Save (Win) or Export (Mac). The Photoshop Export Options dialog box opens. Verify that the Write Layers option button is selected. Click OK to export the layers to a Photoshop document.

Explore view options in the Layers palette

1. Collapse the Electronics and Entertainment layers, then hide them.

2. Press and hold **[Alt]** (Win) or **[option]** (Mac), then click the **Toggles Visibility button**  on the Chair layer.

   All of the layers are displayed.

3. Using the same keyboard commands, click the **Toggles Visibility button** on the Chair layer again.

   All layers, except for the Chair layer, are hidden.

4. Using the same keyboard commands, click the **Toggles Visibility button** on the Chair layer again so that all of the layers are displayed.

5. Move the Foreground layer to the top of the hierarchy.

6. Press **[Ctrl]** (Win) or ⌘ (Mac), then click the **Toggles Visibility button** on the Chair layer.

   The artwork on the Chair layer switches to Outline mode.

7. Using the same keyboard commands, click the **Toggles Visibility button** on the Chair layer again.

8. Press **[Alt][Ctrl]** (Win) or **[option]** ⌘ (Mac), then click the same **Toggles Visibility button**.

   The artwork on every layer, except for the Chair layer, switches to Outline mode, as shown in Figure 25.

9. Using the same keyboard commands, click the **Toggles Visibility button** again.

You learned keyboard commands to explore view options in the Layers palette.

FIGURE 25
The Chair layer shown in Preview mode and all other layers shown in Outline mode

FIGURE 26
Duplicating the Lamp layer

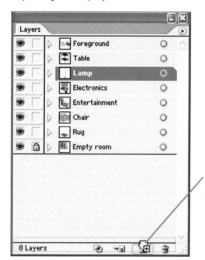

To duplicate a layer and its
contents, drag it on top of the
Create New Layer button

Locate, duplicate, and delete layers

1. Select the Plant 2 artwork on the artboard.

2. Click the **Layers palette list arrow**, then click **Locate Object**.

   The Entertainment layer expands, as does the Plant 2 sublayer.

   | TIP   The Locate Object command is useful when you are working with collapsed layers or with many layers and sublayers.

3. Collapse the Entertainment layer.

4. Select the Lamp layer, then drag it on top of the Create New Layer button ▣ , as shown in Figure 26.

   The Lamp layer and its contents are duplicated.

5. Position the duplicated lamp artwork on the artboard, as shown in Figure 27.

   | TIP   The copy of the lamp is directly on top of the original lamp.

6. Drag the **Lamp copy layer** to the Delete Selection button 🗑 in the Layers palette.

You used the Locate Object command to identify a selected object's position in the Layers palette. You duplicated a layer, then deleted it.

FIGURE 27
Positioning the second lamp

Dim placed images

1. Hide all layers, then create a new layer at the top of the hierarchy, named **Photo**.

2. Click **File** on the menu bar, then click **Place**.

3. Navigate to the drive and folder where your Data Files are stored, click **Living Room Original.tif**, then click **Place**.

   The source for the illustration is placed on its own layer, as shown in Figure 28.

4. Align the photo with the top-left corner of the artboard, if necessary.

5. Double-click the **Photo layer**, click the **Dim Images to check box**, type **50** in the Dim Images to text box, then click **OK**.

   The placed image is less vivid.

   | TIP   Dimming a placed image is useful for tracing.

You created a new layer, placed a photo on the new layer, then used the Layer Options dialog box to dim the photo 50%.

FIGURE 28
The source of the illustration, placed on its own layer

1. Create a new layer at the top of the hierarchy, named **Message**.

2. Using any font you like, type a message for the printer, as shown in Figure 29.

3. Convert the message text to outlines. Double-click the **Message layer**, remove the check mark from the Print check box, then click **OK**.

   The Message layer will not print to any output device.

   TIP When a layer is set to not print, its name is italicized in the Layers palette.

4. Make the Photo layer nonprintable.

5. Hide the Message and Photo layers.

6. Make all the other layers visible.

7. Save your work.

You created a new layer called Message, typed a message for the printer, then designated the Message and Photo layers as nonprintable. You then displayed all of the layers except for the Message and Photo layers.

FIGURE 29
Using a layer for a message to the printer

Printer: Use photo for reference if necessary. Thank you!
Call me at 555-1234 if any problems.

CREATE A
CLIPPING SET

What You'll Do

In this lesson, you will create a clipping mask on a sublayer that will mask the other sublayers in the layer.

Working with Clipping Sets

Adobe uses the terms "clipping mask" and "clipping path" interchangeably. The term **clipping set** is used to distinguish clipping paths used in layers from clipping paths used to mask nonlayered artwork. There's no difference; it's just terminology. Essentially, the term "clipping set" refers to the clipping mask *and* the masked sublayers as a unit.

The following rules apply to clipping sets:
- The clipping mask and the objects to be masked must be in the same layer.
- You cannot use a sublayer as a clipping mask, unless it is a <Group> sublayer. However, the top sublayer in a layer becomes the clipping mask if you first select the layer that the sublayer is in, then create the clipping mask.
- The top object in the clipping set becomes the mask for every object below it in the layer.
- A <Group> sublayer can be a clipping set. The top object in the group will function as the mask.
- Dotted lines between sublayers indicate that they are included in a clipping set.

Flattening Artwork

When you apply the Flatten Artwork command, all visible objects in the artwork are consolidated in a single layer. Before applying the command, select the layer into which you want to consolidate the artwork. If you have a layer that is hidden, you will be asked whether to make the artwork visible so that it can be flattened into the layer, or whether to delete the layer and the artwork on it.

FIGURE 30

The new <Path> sublayer

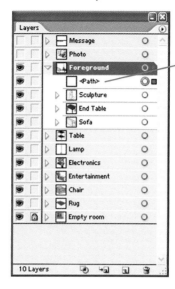

The rectangle is placed on a new sublayer called <Path>, on top of the other sublayers in the Foreground layer

Create clipping sets

1. Select the Foreground layer, click the **Rectangle Tool** ▢ , then create a rectangle that is 6.5" × 6".

2. Position the rectangle so that it aligns exactly with the edges of the artboard.

3. Apply a black stroke to the rectangle and no fill color.

4. Expand the Foreground layer.

   The rectangle, identified as <Path>, is at the top of the sublayers, as shown in Figure 30.

5. Click the **Make/Release Clipping Mask button** ▢ in the Layers palette.

   Any path on the Foreground layer that is positioned off the artboard is masked. The part of the rug that extends beyond the artboard is not masked, because it is not in the same layer as the clipping path. The lamp, too, extends beyond the artboard and is not masked, as shown in Figure 31.

You created a rectangle, then used it as a clipping path to mask the sublayers below it in its layer.

FIGURE 31

Clipping path masks only the objects on its own layer

Clipping path

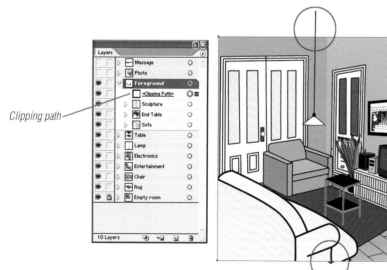

Copy a clipping mask and flatten artwork

1. Click the **<Clipping Path> layer** to select it.

2. Click **Edit** on the menu bar, click **Copy**, click **Edit** on the menu bar again, then click **Paste in Front**.

    A new sublayer named <Path> is created. The rectangle on the <Clipping Path> sublayer is duplicated on the new <Path> sublayer and can be used to mask other layers.

3. Drag the **Indicates Selected Art button** on the <Path> sublayer down to the Rug layer, as shown in Figure 32.

4. Expand the Rug layer to see the new <Path> sublayer, select the Rug layer, then click the **Make/Release Clipping Mask button** 🔲 .

    Compare your Layers palette to Figure 33. The <Path> sublayer becomes the <Clipping Path> sublayer, and the rectangle on the <Clipping Path> sublayer is used to mask the rug on the artboard.

    (continued)

FIGURE 32

Moving the copy of the rectangle to the Rug layer

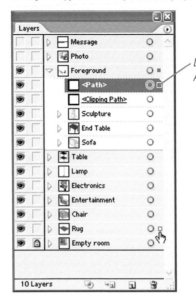

Drag the Indicates Selected Art button to the Rug layer

FIGURE 33

Using the duplicate rectangle to mask the rug

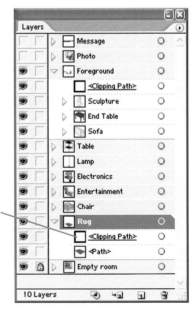

The <Path> sublayer becomes the <Clipping Path> sublayer, and the rectangle on the <Clipping Path> sublayer is used to mask the rug on the artboard

FIGURE 34
Completed illustration

5. Select the lamp artwork on the artboard, drag the **Indicates Selected Art button** on the Lamp layer to the Sculpture sublayer of the Foreground layer, then deselect all.

The lamp artwork moves to the Sculpture sublayer and is therefore masked. Your illustration should resemble Figure 34.

> TIP When you drag the Indicates Selected Art button from one layer to another, the selected artwork moves to the new layer, but the layer does not move.

6. Select the empty Lamp layer, then click the **Delete Selection button** in the Layers palette.

7. Select the Foreground layer, click the **Layers palette list arrow**, click **Flatten Artwork**, then click **Yes** when you are asked whether or not you want to discard the hidden art on the hidden layers.

8. Click **File** on the menu bar, click **Save As**, then save the file as **Living Room Flat**.

You made a copy of the rectangle, moved the copied rectangle to the Rug layer, then made it into a clipping path to mask the rug artwork. You then moved the lamp artwork into the Sculpture sublayer, which masked the lamp. You deleted the empty Lamp layer and flattened all of the artwork on the Foreground layer.

Create and modify layers.

1. Open AI 5-3.ai, then save it as **Gary Garlic**.
2. Create a new layer at the top of the layer hierarchy, named **Text**.
3. Create a new layer at the top of the hierarchy, named **Gary Garlic**.
4. Rename Layer 2 **Body Parts**.
5. Save your work.

Manipulate layered artwork.

1. Move the garlic artwork into the Gary Garlic layer.
2. Move the three text groups into the Text layer.
3. Merge the Background layer with the Box Shapes layer so that the Box Shapes layer is the name of the resulting merged layer. (*Hint*: Click the Background layer, press [Ctrl] (Win) or ⌘ (Mac), click the Box Shapes layer, click the Layers palette list arrow, then click Merge Selected.)
4. Move the Body Parts layer to the top of the layer hierarchy.
5. Save your work.

Work with layered artwork.

1. View each layer separately to identify the artwork on each.
2. Using Figure 35 as a guide, assemble Gary Garlic.
3. Merge the Gary Garlic and Body Parts layers so that the resulting merged layer will be named Body Parts.
4. Select all the artwork on the Body Parts layer, then group the artwork.
5. Save your work.

Create a clipping set.

1. Select the Box Shapes layer.
2. Create a rectangle that is 5" wide by 8" in height.
3. Position the rectangle so that it is centered on the artboard.
4. Apply the Make Clipping Mask command.
5. Reposition the masked elements (text and box parts) so that your illustration resembles Figure 35.
6. Save your work, then close Gary Garlic.

FIGURE 35
Completed Skills Review

You are designing an outdoor sign for Xanadu Haircutters, a salon that recently opened in your town. You are pleased with your concept of using scissors to represent the X in Xanadu, and decide to design the logo with different typefaces so that the client will feel she has some input into the final design.

1. Open AI 5-4.ai, then save it as **Xanadu**.
2. Create a new layer, then move the ANADU headline into that layer.
3. Make four duplicates of the new layer.
4. Change the typeface on four of the layers, for a total of five versions of the logo type.
5. Rename each type layer, using the name of the typeface you chose.
6. Rename Layer 1 Xanadu Art.
7. View the Xanadu Art layer five times, each time with one of the typeface layers, so that you can see five versions of the logo.
8. Save your work, compare your illustration with Figure 36, then close Xanadu.

FIGURE 36
Completed Project Builder 1

You are the Creative Director for a Los Angeles design firm that specializes in identity packages for television networks. One of your most important projects this week is delivering the first round of comps for a new cable channel, Milty TV. Your art directors have come up with two concepts—one dark, one light. You decide to bring each to the client with two options for typography, for a total of four comps.

1. Open AI 5-5.ai, then save it as **Milty TV**.
2. Select the four pieces of artwork at the top of the artboard, then group them.
3. Group the four pieces of artwork at the bottom of the artboard, then cut them.
4. Create a new layer, name it **Orange**, then paste the artwork.
5. Position the orange artwork exactly on top of the blue artwork on the artboard so that it is covered.
6. Rename Layer 1 **Blue**, then duplicate the layer and name it **Blue Two**.
7. Duplicate the Orange layer, then name it **Orange Two**.
8. Deselect all, use the Direct Selection Tool to select the large M, change its typeface to Algerian, then hide the two Orange layers. (*Hint*: If you do not have Algerian as a typeface, choose another one.)
9. Select the Blue Two layer, change the M to Algerian, then hide it.
10. View each of the four layers separately.
11. Save your work, compare your illustration to Figure 37, then close Milty TV.

FIGURE 37
Completed Project Builder 2

You are a freelance designer, working out of your house. The owner of the town's largest plumbing company, Straight Flush, has hired you to redesign his logo. He gives you an Illustrator file with a design created by his son. You study the logo, then decide that it lacks cohesion and focus.

1. Open **AI 5-6.ai**, then save it as **Straight Flush**.
2. Group the elements of each playing card together.
3. Create four new layers.
4. Move each card to the layer with the corresponding number in the layer name.
5. Select all the layers, click the Layers palette list arrow, then click Reverse Order.
6. Reposition the cards on each layer so that they are in order, directly behind the ace.
7. Adjust the layout of the cards to your liking to create a new layout for the logo.
8. Save your work, compare your illustration with Figure 38, then close Straight Flush.

FIGURE 38
Completed Design Project

You are a fabric designer for a line of men's clothing. You are asked to supervise a team that will design new patterns for men's ties. Now that you have studied working with layers, how would you approach building a file that shows three patterns for a tie?

1. Open AI 5-7.ai, then save it as **Ties**.
2. Have one group member select objects in the document while the group watches.
3. Have the group discuss how each tie illustration has been created.
4. Have the group discuss how the document would be more practical if built with layers. How many masks would be required to show the three patterns?
   How many layers would be required?
5. Have the group redesign the document with layers so that the three patterns are all in one clipping set with one tie shape functioning as the mask.
6. Save your work, compare your Layers palette with Figure 39, then close Ties.

FIGURE 39
Completed Group Project

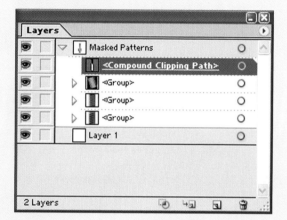

6

WORKING WITH PATTERNS
AND BRUSHES

1. Use the Move command.

2. Create a pattern.

3. Design a repeating pattern.

4. Work with the Brushes palette.

5. Work with scatter brushes.

Working with Patterns and Brushes

Artwork that you create in Illustrator is, of course, an end in and of itself—the result of your efforts in conceiving an image and rendering it, using your skills and talents. As you become more familiar with Illustrator, you will learn to use completed artwork as a component of new illustrations.

Using patterns and brushes is a fine example of this working method. You can design artwork and then use it as a pattern to fill and stroke new artwork. This would be very useful if you were drawing a field of flowers, or stars in the night sky, or trees on a mountainside.

The powerful options in Illustrator's Brushes palette extend this concept even further. Using brushes, you can extend the role of completed artwork as a stroke, a pattern, or a freestanding illustration of greater complexity. For example, you could create a custom brush stroke, such as a leaf, and then use the Paintbrush Tool to paint with the leaf brush stroke. Instead of being limited to filling or stroking an object with leaves, you could paint leaves wherever you wanted on the artboard.

Tools You'll Use

Brushes palette
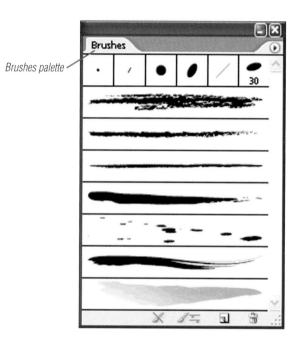

USE THE MOVE COMMAND

What You'll Do

 In this lesson, you will use the Move command to copy an object at precise offsets and create a simple pattern.

Using the Move Command

The word **offset** comes up when you explore the Move command. Quite simply, the term refers to the distance that an object is moved or copied from a starting location to an ending location. In a simple drop shadow, for example, you can describe the effect by saying, "The black copy behind the original has been offset three points to the left and three points down."

The Move command provides the most effective method for moving an object—or a copy of an object—at precise offsets. In the Move dialog box, you enter the horizontal distance and the vertical distance that you want a selected object to move. A positive value moves the object horizontally to the right, and a negative value moves it to the left. A positive value moves the object vertically up, and a negative value moves it down.

An alternate (and seldom used) method for using the Move dialog box is to enter a value for the distance you want the object to move and a value for the angle it should move on. Entering a distance and an angle is the same as specifying the move in horizontal and vertical values. When you enter values in the Distance and Angle text boxes, the Horizontal and Vertical text boxes update to reflect the move.

Conversely, when you enter values in the Horizontal and Vertical text boxes, the Distance and Angle text boxes update to reflect the move. The Move dialog box is shown in Figure 1.

FIGURE 1
Move dialog box

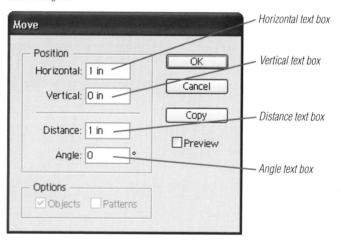

Horizontal text box

Vertical text box

Distance text box

Angle text box

Copy and move objects using the Move dialog box

1. Create a new 4" × 4" CMYK Color document, then save it as **Checkerboard**.

2. Click **Edit** (Win) or **Illustrator** (Mac) on the menu bar, point to **Preferences**, then click **Units & Display Performance**.

3. Verify that the General units of measure are Inches, then click **OK**.

4. Create a ½" square, apply a red fill and no stroke, then position it at the upper-left corner of the artboard.

5. Click **Object** on the menu bar, point to **Transform**, then click **Move**.

6. Enter **.5** in the Horizontal text box, press **[Tab]**, enter **0** in the Vertical text box, then press **[Tab]** again.

   TIP Values in the Distance and Angle text boxes automatically appear, based on the values entered in the Horizontal and Vertical text boxes.

7. Click **Copy**.

   A copy of the square is positioned immediately to the right of the original.

8. Change the fill on the second square to black, select both squares, click **Object** on the menu bar, point to **Transform**, then click **Move**.

9. Enter **1** in the Horizontal text box, then click **Copy**.

10. Click **Object** on the menu bar, point to **Transform**, click **Transform Again**, then repeat this step.

    Your work should resemble Figure 2.

    (continued)

FIGURE 2
A simple pattern created using the Move command

Working with Patterns and Brushes

FIGURE 3

A checkerboard created with a single starting square and the Move dialog box

11. Select all, open the Move dialog box, enter **0** in the Horizontal text box, enter **-.5** in the Vertical text box, then click **Copy**.

> TIP Apply a negative value to move an object down.

12. Double-click the **Rotate Tool** ⟳, enter **180** in the Angle text box, then click **OK**.

13. Select all, open the Move dialog box, enter **-1** in the Vertical text box, then click **Copy**.

14. Apply the Transform Again command twice, then save your work.

   Your screen should resemble Figure 3.

15. Close the Checkerboard document.

Starting with a single square, you used the Move command to make multiple copies at precise distances, to create a checkerboard pattern.

Exporting Illustrator CS2 files

You can export your Illustrator files in a variety of formats. For example, you can export your artwork as a JPEG, which is a Web file format, or as a Photoshop (.PSD) file. To export, click File on the menu bar, point to Export, type a new name for the exported file in the File name text box, then choose the file type from the Save as type list arrow. Depending on the file format that you choose, you may have another Options dialog box appear offering you more settings for your exported file. For example, if you export your illustration as Macromedia Flash (SWF), you'll be able to choose a background color, a lossy or lossless compression, and whether you want the Illustrator layers to be converted to Flash layers or to individual Flash files. These are only a few of the many options in the Macromedia Flash (SWF) Format Options dialog box. When you plan to use your artwork on the Web, you should export it as a JPEG if it contains photographic images or continuous tones, or a GIF, if it contains large areas of soild colors. Exporting your Illustrator document as a PDF creates a file that can be opened and read on computers that have Adobe Acrobat Reader installed. This is a handy way to share your work with someone who may not have Illustrator installed. You can open and manipulate PSD files in Photoshop, where they can even retain their original layer structure. Finally, the SVG (Scalable Vector Graphics) format is a language for describing two-dimensional graphics in XML.

CREATE A
PATTERN

What You'll Do

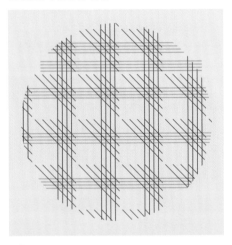

In this lesson, you will create a pattern from a simple illustration, add it to the Swatches palette, name it, and then fill an object with it.

Creating Patterns

In Illustrator you can design patterns that can be used to fill objects or that can be applied as outlines for objects. You can design patterns that are simple or complex, abstract or specific, and you can save them for future use and applications. The Swatches palette comes preloaded with two patterns—Starry Sky and Grid on Grid—which you can modify to create your own versions.

To create a pattern, you first create artwork for the pattern, then drag that artwork into the Swatches palette, where it is automatically defined as a pattern swatch. You can use paths, compound paths, or text in patterns. The following cannot be used as artwork for a pattern: gradients, blends, brush strokes, meshes, bitmap images, graphs, masks, or other patterns.

Designing a Pattern

Patterns repeat. A pattern fills an object by repeating the original pattern, a process called **tiling**. The word is used intentionally as a reference to floor tiles. Illustrator creates pattern fills in much the same way that you would use multiple tiles to cover a floor. Think of the pattern as the floor tile and the object to be filled as the floor.

You design fill patterns by designing one tile. For efficiency with previewing and printing, a pattern tile should be a ½" to 1" square. When saved as a pattern and applied as a fill, the tile will repeat as many times as necessary to fill the object, as shown in Figure 4.

Many times, you will create a pattern that contains no rectangular objects, such as a polka dot pattern, or a pattern of lines. In these cases, you create a **bounding box** to define the perimeter of the pattern tile. Position an unfilled, unstroked rectangular object at the back of the stacking order of the pattern tile. Illustrator will regard this as the bounding box. All of the objects within the bounding box will be repeated as part of the pattern.

The pattern in Figure 5 is composed of lines only. The square is used as a bounding box. It defines the perimeter of the tile, and the pattern is created by repeating only the elements that fall within the bounding box. Again, a bounding box must have no fill and no stroke, it must be a rectangle or a square, and it must be the backmost object of the pattern tile.

Controlling How a Pattern Fills an Object

The way a pattern fills an object is tricky to understand. The pattern begins from the origin of the ruler, which is by default at the bottom-left corner of the artboard. In other words, by default, the pattern begins at the bottom-left of the artboard, not the bottom-left corner of the object.

When an object is filled with a pattern, if you move the object, the pattern changes within the object. If you understand the concept of a clipping mask, the pattern fill is easier to understand. Think of it this way: The pattern covers the *entire* artboard; the object that is filled with the pattern functions like a clipping mask—you can see the pattern only through the object.

FIGURE 4

The tile repeats to fill the object

FIGURE 5

Bounding box determines the perimeter of the pattern tile

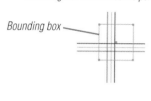

Bounding box

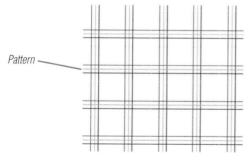

Pattern

The best method for controlling how a pattern appears within an object is to align the ruler origin with the bottom-left corner of the object. To do this, display the rulers, then position your cursor at the top-left corner of the window, where the two rulers meet. The cross hairs are the ruler origin. Drag the cross hairs to the bottom-left corner of the filled object, as shown in Figure 6. Because the ruler origin and the bottom-left corner of the square are the same point, the first tile is positioned evenly in the corner. The pattern fills the object left to right, bottom to top.

Transforming Patterns

When an object is filled with a pattern, you can choose to transform only the object, only the pattern, or both the object and the pattern. For example, the Scale Tool dialog box, shown in Figure 7, contains options for determining whether or not the transformation will affect a pattern fill.

QUICKTIP

The options that you choose in one transform tool dialog box will be applied to all transform tool dialog boxes.

When you transform a pattern, all subsequent objects that you create will be filled with the transformed pattern. To return a pattern fill to its nontransformed appearance, fill an object with a different swatch, then reapply the pattern swatch.

FIGURE 6

Aligning the ruler origin with the bottom-left corner of the filled object

FIGURE 7

Options for patterns in the Scale dialog box

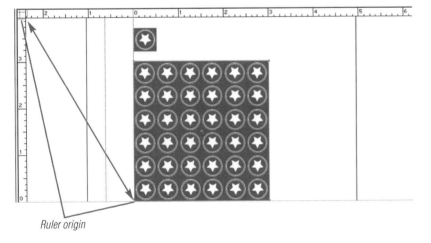

Ruler origin

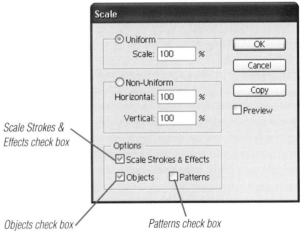

Scale Strokes & Effects check box

Objects check box

Patterns check box

FIGURE 8
Artwork to be used as a pattern tile

FIGURE 9
Artwork applied as a pattern fill

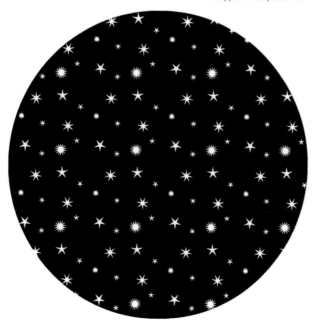

Create a pattern swatch

1. Open AI 6-1.ai, then save it as **Starry Night**.
2. Position the ten stars randomly over the black box.

   | TIP   Enlarge your view of the artboard.
3. Change the fill color of the stars to White.

   Compare your screen to Figure 8.
4. Group the white stars.
5. Select all, then drag the **artwork** into the Swatches palette.

   The Swatches palette automatically identifies and defines the new swatch as a pattern swatch.
6. Double-click the **new swatch** called New Pattern Swatch 1, name it **Starry Night** in the Swatch Options dialog box, then click **OK**.
7. Delete all the artwork on the artboard.
8. Create a circle that is 4" in diameter.
9. Apply the Starry Night swatch to fill the circle, if necessary.

   | TIP   The Starry Night swatch may have automatically been applied to your circle when you created it because it is still selected in the Swatches palette.

   Your screen should resemble Figure 9.

You created a 1"× 1" collection of objects, selected all of them, then dragged them into the Swatches palette. You named the new pattern swatch, then applied it as a fill for a circle.

Transform pattern-filled objects

1. Select the circle, then double-click the **Scale Tool** .

2. Type **50** in the Scale text box, verify that only the Objects check box is checked in the Options section of the dialog box, then click **OK**.

   The object is scaled 50%; the pattern is not scaled.

3. Drag and drop a copy above the original circle.

4. Double-click the **Scale Tool** .

5. Type **200** in the Scale text box, verify that only the Patterns check box is checked, then click **OK**.

   The pattern is scaled 200%; the object is not scaled. Your screen should resemble Figure 10.

6. Save your work, then close the Starry Night document.

You experimented with options for scaling a pattern fill and an object independently using the Scale dialog box.

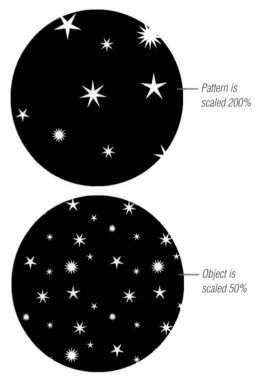

FIGURE 10

Patterns can be transformed independently of the objects that they fill

Pattern is scaled 200%

Object is scaled 50%

FIGURE 11

Position a bounding box to define a pattern

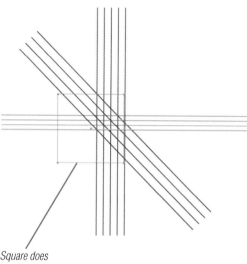

*Square does
not have a fill
or stroke color*

FIGURE 12

A yellow square behind a line pattern

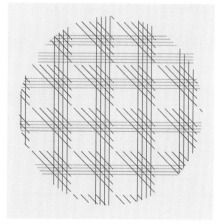

Create a pattern using open paths

1. Open AI 6-2.ai, then save it as **Line Pattern**.

2. Create a 1" square.

3. Position the square over the lines, then remove both the fill and the stroke colors, as shown in Figure 11.

   Note that the rightmost purple line is not within the perimeter of the square.

4. Send the square to the back.

   TIP   If you deselect the square, switch to Outline mode so that you can see the outline of the square to select it, then switch back to Preview mode.

5. Select all, then drag the **objects** into the Swatches palette.

6. Hide the objects on the artboard.

7. Create a 4" circle, then fill it with the new pattern.

8. Create a 5" square, fill it with yellow, remove the stroke color if necessary, send it to the back, then position it behind the circle, as shown in Figure 12.

   The yellow square is visible behind the pattern because the pattern is composed of lines only.

9. Save your work, then close the Line Pattern document.

You placed a 1" square with no fill or stroke behind a group of straight paths. You used all the objects to create a pattern swatch, with the square defining the perimeter of the pattern tile. You filled a circle with the pattern, then positioned a yellow square behind the circle, creating the effect of a circle pattern within a square.

DESIGN A REPEATING
PATTERN

What You'll Do

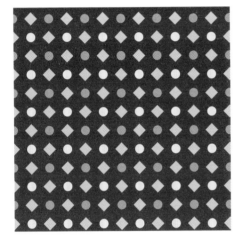

In this lesson, you will design a visually repetitive pattern. You will then explore options for modifying the pattern after it has been applied as a fill.

Designing Patterns

Simple patterns can be tricky to design. Understanding how patterns tile is important for achieving a desired effect. You will often be surprised to find that the tile you design does not create the pattern that you had in mind.

In Figure 13, it at first seems logical that the tile on the left could produce the pattern below. However, it requires the more complex tile on the right to produce what appears to be a "simple" pattern.

Another consideration when designing patterns is whether or not you want the pattern to be apparent. If you were designing a plaid pattern, you would by definition want the pattern to be noticed. However, if you were designing artwork for a field of flowers, you might want the pattern to be subtle, if not invisible. An invisible pattern is difficult to create, especially when it's based on a 1" tile!

In every case, precision is important when creating a pattern. If two objects are meant to align, be certain that they do align; don't rely on just your eye. Use dialog boxes to move and transform objects; don't try to do it by hand.

Modifying Patterns

You modify a pattern by editing the artwork in the pattern tile, then replacing the old pattern in the Swatches palette with the new pattern. When you replace the old pattern, any existing objects on the artboard that were filled with the old pattern will automatically update with the new pattern. Of course, you can always leave the original pattern as is and save the edited pattern as a new swatch. This is often a wise move, because you may want to use that original pattern again sometime.

FIGURE 13
Only the top-right tile could create the pattern

This tile could not create the pattern

Note the four quarter circles in each corner

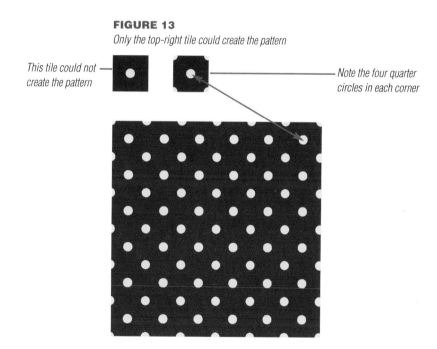

Create a repeating pattern with precision

1. Open AI 6-3.ai, then save it as **Repeating Pattern**.

2. Select the purple circle, click **Object** on the menu bar, point to **Transform**, then click **Move**.

3. Enter **1** in the Horizontal text box, enter **0** in the Vertical text box, then click **Copy**.

   A copy of the purple circle is created at the upper-right corner of the square.

4. Select both purple circles, open the Move dialog box, enter **0** in the Horizontal text box and **-1** in the Vertical text box, then click **Copy**.

   Your screen should resemble Figure 14.

5. Select the blue diamond, then apply the Transform Again command.

   A copy of the blue diamond is created at the bottom edge of the square.

6. Select both blue diamonds, double-click the **Rotate Tool** 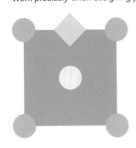, enter **90** in the Angle text box, then click **Copy**.

   Your work should resemble Figure 15.

   (continued)

FIGURE 14
Work precisely when designing pattern tiles

FIGURE 15
Use dialog boxes to make transformations when designing pattern tiles

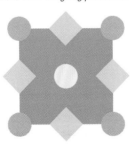

Working with Patterns and Brushes

FIGURE 16

Designing pattern tiles can be tricky work

FIGURE 17

A "simple" pattern

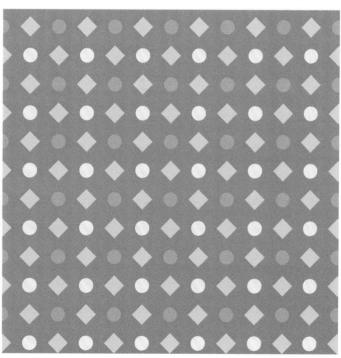

7. Select all, then click the **Divide button** 🔲 in the Pathfinder palette.

8. Deselect, click the **Direct Selection Tool** ▶, click the **artboard**, then delete the areas of the diamonds and circles that are outside the perimeter of the square, so that your design resembles Figure 16.

9. Click the **Selection Tool** ▶, select all, drag the **artwork** into the Swatches palette, then name the new pattern **Alpha Shapes**.

10. Delete the artwork on the artboard.

11. Create a 6" × 6" square, fill it with the Alpha Shapes pattern, then center it on the artboard.

12. Compare your screen to Figure 17.

You used the Move command to position multiple objects in a symmetrical pattern over a 1" square. You then used the Divide pathfinder, which allowed you to select and then delete the areas of objects that were positioned outside the square. You dragged the pattern into the Swatches palette. You named the pattern, then created a square with the pattern as its fill.

Modify a pattern

1. Drag the **Alpha Shapes pattern** from the Swatches palette to the scratch area at the upper-right corner of the artboard.

2. Click the **Direct Selection Tool**, click the **artboard** to deselect the pattern, then click the **pink section** on the pattern.

3. Change the pink fill to a red fill.

4. Switch to the **Selection Tool**, then select the entire pattern.

5. Press and hold [**Alt**] (Win) or [**option**] (Mac), then drag the **modified pattern** on top of the Alpha Shapes pattern in the Swatches palette.

   The Alpha Shapes pattern is replaced in the Swatches palette, and the fill of the square is updated, as shown in Figure 18.

   (continued)

FIGURE 18
Changing the background color of the pattern

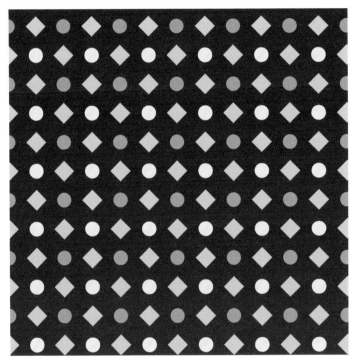

FIGURE 19

Updated pattern without the red background

6. Using the Direct Selection Tool ⬚, select all of the pattern pieces in the scratch area, except for the red section.

7. Press and hold [**Alt**] (Win) or [**option**] (Mac), then drag the **selected objects** on top of the Alpha Shapes swatch in the Swatches palette.

   Your screen should resemble Figure 19.

8. Save and close the Repeating Pattern file.

You dragged the Alpha Shapes pattern swatch out of the Swatches palette and onto the scratch area in order to modify it. You changed a color in the pattern, then replaced the old pattern swatch with the new pattern. The object filled with the original pattern was updated to reflect the changes to the pattern. You modified the pattern again by dragging only parts of it to the Swatches palette.

WORK WITH THE
BRUSHES PALETTE

What You'll Do

In this lesson, you will create a calligraphic brush, a scatter brush, an art brush, and a pattern brush.

Working with the Brushes Palette

The Brushes palette offers six Calligraphic brushes and seven sample Art brushes that you can use to add artwork to paths or that you can paint with, using the Paintbrush Tool. Figure 20 shows the Brushes palette. Using your own artwork, you can create Scatter brushes and Pattern brushes and add them to the Brushes palette. You can work with the brushes that have been preloaded, you can modify them, or you can create new brushes.

Calligraphic brushes apply strokes that resemble those drawn with a calligraphic pen. Figure 21 is an example.

Scatter brushes disperse copies of an object along a path, as shown in Figure 22.

You can apply artwork—such as an arrow or a feather—to a path with an art brush. **Art brushes** stretch an object along the length of a path, as shown in Figure 23.

FIGURE 20
Brushes palette

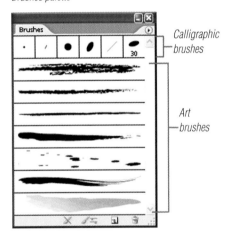

Calligraphic brushes

Art brushes

Pattern brushes repeat a pattern along a path. Pattern brushes are made with tiles that you create. You can define up to five tiles as components of the pattern: one tile for the side, one for the inner corner, one for the outer corner, and one each for the beginning and ending of the path. Figure 24 shows five tiles and a pattern that was created with them.

You can create any of the four types of brushes. Artwork for brushes must be composed of simple paths—no gradients, blends, mesh objects, bitmap images, masks, or other brush strokes can be used. Art and pattern brushes cannot include text. You must convert text to outlines before it can be used as artwork for these types of brushes.

FIGURE 21
A calligraphic brush applied to a path

FIGURE 22
A scatter brush applied to a path

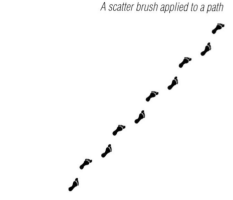

FIGURE 23
An art brush applied to a path

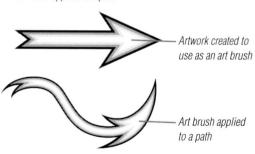

Artwork created to use as an art brush

Art brush applied to a path

FIGURE 24
Five tiles used for a pattern brush

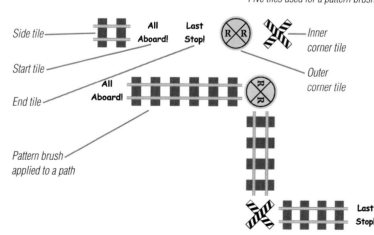

Side tile

Start tile

End tile

All Aboard!

Last Stop!

Inner corner tile

Outer corner tile

Pattern brush applied to a path

All Aboard!

Last Stop!

Create a calligraphic brush

1. Open AI 6-4.ai, then save it as **Four Brushes**.
2. Click **Window** on the menu bar, then click **Brushes**.
3. Click the **Brushes palette list arrow**, then click **New Brush**.
4. Click the **New Calligraphic Brush option button** in the New Brush dialog box, then click **OK**.
5. Type **Twelve Points** in the Name text box, **45** in the Angle text box, and **12** in the Diameter text box, as shown in Figure 25, then click **OK**.

   The Twelve Points brush is added to the calligraphy brush section and is selected in the Brushes palette.
6. Click the **Selection Tool** ▶, select the first curved line on the artboard, then click the **Twelve Points brush** in the Brushes palette.

   (continued)

FIGURE 25

Calligraphic Brush Options dialog box

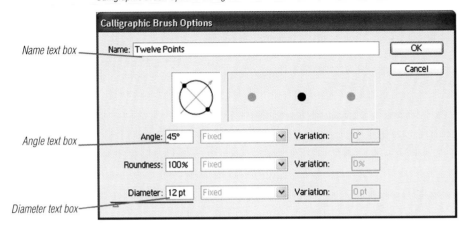

Name text box

Angle text box

Diameter text box

Using the Paintbrush Tool

You can apply any brush in the Brushes palette to any path simply by selecting the path then clicking the brush swatch. Many designers draw a shape with the Pen Tool, then apply their brush of choice. Other designers, however, prefer a more "freehand" approach and use the Paintbrush Tool. The Paintbrush Tool creates paths that are painted with a brush that you preselect in the Brushes palette. In addition to drawing freehand with the tool, you can set options in the tool's dialog box that determine the smoothness of the stroke or the curve and how far the artwork can stray or scatter from the path you draw.

FIGURE 26
Applying a calligraphic brush to paths

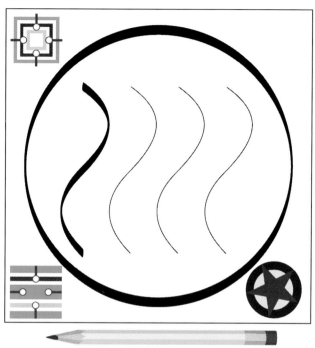

7. Double-click the **Twelve Points brush** in the Brushes palette.

8. Click the **Preview check box** in the Calligraphic Brush Options dialog box, change the Roundness to **20%**, then click **OK**.

9. Click **Apply to Strokes** in the Brush Change Alert dialog box.

    The curved line updates to reflect the changes.

10. Apply the Twelve Points brush to the circle, then deselect all.

    Your screen should resemble Figure 26.

You created and set the parameters for a new calligraphic brush, which you applied to a curved path and to a circle.

The Pencil, Smooth, and Erase Tools

The Pencil, Smooth, and Erase Tools are grouped together in the toolbox. You can draw freehand paths with the Pencil Tool and then manipulate them using the Direct Selection Tool, the Smooth Tool, and the Erase Tool. The Smooth Tool is used to smooth over line segments that are too bumpy or too sharp. The Erase Tool looks and acts just like an eraser found at the end of a traditional pencil; dragging it over a line segment erases that part of the segment from the artboard.

Create a scatter brush

1. Select the star target in the lower-right corner of the artboard, click the **Brushes palette list arrow**, click **New Brush**, click the **New Scatter Brush option button**, then click **OK**.

2. Name the brush **Star Target**, type **20** in the Size text box, type **60** in the Spacing text box, then click **OK**.

   The Star Target brush is selected in the Brushes palette.

3. Hide the star target artwork on the artboard.

4. Apply the Star Target brush to the second curved line, then apply it to the circle.

   TIP To remove a brush stroke from a path, select the path, then click the Remove Brush Stroke button ✖ in the Brushes palette.

5. Double-click the **Star Target brush**, change the spacing to **20%**, click **OK**, then click **Apply to Strokes** in the Brush Change Alert dialog box.

6. Save your work, then compare your screen to Figure 27.

You used a group of simple objects as the artwork for a scatter brush, which you applied to a curved path and to a circle.

FIGURE 27
Applying a scatter brush to paths

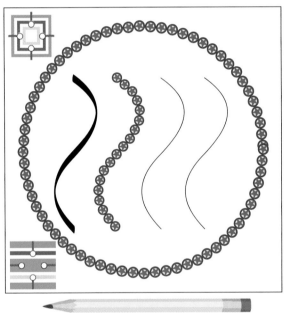

FIGURE 28
Applying an art brush to paths

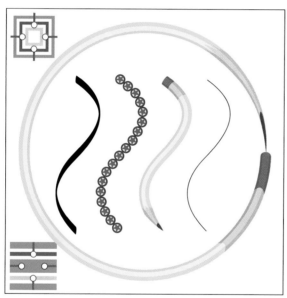

1. Select the pencil artwork, click the **Brushes palette list arrow**, click **New Brush**, click the **New Art Brush option button**, then click **OK**.

2. Click the **Stroke From Right To Left arrow** ← in the Art Brush Options dialog box.

   The direction arrow in the preview window updates and points in the same direction as the point of the pencil.

3. Enter **75** in the Width text box, then click **OK**.

   The pencil brush is selected in the Brushes palette.

4. Hide the pencil artwork on the artboard.

5. Apply the pencil brush to the third curved line, then apply it to the circle.

6. Save your work, then compare your screen to Figure 28.

You used an illustration of a pencil as the art for an art brush. You defined the parameters of the art brush—its direction and its size—then applied the brush to a curved path and to a circle.

Create a pattern brush

1. Verify that your Swatches palette is visible.

2. Select the artwork in the lower-left corner of the artboard, drag it into the Swatches palette, then name it **Green Side**.

3. Hide the artwork used for the Green Side swatch on the artboard.

4. Select the artwork in the top-left corner, drag it into the Swatches palette, then name it **Green Corner**.

5. Hide the artwork used for the Green Corner swatch on the artboard.

6. Click the **Brushes palette list arrow**, click **New Brush**, click the **New Pattern Brush option button**, then click **OK**.

7. Name the new brush **Tomato Worm**.

8. Click the **Side Tile box**, then click **Green Side** in the list of patterns.

9. Click the **Outer Corner Tile box**, then click **Green Corner** in the list of patterns, as shown in Figure 29.

10. Type **40** in the Scale text box, then click **OK**.

    The Tomato Worm brush is selected in the Brushes palette.

You dragged the two pieces of artwork into the Swatches palette and named them. You then created a new pattern brush and, in the dialog box, defined the first piece of artwork as the side tile of the brush, and the second as a corner tile.

FIGURE 29
Pattern Brush Options dialog box

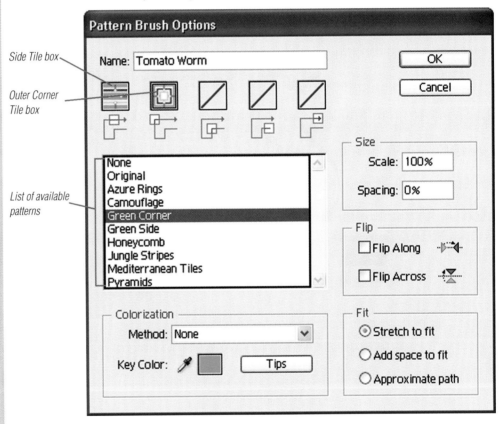

ILLUSTRATOR 6-26

Working with Patterns and Brushes

FIGURE 30
Applying the pattern brush to paths

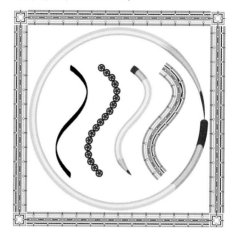

Modify a pattern brush

1. Apply the Tomato Worm brush to the fourth curved line, then apply it to the square.

   Your screen should resemble Figure 30.

2. Double-click the **Tomato Worm brush** in the Brushes palette.

3. Click the **Start Tile box**, then click **Green Corner** in the list of patterns.

4. Click the **End Tile box**, click **Green Corner** in the list of patterns, click **OK**, then click **Apply to Strokes** in the Brush Change Alert dialog box.

   The curved line now begins and ends with the corner artwork, as shown in Figure 31.

5. Save your work.

6. Close the Four Brushes document.

You applied the pattern brush to a curved path and to a square. You then modified the brush, adding artwork for a start tile and an end tile.

FIGURE 31
Modifying the pattern brush

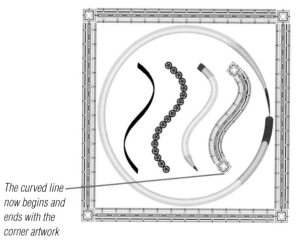

The curved line now begins and ends with the corner artwork

WORK WITH
SCATTER BRUSHES

What You'll Do

▶ *In this lesson, you will work with scatter brushes, enter fixed and random values in the Scatter Brush Options dialog box, and view how those values affect your artwork.*

Working with Scatter Brushes

The role of brushes in creating artwork is easy to underestimate. Many designers identify them as a method for creating really cool strokes and leave it at that. What they are missing is that brushes can themselves be the best option for creating an illustration.

Of the four types of brushes, the scatter brush best illustrates this point. For example, if you were drawing a pearl necklace, a scatter brush would be your smartest choice for creating the illustration, as opposed to dragging and dropping copies of a single pearl illustration along a path, or creating a blend between two pearls.

Why? The reason is that with the scatter brush, you can manipulate the path endlessly, with precise control of the size, spacing, and rotation of the elements along the path. In addition, you can input a scatter value, which determines how far the objects can be positioned from the path, an option that blending does not offer.

The scatter brush is even more powerful for creating the effect of "randomness." Figure 32 shows a fine example of this effect using a flying beetle as the artwork for the scatter brush. In the scatter Brush Options dialog box, you can apply a random range for size, spacing, scatter, and rotation and create the effect of a three-dimensional swarm of beetles flying in different directions—some of them closer to you and larger, some of them farther away and smaller.

For each setting in the Brush Options dialog box, you can choose fixed or random values. When you apply random settings to a scatter brush, the positioning of the objects on the path will be different every time you apply the brush.

FIGURE 32

A swarm of beetles created with a flying beetle scatter brush

Modify a scatter brush

1. Open AI 6-5.ai, then save it as **Random Flies**.

2. Select the circle, then apply the Flying Beetle scatter brush.

3. Double-click the **Flying Beetle brush** in the Brushes palette, click the **Preview check box** to add a check mark (if necessary), then move the Scatter Brush Options dialog box so that you can see as much of the artboard as possible.

4. Click the **Size list arrow**, then click **Fixed**.

   The beetles become the same size.

   | TIP   Press [Tab] to see changes made to the artwork after you change a value in the dialog box.

5. Type **50** In the Size text box.

   The beetles are 50% the size of the original flying beetle artwork.

6. Click the **Scatter list arrow**, click **Fixed**, then type **0** in the Scatter text box.

   The beetles are positioned on the path.

7. Click the **Spacing list arrow**, click **Fixed**, then type **50** in the Spacing text box.

   The beetles are evenly spaced along the path.

8. Click the **Rotation list arrow**, click **Fixed**, then type **0** in the Rotation text box, as shown in Figure 33.

   The beetles rotate 360° as they move from the beginning to the end of the path.

   (continued)

FIGURE 33
Scatter Brush Options dialog box

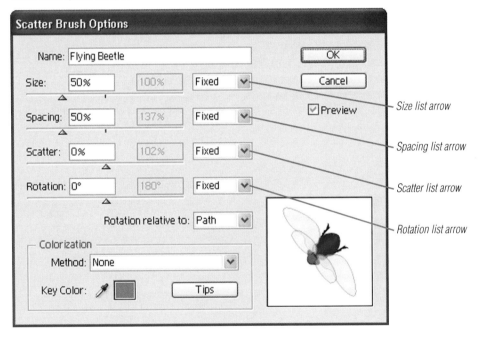

Size list arrow

Spacing list arrow

Scatter list arrow

Rotation list arrow

Working with Patterns and Brushes

FIGURE 34

The Flying Beetle scatter brush, using fixed values

9. Click the **Rotation relative to list arrow**, then click **Page**.

   The beetles no longer rotate along the path.

10. Click the **eyedropper button** in the Scatter Brush Options dialog box, then click the **black leg** of the beetle artwork in the preview window of the dialog box.

    The Key Color box turns black.

11. Click the **Method list arrow**, then click **Tints**.

    The beetles are tinted with the new key color. Your work should resemble Figure 34.

12. Click **OK**, then click **Apply to Strokes** in the Brush Change Alert dialog box.

You explored the parameters that define a scatter brush. You started with scatter brush artwork that was random in size, spacing, scatter, and rotation. By removing the parameters that defined the randomness of the artwork, you gained an understanding of how those parameters created the random effects in the original artwork.

Manipulate random values in a scatter brush

1. Double-click the **Flying Beetle brush** in the Brushes palette.

2. Click the **Size list arrow**, click **Random**, then type **20** in the first Size text box and **100** in the second.

   The beetles will be randomly assigned a size anywhere between 20% and 100% of the original artwork.

3. Click the **Spacing list arrow**, click **Random**, then type **50** in the first Spacing text box and **200** in the second, as shown in Figure 35.

   The beetles are spaced randomly along the path within the set range of values.

4. Click the **Scatter list arrow**, click **Random**, then type **-100** in the first Scatter text box and **100** in the second.

   These values define the distance from each side of the path that the artwork can be positioned. In the case of a circular path, the first value determines how far into the circle the artwork can be positioned, and the second value determines how far outside the circle.

   (continued)

FIGURE 35
Scatter Brush Options dialog box

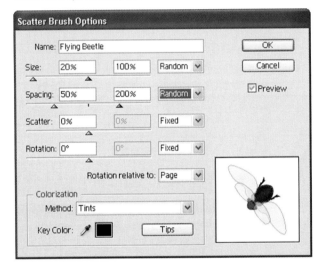

FIGURE 36

Scatter artwork using random values

5. Click the **Rotation list arrow**, click **Random**, then type **-180** in the first Rotation text box and **180** in the second.

   The artwork can be rotated to any position within a full 360°.

6. Click the **Method list arrow**, click **None**, click **OK**, then click **Apply to Strokes**.

   Figure 36 is an example of this brush setting.

7. Click the **Remove Brush Stroke button** ☒ on the Brushes palette, then reapply the Flying Beetle brush.

   The artwork will be different each time you reapply the brush, because the values are determined randomly with each application.

8. Save and close the Random Flies document.

Starting with symmetrical, evenly spaced scatter brush artwork, you manipulated parameters to create artwork that was random in size, spacing, scatter, and rotation values.

Use the Move command.

1. Create a new 6" × 6" CMYK Color document, then save it as **Polka Dot Pattern**.
2. Create a 2" square, then fill it with a green fill, and remove any stroke if necessary.
3. Create a .25" circle, then fill it with white.
4. Align the circle and the square by their center points. (*Hint*: Select both the circle and the square, then click the Horizontal Align Center button and the Vertical Align Center button in the Align palette.)
5. Deselect all, select the white circle, click Object on the menu bar, point to Transform, then click Move.
6. Type **-.5** in the Horizontal text box, type **.5** in the Vertical text box, then click Copy.
7. Keeping the new circle selected, click Object on the menu bar, point to Transform, then click Move.
8. Type **1** in the Horizontal text box, type **0** in the Vertical text box, then click Copy.
9. Select the two new circles, then move a copy of them 1 inch below by typing **0** in the Horizontal text box, **-1** in the Vertical text box, then clicking Copy.
10. Fill the center circle with any blue swatch that you like.
11. Save your work.

Create a pattern.

1. Select all the artwork, then drag it into the Swatches palette.
2. Name the new swatch **Green Polka**.
3. Delete the artwork on the artboard.
4. Create a 4" square, then fill it with the Green Polka pattern.
5. Double-click the Scale Tool, then scale only the pattern 25%.
6. Save your work.

Design a repeating pattern.

1. Hide the 4" square.
2. Drag the Green Polka pattern swatch from the Swatches palette onto the artboard.
3. Deselect the pattern swatch, draw a diagonal 1 point black line from the bottom-left corner to the top-right corner of the green square.
4. Change the stroke color of the line to Sea Green.
5. Deselect, select the line with the Selection Tool, then rotate a copy of the line 90°. (*Hint*: Be sure to click the Objects check box in the Rotate dialog box.)
6. Click the Direct Selection Tool, select the five circles, then cut them.
7. Click the Selection Tool, select the two Sea Green lines, then paste in front.
8. Select the green square, click Object on the menu bar, point to Path, click Offset Path, type **-.5** in the Offset text box, then click OK.
9. Cut the new green square, then paste it in back of the blue circle.
10. Select all the artwork, press and hold [Alt] (Win) or [option] (Mac), then drag the artwork on top of the Green Polka swatch to replace the old pattern with the new one.
11. Delete the artwork from the artboard.

12. Show all, then save your work. Your square should resemble Figure 37.

Work with the Brushes palette.

1. Open AI 6-6.ai, then save it as **Brushes Review**.

2. Select the snowflake artwork on the artboard, click the Brushes palette list arrow, then click New Brush.

3. Click the New Scatter Brush option button, then click OK.

4. Name the new brush **Snowflake**.

5. Set the size to 30%.

6. Set the spacing to 40%, then click OK.

7. Hide the snowflake artwork on the artboard.

8. Create a circle that is 4" in diameter, then apply the Snowflake brush to the circle.

9. Save your work.

Work with scatter brushes.

1. Double-click the Snowflake brush in the Brushes palette.

2. Set all the Scatter and Rotation options to Random.

3. Set the scatter range between 10% and 20%.

4. Set the rotation range between 45° and 25°.

5. Click OK, then click Apply to Strokes.

6. Save your work, deselect all, compare your screen with Figure 38, then close the Brushes Review document.

FIGURE 37
Completed Skills Review, Part 1

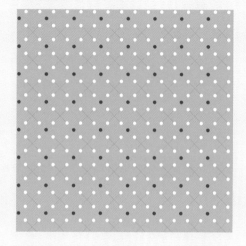

FIGURE 38
Completed Skills Review, Part 2

Working with Patterns and Brushes

You work in the textile industry as a pattern designer. Your boss asks you to design a pattern for a new line of shower curtains. Her only direction is that the pattern must feature triangles and at least eight colors.

1. Create a new 6" × 6" CMYK Color document, then save it as **Shower Curtain**.

2. Create a 1" square with a blue fill and no stroke.

3. Copy the square, paste in front, then fill the new square with green.

4. Click Object on the menu bar, point to Path, click Add Anchor Points, then click the Delete Anchor Point Tool. (*Hint*: The Delete Anchor Point Tool is hidden beneath the Pen Tool.)

5. Delete the top-left corner, top-right corner, left side, and right side anchor points, so that the square is converted to a triangle.

6. Use the Move command to create a copy of the two shapes to the right, then two copies below, so that, together, the area of the four tiles is 2" × 2".

7. Change the colors in each tile.

8. Scale the four tiles 15%.

9. Make a new pattern swatch out of the four tiles, name it **Triangle Pattern**, then apply the pattern to a 4" square.

10. Save your work, then compare your pattern to Figure 39.

FIGURE 39
Completed Project Builder 1

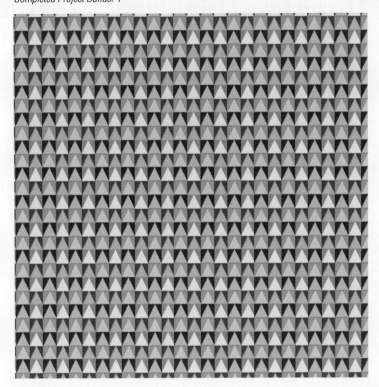

You are a jewelry designer, and you've been hired to create the original design for a new line of necklaces that will be targeted to teenage girls. The necklaces will be made with flat, tinted metals, and you are asked to use bright colors. One catch: Your client tells you that he's "unsure" of what he's looking for and hints that he may make many changes to your design before he's satisfied.

1. Open AI 6-7.ai, then save it as **Teen Jewelry**.
2. Create a new scatter brush with the artwork provided.
3. Name the new brush **Smile**.
4. Set the size to 20%.
5. Set the spacing to 25%.
6. Set the rotation to Random.
7. Set the rotation range from -92° to 92°, make it relative to the page, then click OK.
8. Hide the original artwork.
9. Draw a path resembling the arc of a necklace, then apply the Smile scatter brush to the path.
10. Save your work, then compare your pattern to Figure 40.

FIGURE 40
Completed Project Builder 2

You own a gallery in Key West called Funky Frames. You are known for designing unusual and festive frames of various sizes. The process of designing the frames is complex, as you use many different kinds of materials. However, they all begin with a brush pattern that you create in Illustrator.

1. Open AI 6-8.ai, then save it as **Funky Frames**.
2. Select the left tile, drag it into the Swatches palette, then name it **Side Tile**.
3. Select the right tile, drag it into the Swatches palette, then name it **Corner Tile**.
4. Hide the artwork on the artboard.
5. Create a new pattern brush.
6. Name the new brush **Funky**.
7. Apply the Side Tile swatch as the side tile and the Corner Tile swatch as the outer corner tile.
8. Set the scale value to 50%, then click OK.
9. Apply the Funky pattern brush to a 6" square.
10. Save your work, then compare your pattern to Figure 41.

FIGURE 41
Completed Design Project

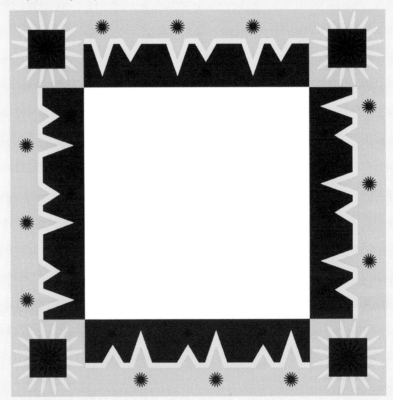

Working with Patterns and Brushes

Your team of graphic designers has been commissioned to design an original plaid pattern, which will be used to produce kilts for the wedding of a famous singer and her Scottish groom. Your only direction is that it must be an original pattern, and it must have at least three colors.

1. Create a new CMYK Color document, then save it as **Original Plaid**.
2. Assign two team members to research the history of plaid patterns and their association with specific groups, families, and organizations.
3. Assign two team members to search the Internet for plaid patterns.
4. Assign two other team members to research the Burberry pattern, one of the most famous patterns ever created.
5. Assign half of the remaining team members to create swatches to compare colors, and the other half to design the pattern.
6. Fill a 6" × 6" square with the new pattern.
7. Save your work, then compare your pattern to Figure 42.

FIGURE 42
Completed Group Project

chapter 7

WORKING WITH FILTERS
GRADIENT MESHES, ENVELOPES, AND BLENDS

1. Work with filters.

2. Work with gradient meshes.

3. Work with envelopes.

4. Create blends.

7 WORKING WITH FILTERS
GRADIENT MESHES, ENVELOPES, AND BLENDS

Illustrator software comes programmed with built-in operations—mathematical algorithms—that create specific effects when applied to objects. These include filters, gradient meshes, envelopes, and blends. A variety of color filters are available that affect the color of objects and create color blends between objects. Distort filters twist, pucker, and bloat objects, among other operations. The Create Gradient Mesh command produces a multicolored object on which colors can transition smoothly and flow in different directions. Envelopes are objects that you use to distort other objects. Blends create a series of intermediate objects and colors between two or more selected objects.

When you are working with filters, meshes, envelopes, and blends, you are working at the intermediate level in Illustrator. All are challenging—less in learning how to use them than in activating your imagination for ideas of how to *best* use them. Of the four, meshes and blends are the broadest in scope, offering powerful options for adding color, shape, depth, and perspective to an illustration.

Tools You'll Use

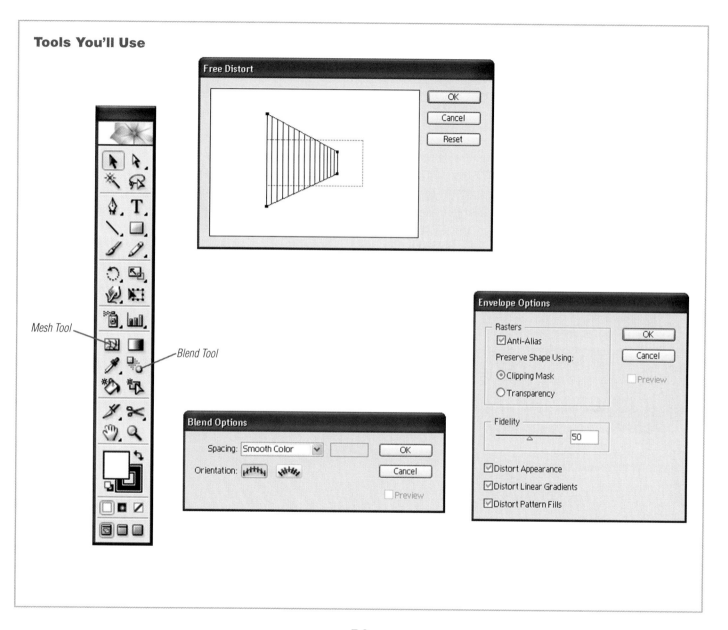

Free Distort

OK
Cancel
Reset

Mesh Tool

Blend Tool

Envelope Options

Rasters
☑ Anti-Alias
Preserve Shape Using:
◉ Clipping Mask
○ Transparency

OK
Cancel
☐ Preview

Fidelity
△ 50

☑ Distort Appearance
☑ Distort Linear Gradients
☑ Distort Pattern Fills

Blend Options

Spacing: Smooth Color

Orientation:

OK
Cancel
☐ Preview

WORK WITH FILTERS

What You'll Do

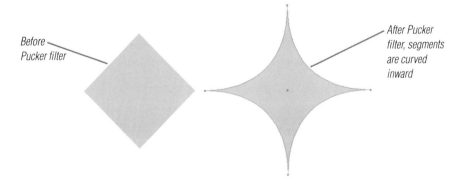

In this lesson, you will explore options for manipulating colors and basic shapes with filters.

Modifying Shapes with Filters

Illustrator provides a number of filters that you can use to alter the shape of an object. These filters provide simple operations that you can use as a final effect or that you can tweak to create a unique effect. Of the many filters that affect shapes, some are essential operations that you will want to have in your skill set.

The Free Distort filter functions much like the Free Transform Tool. A bounding box is applied to a selected object or objects in a preview window. You can alter any of the four handles on the bounding box to distort the selection. The Free Distort filter is very useful for distorting perspective.

The Pucker & Bloat filter adjusts the segments between an object's anchor points.

FIGURE 1
Pucker filter applied

Before
Pucker filter

After Pucker filter, segments are curved inward

With a pucker effect, the segments are moved inward, toward the center of the object, while the anchor points are moved outward, as shown in Figure 1. The bloat effect is achieved by moving the segments outward and the anchor points inward, as shown in Figure 2.

The Twist filter rotates an object more sharply in the center than it does at the edges, creating a whirlpool effect, as shown in Figure 3.

Modifying Color with Color Filters

Illustrator offers a number of filters that alter the color of selected objects. You can use color filters to saturate an illustration, which makes its colors more intense. Conversely, you can reduce the saturation of an image, making its colors duller, with a washed-out appearance. Use the Convert to Grayscale filter to completely desaturate an illustration and create the effect of a black-and-white image.

You can also use color filters to make color blends between objects. The Blend Front to Back filter creates a color blend through all the objects in the stacking order, using the frontmost object as the starting color and the backmost object as the ending color. This filter can be very useful for adding the effect of color depth to an illustration.

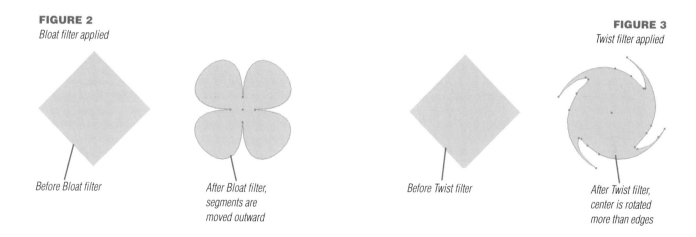

FIGURE 2
Bloat filter applied

Before Bloat filter

After Bloat filter, segments are moved outward

FIGURE 3
Twist filter applied

Before Twist filter

After Twist filter, center is rotated more than edges

Use the Free Distort filter

1. Open AI 7-1.ai, then save it as **Free Distort**.

2. Select all, click **Filter** on the menu bar, point to **Distort** at the top of the Filter menu, then click **Free Distort**.

   A preview of the selected objects appears in the Free Distort dialog box with a bounding box around them.

3. Using Figure 4 as a guide, drag the **four bounding box handles** to the locations shown in the figure to distort the lines in perspective, click **OK**, then deselect.

4. Select all, click **Filter** on the menu bar, point to **Distort**, then click **Free Distort**.

5. Click **Reset**, drag the **bounding box handles** to the locations shown in Figure 5, click **OK**, then deselect.

   Your work should resemble Figure 6.

   You used the Free Distort filter twice to distort a series of paths in perspective.

FIGURE 4
Free Distort dialog box

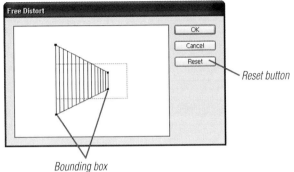

Reset button

Bounding box handles

FIGURE 5
Move handles independently in the Free Distort dialog box

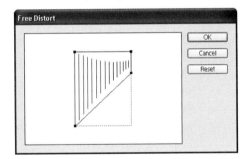

FIGURE 6
A perspective effect, created with the Free Distort filter

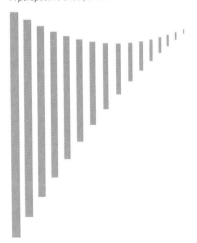

Working with Filters, Gradient Meshes, Envelopes, and Blends

FIGURE 7

Blending the colors from dark to light enhances the perspective effect

1. Select all.

2. Click **Object** on the menu bar, point to **Path**, then click **Outline Stroke**.

   The strokes are converted to closed paths.

3. Deselect, then fill the smallest object with yellow.

4. Select all, click **Filter** on the menu bar, point to **Colors**, then click **Blend Front to Back**.

   A color blend is created from the frontmost to the backmost object in the stacking order. Your work should resemble Figure 7.

   TIP   The Blend Front to Back filter does not work on open paths.

5. Save your work, then close the Free Distort document.

You converted the stroked paths to outlines, and then used the Blend Front to Back filter to create the effect that the objects lighten as they recede into the distance.

Saturate and desaturate an illustration

1. Open AI 7-2.ai, then save it as **Saturation**.
2. Select all, click **View** on the menu bar, then click **Hide Edges**.
3. Click **Filter** on the menu bar, point to **Colors**, then click **Saturate**.
4. Click the **Preview check box**, drag the **Intensity slider** all the way to the right, then click **OK**.

   Your work should resemble Figure 8.
5. Click **Filter** on the menu bar, point to **Colors**, then click **Convert to Grayscale**.

   Every object is filled with a shade of gray, as shown in Figure 9.
6. Click **View** on the menu bar, then click **Show Edges**.
7. Deselect all by clicking the artboard.
8. Save your work, then close the Saturation document.

You used the Saturate filter to intensify the color of an image. You then used the Convert to Grayscale filter to remove all chromatic color from the illustration, thereby creating the effect of a black-and-white image.

FIGURE 8
Illustration with saturated colors

FIGURE 9
Illustration with the Convert to Grayscale filter applied

Working with Filters, Gradient Meshes, Envelopes, and Blends

FIGURE 10

The orange shape is bloated, the gray is puckered

FIGURE 11

The blue circle with added anchor points and the Bloat and Twist filters applied

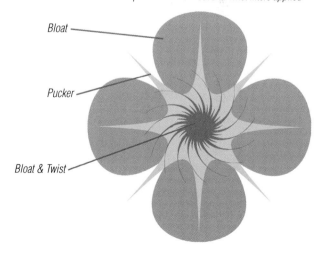

Bloat

Pucker

Bloat & Twist

1. Open AI 7-3.ai, then save it as **Pucker and Bloat**.

2. Select the large orange square, click **Filter** on the menu bar, point to the **first Distort menu**, then click **Pucker & Bloat**.

3. Type **85** in the text box, then click **OK**.

   > TIP   A positive value produces a bloat effect; a negative value produces a pucker effect.

4. Select the gray circle, click **Object** on the menu bar, point to **Path**, then click **Add Anchor Points**.

5. Click **Filter** on the menu bar, then click **Pucker & Bloat** at the top of the Filter menu.

   The Pucker & Bloat dialog box opens with the settings last used.

6. Type **-75**, then click **OK**.

   Your work should resemble Figure 10.

7. Select the blue circle, then apply the Add Anchor Points command twice.

8. Open the Pucker & Bloat dialog box, type **180** in the text box, then click **OK**.

9. Click **Filter** on the menu bar, point to the **first Distort menu**, then click **Twist**.

10. Type **90** in the Angle text box, then click **OK**.

    Your work should resemble Figure 11.

11. Save your work, then close the Pucker and Bloat document.

You applied the Pucker & Bloat filter in varying degrees to each object, producing three distinctly different effects. You also applied the Twist filter.

WORK WITH
GRADIENT MESHES

What You'll Do

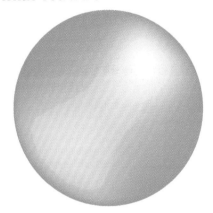

▶ *In this lesson, you will create and manipulate a gradient mesh to add dimension to basic shapes.*

Working with a Mesh Object

The Mesh Tool and the Create Gradient Mesh command can be used to transform a basic object into a mesh object. A **mesh object** is a single, multicolored object in which colors can flow in different directions, and colors transition gradually from point to point. Meshes exceed the ability of simple radial and linear gradients for applying color blends to objects and are very effective for adding contrast and dimension.

When you create a mesh object, multiple **mesh lines** crisscross the object, joined at their intersections by mesh points. **Mesh points** are diamond-shaped and work just like anchor points, with the added functionality of being able to be assigned a color. When you assign a color to a mesh point, the color gradates outward from the point.

The area between four mesh points is a **mesh patch**. You can apply color to all four mesh points simultaneously by apply-ing the color to the patch. Work with this method to apply broad color changes to the object.

Mesh points can be added, deleted, and moved along the mesh line without alter-ing the shape of the mesh.

Anchor points are also part of the mesh, and they function as they do on simple paths. Just as with simple paths, you can manipulate the anchor points' direction lines to alter the shape of the mesh. Figure 12 shows an example of a mesh object.

Creating a Mesh Object

You can create a mesh object from any path. You cannot create a mesh object from compound paths or text objects. You can create a mesh object with the Mesh Tool or by applying the Create Gradient Mesh command.

Generally, you'll be happiest using the Create Gradient Mesh command, which creates a mesh object with regularly spaced mesh lines and mesh points. The Create Gradient Mesh dialog box is shown in Figure 13. The Mesh Tool adds a mesh point and its intersecting mesh lines where you click. The tool is most effective when you want to add a particular mesh point (say, for a highlight) to an existing mesh.

The Create Gradient Mesh command is always the best choice when converting complex objects.

Once a mesh object has been created, it cannot be converted back into a simple path.

Complex mesh objects are a memory drain and may affect your computer's performance. When creating mesh objects, keep in mind that it's better to create a few simple mesh objects than a single complex one.

FIGURE 12
Elements of a mesh object

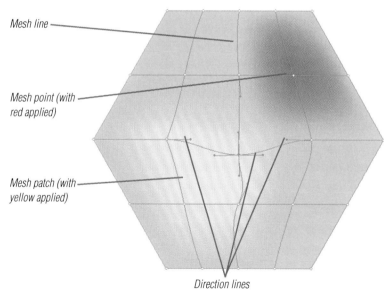

Mesh line

Mesh point (with red applied)

Mesh patch (with yellow applied)

Direction lines

FIGURE 13
Create Gradient Mesh dialog box

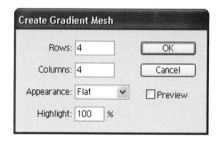

Create a gradient mesh

1. Open AI 7-4.ai, then save it as **Circle Mesh**.

2. Select the circle, click **Object** on the menu bar, then click **Create Gradient Mesh**.

3. Type **2** in the Rows text box and **2** in the Columns text box, then click **OK**.

4. Deselect, then click the **edge of the circle** with the Direct Selection Tool ▸ .

5. Select the center mesh point, then click a **yellow swatch** in the Swatches palette.

6. Move the center mesh point to the green X, as shown in Figure 14.

7. Move the direction lines at the top, bottom, left, and right of the circle's edge, as shown in Figure 15.

(continued)

FIGURE 14
Mesh points can be moved, just like anchor points

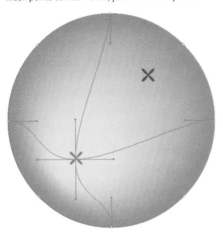

FIGURE 15
The shape of the mesh is manipulated by direction lines

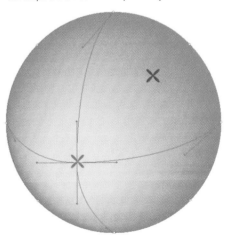

Working with Filters, Gradient Meshes, Envelopes, and Blends

FIGURE 16

Gradient meshes add dimension to an object

8. Click the **Mesh Tool** ⊞ , then click the **blue X**.

   TIP Press [Shift] while you click the Mesh Tool to add a mesh point without changing to the current fill color.

9. Click the **white swatch** in the Swatches palette to change the color of the mesh point to white.

10. Click the **Selection Tool** ▶ , deselect, then hide Layer 2.

    Your work should resemble Figure 16.

11. Save your work, then close the Circle Mesh document.

You applied a gradient mesh to a circle with the Create Gradient Mesh command, changed the color of a mesh point, then moved the mesh point. You then used the Mesh Tool to expand the mesh. You changed the color of the new mesh point to white to add a highlight to the sphere.

Manipulate a gradient mesh

1. Open AI 7-5.ai, then save it as **Heart Mesh**.

2. Select the heart, click **Object** on the menu bar, then click **Create Gradient Mesh**.

3. Type **4** in the Rows text box and **4** in the Columns text box, then click **OK**.

4. Deselect, then click the **edge of the heart** with the Direct Selection Tool ▶.

5. Click the **upper-left mesh point**, as shown in Figure 17, then change the mesh point color to 10% black, using the Color palette.

   The new color gradates out from the mesh point.

6. Click the **Mesh Tool** 🔲.

7. Press and hold **[Shift]**, then drag the **mesh point** along the mesh path to the left, as shown in Figure 18.

(continued)

FIGURE 17
Selecting a mesh point

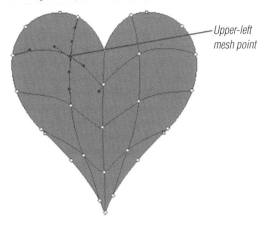

Upper-left mesh point

FIGURE 18

Mesh points can be moved without changing the shape of the mesh

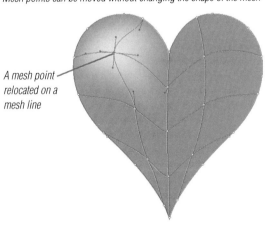

A mesh point relocated on a mesh line

Working with Filters, Gradient Meshes, Envelopes, and Blends

FIGURE 19

The mesh, reconfigured on both sides of the object

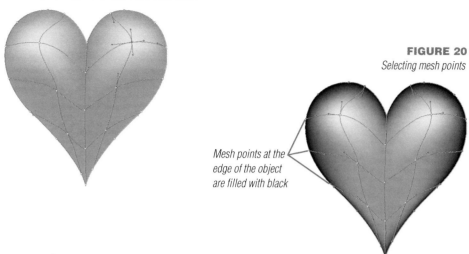

FIGURE 20

Selecting mesh points

Mesh points at the edge of the object are filled with black

FIGURE 21

Mesh points are like anchor points, with the added functionality of accepting color assignments

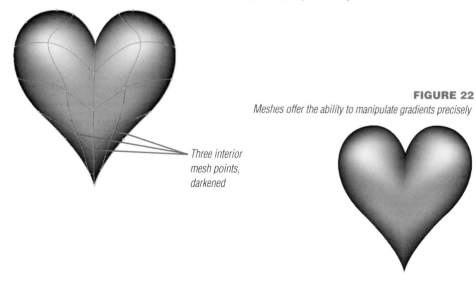

Three interior mesh points, darkened

FIGURE 22

Meshes offer the ability to manipulate gradients precisely

8. Repeat Steps 5-7 for the upper-right mesh point, then deselect so that your work resembles Figure 19.

9. Click the **Direct Selection Tool** ▶, press and hold **[Shift]**, then select the 20 mesh points and anchor points along the edge of the heart.

> TIP   Mesh points appear as diamonds and have the same properties as anchor points, with the added capability of accepting color.

10. Apply a black fill to the selected mesh points.

   The selected anchor points are unaffected. Your work should resemble Figure 20.

11. Deselect, then select the three mesh points at the lower third of the heart, then apply a 60% black fill so that your work resembles Figure 21.

12. Select the mesh point at the center of the heart (between the two 10% black highlights).

13. Apply a 60% black fill, deselect, then compare your work to Figure 22.

14. Save your work, then close the Heart Mesh document.

You applied a gradient mesh to a heart shape, then created highlights by changing the color of two mesh points. Next, you relocated the highlight mesh points without changing the shape of the mesh lines. You then darkened the color of other mesh points to add contrast and dimension to the artwork.

WORK WITH ENVELOPES

What You'll Do

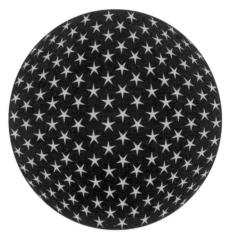

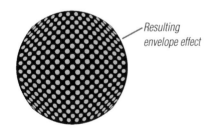 In this lesson, you will create envelope distortions in three ways: using a top object, using a mesh, and using a warp.

Defining Envelopes

Envelopes are objects that are used to distort other selected objects; the distorted objects take on the shape of the envelope object.

Imagine that you have purchased a basketball as a gift, and you want to wrap it with paper that has a polka-dot pattern. If these were objects in Illustrator, the basketball would be the envelope object, and the sheet of wrapping paper would be the object to be distorted. Figure 23 is a good example of what an envelope distortion looks like.

You can make envelopes with objects that you create, or you can use a preset warp shape or a mesh object as an envelope. You can use envelopes with compound paths, text objects, meshes, and blends. Powerful effects can be achieved by applying envelopes to linear gradient fills or pattern fills.

FIGURE 23
An envelope created using a top object

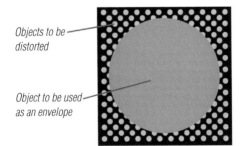

Objects to be distorted

Object to be used as an envelope

Resulting envelope effect

Creating Envelopes with Top Objects, Meshes, and Warps

You create an envelope by using the Envelope Distort command on the Object menu. The Envelope Distort command offers you three options for creating an envelope: Make with Warp, Make with Mesh, and Make with Top Object. The top object is the topmost selected object. Warps are simply 15 premade shapes to choose from, to use as your top object. Warps are especially useful when you don't want to draw your own top object. The envelope in Figure 24 was created using the Flag warp. Meshes are the same as gradient meshes made with the Mesh Tool. Creating an envelope with a mesh allows you to apply a mesh to multiple objects, which is not the case when you create a mesh using the Create Gradient Mesh command or the Mesh Tool. The envelope in Figure 25 was created using a mesh.

Applying Envelopes to Gradient and Pattern Fills

Envelopes can be used to distort objects that have linear gradient fills or pattern fills, but you must first activate the option to do so. In the Envelope Options dialog box, you can check the Distort Linear Gradients or Distort Pattern Fills check box to apply an envelope to either of the fills. Figure 26 shows the options in the Envelope Options dialog box.

FIGURE 24

An envelope created using a warp

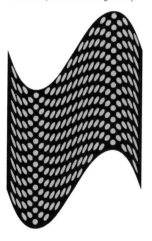

FIGURE 25

An envelope created using a mesh

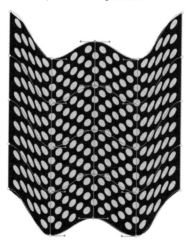

FIGURE 26

Envelope Options dialog box

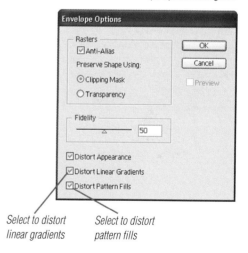

Select to distort linear gradients *Select to distort pattern fills*

Create an envelope distortion with a top object

1. Open AI 7-6.ai, then save it as **Envelope Top Object**.

2. Copy the yellow circle, paste in front, then hide the copy.

3. Select all, click **Object** on the menu bar, point to **Envelope Distort**, then click **Make with Top Object**.

   Your work should resemble Figure 27.

4. Show all, then fill the yellow circle with the Purple Berry gradient in the Swatches palette.

5. Send the circle to the back, so that your work resembles Figure 28.

6. Save your work, then close the Envelope Top Object document.

You used a circle as the top object in an envelope distortion. Because you cannot apply a fill to the circle after it's been used to make the envelope, you filled a copy of the circle with a gradient, then positioned it behind the distorted objects to achieve the effect.

FIGURE 27
A round envelope distorting a flat star pattern

FIGURE 28
A radial blend enhancing the effect of an envelope distortion

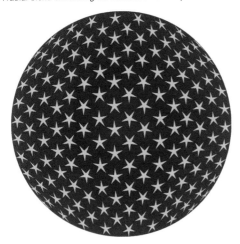

Working with Filters, Gradient Meshes, Envelopes, and Blends

FIGURE 29
Two columns of mesh points, selected

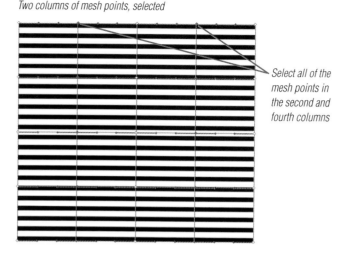

Select all of the
mesh points in
the second and
fourth columns

Create an envelope distortion with a mesh

1. Open AI 7-7.ai, then save it as **Envelope Mesh**.
2. Select all, click **Object** on the menu bar, point to **Envelope Distort**, then click **Make with Mesh**.
3. Type **4** in the Rows text box and **4** in the Columns text box, then click **OK**.

   There are five mesh points on each horizontal line.
4. Deselect, then select the second and fourth column of mesh points, using the Direct Selection Tool ▸ , as shown in Figure 29.
5. Press and hold **[Shift]**, press ↑ two times, then release [Shift].

   Pressing an arrow key in conjunction with [Shift] moves a selected item ten keyboard increments.

   | TIP   The keyboard increment value can be adjusted in the General Preferences dialog box.
6. Select the middle column of mesh points.
7. Press and hold **[Shift]**, press ↓ two times, deselect, then compare your screen to Figure 30.
8. Save your work, then close the Envelope Mesh document.

You applied an envelope distortion with a mesh to a series of rectangles, then moved the mesh points to create a wave effect.

FIGURE 30
An envelope distortion created using a mesh

Create an envelope distortion with a warp effect

1. Open AI 7-8.ai, then save it as **Envelope Warp**.

2. Select all, click **Object** on the menu bar, point to **Envelope Distort**, then click **Make with Warp**.

3. Click the **Style list arrow**, click **Fish**, then click **OK**.

   Your screen should resemble Figure 31.

4. Undo the distort, then make Layer 2 visible.

5. Select all.

(continued)

FIGURE 31
An envelope distortion created using a warp

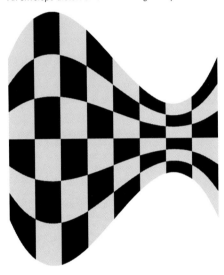

Working with Filters, Gradient Meshes, Envelopes, and Blends

FIGURE 32

An envelope distortion using a premade shape

6. Click **Object** on the menu bar, point to **Envelope Distort**, then click **Make with Top Object**.

    As shown in Figure 32, you get the same result as you did using the fish-style warp. The reason for this is that using the Envelope Distort feature with a warp is the same as using the feature with a top object—the difference is that warps are premade shapes that you can choose, instead of making your own.

7. Save your work, then close the Envelope Warp document.

You applied an envelope distortion with a warp effect—in this case, the Fish warp. You then used an object in the shape of the Fish warp as the top object in a new envelope, with the same result as in the first distortion. Through this comparison, you got a better sense of how Illustrator creates warp effects with envelopes.

Printing color blends and gradient meshes

Print and prepress professionals have long known that some output devices have trouble printing color blends. The most common problem is banding, an effect in which the transitions of the gradient are visibly harsh rather than smooth. This problem was especially common on early PostScript devices. In addition, gradient meshes (which are a newer feature in Illustrator) may print incorrectly, even on PostScript Level 3 printers. If you are having trouble outputting either color blends or meshes, you can print them as bitmaps instead of vectors. To do so, display the Flattener Preview palette, choose settings in the palette, then save the preset with a descriptive name by clicking the Flattener Preview palette list arrow, then clicking the Save Transparency Flattener Preset. When you are ready to print your document, click File on the menu bar, click Print, click the Advanced category on the left side of the Print dialog box, select the Print as Bitmap check box, choose your named preset from the Preset list arrow, then click Print. Anyone who has experience with printing bitmaps knows that the quality can vary greatly. Use this option only if you are having problems, then decide if the output is acceptable. If not, you may need to go to a professional prepress department to output the file.

CREATE BLENDS

What You'll Do

 In this lesson, you will use blends to manipulate shapes and colors for various effects.

Defining a Blend

A **blend** is a series of intermediate objects and colors between two or more selected objects. If the selected objects differ in color—if they have different fills, for example—the intermediate objects will be filled with intermediate colors. Therefore, in a blend, both shapes and colors are "blended." Figure 33 is an example of a blend using shapes and colors.

Blends are created with either the Blend Tool or the Make Blend command. You can make blends between two open paths, such as two different lines. You can make blends between two closed paths, such as a square and a star. You can blend between objects filled with gradients. You can even blend between blends, as shown in Figure 34.

FIGURE 33
In a blend, both shapes and colors are blended

Working with Filters, Gradient Meshes, Envelopes, and Blends

Specifying the Number of Steps in a Blend

The fewer the number of steps in a blend, the more distinct each intermediary object will be. At a greater number of steps, the intermediate objects become indistinguishable from one another, and the blend creates the illusion of being continuous or "smooth."

In the Blend Options dialog box, select from the following options for specifying the number of steps within a blend.

- Specified Steps. Enter a value that determines the number of steps between the start and the end of the blend.
- Specified Distance. Enter a value to determine the distance between the steps in the blend. The distance is measured from the edge of one object to the corresponding edge on the next object.

- Smooth Color. Illustrator determines the number of steps for the blend, calculated to provide the minimum number of steps for a smooth color transition. This is the default option, which poses a bit of a problem in that the minimum number of steps will not always give you the effect you desire, as shown in Figure 35.

FIGURE 34
A blend between blends

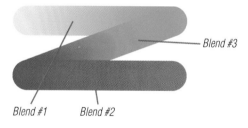

Blend #3

Blend #1   Blend #2

FIGURE 35
Sometimes, the Smooth Color option doesn't produce the blend effect you desire

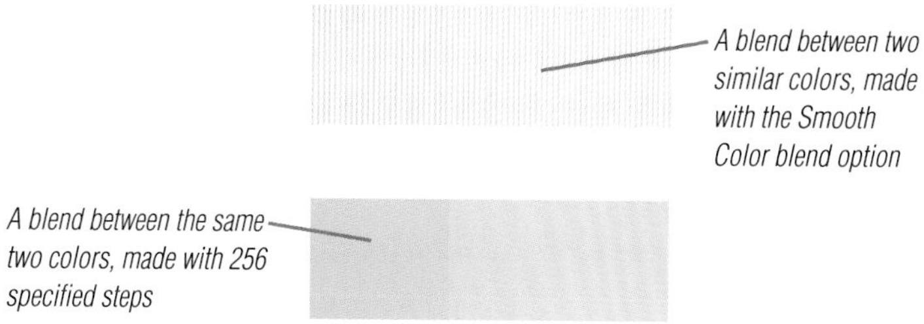

A blend between two similar colors, made with the Smooth Color blend option

A blend between the same two colors, made with 256 specified steps

Manipulating Blends

Once a blend is created, you can change its appearance by making changes to one or more of the original objects. For example, using the Direct Selection Tool, you can select one of the original objects, then change its fill color, stroke color, or stroke weight. Illustrator will automatically update the appearance of the steps to reflect newly added attributes, thus changing the appearance of the entire blend. You can also change a blend by transforming one or more of the original objects, for example by scaling, rotating, or moving them.

You can affect the appearance of a blend by manipulating its spine. When a blend is created, a path is drawn between the starting and ending objects. Illustrator refers to this path as the spine, but it can be manipulated like a path. For example, you can add anchor points to the spine with the Pen Tool, then move them with the Direct Selection Tool. The blend is updated when you alter the spine. Figure 36 shows how a blend's spine can be manipulated.

One of the most stunning manipulations of a blend happens when you replace its spine. Draw any path with the Pen Tool, then select it along with any blend. Apply the Replace Spine command, and the blend replaces its spine with the new path!

FIGURE 36

Manipulating the blend's spine changes the blend

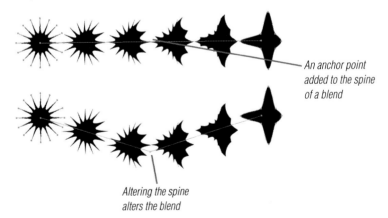

An anchor point added to the spine of a blend

Altering the spine alters the blend

Working with Filters, Gradient Meshes, Envelopes, and Blends

FIGURE 37

The red and blue objects blended with five steps

1. Open AI 7-9.ai, then save it as **Blended Shapes**.

2. Click the **Blend Tool**, click anywhere on the orange square, then click anywhere on the green square.

   | TIP   You can click the Blend Tool on two or more unselected objects to blend them.

3. Click the **Selection Tool**, select the red and blue squares, then double-click the **Blend Tool**.

4. Click the **Spacing list arrow**, click **Specified Steps**, type **5** in the Spacing text box, then click **OK**.

5. Click **Object** on the menu bar, point to **Blend**, then click **Make**.

   Five intermediary squares are created, as shown in Figure 37.

   (continued)

6. Switch to the Selection Tool ▶, then deselect the blend.

7. Click the **Blend Tool** ⬚ₒ, then click the **three purple shapes**.

8. Keeping the purple blend selected, click **Object** on the menu bar, point to **Blend**, then click **Blend Options**.

   TIP You can also access the Blend Options dialog box by double-clicking the Blend Tool.

9. Click the **Spacing list arrow**, click **Specified Steps**, type **2** in the Steps text box, then click **OK**.

   The intermediary steps are reduced to two.

10. Deselect the purple blend.

11. Select the Heart view on the View menu.

12. Double-click the **Blend Tool** ⬚ₒ, change the Specified Steps to 256, then click **OK**.

13. Click the **heart**, click the **small pink circle** in the center of the heart, then deselect.

   The 256 intermediary steps blend the heart to the circle in both color and shape. Your screen should resemble Figure 38.

14. Save your work, then close the Blended Shapes document.

You used the Blend Tool to create a smooth blend and evenly distributed shapes between two sets of squares. You created a blend between differing shapes, then used the Blend Options dialog box to change the number of steps in the blend. You also used a smooth blend to add dimension to the heart.

FIGURE 38
Blends are very effective for adding dimension to objects

FIGURE 39
A blend between two open paths

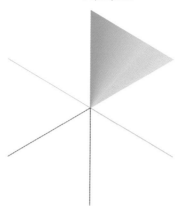

FIGURE 40
This color effect could not be reproduced with a gradient

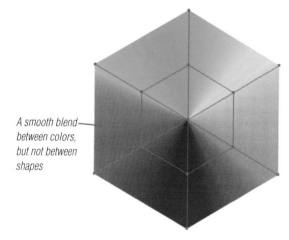

A smooth blend between colors, but not between shapes

FIGURE 41
The blended paths are masked by a circle

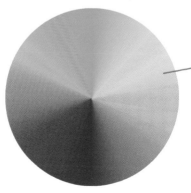

The use of 256 specified steps improves the appearance of the blend

Lesson 4   Create Blends

Create a clockwise color blend

1. Open AI 7-10.ai, then save it as **Clockwise Blend**.

2. Double-click the **Blend Tool** , click the **Spacing list arrow**, click **Specified Steps**, type **256** in the Spacing text box, then click **OK**.

3. Click the top of the green line, then click the top of the yellow line to create a blend, as shown in Figure 39.

   TIP   The Blend Tool pointer turns black when it is successfully positioned over an anchor point.

4. Click the remaining five lines, ending with the green line, to make five more blends, so that your work resembles Figure 40.

5. Draw a circle over the blend that does not exceed the perimeter of the blend.

6. Select all, click **Object** on the menu bar, point to **Clipping Mask**, then click **Make**.

7. Click the **Selection Tool** , deselect, then compare your image to Figure 41.

8. Save your work, then close the Clockwise Blend document.

You created blends between six lines. You specified the number of steps between each pair of paths to be 256, which resulted in a visually uninterrupted blend. You then masked the blend with a circle.

Edit blends

1. Open AI 7-11.ai, then save it as **Blends on a Path**.

2. Click the **blended objects** with the Selection Tool ⬏.

3. Click **Object** on the menu bar, point to **Blend**, then click **Reverse Front to Back**.

   The stacking order of the blended objects is reversed.

4. Click **Object** on the menu bar, point to **Blend**, then click **Reverse Spine**.

   The order of the objects on the path is reversed.

5. Select all.

6. Click **Object** on the menu bar, point to **Blend**, click **Replace Spine**, then deselect.

   The curved path becomes the new spine for the blend, as shown in Figure 42.

7. Save your work, then close the Blends on a Path document.

You reversed the stacking order of a blend, then reversed its spine. You then replaced the spine with a curved path to create a 3-D effect.

FIGURE 42
Blends can be applied to paths

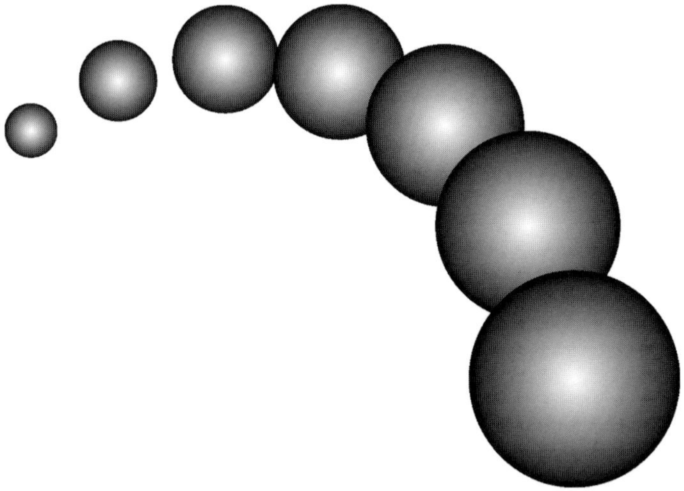

FIGURE 43

A simple blend between open paths

Create color effects with blends

1. Open AI 7-12.ai, then save it as **Chrome**.

2. Double-click the **Blend Tool** , then change the number of specified steps to **256**, if necessary.

3. Switch to Outline mode, click the **Selection Tool** , then select the five paths at the bottom of the artboard.

    Two of the paths are stroked with white and cannot be seen in Preview mode.

4. Switch to Preview mode, click the **Blend Tool** , then, starting from the bottom of the artboard, create a blend between each pair of paths, so that your work resembles Figure 43.

5. Position the text over the blend.

6. Keeping the text selected, click **Object** on the menu bar, point to **Compound Path**, then click **Make**.

7. Select all, click **Object** on the menu bar, point to **Clipping Mask**, then click **Make**.

8. Deselect all, click **Select** on the menu bar, point to **Object**, then click **Clipping Masks**.

9. Apply a 2-point black stroke to the mask.

10. Deselect, save your work, compare your screen to Figure 44, then close the Chrome document.

You created blends between five paths, then masked the blend with text.

FIGURE 44

Chrome letters created with a blend and a mask

Work with filters.

1. Create a new 6" × 6" CMYK Color document, then save it as **Filter Skills**.
2. Create a 4" circle with a yellow fill and no stroke.
3. Apply the Add Anchor Points command.
4. Apply the Bloat filter at 35%.
5. Apply the Twist filter at 50°.
6. Use the Scale Tool dialog box to make a 50% copy of the object.
7. Apply the Transform Again command twice.
8. Fill the top object with Starry Night Blue.
9. Select all, then use the Colors filter to blend the objects from front to back.
10. Save your work, deselect, compare your illustration with Figure 45, then close the Filter Skills document.

Work with gradient meshes.

1. Open AI 7-13.ai, then save it as **Mesh Skills**.
2. Select the yellow hexagon.
3. Apply the Create Gradient Mesh command with 4 rows and 4 columns.

4. Click the Direct Selection Tool, deselect the hexagon, then click the edge of it.
5. Select the top row of mesh points, then click orange in the Swatches palette. (*Hint*: Click and drag the Direct Selection Tool on the artboard to create a selection box that includes the top row of mesh points.)
6. Select the middle row of mesh points, then click red in the Swatches palette.
7. Select the four mesh patches at the bottom of the hexagon, then click Orange in the Swatches palette. (*Hint*: Select each mesh patch one at a time.)
8. Select the five mesh points at the bottom of the hexagon, then click Red in the Swatches palette.
9. Save your work, deselect, then compare your mesh object with Figure 46.
10. Close the Mesh Skills document.

Work with envelopes.

1. Open AI 7-14.ai, then save it as **Envelope Skills**.
2. Click Object on the menu bar, point to Envelope Distort, then click Envelope Options.

3. Verify that there is a check mark in the Distort Pattern Fills check box and in the Distort Appearance check box, then click OK.
4. Position a triangle above the square with the pattern fill. (*Hint*: Click the Polygon Tool, click the artboard, type 3 in the Sides text box, then click OK.)
5. Scale the triangle so that it covers most of the square below it, if necessary.
6. Select all, click Object on the menu bar, point to Envelope Distort, then click Make with Top Object.
7. Enlarge the size of the illustration, if you wish to.
8. Save your work, deselect, compare your illustration to Figure 47, then close the Envelope Skills document.

Create blends.

1. Open AI 7-15.ai, then save it as **Star**.
2. Create a 15% copy of the star.
3. Fill the copy with White.
4. Double-click the Blend Tool, then change the Specified Steps value to 256 if necessary.
5. Blend the two stars.
6. Save your work, deselect, then compare your illustration to Figure 48.
7. Close the Star document.

FIGURE 45
Completed Skills Review

FIGURE 46
Completed Skills Review

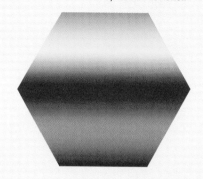

FIGURE 48
Completed Skills Review

FIGURE 47
Completed Skills Review

Working with Filters, Gradient Meshes, Envelopes, and Blends

The owner of Tidal Wave Publishing hires your design firm to redesign their logo. She shows you her original logo—a meticulous line drawing of a wave. She explains that the line drawing has been their logo for more than 25 years, and she feels that it's time for something "more contemporary." She cautions you that she doesn't want anything that feels "too artificial" or looks like "cookie-cutter computer graphics."

1. Create a new 6" × 6" document, then save it as **Tidal Wave**.
2. Create an ellipse that is .5" wide and 4.5" tall, then fill it with any color and no stroke.
3. Apply the Add Anchor Points command five times.
4. Apply the Twist filter at 45°.
5. Apply the Twist filter six more times using 45° each time. (*Hint*: Click Filter on the menu bar, then click Apply Twist at the top of the menu.)
6. Deselect, save your work, compare your illustration to Figure 49, then close the Tidal Wave document.

FIGURE 49
Completed Project Builder 1

Working with Filters, Gradient Meshes, Envelopes, and Blends

Miltie Berger, a famous journalist from Los Angeles, commissions your design firm to create a logo for her new column, which will be titled "Poison Pen." She explains that it will be a gossip column that will "skewer" all the big names in Hollywood. Refer to Figure 50 as you perform the steps.

1. Open AI 7-16.ai, then save it as **Poison Pen**.
2. Double-click the Blend Tool, set the number of specified steps to 40, click OK, then click anywhere on the two white objects on the right side of the artboard to blend them. (*Hint*: They do not need to be selected first.)
3. Deselect, then click the Direct Selection Tool.
4. Select only the bottom object of the blend, then change its fill color to Black and its stroke color to White. (*Hint*: Refer to this new object as the "feather" blend.)
5. Click the Selection Tool, select the very narrow white curved stroke at the center of the artboard, copy it, paste in front, then hide the copy.
6. Select the white stroke again, click Object on the menu bar, point to Path, then click Outline Stroke.
7. Deselect all, double-click the Blend Tool, change the number of steps to 256, then blend the white outlined stroke with the pointy black quill shape that is behind it.

8. Lock the new blend, then show all. The hidden white stroke appears and is selected.
9. Click the Selection Tool, press and hold [Shift], then click the "feather" blend to add it to the selection.

FIGURE 50
Completed Project Builder 2

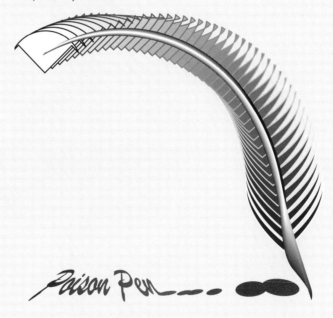

10. Click Object on the menu bar, point to Blend, then click Replace Spine.
11. Save your work, compare your illustration with Figure 50, then close the Poison Pen document.

You create graphics for a video game company. Your assignment for the morning is to create an illustration for a steel cup that will be used to store magical objects in a game.

1. Open AI 7-17.ai, then save it as **Steel Cup**.
2. Select the gray object, then apply the Create Gradient Mesh command using 7 rows and 3 columns.
3. Deselect, then click the edge of the mesh object with the Direct Selection Tool.
4. Press and hold [Shift], then click the four vertical mesh points, fourth in the third row from the left edge of the cup.
5. Click the Color palette list arrow, then click Grayscale, if necessary.
6. Make sure the Fill button is active in the toolbox, then drag the K slider in the Color palette to 20% to lighten the selected mesh points.
7. Select the top right mesh patch and darken it, using the Color palette.
8. Select the mesh points along the left edge and the bottom edge of the "steel cup," then click Black.
9. Continue selecting vertical rows of mesh points and lighten or darken them to create a stainless steel effect. (*Hint*: The mesh points at the bottom edge of the cup should remain black.)
10. Hide the gradient mesh object.

11. Click the edge of the black object with the Direct Selection Tool, then select the five horizontal mesh points in the second row from the top.
12. Fill the row of mesh points with White.

FIGURE 51
Completed Design Project

13. Deselect, then show all.
14. Save your work, compare your steel cup with Figure 51, then close the Steel Cup document.

You own a small design firm in the Caribbean, and your group has just been contracted to do a major project for the island of Saint Claw, a new nation in the West Indies. Having recently gained independence, Saint Claw wants you to consult with their new government on the design of their flag. After the first meeting, you begin working on a composite illustration. Your only direction from the government group is that the flag must be composed of abstract shapes—no words, stars, symbols, etc.

1. Create a new 6" × 6" CMYK Color document, then save it as **Saint Claw Flag**.
2. Assign two group members to the job of inventing the history of Saint Claw and its recent struggle for independence.
3. Assign two group members to search the Internet and collect pictures of as many flags from Caribbean nations as they can find.
4. Have your designers experiment with different width-to-height ratios in determining the shape of the banner.
5. Assign two group members to garner fabric samples from local merchants and textile designers.
6. After you've sketched a design, recreate the design in Illustrator with an envelope distort so that the flag appears to be waving.
7. Save your work, compare your illustration to Figure 52, then close the Saint Claw Flag document.

FIGURE 52
Completed Group Project

Working with Filters, Gradient Meshes, Envelopes, and Blends

chapter 8

WORKING WITH
TRANSPARENCY, EFFECTS, AND GRAPHIC STYLES

1. Use the Transparency palette and the Color Picker.

2. Apply effects to objects.

3. Use the Appearance palette.

4. Work with graphic styles.

8 WORKING WITH
TRANSPARENCY, EFFECTS, AND GRAPHIC STYLES

Appearance attributes are properties that you apply to an object that affect only the look of the object; its underlying structure is not affected. After you apply an appearance attribute to an object, you can later remove it, leaving the original object—and any other attributes—unaltered.

The Transparency palette allows you to control the **opacity** of an object—the degree to which it is "see through." The Transparency palette also includes a list of **blending modes** to choose from. Blending modes are fun, preset filters that control how colors blend when two objects overlap.

Effects are a type of appearance attribute and are listed on the Effect menu. Many effects have the same name as other Illustrator commands and filters. However, unlike commands and filters, effects can be applied to and removed from objects without changing them.

Many effect dialog boxes include a color box that, when clicked, opens up the Color Picker dialog box, or simply the Color Picker. Of all the ways to choose colors in Illustrator, using the Color Picker is the most sophisticated. In this dialog box, you can specify colors numerically as CMYK, RGB, HSB, or hexadecimal (a numbering system based on 16). You can also access the Color Picker by double-clicking the Fill or Stroke buttons in the toolbox.

Many effects listed on the Effect menu are available only for documents in the RGB Color mode. If you are working in CMYK Color mode, these effects will be unavailable. If you apply one of these effects, and then convert the document to CMYK Color mode, you will lose the effect. For these reasons, be aware that some effects that you apply in RGB Color mode may be difficult—if not impossible—to print. If you plan to print the illustration, download the file to your printer in RGB Color mode as a test.

Graphic styles are named sets of appearance attributes. In much the same way that you can create a new color and then name it and save it in the Swatches palette, you can name and save a set of appearance attributes in the Graphic Styles palette. As a style, that set of appearance attributes can be easily—and consistently—applied to other objects.

Tools You'll Use

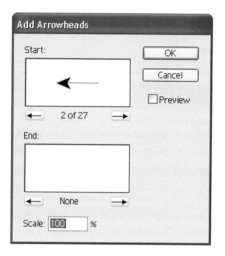

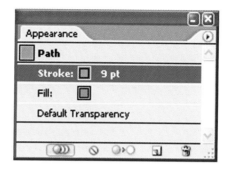

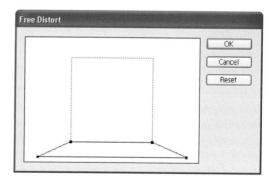

USE THE TRANSPARENCY
PALETTE AND THE
COLOR PICKER

What You'll Do

In this lesson, you will use the Transparency palette to change the opacity and blending modes of objects, and you will use the Color Picker to specify a new fill color.

Understanding Opacity

The term **opacity** derives from the word "opaque," which describes an object that is neither transparent nor translucent, that is not "see through." By default, objects in Illustrator are created with 100% opacity—that is, they are opaque. Whenever one object overlaps another on the artboard, the top object hides all or part of the object behind it. If you were drawing a face behind a veil, clouds in a blue sky, or fish in a tinted goldfish bowl, the ability to affect the opacity of objects would be critical to creating the illustration. Figure 1 shows an example of opacity.

Working with the Transparency Palette

The Transparency palette allows you to control the degree to which an object is transparent. You can change the opacity amount by dragging the Opacity slider in the palette. The Opacity slider works with percentages, with 100% being completely opaque and 0% being completely transparent, or invisible.

Working with Blending Modes

Blending modes are preset filters in the Transparency palette that vary the way that the colors of objects blend with the colors of underlying objects when they overlap them. You cannot determine the amount or intensity of a blending mode; you can simply choose whether or not to apply one. Thus, you will find yourself working with blending modes by trial and error. Blending modes are fun to experiment with. Apply a blending mode—if you like it, keep it. If not, try another.

Of all the blending modes, the most essential is Multiply. The Multiply blending mode makes the top object transparent and blends the colors of the overlapped and overlapping objects in an effect that is similar to overlapping magic markers. Objects that overlap black become black, objects that overlap white retain their original color, and as with magic markers, objects with color darken when they overlap other colors.

Imagine you were drawing a puddle of pink lemonade spilled on a black, white, and yellow tiled floor. You would use the Multiply blending mode on the object you draw to represent the lemonade, as shown in Figure 2. The color of the lemonade would not change where it overlapped the white tiles, because multiplying a color with white produces no change in the color. The lemonade would appear black where it overlapped the black tiles, because any color multiplied with black produces a black result. Where the pink lemonade overlapped the yellow tiles, the area would appear as a dark orange.

Because the Multiply blending mode reproduces real-world color situations, it is important for you to identify it as an essential component of your skills set. Don't forget that it's there!

FIGURE 1
Reducing opacity causes objects to appear translucent

FIGURE 2
Multiply blending mode mimics the effect of overlapping transparent ink, like a magic marker

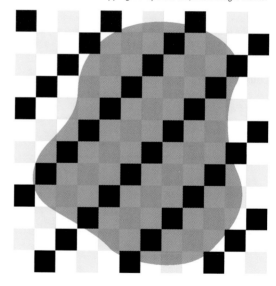

Working with the Color Picker

You use the Color Picker to specify new colors to be used as fills, strokes, or part of effects, such as drop shadows. The easiest way to access the Color Picker is to double-click the Fill or Stroke button in the toolbox.

In addition to allowing you to choose a new color, the Color Picker offers a valuable opportunity for studying the most fundamental color model, HSB, or Hue, Saturation, and Brightness.

The **hue** is the color itself. Blue, red, orange, and green are all hues. The Color Picker identifies hues based on the concept of a color wheel. Because there are 360 degrees to a circle, the hues on the color wheel are numbered 0–360. This is why you see a small degree symbol beside the H (hue) text box in the Color Picker dialog box. The color wheel is represented in the Color Picker by the vertical color slider. Move the triangles along the color slider and watch the number in the H (hue) text box change to identify the corresponding hue on the color slider.

Does this mean that only 360 colors can be specified in the Color Picker? No, because each hue is modified by its saturation and brightness value.

Saturation refers to the intensity of the hue. A comparison of the colors of a tomato and a cranberry would be a fine illustration of different saturation values. Both have hues that fall within a "red" range. However, the tomato's red is far more intense, or saturated. In the Color Picker, 100% is the highest degree of saturation. A saturation value of 0% means that there is no hue, only a shade of gray. A black-and-white photo, for example, has no saturation value.

The reds of the tomato and cranberry also differ in brightness. The tricky thing about understanding the brightness component of a color is that the term "brightness" is so common that it's difficult to know how it applies specifically to colors. A good example is a room with no windows filled with furniture and artwork. If you flood the room with light, all of the colors of the objects in the room will appear at their most vivid. If you have only a single, dim light source (like a flickering candle), the colors will appear less vivid, and many hues will be indistinguishable from others. If there were no light source whatsoever, no colors would appear, because in the absence of light there is no color.

In the Color Picker, 100% is the highest degree of brightness. A brightness of 0% is always black, regardless of the hue or saturation value specified. Thus, 100% saturation and 100% brightness produce a "pure" hue. Any lesser amount of saturation or brightness is a degradation of the hue.

The Color Picker, shown in Figure 3, is made up of a large color field. The color field represents the current hue and all of its variations of saturation and brightness. By dragging the circle around in the color field, you can sample different saturation and brightness values of the selected hue. Saturation values lie on the horizontal axis; as you move the circle left to right, the saturation of the color increases from 0% to 100%. Note that the colors along the left edge of the color field are only shades of gray. This is because the colors along the left edge have 0% saturation.

Brightness values lie on the vertical axis. All the colors at the bottom of the field are black (0% brightness). The color's brightness increases as you move up. Thus, the pure hue (100% saturation and 100% brightness) is at the top-right corner of the field.

For a hands-on example of these essential color concepts, you can drag the circle cursor around the color field. As the sampled color changes, you'll see that the H (hue) number remains constant while the S (saturation) and B (brightness) numbers change. You can change the hue by dragging the triangles along the color slider.

FIGURE 3
Color Picker dialog box

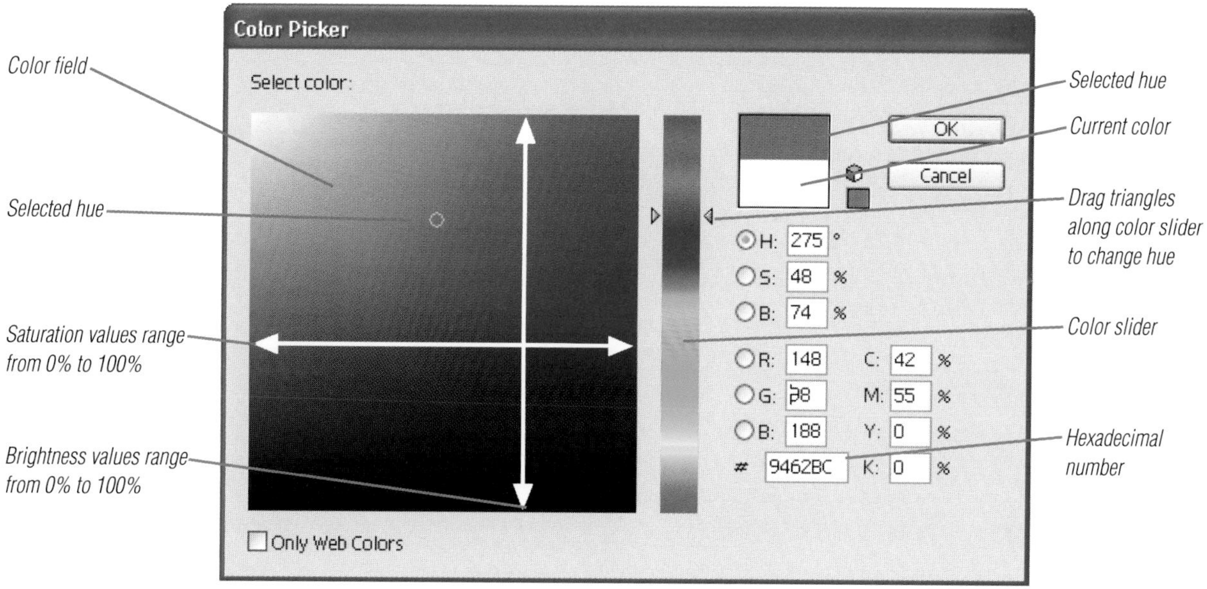

Color field

Selected hue

Saturation values range from 0% to 100%

Brightness values range from 0% to 100%

Select color:

Only Web Colors

H: 275 °
S: 48 %
B: 74 %
R: 148   C: 42 %
G: 98   M: 55 %
B: 188   Y: 0 %
#: 9462BC   K: 0 %

OK
Cancel

Selected hue

Current color

Drag triangles along color slider to change hue

Color slider

Hexadecimal number

Change the opacity and blending mode of objects

1. Open AI 8-1.ai, then save it as **Transparency**.
2. Click **Window** on the menu bar, then click **Transparency**.
3. Select both the yellow circle and the letter T.

   The selection appears in the Transparency palette.
4. Click the **Opacity list arrow**, then drag the **Opacity slider** to 50.
5. Select the cyan and magenta circles, click the **Opacity list arrow**, then drag the **Opacity slider** to 20 so that your screen resembles Figure 4.
6. Select the T and the three circles, then change the opacity to 100%.
7. Click the **Blending Mode list arrow**, click **Multiply**, then deselect all so that your screen resembles Figure 5.
8. Save your work, then close the Transparency document.

You explored the results of changing the opacity of objects and the color effects achieved when you applied the Multiply blending mode to overlapping objects.

FIGURE 4
The three circles and the T at reduced opacity

FIGURE 5
Effect of the Multiply blending mode on overlapping objects

Working with Transparency, Effects, and Graphic Styles

FIGURE 6

Small circle indicates the saturation and brightness values of the selected hue

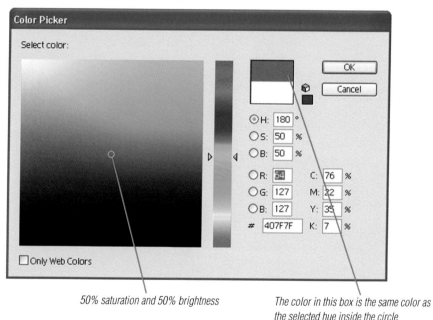

50% saturation and 50% brightness

The color in this box is the same color as
the selected hue inside the circle

1. Open AI 8-2.ai, then save it as **Limeade**.

2. Click **File** on the menu bar, click **Document Color Mode**, then verify that RGB Color is checked.

3. Double-click the **Fill button** in the toolbox to open the Color Picker.

4. Type **180** in the H (hue) text box.

5. Type **50** in the S text box, then press [**Tab**].

   The circle in the color field moves to 50% of the width of the color field, and the values in the CMYK and RGB text boxes are updated to reflect the change.

6. Type **50** in the B text box, then press [**Tab**].

   The color circle moves down to 50% of the height of the color field, as shown in Figure 6.

7. Type **40** in the R text box, type **255** in the G text box, type **0** in the B text box, then click **OK**.

8. Add the new color to the Swatches palette, name it **Lime Green**, then save your work.

You used the Color Picker to select a new fill color. You entered specific values for hue, saturation, and brightness, and entered specific values for red, green, and blue. You then added the new color to the Swatches palette.

APPLY EFFECTS
TO OBJECTS

What You'll Do

In this lesson, you will work with a series of useful effects, using the Effect menu.

Working with Effects

The commands listed on the Effect menu can be applied to objects to alter their appearance without altering the object itself. You can apply effects that distort, transform, outline, and offset a path—among other effects—without changing the original size, anchor points, and shape of the object. The object in Figure 7 is a simple square with a number of effects applied to it, creating the appearance of a complex illustration.

So what is the point of working with effects? The best answer is that working with effects offers you the ability to change

your mind and change your work at any point, because each effect can be easily removed from an object without disturbing other effects that may be applied to it.

When you work with effects, all of your actions are recorded and listed in the Appearance palette. You can, at any time, select an effect in the palette and modify its settings or delete it. When you work without effects—let's say, when you apply the Twist filter—the twist is applied to the object and affects the object. As you continue working, you continue to affect and alter your work. But what happens if, 20 steps later, you decide that you want to decrease the amount of the twist that you applied? You will have to undo everything you've done since applying the twist, then start all over again. If you had applied the Twist effect instead of the Twist filter, you could simply double-click the effect in the Appearance palette, then decrease the amount at which the twist is applied.

The Appearance palette is also a record of what you've done to create an illustration thus far—another benefit of working with effects.

You will note that many of the Effect commands are the same as other commands that you will find on the Filter menu. This can be a bit confusing. Remember that effects are different because they change only the look of the object, not the object itself.

QUICKTIP

For a really fun way to preview filters and effects, check out the Filter Gallery on the Filter menu and the Effect Gallery on the Effect menu. Be sure you are working in RGB Color mode, select your artwork, then click either Filter Gallery or Effect Gallery from the appropriate menu. You'll be able to preview your artwork with specific filters or effects applied. Each style offers additional settings that you can manipulate in the Gallery window.

FIGURE 7
One square with multiple effects applied

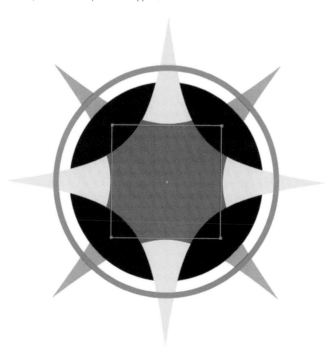

Apply a Bloat effect

1. Click **Window** on the menu bar, then click **Appearance**.

2. Click the **Selection Tool** ▶, then click each letter object in LIMEADE so that they are all selected.

   The Appearance palette displays a new entry called Mixed Objects, meaning that mixed objects are selected. The A and the D are compound paths, while the remaining letters are regular paths.

3. Click **Effect** on the menu bar, point to **Distort & Transform** in the Illustrator Effects section, then click **Pucker & Bloat**.

4. Type **11** in the text box, then click **OK**.

   The Pucker & Bloat item is listed in the Appearance palette.

5. Compare your image to Figure 8.

   The selection marks represent those of the letters *before* the Bloat effect was applied, reflecting the fact that the original objects have not been actually changed by the effect.

You applied a Bloat effect to letter objects. You noted that the effect was listed in the Appearance palette and that the selection marks of the object did not change as a result of the applied effect.

FIGURE 8
Pucker & Bloat effect applied to letter objects

Selection marks show that the original objects have not been changed by the Bloat effect

Working with Transparency, Effects, and Graphic Styles

FIGURE 9
Inner Glow effect affects the black stroke

FIGURE 10

Inflate Warp effect

Apply an Inner Glow and a Warp effect

1. Fill the LIMEADE letter objects with Lime Green.
2. Click **Effect** on the menu bar, point to **Stylize** in the Illustrator Effects section, then click **Inner Glow**.
3. Type **.15** in the Blur text box.

   TIP If your dialog box does not show inches, type .15 in in the Blur text box.
4. Click the **color box** next to the Mode list arrow to open the Color Picker.
5. Type **10** in the C text box, **0** in the M text box, **100** in the Y text box, and **0** in the K text box, then click **OK**.
6. Click **OK** again to close the Inner Glow dialog box.
7. Apply a 3-pt Black stroke to the letters so that your work resembles Figure 9.

   The stroke does not appear black because the Inner Glow effect is altering its appearance.
8. Click **Effect** on the menu bar, point to **Warp** in the Illustrator Effects section, then click **Inflate**.
9. Type **30** in the Bend text box.
10. Type **-30** in the Horizontal text box, click **OK**, then deselect.

    Your work should resemble Figure 10.

You applied the Inner Glow effect to the letter objects, increased the Blur value, then specified the color of the glow, using the Color Picker. You applied a 3-pt Black stroke, creating an interesting effect in conjunction with the Inner Glow effect. You then applied the Inflate Warp effect.

Apply a Drop Shadow effect

1. Select all of the LIMEADE letter objects.

2. Click **Effect** on the menu bar, point to **Stylize** in the Illustrator Effects section, then click **Drop Shadow**.

3. Click the **Mode list arrow**, then click **Normal**.

4. Click the **Opacity list arrow**, then drag the **Opacity slider** to 100.

5. Click the **Color option button**, then click the **color box** to open the Color Picker.

6. Type **240** in the H text box, type **100** in the S and B text boxes, then click **OK**.

   The new color appears in the color box in the Drop Shadow dialog box.

7. Click **OK** to close the Drop Shadow dialog box.

   The Drop Shadow effect is listed in the Appearance palette.

8. Compare your screen to Figure 11.

You applied the Drop Shadow effect, using the Normal blending mode. You also accessed the Color Picker from within the Drop Shadow dialog box to determine the color of the shadow.

FIGURE 11
Drop Shadow effect with a Normal blending mode

Normal blending mode produces an opaque drop shadow

FIGURE 12
Grain effect, isolated on its own layer

FIGURE 13
Grain effect, multiplied at 25% opacity

Apply a Grain effect

1. Verify that the LIMEADE letter objects are still selected, copy them, then paste in front.

2. Verify that the Layers palette is displayed, create a new layer, then move the selected art to the new layer.

   TIP Move the selected art by dragging the Indicates Selected Art button on Layer 1 to the new layer.

3. Click **Effect** on the menu bar, point to **Texture** in the Illustrator Effects section, then click **Grain**.

4. Type **71** in the Intensity text box, type **61** in the Contrast text box, then click **OK**.

5. Click the **Toggles Visibility button** 👁 on Layer 1 to hide Layer 1 so that you can see the results of the effect on Layer 2, as shown in Figure 12, then click the **Toggles Visibility button** ☐ again to show the layer.

   Note that the drop shadow areas were included when the Grain effect was applied.

6. Click the **Opacity list arrow** on the Transparency palette, then drag the **Opacity slider** to 25.

   TIP When you change the opacity of a layer, all objects on the layer are affected.

7. Click the **Blending Mode list arrow**, then click **Multiply**.

8. Deselect, save your work, then compare your screen to Figure 13.

You viewed LIMEADE on a new layer to view the Grain effect independently. You changed the opacity of the copied letters, then changed the blending mode to Multiply, allowing the original letters to be seen through the effect.

USE THE
APPEARANCE PALETTE

What You'll Do

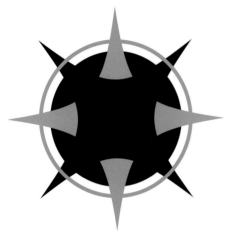

▶ *In this lesson, you will explore the role of the Appearance palette in controlling the appearance attributes of objects.*

Working with the Appearance Palette

The Appearance palette does far more than simply list appearance attributes. It is the gateway for controlling and manipulating all of the appearance attributes of your artwork. The Appearance palette, as shown in Figure 14, shows you the fills, strokes, and effects that have been applied to your artwork and offers you the ability to manipulate those attributes.

When you select an object on the artboard, the Appearance palette lists the associated attributes. Fills and strokes are listed according to their stacking order (front to back), and effects are listed in the order in which they are applied. You can double-click an effect in the Appearance palette to open the effect's dialog box, which will show the settings you used to apply the effect. This is an extremely valuable function of the palette. Imagine opening an illustration after six months and trying to remember how you built it! The Appearance palette provides a trail.

When you have applied a set of attributes to an object, and you then draw a new object, the new object will automatically "inherit" the set of attributes. If you want to remove them, simply click the Reduce to Basic Appearance button in the Appearance palette. You can also click the New Art Maintains Appearance button in the Appearance palette. When selected, the button converts to the New Art Has Basic Appearance button, which means that any newly created art will not inherit any attributes.

Duplicating Items in the Appearance Palette

A strange operation that you can execute with the Appearance palette is the application of multiple fills (and strokes) to a single object. Simply select the Fill attribute in the Appearance palette, then click the Duplicate Selected Item button in the palette. You can also duplicate an attribute by clicking the Appearance palette list arrow, then clicking Duplicate Item.

The Appearance palette is the only place where you can duplicate a fill. One would likely ask oneself, "Why would I need two fills anyway?" The answer is that you don't need two fills. The Appearance palette uses the second fill as a means to create a new object as part of the illustration. The second fill can be distorted and transformed and made to appear as an additional object, as shown in Figure 15. In this figure, the black circle is the original fill, and the yellow and pink objects are duplicate fills. Note that the distortion (Pucker) and transformation (Rotate) of the duplicate fills are *effects* and were not created with a filter or a transform tool. Thus, this is a single object despite its appearance.

Duplicating an effect in the Appearance palette intensifies the effect.

Changing the Order of Appearance Attributes

You can change the order of attributes in the Appearance palette simply by dragging them up or down. The hierarchy of attributes directly affects the appearance of the object. For example, if you dragged the yellow fill attribute in the Appearance palette above the pink fill attribute, the illustration would appear as shown in Figure 16.

FIGURE 14
Appearance palette

Appearance thumbnail

An effect

Appearance palette list arrow

Clear Appearance button

Reduce to Basic Appearance button

Duplicate Selected Item button

Delete Selected Item button

New Art Has Basic Appearance button

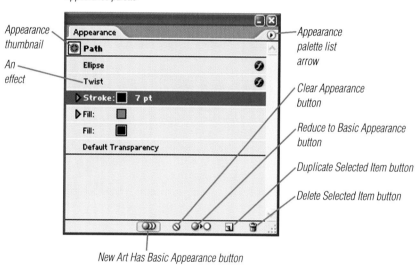

FIGURE 15
Pink and yellow attributes are copies of the black fill

FIGURE 16
The pink attribute is moved behind the yellow attribute

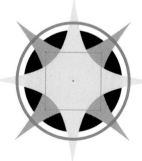

Modify effects

1. Hide Layer 2.

2. Select the LIMEADE letter objects on Layer 1, then double-click **Drop Shadow** in the Appearance palette.

3. Click the **Mode list arrow**, then click **Multiply**.

4. Type **.15** in the X Offset text box, then click **OK**.

   Your work should resemble Figure 17.

5. Select Inner Glow in the Appearance palette, click the **Appearance palette list arrow**, then click **Duplicate Item**.

   The Inner Glow effect is intensified.

6. Deselect, then compare your work to Figure 18.

You double-clicked the Drop Shadow item in the Appearance palette to access the effect's dialog box, which listed the parameters of the effect as you previously applied it. You changed the blending mode of the effect to Multiply, which allowed you to see the lime wallpaper through the blue shadow. You also changed the horizontal offset of the drop shadow. In the Appearance palette, you duplicated the Inner Glow effect.

FIGURE 17
Drop Shadow effect with a Multiply blending mode

Multiply blending mode produces transparent drop shadow

FIGURE 18
Inner Glow effect is intensified when duplicated in the Appearance palette

Working with Transparency, Effects, and Graphic Styles

FIGURE 20
Add Arrowheads dialog box

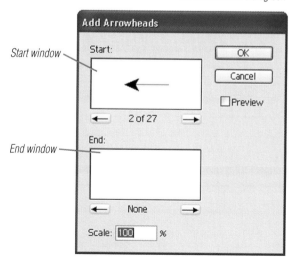

Start window

End window

Remove effects from new art

1. Verify that you see the New Art Maintains Appearance button ⬭ in the Appearance palette.

   TIP If you do not see the New Art Maintains Appearance button, click the New Art Has Basic Appearance button to switch to the New Art Maintains Appearance button.

2. Change the fill to [None] and the stroke to Black in the toolbox.

3. Click the **Pen Tool** ✎., click to the left of the number 5, press [**Shift**], then click directly below the L so that your work resembles Figure 19.

   Notice that the line automatically inherits the effects in the Appearance palette.

4. Click the **Reduce to Basic Appearance button** ⬤▸○ in the Appearance palette.

   The effects are removed from the new line.

5. Using the Stroke palette, click the **Round Cap button** ⬛, click the **Dashed Line check box**, type **6** in the first dash text box, then press [**Enter**] (Win) or [**return**] (Mac).

6. Click **Effect** on the menu bar, point to the **first Stylize command**, then click **Add Arrowheads**.

7. Click the **right arrow** below the Start window until you see arrowhead 2 of 27.

8. Click the **left arrow** below the End window until you see None, as shown in Figure 20, then click **OK**.

   The Add Arrowheads effect is listed in the Appearance palette.

   (continued)

TIP If the arrowhead is overlapping the "5," move the line to the left.

9. Click the **New Art Maintains Appearance button** in the Appearance palette so that you see the New Art Has Basic Appearance button .

   When you click the New Art Maintains Appearance button, it becomes the New Art Has Basic Appearance button. When the New Art Has Basic Appearance button is active, newly created art will not inherit the current attributes.

10. Click the **Rectangle Tool** , draw a rectangle around the lime wallpaper background, then remove the dashes so that the stroke is solid.

    The rectangle does not inherit the Add Arrowheads effect.

11. Show Layer 2, then deselect so that your screen resembles Figure 21.

12. Save your work, then close the Limeade document.

You created a simple line, noting that it automatically inherited the effects in the Appearance palette, then you removed the effects. You added the Add Arrowheads effect. You then chose the New Art Has Basic Appearance button in the Appearance palette, and, when you drew a rectangle, noted that it did not inherit any effects.

FIGURE 21
Black rectangle has a basic appearance

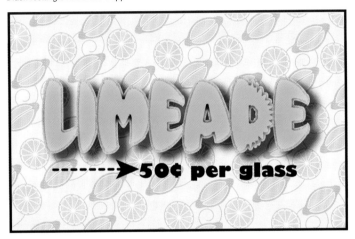

Working with Transparency, Effects, and Graphic Styles

FIGURE 22

Appearance palette

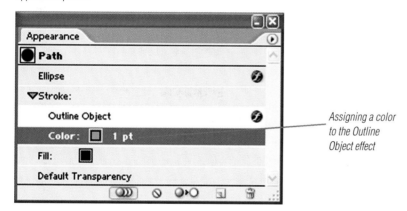

Assigning a color
to the Outline
Object effect

**Create a complex
appearance from a
single object**

1. Create a new 6" × 6" CMYK Color document, then save it as **Triple Fill**.

2. Create a 2" square with a black fill and no stroke.

3. Click **Effect** on the menu bar, point to **Convert to Shape**, then click **Ellipse**.

4. Verify that the Relative option button is selected, type **.25** in the Extra Width text box, type **.25** in the Extra Height text box, then click **OK**.

   The square appears as a larger circle.

5. Click the **Stroke item** in the Appearance palette, click **Effect** on the menu bar, point to **Path**, then click **Outline Object**.

   The Outline Object effect is listed under the Stroke item.

6. Click the **Color attribute** under the Stroke item in the Appearance palette, then click **Green** in the Swatches palette.

   Compare your Appearance palette with Figure 22.

   (continued)

7. In the Stroke palette, change the weight of the stroke to 7 pt.

8. Click **Effect** on the menu bar, point to **Path** in the Illustrator Effects section, click **Offset Path**, type **.25** in the Offset text box, then click **OK**.

   Your screen should resemble Figure 23.

9. Click the **triangle** ▽ next to the Stroke item in the Appearance palette to collapse the detail in the Stroke section.

10. Click the **Fill item** in the Appearance palette, then click the **Duplicate Selected Item button** ⬙ in the Appearance palette.

11. Keeping the original Fill item selected, click **Green** in the Swatches palette.

12. Click **Effect** on the menu bar, point to **Distort & Transform** in the Illustrator Effects section, click **Pucker & Bloat**, type **-65** in the text box, then click **OK**.

   The green fill is distorted above the black fill, as shown in Figure 24.

   (continued)

FIGURE 23
Outer circle is created with the Offset Path effect

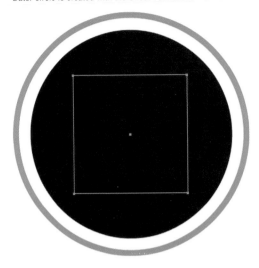

FIGURE 24
Duplicated fill effect is distorted

Duplicated effect ⎯⎯⎯⎯⎯

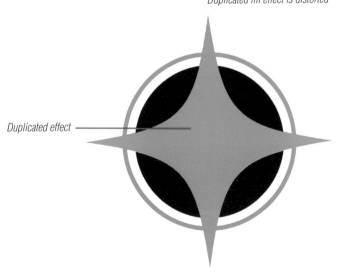

Working with Transparency, Effects, and Graphic Styles

FIGURE 25
Rotation on the third fill is an effect

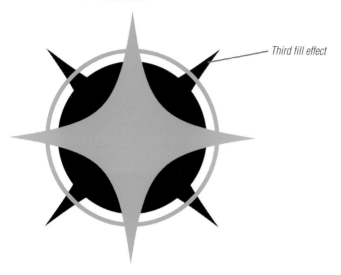

Third fill effect

FIGURE 26
Changing the order of effects changes appearance

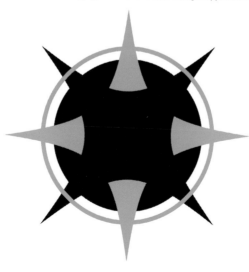

13. Click the **top Fill item** in the Appearance palette, then click the **Duplicate Selected Item button** ⬜ in the Appearance palette.

14. Click the **middle Fill item**, click **Effect** on the menu bar, point to **Distort & Transform**, click **Transform**, type **45** in the Angle text box, then click **OK**.

15. Click the **Color attribute** under the middle Fill item, then change it to black so that your work resembles Figure 25.

16. Click the **middle Fill item**, drag it above the top Fill item so that your work resembles Figure 26, then save and close the Triple Fill document.

Note that the illustration is a single object—as such, it can be used as a style.

You applied a number of effects to a simple square, creating the appearance of multiple objects. You also changed the appearance of the illustration by changing the order of the items in the Appearance palette.

WORK WITH
GRAPHIC STYLES

What You'll Do

In this lesson, you will create and apply graphic styles.

Creating and Applying Graphic Styles

Graphic styles are named sets of appearance attributes that are accessed in the Graphic Styles palette. To create a new style, select the artwork whose attributes you want to save as a style, then do one of the following:

- Click the New Graphic Style button in the Graphic Styles palette.
- Drag a selected object from the artboard into the Graphic Styles palette.

- Drag a thumbnail from the Appearance palette into the Graphic Styles palette.

A graphic style can include fills, strokes, effects, patterns, opacity settings, blending modes, gradients, and effects. However, a graphic style can be created from a *single* set of attributes only. Only one object needs to be selected in order to create a new graphic style. The Graphic Styles palette is shown in Figure 27.

Merging graphic styles

You can create new graphic styles by merging two or more graphic styles in the Graphic Styles palette. [Ctrl] click (Win) or ⌘ click (Mac) to select all the graphic styles that you want to merge, click the Graphic Styles palette list arrow, then click Merge Graphic Styles. The new graphic style will contain all of the attributes of the selected graphic styles and will be added to the Graphic Styles palette as a new graphic style.

When you apply a graphic style to an object, the new graphic style overrides any graphic style that was previously applied to the object. When you apply a graphic style to a group or a layer, all objects in the group or on the layer take on the graphic style's attributes. Graphic styles are associated with the layers they are applied to. If you remove an object from a layer that has a graphic style applied to it, the object will lose the graphic style attributes.

FIGURE 27
Graphic Styles palette

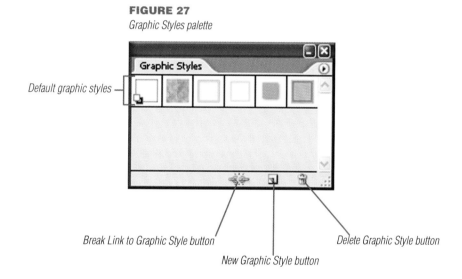

Default graphic styles

Break Link to Graphic Style button

New Graphic Style button

Delete Graphic Style button

Create a new graphic style

1. Open AI 8-3.ai, then save it as **Dolphin Blue**.

2. Create a rectangle that is 1" wide and 2" tall.

3. Fill the rectangle with the Blue Radial swatch and remove any stroke.

4. Click the **Gradient Tool** , then drag the **Gradient Tool pointer** from just below the top-left corner to the bottom-right corner of the rectangle.

   Try to make your fill resemble Figure 28.

5. Click **Effect** on the menu bar, point to **Stylize** in the Illustrator Effects section, click **Round Corners**, type **.15** in the Radius text box, then click **OK**.

6. Click **Effect** on the menu bar, point to **Stylize** in the Illustrator Effects section, then click **Outer Glow**.

7. Change the color to black in the Color Picker, if necessary, click **OK**, type **.1** in the Blur text box, then click **OK**, so that your work resembles Figure 29.

8. Click **Window** on the menu bar, then click **Graphic Styles**.

9. Select all, then drag the **thumbnail** next to Path: Graphic Style in the Appearance palette to the Graphic Styles palette, as shown in Figure 30.

10. Double-click the **new swatch** in the Graphic Styles palette, then name it **Dolphin Blue**.

You created an illustration with the Round Corners and Outer Glow effects, then saved the appearance attributes as a new graphic style in the Graphic Styles palette.

FIGURE 28
Applying the gradient to the rectangle

FIGURE 29
An Outer Glow effect added to the rectangle

FIGURE 30
Creating a new graphic style

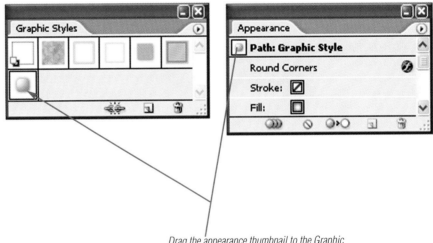

Drag the appearance thumbnail to the Graphic
Styles palette to create a new graphic style

Working with Transparency, Effects, and Graphic Styles

FIGURE 31

Dolphin Blue graphic style applied to an object

Dolphin blue

Apply a graphic style to an object

1. Cut the rectangle from the artboard.
2. Click **Object** on the menu bar, then click **Show All**.

   A dolphin object and the words Dolphin blue appear.
3. Deselect all, select the dolphin artwork, then click **Dolphin Blue** in the Graphic Styles palette.

   Your work should resemble Figure 31.

You applied a graphic style to a simple object.

Apply a graphic style to text

1. Click the **Graphic Styles palette list arrow**; if there is a check mark to the left of Override Character Color, click **Override Character Color** to remove the check mark.

2. Select the text, then click **Dolphin Blue** in the Graphic Styles palette.

   The text takes on all the attributes of the graphic style except the fill color, which remains black.

3. Undo your last step.

4. Click the **Graphic Styles palette list arrow**, click **Override Character Color**, then apply the Dolphin Blue graphic style to the Dolphin blue text.

   Your work should resemble Figure 32.

5. Undo your last step, click **Type** on the menu bar, then click **Create Outlines** to convert the text to outlines.

6. Ungroup the outlines, then apply the Dolphin Blue graphic style to the objects so that your work resembles Figure 33.

7. Compare the text fills in Figure 33 to those in Figure 32.

You explored three ways of applying a graphic style to text and text outlines for different effects.

FIGURE 32
Dolphin Blue graphic style applied to text

FIGURE 33
Dolphin Blue graphic style applied to each object

FIGURE 34

Artwork modified with a stroke and a second Outer Glow effect

Duplicate outer glow
added to dolphin

1. Select all, then apply a 1.5-pt. green stroke to the dolphin and the letters.

2. Deselect, select only the dolphin, click the **Outer Glow item** in the Appearance palette, then click the **Duplicate Selected Item** button ⬔ .

3. Double-click the **duplicate Outer Glow item** in the Appearance palette, then change the opacity to 17% in the Outer Glow dialog box.

4. Click the **color box** in the Outer Glow dialog box to open the Color Picker.

5. Type **32** in the H (hue) text box, **100** in the S (saturation) text box, and **100** in the B (brightness) text box, then click **OK**.

6. Click **OK** again to close the Outer Glow dialog box, then deselect all.

   Your work should resemble Figure 34.

7. Press and hold [**Alt**] (Win) or [**option**] (Mac), then drag the **thumbnail** from the Appearance palette directly on top of the Dolphin Blue graphic style in the Graphic Styles palette.

   The Dolphin Blue graphic style is updated to include the green stroke and the orange outer glow.

8. Save your work, then close Dolphin Blue.

You modified the Dolphin Blue graphic style by changing the settings in the Appearance palette, then replacing the old graphic style with the new appearance attributes.

Use the Transparency palette and the Color Picker.

1. Open AI 8-4.ai, then save it as **Channel Z**.
2. Double-click the Fill button in the toolbox to open the Color Picker, create a color using the following values: hue = 59, saturation = 34, and brightness = 74, then drag the new color to the Swatches palette.
3. Select the square on the artboard, show the Gradient palette, if necessary, click the black color stop on the gradient slider, press [Alt] (Win) or [option] (Mac), then click the new color swatch in the Swatches palette.
4. Change the opacity of the square to 60%.
5. Save your work.

Apply effects to objects.

1. In the Appearance palette, duplicate the Fill item.
2. Keep the original Fill item selected, click Effect on the menu bar, point to Texture, click Grain, click the Grain Type list arrow, then click Regular.
3. Type **70** for the Intensity and **60** for the Contrast, then click OK.

4. Click the Stroke item in the Appearance palette, then add a 1-point orange stroke. (*Hint*: Use any orange swatch.)
5. Click Effect on the menu bar, point to Path, click Offset Path, type **.1** in the Offset text box, then click OK.
6. Save your work.

Use the Appearance palette.

1. Select the top Fill item in the Appearance palette.
2. Click Effect on the menu bar, point to the first Stylize command, click Round Corners, type **1** in the Radius text box, then click OK.
3. In the Transparency palette, change the blending mode to Multiply.
4. Select the bottom Fill item, then apply the Grain effect using the same settings that you previously used.
5. Expand the top Fill item, if necessary, double-click Grain to open the Grain dialog box, then change the Intensity to 100.

6. Duplicate the top Fill item, then change the Color attribute of the middle Fill item to the Orange Black gradient in the Swatches palette.
7. Remove the Round Corners effect from the top Fill item.
8. Collapse the three Fill items and the Stroke item in the Appearance palette.
9. Delete the Opacity: 60% Multiply item from the palette.
10. Save your work.

Work with graphic styles.

1. Show the Graphic Styles palette, if necessary.
2. Drag the thumbnail from the Appearance palette to the Graphic Styles palette.
3. Name the new graphic style **Noise**.
4. Cut the artwork from the artboard.
5. Click Object on the menu bar, then click Show All.
6. Verify that Override Character Color is checked in the Graphic Styles palette menu.
7. Apply the Noise style to the text.

8. Expand the Stroke item in the Appearance palette, then change its color to Black and its weight to 1.5 pt.

9. Double-click the Offset Path item, then change the offset to .15.

10. Update the Noise graphic style with the new attributes by pressing [Alt] (Win) or [option] (Mac) as you drag the thumbnail in the Appearance palette on top of the Noise style in the Graphic Styles palette.

11. Save your work, compare your screen to Figure 35, then close Channel Z.

FIGURE 35
Completed Skills Review

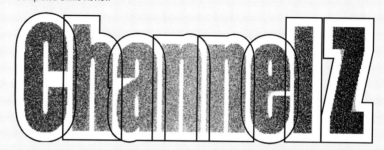

The local VFW has contracted you to design their monthly newsletter. You are happy, because it means a regular monthly payment. However, since their budget is modest, you want to streamline your work as much as possible. One design element of the newsletter that is used every month is a red and blue frame positioned around pictures. You decide to create this as a graphic style in Illustrator.

1. Open AI 8-5.ai, then save it as **Frame**.
2. Show the Brushes palette, then apply the 10 pt Round brush to the square.
3. Click Effect on the menu bar, point to Stylize, then click Feather.
4. Accept the default settings in the Feather Radius text box, then click OK.
5. In the Appearance palette, duplicate the stroke, then change the duplicate stroke color to blue.
6. Click the Offset Path command on the Effect menu. (*Hint*: Point to Path.)

7. Type **.18** in the Offset text box, then click OK.
8. Save the appearance attributes as a new graphic style in the Graphic Styles palette.

FIGURE 36
Completed Project Builder 1

9. Name the new graphic style **Picture Frame**.
10. Save your work, compare your screen to Figure 36, then close the Frame document.

Northstar Couriers has contracted you to design their logo, which is simply their name, NORTHSTAR. They tell you that your design will be applied to everything from their mail packs to their letterhead to their shipping vans.

1. Open AI 8-6.ai, then save it as **Northstar**.
2. Select the square, then duplicate its fill in the Appearance palette.
3. Change the fill color of the top Fill item in the Appearance palette to White, then click the Pucker & Bloat command on the Effect menu. (*Hint*: Point to Distort & Transform.)
4. Type **-100** in the text box, then click OK.
5. Select the top Fill item in the Appearance palette, then click the Transform command on the Effect menu. (*Hint*: Point to Distort & Transform.)
6. Type **-25** in both the Horizontal and Vertical text boxes of the Scale section, then click OK.
7. Double-click Transform in the Appearance palette.
8. Type **-.25** in the Horizontal text box and **.25** in the Vertical text box of the Move section, then click OK.
9. Save the attributes as a new graphic style named **Star** in the Graphic Styles palette.
10. Cut the artwork from the artboard.

11. Type the word **NORTHSTAR** in 72-point. Impact (or a similar font), then convert the text to outlines. (*Hint*: Click Type on the menu bar, then click Create Outlines.)
12. Ungroup the outlines.

FIGURE 37
Completed Project Builder 2

13. Apply the Star graphic style to the text objects.
14. Save your work, compare your illustration to Figure 37, then close Northstar.

Starlight.com, a local Web site that lists the schedules of the city's nightlife, has hired you to redesign their site. Part of that redesign will require a new masthead. They give you no specific direction on how they want their name displayed, but they do tell you that whatever design you create will be applied to other headlines throughout the site.

1. Open AI 8-7.ai, then save it as **Starlight**.
2. Select the black square, then duplicate its fill in the Appearance palette.
3. Click the Free Distort command on the Effect menu. (*Hint*: Point to Distort & Transform.)
4. Move the top two selection handles down and outward, as shown in Figure 38, then click OK.
5. Select the top Fill item in the Appearance palette, click Effect on the menu bar, point to Stylize, click Feather, type **.05** in the Feather Radius text box, then click OK.
6. Change the color of the top Fill item to 40% Black.
7. Select the bottom Fill item in the Appearance palette, then click Inner Glow on the Effect menu. (*Hint*: Point to Stylize.)
8. Specify the color for the glow as hue = 56, saturation = 100, and brightness = 84, change the blending mode to Normal and the Blur to .1, then click OK.
9. Save the attributes as a new graphic style named Starlight Glow in the Graphic Styles palette.

10. Cut the artwork from the artboard.
11. Type the word **STARLIGHT** in 72-point Impact.

FIGURE 38
Free Distort dialog box

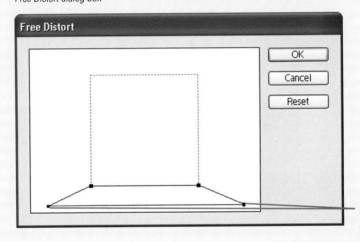

Drag top two selection handles down and outward to these positions

12. Apply the Starlight Glow graphic style to the text.
13. Save your work, compare your screen to Figure 39, the close Starlight.

FIGURE 39
Completed Design Project

STARLIGHT

Working with Transparency, Effects, and Graphic Styles

This group project is designed to test your understanding of the workings of the Appearance palette and the way effects are applied. The challenge is to look at a piece of finished artwork and determine how and why the final effect was achieved.

Note: This exercise requires that you have already completed Project Builder 2 on page 8-33.

1. Open Northstar.ai (the finished file that you created in Project Builder 2), then save it as **Appearance palette test**.
2. Draw a rectangle around the word Northstar, fill the rectangle with red, send it to the back, then deselect so that your image resembles Figure 40.
3. Note that the white "stars" are more visible against the red background.
4. Poll the group: When you executed the steps from Project Builder 2, how many noticed that the "stars" were letters?
5. Here's the test: Have each member of the group write down an explanation—as long as need be—of how the effects applied in the steps yielded this result. The group member should reiterate steps and explain how each contributed to the final result.

FIGURE 40
Completed Group Project

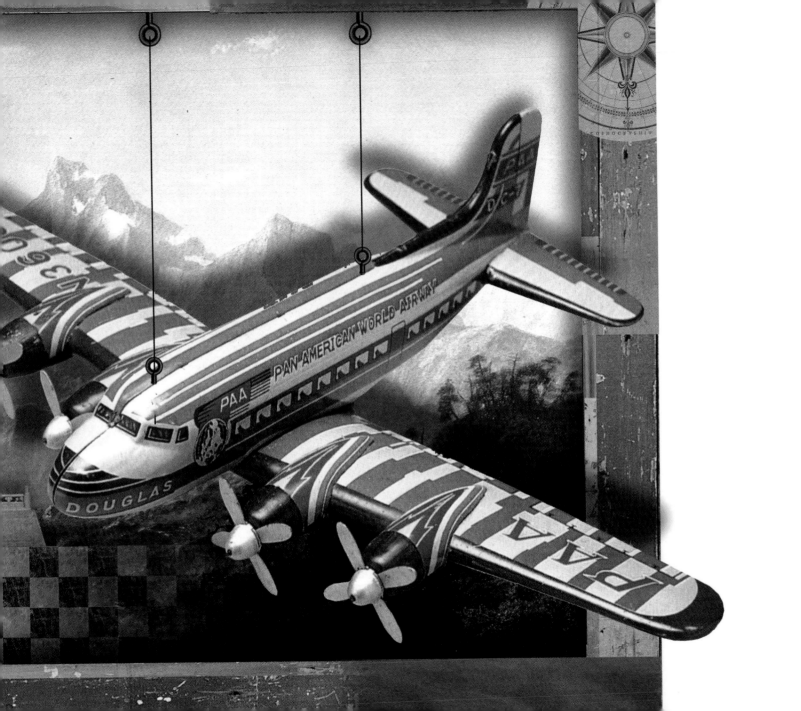

chapter 9

CREATING GRAPHS
IN ILLUSTRATOR

1. Create a graph.

2. Edit a graph using the Graph Data Window.

3. Use the Group Selection Tool.

4. Use the Graph Type dialog box.

5. Create a combination graph.

6. Create a custom graph design.

7. Apply a custom design to a graph.

8. Create and apply a sliding-scale design.

9 CREATING GRAPHS
IN ILLUSTRATOR

When you think of graphs, you probably think of those premade, click-a-button graphs that you can make with any presentation or financial software package. As a designer, you'll be really excited by the graphs that you can create with Illustrator's graph tools. When your project calls for a graph, you can enter the data directly into Illustrator, then have all of Illustrator's design and drawing power behind you when it comes to designing the graph.

For the right project, visually interesting and smartly designed graphs are a very powerful tool for conveying information. Think of using graphs as an opportunity for expressing data artistically. Since people naturally pay more attention to a well-designed graph than to blocks of text, using graphs in a presentation will help you to make your points more persuasively.

Tools You'll Use

Group
Selection
Tool

Graph tools

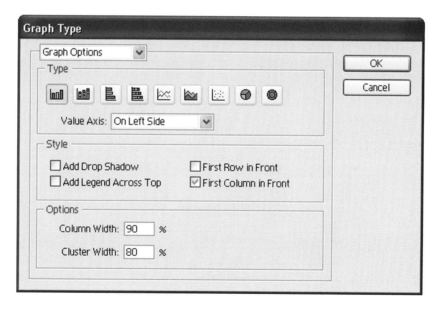

CREATE
A GRAPH

What You'll Do

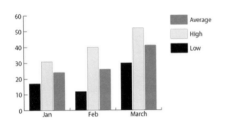

In this lesson, you will enter data and create a column graph.

Defining a Graph

A **graph** is a diagram of data that shows relationships among a set of numbers. A set of data can be represented by a graphic element, such as a bar, line, or point. Different types of graphs are used to emphasize different aspects of a display.

Illustrator offers nine types of graphs:

- Column
- Stacked column
- Bar
- Stacked bar
- Line
- Area
- Scatter
- Pie
- Radar

The right type of graph can help you to simplify complex data and communicate a message more effectively. In Illustrator, you can convert one type of graph into another type and create custom designs that you can then apply to the graph.

Changing the number of decimal points in graph data

Numbers in the Graph Data window are initially displayed with two decimals. For example, if you type the number 86, it appears as 86.00. To modify the number of decimals in any or all cells in the Graph Data window, click the cell(s) that you want to change, then click the Cell style button in the Graph Data window. The Cell Style dialog box opens. Increase or decrease the number in the Number of decimals text box to change the decimal place (set it to 0 if you do not want any decimal place), then click OK. You can also increase or decrease the column width in the Cell Style dialog box by changing the value in the Column width text box.

Creating a Graph

Before you create a graph, it is important to understand how data is plotted in Illustrator's Graph Data window. The first column (vertical axis) of the Graph Data window is reserved for category labels, while the first row (horizontal axis) is reserved for legend labels. See Figure 1.

Category labels describe non-numeric data, such as the months of the year, the days of the week, or a group of salespersons' names.

Legend labels describe numeric data that may change, such as weekly sales totals, payroll amounts, or daily temperatures; they appear in a box next to the graph, called the legend.

The legend, like a map legend, contains the legend labels and small boxes filled with colors that represent the columns on the graph.

FIGURE 1

Entering category labels and legend labels

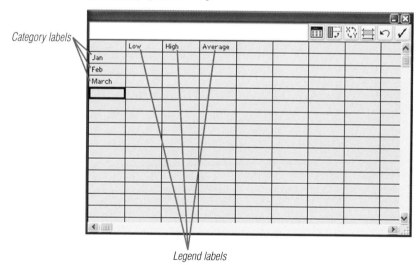

Category labels

Legend labels

Create a column graph

1. Open AI 9-1.ai, then save it as **Graph**.

2. Verify that you are using inches as your General unit of measure by checking your Units & Display Performance Preferences.

3. Click the **Column Graph Tool** 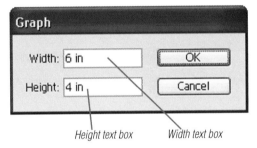, then click the center of the artboard.

4. Type **6** in the Width text box and **4** in the Height text box, as shown in Figure 2, then click **OK**.

   The Graph Data window appears in front of the graph. The Graph Data window consists of rows and columns. The intersection of a row and a column is called a **cell**. The first cell, which is selected, contains the number 1.00 as sample data to create a temporary structure for the graph. The appearance of the graph will change after you enter your own data.

5. Press [**Delete**] (Win) or [**delete**] (Mac), then press [**Tab**] to eliminate the 1.00 from the first cell and select the next cell in the first row.

   You must always remove the number 1.00 from the first cell before entering new data.

6. Type **Low**, press [**Tab**], type **High**, press [**Tab**], then type **Average**.

   You have entered three legend labels.

   (continued)

FIGURE 2
Graph dialog box

Width text box

Height text box   Width text box

FIGURE 3
Graph Data window

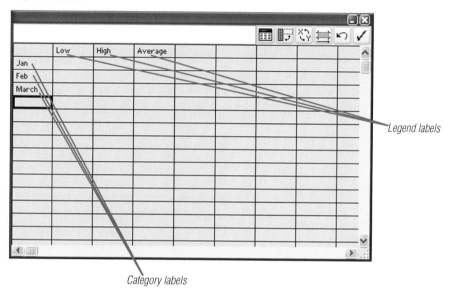

Legend labels

Category labels

FIGURE 4
Column graph

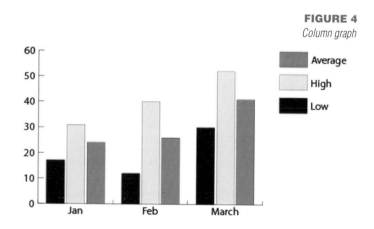

7. Click the **second cell** in the first column, type **Jan**, press [**Enter**] (Win) or [**return**] (Mac), type **Feb**, press [**Enter**] (Win) or [**return**] (Mac), type **March**, then press [**Enter**] (Win) or [**return**] (Mac).

You have entered three category labels. Compare the positions of your labels with those shown in Figure 3.

   TIP   Category labels are listed vertically and legend labels are listed horizontally in the Graph Data window. If you enter your labels incorrectly, you can click the Transpose row/column button in the Graph Data window to switch them.

8. Enter the remaining data shown on the artboard, using [Tab] and [Enter] (Win) or [Tab] and [return] (Mac), and the four arrow keys on your keyboard to move between cells.

   TIP   Often you will want to create labels that consist of numbers, such as a ZIP code or the year 2008. Since these labels are meant to describe categories, they must be set in quotes ("2002") so that Illustrator will not mistake them for data that should be plotted.

9. Close the Graph Data window, saving the changes you made, then reposition the graph on the artboard (if necessary).

10. Deselect, save your work, then compare your graph to Figure 4.

You defined the size of the graph, then entered three legend labels, three category labels, and numbers in the Graph Data window.

EDIT A GRAPH USING THE
GRAPH DATA WINDOW

What You'll Do

	Low	High	Average			
Jan	17.00	31.00	24.00			
Feb	12.00	40.00	26.00			
March	30.00	52.00	41.00			

 In this lesson, you will change the data that is the basis of the column graph, then update the graph to reflect the new data.

Editing Data and Graphs

A project that calls for a graph often calls for edits to the graph. Fortunately, it is easy to make changes to the data that defines the graph . . . and just as easy to update the graph. For every graph in Illustrator, the data that was used to plot it is stored in the Graph Data window. The data is editable; when you make changes to the data, simply click the Apply button in the Graph Data window to preview the changes to the graph.

When you create text and data in another program that you want to use in an Illustrator graph, the document must be saved as a text-only file with commas separating each number from the next. If you are importing an Excel worksheet, it must be saved as a text (tab-delimited) file for Illustrator to support it.

Importing data from other software programs
You can import graph data from a text file or a Microsoft Excel worksheet into the Graph Data window in Illustrator. To import data, you must have the Graph Data window open and selected. Click the Import data button. You will then be prompted to open the file you wish to import.

FIGURE 5

Changing data in the Graph Data window

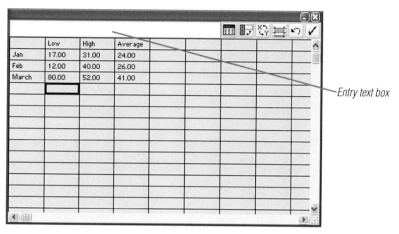

—Entry text box

FIGURE 6

Viewing the new graph

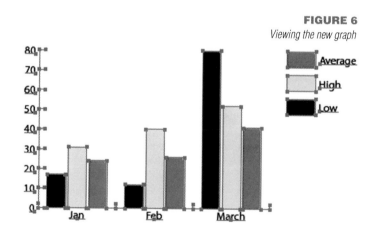

Edit data in a graph

1. Click **View** on the menu bar, then click **Hide Page Tiling**, if necessary.

2. Click the **Selection Tool** ▸, then select and delete the text at the top of the artboard.

3. Click the **graph**, click **Object** on the menu bar, point to **Graph**, then click **Data**.

   TIP   The separate objects that make up the graph are automatically grouped when the graph is created.

4. Click the cell that contains the number 30.00, type **80**, press [**Enter**] (Win) or [**return**] (Mac), then compare your screen to Figure 5.

   When you click a cell, the number in the cell becomes highlighted in the entry text box of the Graph Data window, allowing you to change it to a new number.

5. Click the **Apply button** ✓ in the Graph Data window, then compare your graph to Figure 6.

6. Change the number 80.00 to 34, click the cell that contains the number 41.00, type **43**, then press [**Enter**](Win) or [**return**](Mac).

7. Close the Graph Data window, then save changes when prompted.

   TIP   To remove data from cells in the Graph Data window select the cells from which you want to delete the data, click Edit on the menu bar, then click Clear.

You edited the graph's data in the Graph Data window, then clicked the Apply button to view the changes to the graph.

USE THE GROUP
SELECTION TOOL

What You'll Do

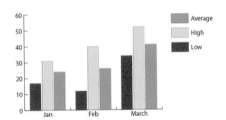

In this lesson, you will use the Group Selection Tool to easily select different areas of the graph for modification.

Using the Group Selection Tool

Graphs are grouped objects, consisting of many individual groups grouped together. Each set of colored columns represents an individual group within the larger group. For example, all of the black columns in Figure 7 represent the low temperatures for each month. The gray columns are the average-temperature group, and the light gray columns are the high-temperature group.

The Group Selection Tool allows you to select entire groups within the larger group for the purpose of editing them with the Illustrator tools and menu commands.

FIGURE 7
Individual groups within a graph

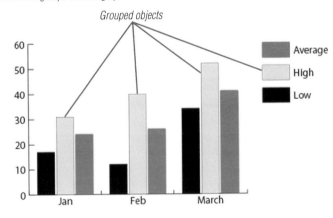

Creating Graphs in Illustrator

FIGURE 8

Changing the color of the low-temperature group to red

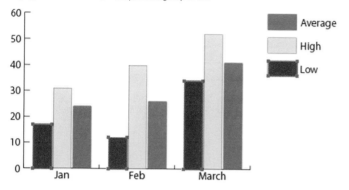

FIGURE 9

Column graph with new colors applied

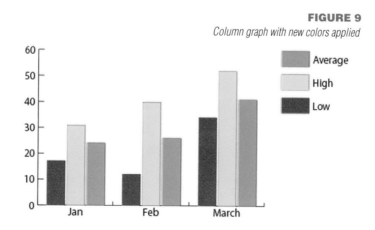

Use the Group Selection Tool

1. Click the artboard to deselect the graph.

2. Click the **Group Selection Tool** ▸⁺ .

   The Group Selection Tool is hidden beneath the Direct Selection Tool.

3. Click the **first black column** above the Jan label, then click again.

   The first click selects the first black column, and the second click selects the two remaining black columns.

4. Click the **first black column** a third time to select the low-temperature legend box.

   If you click too many times, you will eventually select the entire graph instead of an individual group. In that case, deselect and try again.

5. Change the fill color of the selected columns to red, as shown in Figure 8.

6. Click the **first light gray column** above the Jan label, click it again, click it a third time, then change the fill color of the high-temperature columns and legend box to yellow.

7. Select the gray columns and legend box, change the fill color to green, then deselect all.

   Your graph should resemble Figure 9.

8. Save your work.

   TIP   The text labels, value axis labels, and legend labels are also individual groups within the larger graph group. Click twice to select them, then change their font, size, or color as desired.

You used the Group Selection Tool to select groups within the graph quickly and easily, then changed the colors of the columns and the legend boxes.

USE THE GRAPH
TYPE DIALOG BOX

What You'll Do

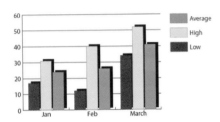

In this lesson, you will modify the graph using the Graph Type dialog box.

Using the Graph Type Dialog Box

The Graph Type dialog box provides a variety of ways to change the look of your graph. For example, you can add a drop shadow behind the columns in a graph or change the appearance of the tick marks.

Tick marks are short lines that extend out from the value axis, which is the vertical line to the left of the graph. Tick marks help viewers interpret the meaning of column height by indicating incremental values on the value axis. You can also move the value axis from the left side of the graph to the right side, or display it on both sides.

Values on the value axis can be changed, and symbols such as $, %, and ° can be added to the numbers for clarification.

Choosing a chart type

Keep in mind the following guidelines when choosing a chart type:

- Pie or column charts are typically used to show quantitative data as a percentage of the whole.
- Line or bar charts are used to compare trends or changes over time.
- Area charts emphasize volume and are used to show a total quantity rather than to emphasize a portion of the data.
- Scatter or radial charts show a correlation between variables.

FIGURE 10
Graph Type dialog box

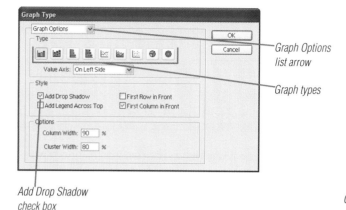

Graph Options
list arrow

Graph types

Add Drop Shadow
check box

FIGURE 11
Choosing options for the value axis

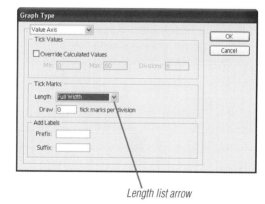

Length list arrow

FIGURE 12
Graph with full-width tick marks and a drop shadow

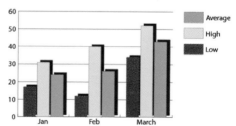

Use the Graph Type dialog box

1. Click the **Selection Tool** ▶, then click the **graph**.

   The entire graph must be selected to make changes in the Graph Type dialog box.

2. Click **Object** on the menu bar, point to **Graph**, then click **Type**.

3. Click the **Add Drop Shadow check box**, as shown in Figure 10.

4. Click the **Graph Options list arrow**, then click **Value Axis**.

   All of the options in this window now refer to the value axis, which is the vertical line located to the left of the columns on the graph.

5. Click the **Length list arrow** in the Tick Marks section of the window, click **Full Width**, compare your Graph Type dialog box to Figure 11, then click **OK**.

6. Deselect the graph, save your work, then compare your graph to Figure 12.

   TIP   The Graph Type dialog box does not provide an option for displaying the number or value that each column in the graph represents. For example, it will not display the number 32 on top of a column that represents 32°. If you want to display the actual values of the data on the chart, you must add those labels manually, using the Type Tool.

You used the Graph Type dialog box to add a drop shadow to the graph and to extend the tick marks to run the full width of the graph.

CREATE A
COMBINATION GRAPH

What You'll Do

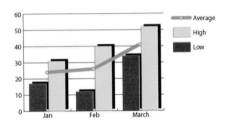

 In this lesson, you will create a combination graph to show one set of data as compared to other data.

Defining a Combination Graph

A **combination graph** is a graph that uses two graph styles to plot numeric data. This type of graph is useful if you want to emphasize one set of numbers in comparison to others. For example, if you needed to create a column graph showing how much more paper than glass, plastic, or aluminum is recycled in a major city over a one-year period, you could plot the paper recycling data as a line graph, leaving the other recycling categories as columns. Your audience would be able to compare how much more paper is recycled than the other three products by looking at the line in relationship to the columns on the graph.

FIGURE 13
Graph Type dialog box

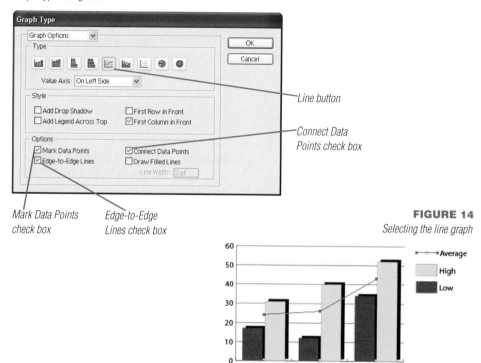

Line button

Connect Data
Points check box

Mark Data Points
check box

Edge-to-Edge
Lines check box

FIGURE 14
Selecting the line graph

FIGURE 15
Formatting the line graph

Markers

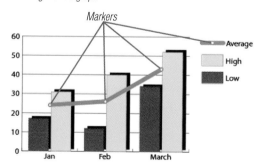

Create a combination graph

1. Click the **Group Selection Tool** [icon], then select all four items of the Average (green) group.

2. Click **Object** on the menu bar, point to **Graph**, then click **Type**.

3. Click the **Line button** [icon], then click the **Add Drop Shadow check box** to remove the check mark.

4. Click the **Edge-to-Edge Lines check box**, make sure that there are check marks in the Mark Data Points and Connect Data Points check boxes, as shown in Figure 13, then click **OK**.

   The four green columns are replaced by four small square markers.

5. Click the **artboard** to deselect the graph.

6. Click the **Group Selection Tool** [icon], then click the first line segment connecting the markers three times to select the entire line and the corresponding information in the legend, as shown in Figure 14.

7. Click **Object** on the menu bar, point to **Arrange**, then click **Bring to Front**.

8. Change the stroke weight to 10 pt, the fill color of the line to [None], the stroke color of the line to green, and the cap to a round cap.

9. Deselect, select the four gray markers using the Group Selection Tool [icon], change their fill color to White, then deselect again.

10. Save your work, compare your graph to Figure 15, then close the Graph document.

You created a combination graph.

CREATE A CUSTOM
GRAPH DESIGN

What You'll Do

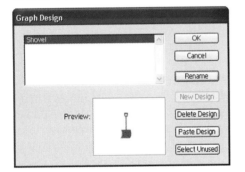

 In this lesson, you will define artwork that will be used for a custom graph.

Creating a Custom Graph Design

A **custom graph design** is simply a picture of something used to replace traditional columns, bars, or markers in Illustrator graphs. For example, when reporting on financial news, newspapers such as *USA Today* often print graphs made with custom designs of coins or dollars instead of columns and bars.

Only vector-based objects can be used for custom graph designs. You cannot use bitmaps, objects created with the Paintbrush Tool, or objects filled with gradients.

Illustrator contains predefined column and marker designs as well as graph designs. These files are located in Adobe Illustrator CS2/Cool Extras/Sample Files. To use these designs, first open one of the sample files, create a new document and then create a new graph. Select the graph, click Object on the menu bar, point to Graph, then click Column. All of the column designs will appear in the Graph Column dialog box.

Using supplied custom graph designs

Illustrator comes with two documents full of custom designs that you can apply to graphs. These designs include flags, cats, hammers, diamonds, dollar signs, stars, and men and women. In addition, three-dimensional objects such as cylinders, hexagons, cubes, arrows, and pyramids are available.

FIGURE 16

Creating a custom graph design

Part A

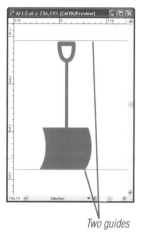

Two guides

Part B

Rectangle is the same height as the shovel and sent behind the shovel

Part C

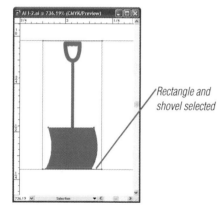

Rectangle and shovel selected

FIGURE 17

Graph Design dialog box

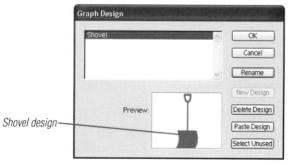

Shovel design

Create a custom graph design

1. Open AI 9-2.ai, then save it as **Snow**.

2. Click **View** on the menu bar, then click **Shovel**.

3. Show the rulers (if necessary), then align two guides with the top and bottom of the shovel, as shown in Part A of Figure 16.

4. Change the fill and stroke colors to [None] in the toolbox.

5. Click the **Rectangle Tool** ▱ , then create a rectangle around the shovel that snaps to the top and bottom guides, as shown in Part B of Figure 16.

   The height of the rectangle should exactly match the height of the custom design, to ensure that data values are represented correctly on the graph.

6. While the rectangle is still selected, click **Object** on the menu bar, point to **Arrange**, then click **Send to Back**.

   The rectangle must be behind the illustration.

7. Select both the rectangle and the shovel, as shown in Part C of Figure 16, click **Object** on the menu bar, point to **Graph**, then click **Design**.

8. Click **New Design**, click **Rename**, name the design **Shovel**, then click **OK**.

   The shovel design appears in the Graph Design dialog box, as shown in Figure 17.

9. Click OK to close the Graph Design dialog box, then save your work.

You created a custom design for graphs, using the Graph Design dialog box.

APPLY A CUSTOM
DESIGN TO A GRAPH

What You'll Do

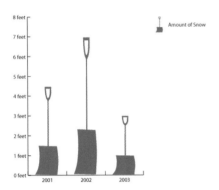

In this lesson, you will apply the shovel custom design to a graph.

Applying a Custom Design to a Graph

Custom designs are typically applied to column graphs and line graphs. Illustrator provides four options for displaying custom designs on a graph: uniformly scaled, vertically scaled, repeating, and sliding.

Uniformly scaled designs are resized vertically and horizontally, whereas vertically scaled designs are resized only vertically. Figure 18 shows an example of a uniformly scaled design, and Figure 19 shows an example of a vertically scaled design. Repeating designs assign a value to the custom design and repeat the design as many times as necessary. For example, if the shovel is assigned a value of 1 foot of snow, 3 shovels would represent 3 feet of snow. Sliding-scale designs allow you to define a point on the custom design from which the design will stretch, thereby leaving everything below that point uniform.

FIGURE 18

A uniformly scaled custom design

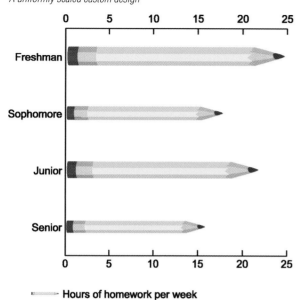

Hours of homework per week

FIGURE 19

A vertically scaled custom design

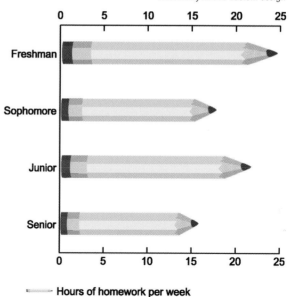

Hours of homework per week

Apply a custom graph design

1. Click **View** on the menu bar, then click **Fit in Window**.

2. Select the **graph** with the **Selection Tool** ▶.

3. Click **Object** on the menu bar, point to **Graph**, then click **Column**.

   The Graph Column dialog box shows a list of custom designs you can apply to your graph.

4. Click **Shovel**, then verify that Vertically Scaled is selected for the Column Type, and that the Rotate Legend Design check box is not checked, as shown in Figure 20.

   (continued)

FIGURE 20
Graph Column dialog box

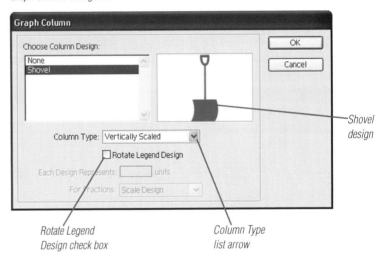

Shovel design

Rotate Legend Design check box

Column Type list arrow

FIGURE 21

Shovel custom design applied to the graph

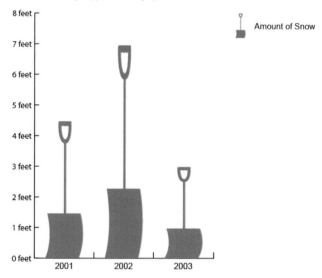

5. Click **OK**.

   The three columns on the graph are replaced with shovels, each a different length, indicating how many feet of snow fell in each year.

6. Click the **artboard to** deselect the graph, so that your work resembles Figure 21.

7. Save your work.

   TIP To remove a custom design from a graph, select the graph, then click None in the Graph Column dialog box.

You selected a custom design in the Graph Design dialog box, you selected Vertically Scaled for the column type, and then you applied the custom design to a graph. The artwork is scaled vertically—taller or shorter—to represent the graph data.

CREATE AND APPLY A
SLIDING-SCALE DESIGN

What You'll Do

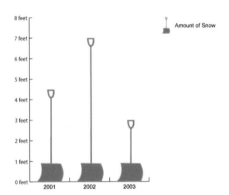

 In this lesson, you will define the area on the shovel design that will be affected by a sliding-scale design. Then you will apply a sliding-scale design to the existing graph.

Creating a Sliding-Scale Design and Applying It to a Graph

When you apply a vertically scaled design style to a column graph, the entire design stretches to accommodate the value assigned to it. This expansion may present a problem if the custom design needs to maintain an aspect ratio. For example, a custom logo design might become unreadable if it is stretched too far. For this reason, a vertically scaled design can sometimes be unsatisfactory.

The answer to the problem is the sliding-scale design, which allows you to define a point on the custom design from which the graph will stretch. Thus a portion of the design can be specified to remain at its original size and not stretch. Figure 22 shows an example of a sliding-scale design.

FIGURE 22

A sliding-scale design

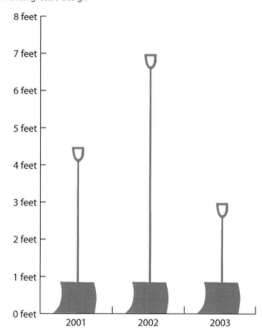

Create and apply a sliding-scale design

1. Return to the Shovel view, click **View** on the menu bar, point to **Guides**, click **Clear Guides**, then set the stroke color to Black in the toolbox.

2. Using the **Pen Tool** 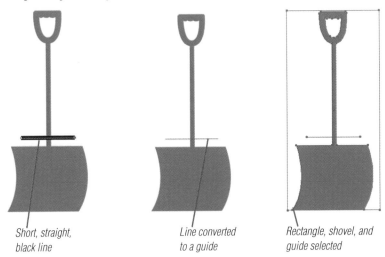, draw a black line across the shovel, as shown in Figure 23.

3. Click the **Selection Tool** , select the entire line, click **View** on the menu bar, point to **Guides**, then click **Make Guides**.

   The black line turns into a guide, as shown in Figure 23.

4. Click **View** on the menu bar, point to **Guides**, then verify that there is not a check mark to the left of Lock Guides.

5. Select the shovel, the rectangle, and the guide, so that all three objects are selected, as shown in Figure 23.

   TIP Drag a selection box around the shovel to make sure you select the rectangle too, or switch to Outline view to see the outline of the rectangle. Because the rectangle has no fill or stroke, it is "invisible" in Preview view.

   (continued)

FIGURE 23
Creating a sliding-scale design

Short, straight, black line

Line converted to a guide

Rectangle, shovel, and guide selected

FIGURE 24

Graph Column dialog box

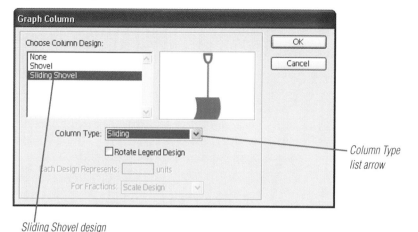

Sliding Shovel design

Column Type list arrow

6. Click **Object** on the menu bar, point to **Graph**, then click **Design**.

7. Click **New Design**, click **Rename**, name the design **Sliding Shovel**, click **OK**, then click **OK** again to close the Graph Design dialog box.

8. Hide the guides, fit the document in the window, then select the graph.

9. Click **Object** on the menu bar, point to **Graph**, click **Column**, click **Sliding Shovel**, click **Sliding** from the Column Type list, as shown in Figure 24, then click **OK**.

10. Deselect, then save your work.

Notice that the scoop of the shovel remains equal in all three columns, as shown in Figure 25.

11. Close the Snow document.

You created a guide on top of the shovel design to identify the area of the artwork that will not be scaled in the graph. You then saved the new artwork as a new sliding-scale design.

FIGURE 25

Completed graph

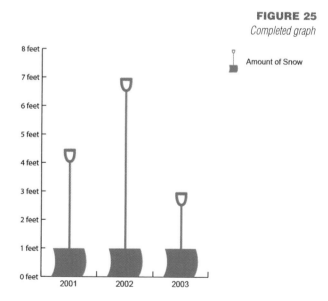

Amount of Snow

Create a graph.

1. Open AI 9-3.ai, then save it as **Weather**.
2. Click the Column Graph Tool, then click the artboard.
3. Type **6** in the Width text box, type **4** in the Height text box, then click OK.
4. Delete the number 1.00 from the first cell in the Graph Data window.
5. Press [Tab] to select the next cell in the first row.
6. Type **Rain**, press [Tab], type **Sun**, press [Tab], type **Clouds**, then press [Tab].
7. Click the second cell in the first column, type **June**, press [Enter] (Win) or [return] (Mac), type **July**, press [Enter] (Win) or [return] (Mac), type **August**, then press [Enter] (Win) or [return] (Mac).
8. Enter the rest of the data that is supplied in the upper-left corner of the artboard to fill in the cells underneath Rain, Sun, and Clouds.
9. Close the Graph Data window, saving your changes to it.

10. Move the graph onto the artboard, if necessary.

Edit a graph using the Graph Data window.

1. Hide the page tiling, if necessary.
2. Delete the text at the top of the artboard.
3. Click the graph to select it.
4. Click Object on the menu bar, point to Graph, then click Data.
5. Click the cell that contains the number 7, and change it to 8.
6. Click the cell that contains the number 20, and change it to 19.
7. Drag the Graph Data window down slightly to view the artboard, then click the Apply button in the Graph Data window.
8. Close the Graph Data window.
9. Save your work.

Use the Group Selection Tool.

1. Deselect the graph, then click the Group Selection Tool.
2. Click the first black column above the June label, click a second time, then click a third time to select the Rain group.
3. Change the fill color of the selected columns to green.
4. Change the fill color of the Sun group to yellow.
5. Change the fill color of the Clouds group to a shade of blue.
6. Save your work.

Use the Graph Type dialog box.

1. Click the Selection Tool, then click the graph.
2. Click Object on the menu bar, point to Graph, then click Type.
3. Click the Add Drop Shadow check box, if necessary, to add a drop shadow.
4. Click the Graph Options list arrow, then click Value Axis.
5. Click the Length list arrow in the Tick Marks section of the window, then click Full Width.
6. Click OK.
7. Save your work.

Create a combination graph.

1. Deselect the graph, then, using the Group Selection Tool, select the entire Sun group.
2. Click Object on the menu bar, point to Graph, then click Type.
3. Click the Line button.
4. Click the Add Drop Shadow check box to deselect the option.
5. Click the Edge-to-Edge Lines check box.
6. Verify that both the Mark Data Points and Connect Data Points check boxes are checked, then click OK.
7. Click the artboard to deselect the graph.
8. Using the Group Selection Tool, select the line that connects the markers and the small corresponding line in the legend.
9. Change the stroke weight of the line to 10 pt.
10. Remove the fill color from the line, then change the stroke color of the line to yellow.
11. Save your work, compare your graph to Figure 26, then close the Weather document.

Create a custom graph design.

1. Open AI 9-4.ai, then save it as **Flowers**.
2. Click View on the menu bar, then click Flower.
3. Click View on the menu bar, then click Show Rulers, if necessary.
4. Drag two guides from the horizontal ruler; position one at the very top of the flower, and the other at the bottom of the stem.
5. Lock the guides, then set the fill and stroke colors to [None] in the toolbox.

6. Create a rectangle that is slightly wider than the width of the flower, and that snaps to the top and bottom of the guides.
7. Send the rectangle to the back. (*Hint:* If you deselect the rectangle and cannot see it, switch to Outline view, repeat Step 7, then switch back to Preview view.)
8. Select the flower and the rectangle.
9. Click Object on the menu bar, point to Graph, then click Design.
10. Click New Design, click Rename, name the design **Flower**, click OK, then click OK again.
11. Delete the flower artwork at the top of the document window, then hide the guides.

FIGURE 26
Completed Skills Review, Part 1

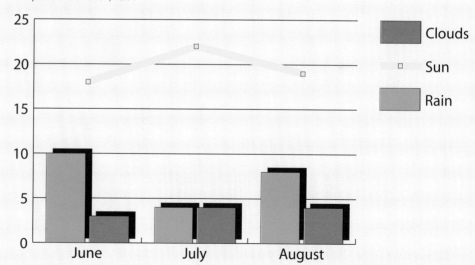

Apply a custom design to a graph.

1. Click View on the menu bar, then click Graph.
2. Select the graph with the Selection Tool.
3. Click Object on the menu bar, point to Graph, then click Column.
4. Click Flower, then make sure that Vertically Scaled is chosen for the Column Type.
5. Click the Rotate Legend Design check box to remove the check mark, then click OK.
6. Click the artboard to deselect the graph.
7. Save your work, then compare your graph to Figure 27.

Creating Graphs in Illustrator

Create a repeating graph design.

1. Click the graph with the Selection Tool.
2. Click Object on the menu bar, point to Graph, then click Column.
3. Click the Column Type list arrow, then click Repeating.
4. Type **10** in the units text box next to "Each Design Represents".
5. Verify that there is not a check mark in the Rotate Legend Design check box.
6. Click the For Fractions list arrow, then click Chop Design.
7. Click OK, then save your work.
8. Deselect the graph, compare your graph to Figure 28, then close the Flowers document.

FIGURE 27

Completed Skills Review, Part 2

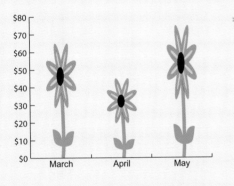

FIGURE 28

Completed Skills Review, Part 3

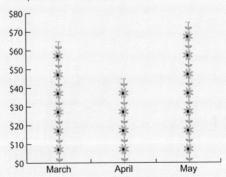

You are applying for financial aid to pursue a master's degree in nutrition and have been asked to submit your monthly living expenses. You decide to present the information in a simple column chart.

1. Open AI 9-5.ai, then save it as **Expenses**.
2. Create a 6" wide by 4" tall column graph.
3. Delete 1.00 from the first cell, then press [Tab].
4. Type **Monthly Expenses**. (*Hint*: Don't worry if the title is not in full view.)
5. Enter the data as shown in Figure 29.
6. Close the Graph Data window, saving your changes to the data.
7. Change the fill color of the graph columns and legend box to the Grid on Grid pattern swatch.
8. Place a drop shadow behind the columns.
9. Click Object on the menu bar, point to Graph, click Type, click the Graph Options list arrow, click Value Axis, type **$** in the Prefix text box, then click OK.
10. Click Object on the menu bar, point to Graph, click Type, click the Graph Options list arrow, click Value Axis, click the Length list arrow under Tick Marks, click Full Width, then click OK.
11. Compare your graph to Figure 30, save your work, then close the Expenses document.

FIGURE 29
Project Builder 1 data

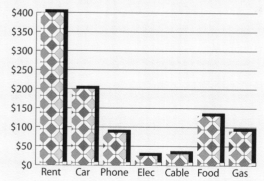

	Monthly						
Rent	400.00						
Car	200.00						
Phone	85.00						
Elec	25.00						
Cable	30.00						
Food	130.00						
Gas	90.00						

FIGURE 30
Completed Project Builder 1

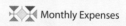
Monthly Expenses

You own an independent market research consulting business that specializes in the television industry. You have recently conducted a survey of 1000 people who describe their television-watching habits as "regularly watch television." The question they were asked was "What is your favorite TV program?" Your research assistants have tabulated the data and supplied the breakdown to you as a column graph in an Illustrator file. You note that the words under the columns are running into each other, and you decide the graph would work better as a pie chart.

1. Open AI 9-6.ai, then save it as **TV Pie**.
2. Create a 6" wide by 4" tall column graph.
3. Delete 1.00 from the first cell, then press [Tab].
4. Type **What is your favorite TV program?**
5. Using the information at the top of the artboard, enter the rest of the data.
6. Close the Graph Data window, saving your changes to the data.
7. Verify that the graph is selected, click Object on the menu bar, point to Graph, then click Type.
8. Click the Pie button, remove the check mark in the Add Drop Shadow check box, if necessary, then click OK.
9. Click Object on the menu bar, point to Graph, then click Data.
10. Click the Transpose row/column button in the Graph Data window. (*Hint*: The Transpose row/column button is the second button in the Graph Data window.)
11. Close the Graph Data window, save changes, then delete the information at the top of the artboard.
12. Choose colors that you like for each section of the pie graph and the corresponding legend box.
13. Save your work, compare your graph to Figure 31, then close the TV Pie document.

FIGURE 31
Completed Project Builder 2

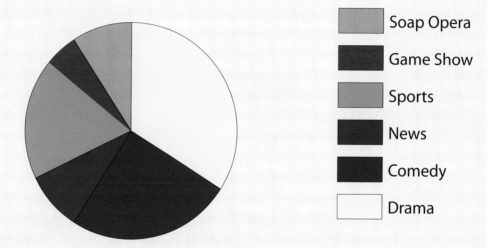

Soap Opera

Game Show

Sports

News

Comedy

Drama

What is your favorite TV program?

You are a freelance designer, and you are hired by a small market research company that specializes in television. They are submitting an annual report to one of their network clients. The report contains a number of pie charts. They want you to design a look that is more "eye catching."

1. Open AI 9-7.ai, then save it as **Designer Pie**.
2. Click the Group Selection Tool, then click the largest wedge two times. (*Hint*: The largest wedge and the Drama legend box are selected.)
3. Change the fill of the two objects to any red.
4. Moving clockwise, fill the remaining wedges and legend boxes with any of the orange, yellow, green, blue, and violet swatches, respectively.
5. Deselect all, click the Direct Selection Tool, drag a marquee to select the pie chart only, then scale the chart 150%.
6. Deselect, click the Type Tool, type **34%** on top of the red wedge, change the font size to 27 pt, then set the fill color to White.
7. Moving clockwise, type the following percentage values on the remaining wedges: **25**, **9**, **18**, **5**, and **9**. (*Hint*: Change the fill color of the values on top of the yellow and orange wedges to Black.)
8. Using the Direct Selection Tool, move each word from the legend over its corresponding wedge. (*Hint*: The words "Game Show"

and "Soap Opera" must be positioned outside of their corresponding wedge because they are too long.)
9. Change the fill color of Sports and Drama to White.
10. Hide the legend boxes, then reposition the What is your favorite TV program? text, and any other objects if necessary.
11. Select only the wedges of the graph, using the Direct Selection Tool.

12. Click Effect on the menu bar, point to Stylize, click Round Corners, type **.139**, then click OK.
13. Apply a 2-point Black stroke to the pie wedges.
14. Save your work, compare your graph to Figure 32, then close Designer Pie.

FIGURE 32
Completed Design Project

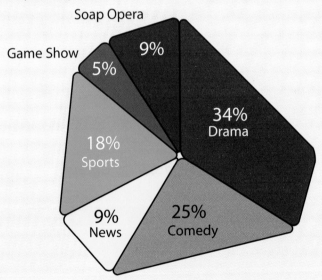

What is your favorite TV program?

You are the chief designer of an in-house design group in a large department store. The head of the Digital Department has asked you to help with a presentation that shows how computers, scanners, and printers have been selling in comparison to one another over the last four weeks. Specifically, she wants you to create a graph that emphasizes how many more scanners she sells each week than computers or printers.

1. Gather the weekly sales data from each of the three departments, which is as follows:

	Computers	Printers	Scanners
Week One	11	13	55
Week Two	12	15	40
Week Three	14	6	61
Week Four	9	11	35

2. Draw a simple bar graph on the chalkboard, showing the sales relationships among the three products.

3. Have some members of the group discuss what would be the best type of graph to convey the data.

4. Have other members of the group decide the colors and fonts that will be used in the graph.

5. Create a new CMYK Color document, then save it as **Sales**.

6. Create a column graph that is 4" wide by 4" high.

7. Enter the data (from Step 1) in the Graph Data window.

8. Close the Graph Data window, saving changes to it.

9. Select the Scanners group, using the Group Selection Tool, then apply the line graph type to it.

10. Change the color and thickness of the line graph so that it is easy to see.

11. Format the rest of the graph (labels, Printers group, and Computers group) if desired.

12. Save your work, compare your graph to Figure 33, then close the Sales document.

FIGURE 33
Completed Group Project

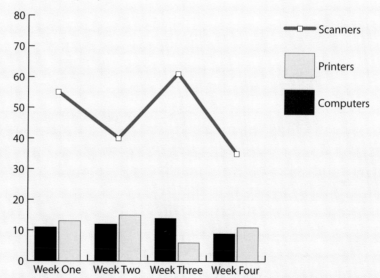

10

DRAWING
WITH SYMBOLS

1. Create symbols.

2. Place symbol instances.

3. Modify symbols and symbol instances.

4. Create symbol instance sets.

5. Modify symbol instance sets.

chapter 10 DRAWING WITH SYMBOLS

In Illustrator, the file size of a document is largely determined by the number and complexity of objects in the document. The greater the number of objects in the document, the greater the file size. A large number of objects with gradients, blends, and effects *greatly* increases the file size. When you are creating graphics for the World Wide Web, file size becomes a serious concern.

Illustrator CS2 offers symbols as a solution for creating complex files while maintaining a relatively low file size. Symbols are art objects that you create and store in the Symbols palette.

Imagine that you were drawing a field of flowers, and you have drawn a pink, a blue, and a yellow flower. Each flower has a radial gradient in its center and color blends to add dimension to the petals and green leaves. Now imagine that you must drag and drop 200 copies of each to create

your field of flowers! Along with a cramp in your hand, you would have an unusually large Illustrator file.

With the three flowers defined as symbols, you can create 200 symbol instances of each flower symbol quickly and easily. The key is: You haven't actually added the complex artwork multiple times, because the instances don't really exist as artwork. They are merely a reference to the original artwork that is the symbol; the instances function only to show the positioning of the symbol artwork on the artboard. Think of it this way: Symbol instances are merely virtual representations of a symbol.

Symbolism tools allow you to edit large numbers of symbol instances quickly and effectively. Whenever you are using the same artwork multiple times in a document, consider using symbols to save time and disk space.

Tools You'll Use

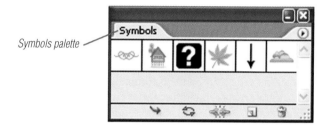

Symbols palette

Symbolism tools

CREATE SYMBOLS

What You'll Do

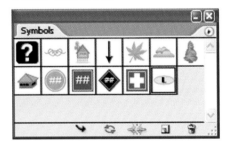

 In this lesson, you will create symbols from Illustrator artwork and save them in the Symbols palette.

Creating Symbols

A **symbol** is artwork that you store in the Symbols palette and reuse in the document. You can create symbols from any Illustrator artwork, including text, compound paths, and grouped paths. Symbols may also include blends, effects, brush strokes, gradients, and even other symbols. The Symbols palette, as shown in Figure 1, is a great place to store artwork that you plan to use again. When you use symbol artwork, you can modify it on the artboard, while retaining its original appearance in the palette. In this way, you can think of the Symbols palette as a database of your original art.

FIGURE 1
Symbols palette

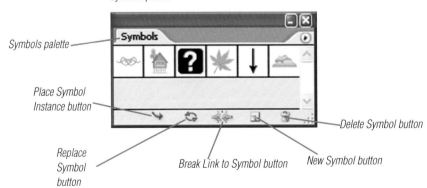

Symbols palette

Place Symbol Instance button

Replace Symbol button

Break Link to Symbol button

New Symbol button

Delete Symbol button

FIGURE 2

Drag artwork into Symbols palette to create a new symbol

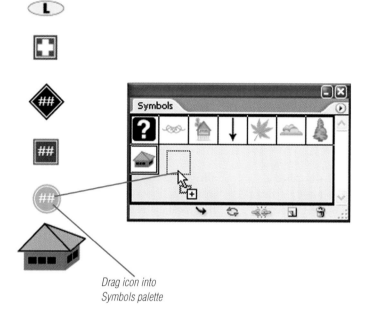

Drag icon into
Symbols palette

FIGURE 3

Symbols palette with new symbols added

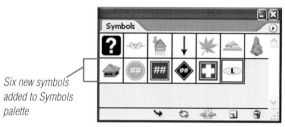

Six new symbols
added to Symbols
palette

Create symbols

1. Open AI 10-1.ai, then save it as **Trail Map**.

2. Click **Window** on the menu bar, then click **Symbols**.

3. Select the brown house picture in the scratch area.

4. Click the **Symbols palette list arrow**, then click **New Symbol**.

5. Type **Ski Lodge** in the Name text box of the Symbol Options dialog box, then click **OK**.

   The Ski Lodge symbol becomes a new symbol in the Symbols palette.

6. Select the green circle icon in the scratch area, then drag it into the Symbols palette, as shown in Figure 2.

7. Double-click the **green circle icon** in the Symbols palette, then name it **Novice**.

8. Add the blue square icon to the Symbols palette, then name it **Intermediate**.

9. Add the black diamond icon to the Symbols palette, then name it **Expert**.

10. Add the red square icon to the Symbols palette, then name it **First Aid**.

11. Add the yellow oval icon to the Symbols palette, then name it **Chairlift**.

    Your Symbols palette should resemble Figure 3.

12. Delete the Ski Lodge, Novice, Intermediate, Expert, First Aid, and Chairlift icons in the scratch area, then save your work.

You created new symbols by using the Symbols palette menu and by dragging and dropping.

PLACE SYMBOL
INSTANCES

What You'll Do

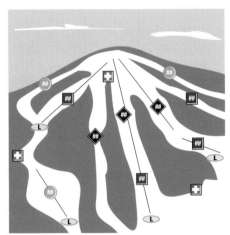

In this lesson, you will place symbol instances on the artboard.

Placing Instances of Symbols

If a symbol is artwork that is stored in the Symbols palette, then the artwork—when put to use in the document—is called a **symbol instance**. You can place a symbol instance on the artboard by first selecting the symbol in the Symbols palette, then dragging it to the artboard, or by selecting it, then clicking the Place Symbol Instance button in the Symbols palette or the Place Symbol Instance command on the Symbols palette menu, as shown in Figure 4.

Symbol instances are "linked" to their corresponding symbols in the palette. This relationship introduces powerful functionality when you work with symbol instances. For example, you can select all the instances of a symbol by selecting the symbol in the palette and then clicking the Select All Instances command on the palette menu.

FIGURE 4

Placing a symbol instance

Symbol instance placed on artboard

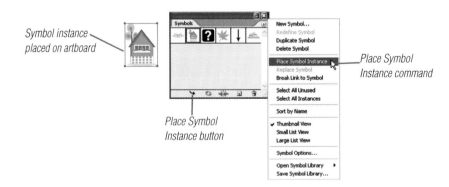

Place Symbol Instance button

Place Symbol Instance command

FIGURE 5

Positioning symbol instances

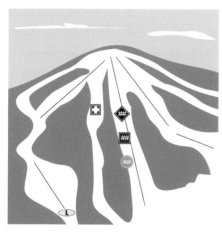

FIGURE 6

Positioning copies of the Chairlift symbol instance

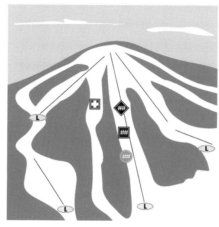

FIGURE 7

Positioning the Novice, Intermediate, Expert, and First Aid symbol instances

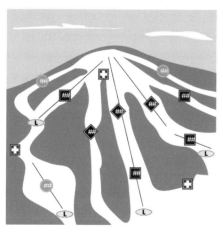

Place instances of a symbol

1. Click the **Novice symbol** in the Symbols palette.

2. Click the **Symbols palette list arrow**, then click **Place Symbol Instance**.

   A single Novice symbol instance appears on the artboard.

3. Drag the **Novice symbol instance** to the location shown in Figure 5.

4. Click the **Intermediate symbol** in the Symbols palette, then drag it to the artboard above the Novice symbol instance.

5. Drag a **symbol instance** of the Expert, First Aid, and Chairlift symbols onto the artboard, then position them as shown in Figure 5.

6. Click the **Chairlift symbol instance** on the artboard, press and hold **[Alt]** (Win) or **[option]** (Mac), drag and drop three copies, then position the copies as shown in Figure 6.

7. Copy and reposition the Novice, Intermediate, Expert, and First Aid symbol instances so that your screen resembles Figure 7.

   Dragging and dropping copies is the easiest way to duplicate the symbol instances.

8. Save your work.

You placed symbol instances of five symbols on the artboard. You then duplicated the symbol instances and positioned them on the artboard.

MODIFY SYMBOLS AND
SYMBOL INSTANCES

What You'll Do

Modifying Symbol Instances

When working with symbol instances, approach them as you would any other Illustrator artwork. You can transform symbol instances by using commands on the Object menu or by using any of the transform tools. You can cut, copy, and drag and drop copies of symbol instances. You can perform any operation from the Transparency, Appearance, and Styles palettes. For example, you can reduce the opacity of a symbol instance and you can apply effects, such as a drop shadow or a distortion.

Symbols are most often composed of multiple objects, such as you would expect to find in a drawing of a butterfly or a flower, for example. When you select a symbol instance on the artboard, its selection marks show only a simple bounding box, as shown in Figure 8; the individual elements of the artwork are not selected.

You can, however, select the individual components of a symbol instance by using the Expand command on the Object menu. The bounding box disappears, and the individual elements of the artwork are available to be selected (and modified), as shown in Figure 9.

Modifying Symbols

Once you have modified a symbol instance, you can use the modified artwork on the artboard to redefine the associated symbol in the palette. When you do so, all existing symbol instances are updated and reflect the changes to the symbol. If you don't want a particular symbol instance to be updated, you can select the instance and break the link to the symbol. The symbol instance will no longer be associated with the symbol.

You can also modify a symbol instance on the artboard and use it to create a new symbol without affecting the original symbol that it is based on. Thus, the Symbols palette is very useful for storing subtle or dramatic variations of artwork. For example, if you are drawing a landscape that features a wind farm, you can draw a single windmill, save it as a symbol, rotate the blades on the original artwork, then save a new symbol, and so on.

FIGURE 8

When you select a symbol instance, the individual elements of the artwork are not selected

FIGURE 9

The Expand command allows you to select the individual elements of the artwork

Edit symbol instances

1. Select the green Novice symbol instance in the lower-left corner of the artboard.

   A bounding box identifies the selection. The elements of the artwork cannot be selected individually.

2. Click **Object** on the menu bar, then click **Expand**.

3. In the Expand dialog box, verify that the Object check box is checked and the Fill check box is not checked, then click **OK**.

   The elements of the symbol instance are selected individually.

4. Deselect the symbol instance, click the **Type Tool** T., highlight the two # signs in the symbol instance, then type **1**.

   Your screen should resemble Figure 10.

   TIP If you receive a message stating that the text was created in a previous version of Illustrator, click OK.

5. Using the same method, expand the Novice, Intermediate, and Expert symbol instances, then change their numbers to those shown in Figure 11.

6. Select all of the symbol instances and each of the blue lines, then hide them.

   TIP Do not use the Select All command to select the symbol instances and the blue lines.

   Your screen should resemble Figure 12.

You used the Expand command to allow you to select individual elements of a symbol instance and edit those elements.

FIGURE 10
Editing a symbol instance

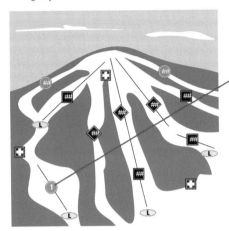

Replace ## with 1

FIGURE 11
Adding numbers to symbol instances

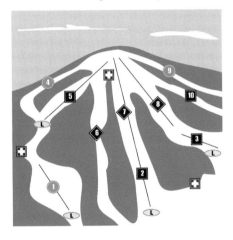

FIGURE 12
The artboard with the symbol instances hidden

FIGURE 13

Positioning four symbol instances of the Ski Lodge symbol

FIGURE 14

Updated instances of the Ski Lodge symbol

This ski lodge graphic is not updated because it is no longer linked to the Ski Lodge symbol

Edit a symbol

1. Position four symbol instances of the Ski Lodge symbol, as shown in Figure 13.

2. Select the bottom-right Ski Lodge symbol instance, then click the **Break Link to Symbol button** in the Symbols palette.

3. Select the top Ski Lodge symbol instance, then click the **Break Link to Symbol button** .

4. Scale the top ski lodge artwork 50%.

5. Press and hold [**Alt**] (Win) or [**option**] (Mac), then drag the **scaled artwork** on top of the Ski Lodge symbol in the Symbols palette.

    The three symbol instances of the Ski Lodge symbol are updated, as shown in Figure 14. The bottom ski lodge artwork does not change.

6. Click the **Sequoia symbol**, then place one instance of the symbol in the scratch area.

7. Click the **Break Link to Symbol button** .

8. Deselect, click the **Direct Selection Tool** , remove the brown "tree trunk" areas from the symbol instance, then reduce the artwork 50%.

9. Press and hold [**Alt**] (Win) or [**option**] (Mac), then drag the **edited tree artwork** on top of the Sequoia symbol in the Symbols palette.

10. Delete the Sequoia symbol instance in the scratch area.

You edited symbols by modifying instances, then replacing the original symbols with the edited artwork. You protected a symbol instance from modification by breaking its link.

Transform symbol instances

1. Select the six green objects within the snow area of the artboard, then change their fill color to the Tree Shadow swatch so that your screen resembles Figure 15.

2. Click the **Sequoia symbol** in the Symbols palette.

3. Click the **Place Symbol Instance button** ↘ in the Symbols palette, then position the instance on the artboard, as shown in Figure 16.

4. Drag and drop nine copies of the Sequoia symbol instance on the artboard, so that your screen resembles Figure 17.

(continued)

FIGURE 15
Six objects filled with the Tree Shadow color

FIGURE 16
Positioning the Sequoia symbol instance

FIGURE 17
Positioning nine copies of the Sequoia symbol instance

FIGURE 18

Positioning 14 copies of the Sequoia symbol instance

5. Verify that the Sequoia symbol is still selected in the Symbols palette, click the **Symbols palette list arrow**, then click **Select All Instances**.

   All instances of the Sequoia symbol are selected on the artboard.

6. Scale the symbol instances 75%.

7. Drag and drop 14 copies of the newly scaled Sequoia symbol instance to the opposite side of the artboard, as shown in Figure 18.

   | TIP   Press [Alt](Win) or [option](Mac) while dragging to create copies.

8. Save your work.

You positioned one instance of a symbol on the artboard, then copied it nine times. You used the Select All Instances command to quickly select the ten instances of the symbol, scaled them 75%, then positioned 14 copies of the scaled symbol instance.

CREATE SYMBOL
INSTANCE SETS

What You'll Do

 In this lesson, you will use the Symbol Sprayer Tool to create sets of symbol instances and mixed symbol instance sets.

Creating a Symbol Instance Set

Instead of creating symbol instances one at a time using the Symbols palette, you can use the Symbol Sprayer Tool to create multiple symbol instances quickly. Imagine that you have a symbol of a star and you want to draw a night sky filled with stars. The Symbol Sprayer Tool would be a good choice for applying the star symbol multiple times.

Symbol instances created with the Symbol Sprayer Tool are called **symbol instance sets**. Incorporate the term "set" into your work with symbols to differentiate the multiple symbol instances created with the Symbol Sprayer Tool from individual instances of a symbol that you create using the Symbols palette.

To create a symbol instance set, click the symbol that you want to use in the Symbols palette, then drag the Symbol Sprayer Tool where you want the symbols to appear on the artboard.

Working with Symbol Instance Sets

When you create a symbol instance set with the Symbol Sprayer Tool, the entire set of symbols is identified within a bounding box, as shown in Figure 19. If the set is selected and you begin clicking and dragging the Symbol Sprayer Tool again, the new symbol instances will be added to the selected set—even if the new symbol instances are outside of the existing set's bounding box. (The bounding box will expand to encompass the new symbol instances.)

You can also create mixed symbol instance sets. Mixed symbol instance sets include symbol instances based on more than one symbol. To create a mixed symbol instance set, create your first set of symbol instances, click a different symbol in the Symbols palette, then click and drag the Symbol Sprayer Tool where you want the new symbols to appear on the artboard. The new symbol instances will be added to the existing set, as shown in Figure 20.

Even though a symbol instance set, by definition, appears as multiple objects, it is best to think of it as a single object. A symbol instance set can be modified and transformed (as a whole). Figure 21 shows a symbol instance set that has been reflected using the Reflect Tool.

FIGURE 19
A symbol instance set created with the Symbol Sprayer Tool

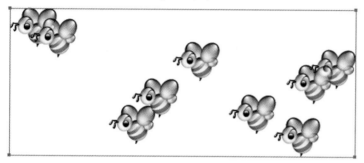

FIGURE 20
A mixed symbol instance set

FIGURE 21
A symbol instance set transformed with the Reflect Tool

Setting Options for the Symbol Sprayer Tool

The Symbol Sprayer Tool has many options to help you control the dispersion of symbol instances. You can access these options in the Symbolism Tools Options dialog box by double-clicking the Symbol Sprayer Tool in the toolbox.

The Diameter setting determines the brush size of the tool. Use a larger brush size to disperse symbol instances over a greater area of the artboard. Note that the brush size does not determine the size of the symbol instances themselves.

The Intensity setting determines the number of instances of the symbol that will be sprayed. The higher the intensity setting, the greater the number of symbol instances that will be dispersed in a given amount of time.

The Symbol Set Density setting determines how closely the symbol instances will be positioned to each other. The higher the density setting, the more closely packed the instances will appear. Figure 22 shows a symbol instance set with a high symbol set density, and Figure 23 shows a symbol instance set with a low symbol set density.

FIGURE 22

A symbol instance set with a high symbol set density

FIGURE 23

A symbol instance set with a low symbol set density

Drawing with Symbols

Expanding a Symbol Set

Despite the many options available with the Symbol Sprayer Tool, it is often difficult to position multiple symbols exactly where you want them. For this reason alone, it is best to think of the Symbol Sprayer Tool as a means to quickly disperse symbol instances but not as a tool to position symbols precisely.

Once you have created a symbol instance set that contains roughly the number of symbol instances you want to work with and have positioned them roughly where you want them to be on the artboard, you can then apply the Expand command to release the set into individual symbol instances. Figure 24 shows a symbol instance set expanded into individual symbol instances.

The power of this operation cannot be overstated. Once expanded, all the symbol instances of the set are available to you to be transformed, repositioned, duplicated, or deleted. Expand the individual symbol instances to be able to select their component parts.

FIGURE 24

A symbol instance set expanded into individual symbol instances

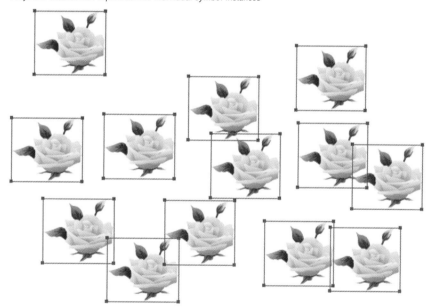

Use the Symbol Sprayer Tool

1. Click the **Sequoia symbol** in the Symbols palette, if necessary.

2. Double-click the **Symbol Sprayer Tool**.

3. Type **.5** in the Diameter text box, type **3** in the Intensity text box, type **5** in the Symbol Set Density text box, then click **OK**.

4. Click and drag the **Symbol Sprayer Tool** to spray instances of the Sequoia symbol over the gray areas so that your artboard resembles Figure 25.

   TIP   Don't try to create all the instances in one move. Click and drag the Symbol Sprayer Tool multiple times in short bursts. Your results will vary from the figure.

5. Press and hold [**Alt**] (Win) or [**option**] (Mac), then click the **Symbol Sprayer Tool** over symbol instances that you do not want to include to remove them, if necessary.

6. Select the symbol set, click **Object** on the menu bar, click **Expand**, verify that only the Object check box is checked, then click **OK**.

7. Deselect, then using the Direct Selection Tool, move the individual Sequoia symbol instances so that your work resembles Figure 26.

   You may also copy and/or delete instances, if necessary.

8. Click **Object** on the menu bar, click **Show All**, then while the hidden objects are still selected, bring them to the front, then deselect.

   Your screen should resemble Figure 27.

9. Save your work, then close Trail Map.

You defined the diameter, the intensity, and the symbol set density for the Symbol Sprayer Tool. You then used the Symbol Sprayer Tool to create a set of Sequoia symbols.

FIGURE 25
Instances of the Sequoia symbol created with the Symbol Sprayer Tool

FIGURE 26
Moving and deleting symbol instances from the set

FIGURE 27
The majority of the trail map artwork is created with symbol instances

FIGURE 28

Spraying instances of the Red Stone symbol

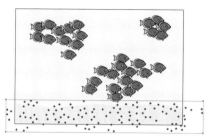

FIGURE 29

Spraying instances of the Purple Stone symbol

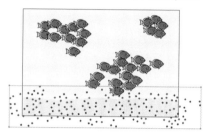

FIGURE 30

Spraying instances of the Green Stone, Orange Stone, and Tan Stone symbols

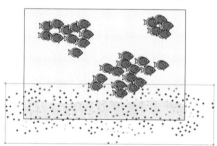

FIGURE 31

Masking the mixed symbol instance set

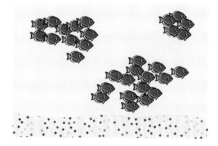

Create a mixed symbol instance set

1. Open AI 10-2.ai, then save it as **Fish Tank**.
2. Click the **Red Stone symbol** in the Symbols palette.
3. Double-click the **Symbol Sprayer Tool** 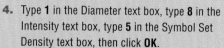.
4. Type **1** in the Diameter text box, type **8** in the Intensity text box, type **5** in the Symbol Set Density text box, then click **OK**.
5. Click and drag the **Symbol Sprayer Tool** over the "sand," as shown in Figure 28.
6. Click the **Purple Stone symbol**, then drag the **Symbol Sprayer Tool** over the "sand," as shown in Figure 29.

   The Purple Stone symbols are added to the set, creating a mixed symbol instance set.
7. Add the Green Stone, Orange Stone, and Tan Stone symbols to the set, so that your screen resembles Figure 30.
8. Select the sand object, copy it, paste in front, then bring the copy to the front.
9. Press and hold [**Shift**], then click the **mixed symbol instance set** so that the sand and the set of rocks are selected.
10. Click **Object** on the menu bar, point to **Clipping Mask**, click **Make**, deselect, then save your work.

   The sand acts as a mask to hide the rocks that extend beyond the sand object, as shown in Figure 31.

You used five different symbols and the Symbol Sprayer Tool to create a mixed set of symbol instances.

MODIFY SYMBOL
INSTANCE SETS

What You'll Do

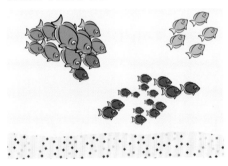

In this lesson, you will use various symbolism tools to modify symbol instance sets.

Using Symbolism Tools

Illustrator offers seven symbolism tools that you can use to modify symbol instances or sets of symbol instances. You will most often use the symbolism tools to affect symbol instances within a set, since individual symbol instances are easy to select and modify directly with transform tools and menu commands. Table 10-1 lists each symbolism tool and its function. Figure 32 shows an illustration of a symbol instance set with each tool applied to the set.

TABLE 10-1: Symbolism Tools

symbolism tool	function
Symbol Sprayer Tool	Places symbol instances on the artboard.
Symbol Shifter Tool	Moves symbol instances and/or changes their stacking order in the set
Symbol Scruncher Tool	Pulls symbol instances together or apart
Symbol Sizer Tool	Increases or decreases the size of symbol instances
Symbol Spinner Tool	Rotates symbol instances
Symbol Stainer Tool	Changes the color of symbol instances gradually to the current fill color in the toolbox
Symbol Screener Tool	Increases or decreases the transparency of symbol instances
Symbol Styler Tool	Applies the selected style in the Styles palette to symbol instances

When you apply symbolism tools to mixed symbol instance sets, each corresponding symbol must be selected in the Symbols palette in order for each type of symbol instance to be modified by the tool. For example, imagine you have created a mixed symbol instance set of four types of flowers (daisy, tulip, rose, and lily) and only the daisy symbol is selected in the Symbols palette. If you apply a symbolism tool to the mixed symbol instance set, only the instances of the daisy symbol will be modified.

When working with symbolism tools, it is also important that you set realistic goals. The symbolism tools are particularly useful if you have created a symbol set that is intended to appear random. For example, if you use symbol instances to render multiple stars in the night sky, the symbolism tools will be an excellent choice for modifying their orientation on the artboard. However, if your goal is to position symbol instances precisely in your artwork, you should expand the symbol set and use the selection tools and transform tools to modify each instance directly.

FIGURE 32
Applying the symbolism tools

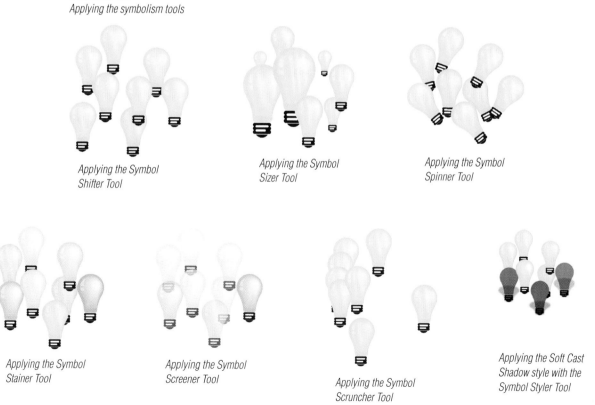

Applying the Symbol Shifter Tool

Applying the Symbol Sizer Tool

Applying the Symbol Spinner Tool

Applying the Symbol Stainer Tool

Applying the Symbol Screener Tool

Applying the Symbol Scruncher Tool

Applying the Soft Cast Shadow style with the Symbol Styler Tool

Use the Symbol Stainer Tool

1. Click **Object** on the menu bar, then click **Unlock All**.

2. Deselect, then select the set of fish symbol instances.

3. Change the fill color in the toolbox to green.

4. Click the **Symbol Stainer Tool**.

   The Symbol Stainer Tool is hidden beneath the Symbol Sprayer Tool.

   > TIP Press and hold the current Symbol tool until you see all of the Symbol tools, then click the Tearoff tab at the end of the row of tools to create a floating palette of all of the symbolism tools.

5. Click and drag the **Symbol Stainer Tool** over the 11 fish symbol instances in the upper-left region of the artboard so that your work resembles Figure 33.

   > TIP Using the Symbol Stainer Tool results in increased file size and may tax your computer's performance.

6. Position the Symbol Stainer Tool over the bottommost fish symbol instance in the same group.

   (continued)

FIGURE 33
Applying the Symbol Stainer Tool with a green fill

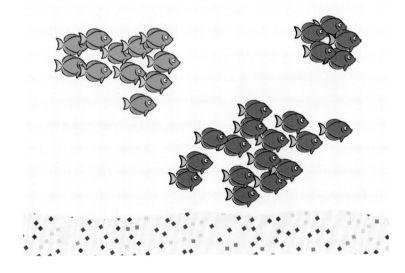

Drawing with Symbols

FIGURE 34

Applying the Symbol Stainer Tool with a yellow fill

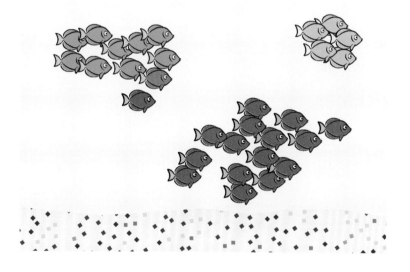

7. Press and hold [**Alt**] (Win) or [**option**] (Mac), then press and hold your mouse button for approximately two seconds.

   Pressing [Alt] (Win) or [option] (Mac) while using the Symbol Stainer Tool gradually removes color applied by the Symbol Stainer Tool. The symbol instance that you clicked returns to its original blue color. The surrounding symbol instances are not affected as directly; their color changes toward the original blue color, but remains somewhat green. Your results may vary.

8. Change the fill color in the toolbox to yellow.

9. Drag the **Symbol Stainer Tool** over the five fish symbol instances in the upper-right region of the artboard, so that your work resembles Figure 34.

You used the Symbol Stainer Tool to modify the color of symbol instances within a set.

Use the Symbol Shifter Tool

1. Double-click the **Symbol Shifter Tool** to open the Symbolism Tools Options dialog box.

   The Symbol Shifter Tool is hidden beneath the current symbolism tool.

2. Type **.25** in the Diameter text box, then click **OK**.

3. Position the Symbol Shifter Tool over any of the green fish, press and hold [**Shift**], then click the **fish instance**.

   The symbol instance is brought to the front of the set.

   TIP It's usually a good idea to enter a small diameter setting when you want to affect the stacking order of instances in a set. A larger brush will affect the stacking order of surrounding instances.

4. Press and hold [**Shift**][**Alt**] (Win) or [**Shift**][**option**] (Mac), then click a **green fish**.

   The symbol instance is sent to the back. Figure 35 shows an example of the green fish instances after the stacking order has been affected by the Symbol Shifter Tool. Compare your choices and results.

5. Change the diameter setting of the Symbol Shifter Tool to 2.5.

6. Click and drag the **Symbol Shifter Tool** over the yellow fish until they no longer touch each other, as shown in Figure 36.

   Your results may vary.

You used the Symbol Shifter Tool to change the stacking order of instances within the symbol set and to move symbol instances within the set.

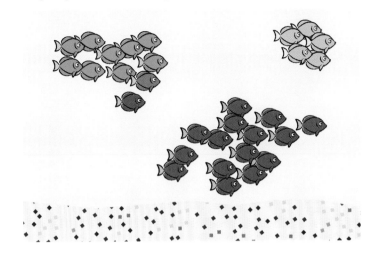

FIGURE 36
Using the Symbol Shifter Tool to reposition instances within the set

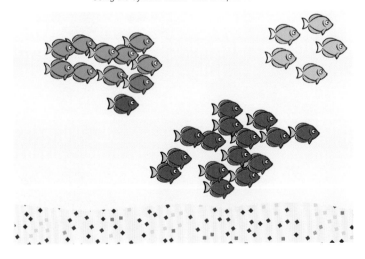

Drawing with Symbols

FIGURE 37

Using the Symbol Spinner Tool on the green fish

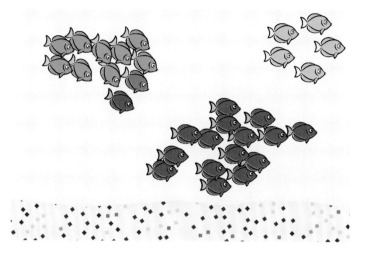

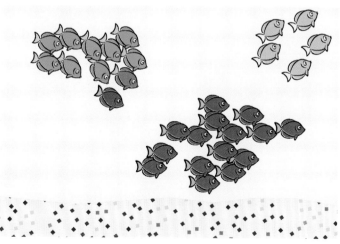

FIGURE 38

Using the Symbol Spinner Tool on the yellow fish

Use the Symbol Spinner Tool

1. Double-click the **Symbol Spinner Tool** .

2. Type **2.6** in the Diameter text box, type **10** in the Intensity text box, then click **OK**.

3. Position the Symbol Spinner Tool over the center of the green fish group.

4. Click and drag slightly to the right, so that the fish rotate, as shown in Figure 37.

   Your results may vary.

   > TIP The blue arrows that appear when you click and drag the Symbol Spinner Tool are not always reliable predictors of the final rotation of the symbol instances. The diameter and intensity settings and the location of the tool in regard to the instances all affect the impact of the rotation.

5. Position the Symbol Spinner Tool over the center of the yellow fish group.

6. Click and drag slightly to the upper-left so that the yellow fish rotate, as shown in Figure 38.

   Your results may vary.

You used the Symbol Spinner Tool to rotate symbol instances within the set.

Use the Symbol Sizer Tool

1. Double-click the **Symbol Sizer Tool** 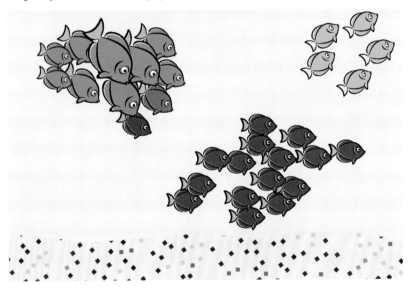.

2. Type **2** in the Diameter text box, type **8** in the Intensity text box, then click **OK**.

3. Position the Symbol Sizer Tool over the center of the green fish group.

4. Press and hold the mouse button for approximately two seconds so that your work resembles Figure 39.

   Your results may vary.

5. Position the Symbol Sizer Tool over the center of the blue fish group.

(continued)

FIGURE 39

Using the Symbol Sizer Tool to enlarge symbol instances

Drawing with Symbols

6. Press and hold [**Alt**] (Win) or [**option**] (Mac), then press and hold the mouse button for approximately three seconds.

7. Deselect all, then save your work.

   Your screen should resemble Figure 40. Your results may vary.

8. Close the Fish Tank document.

You used the Symbol Sizer Tool to change the size of symbol instances within the set.

FIGURE 40
Using the Symbol Sizer Tool to reduce symbol instances

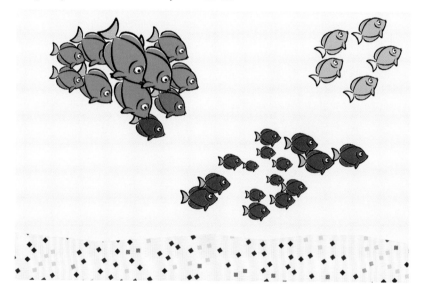

Create symbols.

1. Open AI 10-3.ai, then save it as **Winter Ball**.
2. Show the Brushes palette, then drag the Radiant Star brush onto the artboard.
3. Verify that the Symbols palette is displayed, then drag the Radiant Star artwork into the Symbols palette.
4. Name the new symbol **Snowflake**.
5. Delete the Radiant Star artwork from the artboard.

Place symbol instances.

1. Click the Snowflake symbol in the Symbols palette.
2. Click the Place Symbol Instance button on the Symbols palette.
3. Position the symbol instance between the words ball and December.

Modify symbols and symbol instances.

1. Scale the Snowflake symbol instance 35%, then reposition the Snowflake symbol instance, if necessary.
2. Click Effect on the menu bar, point to Distort & Transform, click Pucker & Bloat, type **50** in the text box, then click OK.
3. Change the opacity of the symbol instance to 75%.
4. Click the Break Link to Symbol button on the Symbols palette.
5. Press [Alt] (Win) or [option] (Mac), then drag the modified snowflake artwork directly on top of the Snowflake symbol in the Symbols palette.

Create symbol instance sets.

1. Double-click the Symbol Sprayer Tool.
2. Type **1** for the Diameter, **2** for the Intensity, and **1** for the Symbol Set Density in the Symbolism Tools Options dialog box.
3. Spray approximately 25 symbol instances of the Snowflake symbol evenly over the artboard.

Modify symbol instance sets.

1. Use the Symbol Sizer Tool to enlarge and reduce symbol instances.
2. Expand the symbol set.
3. Move or delete symbols to your liking.
4. Save your work, then compare your illustration to Figure 41. (*Hint*: Your results will vary from the figure.)
5. Close Winter Ball.

FIGURE 41
Completed Skills Review

You work in the design department of a major Internet portal site. As part of the promotion of this year's Hooray for Hollywood Awards, your site will link to the Awards' site. You are asked to create a banner that says "click here to meet the stars" against a starry sky.

1. Open AI 10-4.ai, then save it as **Hollywood**.
2. Double-click the Symbol Sprayer Tool.
3. Type **2** for the Diameter, **1** for the Intensity, and **10** for the Symbol Set Density.

4. Click the 5 Point Star symbol in the Symbols palette, then drag the Symbol Sprayer Tool across the gradient-filled rectangle.
5. Repeat Step 4, using the 8 Point Star symbol in the Symbols palette.
6. Expand the symbol set.
7. Use the Symbol Shifter Tool to move or delete symbol instances that overlap each other.

8. Use the Symbol Sizer Tool to enlarge and reduce symbol instances to add depth and variety.
9. Show all to reveal the semitransparent text.
10. Save your work, compare your illustration to Figure 42, then close the Hollywood document.

FIGURE 42
Completed Project Builder 1

You work at a busy design firm. Your boss e-mails you an Illustrator file. He tells you that the file contains a symbol of the American flag that he saved some months ago. He wants you to update the existing symbol in the Symbols palette so that the flag is scaled 25% and the opacity of the flag is 50%. He also wants the new symbol to show the flag waving.

1. Open AI 10-5.ai, then save it as **Flag Symbol**.
2. Show the Symbols palette, if necessary, then place an instance of the American Flag symbol on the artboard.
3. Break the link between the symbol instance and the symbol.
4. Click Object on the menu bar, point to Envelope Distort, then click Make with Warp.
5. Click the Style list arrow, then click Flag.
6. Type **-35** for the Bend value, then click OK.
7. Scale the artwork 25%.
8. Show the Transparency palette, if necessary, then change the opacity of the artwork to 50%.
9. Replace the original American Flag symbol with the modified artwork, then remove the flag artwork from the artboard.
10. Save your work, then compare your Symbols palette with Figure 43.
11. Close the Flag Symbol document.

FIGURE 43
Completed Project Builder 2

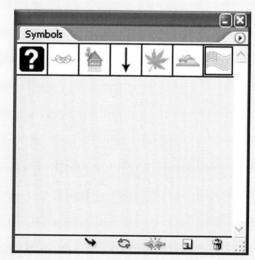

Drawing with Symbols

The nice lady who works at your town's Chamber of Commerce has created a poster for this year's Memorial Day parade and asks you if you could jazz it up. Since your firm is very busy, your improvements must be quick and simple. You e-mail a file containing a symbol of the American flag to an employee with instructions for updating the symbol. He e-mails the file back to you with the updated symbol, and you paste the parade text into the file.

1. Open AI 10-6.ai, then save it as **Memorial Day**.
2. Fill the black rectangle with orange, then hide it.
3. Select all the elements on the artboard, then hide them.
4. Place an instance of the American Flag symbol in the lower-left corner of the artboard.
5. Create a pattern out of the American Flag symbol instances that covers the entire artboard. (*Hint*: Refer to Figure 44 for ideas.)
6. Select all the symbol instances, group them, then send them to the back.
7. Show all, then deselect all.
8. Select the orange rectangle and the symbol instances, then make a clipping mask.
9. Apply a 10% cyan fill and a 3-point Black stroke to the clipping mask.
10. Save your work, compare your screen to Figure 44, then close Memorial Day.

FIGURE 44
Completed Design Project

You own a design firm in Silicon Valley that specializes in solutions for Web sites. You are approached by a representative of Black Swan Technologies, a global company noted for engineering breakthrough devices in the medical field. The representative tells you that he wants you to redesign the splash page of their Web site to convey the fact that they work with all sectors of the medical industry. The company's motto is "We Are Everywhere."

1. Open AI 10-7.ai, then save it as **Black Swan Technologies**.
2. Assemble your design team to discuss the Black Swan Technologies logo.
3. Does anybody think that parts of the logo suggest a bat more than a bird?
4. How does the group think that the concept "We Are Everywhere" can be incorporated visually into the splash page?
5. Discuss how reproducing the logo as a symbol presents possibilities for a splash page design based on the phrase "We Are Everywhere."
6. Create a new symbol using the swan artwork. (*Hint*: Modify the artwork using any Illustrator tools or features that you want before adding the new symbol to the Symbols palette.)
7. Use the swan symbol and the symbolism tools to create a new splash page for Black Swan Technologies.

FIGURE 45
Completed Group Project

8. Save your work, then compare your results with Figure 45.
9. Close Black Swan Technologies.

chapter

11

CREATING
3D OBJECTS

1. Extrude objects.

2. Revolve objects.

3. Manipulate surface shading and lighting.

4. Map artwork to 3D objects.

11 CREATING
3D OBJECTS

Creating 3D objects is one of the more exciting features in Illustrator CS2. With unprecedented ease, you can transform a simple two-dimensional (2D) object into an eye-popping three-dimensional (3D) graphic. You can extrude 2D objects to give them depth, and you can add interesting details by applying a bevel edge. You can revolve 2D objects around an axis to create stunning 3D graphics, complete with surface shading and highlights. You have a number of options for manipulating that surface shading. Apply diffuse shading for subtle highlights, or apply plastic shading to make the object reflect light as though its surface were shiny. You can even add and delete light sources to dramatically change the way a 3D graphic is lit. If that's not enough, once you've designed the 3D object, you can "map" 2D graphics, making them appear to "wrap around" the 3D object. Very cool!

Tools You'll Use

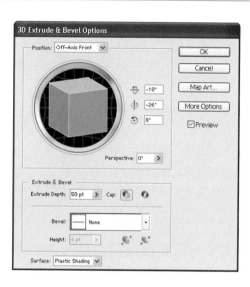

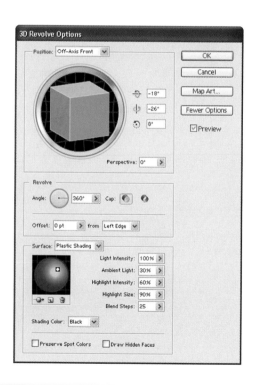

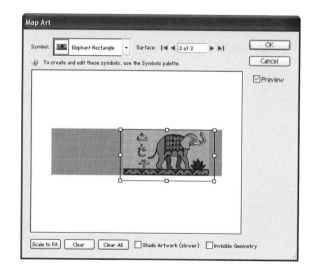

EXTRUDE
OBJECTS

What You'll Do

▶ In this lesson, you will use the 3D Extrude & Bevel effect to extrude objects.

Extruding Objects

Illustrator's **Extrude & Bevel** effect applies a three-dimensional effect to two-dimensional objects. A two-dimensional object has two axes: an X axis representing the width and a Y axis representing the height. When you **extrude** an object you add depth to an object by extending it on its Z axis, as shown in Figure 1. An object's Z axis is always perpendicular to the object's front surface.

Figure 2 shows four 2D objects before and after being extruded. Note the changes to

each object's fill color on the front surface and the light and dark shadings on the other surfaces. These shadings create the 3D effect and are applied automatically when the Extrude & Bevel effect is applied.

QUICKTIP

3D effects may produce fills with flaws. These are usually screen aberrations—an issue with your monitor—and don't show when you print the document.

FIGURE 1
Identifying the Z-axis on an extruded object

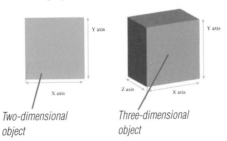

Two-dimensional object

Three-dimensional object

FIGURE 2
Four objects before and after being extruded

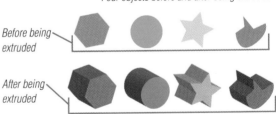

Before being extruded

After being extruded

You determine the degree of extrusion by changing the Extrude Depth value in the 3D Extrude & Bevel Options dialog box, shown in Figure 3. Extrusion depth is measured in points. The greater the value, the more the object is extended on its Z axis, as shown in Figure 4.

Use the Cap buttons in the 3D Extrude & Bevel Options dialog box to make extruded objects appear solid or hollow. The Turn cap on for solid appearance button is the default setting. It produces an object in which the front and back faces (surfaces) are solid, as shown in Figure 5. The Turn cap off for

FIGURE 3
3D Extrude & Bevel Options dialog box

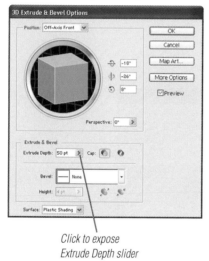

*Click to expose
Extrude Depth slider*

FIGURE 4
Two objects extruded to different depths

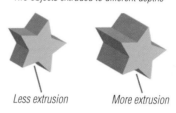

Less extrusion   *More extrusion*

FIGURE 5
Activating the "solid cap" button

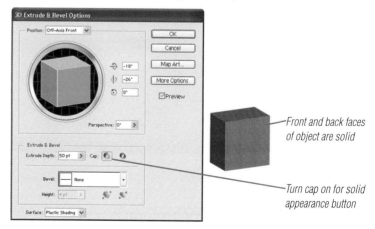

*Front and back faces
of object are solid*

*Turn cap on for solid
appearance button*

hollow appearance button makes the front and back faces invisible, producing an object that appears hollow, as shown in Figure 6.

Rotating 3D Objects

The 3D Extrude & Bevel Options dialog box offers controls for rotating extruded objects.

You can rotate the object manually by dragging the rotation cube, shown in Figure 7. The three text boxes to the right of the cube represent the selected object's X, Y, and Z axes. When you rotate the cube, the values in these text boxes update to reflect the changes you make. You may also enter

values in these text boxes to rotate the selected object at specific angles.

Once an object has been extruded, you can use the rotation cube to view any surface of the object—front, back, left, right, etc. The surface shading will update whenever you rotate an object.

FIGURE 6

Activating the "hollow cap" button

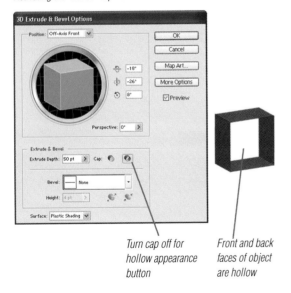

Turn cap off for hollow appearance button

Front and back faces of object are hollow

FIGURE 7

Options for rotating 3D objects

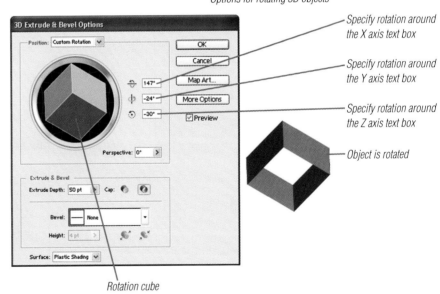

Specify rotation around the X axis text box

Specify rotation around the Y axis text box

Specify rotation around the Z axis text box

Object is rotated

Rotation cube

Creating 3D Objects

Extruding Compound Paths

Applying the Extrude & Bevel effect to a compound path can yield results that are visually very interesting. Figure 8 shows a simple compound path—a circle with a square "knocked out" from its center—positioned in front of a light blue square. Figure 9 shows the same object after being extruded.

Generally speaking, the more surfaces that an object has, the more interesting the 3D effect will be. Figure 10 shows a complex compound path, and Figure 11 shows the results when the Extrude & Bevel effect is applied.

FIGURE 8
Simple compound path

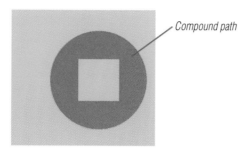

Compound path

FIGURE 10
Complex compound path

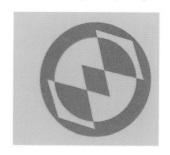

FIGURE 9
Simple compound path, extruded

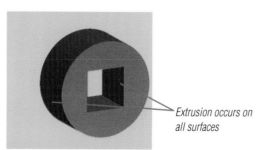

Extrusion occurs on all surfaces

FIGURE 11
Complex compound path, extruded

Applying a Bevel Edge to an Extruded Object

The dictionary defines the term **bevel** as the angle that one surface makes with another when they are not at right angles.

Figure 12 shows an example of a graphic with a bevel edge.

The Bevel menu, shown in Figure 13, offers ten pre-defined bevel shapes that you can apply to the edges of extruded objects.

The width of the bevel edge is controlled by the Height slider. Figure 14 shows six objects, each with a different bevel shape applied to its edge. Each bevel has a width of 4 points.

FIGURE 12
Identifying a bevel edge

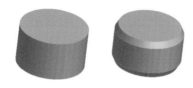

FIGURE 13
Viewing the Bevel menu

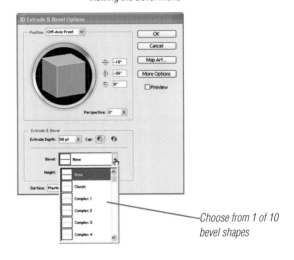

Choose from 1 of 10 bevel shapes

FIGURE 14
Six objects with bevel shapes applied to edges

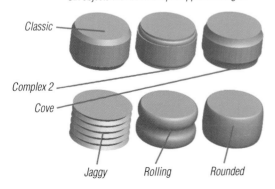

Classic

Complex 2

Cove

Jaggy   Rolling   Rounded

As shown in Figure 15, text can be extruded without first having to convert it to outlines. Once extruded, you can add a bevel edge to text. Figure 16 shows the same text with the Rounded bevel shape.

Because many letters are complex shapes, applying a bevel to extruded text often causes problems. Simply put, the shapes are too intricate to be rendered with a bevel edge. In Figure 16, the two Ts and the E handle the

bevel edge quite well, but you can see that the X is becoming disfigured. In Figure 17, the Classic bevel shape has been applied. The X isn't rendered properly with the Classic bevel shape applied to its edge.

FIGURE 15
Extruding text

FIGURE 16
Extruded text with the Rounded bevel shape applied

The "X" is becoming disfigured

FIGURE 17
Identifying problems with a bevel edge

The "X" isn't rendered properly

Whenever Illustrator is having difficulty rendering an object with a bevel edge, a warning appears in the 3D Extrude & Bevel Options dialog box, shown in Figure 18. When problems do occur, sometimes there is no solution. Your best bet, however, is to reduce the width of the bevel. Figure 19 shows the same text with the same Classic bevel shape shown in Figure 17, but in this figure, the bevel width has been reduced from four points to three points. The dialog box continues to warn that there may be problems with the bevel edge. Though that may be the case, the problems are less obvious.

FIGURE 18

Warning regarding a bevel edge

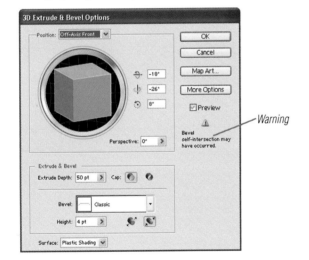

Warning

FIGURE 19

Reducing the width of a bevel edge

The "X" is rendered fairly well

When you apply a bevel shape to an object's edge, you can decide how the bevel will be applied to the object using the Bevel Extent In and Bevel Extent Out buttons in the 3D Extrude & Bevel Options dialog box. The Bevel Extent In button produces a bevel edge that carves away from the edge of the existing object. The Bevel Extent Out button adds the bevel edge to the object. Figure 20 shows the Bevel Extent Out and Bevel Extent In buttons. Generally speaking, the Bevel Extent In option is the better choice, because it stays within the already-established boundaries of the object.

FIGURE 20

Bevel Extent Out and Bevel Extent In buttons

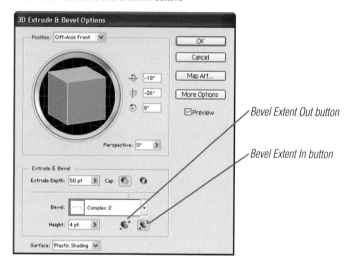

Bevel Extent Out button

Bevel Extent In button

Extrude an object

1. Open AI 11-1.ai, then save it as **Extrude Objects**.
2. Click **View** on the menu bar, then click **Blue Square**.
3. Click the **Selection Tool** ▶, select the **blue square**, click **View** on the menu bar, then click **Hide Edges**.
4. Click **Effect** on the menu bar, point to **3D**, then click **Extrude & Bevel**.
5. Position the 3D Extrude & Bevel Options dialog box so that you can see the blue square, then click the **Preview check box**.

   As shown in Figure 21, the blue square is extruded 50 points on the Z axis.
6. Click the **Extrude Depth list arrow**, drag the **slider** to 96 pt, then click **OK**.

   (continued)

FIGURE 21
Applying the 3D Extrude & Bevel effect

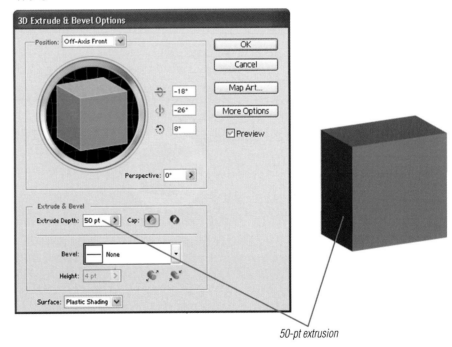

50-pt extrusion

FIGURE 22
Viewing the effect in the Appearance palette

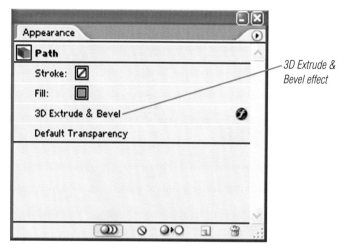

3D Extrude &
Bevel effect

7. Click **Window** on the menu bar, then click
   Appearance.

   As shown in Figure 22, the Appearance
   palette lists the 3D Extrude & Bevel effect
   applied to the object.

8. Double-click **3D Extrude & Bevel** in the
   Appearance palette to open the dialog box,
   then click **Preview**.

9. Click the **Turn cap off for hollow appearance
   button** 〇.

   The object's front and back "capping faces"
   become transparent, making the object
   appear hollow.

10. Click **OK**, then compare your work to
    Figure 23.

*You applied the 3D Extrude & Bevel effect to a
selected object, increased the depth of the extrusion,
then changed the cap so that the 3D object would
appear hollow.*

FIGURE 23
Viewing the extrusion with hollow caps

Extrude and rotate an object

1. Click **View** on the menu bar, then click **Orange Star**.

2. Select the star, click **Effect** on the menu bar, point to **3D**, then click **Extrude & Bevel**.

3. Click the **Preview check box**, then change the Extrude Depth value to 60 pt.

4. Position your cursor over the top-front edge of the rotation cube so that a rotate cursor appears, as shown in Figure 24.

5. Click and drag to rotate the cube, noting that the value in the Specify rotation around the X axis text box is the only value that changes as you drag.

(continued)

FIGURE 24

Manipulating the rotation cube manually

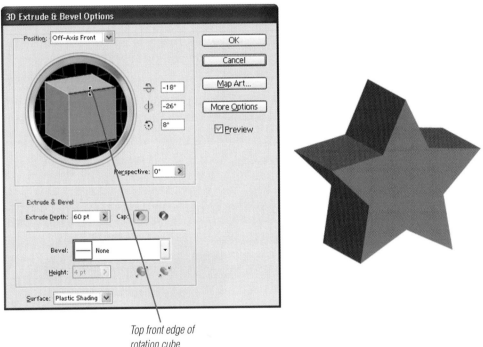

Top front edge of
rotation cube

Creating 3D Objects

FIGURE 25
Entering rotation values

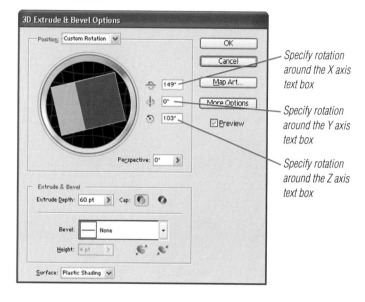

Specify rotation around the X axis text box

Specify rotation around the Y axis text box

Specify rotation around the Z axis text box

6. Experiment with different rotations by dragging the rotation cube from all sides, and note the changes to the orange star object on the page.

7. Double-click the **Specify rotation around the X axis text box** to select its contents, type **149**, then press **[Tab]**.

   TIP Include the negative sign when you select the contents in the Specify rotation around the X axis text box.

8. Type **0** in the Specify rotation around the Y axis text box, press **[Tab]**, type **103** in the Specify rotation around the Z axis text box, press **[Tab]**, then compare your dialog box to Figure 25.

9. Click **OK**, then compare your work to Figure 26.

You applied the 3D Extrude & Bevel effect to a star-shaped object, then manipulated the rotation cube to rotate the object.

FIGURE 26
Viewing the rotated star

Extrude a compound path

1. Click **View** on the menu bar, then click **Target**.

2. Select all three circles, click **Object** on the menu bar, point to **Compound Path**, then click **Make**.

3. Click **Effect** on the menu bar, point to **3D**, then click **Extrude & Bevel**.

4. Click the **Preview check box**, then change the Extrude Depth value to 100 pt.

5. Experiment with different rotations by dragging the rotation cube from all sides.

6. Double-click the **Specify rotation around the X axis text box**, type **28**, then press **[Tab]**.

   TIP If the negative sign is not selected when you double-click the value in the Specify rotation around the X axis text box, make sure you select it before you type 28.

7. Type **-26** in the Specify rotation around the Y axis text box, press **[Tab]**, type **8** in the Specify rotation around the Z axis text box, then press **[Tab]**.

8. Click **OK**, then compare your work to Figure 27.

You created a compound path, applied the 3D Extrude & Bevel effect, then rotated the graphic, all the time noting the visual effect created by applying the effect to a compound path.

FIGURE 27
Viewing the 3D Extrude & Bevel effect applied to a compound path

FIGURE 28

Text outlines with the Classic bevel shape applied

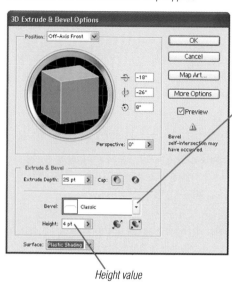

Choose bevel shape list arrow

Height value

FIGURE 29

Viewing the result of applying the Bevel Extent Out button

FIGURE 30

Identifying a possible self-intersection problem

Bevel Extent In
button applied

A minor self-intersection
problem

Apply a bevel shape to an object's edge

1. Click **View** on the menu bar, then click **DOG**.

   The text has been converted to outlines and made into a compound path.

2. Click the **Selection Tool** ▶, click any letter of the text, click **Effect** on the menu bar, point to **3D**, then click **Extrude & Bevel**.

3. Click the **Preview check box**, then change the Extrude Depth value to 25 pt.

4. Click the **Choose bevel shape list arrow**, click **Classic**, verify that the Height value is set to 4 pt, then compare your screen to Figure 28.

5. Note that the Bevel Extent In button is pressed, click the **Bevel Extent Out button** , then note the change to the graphic, as shown in Figure 29.

6. Click the **Bevel Extent In button** , click the **Choose bevel shape list arrow**, then click **Complex 2**.

7. Note the warning in the dialog box that says Bevel self-intersection may have occurred, then compare your graphic to Figure 30.

8. Click **OK**, save your work, then close Extrude Objects.

You applied two bevel shapes to extruded text outlines. You also experimented with the Bevel Extent In and Bevel Extent Out buttons.

REVOLVE OBJECTS

What You'll Do

In this lesson, you will use the 3D effect to revolve objects.

Revolving Objects

In addition to extruding, **revolving** is another method that Illustrator CS provides for applying a 3D effect to a 2D object. Imagine taking a large, hard cover book and opening it so much that its front and back covers touch. The pages would fan out from one cover to the other, all of them with their inside edges adhering to the spine of the book. This example is similar to what happens when the Revolve effect is applied to an object.

Revolving an object "sweeps" a path in a circular direction around the Y axis. Figure 31 shows a familiar shape—the letter E—before and after the Revolve effect is applied. The blue selection

FIGURE 31
The letter E before and after being revolved

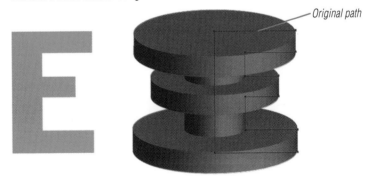

Original path

Creating 3D Objects

marks show the original path, and the left edge of that path is the Y axis around which the path was revolved. The surface shading is applied automatically with the effect.

By default, an object is revolved around a vertical axis that represents its leftmost point. An example of this is shown in Figure 32. The 3D Revolve Options dialog box, shown in Figure 33, also offers the option to revolve the object from its right edge. Revolving the object from its right edge yields an entirely different result, shown in Figure 34.

FIGURE 32
Revolving an object around its left edge

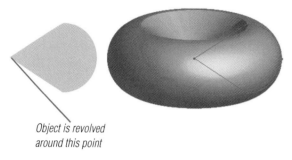

Object is revolved
around this point

FIGURE 33
Choosing the edge for the revolution

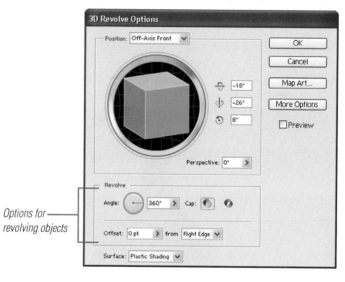

Options for
revolving objects

FIGURE 34
Revolving an object around its right edge

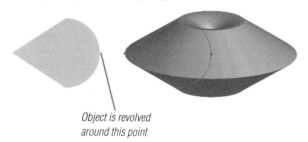

Object is revolved
around this point

Because a revolution occurs around a vertical axis, in most cases, the starting path will depict half of the object you want to revolve. This is more easily explained with examples. Figure 35 shows the original path and the result of applying the Revolve effect to that path. Note how the original path is a two-dimensional half of the revolved three-dimensional object.

Once revolved, an object can be rotated by manipulating the rotation cube in the 3D Revolve Options dialog box. This feature is extremely powerful with a revolved graphic. You can use the rotation cube to present all surfaces of the graphic. Figure 36 shows four sides of the bottle graphic, all of them created by manipulating the rotation cube.

Revolving Multiple Objects

You can apply the Revolve effect to multiple paths simultaneously. Paths to be revolved

FIGURE 35

Identifying the path used to produce the revolved 3D graphic

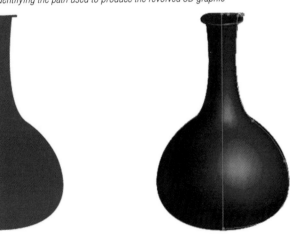

FIGURE 36

A revolved graphic rotated four ways

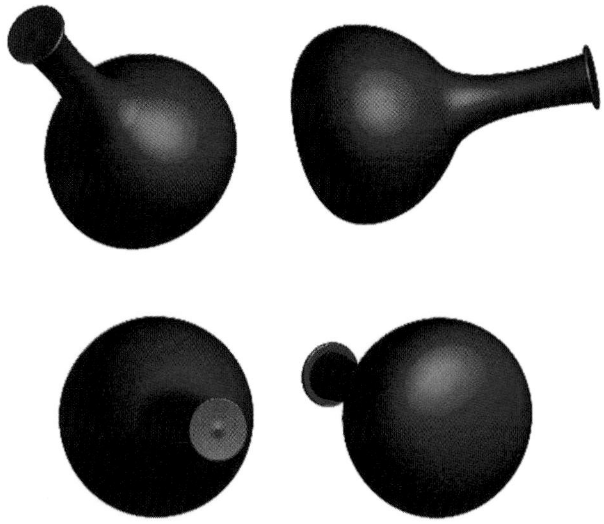

can be open or closed paths. As shown in Figure 37, when multiple paths are selected and the Revolve effect is applied, each path is revolved around its own axis. For this reason, it is often best to align the left edges of multiple paths on the same Y axis, as shown in Figure 38.

As the figure shows, aligning separate paths on the same Y axis can be useful when revolving. However, unwanted results can occur when rotating those paths, even when they are aligned on the same Y axis. Figure 39 shows the same two paths being rotated. Note that because they are separate paths, they rotate separately—each on its own axis. This problem can be resolved by grouping the paths.

FIGURE 37
Multiple paths revolved on their own axis

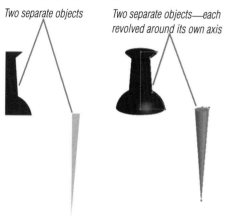

Two separate objects

Two separate objects—each revolved around its own axis

Separate, ungrouped paths rotate separately

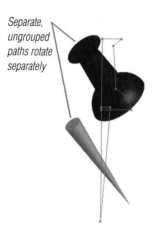

FIGURE 39
Multiple paths rotated on their own axis

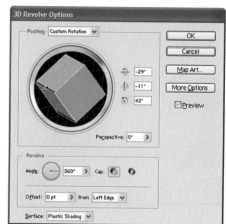

FIGURE 38
Multiple paths aligned on the same axis then revolved

Two separate objects aligned on their left edges

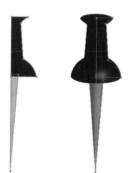

Two separate objects—each revolved around their own axis

Revolving Grouped Objects

When grouped, multiple paths are revolved around a single axis. This can yield unexpected results. In Figure 40, the two paths (left) are grouped, but they don't share the same Y axis. When revolved, both paths revolve around the leftmost axis.

When multiple paths are grouped and revolved, they will also rotate together. Figure 41 shows four versions of two grouped and revolved paths after they have been rotated in the Revolve Options dialog box. In every case, the two paths rotate together because they are grouped. Compare this to Figure 39, in which the two ungrouped paths rotated separately, each on their own axes.

Applying an Offset to a Revolved Object

By default, an object is revolved around a vertical axis that represents its leftmost point. Figure 42 illustrates this point.

FIGURE 40
Two grouped paths revolved around a single Y-axis

Two paths, grouped

Grouped paths revolved around the leftmost axis

Leftmost axis

FIGURE 41
Four grouped paths after being revolved and rotated

FIGURE 42
Object revolved around its leftmost point

Leftmost point

Leftmost point

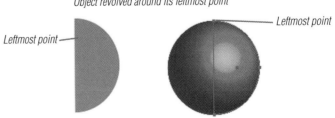

Increasing the Offset value in the Revolve Options dialog box, shown in Figure 43, increases how far from the Y axis the object is revolved. Figure 44 shows the same revolved object from 42 with a 90-point offset value. The path revolves around the same Y axis, but it does so at a distance of 90 points. Figure 45, in which the object has been rotated, shows the offset more clearly. Try to visualize that the object is a series of half circles rotated around a single vertical axis—90 points from that vertical axis.

FIGURE 43
Offset slider in the 3D Revolve Options dialog box

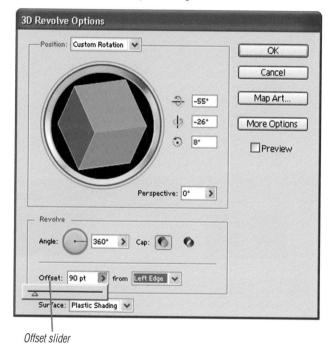

Offset slider

FIGURE 44
Object revolved with a 90-point offset from its Y-axis

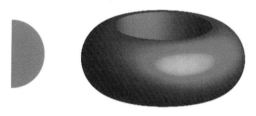

FIGURE 45
Rotated object shows 90-point offset more clearly

Revolve an object

1. Open AI 11-2.ai, then save it as **Green Bottle**.

2. Click the **Selection Tool**, click the **green object**, click **View** on the menu bar, then click **Hide Edges** (if necessary).

3. Click **Effect** on the menu bar, point to **3D**, click **Revolve**, then click the **Preview check box**.

   As shown in Figure 46, the object is revolved on its axis and appears as a bottle. Highlights and shadows are applied automatically.

4. Click **OK**, save your work, then close Green Bottle.

You revolved a simple object to produce a three-dimensional graphic.

Revolve multiple objects

1. Open AI 11-3.ai, then save it as **Revolve Objects**.

2. Select the second row of blue objects, click **Effect** on the menu bar, point to **3D**, then click **Revolve**.

3. Click the **Preview check box**.

   Each object is revolved on its own axis.

4. Click **OK**, then compare your work to Figure 47.

   The graphic on the left has a hard edge because the original object was a rectangle. The round edge of the original object on the right produced a 3D graphic that also has a round edge.

(continued)

FIGURE 46
Revolving an object

Highlights and shadows applied automatically

FIGURE 47
Revolving multiple objects

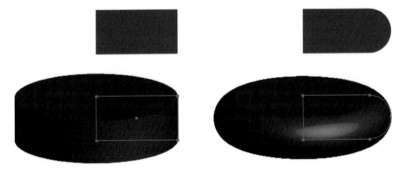

FIGURE 48
Revolving three objects

5. Select the **second row of red objects**, click **Effect** on the menu bar, point to **3D**, then click **Revolve**.

6. Click **OK**, deselect all, then compare your work to Figure 48.

   The first two graphics produced spheres when revolved, but only the middle graphic is a perfect sphere. The two crescent shapes, because they face in opposite directions, produce two drastically different results when revolved.

7. Deselect all, select the **rightmost red object**, double-click **3D Revolve** in the Appearance palette, manipulate the rotation cube to rotate the graphic any way that you like, then click **OK**.

   Figure 49 shows one possible result.

8. Save your work, then close Revolve Objects.

You selected multiple objects, applied the 3D Revolve effect, then noted that each object was revolved on its own axis. You compared the results with the original objects, then rotated one of the revolved objects.

FIGURE 49
Rotating a revolved object

Revolve grouped objects

1. Open AI 11-4.ai, then save it as **Push Pins**.
2. Click **View** on the menu bar, click **Green Pin**, then select the two objects in the Green Pin view.

   TIP The two objects in Green Pin view are not grouped.

3. Click **Effect** on the menu bar, point to **3D**, then click **Revolve**.
4. Click the **Preview check box**, then note the effect on the objects on the page.
5. Manipulate the rotation cube in any direction.

   As shown in Figure 50, the two objects are each rotated on their own axis and the illustration is no longer realistic.

   TIP Because your rotation will differ, your results will differ from the figure.

6. Click **OK**, click **View** on the menu bar, click **Red Pin**, click one of the objects in the Red Pin view.

   TIP The two objects are grouped.

7. Click **Effect** on the menu bar, point to **3D**, click **Revolve**, then click the **Preview check box**.

   As shown in Figure 51, because the two objects are grouped, they are both revolved around the same axis.

   (continued)

FIGURE 50
Rotating revolved objects that are not grouped

FIGURE 51
Two grouped objects revolved around the same axis

Creating 3D Objects

FIGURE 52

Two grouped objects revolved around the same axis

FIGURE 53

Rotating revolved objects that are grouped

8. Click **OK**, click **View** on the menu bar, click **Blue Pin**, select the two objects, click **Object** on the menu bar, then click **Group**.

9. Click **Effect** on the menu bar, point to **3D**, click **Revolve**, then click the **Preview check box**.

   As shown in Figure 52, the two grouped objects are revolved around the same axis. Because they both share the same axis (their left edge) the illustration is realistic.

   TIP The selection edges are showing in the figure so that you can see the left edge that both graphics share.

10. Manipulate the rotation cube in any direction that you like.

   Figure 53 shows one possible result.

11. Click **OK**, save your work, then close Push Pins.

You explored the results of revolving grouped and ungrouped objects. With the green pin, you noted that ungrouped objects cannot be rotated together. With the red pin, you noted that grouped objects are revolved around the same axis. With the blue pin, you noted that grouped objects can be rotated together.

Offset a revolved object

1. Open AI 11-5.ai, then save it as **Desk Lamp**.

2. Select the silver object, click **Effect** on the menu bar, point to **3D**, click **Revolve**, then click **OK**.

3. Select the gold diagonal line, click **Effect** on the menu bar, point to **3D**, click **Revolve**, then click the **Preview check box**.

   As shown in Figure 54, the object's leftmost point is the axis around which it is revolved.

   (continued)

FIGURE 54
Revolving an object around its leftmost point

Leftmost point of
original object

Creating 3D Objects

FIGURE 55

Revolving an object with a 50-pt offset from its axis

50-pt offset from
leftmost point

4. Double-click the **Offset text box**, type **50**, press **[Tab]**, then compare your work to Figure 55.

   The object is revolved at a radius that is 50 points from its axis.

5. Click **OK**, save your work, then close Desk Lamp.

You used an increased offset value to manipulate how an object is revolved in relation to its axis.

MANIPULATE SURFACE
SHADING AND LIGHTING

What You'll Do

▶ *In this lesson, you will familiarize yourself with the controls that allow you to manipulate the highlight effects of a 3D object.*

Applying Surface Shading

When the Extrude & Bevel effect or the Revolve effect is applied to an object, surface shading and lighting are applied automatically. However, you can manipulate these effects.

Surface shading controls how the object's surface appears. When an object is revolved, four surface shadings are available: Wireframe, No Shading, Diffuse Shading, and Plastic Shading. Examples of all four are shown in Figure 56.

Plastic shading is the default surface shade. With plastic shading, the object reflects light as though it were made of a shiny plastic material. Distinct highlight areas appear on the surface of an object.

Diffuse shading offers a surface that reflects light in a soft, diffuse pattern. With Diffuse Shading, no distinct highlights appear on the surface of the object.

The Wireframe option makes all surfaces transparent and shows the object's geometry. The No Shading option, as its name suggests, applies no new shading to the object. Its surface is identical to that of the 2D object.

Creating 3D Objects

Manipulating Lighting Controls

When you choose Diffuse Shading or Plastic Shading, a number of lighting controls are available for you to manipulate the lighting effects that are applied to the object automatically.

- Lighting Intensity controls the strength of the light on the object. The range for lighting intensity is 0-100, with 100 being the default.
- Ambient Light is a very useful control. It determines how the object is lit globally. The range for Ambient Light is 0-100. Any changes that you make with the Ambient Light slider affect the brightness of the object uniformly, though the effect is much more pronounced in the shadow areas than in the highlights. Decreasing the ambient light noticeably makes the shadow areas darker, which increases the overall contrast of the object, from shadow to

FIGURE 56
Four surface shading choices

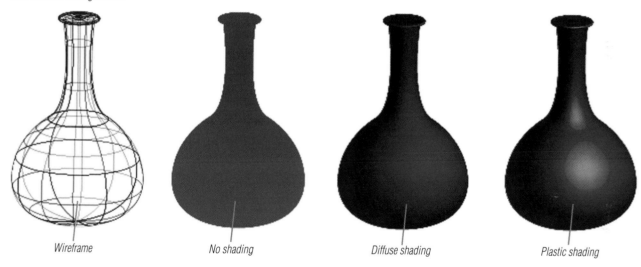

Wireframe   No shading   Diffuse shading   Plastic shading

highlight. Figure 57 shows two objects, one with 60% ambient light and one with 20% ambient light.

- As its name implies, **Highlight Intensity** controls how intense a highlight appears. The more intense the highlight, the more white it appears. Figure 58 shows two objects, one with 100% highlight intensity and one with 60%

highlight intensity. Note that at 100%, the highlight is too white and "glaring." At 60%, the highlight is a good mixture of white and the object's color.

- Highlight Size controls how large the highlights appear on the object.
- Blend Steps controls how smoothly the shading appears on the object's surface and is most visible in the transition

from the highlight areas to the diffusely lit areas. The range for blend steps is 1-256, with higher numbers producing more paths and therefore smoother transitions. If your computer can handle it, use 256 blend steps, but be aware that the higher the number, the more computer memory will be required to render the object.

FIGURE 57
Comparing ambient lighting

60% ambient lighting

20% ambient lighting

FIGURE 58
Comparing highlight intensity

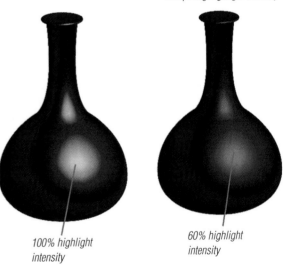

100% highlight intensity

60% highlight intensity

Creating 3D Objects

Manipulating Light Sources

In addition to manipulating lighting controls, you can manipulate the light itself. When Diffuse Shading or Plastic Shading is chosen as the surface shading, a default light source, shown in Figure 59, is applied.

You can drag the light source to a new location to light the object from a different angle, as shown in Figure 60. This can be very effective for manipulating the overall lighting of the object.

In addition to relocating the default light source, you can add additional light sources by clicking the New Light button. By default, the new light source appears at the center of the lighting key, but it too can

FIGURE 59
Viewing default light source settings

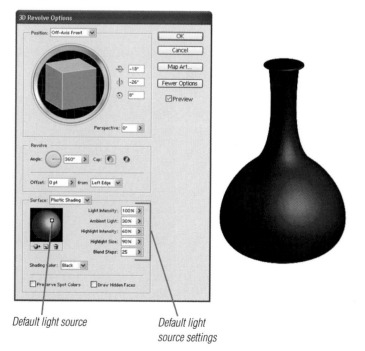

Default light source

Default light source settings

FIGURE 60
Relocating a light source

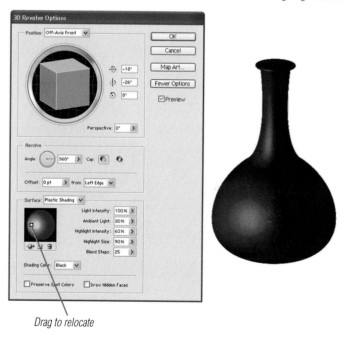

Drag to relocate

be relocated, as shown in Figure 61. You can apply different light intensity values to individual light sources. It is often a good idea for one light source to be more dominant than the other(s).

You delete a light source by selecting it and then clicking the Delete Light button. The Move selected light to back of object button moves the light source to the back of the object. This is often most effective when

there's a background object that allows the back light to be more apparent. In Figure 62, the second light has been moved behind the object; the highlights on the right side of the object are from the back light.

FIGURE 61
Relocating a second light source

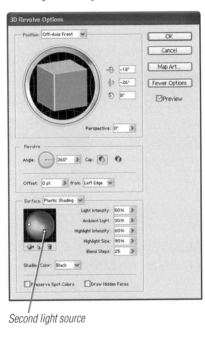
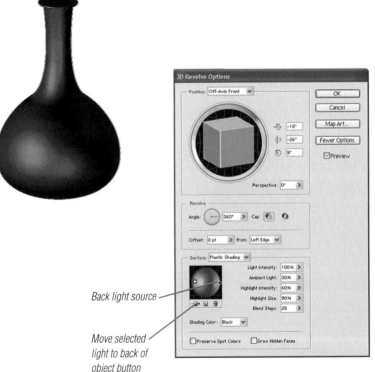

Second light source

FIGURE 62
Using a light source as a back light

Back light source

Move selected light to back of object button

Highlight from back light source

FIGURE 63
Viewing the object with the Plastic Shading surface applied

Apply surface shading to a 3D object

1. Open AI 11-6.ai, then save it as **Surface Lighting**.

2. Click the **object** to select it, then double-click **3D Revolve** in the Appearance palette.

3. Click the **Preview check box**, then note the subtle lighting effects on the object.

   The Diffuse Shading surface type is applied to the object.

4. Click the **Surface list arrow**, then click **No Shading**.

5. Click the **Surface list arrow**, then click **Wireframe**.

6. Click the **Surface list arrow**, click **Plastic Shading**, then compare your artwork to Figure 63.

You examined four types of surface shadings as applied to a revolved object.

Manipulate lighting controls

1. Click **More Options** in the dialog box.
2. Click the **Ambient Light list arrow**, then drag the **slider** to 20.
3. Click the **Highlight Intensity list arrow**, then drag the **slider** to 75.
4. Click the **Highlight Size list arrow**, then drag the **slider** to 75.
5. Click the **Light Intensity list arrow**, drag the **slider** to 50, note the change in the object, then drag the **slider** to 100.
6. Click the **Blend Steps list arrow**, then drag the **slider** to 128.
7. Click **OK**, then compare your artwork to Figure 64.

You manipulated five surface shading controls, noting their effect on a 3D object.

Manipulate light sources

1. Verify that the green object is selected, double-click **3D Revolve** in the Appearance palette, then click the **Preview check box**.
2. Drag the **light** to the top center of the sphere, as shown in Figure 65.

(continued)

FIGURE 64
Manipulating surface shading on a 3D object

FIGURE 65
Relocating a light

Relocated light source

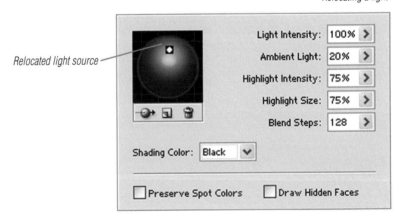

Creating 3D Objects

FIGURE 66
Relocating the new light

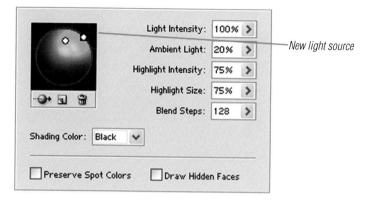

New light source

3. Click the **New Light button** 🔳 to add a second light.

   TIP By default, a new light is positioned at the center of the sphere.

4. Drag the **new light** to the top-right corner of the sphere, as shown in Figure 66.

5. Click the **New Light button** 🔳 to add a third light, then move it to the location shown in Figure 67.

6. Click **OK**, compare your work to Figure 68, then compare Figure 68 to Figure 64 to see the results of adding the two lights.

7. Save your work, then close Surface Lighting.

You added and positioned lights to modify the lighting effects applied to the 3D object.

FIGURE 67
Relocating the third light

Third light source

FIGURE 68
The object with different lighting

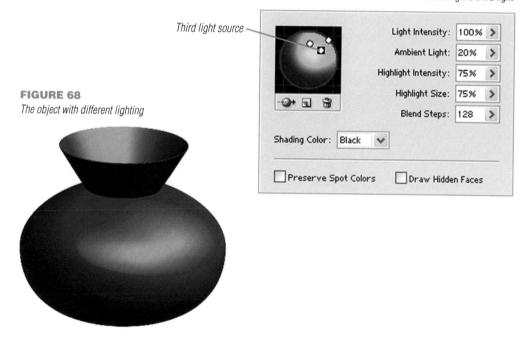

Lesson 3   Manipulate Surface Shading and Lighting

MAP ARTWORK TO
3D OBJECTS

Mapping Artwork

Once you have created a three-dimensional object, you can "map" two-dimensional artwork to the three-dimensional object. A good example of this concept is a soup can and a soup label. The two dimensional soup label is designed and printed. It is then wrapped around the three-dimensional soup can.

The process of mapping a 2D object to a 3D object first includes converting the 2D object to a symbol. Figure 69 shows a revolved 3D object and 2D artwork that will be mapped to it.

To map the artwork, you first select the 3D object, then click Map Art in the 3D Revolve Options dialog box. In the Map

What You'll Do

In this lesson, you will map 2D artwork to a 3D object .

FIGURE 69
Viewing 3D artwork and 2D artwork to be mapped

2D Illustrator artwork

3D object

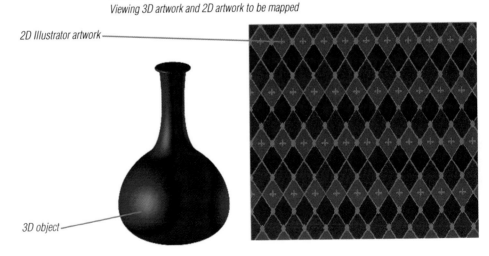

Creating 3D Objects

Art dialog box, shown in Figure 70, you must first choose which surface you intend to map the art to. When you click the surface buttons, the active surface is shown in red wireframe on the 3D object. In this example, we are mapping the wrapping paper to surface 1 of 4, which is shown in Figure 71.

The grid pattern represents the *complete* surface of surface 1 of 4. Understand that this means not only the surface that you see—the front surface—but the entire surface, all the way around. For this exercise, we're interested in mapping the wrapping paper to the surface that we can see—the front surface. That area is defined by the curved lines, identified in Figure 71.

Map Art dialog box

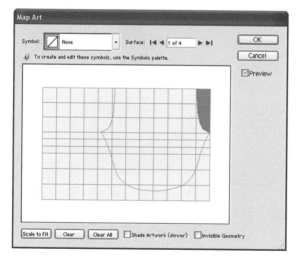

Identifying the surface to be mapped

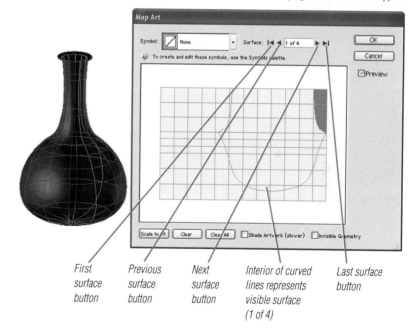

First surface button

Previous surface button

Next surface button

Interior of curved lines represents visible surface (1 of 4)

Last surface button

Once you have chosen the surface, you then choose the symbol to be mapped by clicking the Symbol list arrow and selecting the appropriate symbol. When you do so, the symbol artwork is centered on the grid. In this example, the symbol is named Wrapping Paper. For this exercise, we drag the artwork so that it completely covers the curved lines that represent the front face, as shown in Figure 72.

Once the artwork is mapped, it reshapes itself to the three-dimensional object, as shown Figure 73.

FIGURE 72

Positioning the symbol artwork

FIGURE 73

Viewing the mapped art

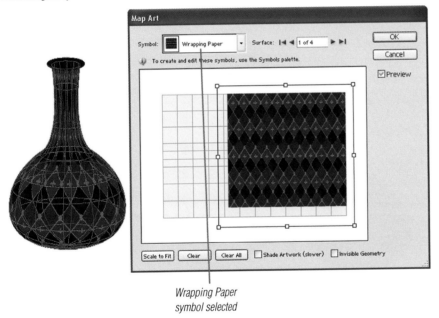

*Wrapping Paper
symbol selected*

Creating 3D Objects

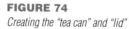

FIGURE 74

Creating the "tea can" and "lid"

1. Open AI 11-7.ai, then save it as **Tea Can**.

2. Select all, click **Effect** on the menu bar, point to **3D**, click **Revolve**, then click **OK**.

   Your artwork should resemble Figure 74.

3. Open AI 11-8.ai, select all, click **Edit** on the menu bar, click **Copy**, close the document, then return to Tea Can.ai.

4. Click **Window** on the menu bar, click **Symbols**, click **Edit** on the menu bar, click **Paste**, then drag the pasted artwork into the Symbols palette to create a new symbol.

5. Delete the pasted artwork from the artboard.

6. Double-click the **new symbol** in the Symbols palette, type **Elephant Rectangle** in the Symbol Options dialog box, then click **OK**.

7. Open AI 11-9.ai, select all, copy the artwork, close the document, return to Tea Can.ai, then paste the artwork.

8. Drag the pasted artwork into the Symbols palette to create a new symbol, then delete the pasted artwork from the artboard.

9. Name the new symbol **Elephant Circle**.

You used the 3D Revolve effect to create the artwork to which the 2D artwork will be mapped. You then created two symbols, one for each part of the 2D artwork.

Map rectangular artwork

1. Click the **Selection Tool** 🔈, click the **silver-object**, then press ↑ eight times so that the silver artwork is fully "under" the purple lid.

2. Double-click **3D Revolve** in the Appearance palette to open the 3D Revolve Options dialog box, click the **Preview check box**, then click **Map Art**.

3. Note that the Surface text box reads 1 of 3 and that a red line indicates that surface on the object, as shown in Figure 75.

4. Click the **Next Surface button** ▶ two times, so that the Surface text box reads 3 of 3.

   The light gray areas of the layout grid represent the visible area of the silver object at this viewing angle.

5. Click the **Symbol list arrow**, then click **Elephant Rectangle**.

6. Drag the **top-left and bottom-right resizing handles** on the symbol's bounding box so that the artwork fits into the light gray areas of the layout grid, as shown in Figure 76.

(continued)

FIGURE 75
Viewing surface 1 of 3 in the Map Art dialog box

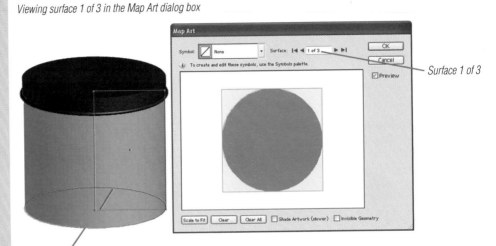

Surface 1 of 3

Red line identifies surface

FIGURE 76
Resizing the artwork to the visible area

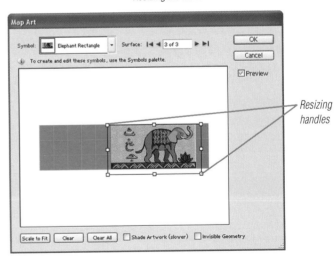

Resizing handles

Creating 3D Objects

FIGURE 77
Adjusting surface shading and lighting

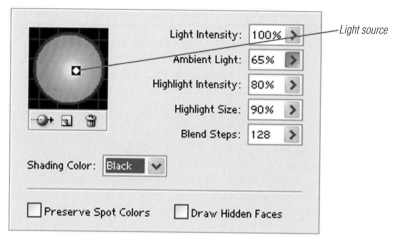

Light source

7. Drag the **bottom-middle resizing handle** up slightly so that the silver "can" will show beneath the "elephant label."

8. Click the **Shade Artwork (slower) check box**.

9. Click **OK**, change the ambient light setting to 65%, change the highlight intensity setting to 80%, change the number of blend steps to 128, then move the light to the location shown in Figure 77.

10. Click **OK**, deselect all, then compare your work to Figure 78.

In the Map Art dialog box, you selected the symbol that you wanted to map and the surface that you wanted to map it to. You resized the symbol artwork so that it fit onto the surface properly, then you activated the shading option to make the artwork appear more realistic as a label. You modified surface shading settings and lighting to improve the appearance of the artwork.

FIGURE 78
Viewing the mapped art

Map round artwork

1. Click the **purple "cover" object**, double-click **3D Revolve** in the Appearance palette, click the **Preview check box**, then click **Map Art**.

2. Click the **Next Surface button** ▶ once, so that the Surface text box reads 2 of 5.

3. Click the **Symbol list arrow**, then click **Elephant Circle**.

4. Point to the **upper-right resizing handle** until a rotate cursor appears, then drag to rotate the graphic to the position shown in Figure 79.

5. Click **OK** to close the Map Art dialog box, click **OK** again, deselect all, then compare your artwork to Figure 80.

You mapped a circular piece of 2D artwork to an oval 3D object.

FIGURE 79
Rotating the mapped art

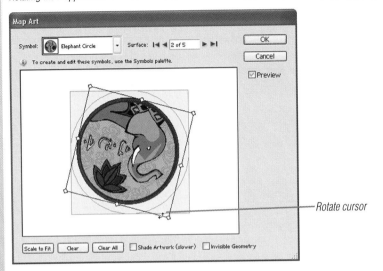

— Rotate cursor

FIGURE 80
Viewing the mapped art

Creating 3D Objects

FIGURE 81
Positioning the artwork

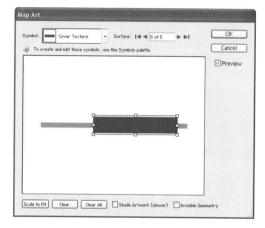

FIGURE 82
Relocating the light

FIGURE 83
Viewing the finished artwork

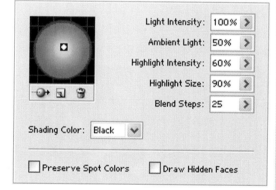

1. Open AI 11-10.ai, select all, copy the artwork, close the document, then return to Tea Can.ai.

2. Verify that the Symbols palette is visible, click **Edit** on the menu bar, click **Paste**, then drag the pasted artwork into the Symbols palette to create a new symbol.

3. Delete the pasted artwork from the artboard.

4. Double-click the **new symbol** in the Symbols palette, type **Cover Texture**, then click **OK**.

5. Click the **purple "cover" object**, double-click **3D Revolve (Mapped)** in the Appearance palette, click the **Preview check box**, then click **Map Art**.

6. Click the **Next Surface button** ▶ until the Surface text box reads 5 of 5.

7. Click the **Symbol list arrow**, then click **Cover Texture**.

8. Position the symbol artwork so that it covers the entire light gray area, shown in Figure 81.

9. Click **OK** to close the Map Art window, then drag the light to the location shown in Figure 82.

10. Click **OK**, deselect all, then compare your work to Figure 83.

11. Save your work, then close Tea Can.

You mapped artwork to the front face of a 3D object to add texture.

Extrude objects.

1. Open AI 11-11.ai, then save it as **Extrude & Bevel Skills**.

2. Click the Selection Tool, select the blue octagon, click View on the menu bar, then click Hide Edges.

3. Click Effect on the menu bar, point to 3D, click Extrude & Bevel, then click the Preview check box.

4. Click the Extrude Depth list arrow, then increase the depth to 75 pt.

5. Click the Turn cap off for hollow appearance button, then click OK.

6. Select the orange letter H, click Effect on the menu bar, point to 3D, then click Extrude & Bevel.

7. Click the Preview check box, then change the Extrude Depth value to 60 pt.

8. Double-click the Specify rotation around the X axis text box to select its contents, type **17**, then press **[Tab]**.

9. Type **-17** in the Specify rotation around the Y axis text box, press [Tab], type **-31** in the Specify rotation around the Z axis text box, then click OK.

10. Select the green octagon and the two objects inside it, click Object on the menu bar, point to Compound Path, then click Make.

11. Click Effect on the menu bar, point to 3D, then click Extrude & Bevel.

12. Click the Preview check box, then experiment with different rotations by clicking and dragging the rotation cube from all sides.

13. Double-click the Specify rotation around the X axis text box, type **26**, then press [Tab].

14. Type **-9** in the Specify rotation around the Y axis text box, press [Tab], then type **5** in the Specify rotation around the Z axis text box.

15. Click OK.

16. Select the hollow blue octagon at the top of the artboard, then double-click 3D Extrude & Bevel in the Appearance palette.

17. Click the Preview check box, then click the Turn cap on for solid appearance button.

18. Click the Bevel list arrow, click Complex 3, then drag the Height slider to 6.

19. Click the Bevel Extent Out button, click Ok, then compare your work to Figure 84.

20. Save your work, then close Extrude & Bevel Skills.

FIGURE 84

Completed Skills Review, Part 1

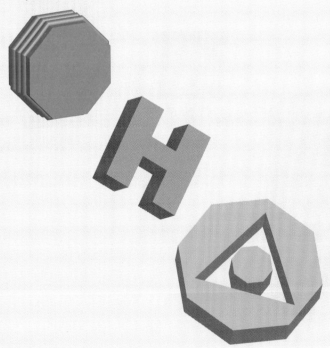

Revolve objects.

1. Open AI 11-12.ai, then save it as **Gold Urn**.
2. Click the Selection Tool, select all, click View on the menu bar, then click Hide Edges (if necessary).
3. Click the Horizontal Align Left button in the Align palette.
4. Click Effect on the menu bar, point to 3D, click Revolve, then click the Preview check box.
5. Manipulate the rotation cube in any direction, note that the three objects all rotate on their own axes, then click Cancel.
6. Click Object on the menu bar, then click Group.
7. Click Effect on the menu bar, point to 3D, click Revolve, then click the Preview check box.
8. Manipulate the rotation cube in any direction.
9. Click Cancel.
10. Click Effect on the menu bar, point to 3D, click Revolve, then click the Preview check box.
11. Click the Offset list arrow, change the offset value to 48, then click OK.

Manipulate surface shading and lighting.

1. Double-click 3D Revolve in the Appearance palette.
2. Click the Preview check box, click the Surface list arrow, then click No Shading.
3. Click the Surface list arrow, then click Diffuse Shading.
4. Click the Surface list arrow, then click Plastic Shading.
5. Click More Options, if necessary, click the Ambient Light list arrow, then drag the slider to 45.
6. Drag the light to the top center of the sphere.
7. Click the New Light button to add a second light.
8. Drag the Light Intensity slider to 30.

Map artwork to 3D objects.

1. Drag the Offset slider to 0, then click Map Art.
2. Click the Next Surface button until the Surface text box reads 5 of 13.

3. Click the Symbol list arrow, then click Wrapping Paper.
4. Click OK.
5. Click OK, then compare your work to Figure 85.
6. Save your work, then close Gold Urn.

FIGURE 85
Completed Skills Review, Part 2

You are a freelance illustrator, and you have been hired to draw an old-fashioned lava lamp to be part of a montage. To begin work on the illustration, you decide to draw three paths, then use the 3D Revolve effect.

1. Open AI 11-13.ai, then save it as **Lava Lamp**.
2. Click the Selection Tool, then drag the three path segments so that they are aligned with the blue guide.
3. Hide the guides.
4. Select all, click Effect on the menu bar, point to 3D, then click Revolve.
5. Click the Preview check box, note the results, then click Cancel.
6. Group the three paths, apply the Revolve effect again, then click the Preview check box.
7. Click More Options, if necessary, apply Plastic Shading as the surface shading, then drag the Ambient Light slider to 45.
8. Click OK, deselect all, then compare your work to Figure 86.
9. Save your work, then close Lava Lamp.

FIGURE 86
Completed Project Builder 1

Creating 3D Objects

You are a designer for a game company, and you are designing the packaging for a chess game. You decide to use basic shapes and the 3D Revolve effect to create a graphic for the cover art.

FIGURE 87

Completed Project Builder 2

1. Open AI 11-14.ai, then save it as **Chess Pawn**.
2. Click the Selection Tool, then align each shape with the black rules.
3. Hide the Assembled layer, then verify that the Pawn Parts layer is targeted.
4. Select all on the Pawn Parts layer, then hide edges.
5. Click Effect on the menu bar, point to 3D, then click Revolve.
6. Click the Preview check box, note the results, then click Cancel.
7. Click the Horizontal Align Left button in the Align palette.
8. Press and hold [Alt] (Win) or [option] (Mac), then click the Add button in the Pathfinder palette.
9. Click Effect on the menu bar, point to 3D, click Revolve, then click the Preview check box.
10. Select the contents of the Specify rotation around the X axis text box, type **-57**, then click OK.
11. Click the White Pawn swatch in the Swatches palette, then compare your work to Figure 87.
12. Save your work, then close Chess Pawn.

Creating 3D Objects

You are a designer for a T-shirt company. Presently, your assignment is to develop shirts that feature peoples' names in 3D. To come up with a design, you experiment using your own name.

1. Create a new 8" × 8" document, then save it as **T-Shirt Text**.
2. Type your first name in a bold font at a large point size. (*Hint*: The typeface used in Figure 88 is 216 pt Antique Olive Bold Condensed.)
3. Change the fill color to something other than black.
4. Click Effect on the menu bar, point to 3D, then click Extrude & Bevel.
5. Click the Preview check box, then change the Extrude Depth value to one of your liking.
6. Choose a bevel shape that you like.
7. Click OK, then compare your work to Figure 88, which shows one possible result.
8. Save your work, then close T-Shirt Text.

FIGURE 88
Sample Completed Design Project

This group project is designed to challenge the group's ability to visualize simple paths and how they will appear when the 3D Revolve effect is applied. The group will look at nine graphics, all of which are simple paths to which the 3D Revolve effect has been applied. Each member of the group should take a piece of paper and a pencil and try to draw the simple path that is the basis for each graphic. Note that for each 3D graphic, no rotation or offset has been applied—each is the result of simply applying the 3D Revolve effect to a simple path. Note also that two of the simple paths are open paths, and the other seven are all closed paths.

1. Refer to Figure 89.
2. Look at Graphic #1, and try to visualize what it would look like if the 3D Revolve filter were removed.
3. Using a pencil and paper, draw the original path that was used to create the graphic.
4. Do the same for the remaining eight graphics.
5. Open AI 11-15.ai, then save it as **Mystery Shapes**.
6. Select each graphic, then delete the 3D Revolve effect from the Appearance palette.
7. Compare your pencil drawings to the graphics in the file.
8. Save Mystery Graphics, then close the file.

FIGURE 89
Reference for Group Project

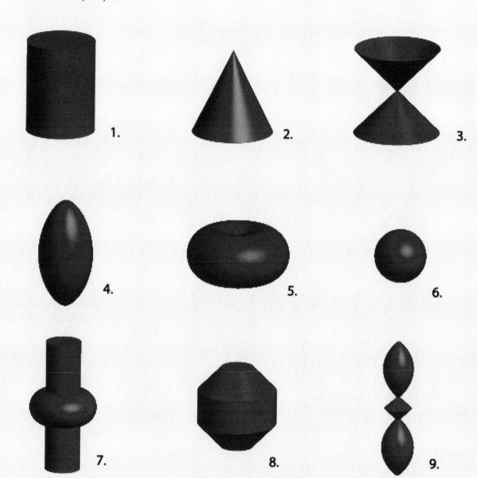

1.
2.
3.
4.
5.
6.
7.
8.
9.

chapter

12

PREPARING A DOCUMENT
FOR PREPRESS
AND PRINTING

1. Explore basic color theory.

2. Work in CMYK mode.

3. Specify spot colors.

4. Create crop marks.

5. Create bleeds.

12 PREPARING A DOCUMENT
FOR PREPRESS
AND PRINTING

Illustrator is so widely praised for its excellence as a drawing tool, it's easy to forget that the application is also a top-notch page layout solution. Illustrator CS2 is a powerhouse print production utility, a state-of-the-art interface with the world of professional prepress and printing. Everything that you need to produce an output-ready document is there—crop marks, trim marks, reliable process tints, the full PANTONE library of non-process inks—all backed by a sophisticated color separations utility. If you are new to the world of prepress and printing, Illustrator CS2 makes for an excellent training ground, with straightforward, easy-to-use palettes and dialog boxes. If you are experienced, you will admire how Illustrator seamlessly transitions from design and drawing to layout and output, thoughtfully and thoroughly encompassing the gamut of a printer's needs, demands, and wishes.

Tools You'll Use

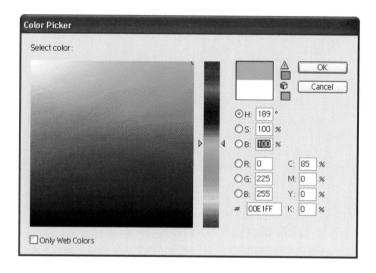

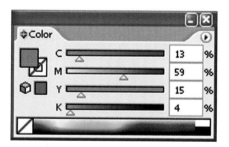

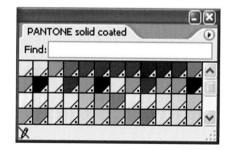

EXPLORE BASIC
COLOR THEORY

What You'll Do

 In this lesson, you will learn basic color theory to gain an understanding of the role of CMYK ink in offset printing.

Exploring Basic Color Theory

All of the natural light in our world comes from the sun. The sun delivers light to us in waves. The entirety of the sun's light, the electromagnetic spectrum, contains an infinite number of light waves—some at high frequencies, some at low frequencies—many of which will sound familiar to you. X-rays, gamma rays, and ultraviolet rays are all components of the electromagnetic spectrum.

The light waves that we see in our world are only a subset of the electromagnetic spectrum. Scientists refer to this subset—this range of wavelengths—as visible light. Because this light appears to us as colorless (as opposed to, say, the red world of the planet Mars), we refer to visible light as "white light."

From your school days, you may remember using a prism to bend light waves to reveal what you probably referred to as a rainbow. It is through this bending, or "breaking down" of white light, that we see color. The rainbow that we are all so familiar with is called the visible spectrum, and it is composed of seven distinct colors: red, orange, yellow, green, blue, indigo, and violet. Though the colors are distinct, the color range of the visible spectrum is infinite; for example, there's no definable place in the spectrum where orange light ends and yellow light begins.

Colors in the visible spectrum can themselves be broken down. For example, because red light and green light, when combined, produce yellow light, yellow light can, conversely, be broken down, or reduced, to those component colors.

Red, green, and blue light (RGB) are the additive primary colors of light, as shown in Figure 1. The term **primary** refers to the fact that red, green, and blue light cannot themselves be broken down or reduced. The term **additive** refers to the fact that these same colors combine to produce other colors. For example, red and blue light, when combined, produce violet hues. As primary colors, red, green, and blue light are the irreducible component colors

of white light. Therefore, it logically follows that when red, green, and blue light are combined equally, they produce white light.

Finally, you'll note that nowhere in this paradigm is the color black. That is because, in the natural world, there is no such color as black. True black is the absence of all light.

FIGURE 1

Red, green, and blue are the additive primary colors of light

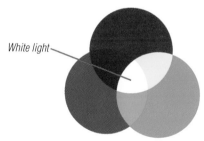

White light

Understanding Subtractive Primary Colors

Three things can happen when light strikes an object: the light can be reflected, absorbed, or transmitted, as shown in Figure 2.

Reflection occurs when light strikes an object and "bounces" off the object. Any object that reflects all of the light that strikes it appears as pure white.

Absorption occurs when light strikes an object and is not reflected, but instead is absorbed by the object. Any object that absorbs all of the light that strikes it appears as pure black.

Transmission occurs when light strikes an object and passes through the object. Any object that transmits all of the light that strikes it becomes invisible.

There are no truly invisible objects in our world (only some gasses are invisible). Nor are there any purely white or purely black objects. Instead, depending on the physical properties of the object, varying amounts of light are reflected, absorbed, and transmitted.

If an object absorbs some light, it logically follows that not all the white light that strikes the object will be reflected. Put another way, red, green, and blue light will not be reflected in full and equal amounts. What we perceive as the object's color is based on the percentages of the red, green, and blue light that are reflected and the color that that combination of light produces.

An object appears as cyan if it absorbs all of the red light that strikes it and also reflects or transmits all of the green and all of the blue light. An object that absorbs all of the green light that strikes it and also reflects or transmits all of the red and all of the blue light appears as magenta. An object that absorbs all of the blue light that strikes it and also reflects or transmits all of the red and all of the green light appears as yellow, as shown in Figure 3.

Cyan, magenta, and yellow are called **subtractive primary colors**. The term subtractive refers to the fact that each is produced by removing or subtracting one of the additive primary colors, and overlapping all three pigments would absorb all colors.

FIGURE 2

Visual representations of reflection, absorption, and transmission

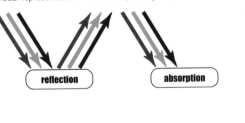
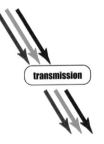

FIGURE 3

Printers often refer to cyan as "minus red," magenta as "minus green," and yellow as "minus blue"

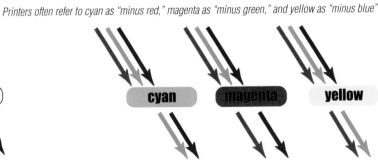

Understanding the Theory of Four-Color Process Printing

Color printing uses the three subtractive primary colors (plus black) to produce a color image or tint. To understand this, read the two points below carefully:

- The standard color for paper is white. The paper appears as white because it is manufactured to reflect RGB light in equal amounts.
- Cyan, magenta, and yellow inks are transparent—they are manufactured so that light passes through them. For example, cyan ink is manufactured to absorb red light and transmit green and blue light.

Here is the key to the whole theory: The color that you see when you look at a printed page is *not* reflected off the inks; it is light reflected off the paper. The light that is reflected off the paper is that which has not been absorbed (or *subtracted*) by the inks. Figure 4 demonsrates this concept.

FIGURE 4

The color of the printed image is reflected off the paper, not the inks

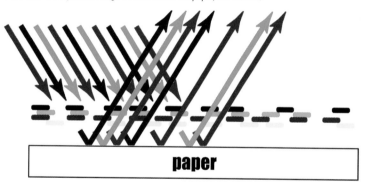

Creating a rich black

For many designers, black is the most powerful "color" in the palette. No other color can provide such contrast. Black can be used to trigger emotions. Black is neutral, but it's never silent. Use black ink (K) for text and lines and small areas of your artwork. When you have designed artwork with large black areas that you want to be dramatically black, keep in mind that black ink alone may not be enough to produce the effect. To produce deep blacks, printers create a process tint that is 100% K plus 50% C. The cyan ink overlapped with the black produces a dark, rich black . . . which is why printers refer to this tint as a "rich black." Keep the idea in mind when you are working with black, but remember also that rich blacks are never used for text or lines.

Understanding CMYK Inks

CMYK inks are called process inks. Process inks are manufactured by people, so by definition, they're not perfect. For example, no cyan ink can be manufactured so that it absorbs 100% of the red light that strikes it. Some is reflected, and some is transmitted, as shown in Figure 5. Perfect magenta and yellow inks cannot be manufactured either. In addition, an ink's ability to transmit light is not perfect. That same cyan ink should, if it were a true cyan, transmit both blue and green light. Manufactured cyan inks actually absorb a small percentage of blue and green light.

These imperfections become crucial when you try to use cyan, magenta, and yellow (CMY) to print dark areas of an image. In theory, if you overlapped all three inks, the area would appear black because each would absorb an additive primary, and no light would be reflected off the paper, as shown in Figure 6.

FIGURE 5
Cyan ink in theory vs. reality

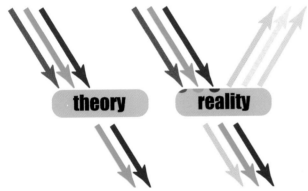

FIGURE 6
If "perfect" inks were overlapped, no light would be reflected; the area of the overlap would appear black

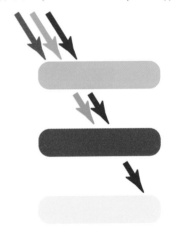

Because, in reality, the inks are unable to achieve 100% absorption and some light gets through and is reflected off the paper, CMY inks are unable to produce satisfactory shadows and dark areas of an image, as shown in Figure 7.

FIGURE 7

In reality, CMY inks are insufficient to produce black areas

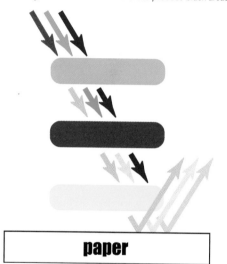

To compensate, black ink is used to produce deep shadows and fine detail. Printers refer to black ink as "K." They do not refer to it as "B" because "B" could be confused with blue, and blue could be confused with cyan. Also, printers have long referred to black as the "key" for aligning (registering) the four colors. Thus, the K in CMYK, though not a subtractive primary, is nevertheless essential to the subtractive printing process, as shown in Figure 8.

FIGURE 8

The image on the left was printed with only CMY inks; black ink adds contrast and depth to the image on the right

Coping with color confusion

If all of this color theory talk is making your head spin, don't worry about it. Working in Illustrator and producing a printed project *does not require* that you have these theories in your head. As you become more experienced with the printing process (and if you generally like this kind of stuff), these concepts will make more sense. Until then, remember the two essential points of this discussion: The offset printing process uses transparent CMYK inks; the color you see on a printed page is reflected off the paper, not the inks.

WORK IN
CMYK MODE

What You'll Do

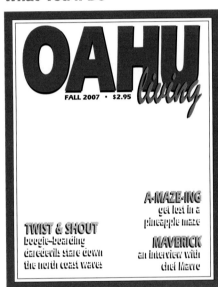

In this lesson, you will use Illustrator's Color Picker, Color palette, and print options in CMYK Color mode.

Understanding Color Gamut

RGB, CMYK, and HSB are all known as **color models**. The **color mode** determines the color model used to display and print Illustrator documents. Illustrator offers two color modes for documents: RGB and CMYK.

As we've discussed, offset color printing is based on the CMYK color model. All light-emitting devices, such as your television or your monitor, produce color based on the RGB color model. If you flick a drop of water at your television screen, you will be able to see that the image is composed of very small red, green, and blue pixels. The full range of color that you perceive when you watch TV is the result of the additive properties of light; the red, green, and blue light are combining to produce the image.

Color gamut refers to the range of colors that can be printed or displayed by a given color model. A good monitor, based on the RGB color model, can produce a color gamut of more than 16 million colors. However, the spectrum of colors that can be viewed by the human eye is wider than any man-made method for reproducing color.

Setting up color management

For the print and prepress professional, Illustrator's Color Settings dialog box simplifies the goal of setting up a color-managed workflow by bringing most of the standard color management controls to a single place. The predefined configurations offer a set of color management options that are designed to achieve color consistency in a production workflow. In most cases, the predefined color settings will provide enough color management controls to meet the demands of a prepress environment.

The CMYK color model is substantially smaller than the RGB color model. Therefore, when you are creating computer graphics, remember that some colors that you can see on your monitor cannot be reproduced by the CMYK printing process.

Illustrator addresses this reality in different ways. For example, if you are working in RGB mode and choosing colors in the Color Picker or the Color palette, Illustrator will warn you if you have chosen a color that is "out-of-gamut"—that is, a color that cannot be printed. Also, if you have created an image in RGB mode and you convert to CMYK mode, Illustrator will automatically replace the out-of-gamut colors applied to images with their closest CMYK counterparts.

As shown in Figure 9, the colors in RGB that are out-of-gamut for the CMYK color model are the brightest, most saturated, and most vibrant hues.

Don't despair. As you have certainly noted from looking at art books, posters, and even some high-quality magazines, the CMYK color model can be used to reproduce stunning color images. (Note: Because this book is a printed product and therefore based on the CMYK color model, we are unable to show you examples of out-of-gamut colors.)

FIGURE 9
CMYK color model is unable to reproduce the brightest and most saturated hues that you can see on your screen

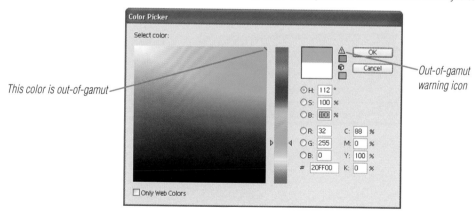

Specifying CMYK Tints

Tints are, quite simply, colors that you print by mixing varying percentages of CMYK inks. The lightest colors are produced with small percentages of ink, and darker colors with higher percentages. You can purchase process tint books that show you—with a high degree of fidelity—a large number of the color combinations available in the CMYK gamut.

In Illustrator, you specify CMYK tints by entering percentages in the Color Picker and the Color palette, as shown in Figure 10. If this idea is setting off alarms in your head . . . good for you! All the color produced by your monitor is based on the RGB color model. By definition, you cannot "see" the CMYK color model (or real CMYK tints, for that matter) on your monitor.

In the early days of desktop publishing, this contradiction generated enormous fear in the hearts of print professionals and created an entire cottage industry of color calibration hardware and software. Despite the dire

FIGURE 10

Specifying a process tint in the Color palette

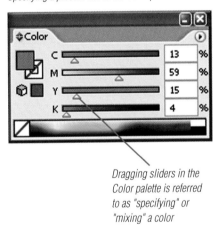

Dragging sliders in the Color palette is referred to as "specifying" or "mixing" a color

Preparing a Document for Prepress and Printing

warnings, however, color calibration problems turned out to be a phantom menace; simply put, the majority of print work produced is not so color-critical that variation in color is a problem (if the variation is even noticed).

Practically speaking, you must accept that the colors in your illustration on-screen will *never* be an exact match to the printed version. However, the numbers that you enter when specifying percentages of CMYK are *exactly* the percentages that will be output when the illustration goes to the printer. Therefore, if you *must* have a specific tint, find the color in a process tint book, and enter the percentages as specified. Then, don't worry about how the tint looks on your screen. If it looks close, that's great. If not, it doesn't matter. The printer is contractually responsible to be able to reproduce the tint that you specified.

Printing transparent artwork

Whenever you have a document with transparent objects (objects whose opacity is set to less than 100%), you should be sure to check the transparency preferences before printing the file. When you print or save artwork that contains transparency, Illustrator performs a process called flattening. When flattening, Illustrator identifies transparent artwork, then isolates the areas that are overlapped by the transparent object by dividing the areas into components. Illustrator then analyzes those components to determine if they can be output with vector data or if they must be rasterized (converted to pixels). The flattening process works very well in most cases. However, if you are unsatisfied with the appearance of the high-resolution output, you may want to step in and rasterize the artwork yourself. Before outputting the file, you can use Illustrator's Overprint Preview mode (found on the View menu), which approximates how transparency and blending will appear in color-separated output.

Specify process tints in the Color Picker

1. Open AI 12-1.ai, then save it as **Oahu**.

2. Select the placed image, then hide it.

3. Double-click the **Fill or Stroke button** in the toolbox to open the Color Picker, then type **189** for the hue, **100** for the saturation, and **100** for the brightness.

   The out-of-gamut warning icon appears, as shown in Figure 11.

4. Click the **blue square** under the out-of-gamut warning icon.

   The closest process color is specified as the new fill color.

5. Click **OK** to close the Color Picker dialog box.

6. Add the new color to the Swatches palette, then name it **Maverick**.

You chose a color in the Color Picker that was out-of-gamut for CMYK. You chose the process match that the out-of-gamut warning offered as a new fill color, then added it to the Swatches palette.

FIGURE 11
Out-of-gamut warning in the Color Picker

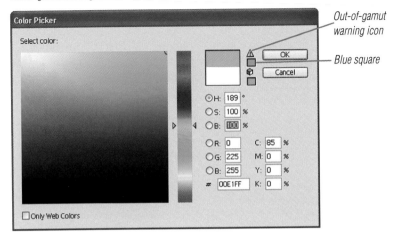

Out-of-gamut warning icon

Blue square

Using Type 1, TrueType and OpenType fonts

Type 1, TrueType and OpenType fonts are outline fonts used in both Macintosh and Windows operating systems. TrueType and Type 1 fonts offer great quality and are easy to use; however, they are incompatible on Macintosh and Windows platforms. For example, a Macintosh TrueType font is different from a Windows TrueType font and they are not cross-platform compatible. Adobe and Microsoft came up with OpenType fonts as the solution to font sharing. OpenType fonts use a single font file for Macintosh and Windows computers. This eliminates font substitution and text reflow problems. To make sure your fonts are compatible on both systems, open your Illustrator document on both a Macintosh and a Windows computer before you output the file.

Preparing a Document for Prepress and Printing

FIGURE 12

Applying process tints to the artwork

Mix process tints in the Color palette

1. Click **Window** on the menu bar, then click **Color** to show the Color palette, if necessary.

2. Click the **Color palette list arrow**, then click **CMYK**, if necessary.

3. Using the sliders on the palette, mix a process tint that is 5C/70M/100Y, then press [**Enter**] (Win) or [**return**] (Mac).

   In standard notation for process tints, zero is not specified. As there is no black in this tint, the K percentage is not noted.

   > TIP You will not see the new color in the Color palette if the cursor is still flashing in the last text box that you entered a new value in. Pressing [Tab] advances your cursor to the next text box.

4. Add the new color to the Swatches palette, then name it **Living**.

5. Mix a new process tint that is 5C/40M/5Y.

6. Add the new color to the Swatches palette, then name it **Amazing**.

7. Mix a new process tint that is 30M/100Y.

8. Add the new color to the Swatches palette, then name it **Twist**.

9. Apply the four new tints that you have added to the Swatches palette to the artwork, as shown in Figure 12.

10. Save your work.

You mixed three different process tints in the Color palette, saved them in the Swatches palette, then applied the four tints you have created so far in this chapter to the artwork.

SPECIFY SPOT COLORS

What You'll Do

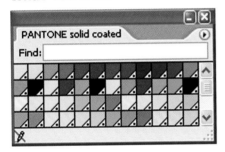

In this lesson, you will create and apply spot colors.

Understanding Spot Colors

Though printing is based on the four process colors CMYK, it is not limited to them.

Imagine that you are an art director designing the masthead for the cover of a new magazine. You have decided that the masthead will be an electric blue, vivid and eye-catching. If you were working with process tints only, you would have a problem. First, you would find that the almost-neon blue that you want to achieve is not within the CMYK gamut; it can't be printed. Even if it could, you would have an even bigger problem with consistency issues. You want that blue to be the same blue on every issue of the magazine, month after month. But process tints will vary on press; as the cover is printed, the blue color in the masthead will shift in tone, sometimes sharply.

Designers and printers use non-process inks to solve this problem. Non-process inks are special premixed inks that are printed separately from process inks. The color gamut of non-process inks available far exceeds that of CMYK. Non-process inks also offer consistent color throughout a print run.

Tabbing through the Color palette

The easiest way to mix process tints in the Color palette is to start out by double-clicking the C text box to select the current value, then enter the percentage of cyan that you want for the new tint. Press [Tab] to advance to the next text box, enter the new percentage, and so on. After you have entered the percentage in the B (black) text box, be sure to press [Tab] again. If you want to reverse direction, press and hold [Shift] while tabbing.

The print world refers to non-process inks by a number of names:

- Spot colors: Refers to the fact that non-process inks print on the "spots" of the paper where the process inks do not print.
- Fifth color: Refers to the fact that the non-process ink is often printed in addition to the four process inks. Note, however, that non-process inks are not necessarily the "fifth" color. For example, many "two-color" projects call for black plus one non-process ink.
- PANTONE color: Pantone is a manufacturer of non-process inks.
- PMS color: An acronym for PANTONE Matching System.

Loading Spot Colors

In Illustrator, you use the Swatch Libraries menu item to select from a range of color systems (or libraries), including PANTONE, the standard library for non-process inks. When you import the PANTONE library, it appears as a separate palette, as shown in Figure 13.

FIGURE 13
PANTONE solid coated library appears as a separate palette

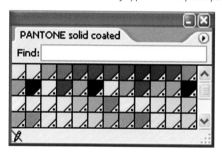

Rasterizing artwork

Illustrator is a vector-based drawing program; the graphics you create are called vector graphics. However, Illustrator is not exclusively vector-oriented, nor are Illustrator graphics limited to vectors. For a number of reasons, you may wish to convert a vector graphic into a bitmap graphic, a process called rasterization. If your Illustrator file is very complex, rasterizing it will convert it to a simple bitmap image. Output devices sometimes have trouble with complex objects and effects, such as gradient meshes and transparent objects. If you rasterize the graphic, you will see immediately if the effects translated properly. If so, the artwork is ready to print, as a simple, standard bitmap image. When rasterizing a vector graphic for output, whether for high-resolution printing or to appear on the Internet, you must determine the resolution (the number of pixels per inch) that the resulting bitmap will contain. You can input the desired resolution for the resulting bitmap file using the Document Raster Effects Settings dialog box. Click Document Raster Effects Settings on the Effect menu.

Outputting Documents with Spot Colors

All spot colors in the PANTONE library have a process match, which is of course a misnomer: if the process tint *matched* the spot color, there would be no need for the spot color in the first place. Some process tints—especially in the yellow hues—can come close to matching a spot color. Others—especially deep greens and blues—don't even come close.

When a four-color document is printed on a printing press, each of the four colors is printed separately: first yellow, then magenta, then cyan, then black. When an Illustrator document is output for printing, the document must be output as separations. Separations isolate each of the four process colors on its own "plate."

Clarifying resolution issues

The reckless misuse of the terms "resolution" and "DPI" by designers, printers, and even software programmers has resulted in widespread confusion over this concept and countless dollars and hours lost in struggling with files whose resolution settings are incorrect. And despite all of the confusion, the concepts are surprisingly simple and easy to understand. In general, when the term "resolution" is used, it is in reference to the number of pixels per inch in a bitmap image, or PPI. Unfortunately, seemingly everybody uses the term DPI instead of PPI; PPI is the only correct term for the resolution of a bitmap image. DPI stands for "dots per inch," which is the resolution of an output device. Dots are dots, and pixels are pixels; they are mutually exclusive. The resolution of your laser printer is probably 600 DPI or 1200 DPI, which is a satisfactory number of printing device dots to print text and lines that appear to be smooth. For bitmap images and blends, a minimum resolution of 2400 DPI is required for the output device to produce the smooth transitions of tone. Add to this confusion a third type of resolution, the resolution of a printed document. Lines per inch, LPI, or "line screen" is the number of lines of halftone dots (ink dots) in a printed image (professionally printed, not output from a desktop printer). Many printers refer to this resolution as, you guessed it, DPI, which is wholly incorrect. Lines are lines, and dots are dots. LPI is the only correct term for the resolution of a printed image. Standard line screens for color printing are 133 LPI and 150 LPI. A fluency with resolution terminology will help you in Illustrator when you want to rasterize a vector graphic (convert it to a bitmap image). When doing so, you must determine the resolution of the resulting bitmap image, the PPI. The PPI for a bitmap graphic that is to be used on the Internet is 72 PPI. The PPI for a bitmap graphic that is to be printed is twice the LPI.

When a color document is printed with four colors and a spot color, the spot color requires its own plate on the printing press so that the non-process ink can be laid down separately from the process inks.

In Illustrator, all spot colors that you use in a document will automatically be converted to their process match when separated, unless you *deselect* the Convert to Process option in the Separation Setup dialog box, which you access through the Print dialog box. See Figure 14.

See Figure 14.

FIGURE 14

Spot colors are converted to their process match when seperated

Understanding the output resolution of a vector graphic

Curved lines that you draw in Illustrator are, in terms of output, defined by small straight lines. "Curves" are made up of lines so small that your eye blends them together to create the appearance of a smooth curve. Therefore, the smaller the line segments, the smoother the curve. Of course, if the line segments are smaller, more of them are needed to draw the curve. Therefore, vector graphics have an output resolution, the number of line segments that will be used to draw the curve. Yet another term comes into play, and that is "flatness." The output resolution determines the flatness of the curve. A lower output resolution results in longer and fewer line segments to draw a curve. A higher output resolution increases the number of line segments and the file size. Sometimes, you will get a printer error if a document contains many long curved paths, simply because the file information is too much for the printer's processor to handle. In that case, you may want to reduce the default output resolution. Illustrator's default output resolution setting is 800 dots per inch (DPI). You can modify the flatness setting in the Graphics windows of the Print dialog box. In the Paths section of the window, drag the slider toward Quality for a lower flatness setting and a higher quality.

Import and apply spot colors

1. Click **Window** on the menu bar, point to **Swatch Libraries**, then click **PANTONE solid coated**.

   A new palette appears with small sample colors of each color in the library, as shown in Figure 15.

   > TIP You can purchase PANTONE swatch books from the Pantone Web site at *www.pantone.com*.

2. Click in the Find text box in the PANTONE solid coated palette.

   > TIP If the Find text box is not available, click the PANTONE solid coated palette list arrow, then click Show Find Field.

3. Type **663** in the Find text box.

   Color number 663 C is selected in the PANTONE solid coated palette.

   > TIP To display the number for each PANTONE color, click the PANTONE solid coated palette list arrow, then click List View.

   (continued)

FIGURE 15
PANTONE solid coated palette

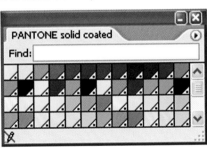

Preparing a Document for Prepress and Printing

FIGURE 16

Spot color applied to the artwork

4. Click the **OAHU letters**, then click the **PANTONE 663 C color swatch**.

   The PANTONE 663 C color swatch is added to the standard Swatches palette.

5. Double-click the **PANTONE 663 C swatch** in the standard Swatches palette.

6. Click the **Color Mode list arrow**, then click **CMYK**.

7. Note that Spot Color is listed as the Color Type in the Swatch Options dialog box.

8. Note the CMYK values.

   The CMYK values represent the values you would use to create the closest possible match of PANTONE 663 C with process inks.

9. Click **Cancel** to close the Swatch Options dialog box.

10. Change the fill of the red frame to PANTONE 663 C.

11. Show all, then send the placed image to the back.

   Your work should resemble Figure 16.

12. Save your work, then close the Oahu document.

You displayed the PANTONE solid coated library of swatches. You then applied a spot color to artwork.

CREATE CROP MARKS

What You'll Do

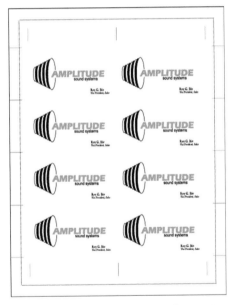

In this lesson, you will set up documents to print with crop marks and trim marks.

Creating Crop Marks

The **trim size** of a document refers to the size of the finished document. **Crop marks** are short, thin lines that define where the object is trimmed after it is printed. Figure17 shows crop marks around an image.

You can create custom-sized crop marks on the artboard by drawing a rectangle that is precisely the same size as the document's trim size. Then, keeping the rectangle selected, click Object on the menu bar, point to Crop Area, then click Make. Crop marks will replace the rectangle.

When the trim size and the document size (the size of the artboard) are the same, you don't need to create your own crop marks. In this case, you can add crop marks in the Print dialog box. Go to the Marks and Bleeds window in the Print dialog box, then check All Printer's Marks in the Marks section.

Editing Crop Marks

Once you've created crop marks, you cannot directly select them to edit them. Instead, you release them using the Release Crop Area command, edit the rectangle that defined the crop marks, then reapply the Make Crop Area command.

Using the Create Crop Marks Filter

Crop marks define where a printed image should be trimmed. You can create multiple marks using the Create Crop Marks filter on the Filter menu. For example, when printing business cards, printers use a standard-sized 8.5" × 11" sheet of paper. Printing a single business card on that size paper would be an absurd waste, so printers position multiple copies of the card, usually eight or ten, on the same sheet. Each of those copies must be trimmed as shown in Figure 18.

To create multiple crop marks, select the object whose size represents the trim size, then apply the Create Crop Marks filter. Use the same method to apply crop marks to the remaining artwork on the page, one at a time.

FIGURE 17

Crop marks define the trim size of the artwork

FIGURE 18

Create Crop Marks filter creates marks for multiple cuts

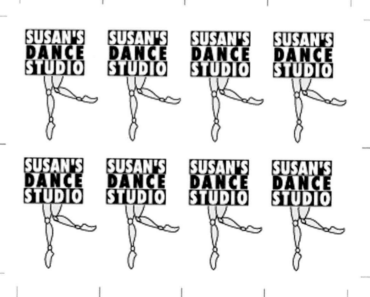

Create crop marks

1. Open AI 12-2.ai, then save it as **Crop Marks**.

2. Click **View** on the menu bar, then click **Business Card**.

   The view of the artwork is enlarged.

3. Select the 2" × 3.5" rectangle.

   2" × 3.5" is the standard size for business cards.

   > TIP Switch to Outline mode if you have trouble selecting the rectangle.

4. Click **Object** on the menu bar, point to **Crop Area**, then click **Make**.

   The rectangle is converted into crop marks that define the trim size as that of the rectangle. Your screen should resemble Figure 19.

5. Save your work, then close the Crop Marks document.

You selected a rectangle, then you applied the Make Crop Area command.

FIGURE 19
Applying crop marks

Roy G. Biv
Vice President, Sales

Preparing a Document for Prepress and Printing

FIGURE 20

Applying crop marks

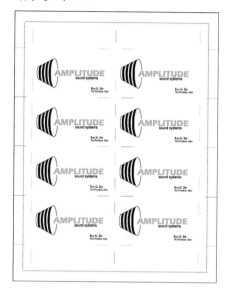

FIGURE 21

Delete crop marks that lie on trim lines

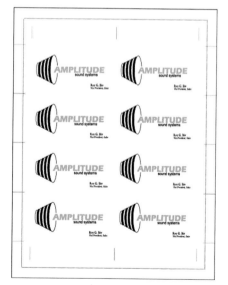

1. Open AI 12-3.ai, then save it as **Multiple Crop Marks**.

2. Select all, cut the objects, then paste them.

   | TIP   Cutting and pasting artwork centers it on the artboard.

3. Switch to Outline mode, deselect, then select the rectangle of the top-left card.

4. Click **Filter** on the menu bar, point to **Create**, then click **Crop Marks**.

   Unlike the Make Crop Area command, when the Create Crop Marks filter is applied, the selected rectangle is not deleted and the trim marks can be selected.

5. Delete the rectangle only.

6. Select the next rectangle down, click **Filter** on the menu bar, click **Apply Crop Marks** at the top of the menu, then delete the rectangle.

   The last filter used always appears at the top of the Filter menu.

7. Repeat the instructions in Step 6 to create crop marks for the six other business cards.

8. Switch to Preview mode, then compare your screen to Figure 20.

9. Use the Direct Selection Tool ▸ to delete all of the crop marks that are positioned on the inner trim of the business cards, leaving only the outer marks, as shown in Figure 21.

   Crop marks should be positioned only "off the artwork."

10. Save your work, then close the document.

You applied crop marks to eight objects.

CREATE
BLEEDS

What You'll Do

In this lesson, you will modify artwork to accommodate bleeds.

Creating Bleeds and Safety Guides

Artwork that extends to the trim is referred to as a "bleed" element, or simply a **bleed**, based on printer lingo meaning that to print correctly, the ink must bleed off the page.

Imagine that you have designed a business card that shows white lettering against a black background. You have used the Make Crop Area command so that the marks define the "live area" as 2" × 3.5". When the cards are trimmed, if the cutter is off by the slightest amount, $\frac{1}{10}$ of an inch, for example, your black business card will have a white line on one edge.

To accommodate variations in trimming, a printer will ask you to "build a bleed." What he or she is asking you to do is to extend bleed artwork so that it exceeds the cropped area by a minimum of .125". Artwork can bleed off any one or all four sides of the trim. Two of the most straightforward ways of doing this are to create a bleed object with the Offset Path command, or to extend the existing artwork off the artboard using the Move command for precision. Figure 22 shows an example of using bleeds.

In addition to bleeds, as a designer you should be conscious of your safety margin. All elements that aren't designed to bleed should be kept a minimum of .125" from the trim edge. This practice is known as maintaining safety or type safety. As with bleeds, safety guides anticipate variations in the trim cut and are designed to keep artwork from being accidentally trimmed off the page.

FIGURE 22
Bleeds extend the crop marks to accommodate variations when trimming

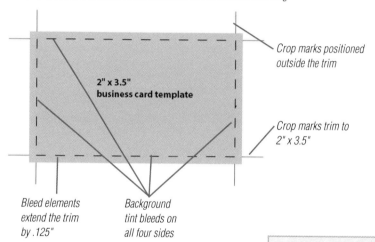

2" x 3.5"
business card template

Crop marks positioned
outside the trim

Crop marks trim to
2" x 3.5"

Bleed elements
extend the trim
by .125"

Background
tint bleeds on
all four sides

Exporting Illustrator files to QuarkXPress and InDesign
Throughout this book, we have been regarding Illustrator as a drawing tool—software that you can use to create an illustration. Adobe has designed Illustrator to also play the role of a page layout application. However, despite Illustrator's excellence, Adobe InDesign and QuarkXPress hold the distinction of being the preeminent page layout applications. Both InDesign and Quark import Illustrator files easily. Because InDesign, like Illustrator, is an Adobe product, InDesign will import an Illustrator file in its "native" Illustrator ".ai" format. To save an Illustrator file that is to be placed in QuarkXPress, save the Illustrator file as an Illustrator EPS (Encapsulated Post Script). QuarkXPress recognizes Illustrator files only in the Illustrator EPS format. If you have used spot colors in the Illustrator file, Quark will recognize this and automatically list the spot colors in its own color palette.

Create a bleed using the Offset Path command

1. Open AI 12-4.ai, then save it as **Oahu Bleed**.

2. Select the frame of the artwork that is filled with PANTONE 663 C.

3. Click **Object** on the menu bar, point to **Path**, then click **Offset Path**.

4. Type **.125** in the Offset text box, then click **OK**.

   The Offset Path command creates a new object, in this case, a bleed object that extends the artboard .125" on all sides. Your artwork should resemble Figure 23.

5. Verify that the new bleed object is still selected, then send it to the back.

6. Save your work, then close the Oahu Bleed document.

You used the Offset Path command to extend the edges of a bleed object .125".

FIGURE 23

A bleed object created with the Offset Path command

.125" bleed —

FIGURE 24
Three sides of the blue rectangle must bleed

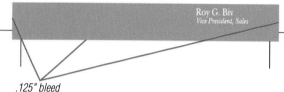

.125" bleed

FIGURE 25
The rule, too, must bleed

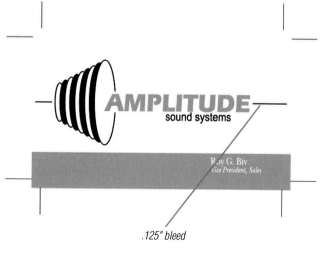

.125" bleed

Create a bleed using the Move command

1. Open AI 12-5.ai, then save it as **Three Sided Bleed**.

2. Click **View** on the menu bar, then click **Business Card**.

3. Select the black-stroked rectangle, click **Object** on the menu bar, point to **Crop Area**, then click **Make**.

4. Click the **Direct Selection Tool** , then click the bottom edge of the blue rectangle.

5. Click **Object** on the menu bar, point to **Transform**, click **Move**, type **0** in the Horizontal text box, type **-.125** in the Vertical text box, then click **OK**.

6. Select the left edge of the blue rectangle, then move it -.125" to the left.

7. Select the right edge of the blue rectangle, then move it .125" to the right.

   The blue rectangle bleeds on all three sides, as shown in Figure 24.

8. Select *only* the left anchor point of the black line, then move the point -.125" horizontally.

9. Select *only* the right anchor point of the black line, then move the point .125" horizontally, so that your work resembles Figure 25.

10. Save your work, then close the Three Sided Bleed document.

You extended individual lines and anchor points outside the crop marks as bleeds.

Explore basic color theory.

1. List the seven distinct colors of the visible spectrum.
2. What are the three additive primary colors?
3. What are the three subtractive primary colors?
4. When red, green, and blue light are combined equally, what color light do they produce?
5. Explain the term "subtractive" in terms of the subtractive primary colors.
6. Explain the term "transmission" in terms of light striking an object.
7. Which additive primary color would be 100% absorbed by a perfect cyan ink?
8. Which additive primary color would be 100% absorbed by a perfect magenta ink?
9. Which additive primary color would be 100% absorbed by a perfect yellow ink?
10. What is the fourth color in the four-color printing process, and why is it necessary?

Work in CMYK mode.

1. Open AI 12-6.ai, then save it as **Sleep Center**.
2. Using the Color palette, create a new process tint that is 55M/75Y.
3. Save the process tint in the Swatches palette as **Tagline color**.
4. Fill the words THE SLEEP CENTER with the Tagline color swatch.
5. Deselect the text, then save your work.

Specify spot colors.

1. Click Window on the menu bar, point to Swatch Libraries, then click PANTONE solid coated.
2. Select the object with the gradient on the artboard.
3. Select the black color stop on the gradient slider in the Gradient palette.
4. Press [Alt] (Win) or [option] (Mac), then click a purple swatch in the PANTONE solid coated palette.
5. Save your work.

Create crop marks.

1. Copy the rectangle with the gradient fill, then paste in front.
2. Select the copied rectangle, click Object on the menu bar, point to Crop Area, then click Make.
3. Save your work.

Create bleeds.

1. Click the left edge of the rectangle with the Direct Selection Tool.
2. Click Object on the menu bar, point to Transform, then click Move.
3. Type **-.125** in the Horizontal text box, type **0** in the Vertical text box, then click OK.
4. Select the top edge of the rectangle.
5. Open the Move dialog box, type **0** in the Horizontal text box, type **.125** in the Vertical text box, then click OK.
6. Select the right edge of the rectangle.
7. Open the Move dialog box, type **.125** in the Horizontal text box, type **0** in the Vertical text box, then click OK.
8. Save your work, then compare your illustration to Figure 26.

FIGURE 26
Completed Skills Review

Preparing a Document for Prepress and Printing

You work in the computer department at a small print shop. Your boss brings you an Illustrator file for a business card for USAchefs, an Internet company that works with the top chefs and restaurants in the city. Your boss asks you to create a print proof, which she will show to the customer. She asks you to create a rich black, add crops, and build a bleed, then says, with a wink, "But not necessarily in that order." You realize that she's challenging you to figure out the right order in which to get all three processes accomplished.

1. Open AI 12-7.ai, then save it as **USAchefs**.
2. Copy the black rectangle, then paste in front.
3. Use the copied black rectangle to make crop marks.
4. Select the new black rectangle, then use the Offset Path command to offset the path .125".
5. Keeping the new object selected, increase the cyan portion of its fill color 50% to create a rich black.
6. Delete the original (smaller) black rectangle.
7. Save your work, then compare your illustration to Figure 27.
8. Close the USAchefs document.

FIGURE 27
Completed Project Builder 1

You own a design firm in a small town. A new client delivers his logo to you on disk, telling you that it has two colors: PANTONE 255 and 70% PANTONE 5767. He tells you, "It's all set to go." You know that this client knows only enough to be dangerous. You open his file and, sure enough, you note immediately that all of the tints are process tints. You must change the fills and strokes to the proper PANTONE colors. Because this is a complex logo, and because you know that your client's knowledge of Illustrator is limited, you are aware that you must be very careful not to miss any elements.

1. Open AI 12-8.ai, then save it as **City Square Associates**.
2. Apply the Show All command, just to avoid any potential surprises.
3. Delete the green letters.
4. Display the PANTONE solid coated palette.
5. Select the letter C in the center.
6. Click Select on the menu bar, point to Same, then click Fill Color.
7. Apply PANTONE 255 C to the fill, then hide the selection (*Hint*: If the Find Field text box does not work, you'll have to scroll around to find the correct swatch.)
8. Select the top white rectangle.
9. Click Select on the menu bar, point to Same, then click Stroke Color.
10. Apply PANTONE 255 C to the stroke, then hide the selection.

11. Click the green square in the center, then change the black stroke to PANTONE 255 C.
12. Click Select on the menu bar, point to Same, then click Fill Color.
13. Apply PANTONE 5767 C to the fill.
14. Display the Color palette, if necessary, then drag the slider to 80%.

FIGURE 28
Completed Project Builder 2

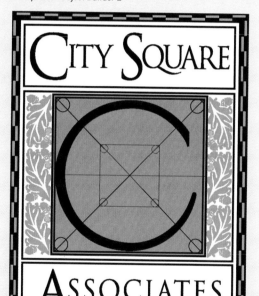

15. Hide the selection.
16. Select all and note that all the remaining items have a white fill.
17. Show all, save your work, then compare your illustration with Figure 28.
18. Close the City Square Associates document.

Preparing a Document for Prepress and Printing

You are the assistant art director for OAHU magazine. The art director tells you that, at the last minute, the editor in chief has changed the cover photo. You place the new photo in the Illustrator file and realize immediately that the colors that worked so well with the previous photo no longer work with this new photo.

1. Open AI 12-9.ai, then save it as **Oahu 2**.
2. Choose a new PANTONE color for the title and the frame.
3. Mix a new process tint, then apply it to the word "living".
4. Mix three new process tints, then apply them to the three subheads.
5. Save your work, compare your illustration with Figure 29, then close Oahu 2.

FIGURE 29
Completed Design Project

You are the head of the film output department for a small printer. You receive an Illustrator file for the business card for USAchefs. The file is complete with a rich black, crop marks, and bleeds. With so many years' experience, you know how best to lay out and print standard-sized business cards for maximum cost-effectiveness. However, you have a group of six new workers whom you hired for the third shift, and you realize that the issues involved with preparing this job would make for a great lesson.

1. Open AI 12-10.ai, then save it as **Chef Output**.
2. Have two group members discuss the most cost-efficient layout for the card on an 8.5" × 11" sheet. How many cards can be positioned on the sheet while still keeping a minimum .25" margin on all sides?
3. Once the group has calculated the number of cards that can fit on the page, ask them to calculate the size of the total area (without bleeds) covered by the artwork.
4. Note for the group that a bleed and crop marks have already been created in the file. Ask two group members to explain why both will need to be removed for the new layout.
5. Ask two other group members to study the parameters as listed above and then to explain to the group the best strategy for creating the bleed once the cards are laid out and the crop marks are in place.
6. Position 12 cards (4 across, 3 down) on the 8.5" × 11" page, then add crop marks and bleeds.
7. Change the document size to 11" × 17"
8. Save your work, then compare your document to Figure 30.
9. Close the Chef Output document.

FIGURE 30
Completed Group Project

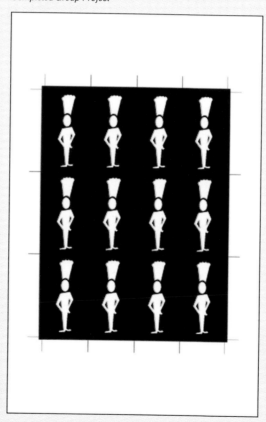

13

PREPARING GRAPHICS
FOR THE WEB

1. Create slices.

2. Specify slice type and slice options.

3. Use the Save for Web dialog box.

4. Create an image map.

13 PREPARING GRAPHICS
FOR THE WEB

Illustrator CS2 represents a giant step forward for creating Web graphics. We have all become familiar with the standard look for a Web page: headline across the top, a colored margin with links on the left, standard typefaces, and large blocks of HTML text flowing down the page. Illustrator CS2 shatters this standard and introduces nothing less than a new concept for a Web page: an artboard! Illustrator CS2 offers you the freedom to create a Web page entirely in Illustrator, with all the power

and sophistication that the application has to offer. You can then save your artwork—export your document—as a Web page, complete with links, HTML text, and bitmap images. Illustrator has defined a new approach for Web design, one that is free from the constraints of producing a page from scratch with HTML code. For the designer, this approach offers a dramatic advance for originality and personal expression on the Web.

Tools You'll Use

Slice Tool — Slice Selection Tool

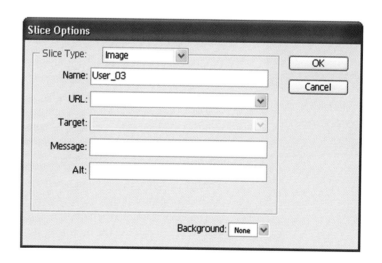

CREATE SLICES

What You'll Do

In this lesson, you will create slices using guides. You will also combine slices.

Understanding Web Graphics

When you create graphics for the Web, you will need to pay attention to different considerations than you would when designing graphics for print. The Web is an entirely different medium, and you will be required to become familiar with, if not fluent in, many issues.

Color is an essential consideration when producing Web graphics. Since a computer's monitor functions as a light source, it produces color based on the additive model; color is created by combining light. Thus, graphics that you create must be saved in RGB mode.

For the designer, this is good news: The RGB color gamut is much larger than the CMYK color gamut. When designing for the Web, you can use the brightest, most saturated colors. However, the colors you see on your artboard aren't necessarily the colors that will appear in your Web browser. Color choices, file formats, and the degree of compression all affect the appearance of color.

Resolution is an essential consideration when using bitmap graphics on the Web. If you place a bitmap graphic in your Illustrator file, remember that 72 pixels per inch (PPI) is the standard resolution for bitmap graphics on the Web.

Two essential considerations when choosing the correct file format for your Web graphics are file size and display characteristics. Two standard compression file formats for bitmap graphics—JPEG and GIF—both reduce file size significantly, but through dramatically different processes. Knowing which to choose, and then choosing the degree to which each compresses the file, require understanding and experience.

Understanding Sliced Artwork

When you create graphics for the Web, file size is a fundamental consideration. Smaller file sizes enable Web servers to store and transmit images more efficiently, and allow viewers to download images more quickly.

When creating graphics for the Web, you often find that the file size of the entire document is far too large to be acceptable. For this reason, Illustrator allows you to divide your work into slices: You literally divide the artwork into areas to be output as individual—and therefore smaller—files.

Imagine a 100-piece puzzle whose pieces are all rectangular. Imagine that the entire puzzle, when put together, weighs exactly one pound. It would stand to reason that each of the 100 pieces weighs far less than one pound. This is a good analogy for understanding sliced artwork. Each slice is like a piece of the puzzle, smaller in area and—more importantly—smaller in size.

The analogy is not apt in one area: When a puzzle is completed, you can see the lines between the pieces. With sliced artwork, the slices in the work are invisible when it is viewed in a Web browser.

Slices provide another important function. Web pages can contain many different kinds of elements, such as HTML text and bitmap images. In Illustrator, if you use slices to divide the different elements, you can then output them differently. For example, if you create a slice that contains a bitmap image and another that contains HTML text, you can output the bitmap slice as a JPEG file and the text slice as an HTML file.

QUICKTIP

You can save illustrations as SVG Tiny. SVG Tiny is a smaller, more limited version of the SVG file format. SVG Tiny is the file format used in small devices, such as mobile phones. This file format does not support gradients, SVG filters, symbols, clipping masks, and transparency. You save a file as SVG Tiny by first saving it as an SVG format, then clicking More Options in the SVG Options dialog box.

Creating Slices with the Make Slice Command and the Slice Tool

The Make Slice command creates a slice whose dimensions match those of the bounding box of the object. This command also creates a slice that captures text with its basic formatting characteristics. With the Make Slice command, the object is the slice, and vice versa. If you move or modify the object, the slice automatically adjusts to encompass the new artwork.

The Slice Tool allows you to draw a rectangular slice anywhere on the artboard. Slices that you create with the Slice Tool are independent of the underlying artwork. In other words, if you move the artwork, the slice does not move with the artwork.

Whether you use the Make Slice command or the Slice Tool to create slices, Illustrator generates automatic slices that cover the remainder of the artboard. Illustrator does this to create a complete HTML table, in case the document is saved as a Web page.

In Figure 1, slice 3 was drawn with the Slice Tool. Slices 1, 2, and 4 were generated automatically.

Put quite simply, automatic slices are cumbersome, tricky, and hard to work with. Every time you add or edit slices, Illustrator must regenerate automatic slices; thus, the slice pattern on the artboard continues to change.

FIGURE 1
Slice 3 was created with the Slice Tool; slices 1, 2, and 4 were generated automatically

Creating Slices from Guides

You can use standard ruler guides to define how you want artwork to be divided into slices. Figure 2 shows three guides that were positioned so as to isolate the graphic of the dog.

By definition, guides extend across and beyond the artboard. Therefore, when you use guides to define areas to be sliced, the length of the guide can get in the way. For example, the two vertical guides in Figure 2 extend up beyond the dog area into the headline. Thus, the headline is unnecessarily divided into three sections.

This problem can sometimes seem extreme. Figure 3 shows two additional horizontal guides positioned on the artwork to isolate each of the three photos and their corresponding text on the right. Each will be used as a link that will take the viewer to a different page. Therefore, it is necessary to create a slice for each link. Note, however, that the horizontal guides extend across the dog area, dividing that artwork into three parts.

FIGURE 2
Guides isolate the dog graphic into its own area

Horizontal guide

Two vertical guides

FIGURE 3
Two additional horizontal guides divide the dog graphic into three sections

When you apply the Create from Guides command, Illustrator generates slices for each area defined by a guide, as shown in Figure 4. Twelve slices are unnecessary to save this artwork for the Web. For example, slices 04, 07, and 10, if combined, could be saved as a very small file. Also, one might want to try to save the dog graphic as one file. Breaking the dog artwork into three slices runs the risk that each slice might vary slightly in color because of the file format and the compression that is applied.

FIGURE 4
The Create from Guides command generates only slices—no automatic slices

Note, however, that each slice . . . is a slice! The Create from Guides command generates only slices—no automatic slices. Each slice can be selected with the Slice Selection Tool. Therefore, slices can be easily combined, as shown in Figure 5.

Of the three main ways that Illustrator offers for making slices, using guides and then combining excess slices is the simplest, most straightforward, and hassle-free method.

FIGURE 5
Slices can be combined easily

Make slices

1. Open AI 13-1.ai, then save it as **SDS**.

2. Close all palettes except for the toolbox.

3. Change the style of the guides to Dots and the color of the guides to Yellow.

   TIP If you are using Macintosh OS 10, your preference settings are on the Illustrator menu.

4. Show the rulers, then position a guide on all four sides of the photo, as shown in Figure 6.

5. Position a vertical guide to the left of the three text buttons, then position another guide to the right of the three text buttons.

6. Position a horizontal guide above the purple text as shown in Figure 7.

7. Position a horizontal guide above and below the "purchase show tickets" button, as shown in Figure 8.

8. Verify that your guides are unlocked.

9. Select all, click **Object** on the menu bar, point to **Slice**, then click **Create from Guides**.

   Thirty slices are generated, as shown in Figure 9.

   TIP The View menu has commands to hide and show slices.

You positioned guides, then used them to create slices.

FIGURE 6
Positioning guides on all four sides of the photo

Position guides on all four sides of this photo

FIGURE 7
Positioning a guide above the text

Horizontal guide above text

FIGURE 8
Positioning guides above and below the "purchase show tickets" button

Purchase show tickets button

FIGURE 9
Thirty slices generated from guides

Preparing Graphics for the Web

FIGURE 10

Slices 06, 11, and 16 selected

Slices 06, 11, and 16

Combine slices

1. Click the **Selection Tool** ▸ , then click anywhere in the scratch area to deselect the slices.

2. Click the **Slice Selection Tool** ✄ .

   TIP The Slice Selection Tool is hidden beneath the Slice Tool.

3. Using [Shift], select slices 06, 11, and 16 as shown in Figure 10.

   TIP The easiest way to select a slice is to click the slice number.

4. Click **Object** on the menu bar, point to **Slice**, then click **Combine Slices**.

   The three slices are combined into one slice; all of the slices are renumbered, as shown in Figure 11.

5. Hide the guides.

6. Using the same method, combine the four slices that contain the purple text.

7. Combine the six black slices on the right-hand margin.

8. Combine the three slices that contain the photo.

9. Combine the five slices that contain the logo in the spotlight, so that your slices correspond to Figure 12.

10. Save your work.

You combined slices to create single slices for specific areas of the artwork.

FIGURE 11

Three slices combined into one

Newly combined slice

FIGURE 12

After combining slices, 14 slices remain

SPECIFY SLICE TYPE
AND SLICE OPTIONS

What You'll Do

 In this lesson, you will specify slices as Image or No Image, and you will add URL links to image slices.

Specifying Slice Types

A slice's type and the options assigned to it determine how the artwork contained in the slice will function on a Web page. A slice must be selected in order for you to assign a type and apply options to it. The Slice Options dialog box allows you to specify one of three categories for a slice's type. Basically, a slice's type defines its content.

The Image type is used when you want the content of a slice to become a linked image file on a Web page.

The No Image type is used when you want the area to contain text or a solid color. You enter the text or the color information directly into the Slice Options dialog box. You cannot view No Image slice content in Illustrator; you must use a Web browser to preview it.

Choosing between Image and No Image is not always as straightforward as it would at first seem. Consider slice 2 in Figure 13, for example. It contains no artwork, and

certainly would not function as a link. However, it does contain a background color—the same background color that is shared by all of the slices.

If you were to define the slice type of slice 2 as No Image, it would by default have no background color. If you saved the file for the Web, the content of slice 2 would appear white on the Web page. You could apply a background color in the Slice Options dialog box, and specify the color to have the same RGB values as the background color in the Image slices. This solution may work well. However, you also have the option of specifying slice 2's type as Image—a single color image with no links. In this case, slice 2 would be output using the same file format as the other slices, logically a safer bet for color consistency.

The third type of slice is HTML Text, which you use if you want to capture Illustrator text and its basic formatting. You can only create this type of slice using the Make Slice command.

Generally, you will use Illustrator to create display text—text that is intended to be used as a design element, such as a headline. Rather than saving display text as text for the Web, it is a smart decision to simply save a version of your artwork with display text converted to outlines and defined as an image. With this method, you know for certain that your text will appear exactly as you designed it, with no risk of its being modified by or being in conflict with a browser's preset preferences.

Setting Options for Image Content Slices

When you specify a slice as an Image slice, you have the following options in the Slice Options dialog box:

- **Name**: By default, the slice name is used as the file name when you save the Web page. By default, the slice is named with the slice number. It is a good idea to rename an important slice with a name that is more descriptive of its content.
- **URL**: Specify a URL to make the slice a hotspot on the Web page.
- **Target**: If you've specified a URL, the target specifies the frame that you want the link to target. You can enter the

name of a target frame, or you can use one of the standard targets in the pop-up menu. If you are unfamiliar with frames, note that _parent and _blank are the most common. _blank means that a new browser window will be opened, or "spawned," to show the linked page. _parent, the more standard of the two, means that the current window will change to show the linked page.

- **Message**: The information you type in the Message text box is what will appear in the status bar of a browser

window when you position your cursor over the corresponding image slice. Messages usually convey information about the current image, or information about what the image links to.

- **Alt**: Think of Alt as an "alternative" to an image. Alternative text is for sight impaired Web surfers. They will hear the alt text rather than see the image.
- **Background**: If you are saving a bitmap image with a transparent background, you can specify a color for the background behind the transparent areas.

FIGURE 13

Slice 2 could be specified as an Image or a No Image type

Setting Options for No Image Content Slices

In the Slice Options dialog box, you can set the following options:

- **Text**: In the Text Displayed in Cell text box, you can enter text that will appear in the slice. You can format the text using standard HTML tags. Be careful not to enter more text than can fit in the slice. If you do, the overflow will extend into neighboring slices. Because you cannot view the text in Illustrator, you will need to save the file for the Web and open it in a browser to view your work.

- **Alignment**: Use the Horiz and Vert list arrows to specify the horizontal and vertical alignment of the text.

- **Background**: Choose a background color for the slice.

FIGURE 14
Slice Options dialog box for slice 03

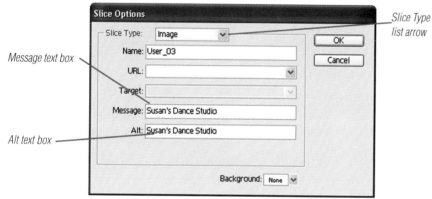

Message text box

Alt text box

Slice Type list arrow

1. Click the **Slice Selection Tool** , then click **slice 03**, if necessary.

2. Click **Object** on the menu bar, point to **Slice**, then click **Slice Options**.

3. Click the **Slice Type list arrow**, then click **Image**, if necessary.

4. Type **Susan's Dance Studio** in both the Message and Alt text boxes, as shown in Figure 14.

5. Click **OK** to close the Slice Options dialog box.

6. Click **File** on the menu bar, then click **Save** to update your slice numbers.

7. Click **slice 14**, click **Object** on the menu bar, point to **Slice**, click **Slice Options**, specify it as an Image slice, type **Fall registration** in the Message and Alt text boxes, click **OK**, then save.

8. Click **slice 01**, define it as No Image, click the **Background list arrow**, click **Black**, click **OK**, then save.

   The black background will be coded in HTML. If you wanted to use the underlying black object as the black background, you would specify the slice type as an image, just as you did the logo.

9. Repeat Step 8 to specify slices 02, 04, 05, 11, and 12 as No Image slices with a black background, one at a time.

   TIP You cannot apply Slice Options to multiple slices simultaneously.

You used the Slice Options dialog box to specify slices as Image slices and No Image slices.

Set options for image content slices

1. Click the **Slice Selection Tool** 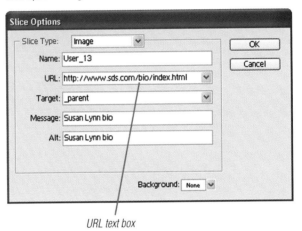, if necessary, click **slice 13**, click **Object** on the menu bar, point to **Slice**, then click **Slice Options**.

2. Click the **Slice Type list arrow**, then click **Image**, if necessary.

3. Type **http://www.sds.com/bio/index.html** in the URL text box.

   In a Web browser, clicking slice 13 will link to an HTML biography page.

4. Click the **Target list arrow**, then click **_parent**.

   In a Web browser, clicking slice 13 will change the current window to the HTML biography page.

5. Type **Susan Lynn bio** in the Message and Alt text boxes, as shown in Figure 15, click **OK**, then save.

   TIP Each time you make changes to a slice or combine slices, the slice numbering is thrown off. Saving your work reapplies the correct slice numbers to the slices.

   (continued)

FIGURE 15

Slice Options dialog box for slice 13

URL text box

FIGURE 16

Slice Options dialog box for slice 07

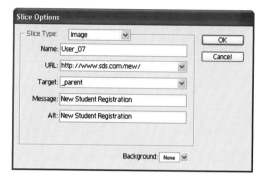

FIGURE 17

Slice Options dialog box for slice 09

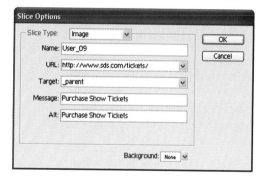

FIGURE 18

Slice Options dialog box for slice 10

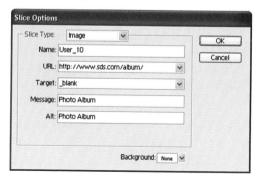

Lesson 2   Specify Slice Type and Slice Options

6. Click **slice 08**, open the Slice Options dialog box, repeat Steps 2–5 so that slice 08 contains the same slice information as slice 13, then save.

7. Click **slice 06**, open the Slice Options dialog box, verify that the Slice Type is set to Image, click **OK**, then save.

8. Click **slice 07**, open the Slice Options dialog box, type the information shown in Figure 16, click **OK**, then save.

9. Specify the slice options for slice 9 as shown in Figure 17, then save.

10. Specify the slice options for slice 10 as shown in Figure 18, then save.

Because the target for slice 10 is _blank, slice 10, when clicked, will open a new browser window for the photo album page.

You used the Slice Options dialog box to specify URLs to which the image slices will link when clicked in a browser application.

USE THE SAVE FOR WEB DIALOG BOX

What You'll Do

 In this lesson, you will optimize slices for the Web, using the Save for Web dialog box.

Optimizing Artwork for the Web

Most artwork, even when sliced, requires optimization. **Optimization** is a process by which the file size is reduced through standard color compression algorithms.

Illustrator CS2 offers a number of optimization features to save artwork in different Web graphics file formats. Your choice of a file format will have the greatest effect on the optimization method that is performed on the artwork.

The Save for Web dialog box presents unprecedented options for previewing images. The tabs at the top of the image area define the display options. The Original display presents the artwork with no optimization. The Optimized display presents the artwork with the current optimization setting applied. The 2-Up display presents two versions of the artwork—the original and the optimized version—side by side, and the 4-Up display presents the original beside three optimized versions.

Optimizing with the GIF File Format

GIF is a standard file format for compressing images with flat color, which makes it an excellent choice for many types of artwork generated in Illustrator. GIFs provide effective compression; for the right type of artwork, GIFs maintain excellent quality with crisp detail. In many cases, the compression has no noticeable effect on the image.

GIF compression works by lowering the number of colors in the file. The trick with GIFs is to lower the number of available colors as much as possible without adversely affecting the appearance of the image. Generally, if the number of colors is too low, problems with the image are obvious, as shown in Figure 19.

Optimizing with the JPEG File Format

JPEG is a standard file format for compressing continuous-tone images, gradients, and blends. JPEG compression relies on "lossy" algorithms—lossy referring to a loss of data. In the JPEG format, data is selectively discarded.

You choose the level of compression in the JPEG format by specifying the JPEG's quality setting. The higher the quality setting, the more detail is preserved. Of course, the more detail preserved, the less the file size is reduced.

When JPEG compression is too severe for an image, the problems with the image are obvious and very unappealing, as shown in Figure 20.

JPEG has emerged as one of the most used, if not the most used, file formats on the Internet. As a result, many designers ignore GIFs in favor of JPEGs, though many times GIFs would be the better choice.

FIGURE 19
A GIF file with too few colors available to render the image adequately

FIGURE 20
Problems with JPEGs are obvious and very unappealing

Optimize a slice as a JPEG

1. Click **File** on the menu bar, then click **Save for Web**.

2. Click the **Optimized tab**, if necessary.

   The Optimized view shows you the artwork with the current optimization settings applied.

3. Click the **Slice Select Tool** ![icon] in the Save for Web dialog box, click **slice 03**, click the **Preset list arrow**, then click **JPEG High**.

   The selected slice is updated.

4. Click the **4-Up tab**.

   The image area is divided into four views of the artwork. The upper-right window is selected.

5. Click the **Hand Tool** ![icon] in the Save for Web dialog box, then drag the upper-right window until all of slice 03 is visible, if necessary, as shown in Figure 21.

   | TIP Use the Zoom Tool to zoom in or out, if necessary.

6. Compare the file size of the original to the other three.

7. Compare the download times and quality settings, as listed in the upper-right and bottom windows.

8. Examine the three images.

   The quality of the lower-right image is unsatisfactory. Distracting pixels are visible at the edges of the logo and on the legs.

9. Click the **lower-left window**, click the **Quality list arrow**, then drag the **slider** to 40.

10. Keep the Save for Web dialog box open.

You used the 4-Up view of the Save for Web dialog box to compare three optimized JPEG files, each with different settings.

FIGURE 21
Save for Web dialog box

File size

Download time

Quality setting

FIGURE 22

Slice 14, optimized as a GIF using 8 colors

Color Table

Change in file size

1. Click the **Optimized tab**.

2. Click the **Slice Select Tool** , click **slice 06**, press and hold [**Shift**], then click **slice 13** to add it to the selection.

3. Click the **Preset list arrow**, then click **GIF 32 Dithered**.

4. Remove the check mark from the Transparency check box.

5. Deselect, click **slice 06** only, then click the **Color Table tab** to the right of the image window.

   The Color Table shows the 32 total colors that are used to represent the artwork.

6. Click **slice 14**, click the **Settings list arrow**, then click **GIF 32 No Dither**.

   Note the change to the swatches in the Color Table. Though the setting is for 32 colors, only 17 colors are required to reproduce the artwork.

7. Note the file size in the lower-left corner.

8. Click the **Colors list arrow**, then click **8**.

   Note the change in the Color Table and the change in file size, as shown in Figure 22. Note also the high quality of the artwork with only eight colors.

9. Remove the check mark from the Transparency check box.

10. Keep the Save for Web dialog box open.

You optimized a slice as a GIF. You lowered the number of colors available to draw the image, noting the changes in image quality and file size.

Lesson 3   Use the Save for Web Dialog Box

Compare and contrast JPEG vs. GIF formats

1. Click the **Slice Select Tool** 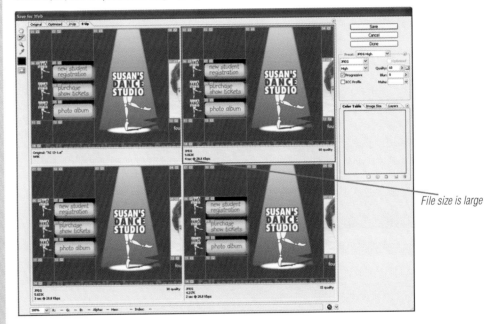, if necessary, click **slice 07**, press and hold [**Shift**],
   then click slices **09** and **10** to add them to
   the selection.

2. Click the **Preset list arrow**, click **JPEG High**,
   then click the **4-Up tab**.

3. Compare the quality of the three JPEGs to
   the original.

   The High quality JPEG in the upper-right
   window is the only version with acceptable
   quality. Note that the file size is over 9K, as
   shown in Figure 23.

   | TIP   Your file size may slightly differ.

4. Click the **Optimized tab**.

5. Click the **Preset list arrow**, click **GIF 128 No
   Dither**, then remove the check mark from
   the Transparency check box.

6. Click the **4-Up tab**, then use the Hand Tool,
   if necessary, to see as much of the three buttons as possible.

   (continued)

FIGURE 23

Slices 07, 09, and 10 optimized as a high-quality JPEG

File size is large

FIGURE 24

Slices 07, 09, and 10 optimized as a GIF

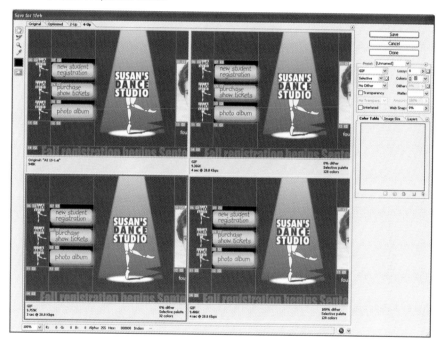

7. Click the **lower-left window**, then note that its Selective palette is 64 colors, one-half that of the image in the upper-right window.

8. Click the **Colors list arrow**, then click **32**.

   The Selective palette of the image in the lower-left corner is reduced by half, yet the quality remains acceptable.

9. Click the **Colors list arrow**, then click **16**.

   The reduced palette does not contain enough colors to represent the buttons' drop shadows smoothly.

10. Click the **Colors list arrow**, then click **32**.

    The file size is around 6 kilobytes—⅔ that of the acceptable JPEG—and the quality is almost indistinguishable from the original, as shown in Figure 24.

11. Keep the Save for Web dialog box open.

You experimented with optimizing a slice as both a JPEG and GIF, comparing file size and image quality. You found that the GIF format was able to optimize the slice with higher quality at a lower file size than the JPEG format.

Lesson 3   Use the Save for Web Dialog Box

Create photo effects with a GIF

1. Click the **Optimized tab**.

2. Click the **Slice Select Tool** 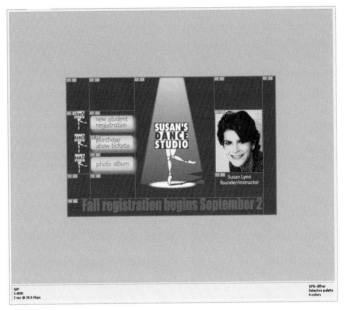, if necessary, then click **slice 08**.

3. Click the **Preset list arrow**, then click **GIF 32 Dithered**.

4. Click the **Color Table tab**, if necessary.

   The Color Table shows the 32 total colors that are used to present the photo in slice 08.

5. Click the **Colors list arrow**, then click **16**.

   The number of colors in the Color Table is reduced.

6. Click the **Colors list arrow**, click **8**, then note the effect on the photo and the file size shown in the lower-left corner of the dialog box.

7. Click the **Colors list arrow**, click **4**, click the **Dither list arrow**, then drag the **slider** to 10%.

8. Click the **Specify the dither algorithm list arrow**, then click **Noise** so that the photo resembles Figure 25.

9. Keep the Save for Web dialog box open.

You specified an Image slice as a GIF, then lowered the number of colors available to reproduce the image, noting the effect on the image. You then added noise as the type of dither algorithm to create a special effect.

FIGURE 25
An effect created by optimizing a photo as a GIF

FIGURE 26

Web page shown in a browser window

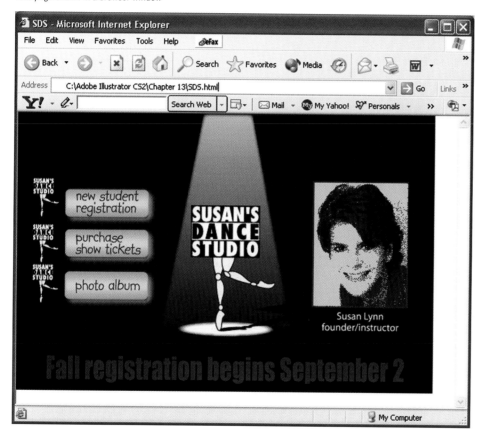

1. Click **Save**, name the file **SDS.html**, then click **Save**.

2. Launch your Web browser, such as Netscape or Internet Explorer.

   TIP If you do not have access to a Web browser, proceed to the next lesson.

3. Open SDS.html in your Web browser application.

4. Point to different images and note the messages that you entered in the Slice Options dialog box, in the status bar of the browser window.

   Your screen should resemble Figure 26.

5. Close (Win) or Quit (Mac) your browser, then save and close the SDS document.

You saved the file with the optimization settings that you specified in the Save for Web dialog box. You then viewed the HTML file in a Web browser application.

CREATE AN IMAGE MAP

What You'll Do

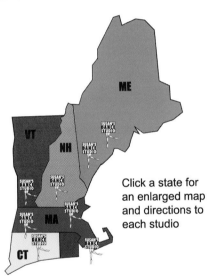

Click a state for
an enlarged map
and directions to
each studio

*In this lesson, you will change the colors
in an illustration to Web safe colors and
create polygonal image maps with URLs
attached to them for use on a Web page.*

Working with Web Safe Colors

Given all of the variables that might affect color display on the Internet—different monitors with different settings, different Web browsers with different settings, among many other conditions—you can never be certain that the colors that you specify in your document will appear the same way when viewed as a Web page. You can't even be certain that they'll be consistent from computer to computer. To alleviate this problem to some degree, Illustrator offers a Web Safe RGB mode in the Color palette and a Web swatch library. The Web swatch library contains predefined colors that are coded so as to be recognized by most computer displays, and by the common Web browser applications. When color is critical, it is best to think of the Web safe gamut as a safe bet for achieving reasonable consistency, understanding that a guarantee is a bit too much to expect.

Creating vector-based Web graphics

Though bitmap images are the most common graphics on the Web, vector-based graphics make for excellent Web graphics. Unlike bitmap graphics, which tend toward higher file sizes and lose quality when enlarged, vector graphics are scalable, compact, and able to maintain their image quality at different resolutions. The Macromedia Flash SWF file format supports vector graphics for the Web. SWF also recognizes symbols in your artwork. When the artwork is saved or exported as an SWF, each symbol is defined only once, which can substantially lower the file size. The SWF format also provides excellent support of complex Illustrator artwork, such as gradients, mesh objects, and patterns.

Understanding Image Maps

Image maps allow you to define an area of an illustration as a link. In a Web browser, when a user clicks the area of the image defined as a link, the Web browser loads the linked file.

Unlike using slices to create links, using image maps stores the artwork and the links in a single file; using slices causes artwork to be exported in different files. Another main difference is that slices are always rectangular, while image maps enable you to create links from polygons and odd-shaped objects, as shown in Figure 27.

Image maps are quite simple to make in Illustrator. The Attributes palette contains an Image list arrow, which allows you to choose a shape for your image map. You can then enter the URL for the link. The resulting image map is not visible—not in Illustrator and not in the browser. The area that the user clicks on the image map is also known as a **hotspot**.

FIGURE 27

Image maps enable you to define odd-shaped areas of an image as links to a URL

Choose Web safe colors

1. Open AI 13-2.ai, then save it as **New England Map**.

2. Show the Color palette, if necessary.

3. Click the **Color palette list arrow**, then click **Web Safe RGB**.

4. Verify that the Fill button is in front of the Stroke button in the toolbox, click the **Selection Tool** ▶, then click the **state of Maine**.

   The Color palette, as shown in Figure 28, shows the current fill color, the Out of Web Color Warning button, and the In Web Color button. The In Web Color button shows the closest possible Web safe color to the green fill.

5. Click the **In Web Color button** ☐ in the Color palette.

   The object's fill color changes to a Web safe color.

6. Click the **state of New Hampshire**, then click the **In Web Color button** ☐ in the Color palette.

7. Using the same method, change the fill color of the state of Vermont to a Web safe color.

You used the In Web Color button in the Color palette to change objects' fills to Web safe colors.

FIGURE 28
Color palette in Web Safe RGB mode

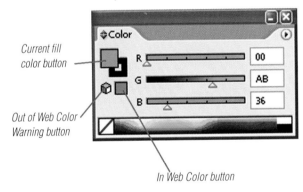

Current fill color button

Out of Web Color Warning button

In Web Color button

FIGURE 29

The image map artwork, optimized as a GIF

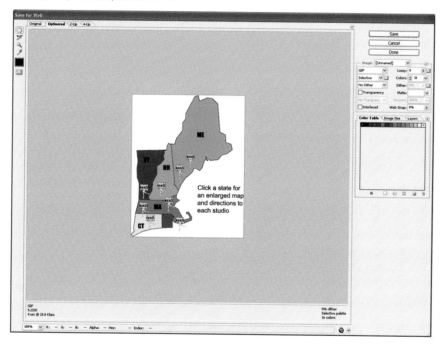

1. Select the state of Maine, click **Window** on the menu bar, then click **Attributes**.

2. Click the **Image list arrow** in the Attributes palette, then click **Polygon**.

   An invisible hotspot that closely follows the outline of the selected object is created.

3. Type **http://www.sds.com/map/me** in the URL text box.

4. Select the state of New Hampshire, click the **Image list arrow**, then click **Polygon**.

5. Type **http://www.sds.com/map/nh** in the URL text box.

6. Add polygon hotspots using the following URLs to Vermont, Massachusetts, and Connecticut. **http://www.sds.com/map/vt**, **http://www.sds.com/map/ma**, and **http://www.sds.com/map/ct**.

7. Click **File** on the menu bar, click **Save for Web**, then click the **Optimized tab**, if necessary.

8. Click the **Preset list arrow**, then click **GIF 32 No Dither**.

9. Click the **Colors list arrow**, then click **16**.

10. Remove the check mark from the Transparency check box. Your screen should resemble Figure 29.

11. Click **Save**, accept the current file name, then click **Save**.

12. Save and close New England Map.

You created five polygonal image maps with corresponding URLs. You then used the Save for Web dialog box to specify the artwork as a GIF file.

Create slices.

1. Open AI 13-3.ai, then save it as **Hana**.
2. Show rulers, then place a horizontal guide just above the five photos. (*Hint*: Change your guides to a darker color.)
3. Place a horizontal guide just below the five photos (above the blue text).
4. Place a vertical guide between each photo and the next, for a total of four vertical guides.
5. Verify that your guides are unlocked.
6. Click Object on the menu bar, point to Slice, then click Create from Guides.
7. Deselect all.
8. Click the Slice Selection Tool.
9. Select slices 01 and 02, click Object on the menu bar, point to Slice, click Combine Slices, then save.
10. Combine slices 02, 03, and 04, then save.
11. Combine slices 08 and 09, then save.
12. Combine slices 10 and 11, then save.
13. Save your work. (*Hint*: It's important that you save after Steps 9, 10, 11, and 12.)

Specify slice type and slice options.

1. Select slice 01, click Object on the menu bar, point to Slice, then click Slice Options.
2. Define slice 01 as an Image slice, click OK, then save.
3. Select slice 02, click Object on the menu bar, point to Slice, then click Slice Options.
4. Define slice 02 as a No Image slice, click the Background list arrow, click White, click OK, then save.
5. Select slice 08, define slice 08 as a No Image slice, click the Background list arrow, click White, click OK, then save.
6. Select slice 09, click Object on the menu bar, point to Slice, then click Slice Options.
7. Define slice 09 as an Image slice, click OK, then save.
8. Select slice 03, define it as an Image slice, then type **http://www.hana.com/photo1** in the URL text box.
9. Click the Target list arrow, then click _blank.
10. Type **Explore by car** in the Message and Alt text boxes, then click OK.
11. Save your work.

Use the Save for Web dialog box.

1. Click File on the menu bar, then click Save for Web.
2. Click the Slice Select Tool, if necessary, click slice 01, click the Preset list arrow, click GIF 32 Dithered, then remove the check mark from the Transparency check box.
3. Click slice 09, click the Preset list arrow, click GIF 32 Dithered, remove the check mark from the Transparency check box, click the Colors list arrow, then click 8.
4. Click slice 03, click the Preset list arrow, then click JPEG High.
5. Click the 4-Up tab, click the Hand Tool, then drag the Hand Tool over the selected window until slice 03 is visible in all four windows.
6. Compare the quality and file sizes of the three optimized images.
7. Click Done.

Create an image map.

1. Click Window on the menu bar, then click Attributes, if necessary.
2. Click the Selection Tool, then click the purple diamond in slice 01.
3. Click the Image list arrow in the Attributes palette, then click Polygon.
4. Type **http://www.hana.com/car** in the URL text box in the Attributes palette.
5. Click the gold diamond.
6. Click the Image list arrow in the Attributes palette, then click Polygon.
7. Type **http://www.hana.com/horse** in the URL text box.
8. Click the green diamond.
9. Click the Image list arrow in the Attributes palette, then click Polygon.
10. Type **http://www.hana.com/foot** in the URL text box.
11. Click the blue diamond.
12. Click the Image list arrow in the Attributes palette, then click Polygon.
13. Type **http://www.hana.com/bike** in the URL text box.
14. Save your work, then compare your window to Figure 30.
15. Close the Hana document.

FIGURE 30
Completed Skills Review

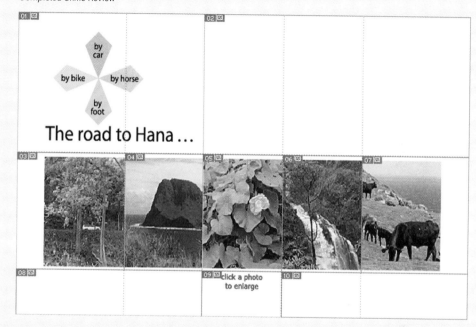

You work in the online department of *OAHU* magazine as an art manager. Every month, when the magazine hits the newsstands, you update the magazine's Web site with the new online issue. The top page always features this month's cover of the magazine (reduced 50% to fit on the page). The print department sends you an Illustrator file. Your job is to prepare the file to be used on the Web. You dislike this month's cover choice—a dark, busy, and out-of-focus image—and note that the subheads must remain bright when they are converted to Web safe colors.

1. Open AI 13-4.ai, then save it as **Oahu Online**.
2. Click File on the menu bar, point to Document Color Mode, then click RGB Color.
3. Click Window on the menu bar, then click Color, if necessary.
4. Click the Color palette list arrow, then click Web Safe RGB.
5. Select the word OAHU. (*Hint*: The magazine cover frame is grouped to the Oahu text.)
6. Click the In Web Color button in the Color palette.
7. Select the word "living."

8. Click the In Web Color button in the Color palette.
9. Change the colors for the three subheads (TWIST & SHOUT, A-MAZE-ING, and MAVERICK) to Web safe colors.

10. Save your work, then compare your document to Figure 31.
11. Close the Oahu Online document.

FIGURE 31
Completed Project Builder 1

You work in the online department of *OAHU* magazine as a Web master. Every month, you receive the color-corrected version of this month's cover, which you position on the top page of the Web site. The cover is one of your favorite features of the *OAHU* magazine Web site: Users can click the three featured cover stories and go immediately to the online article. You create the slices and specify the slice options.

1. Open AI 13-5.ai, then save it as **Oahu Magazine**.
2. Show the rulers, if necessary, then place a vertical guide between the A and H in OAHU.
3. Place a horizontal guide beneath the word *"living."*
4. Place a horizontal guide above the word A-MAZE-ING.
5. Place a horizontal guide above the word MAVERICK.
6. Use the guides to make slices.
7. Combine slices 5 and 7, then save.
8. Define the options for slice 5 as follows:
   Slice Type: Image
   URL: http://www.oahu.com/twist
   Target: _blank
9. Save your work.
10. Define the options for slice 6 as follows:
    Slice Type: Image
    URL: http://www.oahu.com/amazeing
    Target: _blank

11. Save your work.
12. Define the options for slice 7 as follows:
    Slice Type: Image
    URL: http://www.oahu.com/maverick
    Target: _top

FIGURE 32
Completed Project Builder 2

13. Save your work.
14. Define slices 1, 2, 3, and 4 as Image slices.
15. Save your work, then compare your document to Figure 32.

You work in the online department of *OAHU* magazine as an art director. Every month, you personally optimize the cover image for the Web site. You feel strongly that the process of compressing a cover image demands a critical eye to maintain image quality. You note that you'll be able to optimize the image substantially: the photo is so busy and out-of-focus that it will be hard to see any flaws created by compression. Your goal is to compress each slice to approximately 8K or less, while maintaining acceptable quality.

1. Open AI 13-6.ai, then save it as **Oahu Cover**.
2. Click File on the menu bar, then click Save for Web.
3. Click the Optimized tab, if necessary.
4. Select all seven slices.
5. Click the Preset list arrow, then click JPEG High.
6. Click the 4-Up tab.
7. Note that the quality of the JPEG with the quality setting of 30 is unacceptable, then click the Optimized tab.
8. Note the file size and download time of the total image.
9. Deselect by clicking outside the magazine cover, then select each slice, noting the file size of each one in the lower-left corner of the window.
10. Select all of the slices.

11. Click the Preset list arrow, then click GIF 64 Dithered; note the file size.
12. Change the Colors to 32, as shown in Figure 33.
13. Note any changes in quality.

FIGURE 33
Completed Design Project

14. Deselect all, then select each slice, noting the file size of each one.
15. Click Done, then close the Oahu Cover document.

You work for a design consulting group. Lately, your company has enjoyed much new business from Internet companies who want your team to assess the design quality of their Web sites. Your newest client is USAchefs, a national Web site for chefs and the restaurant industry that features high-quality food photography.

1. Connect to the Internet, go to *www.course.com*, navigate to the page for this book, click the Online Companion link, then click Link 1 for this chapter.

2. Print the Web page, make copies, then distribute them to the group.

3. Have each member of the group draw lines on his or her copy that represent guides to be used as slices.

4. Collect the copies, then lay them out on a table.

5. Have the group come to a consensus as to the best grid for slices.

6. Have the group discuss the quality of the graphics on the page—all the graphics, not just the picture of the food.

7. Poll each group member, asking if he or she thinks the food slices are JPEGs or GIFs.

FIGURE 34
Completed Group Project

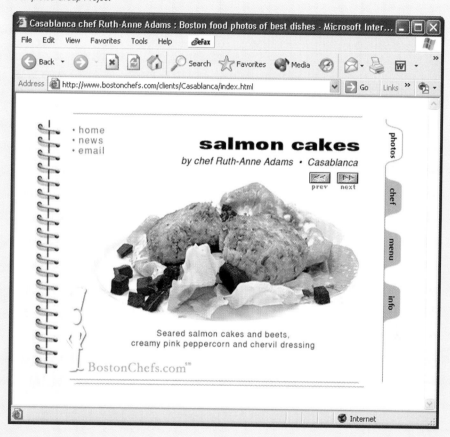

Topic Area	Objectives	Chapter
1. General Knowledge	■ List and describe the benefits of the Control palette.	4
	■ Customize and manage the organization of palettes.	1
2. Laying Out a Document	■ Describe the different components of the work area.	1
	■ Given a scenario, select and configure the appropriate settings in the Document Setup dialog box.	1
3. Working with Shapes and Objects	■ Convert a bitmap file to vector artwork by using the Live Trace command object.	3
	■ Describe how to create artwork by using the Live Paint tools.	3
	■ Align strokes to paths by using the Align Stroke option in the Stroke palette.	3
	■ Transform shapes by using the Transform tools or the Transform palette.	1and 4
	■ Transform shapes by using 3D effects.	11
	■ Create spot colors and add them to the Swatches palette.	2
	■ Apply colors, strokes, fills, and gradients to objects by using the Fill box, Stroke box, or Appearance palette.	1,2, and 8
	■ Create and modify masks, including clipping masks.	4
	■ Create, use, and customize brushes.	6
	■ Modify overlapping objects by using the Transparency palette.	8
	■ Change the appearance of objects by using the Graphic Styles palette.	8
	■ Create, use, and edit symbols by using the Symbols palette and Symbols tools.	10
	■ Create and modify compound shapes by using Pathfinder palette.	4
	■ Select objects by using the selection tools.	1-12
	■ Preview effects by using the Effects Gallery and preview filters by using the Filter Gallery.	8
4. Working with Type	■ Apply an underline or strikethrough to text by using the Character palette.	2
	■ Add type to a document.	2
	■ Create outlines of type by using the Create Outlines command.	2
	■ Change the look of type by using the Envelope command.	7
	■ Insert special characters by using the Type menu and the Glyph palette.	2
	■ Manage the composition of text by using palettes, menus, and preference settings.	2
	■ Create and modify type by using Character and Paragraph styles.	2
	■ List and describe the advantages and disadvantages when using OpenType, TrueType, or Type 1 fonts.	12

Topic Area	Objectives	Chapter
5. Managing Color	■ Discuss the color management workflow process that is used in Adobe Illustrator	12
	■ Set up color management in Illustrator by using the Color Settings dialog box	12
6. Managing assets with Bridge	■ List and describe the functionality Adobe Bridge provides for viewing assets.	1
	■ Explain how to apply metadata and keywords to assets in Adobe Bridge.	1
7. Outputting to Print	■ Apply a spot color to a grayscale image.	1
	■ Apply a spot color to the drop shadow of a drop shadow effect.	1
	■ Prepare a document for printing by choosing and configuring the appropriate resolution and rasterization settings.	12
	■ Explain guidelines associated with printing gradient mesh objects and color blends.	12
	■ Prepare and output a document to be used for color separation.	12
	■ Explain guidelines associated with printing transparencies.	12
8. Saving and Exporting	■ Given a file type, describe the options available when exporting an Illustrator document to that file type.	6
	■ List and describe the options available for saving Illustrator documents by using the Illustrator Legacy Options dialog box.	1
	■ Describe the differences, and explain criteria for when you would output an Illustrator document to various file formats. (formats include: PSD, JPEG, GIF, PDF, SVG)	6
9. Publishing for the Web	■ Describe the benefits of using the SVG-T (SVG Tiny) file format.	13
	■ Discuss options and considerations associated with preparing graphics that will be used on the Web.	13
	■ Export Illustrator images that are optimized for publication on the Web.	13
	■ Output symbols to SWF and SVG formats.	10
	■ Add interactivity to an SVG file by using the SVG Interactivity palette.	13

CERTIFICATION GRID

Files used in this book

Chapter	Data File Supplied	Student Creates File	Used in
1		The Lay of the Land	L1
	AI 1-1.ai		L2
		Basic Shapes	L3–L6
	AI 1-2.ai		L7
		Funky Flag	Skills Review
	AI 1-3.ai		Project Builder 1
		Iris Vision Bid	Project Builder 2
	AI 1-4.ai		Design Project
	AI 1-5.ai		Group Project
2	AI 2-1.ai		L1–L6
	AI 2-2.ai		L2
	AI 2-3.ai		Skills Review
		La Mirage	Project Builder 1
	AI 2-4.ai		Project Builder 2
		Vanishing Point	Design Project
		Firehouse	Group Project
3	AI 3-1.ai		L1
	AI 3-2.ai		L2
	AI 3-3.ai		L2
	AI 3-4.ai		L3–L4
	AI 3-5.ai		L7
	AI 3-6.ai		L7
	AI 3-7.ai		L7
	AI 3-8.ai		L7
		Snowball Assembled	L5–L6
	AI 3-9.ai		Skills Review
		Peppermill Vector	Project Builder 1
		USAchefs Logo	Project Builder 2
		Sleek	Design Project
		Shape	Group Project

Chapter	Data File Supplied	Student Creates File	Used in
4	AI 4-1.ai		L1
	AI 4-2.ai		L1
	AI 4-3.ai		L1
	AI 4-4.ai		L2
	AI 4-5.ai		L2
	AI 4-6.ai		L3
	AI 4-7.ai		L3
	AI 4-8.ai		L4
	AI 4-9.ai		L4
	AI 4-10.ai		L4
	AI 4-11.ai		L4
	AI 4-12.ai		L5
	AI 4-13.ai		L5
	AI 4-14.ai		L5
	AI 4-15.ai		Skills Review
	AI 4-16.ai		Skills Review
	AI 4-17.ai		Project Builder 1
	AI 4-18.ai		Project Builder 2
		Ties	Design Project
		Dartboard	Group Project
5	AI 5-1.ai		L1–L4
	AI 5-2.ai		L1–L4
	AI 5-3.ai		Skills Review
	AI 5-4.ai		Project Builder 1
	AI 5-5.ai		Project Builder 2
	AI 5-6.ai		Design Project
	AI 5-7.ai		Group Project
6		Checkerboard	L1
	AI 6-1.ai		L2
	AI 6-2.ai		L2
	AI 6-3.ai		L3

Chapter	Data File Supplied	Student Creates File	Used in
	AI 6-4.ai		L4
	AI 6-5.ai		L5
		Polka Dot Pattern	Skills Review
	AI 6-6.ai		Skills Review
		Shower Curtain	Project Builder 1
	AI 6-7.ai		Project Builder 2
	AI 6-8.ai		Design Project
		Original Plaid	Group Project
7	AI 7-1.ai		L1
	AI 7-2.ai		L1
	AI 7-3.ai		L1
	AI 7-4.ai		L2
	AI 7-5.ai		L2
	AI 7-6.ai		L3
	AI 7-7.ai		L3
	AI 7-8.ai		L3
	AI 7-9.ai		L4
	AI 7-10.ai		L4
	AI 7-11.ai		L4
	AI 7-12.ai		L4
		Filter Skills	Skills Review
	AI 7-13.ai		Skills Review
	AI 7-14.ai		Skills Review
	AI 7-15.ai		Skills Review
		Tidal Wave	Project Builder 1
	AI 7-16.ai		Project Builder 2
	AI 7-17.ai		Design Project
		Saint Claw Flag	Group Project
8	AI 8-1.ai		L1
	AI 8-2.ai		L1–L3
		Triple Fill	L3
	AI 8-3.ai		L4

Chapter	Data File Supplied	Student Creates File	Used in
	AI 8-4.ai		Skills Review
	AI 8-5.ai		Project Builder 1
	AI 8-6.ai		Project Builder 2
	AI 8-7.ai		Design Project
	Northstar.ai**		Group Project
9	AI 9-1.ai		L1–L5
	AI 9-2.ai		L6–L8
	AI 9-3.ai		Skills Review
	AI 9-4.ai		Skills Review
	AI 9-5.ai		Project Builder 1
	AI 9-6.ai		Project Builder 2
	AI 9-7.ai		Design Project
		Sales	Group Project
10	AI 10-1.ai		L1–L4
	AI 10-2.ai		L4–L5
	AI 10-3.ai		Skills Review
	AI 10-4.ai		Project Builder 1
	AI 10-5.ai		Project Builder 2
	AI 10-6.ai		Design Project
	AI 10-7.ai		Group Project
11	AI 11-1		L1
	AI 11-2		L2
	AI 11-3		L2
	AI 11-4		L2
	AI 11-5		L2
	AI 11-6		L3
	AI 11-7		L4
	AI 11-8*		L4
	AI 11-9*		L4
	AI 11-10*		L4

*Artwork is copied from Files 11-8, 11-9, and 11-10 and pasted into Tea Can file. Students do not save these files.

**Students open the completed Project Builder 2 for the Group Project Data File.

Chapter	Data File Supplied	Student Creates File	Used in
	AI 11-11		Skills Review
	AI 11-12		Skills Review
	AI 11-13		Project Builder 1
	AI 11-14		Project Builder 2
		T-Shirt Text	Design Project
	AI 11-15		Group Project
12	AI 12-1.ai		L2–L4
	AI 12-2.ai		L4
	AI 12-3.ai		L4
	AI 12-4.ai		L5
	AI 12-5.ai		L5
	AI 12-6.ai		Skills Review
	AI 12-7.ai		Project Builder 1
	AI 12-8.ai		Project Builder 2
	AI 12-9.ai		Design Project
	AI 12-10.ai		Group Project
13	AI 13-1.ai		L1–L3
	AI 13-2.ai		L4
	AI 13-3.ai		Skills Review
	AI 13-4.ai		Project Builder 1
	AI 13-5.ai		Project Builder 2
	AI 13-6.ai		Design Project
	NONE		Group Project

Absorption

Occurs when light strikes an object and is absorbed by the object.

Additive primary colors

Refers to the fact that Red, Green, and Blue light cannot themselves be broken down but can be combined to produce other colors.

Adobe Bridge

A sophisticated, stand-alone file browser, tightly integrated with the four CS2 applications. The main role of Bridge is to help you locate, browse and organize files—also called "assets"—more easily.

Ambient light

Determines how an object is lit globally.

Art brushes

A brush style that stretches an object along the length of a path.

Attributes

Formatting which has been applied to an object that affects its appearance.

Bevel

The angle that one surface makes with another when they are not at right angles.

Bevel join

Produces stroked lines with squared corners.

Bitmap images

Graphics created using a grid of colored squares called pixels.

Bleed

Artwork that extends to the trim and must extend the trim size by .125" to allow for variations when trimmed.

Blend

A series of intermediate objects and colors between two or more selected objects.

Blend Steps

Controls how smoothly shading appears on an object's surface and is most visible in the transition from the highlight areas to the diffusely lit areas.

Blending modes

Preset filters that control how colors blend when two objects overlap.

Bridge

See Adobe Bridge.

Brightness

The degree of lightness of a color.

Butt caps

Squared ends of a stroked path.

Calligraphic brushes

Brush style that applies strokes that resemble those drawn with a calligraphic pen.

Caps

The ends of stroked paths.

Clipping mask

An object whose area crops objects behind it in the stacking order.

Clipping set

Term used to distinguish clipping paths used in layers from clipping paths used to mask non-layered artwork.

CMYK

Cyan, Magenta, Yellow, and Black; four inks essential to professional printing.

Color gamut

Refers to the range of colors that can be printed or displayed within a given color model.

Color mode

Illustrator setting determining the color model of a document: RGB or CMYK.

Color model

A system used to represent or reproduce color.

Color Picker

A sophisticated dialog box for specifying colors in Illustrator.

Combination graph

A graph that uses two graph styles to plot numeric data; useful for emphasizing one set of data in comparison to others.

Compound path

Two or more paths that define a single object. When overlapped, the overlapped area becomes a negative space.

Compound shape

A term used to distinguish a complex compound path from a simple one. Compound shapes generally assume an artistic rather than a practical role.

Corner point

An anchor point joining two straight segments, one straight segment, and one curved segment, or two curved segments.

Crop marks

Short, thin lines that define where artwork is trimmed after it is printed.

Custom graph design

Artwork used to replace traditional columns, bars, or markers in Illustrator graphs.

Direction lines

Emanating from an anchor point, they determine the arc of a curved segment.

'Drag & drop' a copy

Pressing [Alt] (Win) or [option] (Mac) when moving an object; creates a copy of the object.

Edge

Similar to a stroke, an edge is a new shape or area created by the overlap of Illustrator objects, when the Live Paint Bucket Tool is applied. Edges appear as strokes but can be filled with color using the Live Paint Bucket Tool.

Effect

A type of appearance attribute which alters an object's appearance without altering the object itself.

Envelopes

Objects that are used to distort other objects into the shape of the envelope object.

Extrude

To add depth to an object by extending it on its Z axis. An object's Z axis is always perpendicular to the object's front surface.

Extrude & Bevel effect

A 3D effect that applies a three-dimensional effect to two-dimensional objects.

Flatten Artwork

Consolidating all layers in a document into a single layer.

GIF

A standard file format for compressing images by lowering the number of colors available to the file.

Gradient / Gradient Fill

A graduated blend between two or more colors used to fill an object or multiple objects.

Graph

A diagram of data that shows relationships among a set of numbers.

Graph type

A dialog box that provides a variety of ways to change the look of an Illustrator graph.

Graphic Styles

Named sets of appearance attributes.

Highlight Intensity

Controls how intense a highlight appears.

Highlight Size

Controls how large the highlights appear on an object.

Hue

The name of a color, or its identity on a standard color wheel.

Image map

A graphic with areas defined as links for the Internet.

Imageable area

The area inside the dotted line on the artboard which represents the portion of the page that a standard printer can print.

Insertion mode
The drawing mode in Illustrator that allows you to add a new object to a live paint group. A gray rectangle surrounding a live paint group indicates Insertion mode is active.

Joins
Define the appearance of the corner where two paths meet.

JPEG
A standard file format for compressing continuous tone images, gradients, and blends.

Kerning
Increasing or decreasing the horizontal space between any two text characters.

Keyboard increment
The distance that a single press of an arrow key moves a selected item; editable as a preference.

Layers
A solution for organizing and managing a complex illustration by segregating artwork.

Lighting Intensity
Controls the strength of the light on the object. The range for lighting intensity is 0-100, with 100 being the default.

Linear gradient
A gradient which can fill an object from left to right, top to bottom, or on any angle.

Live paint group
A live paint group is created when the Live Paint Bucket Tool is applied to selected objects. All of the resulting regions and edges are part of the live paint group and share a dynamic relationship.

Menu bar
At the top of the Illustrator window; a bar which includes all of the Illustrator menus.

Mesh lines
Paths that crisscross a mesh object, joined at their intersections by mesh points.

Mesh object
A single, multicolored object in which colors can flow in different directions and transition gradually from point to point.

Mesh patch
The area between four mesh points.

Mesh points
Diamond shaped points which function like anchor points, with the added ability of being able to be assigned a color.

Miter join
Produces stroked lines with pointed corners.

Miter limit
Determines when a Miter join will be squared off to a beveled edge.

Multiply
An essential blending mode in which the colors of overlapping objects create an effect that is similar to overlapping magic markers.

Non-process Inks
Special pre-mixed inks that are printed separately from process inks.

Offset
(noun) The distance that an object is moved from a starting location to a subsequent location.

Offset path
A command that creates a copy of a selected path repositioned at a specified distance.

Opacity
The degree to which an object is transparent.

Optimization
A process by which a file's size is reduced through standard color compression algorithms.

Outline stroke
A command that converts a stroked path into a closed path that is the same width as the original stroked path.

Outlined text
A command that changes text in a document to standard vector graphics.

Palettes
Windows containing features for modifying and manipulating Illustrator objects.

PANTONE
The standard library of non-process inks.

Pathfinders
Preset operations that combine paths in a variety of ways; useful for creating complex or irregular shapes from basic shapes.

Pattern brushes
A brush style that repeats a pattern along a path.

Pattern fill
Multiple objects used as a fill for an object; the object is filled by repeating the artwork.

Pica
12 points, or $\frac{1}{6}$ of an inch.

Pixel
Picture element. Small, single-colored squares which compose a bitmap image.

Point
$\frac{1}{72}$ of an inch.

Point of origin
The point from which an object is transformed; by default, the center point of an object, unless another point is specified.

Process tints
Colors that can be printed by mixing varying percentages of CMYK inks.

Projecting cap
Produces a squared edge that extends the anchor point of a stroked path by a distance that is ½ the weight of the stroke.

Radial gradient
A gradient which fills an object as a series of concentric circles.

Reflection
Occurs when light strikes an object and 'bounces' off the object.

Region
Similar to a fill, a region is a new shape or area created by the overlap of Illustrator objects. Regions are created when the Live Paint Bucket Tool is applied.

Resolution
The number of pixels in a given inch of a bitmap graphic.

Resolution-independent
Refers to a graphic which can be scaled with no impact on image quality.

Revolve
Another method that Illustrator CS2 provides for applying a 3D effect to a 2D object by "sweeping" a path in a circular direction around the Y axis of the object.

RGB
Red, Green and Blue; the additive primary colors of light.

Rich black
A process tint that is 100% Black plus 50% Cyan; used to print deep, dark black areas of a printed page.

Round cap
Produces a stroked path with rounded ends.

Round join
Produces stroked lines with rounded corners.

Saturation
The intensity of a hue.

Scatter brush
A brush style which disperses copies of an object along a path.

Scratch area
The area outside the artboard where objects may be stored for future use; objects on the scratch area will not print.

Slice
Divided artwork to be output as individual— and therefore smaller—files.

Smart guides
Non-printing words that appear on the artboard and identify visible or invisible objects, page boundaries, intersections, anchor points, etc.

Smooth points
Anchor points created by clicking and dragging the Pen Tool; the path continues uninterrupted through the anchor point.

Snap to point
Automatically aligns points when they get close together.

Stacking order
The hierarchy of objects on the artboard, from frontmost to backmost.

Status bar
A utility on the artboard that contains a list arrow menu from which you can choose a status line with information about the current tool, the date and time, the amount of free memory, or the number of undo operations.

Subtractive Primary Colors
Cyan, Magenta and Yellow; the term subtractive refers to the concept that each is produced by removing or subtracting one of the additive primary colors and that overlapping all three pigments would absorb all colors.

SWF
Macromedia Flash file format that supports vector graphics for the Web.

Symbol instance
A single usage of a symbol.

Symbol instance set
Symbol instances created with the Symbol Sprayer Tool.

Tick marks
Short lines that extend out from the value axis of a graph and aid viewers in interpreting the meaning of column height by indicating incremental values on the value axis.

Tile
Artwork, usually square, used repeatedly in a pattern fill.

Tiling
The process of repeating a tile as a fill for a pattern.

Title bar
At the top of the Illustrator window; contains the name of the document, magnification level, and color mode.

Toolbox
A palette containing Illustrator tools for creating, selecting, and manipulating objects in Illustrator.

Tracking
The process of inserting or removing uniform spaces between text characters to affect the width of selected words or entire blocks of text.

Transmission
Occurs when light strikes an object and passes through the object.

Trim marks
Like crop marks, define where a printed image should be trimmed; trim marks are used to create multiple marks for multiple objects on a page that are to be trimmed.

Trim size
The size to which artwork or a document is to be cut.

Tweaking
Making small, specific improvements to artwork or typography.

Type area select
An Illustrator preference which allows the user to select text simply by clicking anywhere on the text.

Vector graphics
Resolution-independent graphics created with lines, curves, and fills.

Visible light
Light waves that are visible to the human eye.

White light
Refers to the concept that natural light on Earth appears to people as not having any dominant hue.

Zoom text box
A utility in the lower-left corner of the Illustrator window that displays the current magnification level.